CONTENTS.

THE WORK OF THE HOLY GHOST IN OUR SALVATION.

BOOK I.

WORKS OF
THOMAS GOODWIN

Works of
THOMAS GOODWIN

The Work of the
Holy Spirit in Our Salvation

THE BANNER OF TRUTH TRUST

THE BANNER OF TRUTH TRUST
3 Murrayfield Road, Edinburgh EH12 6EL
P.O. Box 621, Carlisle, Pennsylvania 17013, U.S.A.

*

Reprinted from Volume Six of the
Works of Thomas Goodwin, published by James Nichol in 1863

First Banner of Truth Trust edition 1979

ISBN 0 85151 279 8

*

Printed in Great Britain by
photo lithography by W & J Mackay Ltd, Chatham

BOOK IV.

BOOK VII.

BOOK X.

OF THE WORK OF THE HOLY GHOST

(THE THIRD PERSON OF THE TRINITY)

IN OUR SALVATION.

OF THE WORK OF THE HOLY GHOST IN OUR SALVATION.

BOOK I.

A general and brief scheme of the whole of that work committed to the Holy Spirit in bringing us to salvation; in an enumeration of all particulars, and of the glory due unto him for it.—The work of the Holy Spirit in the unction of Jesus to be our Saviour.

CHAPTER I.

Some general observations premised out of the fourteenth, fifteenth, and sixteenth chapters of St John's Gospel.

THERE is a general omission in the saints of God, in their not giving the Holy Ghost that glory that is due to his person, and for his great work of salvation in us, insomuch that we have in our hearts almost lost this third person. We give daily in our thoughts, prayers, affections, and speeches, an honour to the Father and the Son; but who almost directs the aims of his praise (more than in that general way of doxology we use to close our prayers with, ' All glory be,' &c.) unto God the Holy Ghost? He is a person in the Godhead equal with the Father and the Son; and the work he doth for us in its kind is as great as those of the Father or the Son. Therefore, by the equity of all law, a proportionable honour from us is due to him. God's ordination amongst men is, that we should ' render to all their due, honour to whom honour is due,' Rom. xiii. 1. To the magistracy (which there he speaks it of) according to their place and dignity; and this he makes a debt, a due, ver. 8. And the like is enjoined concerning ministers, that are instruments of our spiritual good, that we should ' esteem them very highly for their work's sake,' 1 Thes. v. 13. Let the same law, I beseech you, take place in your hearts towards the Holy Ghost, as well as the other two persons of the Trinity. The Holy Ghost is indeed the last in order of the persons, as proceeding from the other two, yet in the participation of the Godhead he is equal with them both; and in his work, though it be last done for us, he is not behind them, nor in the glory of it inferior to what they have in theirs. And indeed he would not be God, equal with the Father and the Son, if the work allotted to him, to shew he is God, were not equal unto each of theirs. And indeed, no less than all that is done, or to be done in us, was left to the Holy Ghost's share, for the ultimate execution of it ; and it was not left him as the refuse, it being as necessary and as great as any of theirs. But he being the last person, took his own lot of the works about our salvation, which are the last, which is to apply all, and to make all actually ours, whatever the other two had done afore for us. The scope of this treatise is to set forth this work to you in the amplitude of it, to the end you may accordingly in your hearts honour this blessed and holy Spirit. And surely if to neglect the notice and observation of an attribute of God, eminently imprinted on such or such a work of God's, as of power in the creation, justice in governing the world, mercy in bearing with sinners, grace in our salvation ; if this be made so great a sin (Rom. i.) then it must be deemed a greater diminution to the Godhead to neglect the glorifying one of these persons, who is possessed of the whole Godhead and attributes, when he is manifested or interested in any work most gloriously.

In prosecution of my design, to persuade you to honour the Holy Ghost as you do the Father and the Son, I shall consider the 14th, 15th, and 16th chapters of John, and make some general observations upon various passages in those chapters serving to this purpose; and we shall see therein what a valuation the Father and the Son, the other persons with him, have in those chapters put upon him and his work, and what a great and singular matter they make of his work, and what divine esteem of his person, as by Christ's speeches scattered up and down therein appears. Though the Father himself doth not immediately speak, yet the Son doth in his name, as well as in his own. And you may well take their judgments, for they are sharers and co-rivals with him in point of glory about our salvation ; the work of which I shall only treat of.

There are these *general observations* which I shall make upon the whole series of the aforesaid chapters, which serve the design of my discourse.

Obs. 1. *First*, Our Saviour had abundantly in all his former sermons discoursed both his work and hand in our salvation, as also his Father's ; and now at last, just when he was to go out of the world, he then, and not till then, doth more plainly and more fully discover to them this third person, that had an after-work left to him, who to that end was to come when he should be gone, and was to come visibly upon the stage, to act visibly a new scene of works, left by the Father and himself unto him: John xiv. 16, ' I will pray the Father, and he shall give you another Comforter.' He had said, chap. viii. 17, that ' the testimony of two men' (or persons) ' is true ;' and that he himself was one witness of those two there spoken of, and his Father another: ver. 18, ' I am one that bear witness of myself, and the Father that sent me beareth witness of me.' And he tells us here, you see, that there is yet another, distinct from the Father and himself; for in his saying, ' I will pray the Father to give you another Comforter,' he must mean a third person, distinct from them both, to be that other. And moreover this Spirit, as another person, is said likewise to be a third witness of, and unto Christ ; John xv. 26, and so is to be joined as a person, and third witness with these two : ' When the Comforter is come, whom I will send unto you from the Father, even the Spirit of truth, which proceedeth from the Father, he shall testify of me ;' like as of the Father and himself, the same had been spoken in that chap. viii. ver. 18, last cited. And the coherence with ver. 17 argues their being witnesses alike, to be distinct persons each from other, for, ver. 17, he allegeth the law, ' It is written in your law, that the testimony of two men is true.' For therein lies the validity of their testimony, that they must be two men or two persons that make up a legal testimony. And in this 15th chap. ver. 26, there is the Holy Ghost as a third witness brought into court to testify with both ; and therefore he is a person if a witness, for there are three persons if three witnesses, and the law itself he cites says, ' Under the mouth of two or three witnesses shall the matter be established,' Deut. xix. 15, and Matt. xviii. 16. We may also observe how industriously careful Christ is further to characterise this person of the Holy Spirit, the author of these works, and to describe who he was, and what manner of person, that they might be sure to mind him, and have a regard to him, and to know whom and to what name they were to be so much beholden. Thus, ver. 26, ' The Comforter, which is the Holy Ghost' (says he) ; and ver. 17, ' Even the Spirit of truth ;' and chap. xv. 26, ' Whom I will send unto you from the Father, who proceedeth from the Father.' Which last addition is to shew the divine procession of the Holy Ghost, and the original and the consubstantiality of his person, to be out of the substance of the Father, proceeding from him ; as (1 Cor. ii. 12) the apostle signaliseth him, ' The Spirit that is out of God ;' or (which is all one) that hath his subsistence, or his being a person, by proceeding from God the Father, and so being God with God, insomuch as it is not in anywise to be understood that he subsisted *extra Deum*, out of, or separate from God ; for he had said, ver. 11, that he is in God, even as the spirit of a man is said to be in him.

Some would understand that speech of Christ's, ' Who proceedeth from the Father,' to be meant in respect of God's sending him forth to us, and his embassage to us. But that had been said by Christ in the words afore, ' Whom I will send from the Father ;' and therefore to intend the words after—' Who cometh from the Father'—of an ambassador's sending, had been needless, for Christ had said that already ; and therefore if that had been all the meaning of that addition, he had but said the same over a second time. There is therefore, in those speeches, a manifest distinguishing between that dispensatory sending of him from the Father to them, and that substantial proceeding of his from the Father, as a third person ; and this is added to shew the original ground, why it must be from the Father that he sends him, and with his consent first had ; because his very person is by proceeding from the Father, and therefore this his office too. And therefore that latter is spoken in the present time, whereas that other speech of Christ's, ' Whom I will send from the Father,' is in the future ; because the Holy Ghost his dispensatory sending, both from the Father and from Christ, was yet to come ; whereas this personal proceeding of his from the Father was then, when he spake it, and is continually, and had been from eternity.

Now the tendency of these reiterated designations of the person, doth manifest Christ's sedulous intention, and tender regard to, and for the honour of this, so great a person ; and to raise up in their hearts a valuation of this person himself, that should be the Comforter ; and to make them careful to give glory to him, even the Holy Ghost, as a third person, and the Comforter. As likewise to assure them of his coming upon them, when himself was gone ; and that therefore they might honour him in his coming, for his work, as he would have them to honour himself for his own work, and coming in the flesh. It is as if he had said, I would not, for that honour I ever look for from yourselves, that you should so attribute the comfort you shall have, or the revealing of truth to you (from which he is called 'the Spirit of truth'), so unto me or my Father alone, as to neglect or omit to give him his peculiar honour in it; for it properly, and of due, belongs to him.　You are and shall be beholden to me and my Father, for the sending of him; but you are to be especially beholden to himself, for that work he doth in you, being sent by us.　Be sure therefore to take notice of him and his person, distinct both from me and my Father.　For it is 'another Comforter' (says he, ver. 16) 'which is the Holy Ghost,' (ver. 26), and therefore you ought as distinctly to glorify him as you would do us.

Obs. 2. The second observation is concerning the particular works which Christ says are his, and for which we are to honour him.　And an enumeration of his works being the scope of this my discourse, we may find divers particulars that are the most eminent of them, named and specified in these chapters to our hand, which will sufficiently serve for me to take the mention of them, for an example to me to proceed to specify other works that are attributed to him elsewhere.　This I premise, because I would not be obliged to fetch each of them which I shall after name out of these chapters, and so to confine myself thereto.

The particular eminent work indeed on which he insists in these chapters, is, that of being a Comforter to them; for the occasion of these sermons was to relieve and pacify the apostles' minds, against his own leaving them, as they thought, desolate.　But therewith he further brings in other works of his besides, and in effect that he should do all, that they had need of his help in.　He insinuates to them how much already themselves had been obliged unto him for his working hitherto in them, which he calls them to look back upon, for they had received them already in regenerating, converting and calling them out from the world (which was his first and great work in them), and so distinguished them from the world.　Thus chap. xiv. 16, 17, 'The Comforter, the Spirit of truth; whom the world cannot receive, because it seeth him not, neither knoweth him;' that is, knows him not by experience of any saving work upon them, and so they cannot receive him as a comforter, because it is necessary they first receive him as a converter.　'But ye know him,' and have found him to have begotten you again; 'for he dwelleth in you,' hath come and taken possession of you, and acted hitherto in you all that spiritual good that hath been found in you, and thereby hath taken everlasting possession of you, as it follows: 'and shall be in you,' to perfect all that is wanting, and that for ever, as verse 16.

A second work there specified is, that he should be to them a 'Spirit of truth,' 'to lead them into all truth,' which, as a sacred *depositum*, he was by them, as apostles, to leave unto the rest of the world; chap. xiv. 26, 'He shall teach you all things, and bring all things to your remembrance, whatsoever I have said unto you.'　And not only so, but shall suggest new to you, chap. xvi. 12, 13, 'I have many things to say unto you, but ye cannot bear them now.　Howbeit when he, the Spirit of truth, is come, he shall not speak of himself; but whatsoever he shall hear, that shall he speak.'

A third work instanced in is, that 'He will shew you things to come;' and this to that end, that ye may teach and write them to others, chap. xv. 26, 27.　He shall bear witness of me, and you shall bear witness of me.

A fourth work specified is, to sanctify them against sin and corruption. This work is imported in his name, 'the *Holy* Spirit,' as the other, of leading them into all truth, is signified by that other title, 'the Spirit of *truth*;'

for he is termed the Holy Spirit, because he sanctifies : Rom. xv. 16, ' Being sanctified by the Holy Ghost.'

Fifthly, He shall be a Comforter to you, against all sorrows, chap. xiv. 16, 17, 18.

Sixthly, He shall assist and direct you in all your prayers, and be the inditer of them for you ; and so effectually as to obtain what you shall ask, chap. xvi. 23, ' Verily, verily, whatsoever ye shall ask the Father in my name, he will give it you ; hitherto have you asked nothing in my name ;' for the Holy Ghost was not as yet given, as he in these chapters promiseth he should be. ' But in that day,' namely, when the Holy Ghost is come, ' ye shall ask in my name,' then (as in chap. xiv. 20). ' In that day,'— namely, when the Comforter is come, that word in that day refers there-unto—' ye shall know that I am in my Father, and you in me.' These works he specifies as to themselves.

But withal, seventhly, he mentions his works upon the world, by their ministry, unto whom they were sent. He shall be a converter and con-vincer of the world ; that is, the glory of the conversion of the Gentiles is reserved for him, by your ministry : chap. xvi. verses 8, 9, ' When he is come, he will reprove the world of sin, and of righteousness, and of judg-ment : of sin, because they believe not on me,' &c. To which three enumerations the total of the work of conversion is reduced, of which afterwards.

Obs. 3. Thirdly, observe what Christ says, I myself must be gone (saith he) and disappear, to the end it may appear that all this whole work is his, not mine : ver. 7, ' If I go not away, the Comforter will not come.' He will not do these works while I am here, and I have committed all to him. That look, as my Father hath visibly ' committed all judgment unto me,' (John v. 22, 23, ' For the Father judgeth no man, but hath committed all judgment unto the Son ; that all men should honour the Son, even as they honour the Father '), so here : I and my Father will send him, having com-mitted all these things to him, that all men might honour the Holy Ghost, even as they honour the Father and the Son. Even as in like manner the reason why the Spirit was not sent, whilst Christ was on earth, was to shew that not the Father alone sent him, but that he came from Christ, as well as from the Father. And so Christ, he went to heaven to shew that both Father and Son would send the Holy Ghost from thence, Acts ii. 32, 33, ' This Jesus hath God raised up, whereof we all are witnesses. There-fore being by the right hand of God exalted, and having received of the Father the promise of the Holy Ghost, he hath shed forth this which you see and hear.' Thus wary and careful are every of the persons to provide for the honour of each other in our hearts. And as careful should we be to give it to them accordingly.

CHAPTER II.

Some further observations touching the coming of the Holy Ghost.—That he had a signal coming designed to him for his glory at the feast of Pentecost, as Christ had a visible coming in the flesh.—The great change made in the world thereby.

Add to these observations out of those chapters, these also that follow, concerning this his coming promised in those chapters, but observed out of other scriptures.

I. That a signal coming should be appointed to him, to the performance of his work, as well as unto Christ to perform his. This coming of his you have inculcated again and again in these chapters, in these words, ' When he is come,' and the like. Which imported that, although he was given to work regeneration in men afore, even under the Old Testament (as Neh. ix. 20, ' He gave them his good Spirit,' and many other places, shew), that yet to let all the world of believers take notice his coming, and his work, he must have a coming in state, in a solemn and visible manner, accompanied with visible effects, as well as Christ had, and whereof all the Jews should be, and were witnesses (thus Acts, chaps. ii. iv.), and it was also apparent throughout the primitive times, in outward signs and miracles, extraordinary gifts and conversions. And as Christ, though he was under the Old Testament present with that church and with the fathers—Acts vii. 37, 38, ' This is he that was in the church in the wilderness, with the angel which spake to Moses in the mount Sinai, and with our fathers'—yet had a visible coming in flesh to manifest his person; that it was he who had done all those works then, and came now to work more, and far greater works : so there was a visible coming of the Holy Ghost, both in the appearance of him as a dove, descending on Christ at first, and afterwards in the resemblance of cloven tongues.

And there was not a personal union of the Holy Ghost with that dove and those tongues, as in Christ's manifestation in the flesh there was between the eternal Son of God and human nature. Yet these appearances of the Holy Ghost are to be understood by us as visible outward representations and discoveries of him to be the third person ; and that it had been he who was the author of all the whole work of application in the saints then under the Old Testament; as well as now of regeneration and sanctification, and of comforting; and that he had been indwelling in all saints afore this his coming, as well as after.

And this his coming was as clearly prophesied of, and solemn promise made thereof, under the Old Testament, as there was of Christ's coming in the flesh. Which did so much heighten and raise up the expectations of all believers then about him ; as that upon which, and whereby, so great a change should be made in the church and world in the last days. This the apostle Peter commemorates and applies upon the Spirit's visible coming upon himself and the rest of his fellows : Acts ii. 16–18, ' This is that which was spoken by the prophet Joel ; It shall come to pass in the last days, saith God, I will pour out my Spirit upon all flesh : and your sons and your daughters shall prophesy, and your young men shall see visions, and your old men shall dream dreams : and on my servants and on my handmaidens I will pour out in those days of my Spirit ; and they shall prophesy ;' and so on. Yea, this coming of the Spirit I may farther call the great promise of the New Testament. For as Christ's coming was the great promise of the Old Testament, so the sending of the Spirit is entitled the 'promise of the Father' in the New : Luke xxiv. 49, ' And behold I send the promise of my Father upon you.' And he is so styled, not only in that he had been promised in the Old Testament by the prophets (as in that of Joel ii. 28, 29, now cited), and in multitude of other prophecies of old ; but because that Christ himself did now *de novo* (as it were) promulge it as his promise, and the Father's ; and that upon this authority, that this Spirit proceeded from him, as well as from the Father, and that he was first to receive him from* us, and then shed him forth on us, Acts

* Qu. 'for'?—ED.

ii. 33, that so it might be made good, that ' all the promises are yea and amen in him ;' seeing this promise of the Spirit is given upon Christ's account, as he is the Son (according to that, ' God hath sent forth the Spirit of his Son into your hearts,' Gal. iii. 13, 14 compared), and also because now under the New Testament this promise was to be fulfilled in such a manner and measure as was never under the Old ; and so it becomes a promise proper to the New, that next great promise, which was to succeed that of Christ himself, the promise of promises ; the sole great promise now left to be given.   God the Father had but two grand gifts to bestow ; and when once they should be given out of him, he had left them nothing that was great (comparatively) to give, for they contained all good in them ; and these two gifts were his Son, who was his promise in the Old Testament, and his Spirit, the promise of the New.   And the Father doth honour himself to us by this title, that he is the promiser and giver of the Spirit ; and Christ himself, now when he is come, takes the honour too of that, to make the sending of the Spirit his promise also, in saying, ' Behold I send him :' Luke xxiv. 49, and John xiv. 26, ' Whom my Father will send in my name.'   And it is evident that our Saviour, in calling him ' the promise of the Father,' which was spoken by him after his resurrection, Luke xxiv. 49, doth refer to his own words and sermons uttered afore his resurrection, in 14th, 15th, and 16th chapters of John, rather than to the prophets primarily in his intention : Acts i. 4, ' Wait for the promise of the Father, which ye have heard of me.'

Again, Christ had John the Baptist, who ' began the gospel,' to foretell his manifestation in the flesh, and to prepare the way for this Lord.   And besides him, his angels did it.   But the Holy Ghost hath Christ himself to foretell his coming upon flesh : and that to prepare the hearts of men for him whenever he should come.

And, lastly, on purpose to honour his visible coming, he had answerably an extraordinary work left to him, upon that his visible coming : the conversion of the whole Gentile world ; and the raising and building of the churches of the New Testament was reserved of his glory.   To believe in the Holy Ghost, and the holy catholic church, you know how near they stand together in the Creed.   His visible coming at Pentecost was the visible consecration and dedication of that great temple, the mystical body of Christ, to be reared under the gospel (the several members of which body are called ' temples of the Holy Ghost,'* 1 Cor. iii. 16), as that appearance at Christ's baptism was the consecration of the head.   Of this work of the Spirit, that of the psalmist, though spoken literally of the first creation, may yet be used in allusion, and is mystically applied by some of the fathers thereunto : Ps. civ. 30, ' Thou sendest forth thy Spirit, they are created ; thou renewest the face of the earth.'   The whole earth was decked and adorned with a new array, when the Spirit of God moved upon that chaos ; and the whole face of the world was in that age of the gospel's promulgation no other than a chaos, void, and without all form ; ' all nations had walked in their own ways :' but the Spirit was sent forth, and lo this barren wilderness became a fruitful field all the world over.

The feast of Pentecost was under the old law the feast of the first fruits, Lev. xxiii. 10.   Thus it was in the type, and the apostles on that day received for the church of the New Testament ' the first fruits of the Spirit,' Rom. viii. 23.   And the sickle was then first put in, in the conversion of the three thousand out of all nations (whether Jews or Gentiles, or mixed

* Ye are the temples of the Holy Ghost.

with both) ; so to begin that great harvest, whereof these were the first fruits or seeds which consecrated the rest (as the first fruits did under the law) in after ages to come, as Christ told them that their fruit should remain, John xv. 16. And this coming of the Holy Ghost then, and converting such as were inhabitants out of all nations, was by Christ designed to be for the handsel of the conversion of all nations : Acts i. 8, ' Ye shall receive power, after that the Holy Ghost is come upon you ; and ye shall be witnesses unto me, both in Jerusalem, and in all Judea, and in Samaria, and unto the uttermost parts of the earth ;' charging them to stay at Jerusalem, and not to stir one foot out from thence, but ' wait first for the promise of the Father,' ver. 4. For it would have been a vain attempt to have endeavoured to convert the world until the Holy Ghost had come upon them ; and hence it was that this his visible coming was reckoned by the chief apostle the first era, the beginning of the gospel, as the beginning of the creation described by Moses is of the world : Acts xi. 15, ' The Holy Ghost fell upon them Gentiles, as upon us *at the beginning*,' which refers to that at Pentecost. And this yet further answers the type, for the first giving of the law by Moses was on that day, the day of Pentecost ; and so this coming of the Spirit that day was justly reckoned the beginning of the gospel, although the account of the Christian world begins with the nativity of Christ. But the full revelation of the gospel and the mysteries thereof, and the conversion of the world of the Gentiles, this was ordained for the Spirit's glory, and reserved for his coming, John xvi. ; which conversion of the world is magnified as an after-sacrifice, as the saints' sufferings after Christ are styled the after-sufferings of Christ, Col. i., presented unto God by the Holy Ghost ; Christ offered up himself as that alone meritorious sacrifice, but this of the Gentiles did come after, a sacrifice sanctified by the Holy Ghost. The grace vouchsafed to the apostle for his poor instrumentalness therein, he owns, whilst he yet gives the glory of it to the Holy Ghost ; which you may find in Rom. xv. 15, 16, ' To me this grace was given, that I should be the minister of Jesus Christ to the Gentiles, ministering the gospel of God, that the offering up of the Gentiles might be acceptable, being sanctified by the Holy Ghost.' The Gentiles, you know, before had ever been esteemed unclean, and upon that account unmeet to be an offering unto God, as the law shews ; which that vision of all sorts of unclean beasts made to Peter in the sheet (Acts x.), and the comment thereupon which he makes that the Gentiles were meant, doth shew. But these were all purified by the Holy Ghost's converting of them, that thereby all difference was taken away ; and so much as those that were not to be conversed with by a Jew, were now offered up as a sacrifice to God. Thus Acts xv. 8, 9, ' God, which knoweth the hearts, bare them witness, giving them the Holy Ghost, even as he did us ; and put no difference between us and them, purifying their hearts by faith.'

Thus much for some general observations premised.

CHAPTER III.

Of the works of the Holy Ghost upon Christ our Saviour.

The summing up of the works of the Holy Spirit, and laying them altogether in one heap, that we find scattered up and down in the Scriptures, would, if we were able to recollect them all, and every particular, arise to a very great bulk. I shall reduce them which I have gleaned as most eminent unto these three heads,

I. What work and use he is, and was of, to Christ our head.

II. What to the church, taken collectively.

III. What to every saint. And in the filling up of these, I shall not mention anything that may by consequence be argued his, but what the Scriptures do expressly attribute to him.

I. I shall first describe his operations upon Christ our head.

1. It was the Holy Ghost that formed his human nature in the womb : Mat: i. 18, it is said that Mary ' was found with child of the Holy Ghost'; and ver. 20, 'That which is conceived in her is of the Holy Ghost.' So then he made the man Jesus, both body and soul.

2. Some divines do further ascribe unto this Spirit the special honour of tying that marriage knot, or union, between the Son of God and that man Jesus, whom the Holy Ghost formed in the virgin's womb. Now if their meaning be that he, in common with the Father and the Son, did join in that great action, I grant it, according to the measure of that general rule, that *opera ad extra sunt indivisa*, all works outward, or that are wrought not within the Godhead itself (which admit some exception), all the three persons had a joint common hand in. But that which is my proper subject, is, what special honour in those works doth by way of eminency belong to the Holy Ghost in any of these works. And so considered, I have not found a ground why to attribute the personal union more particularly to the Holy Ghost ; but rather (according unto what occurs to my observation in the Scriptures, and to consonant reason), that action is more peculiarly to be attributed to the Son himself, as second person, who took up into one person with himself that human nature. The Father indeed sent the Son into the world, to take flesh ; and the Holy Ghost formed that flesh he assumed ; but it was the Son's special act to take it up into himself, and to assume it. So the apostle tells us, Heb. ii. 16, ' He took on him* the seed of Abraham ;' or he took to himself, *assumpsit ad*, which word denotes the very act of that union. And it was his own single act, and in reason it must have been so ; for it was an act of a person knowing, and actually intelligent in what he did, when it was done by him. And that thing he did was a taking to himself a foreign nature, to be one person with himself; as a person affording his own subsistence unto that nature, to be a person with himself. Himself must communicate that personality, and none other for him, for it is properly his own to bestow ; unto which that in chap. x. accords, ' When he comes into the world, he says, A body hast thou prepared me,' speaking to his Father, who prepared that body by the Holy Ghost; and it was his Father's ordination he should take it; but he, as a person existing afore he took it, as coming into the world by assuming it, says, ' Lo, I come to do thy will, O God,' as ver. 7 it is more expressly added. But,

3. It was the Holy Ghost had the honour of the consecration of him to be the Christ, and that by anointing him ' without' or ' above measure,' as John the Baptist witnessed, John iii. 34. It was with power and all grace that he was anointed : Isa. xi. 2, ' The Spirit of the Lord shall rest upon him, and the Spirit of wisdom and understanding, the Spirit of counsel and might, the Spirit of knowledge and of the fear of the Lord.' What is Messiah, or Χριστὸς, but the Most Holy One anointed ? Dan. ix. Now, with

* Ἐπιλαμβάνεται.

what oil was Jesus anointed, and so made Christ? Acts x. 38, 'God anointed Jesus of Nazareth with the Holy Ghost.' The Holy Ghost is that oil he is anointed with above his fellows; and he hath his name of Christ, which is the chief name of his person, from the Holy Ghost, as he hath that of Jesus for saving us, which is his work. Christ, the anointed, is the name that speaks all his offices. Kings, priests, and prophets, who were only his shadows, were anointed. And it is made the true, proper sign and token of his person's being the Son of God, that the Holy Ghost came visibly on him, and abode upon him: John i. 32–34, 'And John bare record, saying, I saw the Spirit descending from heaven like a dove, and it abode upon him. And I knew him not: but he that sent me to baptize with water, the same said unto me, Upon whom thou shalt see the Spirit descending, and remaining on him, the same is he which baptizeth with the Holy Ghost. And I saw, and bare record, that this is the Son of God;' with which compare John vii. 38, 39, 'He that believeth on me, as the scripture hath said, out of his belly shall flow rivers of living water. (But this spake he of the Spirit, which they that believe on him should receive: for the Holy Ghost was not yet given; because that Jesus was not yet glorified);' whereupon, ver. 40, 41, 'Many of the people, when they heard that saying, Of a truth, said they, this is that Prophet; others, This is the Christ.' This descending visibly of the Spirit (which was done first to him), was the highest evidence of these that could be, excepting only that of the Father: 'This is my beloved Son.' The Baptist makes these his highest characters, that it was he baptized with the Holy Ghost as with fire; and that he received the Spirit without measure, though he was personally full of grace and truth himself, as he was the Son of God.

4. It was the Holy Ghost anointed him to all his offices, as first to be a prophet and preacher of the gospel, which was first spoken by the Lord, Heb. ii. Thus, Luke iv. 18 (and some think it was his first text), 'The Spirit of the Lord is upon me, because he hath sent me to heal the broken-hearted, to preach deliverance to the captives, and recovering sight to the blind, to set at liberty them that are bruised.' Whether you take the words οὗ ἕνεκεν antecedently or consequently, either that *because* by God he was designed to be a preacher, *therefore* the Spirit was on him; or that *because* the Spirit was on him, he *therefore* was fitted to be a preacher, it comes all to one as to my purpose. The Spirit was he that made him a preacher of the gospel, to utter things which man never did, and to speak in such a manner as man never did. And this is evident by the context in that Luke iv., for it was his first sermon after his baptism, when the Holy Ghost had anew fallen on him, and he had returned 'full of the Holy Ghost,' as Luke iv. 1; and again in ver. 14 he returned (or went) 'full of the Holy Ghost' into Galilee, his ordinary standing diocese for his ordinary preaching, as the evangelists shew.

5. The Holy Ghost anointed him with power to do all his miracles, and all the good he did; so in Acts x. 38, 'He was anointed with the Holy Ghost and with power: going about doing good, and healing all that were oppressed of the devil;' whom it is expressly said he cast out 'by the Spirit,' Mat. xii. 28.

6. When Christ was dead, who was it raised him up from the grave? Which work was so great a work, as God himself accounts it as a new begetting, or making him anew, and as it were a second conception of him, a new edition of his Son Christ: Acts xiii. 33, 'He raised up Jesus again: as it is written in the second Psalm, Thou art my Son, this day

have I begotten thee.' God rejoiceth, as having but then recovered and found his Son, that was as it were lost in the likeness of sinful flesh. Now, who was the immediate cause of this new advancement, whereby he was born into the other world ? The Holy Ghost : Rom. viii. 11, ' But if the Spirit of him that raised up Jesus from the dead dwell in you, he that raised up Christ from the dead shall also quicken your mortal bodies, by his Spirit that dwelleth in you.' God by his Spirit raiseth up both Christ and us.

7. When he ascended, who filled him with that glory ? The Holy Ghost : Ps. xlv., he was ' anointed with the oil of gladness above his fellows ;' which oil, Acts x. 38, is said to be the Holy Ghost.

8. It was the Holy Ghost that solemnly anointed him as king in heaven : Acts ii. 33, ' Being at the right hand of God, and having received of the Father the promise of the Holy Ghost,' &c. Peter's inference from this is, ver. 36, ' Therefore let all the house of Israel know assuredly, that God hath made that same Jesus, whom ye have crucified, both Lord and Christ.'

9. It was and is the Holy Ghost that proclaims him Christ in all men's hearts. He sets the crown upon him there also, as well as in heaven, in so much that no man could ever come to acknowledge him the Christ but from the Spirit : 1 Cor. xii. 3, ' No man can say Jesus is the Lord, but by the Holy Ghost.' So as whatever right he had in his person, or by his Father's designation (of which in Acts ii. 36, Rom. xiv. 9), yet it is the Spirit that publicly proclaimed him such, brought him in all his subjects ; or, to use Christ's own words, ' He it is that glorifies me, shewing it to them,' John xvi. 14. All this he hath done to and for Christ our head.

CHAPTER IV.

His operations upon the church, the body of Christ ; and that first as col-
lectively taken, the whole thereof.

II. Let us now consider the operations of the Holy Ghost in and upon the church, collectively taken, as the body of Christ.

1. He was the first founder of the church of the New Testament. The apostle, writing to the Ephesians, who (as you know) had formerly gloried of their temple of Diana as one of the seven wonders of the Gentile world, sets before them, chap. ii., an infinitely far greater and more glorious temple, whereof they themselves, he tells them, were a part, even the church universal of the New Testament, consisting of Jew and Gentile : Eph. ii. 21, ' A building fitly framed together, that groweth up into an holy temple in the Lord.' But then, who is the builder and framer of this fabric, age after age, till all is perfect ? And through whom also is it that this temple, when built, is consecrated unto God for a mansion-house or habitation, who hath the whole world to dwell in ? The 22d verse shews both, ' In whom' (namely, Christ) ' ye' (Ephesians) ' are also builded up together for an habitation of God through the Spirit ;' which in the coherence with the former, is as if he had said, He that made you, the Ephesians, a church (which was as a particular member of that uni-versal body), as ' members in particular,' 1 Cor. xii. 27, the same Spirit was the builder of that great cathedral in which are comprehended all par-ticular churches as smaller oratories ; so as he is the great founder of all,

both in the whole, yea, of every member that worships therein. Thus, in ver. 18, 'Through him' (namely Christ) 'we have both' (Jew and Gentile) 'access to God' (but) 'through the Spirit.' Yea, he is the soul of this one body; Eph. iv. 4, 'There is one body and one Spirit.' Christ bears the relation of head to this body; but who is the universal soul, which is in all, and every part of it? It is the Holy Ghost; and oh! how glorious a church and body shall Christ have, when all are met and set together, and filled full of this Spirit at the latter day! Eph. v. 27. At that day it is he will 'present it to himself a glorious church, not having spot, or wrinkle, or any such thing.' Thus spake the husband, the head, of this spouse. But who is the soul that gives this beauty, that formed this symmetry of all the members, and adds life to all? The Holy Ghost. And now, let us think what a mighty and vast work this of forming and building the universal church is, whereof this Holy Spirit is the former and effecter. There was a perfect pattern and platform of the whole and every member thereof in God's breast, an *idea* also in Christ's (as appears by the last-cited Eph. v.) which this Spirit will bring in the end the whole unto, and frame each living stone in the building to bear a due, suitable, and comely proportion in the whole, and each to other. And this is, and hath been providentially a-doing and a-framing in every part thereof, in all and every age, and hath been wrought from the beginning of the world, in the several parcels apart, even as each piece of tapestry in hangings use to be wrought in little bits and small parcels, which, when finished, are then at last set together. And this Spirit, who is the *dedolator*, the architectonical master-workman, hath in his eye every degree of grace he works in every of these members' hearts who is a stone in this building, according to the pattern which the Father and Christ have in their *idea* and model, of every particular, as also of the whole, and exactly frames each and the whole unto their mind, and misseth not the least of the set proportion in the pattern, which, in so long, so various, and multifarious a work to do (as this therefore must be supposed), what infinite wisdom and power doth it require, and argues him to be God, that is in God, as the spirit of a man within him, and 'searcheth the deep things of God.'

2. All the means of the church's edification (as the word, ministry, and all gospel ordinances) all which are the goods and chattels, the household-stuff of the church universal ('Paul and Apollos are theirs'), these are all of him, and blessed by him. He wrote the Scriptures, 2 Peter i. 21, gave the prophecies, 1 Peter i. 11, revealed the gospel, Eph. iii. 5, in such a manner and measure, and with such an enlargement as never before, to the sons of men.

The care of all that great affair of the ministry, and the work thereof, is incumbent on him, lies on his hands to manage. In the New Testament we find him once immediately speaking in his own person, and taking on him as a person (as the Father had done afore when he said, 'This is my well-beloved Son'); and the occasion was particular about the execution of this work of the ministry, it is in Acts xiii. 2, 'The Holy Ghost said, Separate me Barnabas and Saul for the work whereunto I have called them.' In which effort of his, he speaks as one entered upon an office or work committed to him, and betrusted with him. And it is as if he had said, this is my work proper to me, I am the immediate governor and administrator herein; for all that any way concerns the edification of the church is committed to my management and care. And he says he had designed Paul and Barnabas to one part, as Peter and John to another, Gal. ii., yea, all their gifts are his, in him, and he as a person that is the sovereign thereof, 'distributes them as he will,' 1 Cor. xii. 4, 7. He makes ministers, John xx. 22. And that power to declare that sins are forgiven, and so set free men's consciences, is from their having received the Holy Ghost first, 'Christ breathed on them, and said, Receive ye the Holy Ghost;' and then adds, 'Whose sins ye remit, are remitted.' And as he makes ministers, so he sends out ministers, Acts xiii. 4; and in vain it is for them to go until he comes upon them. The apostles are therefore commanded to stay going forth into the world till they should have received the Holy Ghost, Acts i. 8. He appoints the place and people any of them should go unto, and forbids and hinders where they should not be usefully employed. He gives them orders : he bids Philip go to the eunuch, Acts viii. 29 ; and Acts xi. 12, he sends Peter to Cornelius ; and on the other side, he forbids to preach to such or such. Paul and Timothy were forbidden of the Holy Ghost to preach in Asia, Acts xvi. 6 ; and they again 'essayed to go into Bithynia: but the Spirit suffered them not,' ver. 7. And when they preach, it is he prompts them with their sermons, Mark xiii. 11. The apostles 'spake as the Spirit gave them utterance,' and when they spake, they spake apophthegms, as the word is, weighty sayings : 1 Cor. ii. 13, 'Which things we speak, not in the words which man's wisdom teacheth, but which the Holy Ghost teacheth ; comparing spiritual things with spiritual;' that is, suiting expressions to the gravity and weight of the things delivered. He fires their tongues and hearts, that they should not speak mere empty and powerless words, nor shoot powder, but fiery bullets, such as have warmth and life in them. And when they preach, he makes their sermons to be the ministration of the Spirit, to convey himself unto their hearts, and to make the gospel 'the power of God unto salvation.' All the power of sermons is from the Holy Ghost : 1 Thes. i. 5, 'Our gospel was not in word only, but in power, and in the Holy Ghost;' 1 Peter i. 11, 12, the gospel is said to have been preached 'with the Holy Ghost sent down from heaven,' who waiteth and watcheth when ye come to sermons, and at the speaking such a word as will do your hearts good, he falls upon you : Acts x. 44, 'Whilst they were speaking these words, the Holy Ghost fell on them.' I might shew the same in all the ordinances, but of them after.

For a conclusion. It may be truly said (as it hath been by some of the ancients) that as Christ was the fulfiller of the law, and the end of the law (Rom. x.), so that the Spirit is the complement, the fulfiller, and maker good of all the gospel, * otherwise all that Christ did would have profited us nothing, if the Holy Ghost did not come into our hearts and bring all home to us. Christ made his will by his death, Heb. ix ; but the Spirit is his administrator. Christ's blood and purchase gave us, by his redeeming us, *jus ad rem ;* but the Holy Ghost, by applying it, only *jus in re ;* he gives us possession, livery, and seisin. Himself is the *Arrha :* the earnest and the investiture of all is by him. The promises had been but as blanks eise to us ; but it is the Holy Ghost is the sealer of us by them, the verifier of them, 2 Cor. i. 20, 22. Christ also came, and delivered his commands to his apostles, to teach his church to do them, as in Mat. xxviii. 20 ; but withal it is expressiy said of him, and that after his being risen again, that he gave those his commands to them by the Holy Ghost, Acts i. 2. And then again, those great truths he uttered only by word of mouth ; but it was the Holy Ghost which recovered them when they were almost lost,

---

* Christus legis, Spiritus evangelii complementum.—*Tertul.*

and in a manner clean gone out of the apostles' weak and shallow memories and understandings. And he it was that added a thousand more truths to them, which Christ never uttered ; to whom therefore Christ refers them : John xvi. 12, 13, 'I have yet many things to say unto you, but ye cannot bear them now. Howbeit when he, the Spirit of truth, is come, he will guide you into all truth ; for he shall not speak of himself ; but whatsoever he shall hear, that shall he speak.'

Only by the way, let ministers and Christians take notice what is the glory of the ministry, even the Holy Ghost. Thus Paul himself, 1 Cor. ii. 4, 'My speech and my preaching was not with enticing words of man's wisdom, but in demonstration of the Spirit and of power.' The phrase, 2 Cor. iii. 6, is, 'He hath made us able ministers of the Spirit.' The words in that text are indeed 'ministers of the New Testament,' but it follows in the same verse, 'not of the letter, but of the Spirit.' And this New Testament, or the gospel, says the apostle, ver. 3, is ministered by us ' with the Spirit of the living God.' Our abilities lie in our being made more or less instruments, by whom the Holy Ghost is pleased to communicate himself. Acts xi. 24 it is said, Barnabas was 'a good man, and full of the Holy Ghost,' in his own person ; 'and much people was added to the Lord.' A preacher, in the primitive language, is termed, 'He that ministereth the Spirit,' Gal. iii. 2, 5. And therefore value ministries by this ; and let ministers seek to be filled with the Holy Spirit. It is still prefaced of their preaching, such or such an one was filled with the Holy Ghost, and spake, as Acts iv. 8, and Acts ii. 3, 4.

CHAPTER V.

His operations in every part and member of the church and body of Christ.

III. It is next to be considered what the Holy Ghost doth in every part and member of this body of Christ, the church ; what he doth for every particular saint. For look, what he is to, and in the church universal, that he is first unto, and in, every saint in particular ; for it is the particular individual saint that makes up the church universal ; even as reason is first and principally in every particular and individual man ; and by means thereof it is that reason is found, and so abounds in a body or assembly of men. They meeting together, every one severally brings a portion of it with him thereunto ; so as the main of his work lies and consists in what he doth in and to every member. And when he falls upon assemblies of saints as met, yet it is so as he falls on the whole, by visiting the particular souls so assembled, and out of respect unto each single soul ; as when the rain falls upon a field of corn, it falls upon the whole for every particular blade's sake, watering every stalk at its root, and so all grow up together. Hence therefore, Acts ii., where the fulfilling of those promises made in the 14th and 15th chapters of John, were in the first fruits of them accomplished, it is expressly indigitated that ' the Spirit sat upon each of them :' ver. 3, 'And they were all' (that is, every one of them) ' filled with the Holy Ghost ;' as organ pipes use to be with the common blast of the bellows that breathes wind into them, though by the difference of the pipes there is a differing sound. And thus the Holy Ghost doth, as one Spirit, inform and inspire the whole body of Christ, as the soul doth the whole body of a man. Eph. iv. 4, 'There is one body, and one Spirit,' and the Spirit is the same in every member. Now consider with yourselves, if there were but one common soul (as some have feigned to be in the system of the world) which acted, and enlivened every man and thing in the world, you would acknowledge that it must be a mighty, vast, and burthensome work which is incumbent upon that great soul (whatever it were), and which it undergoes at every moment. But thus it is in reality with this great Spirit, the soul of the whole church, who both informs and enliveneth the whole, and every member of it.

What therefore is next to be considered, is the activity of this Holy Spirit upon us, and in working in us.

1. First, in general; he worketh no less than *all* that is wrought, 1 Cor. xii. 11, ' But *all* these *worketh* that one and self-same Spirit, dividing to every man severally as he will.' As of Christ, who is the Word, it is said in the point of the first creation (John i. 3), that 'without him there was not anything made that was made;' so of the Spirit in this new creation we may say, that without him there is not anything wrought in us that is wrought.

But let us consider particularly his works.

(1.) In regeneration, which is his prime work in us.

He is the author of all the principles or habits of grace, of that whole new creature, of that workmanship created to good works, the spiritual man, which is called *spirit;* that divine nature, which is the mass and lump of all things pertaining to life and godliness; that which is born of the Spirit, John iii. 6; the image of Christ, which is styled ' Christ formed in us,' Gal. iv. 19. That divine nature is the image drawn. But who is the immediate former, the limner? It is the Spirit of God; 2 Cor. iii. 18, ' We are changed into the same image from glory to glory, even as by the Spirit of the Lord.' And that place shews that not only the first draught of that image is of his drawing, the ground colours, but all the additional lines that follow after, to perfect it all along, from one end of the work to the other. For he attributes that continual change wrought after conversion, in every degree of it, ' from glory to glory,' unto this Spirit. And therein he so speaks of himself and these believing Corinthians, yea, all believers. ' We are thus changed ' all along by beholding, &c. All the changes into that image are by the Spirit of the Lord. No hand hath skill or power to add to this work; none able to mingle colours orient and lively enough but he. In the same chapter the believing Corinthians are declared to be ' the epistle of Christ,' so far as they were or shewed themselves Christians in reality. And Christ and his graces are the perfect original and exemplar; and these Corinthians, so far as they had advanced in Christianity, were for essential parts the entire copy, which in some degree does express to the life that original. And there is not a letter or tittle added in the copy which is not found in him, 2 Cor. iii. 3, ' For ye are manifestly declared to be the epistle of Christ, ministered ' (indeed says the apostle) ' by us ' (as the pens), ' but written with the Spirit of the living God; not with ink, nor in tables of stone, but in fleshly tables of the heart:' unto the draught of the least line of which no art or pencil of man can reach, or hath colours orient enough to write it. For all and every tittle, every stroke, is no other than an inward living disposition of heart, like unto the divine life and nature of Christ, the Son of the living God, and therefore requires the living power of the Spirit of the living God (as he is there styled) to concur to the creating of it; Ps. li. 10, 11, ' Create in me a clean heart, O God, and renew a right spirit within me. Cast me not away from

thy presence, and take not thy Holy Spirit from me.' For as he vouchsafes to become the ink, so he bears the part of a hand, too, of a ready
writer. The Spirit is the finger of God (Mat. xii. 28, compared with Luke
xi. 20), the sole artist that guides those pens that cast this ink, as there
also (in ver. 6) it follows : ' God hath made us able ministers of the New
Testament ; not of the letter ' (for even that New Testament hath also letter
to men unregenerate, and is but the dispensation of a notion), ' but of the
Spirit,' or power.

Let us go over the particular actings of the soul, which are as a drawing
out of those created principles, whether at or in our first conversion or
afterwards ; and we shall find that each and every particular thereof are
attributed to this Spirit.

[1.] Hast thou seen thy sinful condition, and been humbled, as to hell,
for it ? It is the Spirit's proper work, for which he was sent. Thus says
Christ, John xvi. 8, ' When he is come he shall convince the world of sin.'
And he says it to his apostles, when he was to send them into the world
to convert men. And this is the first work of the three there rehearsed,
that the Holy Spirit beginneth with, in conversion, viz., a conviction of a
state of sin and unbelief. As it follows, ' of sin, because they believed not
on me,' and consequently, of damnation, as having lived without God and
Christ in the world ; and this work, though it may seem too low for him,
yet he is pleased to bear a title from it, and is termed a Spirit of bondage
to us, as causing us to see our bondage to sin, and death, and hell : Rom.
viii. 15, ' For ye have not received the Spirit of bondage again to fear ; but
ye have received the Spirit of adoption, whereby we cry, Abba, Father.'
It is one and the same Spirit there spoken of, in respect of two contrary
operations, who hath the title there of both. It is the Holy Ghost who is
that Spirit of adoption there spoken of, whereby we (afterwards) cry, Abba,
Father. This you may also see, Gal. iv. 6, and in the next ver. 16 of that
Rom. viii. It is the Spirit who also ' witnesseth to us that we are the sons
of God ;' and by the opposition it will follow that if the Holy Ghost be the
Spirit of adoption spoken of, that he also was that Spirit of bondage ; inasmuch as he doth discover to us our bondage ; even as he is termed the
Spirit of adoption, because he testifies our sonship. And the discovery
of this our bondage is an infinite favour. For do not the great and wise
ones of the world go hoodwinked quick to hell in a moment, and know not
whither they are going until they are there ? And of thyself thou couldst
never have been thoroughly convinced of that ; for the heart is deceitful
above measure, who can know it ? None without the light of this Spirit.
For it is the spirituality of the law whereby he instructs men to know
wisdom in the hidden point of their corrupt nature, as David, confessing it,
speaks, Ps. li., 5th and 6th verses compared together, ' Behold, I was
shapen in iniquity ; and in sin did my mother conceive me. Behold, thou
desirest truth in the inward parts ; and in the *hidden part* thou shalt make
me *to know wisdom.*' And without the light of which law the same David
likewise confesseth, Ps. xix. 12, ' Who can understand his errors ? cleanse
thou me from secret faults.' By which secret sins he understands the immediate ebullitions of corrupt nature. And it is he that ' searcheth the
deep things of God,' 1 Cor. ii. 10 ; the hidden wisdom, ver. 7 ; hid in God,
Eph. iii. 9 ; and reveals it to us, ver. 5. It is he, the same Spirit, that
searcheth the deep deceitfulness of men's hearts, and reveals it to them,
which David called wisdom in the hidden part. And it is THOU (says he
of God) that makest me to know it ; that is, thou by thy Spirit, who

knowest all things, 1 Cor. ii. 10. And this for him to vouchsafe to do for him, to take the same pains to do it, as ever mother or schoolmaster took to teach a child from his alphabet to read, is an act of infinite grace. It is he that gives thee eyes to see, and an heart to understand, who holds the candle to thee, and points with his finger to every sin. Let us all consider the unpleasingness of this work, which were it not that it is necessary for his saving thee, he who is the Holy Spirit would never rake into such foul and filthy jakes and dunghills of lusts and by-ends, unbelief and presumptions. This must needs be a loathsome work to him, by reason of the objects he is exercised in, and tedious in itself. And this is the entrance into conversion.

[2.] It is this Spirit which works repentance upon this discovery of sin, and turns our hearts from sin to God effectually. John the Baptist came preaching ' the baptism of repentance for the remission of sins.' Now by what, or whose power was it, that repentance was wrought in the hearts of multitudes that were his hearers? It was the Holy Spirit. ' He shall come' (says the prophet) ' in the spirit and power of Elias,' Mal. iv. 6. The spirit of Elias was the Holy Ghost, resting on him (2 Kings ii. 15), as he did on the Baptist: Luke i. 15, ' He shall be filled with the Holy Ghost, even from his mother's womb.' And it is spoken to signify the power that should accompany his ministry, to work repentance, as it follows in the next verse ; ' And many of the children of Israel shall he turn to the Lord his God.' And thereupon it is, that this prophecy of Malachi's is alleged, ver. 17, ' He shall come in the spirit and power of Elias, and turn the hearts of the disobedient to the wisdom of the just.' So as that which is spoken of Paul's ministry among the Thessalonians, 1 Thes. i. 5, that it came ' not in word only, but in power, and in the Holy Ghost,' might (though in a lower degree) be said of his. And yet the first and eminent effect of his ministry was seen in the working of repentance, as it is often said, in Acts 13th and 19th chapters. It may likewise be observed, as serving to th's purpose, that when Christ gave that new commission to his apostles, to preach repentance in his name unto all nations, for the remission of sins (as in Luke xxiv. 47), he withal renews ' the promise of the Father,' which was the Holy Ghost; ver. 49, ' Behold, I send the promise of my Father upon you.' And why is that annexed to the former, as the preface thereto, ' And behold,' shews, but because the giving of the Holy Ghost, even after Christ's ascension, was to work repentance in men's hearts by that their preaching? Yea, and he commands them (as with a caution, in the following words), that they should tarry in the city of Jerusalem, until they were endued with power from on high. Without whom, and the power of whom, their preaching repentance would have had no efficacy at all, to move men to turn unto God ; but through whose operation God gave Israel, Acts v. 31, 32, yea, and the Gentiles, repentance unto life, Acts xi. 18.

[3.] The work of faith is of his operation; and therefore he is styled ' The Spirit of faith,' 2 Cor. iv. 13. And the same Spirit that wrought faith in the New Testament, is said to have done it in the Old, as that place shews ; 2 Cor. iv. 13, ' We having the same Spirit of faith,' &c.; the same which David and they in the Old Testament had. It is therefore also, that to be full of the Holy Ghost and of faith are joined; Acts vi. 5, ' Stephen, a man full of faith, and of the Holy Ghost:' also Barnabas is said to be ' a man full of the Holy Ghost, and of faith,' Acts xi. 24.

Let us view some special acts of faith, and see how the working of them is ascribed to the Holy Ghost.

First; He gave thee a spiritual sight of Christ and God's free grace, which drew thy heart unto them.

He gave thee a sight of God's free grace, when thou hadst seen thy sins and thy undone condition, and thy heart was thrown off the hinges of thy former hopes on self-righteousness, and the bladders of presumptions upon God's mercy upon false grounds pricked and fallen; and thou wert left utterly at the loss, and knewest not what to do to be saved. Who was it opened to thee the first ' door of hope' (Hosea ii.), and gave thee the first ken, hint, and glimpse of grace and mercy; and that God would abundantly and freely pardon thee, if thou wouldst seek him and ply thyself to him ? Who was it then that laid before thee that all-sufficient righteousness of faith; and that did set thy heart on work to seek it? Even the good Spirit, who is therefore called ' The spirit of grace and supplication,' Zech. xii. 10. He became a Spirit of grace, in making a discovery of that rich and free grace in God's heart to be inclining towards thee, and therewith became the Spirit of supplication in thee, inflaming thee, as a condemned man for life, to seek after that grace and pardoning mercy in God. And from thence he led thee to the cross of Christ, and made and set such a lively picture of him, as crucified before thine eyes (Gal. iii. 1), as all angels and men could never have pourtrayed, no more, yea, infinitely far less, than they can the sun. It was he, the same Spirit of grace, that did it; and so it follows, Zech. xii. 10, ' And they shall look upon him whom they have pierced.' Thus also, John xvi. 8, it is said, ' When he is come, he shall convince the world of righteousness ' (which Christ there enumerates as the Spirit's second work in calling us); even of that all-sufficient right-eousness of Christ, offered up for satisfaction to the Father; who was ' made sin, that we might be made the righteousness of God in him.' And when the word of faith sounded in thy heart and ears, thou hadst not eyes to see it; therefore this ' fountain for sin and uncleanness to wash in ' must be ' opened' (as it is said, Zech. xiii. 1), or men descry it not. Thou wert ready to perish for thirst, as Hagar was, Gen. xxi., and lifted up thy voice and weptest. But as God opened her eyes, and she saw a well (ver. 19) just by her: so did the Spirit thine, to spy out Christ and his righteousness, which is hid unto the world. As I heard one say on his deathbed, Oh ! where had I been if I had not spied out Christ ! It was this Spirit of grace who caused thee to look towards him, and first set thy eyes and heart to see him, and look on him that was pierced, as all that are saved should be brought to do, as they did on the brazen serpent, John iii. 14, 15.

Secondly; When thou didst find (being come to this fountain) that the well was deep, and thou hadst not wherewith to draw; and while thou wert but looking down into it, with a longing eye after it; but couldst not reach into it, to wash thyself in it; but layest as that poor impotent man did at the pool, utterly without strength (as John v.) to have stepped in : it was then the Holy Ghost sprinkled of it upon thy heart, and caused thine iniquity to pass away (1 Pet. i. 2); ' Through sanctification of the Spirit, and sprinkling of the blood of Jesus Christ.' The blood indeed is the blood of Jesus, but the sprinkling (in that place) is attributed to the Spirit, as well as obedience. It was Christ shed that blood (it is therefore there called the blood of Jesus Christ), but it is the Spirit that sprinkleth it, and he sprinkleth it with both hands, on thy heart, to wash away thy spots; and therefore in ver. 22 they are said to have ' purified their souls in obeying the truth, through the Spirit:' which is spoken of the obedience of faith for justification, as well as sanctification ; as the parallel words of the same apostle, in Acts xv. 8, 9, compared, shew : ' God giving unto them the Holy Ghost, even as he did to us, and put no difference between us and them, purifying their hearts by faith.' And in 1 Cor. vi. 11, justification as well as sanctification is attributed to the Spirit : ' But ye are washed, but ye are sanctified, but ye are justified in the name of the Lord Jesus, and by the Spirit of our God.' ' But ye are washed,' that is the general ; ' but ye are sanctified, but ye are justified ' (two distinct benefits), ' justified in the name of the Lord Jesus, and by the Spirit of our God.' Both of these are by both Christ and the Spirit ; as justification is in the name of the Lord Jesus, so is sanctification too ; and by the like reason they were both justified ' by the Spirit of our God.' It is Jesus Christ's name affords the merit and virtue for both, but the Spirit is the applier of them and all other blessings.

Thirdly ; And when thou hast been brought to close with Christ for justification and righteousness, who was it brought thee to the Father to be justified by him also (' who justifies the ungodly,' Rom. iv. 5), and who gave thee access to him, when thou stoodest trembling, not daring to approach to a consuming fire, and everlasting burnings ? It is ' through Christ we have access ' (manuduction) ' by one Spirit unto the Father,' Eph. ii. 18. It is both *through* Christ, and *by* the Spirit, who leads us, as well as Christ. And indeed, Christ leads us to the Father (as it were) with one hand, and the Holy Ghost by the other. Yea, it was this Spirit that taught thee to call God Father (Rom. viii. 15, Gal. iv. 6), and therewith to seek adoption from him.

Fourthly; When thou art once justified by faith, and hast that righteousness imputed to thee, who is it hath hitherto kept, and continues to keep thine heart fixedly to wait for, and hold to that righteousness alone for thy salvation ? And who is it withholds thee from betaking thyself to any other for justification ? Who settles thy hopes solely on it ? It is even this Spirit : Gal. v. 5, ' For we through the Spirit wait for the hope of righteousness by faith.' Justification by faith (as we know) is the eminent subject of that epistle ; and these words come in in the midst of many other lesser additional persuasives, which he useth last, after the doctrinal arguments in the former chapters, tending all to this, that they should stand fast in that liberty which ver. 1 of this chapter begins with, and which the righteousness of Christ endows us with ; and that they should renounce that of works in the point of justification.

We, says he, that is, the generality of believers, Jew and Gentile, of weak and strong faith, we all do steer this way ; and therefore you that turn aside to the works of the law for your justification do sever yourselves from the faith common to the church. With which accords that of the apostle Peter, 2 Peter i. 1, ' To them that have obtained like precious faith with us ' (apostles, namely), ' through the righteousness ' (ἐν δικαιωσύνῃ) ' of God and our Saviour Jesus Christ.' This was the true and common faith of apostles, and all in those times.

Do wait (says he), that is, we not only did rely upon that righteousness wholly for our first justification (as the papists distinguish), being necessitated unto that alone then, because as then we had no other works to rely upon, but of nature and unregeneracy (which upon conversion are discovered to be dead works), but ever since we abide by it, and depend upon that alone for our justification afterward, and that now, when we have other manner of works of true holiness and sincerity renewed in us, and which increase more and more in us; which (if any works could or might) would entice us over to join them with Christ, as a ground of our confidence for justification. But we are immoveably constant unto this righteousness by faith, and the hope that is from it, for time to come; and this continually, all along the remainder of our lives. 'Do wait,' says he, 'for the hope of the righteousness by faith.' Those words, *of righteousness by faith*, are a distinction, severing it from that of works, and is an indigitation that he meant that to be the righteousness, which had been the subject of his discourse. For otherwise, that word, *to wait*, did sufficiently import that by faith they were expectants of it, without that addition.

Those words, *for the hope of righteousness*, are an extensive speech, and spoken in many respects, especially three.

1. It respects a waiting for justification still to come upon us, from that righteousness. Hope is of what is yet to come; and we not only lay hold on that righteousness to be justified by it at present, but we wait for the hope of justification by it for ever. For we are to be justified continually all along the remainder of our lives; for it is *actus continuus* or *perpetuus;* and therefore our hopes of justification are to be continued and kept up, and we depend wholly on that righteousness which is by faith, as well as when we were converted at first, or do at this day. It is called an 'everlasting righteousness,' Dan. ix. 24. And it is but one and the same righteousness first and last which we wait for.

2. We wait for that eternal life (which is frequently termed our hope, and the hope of glory), both after death and at the day of judgment, as the conjunct consequent of this righteousness; for glory is an inheritance entailed upon that righteousness of justification, as the holy apostle informs us: Tit. iii. 7, 'That being justified by his grace, we should be made heirs according to the hope of eternal life.' And at that day it is that justification and forgiveness of sins is with the solemnity of those words ('Come ye and inherit,' &c.) finally to be pronounced, and admission thereupon is to be given into eternal glory.

3. Among the persons here expressed by the word *we*, whose example he presseth upon these unsettled Galatians, it falls out that there are true believers who have sought God much and long, for the justification by faith through Christ's righteousness, and the assurance of it; and God hath been pleased to defer the manifestation of it to their souls. And there were others that had obtained an assurance of it in some good degree, and yet either through sins renewed, and other sad and dark temptations, have been weakened in their faith about it. And in that case there are other ways for relief and comfort besides this of the righteousness of faith, that are ready to offer themselves unto such souls, or otherwise are apt to faint in waiting (as the Psalmist speaks of himself), and to have their souls 'made sick,' (as Solomon speaks of ' hope deferred '), and are ready to grow weary, and give over waiting for the Lord any longer. Now in such a case, who is it that giveth those poor souls (who make the greatest number of believers) patience of hope to wait? Lam. iii. 29, 'He putteth his mouth in the dust, if so be there may be hope,' and causeth them to wait (as there it is also said), and causeth them to wait on till God shall reveal himself to their souls (which is the thing I cited this place for, and have opened as I have done). It is even the Spirit. And for his great honour, it is added by the apostle, ' We, *through the Spirit*, wait.' It is one of his greatest works in us to hold our hearts constantly fixed to this righteousness, and to settle our whole expectation upon it, and to continue so to do, that we may look

unto no other righteousness for justification and salvation.   These Galatians
having at their first calling embraced Christ nakedly, and him alone, for
justification, as ver. 7 and 8 insinuates, ' Ye did run well,' says he ; ' who
did hinder you, that ye should not obey the truth ?   This persuasion cometh
not of him that calleth you.'   One true cause that so many of them afterward had fallen to the doctrine of works was that they would not wait by
pure faith, at which this place also glanceth.   They would see something
in themselves, as a ground of a believing on Christ, and so had recourse to
themselves, to their own doings and actings, for a foundation of it ; at least
to join them in commission with Christ to justify them.   A new convert in
Christianity, such an one especially, is in a great danger of thus diverting ;
for the spirit that is within us would of itself go that way, unless powerfully detained from it by this other blessed Spirit in us.   The law is ingrafted in every man by nature, and was in pure nature of innocency,
which knew no other way for justification but by a man's own righteousness,
and it was the law of nature to be thereby justified.   And this new nature
that is begotten in a Christian is, in the groundwork of it, materially a conformity to the same law ; and the law is continued under grace to be a tutor
to instruct it how to walk in truth of holiness.   And hence the heart is
apt to listen to the other dictates of it even in the point of justification also.
And again it is man's own righteousness which Paul, after many years' experience of the righteousness of faith, was yet by reason of the propensity
of nature to it, afraid to be found in, Phil. iii.   And the dispositions of
righteousness that are renewed in us, and the duties we perform, do often
offer their help to supply the room of faith, giving us confidence ere Christ
comes.   And Christ, to try us, stays often long (as Samuel did his coming
to Saul) ere he reveals himself.   And as Abraham, waiting long for a child,
turned aside to Hagar, so do we to works.   Now in all these hazards, who
took thee by the hand, and taught thee the way of sheer faith, and then
afterward the way of bare waiting upon God ?   Who instructed thee by a
strong hand, and would not suffer thee to go in the way of the law, but
strengthened and secretly supported thy spirit in waiting till God should 'rain
down righteousness,' as the prophet speaks ?   It was this good Spirit ; and
nothing else could or had been able to have done it in thee, but that Spirit
who moved on the chaos when it was darkness, and but one step from
nothing, and newly come out of nothing, and ready to return unto nothing
again ; and who by his almighty power upheld, hatched, and supported it
from falling into nothing, Gen. i.   It is the same good Spirit who enliveneth
and inspiriteth such a soul in its confessions.   It was he who fostered and
maintained and kept up this resolved purpose in thy heart, to remain comfortless for ever, otherwise than by such comforts as Christ and his righteousness should afford thee.   And though thou didst vehemently hunger
and thirst after righteousness of justification, as well as of sanctification, yet
thou wouldst have starved rather than have lived upon thy own bread ; that
is, have trusted to thine own righteousness ; and none but Christ, and his
righteousness, who is ' the Lord our righteousness,' and his alone, was it
would satisfy thee ; yea, that none else should was the fixed resolve of thy
heart.   It is the Spirit guides and leads thee, thus ver. 18 of this 5th
chapter, ' If ye be led by the Spirit, ye are not under the law,' which is spoken
in point of justification.   He took thee by the hand, and gently led thee the
right way therein, as well as (according to what is spoken in respect of
sanctification) he led thee to walk holily.   The Spirit is the leader and con-
ductor in both, as the coherence with his former and his immediate fore

going discourse do shew, and do suit this of these works to be the scope of these words in common to either.

Fifthly: When thou didst attain unto joy and peace in believing, though Christ was the peace-maker, yet who was the peace-bringer? It was the Holy Ghost: Rom. xv. 13, ' Now the God of hope fill you with all joy and peace in believing, that ye may abound in hope, through the power of the Holy Ghost.' All that ' joy unspeakable and full of glory,' 1 Pet. i. 8, that ' peace which passeth all understanding,' Phil. iv. 7, whereby we ' glory in tribulation,' Rom. v. 2, and are ' more than conquerors,' Rom. viii. 37, to whom is it to be ascribed? Whose operation is it? The Holy Ghost's. It is particularly appropriated to him; and therefore it is styled, ' joy in the Holy Ghost:' Rom. xiv. 17, ' The kingdom of God is not meat and drink; but 'righteousness, and peace, and joy in the Holy Ghost.' As God's kingdom consists of these things, so this joy is a peculiar belonging to his Spirit; it is his jurisdiction, it is styled joy in the Holy Ghost; when yet our joy is in God and in Christ objectively, yet in the Holy Ghost efficiently, which is therefore elsewhere styled, ' The joy of the Holy Ghost:' so 1 Thess. i. 6. And the consolations we have are called ' The comforts of the Holy Ghost,' Acts ix. 31, as being the author and diffuser of them into our hearts, &c. In which sense our praying is in like manner said to be in the Holy Ghost (Jude, ver. 20), as the inditer of our prayers, Rom. viii. And it is also thus termed joy in the Holy Ghost, by way of a superlative eminency, in difference from all other joys which have ever entered into the heart of man; and in compare to which all other joys are but as the crackling of thorns, the fuel they are fed with being earthy and terrene. It is a joy ' not as the world giveth' (saith Christ, speaking of his peace). And it therefore hath the peculiar character of glorious joy, as being joy of another kind, and also unspeakable for degrees and abundance; ' more joy than when their corn and wine,' increasing never so much, afforded, Ps. iv. 7. We use to distinguish things that are excellent, by joining the name of the workman, author, or efficient, when in his workmanship he transcendeth all other artists. And so it is in this. All the sweetmeats of heaven (and this joy is the taste of the hidden manna), he hath the keeping and delivery of them out, where and when he will. And not only so, but he tempers them, and all the cordials out of God the Father's love, and Christ's heart and blood, and mingleth his own love with theirs, and puts them into our hearts, conveying them in promises of the word, and fitly and seasonably applies them, and reserves them for us as we need. And though Christ bequeatheth that peace and joy as his last legacy, he being the purchaser of it by his death, yet it is the Holy Ghost that is his administrator and executor of it, to perform it, and execute his will. He it is that maketh known to us that love which hath lain hid in the heart of God the Father towards a particular soul, in choosing him at first, and then giving him to Christ, and giving his Son to die for him. It is he who displays that love which is laid out in infinite wisdom, contriving and ordering all about every man's particular salvation who is saved. It is he likewise that takes of Christ's, and shews and brings home his love in giving himself for every such soul, and causeth it to ' know the love of Christ, which passeth knowledge ;' which he did vouchsafe to our apostle; ' Who loved me' (says he), ' and gave himself for me,' Gal. ii. 20. He shews these things (as Christ's word is), and tells over the stories of them in a way of application and comfort to a man's own heart in particular; and withal, lets in the taste of them; and makes the loves of all the three pass through and through us, even through our very inwards, as oil that soaks into the bones, and refresheth the marrow within them, even this ' oil of gladness,' which is purely of his making.   And he gives an immediate taste of that love fresh out of the heart of God and Christ, and causeth every faculty in its kind to taste how good the Lord is.   He gives us a relish of the sweetness, of the deliciousness of loves; *loves*, in the plural, as it is expressed in Cant. v. 1; which we are made abundantly to drink and taste of, as it is said Cant. v. 1.   In Rom. v. 5, you have it thus expressed, ' Hope maketh not ashamed; because the love of God is shed abroad in our hearts by the Holy Ghost, which is given unto us.'   *Given* us he had been afore, to endow us with justifying faith, and all those glorious fruits of it, which he setly had enumerated; as peace with God, ver. 1; access by faith into grace, ver. 2; rejoicing in hope of the glory of God; glorying in tribulation; and patience working experience; and experience, hope: and that hope rising up, in the end, to a steadiness, solidity, and constancy, as never to be confounded; no, not in a man's own apprehension or fears.   And this hope is wrought by shedding the love of God abroad in the heart, so as never to be violated or temerated by prevailing doubtings any more.   And this he reckons last, as the sum, the complement of all the foregoing privileges.   And this last, as well as all those other, are the effects of the Spirit given us; for he working those other first, and then this of shedding the love of God over and above.   Now that wherein this love of God and Christ materially or objectively doth consist, the apostle tells us in the following 6th, 7th, and 8th verses, that ' God himself hath commended his love to us, that when we were enemies, Christ died for us;' than which there cannot be a higher strain or note that love could reach unto.   Yet the coherence of this place shews, that if the material part of this love should be declared in words never so illustriously, without the power of the Holy Ghost accompanying it, and his shedding that love abroad in the heart; yea, if these very words were used, whereby God himself commends his love by the Holy Ghost himself, as the penman of them; yea, if these words were preached and enlarged upon by the apostles themselves, ay, and by all the angels in heaven too (if they were sent by God to do it), yet they would avail nothing upon our hearts to affect them therewith, without a transcendent operation of this blessed Spirit, whose work and office is to be ' the Comforter.'   Yea further, where this Holy Spirit doth, by this and such like words as those, setting forth the love of God and Christ, perfume and bedew the souls of believers in his ordinary dispensation of faith with the consolations of the Almighty, more or less; yet the text in Rom. v. 5 means and intends, by that shedding abroad God's love, a higher communication of the love of God than those more commonly vouchsafed.   And as there is promised a pouring forth of this Spirit, so there is a pouring forth joys in the Holy Ghost more extraordinary, which in its measure doth exceed the dispensings by the ordinary light of faith believers are accustomed unto. And the reason for this latter dispensation may be resolved unto this, that this Holy Spirit ' searching the deep things of God,' and knowing the height, depth, breadth, and length of his love, to the extremest dimensions of it, and coming immediately upon men's souls from out of the heart of God and Christ, is enabled from thence to bring this their love warm immediately out of their hearts and convey it into ours, and give us a true and native original taste of and from the things themselves, and the sweetness thereof.   And so he sheds it abroad (as the word here is) into every chink and cranny of the soul, thirsting after this love, and brings it as fresh as the mother's milk comes out of the dug into the child's mouth or stomach ; and his love so shed into us by the Holy Spirit, is digested or turned into love in us, and returned on our parts towards God and Christ again.   This is another manner of thing than all the words that ever have been or can be uttered ; yea, though penned by the Holy Ghost himself, speaking the greatest things that can be uttered of this love, and enlarging our minds to the most extensive conceptions of the dimensions of this love, so far as words or arguments by words will avail to do it, though uttered by the tongues of men or angels.   But, when the Spirit by the word (for I speak not of revelations without that word, or besides it), shall add his condiment and seasoning to that love of God set forth in the word, with diffusing joy which passeth understanding, this doth infinitely surpass even such joys ; as he doth sometimes unto some saints vouchsafe.

Sixthly : If we consider all the fellowship and communion we have with the persons of the Father and the Son, we shall find that this Holy Spirit is the introducer of us into it, and the manager and transacter of it in us, and for them with us.   ' Our fellowship is with the Father, and with the Son,' 1 John i. 3.   By means of which it is that our joy mentioned is a full joy, ver. 4.   And all this fellowship is through the help and manifestations of the Holy Ghost: Phil. ii. 1, ' If there be any comfort in love' (which is peculiarly attributed to the Father) ; ' If any fellowship of the Spirit,' who communicates both these.   This place seems to speak, in the matter of it, somewhat parallel to that of the same apostle : 2 Cor. xiii. 14, ' The grace of our Lord Jesus Christ, and the love of God, and the communion of the Holy Ghost be with you all.'   Now it is the love of the Father which ordained Christ and salvation for us ; it is the grace of Christ which works our salvation by redemption ; as you read how grace is in that sense and respect attributed unto Christ, 2 Cor. viii. 9.   But yet it is the Holy Ghost imparts and conveys all things that the Father or Son hath.   He takes them and reveals them to us, and so glorifies them both unto us : John xvi. 14, 15, ' He shall glorify me,' said Christ, ' for he shall receive of mine, and shall shew it unto you.   All things that the Father hath are mine : therefore, said I, he shall take of mine, and shall shew it unto you.' In saying, *All that the Father hath are mine*, he doth plainly affirm that it is the Spirit that shews all that is the Father's to us, as well as Christ, and what is Christ's.   And in that renowned place in the gospel of John, where Christ promiseth that ' he and his Father will come to us, and make their abode with us,' and that he ' will manifest himself to us,' John xiv. ver. 21–23.   Yet in the verse 20 immediately foregoing, Christ says, ' At that day ye shall know that I am in my Father, and you in me, and I in you ;' *in that day*, namely, when he should give and send his Spirit, as by this verse, being compared with verse 16, appears.   And therefore it is, that that fulness of joy which ariseth from the communion with these persons is termed, ' joy in the Holy Ghost' (that is, through the Holy Ghost) ; and the communion of the Holy Ghost, although the objects of that joy are the love and persons of the Father and Son.

Seventhly ; All the evidence and witnessing of all or any grace wrought in us (though not accompanied with joy unspeakable and full of glory), as a love in us to God the Father, Son, and Holy Ghost, they are all of his working, and from him.

Do our own consciences witness to any eminent holy disposition that is written in our hearts, such as the apostle professeth he found in his own heart, even to a willingness to be accursed from Christ, for the glory of

God, and the salvation of his own countrymen the Jews ? The evidence
of this to his conscience was from the Holy Ghost, without whose testimony joined to that of his conscience, his conscience would not have witnessed it. Natural conscience witnesseth the things of the law naturally in
man, Rom. ii., yet gracious dispositions it cannot. Here the apostle himself speaketh himself concerning this matter : Rom. ix. 1–3, 'I speak the truth
in Christ, I lie not, *my conscience also bearing me witness in the Holy Ghost.*
I could wish that myself were accursed from Christ for my brethren, my kinsmen according to the flesh.' When he says, *my conscience bearing me witness in
the Holy Ghost,* he speaks it not only because the Holy Ghost was he that
had wrought that grace in him, but that, in point of his conscience witnessing of it, it was the Spirit who was the cause of that witness. Conscience
indeed was the faculty that was the substance that witnessed this to his
soul, but it was *in* (that is, *from*) the Holy Ghost so testifying with it.
And therefore if that or any other grace in us be evidenced to us, it is he
that is the eminent witness, and causeth that grace to speak so loud as to
witness it : Rom. viii. 16, ' The Spirit itself beareth witness with our spirit
that we are the children of God.' It may be read ' witnesseth *to* our spirit,'
and ' witnesseth *with* our spirit.' And though man hath a reflecting faculty
as a man, which (1 Cor. ii.) the apostle indigitates, ' None knoweth the
things of a man, but the spirit that is in man,' yet the discerning the
things of God, and of his supernatural working in a man, the apostle in
the same place attributes to the Spirit, as the person who works all, and
makes all in us, and also reveals all that to us which he worketh. He
writes first all graces in us, and then teacheth our consciences to read his
handwriting, which we could never do without his light. In 1 John v. ver.
6 and 7, you read of six witnesses, ' three in heaven,' and ' three on earth,'
who are witnesses of two things : 1, Christ to be the Son of God ; 2, To
believers' hearts of their own salvation, as in ver. 1, ' Whosoever believeth
that Jesus is the Christ is born of God,' which also is evident by comparing ver. 13, where both these two are put together, as the things believers
might know, through what he had written in this epistle, especially now
last written in those immediate foregone verses. Now you find there in
these 6th and 7th verses, that the Spirit, or the Holy Ghost, is mentioned in either catalogue ; first, among the witnesses in heaven, ' The
Father, the Word, and the Holy Ghost ;' and yet again this Spirit, that is
a witness in heaven, is yet numbered with those that bear record on earth,
too. Ver. 8, ' The Spirit, the water, and the blood ;' and he, the first,
and as the principal of these on earth, is set before water and blood. One
among other reasons I have apprehended for this, is that he efficiently is
the grand witness with those other two on earth in their witnessing ; and
to whatsoever they bear their testimony, this Spirit joins with them in it,
and brings home their testimony into our hearts ; as without whom and
which their witness would be of no force. As, for example, if Christ's
blood, when believed on, witnesseth to our hearts, by giving our hearts ease
and peace, it is because this Spirit joins with it in its testimony. If water,
or the new creature (begotten of water and this Spirit, the holy Spirit
working as water in cleansing us), if that do testify to us, it is in virtue of
the Holy Ghost's conjecture with it, and irradiation of it, and it is that
which gives its validity of testimony to it : as Rom. viii. 16, ' He witnesseth
with our spirits ;' that is, our graces (or that which is born of the Spirit,
which is spirit), and in the same 1 John v. 6, the apostle resolves all into
this, as the foundation of the other's testimonies, ' It is the Spirit that

beareth witness, because the Spirit is truth.' It is he therefore that bears the name of witness, κατ᾽ ἐξοχήν, as being the 'Spirit of truth,' as Christ also calls him. And truly in that Rom. viii., where it is rendered, 'The Spirit witnesseth with our spirits,' the Holy Ghost, in the original, hath so composed the words, that they import his witnessing *to* our spirits as well as *with* our spirits ; and that witnessing *with* hath a respect to the witness of the other two persons, the Father and Christ, as with whom this Spirit should witness to our spirits ; they all three, the witnesses in heaven, conjoining their testimonies together to persuade our spirit (that is, our souls and graces in them), 'that we are the children of God.' And if so understood, then the witnessing both of the Father and of Christ unto our salvation is eminently attributed to the Spirit, who only is named, as also in witnessing the truth by Christ, and the especial honour thereof is given to him, which accords with that fore-cited speech of Christ, John xvi. 14, 15. And thus he is the great witnesser, both of heaven and of earth, to this of our being the sons of God.

Eighthly; As thus in respect of evidencing our graces to us, and his joining with God the Father and Christ in their testimonies also to us, the Spirit doth the work so as to lead us into all truths of the word and secrets of God whatever, which in this life are revealed ; it is he whom God sends to discover and convince us of them all : 1 Cor. ii. 10, 'He searcheth all the deep things of God.' He is the keeper of all those archives of eternity, and they are all committed to his custody, and he lets us into the view of them, and reveals what is revealed of them unto us ' as he will.' There is not a thing that God hath prepared for us that love him, ver. 9 (which is spoken of the hidden things of the gospel, ver. 7), but he is the manifester of it to one or other of the saints ; it is he leads into all truth : 2 Tim. i. 13 and 14, 'Hold fast the form of sound words, which is in Christ Jesus.' But, alas ! might they say of ourselves, we are apt to let them slip and leak out (as Heb. ii. 1), and to be ' carried away with every wind of doctrine,' Eph. iv. (this we are prone to be), therefore he adds, ver. 14, 'That good thing' (so he calls the truth of the doctrine of wholesome words, for *bonum et verum convertuntur*), ' keep by the Holy Ghost which dwelleth in us.' Who also brings them home to our remembrance when we have forgotten them, John xiv. 26.

And as these matters, in point of faith, and assurance, and joy, and all communion with God the Father and the Son, are transacted by this Spirit, together with the revelation of all truths, so,

Ninthly ; If we view all and the whole of the work and works of sanctification that are wrought in us, or proceed from us, it will appear that it is he that works them all in us and for us. This is the third part of the application of salvation to us ; according to that distribution which Christ makes, John xvi. 8, 11, and which he attributes to the Spirit, ' when he is come, he shall convince the world of *judgment*,' that is, of true holiness, sanctification, and reformation of heart and life ; as in the Old Testament frequently, and in the New, that word *judgment* is used, as Mat. xii. 20. That Christ shall ' bring forth judgment to victory,' citing ver. 18 out of the Old, viz., out of Isa. xlii. 1, ' He shall shew judgment to the Gentiles.' And in respect of his working herein, he hath this denomination made appropriate to him, viz., ' a Spirit of judgment,' purging away the filth of sin in his people, Isa. iv. 4. And holiness is called ' the sanctification of the Spirit,' 1 Peter i. 2, and 2 Thess. ii. 13. And for this cause he bears the name of the Holy Spirit, as the eminent efficient of holiness in us.

And accordingly as men have grown up into, and increased more and more in, holiness, they have been said to be filled with the Holy Ghost, as, Luke i. 41, it is said of Elizabeth the mother, and her child the Baptist; and his eminent holiness is expressed by this, ' He shall be filled with the Holy Ghost even from his mother's womb,' Luke i. 15. And the same strain of speech goes on in the New Testament: Acts vi. 3, ' Choose men full of the Holy Ghost and wisdom.' Of Barnabas it was said, ' A good man, and full of the Holy Ghost,' Acts xi. 28; and the super-excelling fulness and eminency of Christ's graces is set out by this measure, that he had ' the Spirit above measure;' for this Spirit's indwelling in him was the fountain and standard of his infinitely transcending holiness.

Let us go over the several particulars of that work.

1. Habitual holiness, and all the principles of holiness. I have shewn afore that they are wholly of his operation, and this our baptism (which is the seal of regeneration, or of the new creature) doth signify in a special manner. The letter of that word Βάπτω imports not simply to *wash*, or to *be washed*, but to be *dyed* also. It is also taken from the dyer's vat, into which what clothes are dipped they carry away in them a new habitual tincture. The Holy Ghost takes a man's heart, and dyes it anew, changeth it. As a cloth goes into the vat of one colour and comes out of it of another, ' so is he who is born of the Spirit:' he goes wholly flesh, comes out spirit in a good degree, ' which two are contrary,' Gal. v.

2. Mortification of sin and to the world is ascribed to the Spirit : Rom. viii. 13, ' For if ye live after the flesh, ye shall die ; but if ye, *through the Spirit*, do mortify the deeds of the body, ye shall live.' It was prophesied by Malachi, Mal. ii. 2, 3, that Christ coming after the Baptist, should ' purify the sons of Levi ' by ' fuller's soap, and the refiner's fire.' Now who is that refiner's fire but this Spirit ? as appears by comparing Isa. iv. 4, where he is styled ' the Spirit of burning,' and ' the Spirit of judgment;' the Spirit of burning, consuming and purging out our dross and filth ; and there also is the prophecy of Christ's coming to ' baptize with the Holy Ghost and with fire,' as the Baptist expounded it ; the Holy Ghost, as it is spoken, partly because what remaining filth his baptism of water had not cleansed out, Christ's Spirit, as fire, should do it ; for, Num. xxxi. 23, the fire is made a stronger purifier than water ; and even of the Baptist himself and his ministry (the Spirit of God accompanying it), it was foretold by Isaiah, chap. xl., that the glory and beauty of the whole creation should be blasted, and caused to fade and wither, as flowers of the grass are by a wind, in and to new converts' hearts, and deading their souls, being deadened unto it, when the voice of the crier should come and preach repentance to the people, and the glory of the Lord (Christ, namely) should be revealed. The grass withered, and the flower faded (ver. 7) in such men's hearts as were savingly wrought upon by his voice and cry. And how came this to pass ? It is added, ' The Spirit of the Lord hath blown upon it.' And the apostle Peter expounding this prophecy, says, That all believers wrought upon by his and the apostle's ministry, had ' purified their souls,' 1 Peter i. 22, by the preaching of the gospel, and then referreth us unto this very place in Isaiah, ' Being born again ;' ver. 23, ' For all flesh is as grass, and the glory thereof as the flower of grass. The grass withereth, and the flower thereof falleth away ; but the word of the Lord endureth for ever; and this is the word which by the gospel is preached unto you, ver. 24 and 25.

3. There is in Scripture ascribed to the Holy Ghost the implantation of

all the contrary graces, which are so often compared to flowers and the gardens of them, and unto trees in orchards and beds of spices, planted artificially by a florist (which is an allusion the Holy Ghost delights to use in that book of Canticles) ; the fruits and flowers whereof shall never fade (as the flower of grass doth), but grow up, and flourish to eternal life ; which flowers, &c., because planted in her heart, the spouse there calleth her garden—' upon my garden '—as also Christ calls it his garden, and both in that one verse, Cant. iv. 16, which, as appears by ver. 12, was her own self. ' An enclosed garden is my sister, my spouse,' says Christ of her, ' a spring shut up, a fountain sealed.' And ver. 13 and 14, ' Thy plants are an orchard of pomegranates, a fountain of gardens, a well of living waters, and streams from Lebanon ;' which is certainly an enumeration of particular graces in their distinction and variety, if we knew how aptly to apply those similitudes in each to what is proper to each. But however, it serves in general to instruct us, that there is such a variety of graces in our hearts, as here of trees in the spouse's heart, * and that the heart of every saint is an orchard to such spiritual plants growing therein ; and in like manner, a garden to a like variety of flowers, as in ver. 12. And various graces are meant by either. And the planting and bringing forth these are all ascribed to the Holy Spirit, as Christ's chief planter. Thus I understand that fore-cited ver. 12, ' A garden enclosed, a spring shut up,' to intend that she had two things enclosed in her heart.

(1.) All sorts of graces, planted as in a garden, as the effects.

(2.) The indwelling of the Spirit, as the spring and producer of all these flowers, and accordingly in ver. 15 she is said to be ' a fountain of gardens, a well of living water, and streams from Lebanon.' Now that well of living water is apparently the Spirit : John iv. 14, ' But whosoever drinketh of the water that I shall give him, shall never thirst ; but the water that I shall give him, shall be in him a well of water springing up into everlasting life ;' which is interpreted to be the Holy Ghost (John vii. 38, 39), which comes as a spring from Lebanon, that is, from that high mountain, even from heaven, from the throne of God and of the Lamb, as Rev. xxi. 1, ' And he shewed me a pure river of water of life, clear as crystal, proceeding out of the throne of God and of the Lamb,' which watereth these flowers ; which well the church hath in her belly, as Christ's word is in that of John the Evangelist, chap. vii. 38. And all these plants in Christ's garden, which is the soul of a believer, are of the Spirit's bringing forth and setting ; for as the earth, watered with fructifying water, brings forth plants as at the first creation, so the soul, bedewed with the Spirit, brings forth ' trees of righteousness, of the planting of the Lord, that he might be glorified,' Isa. lxi. 3 ; which (as appears by comparing ver. 1) is recorded as the effect of Christ's having this Spirit given him : ' The Spirit of the Lord is upon me, to preach the gospel,' whereof this is made the immediate effect, viz., the communicating the same Spirit unto his members, for this end, to plant in them trees of righteousness. Thus it is ascribed unto this Spirit, and ver. 11 of the same chapter it is added, ' For as the earth bringeth forth her bud, and as the garden causeth the things that are sown in it to spring forth, so the Lord God will cause righteousness and praise to spring forth before all nations.' In a word, he is styled the Spirit of grace, Heb. x. 29 as the eminent efficient of all our graces ; and therefore, they that apostatise are said to do despite unto this Spirit, as he is the efficient of all graces and gracious workings.

* Qu. ' garden' ?—Ed.

4. As the planting, so the drawing them forthwith into act, both bud and fruit, and causing them to grow, is his work also.

(1.) The drawing them forth into act, or the acting of them, or the causing them to shoot forth, is ascribed to him. He is that wind which, blowing upon our graces, causeth them to flow out, even as his blowing upon the flower of the grass (as you heard out of Isa. xl.) withers and mortifies the flowers or glories of this world to new converts. And this follows in the next words of the same chapter: Cant. iv. 16, 'Awake, O north wind; and come, thou south; blow upon my garden,' says the spouse, 'that the spices thereof may flow out. Let my beloved come into his garden, and eat his pleasant fruits.' There are two prayers in those word: the *first* to the Spirit, 'Come, thou south wind, and blow;' and the *second* to Christ himself, 'Let my beloved come into his garden' when it shall be thus blown upon. *First*, the wind there apparently is the Holy Ghost, Ezek. xxxvii. 3d, 14th verses compared with 5th, 6th: 'As the wind bloweth where it listeth, so is he that is born of the Spirit.' The Spirit is a quickening wind (the breath of the living God and of Christ), who coming upon a man doth regenerate him, and infuse a new spirit into him, as Christ had there said. And after he is thus quickened and born, a soul new born of the Spirit, then by blowing thereon the same Spirit doth cause him to operate and act as such a new creature, who is so high born, should in some measure do. Insomuch as all and the whole of him who is truly born again is from this Spirit, not only his first begetting, but his after actings; which latter Christ also involves in saying, 'so is he that is born of the Spirit,' supposing him first to have been begotten anew.

If any shall object, that the Spirit is but one and the same Spirit, viz., the person, and how can he be termed both the north wind and the south wind, which are not only diverse, but blow contrary ways? the answer is, It is true the person of the Holy Ghost is one and the same person, as in himself considered, but his being said to be a wind is in respect of his operations upon us; and so his blasts may blow several ways, not only in these two points of the compass there mentioned, but several others; and in this respect he is said to be 'seven spirits,' Rev. i. 7, from whom grace is there prayed for as well as from Christ and the Father. And even the natural wind in the air is one and the same wind for the substance of it, whilst yet it turneth itself about, as God pleaseth, unto several quarters, from north to south, &c. And this objection is preoccupated by the apostle: 1 Cor. xii. 3, 4, 'Now there are diversities of gifts, but the same Spirit;' and so on, ver. 6–8, and 'there are differences of administrations,' &c. Now, both these contrary winds are needful to cause the several graces in believers to flow forth: 'Come,' says the spouse, praying to this Spirit, 'come, and blow upon my garden, that the spices thereof may flow out.' So then the Spirit's operations upon those graces is the blowing upon them; and their exerting that hidden virtue or active power that lies latent in them, through the excitement and actings of the Holy Ghost, is that their flowing forth. And it is as if she had said, I indeed have these plants and graces habitually rooted in me by thee, O holy and blessed Spirit; but I am utterly unable so much as so give forth the least scent or virtue of them (which other plants naturally do) without thy breathing on them, and moving and impregnating of them. Yet even earthly plants yield their fragrancy of themselves yet more strongly and abundantly when the wind drives them to and fro, and exhales the scent out of them; but she, in the sense of her utter inability, prays to the Spirit to come and influence her.

And from hence, by the way, we may observe an instance of a warrant to pray distinctly to the person of the Spirit; as if it had been said by her, Awake, and come, thou Holy Spirit. As likewise to pray distinctly to the person of Christ, as she also doth in these next words, 'Let my beloved come;' and that is, Then be thou also pleased to come and visit thy garden, when first thy Spirit, sent by thee, hath drawn out and educed from out of those plants that are growing therein, those pleasant savours so pleasing to thee, which these my graces, when thus acted by the Spirit, do afford. And indeed the many former prayers and petitions, ever and anon found up and down in this book of the Canticles, do put it out of all question that it is useful for us thus to pray to each person.

There is not so much as the least good thought, nor the least bud which we with all our inherent graces are able to bring forth, unless this Holy Spirit efficaciously blows upon us, 2 Cor. iii. 6. It is the Spirit (says he) who is ζωοποιοῦν, that quickens and gives life; and he speaks this of the Holy Spirit joining with the gospel, even the Spirit of the living God, whom he had under that title mentioned afore in ver. 3. And that his quickening relateth unto all and everything of the Spirit of life within us, even unto the production of but one, a single individual one action, though it also be but the least good thought, is expressly said in ver. 5: 'Not that we are sufficient of ourselves to think any thing as of ourselves; but our sufficiency is of God;' that is, unless God (the living God) by his living Spirit (as in ver. 3) do form it in us, and although the matter of a good thought were cast into our minds, yet as seed thrown into a barren soil, it would sow this in our hearts, it would instantly become a dead work, such as all the works of unregenerate men are, Heb. vi. 1. So that our eyes should be fixed upon and entirely ascribe all that is good in us to this Spirit as the author. And though we and our wills do concur in the acting also, yet he is the efficient of that concurrence in us, causing us to do; yea, and is the cause of every degree of that goodness in our actings, 'dividing to every man severally as he will,' 1 Cor. xii. 11.

3. The Spirit produceth all the spiritual strength we receive, when our hearts are ready to be overborne with temptations, or a lust; or when we want strength to do such and such a work or duty; to suffer, that we may be able to endure in such a trial. It is the Spirit gives strength to the inner man (Eph. iii. 16, compared with Coloss. i. 10 and 11), likeas the Spirit fell on Samson, and gave him strength, who of himself was otherwise but as other men. It was he made Elias so bold and courageous, and the prophet Amos* after him, chap. iii. 8, 'Truly,' says he, 'I am full of power, by the Spirit of the Lord, and of judgment, and of might, to declare to Judah his transgression, and to Israel his sin.' The like he gave the Baptist to tell Herod of his sin, which cost him his life. It was because he came in the power and spirit of Elias. Take the weakest heart that is, as weak as water (as the prophet speaks), and let the Spirit join with it, and mingle himself therewith, and it is too hard and strong for all the world; it will snap asunder tentations, as Samson did his withs. There is a supply of the Spirit, Phil. i. 10, comes in with fresh forces, when we are near to a yielding up the fort, and being led captive, and so he rescues and delivers us. In all our walkings with God, he is our guide and faithful companion, to see to us and keep us out of harm's way. And often when

* 'Micah.'—Ed.

we stumble, he puts under his hand, as the psalmist's word is. And a little help keeps up a man that is falling or reeling, or to recover him again when he is falling. And thus the apostle seems to intend that speech, ' who helpeth our infirmities,' Rom. viii. And those infirmities there are not to be limited to the infirmities that belong to and accompany our prayers only, but which accompany us in all our ordinary walkings. The word συναντιλαμβάνεται supposeth it to be the case of a weak man in himself, who yet further hath a weight or a burden hanging on him, which presseth him down (as of our corruptions, especially some, or such as are more proper to us, as the apostle expresseth, Heb. xii.), who yet having a friend to accompany him in his running the race set before him (as there the apostle's allegory is), he perceiving the weakling's aptness to sink under the weight, does continually relieve him ; and not only shores up and sustains the man, but himself takes the other end of his burden (and the far heavier end), and so helps him to bear it, and go on along with it. And this the apostle expressly there attributes to the Spirit ; and if so be it chanceth that we fall, he is still at hand, a present help (as a present help, as David says), to take us up ; yea, then when we fall into the foulest mire and dirt, and grievously defile ourselves, it is the Spirit that cleanseth us, according to that of the apostle : 1 Peter i. 22, ' We through the Spirit purify ourselves.' And according to that of David : Ps. li., ' Create in me a clean heart' (after he had so foully fallen into uncleanness), and ' take not thy Holy Spirit from me,' verses 10, 11. In this case this gracious Spirit says not (as the harsh spirits of men would say), Even lie there still, since you would needs fall, sprawling in your own filth. Not so this good Spirit : but as if a man (a brother) be overtaken with a fault, those that are spiritual are to take on them to restore, and often do restore, such a man in the spirit of meekness ; how much more will and doth this blessed Spirit, who is he that makes spiritual those that are such, and endues them with that spirit of meekness, out of his own dovelike meekness, restore such an one, and take care of him for ever after, lest he fall so again.

4. He is a Spirit of counsel, powerfully instructing and convincingly teaching how to act and walk, for he directs us to set right steps, and to walk with a right foot, and thereby prevents us of many a sin, by seasonable instruction set on upon our hearts with a strong hand, as Isa. viii. 11. For, as the same prophet says, Isa. xi. 2, he is the Spirit of counsel and of might. 1. Of counsel to direct. 2. Of might, to strengthen the inner man. Such he was to Christ the head, of whom it is there spoken. For instance, in that agony (on the determination of which our salvation depended), and conflict in the garden, when he prayed, ' Let this cup pass,' it was this good Spirit that counselled him to die ; and in Ps. xvi. 7 he blesseth God for it, ' I bless the Lord that hath given me counsel.' It was that counsel that in that case caused his heart to say, ' Not my will, but thine.' When we are out of the way he recalls us, and is 'a voice behind us, saying, This is the way, walk in it ;' and not only thus directs us, but taketh us by the arm, and teacheth us to go, Hos. xi. 3. ' Thy Spirit is good, lead me,' says the psalmist, Ps. cxliii. 10. And therefore it is a usual phrase in Rom. viii. and Gal. iv., our being *led* by the Spirit. And not only so as to direct and lead, but effectually to cause us to walk in his statutes and ways. For,

5. As he is a Spirit of counsel to our understanding part, so an effectual persuader and conducter of our wills, with might (as was observed), ' working in us the will and the deed, according to his good pleasure.' For although

the will of a man regenerate is endowed with a new vital principle of spiritual life, so as in its willing and acting spiritually it doth it freely, and as a living principle of its own acts, yet it acts concurring with the movings and influences of the Spirit, according to that most excellent scripture (as to this purpose), Ps. cx. 3, ' Thy people shall be willing in the day of thy power.'   Herein the Holy Spirit hath determined the controversy, and reconciled the freeness of man's will in conversion, as likewise in the afteractings of grace, with the determinating efficacy of the power of God's grace, this being so full and infallible a prophecy, certainly foretelling these events of their willingness.   Now that prophecy doth directly refer to the day of Pentecost (whereof that psalm treateth), and of Christ's ascension and sitting in heaven ; and that passage refers unto the pouring forth the Spirit that day upon the apostles, and unto his coming upon three thousand of the Jews converted the same day, and made willing, by the same Spirit accompanying that great apostle's ministry, as the fulfilling of this prophecy. You read the story in Acts ii., where you find that willingness ascribed unto the Spirit as his work ; and so wonderfully efficacious is his power, as it was styled in that psalm, ' The day of his power ;' not of man's will. Christ's power.had the day of it in overcoming man's will.   And whereas it is said, that ' God worketh in us to will and to do,' it is not by his giving in power only to will or to do, but to will, Tὸ θέλειν, the act of willing, Tὸ θέλειν; and the giving this was the Spirit's gift.   So in those converts it was by the Spirit (as Ps. cx. compared with Acts ii. will inform us), who is indeed the power of the Most High, Luke i. 35.   And to cause us to *do*, and therefore to *will*, is expressly attributed to this Spirit in Ezek. xxxvi., where, first, it is said, ' A new heart also will I give you, and a new spirit I will put within you : and I will take away the stony heart out of your flesh, and I will give you a heart of flesh ;' which words denote the creating of those principles of spiritual life and habitual graces ; and then it is added, ver. 27, ' I will put *my Spirit* within you, and *cause you to walk in my statutes*, and ye shall keep my judgments *and do them*.'   What is this other but the same with that in the Philippians, to ' work in us to will and to do' ?   For if to *do*, then to be sure to *will*.   And this promise of the covenant (and it is the covenant of grace is there promulged) is to work in us an evangelical obedience unto all the commandments, which begins first with to *will*, and then follows to *do*, according unto that of the apostle, ' Not to do, but to be willing,' 2 Cor. viii. 10.

6. As all the principles and the production of the acts and fixing the will, so our whole growth in grace, from first to last, is attributed to this Spirit also : Isa. xliv. 3, 4, ' I will pour water upon him that is thirsty, and floods upon the dry ground : I will pour my Spirit upon thy seed, and my blessing upon thine offspring : and they shall spring up as the grass, as willows by the water courses,' or streams.   There are two things that cause the springing up of grass and growth in willows.   1. Sufficiency and plenty of water, either rain from heaven or streams of rivers, when trees (as willows) are seated by them.   2. The sun and the sweet influences thereof, Deut. xxxii.   And for this latter we have elsewhere our Lord Christ compared to the sun in this very respect: Mal. iv. 2, ' But unto you that fear my name shall the Sun of righteousness arise with healing in his wings ; and ye shall grow up as calves in the stall ;' as the sun causeth trees and plants to grow, so beasts too, which latter allusion he prosecutes there.   But in that of Isa. xliv. he compares the Spirit to the floods and the rain, which, increasing the sap within the root and body of the trees,

causeth them to grow up and bring forth fruits, even to old age: ' I will pour floods upon the dry ground : I will pour my Spirit upon thy seed.'

7. The acceptance of all these fruits by God, and of our persons by God for them, both all along, and specially when all is finished and perfected, is by and from the Holy Ghost. Thus Rom. xv. 16 the apostle speaks, ' That the offerings up of the Gentiles might be acceptable, being sanctified by the Holy Ghost.' In which words he sets out the great function and success of his gospel ministry, under allusions to the Levitical priesthood, as that which succeeded that of the law (Isa. lxvi. 20), in declaring how there had been a far more excellent sacrifice offered up to God by his preaching than had been by them of old. Their sacrifices were but of beasts, but this was of men—the souls of men, which by his preaching had been converted to God, even an innumerable company of the Gentiles, which were the first fruits and foundation of the church of the New Testament. These sacrifices of the gospel also in number far exceed any of the sacrifices of the Old Testament that were at any one time ever offered up ; yea, than there had been by Solomon, at the foundation and consecration of his new-built temple ; and yet all this was as the work but of one apostle. Of those Old Testament sacrifices, it is still noted how and what acceptableness they had with God, as Abel's, Heb. xi. ; as Noah's, Gen. viii. 20, 21, ' God smelt a sweet savour ;' and of Solomon, testified by fire coming down from heaven. Now of this great New Testament oblation here, that which gave the acceptableness is expressly said to be the being sanctified by the Holy Ghost, * as the cause that rendered them acceptable; and our translators favour it, if not imply it, in rendering it, ' Being sanctified by the Holy Ghost ;' that is, *in that*, or *because*, it was sanctified by the Holy Ghost, and *therefore* acceptable. As for the apostle's own part, he professeth himself but the poor instrument ; so in the following 18th verse; and that it was Christ, and his Spirit, had wrought all by him. And as he wrought nothing in those Gentile hearts, so the acceptation of what was wrought was much less from any consideration whatever in him to make this sacrifice accepted by the holy God. Far be that from the least of our thoughts ; for it is to be attributed unto Christ as the worker of it, ver. 18, and unto the Spirit, in this 16th verse, and unto the Spirit as well as unto Christ. Neither is our sanctification, simply in itself, and abstractly considered, as it is in us, of force and virtue alone, to cause this acceptation. This the confessions of David and Daniel, &c., abundantly do declare. It is the matter indeed, or thing, that is accepted, but not the ground or cause of the acceptation. And therefore that word ἐν, *in* (as in the original), which is translated *by* the Holy Ghost, is not added barely to shew that the Holy Ghost was the author of this and all other sanctification that is accepted, but that it might be noticed that it was he who was and is the main and principal cause of that acceptation ; and for which it hath a due value with God, even for this reason, that our sanctification is the work of the Holy Ghost. As we esteem the work for the workman's sake, so doth God our works for the Holy Ghost's sake, as the worker of it.

If it be said that our good works and holiness have their acceptation from Christ ; it is granted, as most true, our persons are accepted in his person, as ' the beloved,' Eph. i. 6, and our works in his works of mediation, the sole meritorious cause of that acceptation, and as by way of mediation between God and us, insomuch as Christ is said to be made sanctification

---

* Acceptationis istius oblationis sive victimæ, causam tribuit sanctificationi.— *Rolloc in verba.*

itself to us, 1 Cor. i. 30, as if it were no sanctification in the sight of God, that is not made accepted for such in Christ. And by him we offer up our sacrifices to God ; and God is well pleased with them, Heb. xiii. 15 and 16. And upon such an account the Holy Ghost is not the cause of this kind of acceptation. This honour is Christ's alone ; yet so as there is left room for this Holy Spirit to have the glory of procuring acceptation to our good works another way, namely, in that he is the efficient of them, and in that they are his works in us. Yea, and our persons also are in such a like respect accepted in and for the Holy Ghost, in that we are the temples of the Holy Ghost, and he dwells in us ; and God hath respect to the temple for his sake that dwells therein. Therefore give and acknowledge that honour to the Spirit, for his work and interest, as well as to the Son for his.

If we have recourse to the metaphor the apostle began with, and continues along to the end of the verse, viz., that the Gentiles were made a sacrifice and an offering to God, and had their lusts slain by the gospel, the sword of the Spirit, as the sacrificing knife, and this by the Holy Ghost, according to that in chap. viii., ' You by the Spirit mortify the deeds of the body,' we may extend the allusion to the acceptation of a sacrifice. There were two things made the sacrifice acceptable, viz., the *altar* upon which the offering was made, which Christ teacheth us, ' The altar sanctifies the gift ;' and that most fitly represented Christ's part in our acceptation : Heb. xiii. 10, ' We have an altar,' namely Christ, by whom we offer our sacrifice of praises, and by whom they are accepted, ver. 12, 15, 16. But then there was *fire* also, which came forth immediately from the Lord, and consumed the burnt offering that was upon the altar. So it was at first in Moses's time, Lev. ix. 24 ; and the second time fire came down from heaven, and did the like in Solomon's time, 2 Chron. vii. 1, when the temple was finished and consecrated. This signified the Holy Spirit, who comes out from God, τὸ πνεῦμα τὸ ἐκ τοῦ Θεοῦ, 1 Cor. ii. 12, even as that fire came forth from the Lord, and came upon the apostles to convert the world, like fire ; according to the promise that they should be ' baptized with the Holy Ghost, as with fire.' And he is termed the ' Spirit of burning,' Isa. iv. 4, as the sacrifices are termed burnt-offerings and fire-offerings. And as the fire caused the sacrifice to ascend in smoke (and therefore the Hebrew word for a burnt-offering is Gnolak, *ascension*), and consumed the offering to ashes, so doth this Spirit cause our sacrifice, as well as the altar : Ps. xx. 3, ' The Lord accept thy burnt sacrifice.' It is in the Hebrew, ' The Lord shall turn to ashes,' which our translators rightly translate *accept*, from the wonted speech of Moses's law, which informs us that the smoke which ascended from the sacrifice by reason of the fire, is termed up and down in the Levitical law ' a rest before the Lord,' and ' a savour of rest,' Lev. vi. 15 ; which the paraphrasts do *in terminis*, in our own phrase and words, render ' a favourable acceptation with the Lord ;' and this sweet savour is expressly attributed to the fire, as that which did thus sanctify the offering, and the acceptation of the sacrifice, its being a fire-offering. He puts it upon account, Lev. i. 9 and 13. It is a burnt offering (says the text there), ' an offering made by fire, of a sweet savour unto the Lord,' as if he would have said, it is therefore of a sweet savour because made by fire. So then as Christ, as the altar and mediator, gives an acceptation, so the Spirit, as the fire that consumes the sacrifice, and causeth it to ascend in smoke, causeth the acceptation also ; but either upon differing accounts, as was explained.

8. The whole edification of every saint, by the means of grace, which are the ordinances and other means whatsoever, all flow from the benign

influences of this Spirit accompanying them, and bedewing men's hearts by them. And for the proof of this in general, you have that passage, Acts ix. 31, 'Then had the churches rest, and *were edified*, walking in the fear of the Lord.' And so it is said of churches walking in all the order and ordinances of Christ ; as of the Colossian church it is spoken (chap. ii.) that they did so ; ' in the comfort of the Holy Ghost,' as the author of that edification and comfort by those ordinances.

I shall instance particularly in the main ordinances of our salvation, and shew how our profiting by them is from the Spirit.

In the preaching of the word we receive not only the fruits of the Holy Spirit, but the Spirit himself, by the hearing of faith, that is, by the hearing the gospel preached, which is the doctrine of truth : ' Our gospel came not to you in word only, but in power, and in the Holy Ghost,' 1 Thess. i. 5 ; 'I create the fruit of the lips, peace, and teach thee to profit,' namely, by the lips of those who by office are said to 'preserve knowledge,' Mal. ii. 7. All which profiting is attributed to the Spirit : 1 Cor. xii. 7, 'But the manifestation of the Spirit is given to every man to profit withal.' It is the profit both of a man's self and others. And the Holy Spirit's care is very great herein ; he is the *Providore General*, to oversee the overseers of the flock, and to see to it, provide the fittest stewards for every flock : Acts xx. 28, 'The flock over which the Holy Ghost hath made you overseers.' And he furnisheth them with such gifts as shall best serve and most suitably agree unto their capacities, and the bore of their understandings, and to work on their hearts ; and in providential grace disposeth of them and their gifts as shall be most agreeable to their spirits and spiritual condition. As some ministers are fitted for the profiting of the weak, so others to the wise ; even as the apostle says he was a debtor to both, Rom. i. And then he takes a further special care of their forehand meditations and preparations, to suggest such materials and notions for their sermons as shall be a food most convenient for men's souls. They are 'stewards, that give meat in due season,' Mat. xxiv. 45. He fills the breasts of ministers (their spiritual nurses) with consolations and other truths, suitable to the temper and constitution of their stomachs, and instructeth them to speak words in season ; and this very often unknown to themselves that speak them, they not having any aim at thee or any other man in particular in such passages, which also are utterly unexpected to or perhaps not prayed for by him whom yet they greatly concern, when yet the Holy Ghost knew whom to direct those passages unto, and had set up thy heart as the mark to shoot those arrows into it.

9. And lastly, to draw to a conclusion, and it is indeed the happy conclusion and crown of the whole work of the Spirit upon us, for we are now come to the brink of eternity, the consummation of all.

(1.) With respect to death, this Holy Spirit, the Comforter, all our life long feeds and maintains by faith, more or less, a lively hope within them that are regenerate : 1 Pet. i. 3, 'Blessed be God, that hath begotten us again to a lively hope ;' which, according to the degree of it in any, allays that fear of death, the king of sorrows, Job xviii. 14 ; the fear of which all men (which have not this Spirit) are subject unto the bondage of all their lifetime, Heb. ii. 15 ; from the dominion of which bondage the Spirit of adoption frees us, Rom. viii. 15, so as to have our spirits supported by faith, so far as ordinarily to be able (when put to it in earnest) to venture or cast our souls into the hands of God as a Father. And this the Scriptures attribute unto this good Spirit. In the 2d Corinthians, 4th and 5th chapters, the apostle treats of a believer's dying, and comforts himself and them against it; for upon occasion, as the times then were, he and other saints were in continual hazard of death; as ver. 11, 'For we that live are always delivered unto death for Jesus' sake.' Now, from whence or from whom had he and they supports and reliefs against this, but from the Spirit, his working and upholding faith in them? 'We having the same Spirit of faith, according as it is written,' &c., and pertinently quotes a saying of David's under the Old Testament in the 116th Psalm, where he had been under apparent apprehensions of death, as in the third verse, upon occasion of which David had uttered that speech, 'I believed, therefore have I spoken,' ver. 10; and spoke it, as it were, in defiance of death and all the fears of it, and dangers about it. Now, whence had David this confidence? From the Spirit, says the apostle, as who wrought and maintained that faith in him. Thus it was in the Old Testament, 'and we' (says he, under the New Testament), 'having the same Spirit of faith,' we, upon the view of such apparent dangers of death, believe and therefore speak, with a far greater confidence, by how much the Spirit that is in the New exceeds in his comforts the same that was in the Old; but, from the same Spirit, both. And what spake he by this Spirit of faith? It follows in ver. 14, 'We knowing that he which raised up the Lord Jesus shall raise up us also by Jesus;' this they spake and believed, and comforted themselves with against dying. Again, in the 5th chapter, what made him confident of a house in heaven when this earthly tabernacle should be dissolved? Even this, and above all this, that God hath given us the earnest of his Spirit, ver. 5, to bind the promise of eternal life. And from thence it is (says he) that 'we are always confident,' &c., ver. 6; *always*, which extends both to all along our lives, and also at our deaths. Which is a second thing, that when we come to die, or that the time of death approacheth, and is coming upon us, this Spirit it is given to support us. For if always, as the apostle even now said, and at all other times of our lives, and upon other occasions of fears and distress, he is given to help our infirmities, Rom. viii. 28, then especially when we are weakest, as at death (to be sure) we shall be, when our flesh fails, &c., Ps. lxxiii. 26.

(2.) And at the last day of the world, who is it shall raise thee up, having kept thy bones, dwelt in thy dust all this while, as Christ's Godhead did his body, which therefore though in the grave David calls the 'Holy One'? Ps. xvi. It is this Spirit: Rom. viii. 11, 'But if the Spirit of him that raised up Jesus from the dead dwell in you, he that raised up Christ from the dead shall also quicken your mortal bodies by his Spirit that dwelleth in you.' It is brought in as the comfortable consequent of this Spirit dwelling in us; and having raised thee, leaves thee not, but is the author of all thy glory and communion with Father, Son, and himself for ever, 1 Pet. iv. 14. He is in that respect termed the Spirit of glory; not of grace only, but of glory: 'Blessed are ye, for the Spirit of glory and of God resteth on you;' that is, you possess for ever this fountain of all glory, this Spirit of God, therefore the promise of the Spirit is made adequate to the whole blessing (as being the mass of blessings) which was given to Abraham: Gal. iii. 14, 'That the blessing of Abraham might come on the Gentiles though Jesus Christ; that we might receive the promise of the Spirit through faith.' The whole is termed the promise of the Spirit.

CHAPTER VI.

The uses of the precedent doctrine.

Use 1. Let me a little affect your hearts with the love of the Spirit, from and upon occasion of all that hath been said. There is a daily intercourse with, and meditation of, the love of the Father and the love of Christ. There is a fellowship of the Father, and a fellowship of the Son, in the souls of every believer. But the Holy Ghost, though he hath been universally aknowledged as a person equal to either, yet we do not hold and pursue after fellowship with him as a distinct person; nor is his love in what he hath done for us set on as a seal upon our hearts. Whereas the Scriptures (though more sparingly, because it was he who wrote them) do urge obligations upon us, drawn from him, as well as the other two persons.

If we believe he is a person in the Trinity, let us treat with him as a person, apply ourselves to him as a person, glorify him in our hearts as a person, dart forth beams of special and peculiar love to, and converse with him as with a person. Let us fear to grieve him, and also believe on him, as a person; which our very Creed directs us to. Do you profess to hold communion and converse with the saints? I beseech you, have it with the maker of them, the Holy Ghost; and this not at second hand, by having fellowship with those he dwells in, but immediately also with himself.

Because the Spirit is *intimior intimo,* is so nearly and intimately united to us, dwells in us as our own souls do in us, therefore we converse not with him (as we do seldom with our own souls), but are most of all strangers thereto. Also because his work is but new beginning, and as yet imperfect, and but a foundation of that building in eternity to be raised: whereas Christ hath perfected his, hath ' perfected for ever those that are sanctified' (Heb. x. 14), by one offering once made ; it is therefore we discern not (mind not) the Holy Ghost, or his works, as we do Christ and his. But what says the apostle, Rom. xv. 30, ' Now I beseech you, brethren, for the Lord Jesus Christ's sake, and for the love of the Spirit, that ye strive together with me,' &c. You see he adjures them by the Spirit, and his love, and their love unto the Spirit, as well as for Christ's sake. The occasion was, ' that ye would pray for me,' says he, that that work of the ministry (which is properly the Holy Ghost's work, Acts xiii. 2), may prosper in my hand. And if you profess love to the Spirit, whose work it is, and so consider his love to you, who hath done so much for you, his honour in this work will be dear to you. And inasmuch as he had urged them just before, ' for the Lord Christ's sake,' and then subjoins, ' for the love of the Spirit,' surely he must mean in like connection of sense, that for the Spirit's sake also, and for his love's sake towards them, who had borne no less love to them than Christ had done, they would do what he exhorted them to. Sure his exhortation falls not lower, nor runs in a lower way, to mean only the love which they bore to the Spirit, but it means that love which the Spirit himself bore to them, and which is equal to that of Christ. And the edge of his persuasive farther lies in this, and is as if he had said, Seeing that when we exhort you for Christ's sake, it useth to take with you, to move and prevail with you; so when we urge you by the love of the Spirit, it will have no less effect, if you do but consider all he hath done for you, or is to you. Now when he moves them for Chrits's sake (as in the first place he doth), the meaning is to obtest them by all the love that Christ had borne them, and by what he had done for them. When, therefore, he adds, ' and for the love of the Spirit' (the Spirit being a person we are obliged to, as well as unto Christ), can you think he had not this as his more especial aim, to move them in like manner by this very love of the Holy Ghost, who indeed deals altogether in the affairs of love from the Father and the Son ? He proceeds from them by way of love, and love in them mutually each to other is the original of his person. And as he is the love that is between them both, so it is he who sheds abroad the love of both into our hearts ; and it is he who is grieved, as a friend or person that loves us (as Eph. iv. 30), when we sin, or neglect that duty which is his care and charge to work in us.

And as this is the apostle's scope, so this love of his ought to be very dear unto us ; for if we single out any thing earnestly to entreat some other thing from another, that thing we entreat them by must be supposed to be most precious to us. Again, when, Rom. viii., he had insisted on this, that there is the Spirit of Christ in us, or we are none of his, he then begins the enumeration of many great things this Spirit doth for us throughout that chapter, by those arguments persuading us not to live after the flesh, but after the Spirit. In the midst of these persuasives he comes in with this, ' Wherefore, brethren, we are debtors, but not to the flesh.' Those words make two entire sentences, one affirmative, that ' we are debtors ;' the other negative, ' but not to the flesh ; ' we are not debtors to the flesh. Now to whom is it he affirms we are debtors ? Evidently the Spirit, as not only the words of opposition, ' not to the flesh' (which two are in this chapter set as ἀντικείμενα, as contraries and opposites, as everywhere else), but as the coherence and the illation—' *therefore* we are debtors'—shew. It was this Spirit he had last spoken of, the Spirit that dwelleth in us as a guide and leader, actor and informer of us, as the soul in our souls : ver. 11, ' If the Spirit of him that raised up Jesus from the dead dwelleth in you, he that raised up Christ from the dead shall also quicken your mortal bodies by his Spirit that dwelleth in you.' And from thence he infers, ' therefore we are debtors.' To whom but to him ? Debtors unto what ? To live after the Spirit and not after the flesh : so ver. 12, 13, ' Not to the flesh, to live after the flesh ; for if ye live after the flesh, ye shall die : but if ye through the Spirit do mortify the deeds of the body, ye shall live.' The obligation here, you see, runs in the Spirit's name, the arrest is at his suit. Debtors then we are, and infinitely indebted to him, and this for dwelling in us ; and because we are led and guided by him, as a person that loves us, are we wonderfully beholden unto him. And those next words, ' As many as are led by the Spirit,' directs us to treat with him as with a person, a familiar, a friend, that walks with us, takes us by the hand, talks to you, adviseth you as the Spirit of counsel (as, Isa. xi. 2, he is called), continually speaking in us, ' This is God's way, walk in it.' Again, when we read 2 Cor. xiii. 14, ' The grace of the Lord Jesus Christ, and the love of God, and the communion of the Holy Ghost, be with you' : that Κοινωνία, which we translate communion, doth it not, and may it not, import the fellowship and converse that the Holy Ghost vouchsafes to us with himself, as well as that with the Father and the Son ? 1 John i. 4. The word in both places is one and the same. And when he moves them (Phil. ii. 1) by all these considerations, ' If there be any consolation in Christ, any fellowship of the Spirit,' &c., why should we not interpret ' fellowship of the Spirit' for converse and intercourse had by us from him as a person, as well as consolation in Christ, is that which is in the person of Christ ?   Out of such an experimental sense of sweet familiarity and converse had with the Spirit of God, doth that speech of Holy David seem to proceed, Ps. cxliii. 10, ' Thy Spirit is good, lead me.'   Methinks he speaks so feelingly of him, and of that sweetness he had found in him as a friend, as if he had said, I have found his counsel and converse so good, O give me more of them.   And when he bids us grieve him not (Eph. iv. 30), doth it not import one whom we converse with daily, that is full of love and kindness to us, full of tenderness, whose love we should take in, and consider, and have a wary, watchful regard to, and grieve with him if we offend him ?

I cannot enlarge upon the work he hath done and is to do for us, which yet is proper to this occasion.   I shall only instance in what, in the doctrinal part, I have been so large in, and in that which, Rom. viii. 11, 12, the apostle putteth this very obligation upon ; our being debtors to the Spirit. He had in that chapter spoken much and great things about the Spirit's indwelling in us, and the fruits thereof: and he spoke thus, ver. 11, ' If the Spirit of him that raised up Jesus from the dead dwell in you, he that raised Jesus from the dead shall also quicken your mortal bodies by his Spirit that dwelleth in you.   Christ's love was in dying, the Spirit's is shewn in his indwelling in us.   His inference from thence is, ver. 12, ' Therefore, brethren, we are debtors, not to the flesh, to live after the flesh.' But that the greatness of his love and grace may appear unto us, and we may put a due value upon it, let us compare it with the love of Christ himself in being incarnate, and dwelling in our nature for us.   You account it infinite love in him to leave the bosom of his Father, to come down from heaven, and become one person with a man, to be made flesh, and so to be made less than his Father in that respect.   Yea, and this love is the greater, inasmuch as he assumed this nature as clothed with all infirmities of flesh and blood, the likeness of sinful flesh, and dwelt among us, and endured such contradictions of sinners, as the apostle speaks.   And this union was the foundation of all his work and satisfaction for us.   And herein God commended his love, as Heb. ii. you have it set forth.   And yet set this grace of the Holy Ghost's indwelling in us by it, and it riseth up unto an equality ; and though it fall lower in some respects, yet exceeding that of Christ in others, the scales will be acknowledged even.

It falls lower in this, that the union between him and us is not personal, as that of Christ's is with his human nature ; but yet it is as near it as possibly may be, for it is an immediate union of our persons to and with his person, so as to have an eternal right personal to each other, and everlastingly to dwell each in other.   And it indeed was well for us we had not a personal union with the Spirit ; for our defilements (if remaining) would then have defiled and been imputed unto his person.

In other things it is equal ;

For, 1. Both are said to come alike down from heaven ; the Spirit (1 Pet. i. 12) as well as Christ.

2. He indwells in us for ever, as was shewn.   He is in us ; and shall be with us married as indivisibly without all divorce, as the Son of God and that human nature also are.   Yea, and as Christ continued his union with the body in the grave, so those words (Rom. viii. 11), ' The Spirit of him that raised up Jesus from the dead shall also quicken your mortal bodies, by his Spirit that dwelleth in you,' import, that the Spirit continueth his union and relation to the body (which, 1 Cor. vi. 19, is also called his temple) even within the grave, and fallen to dust.

But, 3. In these things the love shewn by the Spirit in such his union with us doth exceed.

(1.) That though indeed the Son of God dwelt and dwells thus intimately in a human nature, yet it is a nature made holy, harmless, separate from sin and sinners, Heb. vii.   But this good Spirit's lot and part is to come at first into hearts full of all defilements, into rags of uncleanliness, into flesh that is and hath wholly corrupted itself.   Of old this was made a wonder by Solomon ; ' Will God in very deed dwell on earth, in a house which I have built for him, whom the heaven and the earth cannot contain ?' 2 Chron. vi. 18.   But here is a wonder of wonders, that the holy God (as the Spirit is) should dwell in hearts so unholy and unclean, and make them his temples (as 1 Cor. vi. 19).

(2.) Christ indeed dwelt among us, and conversed with sinful men, whereby he suffered daily such contradictions of sinners.   But it was a contradiction merely from without, and yet this grated on his spirit (nothing more), insomuch as it is said he pleased not himself in the best of his company, Rom. xv. 3.   But the union of the Holy Ghost, and his indwelling in us, is in our sinful hearts ; so as often, where his indwelling is mentioned, it is inserted (Gal. iv. 6), ' He sent the Spirit of his Son into our hearts.' 2 Cor. i. 22, ' He hath given the earnest of his Spirit into our hearts.'   John vii. 38 ; this spring of living water is said to be in the belly, environed about with mud.   All which imports a nearer union than that of Christ within us ; to which this limitation is added, ' He dwells in our hearts by faith.'   But of the Spirit it is said everywhere that he dwells in us.   It is originally his title, 2 Tim. i. 14, to be styled, ' He that dwells within us.' Now the contradiction which he by reason of this near inhabitation endures must needs be much greater and quicker to his sense, from those he dwells thus within, and hath entered into, and hath undertaken such a conjunction withal, than that of outward converse, which Christ only endured.   For if what Christ says in another case be true, what is from without should offend ; then how much more that which is from within, the person one dwells withal ?   And in this respect he alone of all the three persons is said to be grieved, having taken on him the part of an intimate friend.   A father (as God the Father) is offended, but a familiar friend is grieved.   It argues a nearer striking home at the heart.   And in this respect he hath had an hard task of it, and this from the beginning of the world.   He hath been burdened, and felt the weight of the old world (Gen vi.), ' My Spirit shall not always strive with man therein.'   And yet he relieves himself by bringing the flood upon them after an hundred and twenty years.   But against these he thus indwells in, whom he regenerates, he hath no relief; for he hath eternally undertaken for them.

And is it nothing, think you, to have his work continually spoiled ? Never to find the soul as he left it ?   To have that heart he dwells in continually resisting and contradicting of him ?   To have that unspun in the night which he hath woven in the day ?   To have made a good prayer in us, and that swept away, as if it were but a cobweb, by lust that riseth ? To have his greatest enemy, the devil, blaspheme him and his graces, in his own house, in his own hearing ?   If Lot's righteous soul was vexed, or our own graces within us troubled ; then how much more is the author of all grace, dwelling in us, insomuch as he is weary of this world, and the course held in this respect ?

And to that account I have sometimes in my thoughts cast that speech, Rev. xxii., where we find some outcries for Christ's coming, that he would come quickly. ' The Spirit says, Come ' (speaking to Christ), as well as ' the bride says, Come.' She, that she may enjoy her husband ; he, that he may be eased. He groans to be unburdened of this conflict with sinful hearts he dwells in (as our souls are said to do, 2 Cor. v.), as having so long borne the trouble and grief of this work, which till there is an end of all by Christ's coming, he is designed unto.

Use 2. There is another use of this doctrine, which I urge to unregenerate men. Well, God by his providence hath brought thee once more to the word, which the apostle calls the ministration of the Spirit. Now consider, though thou hast been never so empty, dry, and barren of goodness, and art now in thy filthiness, thou mayest carry home the Spirit with thee, and therein thou art passive ; but if thou dost, it will cost thee something in his workings on thee ; he will work strangely on thy heart. Thou mayest now begin to be possessed of the richest gift God hath to bestow. Thou camest to see fashions, a reed shaken with the wind, as John's hearers did ; but thou standest in the wind of the Spirit, and he may seize upon thee, and save thee ; for he comes upon men without preparation, and then works all. I shall open but two or three scriptures to this purpose. In Isa. xliv. 3, there is the promise of the Spirit (which in Gal. iii. is said to have been made to Abraham and his seed), ' I will pour water upon him that is thirsty, and floods upon the dry ground ;' which Isaiah himself interprets, ' I will pour my Spirit upon thy seed, and my blessing upon thine offspring ; and they shall spring up ' (as herbs, namely) ' among the grass,' &c. ' One shall say, I am the Lord's,' &c. And this scripture also did our Saviour Christ allude to in the promise of his Spirit to the woman of Samaria : John iv. 14, ' But whosoever drinketh of the water that I shall give him shall never thirst ; but the water that I shall give him shall be in him a well of water springing up into eternal life.' He alludes also to the same scripture in what he says to his disciples : John vii. 37–39, ' If any man thirst, let him come to me, and drink. He that believeth on me, as the scripture hath said, out of his belly shall flow rivers of living water. But this spake he of the Spirit, which they that believed on him should receive : for the Holy Ghost was not yet given ; because that Jesus was not yet glorified.' The promise in each refers to both places : and yet the occasion was differing, though of one and the same Spirit. If you observe the purport and occasion of the promise of the Spirit in the 4th of John, it was when our Saviour was treating with the woman of Samaria, a great sinner, ver. 18 ; utterly ignorant, ver. 10, 23 ; a flouter of him, ver. 15 ; and as yet (when Christ spake these words) purely in her natural estate. And therefore this promise of the Spirit here all acknowledge to be the Spirit of regeneration, to work conversion at the first ; to become, as at the first he doth, a well of water springing up to eternal life.

Now this was at first poured upon a dry ground, in respect to any such work ; utterly dry, utterly barren, that hath not so much as a desire or thirst after this Holy Spirit, to ask him, as she had not, ver. 10, ' If thou knewest the gift of God, and who it is that saith unto thee, Give me to drink, thou wouldst have asked of him, and he would have given thee living water.' And upon this ignorant, barren soul doth Christ pour out his Spirit whilst he is speaking with her ; and which was the strangeness of it, though poured from without, yet soaking into her, it began (as Christ promised) to become a spring in her heart, which other water poured from without on earth doth never become, bubbling up all that which tended to eternal life. And the promise of the Spirit as regenerating at the first, and to tha end poured out on such souls as here, was part of Isaiah's scope. He had a further also, for it is pouring ' water upon dry ground,' causing herbs to come up where barrenness was (ver. 4), to the end that men that are Gentiles, and strangers to the commonwealth of Israel (as this Samaritan was) might ' call themselves by the name of Jacob, and subscribe unto the Lord, and surname themselves by the name of Israel,' ver. 5. And the first thing we see God doth (as Christ also in the 4th of John promiseth) to such sons, is to pour out his Spirit on them in that very condition, and he becomes a spring within them of all goodness, even then when there is not a drop afore, nor any preparation to it. And again the prophet Isaiah, prophesying of times when Christ should be on earth, thus speaks, chap. xxxv. ver. 5, 6, ' Then the eyes of the blind shall be opened, and the ears of the deaf shall be unstopped. Then shall the lame leap as an hart, and the tongue of the dumb sing.' Then followeth the very same promise, that ' in the wilderness waters should break out, aud streams in the desert, and the parched ground shall become a pool.' Which promise, as Christ interpreted, so he also made it good, fulfilling of it in this Samaritan, the first fruits of Gentile converts ; and this he did whilst he was speaking it to her. Ezekiel speaks to the same purpose and effect (chap. xxxvii.), though under another allusion, of men not only dead, but consumed to bone, and those bones dry; and a wind came from God upon them, even when in this estate, and made them alive. And what is the moral of it ? The Spirit of God (whom Christ compares to the wind, John iii., and who, Acts ii., came as a rushing wind), the Spirit of the living God (as in 2 Cor. iii. 3) came upon these men, and made them alive, even when dead and dry bones. Thus it is said, ver. 14, ' I will put my Spirit in you, and ye shall live.' He puts his Spirit into us, not only pours him on us ere we have the least of life, who therefore must needs come on us, yea, into us when we are dead. He gets into us, and becomes a spring in our bellies, in the heart of this barren earth when it is dry.

Use 3. Is it the Spirit of God who is the author of conversion ? Then ament and bewail the hardness of thy heart, which though it hath so often had good motions put into it by the Spirit (which motions, for aught thou knowest, are the beginnings of this work, and leaders unto repentance), yet it hath not followed them, but given a deaf ear unto them.

1. Consider the heinousness of the sin. It is that which Stephen upbraided the Jews with : Acts vii. 51, ' Ye stiffnecked, who evermore resist the Holy Ghost.' It is the sin for which our Saviour chiefly wept over Jerusalem, Luke xiii. 34. Consider that it is to oppose the Holy Ghost in his own proper work and office, and in as much as in you lies to put him out of office. And though it be not always *that* sin against the Holy Ghost, which is unpardonable (for many have afterwards repented of this), yet it is *a* sin against the Holy Ghost. For as the Scripture, though it makes indeed but one ὁ Ἀντίχριστος, ' *that* antichrist, the man of sin and son of perdition,' the pope, the greatest arch-heretic that ever was, or will be, yet every petty popeling and less notorious heretic is *an* antichrist, ' for there be many antichrists now in the world' (says the apostle of his times, before the great antichrist was risen). So it is in this case : though the Scripture makes but one sin against the Holy Ghost, κατ᾽ ἐξοχὴν, yet the resister of the least motion of the Spirit leading to repentance is a sinner against the Holy Ghost, and there be many such sinners. I appeal to many of you ; how often hath the Holy Ghost come and viewed you ? How often hath he come to your hearts when ye were alone, and even unto your bedside,

beseeching you, and ye have put him off! And you may judge of the greatness of this sin, to resist the least good motion (which is a step to the other), in that the Scripture makes the full act (or grosser act, as I may call it) of that sin to be, *in isto genere* in that kind, the greatest and the only unpardonable one. Now we measure sins in the act they tend to; as murder being a great sin, and the act thereof more heinous than of other sins, therefore thoughts of murder and revenge are worse than any other sinful thoughts. And if you will put this sin of resisting the motions of the Spirit into the balance of the sanctuary, and rightly weigh it with other ways of sinning, I dare affirm it, that the resisting the least good motion tending to conversion is greater than many of those grosser acts against the law of God. And these motions resisted do heighten and aggravate all our other sins committed before and after them. For they tend to turn us from them by causing us to repent of all sins past, and preventing sins to come. Moreover this sin is a sin against the gospel (for the gospel is the ministration of the Spirit, and so of these good motions of the Spirit), and sins against the gospel are greater than those against the law. And therefore (Heb. ii. 23) the very neglecting the salvation of the gospel is made a crime deserving a sorer punishment than any breach of the law. And how much sorer punishment does it deserve to despise it when it is brought home to us by the Holy Ghost, and by him set on upon our hearts? If barely to hear the word, and not be moved by it, be a sin, and a heinous one, then to be moved by it and to neglect it is a greater; for it is despising of the greater mercy, and it is against the Spirit of grace in the gospel.

2. Consider the danger of this sin. You have seen that, for the guilt of it, it is above committing gross sins against the law. And the danger of it is answerable; for sins against the law God threateneth but conditionally with damnation, if men believe not, and repent not; so as that repentance coming between they may escape. But this God threateneth, yea, and punisheth with impenitency itself (and that is the damning sin) for God useth ordinarily to punish sins in their own coin, according to their nature and kind; and this he punisheth with impenitency, because it resists the work of repentance: 'I would have purged thee' (says God in the prophet, unto the people of Israel), 'but thou wouldst not.' When God would they would not, and therefore God never after would. And when God hath used means, and comes unto us to cleanse us, and we would not, he says (as it is, Rev. xxii. 11), 'He that is filthy, let him be filthy still'; and so we shall be long enough, for all him. For at length God grows peremptory, and never makes offer more. God commonly gives such up unto irrecoverable hardness of heart and blindness of mind. And I appeal to their own consciences if they grow not harder after such resistings, as clay doth, the more the sun hath shone upon it, or as ice freezeth harder after it had begun to thaw. Consider but the reason of it. If a man sins against the law, he hath yet the court of the gospel to sue in, and so to obtain pardon; as if a man be cast in one court, he hath a liberty to remove his suit from that court unto a higher; but if he be condemned in the higher, then there is no going backward unto any lower court. So God hath given us two courts, that of the law and that of the gospel. Thou being an unclean or covetous person, or a drunkard, goeth to the law, and that condemns thee. Then the Spirit offers thee to remove thy suit to the highest court of the gospel, and upon faith and repentance to bring thee a pardon. Thou neglects this, and so the gospel itself presently condemns thee; for there, 'he that believes not is condemned already,' John iii. 18. And if mercy and

the offers of it condemn thee, I know not what can save thee ; for that is the highest court, and go backward thou canst not. The work of the Spirit (as you heard) is the last act of man's salvation, and without it neither no evidence of thy election, nor redemption, are to be respected. And if thou run unto God's mercy (as that is the common shift, that God is merciful) or to Christ's redemption, in that he died for sinners, both these send thee to the Spirit. And the Spirit tells thee he hath offered salvation unto thee upon thy repenting many a time, and hath proffered to assist therein, and thou didst still refuse ; and how then canst thou expect salvation ? Ay, but thou wilt say, I hope the Spirit will offer again and again, and when I am on my deathbed, as well as now. I answer,

1. That it is a great hazard, for ' the Spirit blows when and where he listeth ;' and, it may be, he will never move thee more. And,

2. Consider whether thou hast any reason to expect this. For suppose thou shouldst have often, again and again, moved a friend of thine in a matter which concerns himself, and which thou hast most * benefit by, only out of love, thou hast thus moved him in it, and he still gives thee a contrary or froward answer, and goes on doing the contrary, wouldst not thou at last resolve, that seeing thou hast so often moved him in vain, hereafter thou wilt never speak of it to him more ? This is the case between the Spirit and thee. He hath often moved thee in a matter that concerns thine eternal wealth or wo, even to repent, but thou givest him a churlish answer, and goest still on in thine impenitency ; how then canst thou expect he should ever move thee again ? God comes at length to say of thee, as of those in Hosea vi. 4, who had had many good motions, which like the dew were dried up, and reformations which like a cloud passed away, ' O Ephraim, what shall I do unto thee ? O Judah, what shall I do unto thee ? For your goodness is as a morning cloud ; and as the early dew it goeth away.'

3. Yet seeing this is thy plea, that thou hopest the Holy Ghost will move thee again, I charge thee, as thou tenderest thine own salvation, if that now or hereafter he doth move. thee, to take the opportunity of time and tide. If by meditation, reading, or prayer, any sparks be kindled in thee, blow them up ; let those thoughts rest on thee ; welcome them, hug them, as the best guests that ever came to lodge in thine heart. Shall an ambassador extraordinary be sent from the King of heaven unto thee with a message, and wilt thou not give him audience, but put him off from day to day, and tell him (as Felix did Paul) thou wilt hear him another time ? The best men are but green wood, on which, though fire do take hold, it is subject to die again ; and therefore, if thou hast but a few sparks, leave them not till they have taken hold, nor then till they are put into a flame. And above all things, take heed of quenching them by carnal mirth, or company, or recreations, as men use to do.

* Qu. ' no ' ?—Ed.

CHAPTER VII.

How the Holy Ghost is the author of regeneration, or the first application of salvation to us, in a more peculiar manner, comparatively to the other two persons.

Not by works of righteousness which we have done, but according to his mercy he saved us, by the washing of regeneration, and renewing of the Holy Ghost ; which he shed on us abundantly through Jesus Christ our Saviour.—TITUS III. 5, 6.

Regeneration, you see, is attributed to the Spirit as the author. It is termed the ' renewing of the Holy Ghost ' and likewise the ' shedding forth the Holy Ghost ' is magnified as the rich gift and blessing of the New Testament.

I have in a former discourse shewn how all the three persons have shared and distributed the whole work of our salvation amongst them, unto three several parts. 1. Election is appropriated to the Father. 2. Redemption to the Son. 3. Application of both to the Holy Ghost ; who accordingly doth bear several offices suited to these three works.

That which now I have to do, is more particularly to demonstrate both the ὅτι and διότι of this point of great moment ; both *that* and *why* this last part of salvation, viz., application, and so principally this of regeneration, is attributed to the Holy Ghost.

I. I shall produce scriptures to demonstrate this point.

1. The first Scripture is John iii. 5, ' Except a man be born of the Spirit, he cannot enter into the kingdom of God.' This scripture shews not only the necessity of being born again, but withal that it must be the Spirit, who must do it, or it will not be done. ' For no man can so much as say, Jesus is the Lord, but by the Holy Spirit,' 1 Cor. xii. 3.

2. The near kindred and dependence the new creature hath with and upon the Spirit, as the child begotten hath of and with its proper father, doth evidence the same truth.

(1.) The new creature is in the same third of John, ver. 6, styled *spirit* (as elsewhere it is called a spiritual man, 1 Cor. ii.), ' That which is born of the Spirit is spirit.' It is therefore professedly baptized into the same name, because the father of this new birth and baptism is the Spirit. With men the begotten bears the name of the most immediate parent ; and so in this case, though this work of the Spirit be in common termed the divine nature (2 Peter i. 4) because it is the image of the Godhead, of which all three persons are partakers, yet to shew that in a more peculiar manner it is the child of the Spirit, it is called spirit.

(2.) For the very same reason this Spirit of God, the author, relatively bears the name of *Holy* in the New Testament, where it is (though not first) yet more frequently used as his special title, to be called ' The Holy Ghost,' as our old English hath rendered it to us. Is not the Father holy, and the Son holy, and both equally holy with this Holy Spirit ? Yes, essentially and personally also in themselves ; ' Holy, holy, holy,' they are all proclaimed, Isa. vi. How came these other two to bear it, that he, the third person, should have the peculiar style of *Holy?* It is not neither in a peculiar, neither in a personal or essential respect, but relatively unto that which is his proper and peculiar work, because he sanctifies and makes us holy, and so merits that name ; as Christ doth of our *Saviour*, and the Father of God the Father and *Maker*. And here let me return to the necessity of this person's making us holy. As it is necessary for Christ to redeem us, there is an absolute necessity that we all be a sanctified holy sacrifice offered up to God, if we look to be saved, or otherwise we must be made a sacrifice of his wrath, as Christ hath told us, Mark ix. 49. Where he having threatened, if lust be not killed, men shall be cast into the fire that is unquenchable (ver. 47, 48), he adds this as a reason, that every man is to be a sacrifice to God one way or other. According to the old law some sacrifices were consumed with fire, as the burnt-offerings ; some seasoned with salt, to sink up the corrupt moisture in them, Lev. ii. 13. One sort of these sacrifices all men must become ; if not sanctified by the Spirit, so as to have salt in them, then with hell-fire, which also is a sacrifice to God. Now Christ for our redemption offered up himself a sacrifice to God, for a sweet smelling savour, Eph. v. 2 ; and it was necessary he should be so. And to that end he sacrificed himself, as in his sacrificial prayer he speaks, John xvii. 19. And it is as necessary, if we be saved, that our persons be offered up unto God as a sacrifice also, Rom. xii. 1, even a living sacrifice, holy and acceptable to God. It was necessary, therefore, we should have a sanctifier of us to be an offering unto God, as well as a redeemer, that offered up himself for us. And who is that ? You are directed to him in Rom. xv., ' This is the issue of my ministry,' (says Paul, speaking of his converting the nations, ver. 18, 19) ' that the Gentiles ' (being converted) ' might be an offering acceptable, being sanctified by the Holy Ghost.' Else never to be acceptable to God. Christ was sanctified immediately by himself, by the personal union with the Son of God—'I sanctify myself '—even as he also ' offered up himself by the eternal Spirit,' or Godhead dwelling in him, Heb. ix. ; but we by the Holy Ghost. And as in that other speech, ' That which is born of the Spirit is spirit,' the new creature bears his name ; so here, he is called the Holy Spirit, or bears the name of *holy*, because the sanctifier of us : ' Being sanctified by the Holy Ghost.'

3. The work of conversion, not only in the whole, but in every part thereof, is attributed to him, John xvi. 8, 9, 10. It is (as I hinted afore, and shall shew hereafter) divided into three parts. 1. Conviction of sin. 2. Of righteousness for justification. 3. Of judgment, holiness, and reformation ; and the Spirit is there made the author of these three. And according to this division of the parts thereof, he hath titles also given him, as in relation to his immediate working of these three.

(1.) He condescends to be termed ' the Spirit of bondage ;' I say, he condescends but to the work and name ; for otherwise, and in himself, he is ' the free Spirit,' (Ps. li. 11, 12), and delights in comforting us, not in grieving us. And he is therefore also called ' the Comforter ;' but yet to affect our salvation, and the effectual application of it to us, he (contrary to his nature) becomes our jailor, takes the keys of death and damnation into his custody, and shuts up our spirits under the law, as it is a schoolmaster to Christ, rattles the chains, lets us see the sin and punishment we deserve. He convinceth of sin, John xvi., and becomes a ' Spirit of bondage,' Rom. viii. 15.

(2.) But then, secondly, in regard of the revealing God's love to us, and Christ and his righteousness, by whom we are adopted, and by which justified, he is called in the same place ' the Spirit of adoption,' ' the Spirit of

faith,' as some interpret, 2 Cor. iv. 13.   Barnabas was 'full of the Holy
Ghost, and of faith,' Acts xi. 24.

(3.) In regard of sanctifying us, and convincing of judgment, he is in the
Old Testament enstyled the 'Spirit of judgment,' Isa. iv. 4, in respect of
washing away the filth of sin : ' When the Lord shall have washed away
the filth of Zion, by the Spirit of judgment,' &c.   And in the New he is
entitled ' the Spirit of grace :' Heb. x. 29 ' Have done despite to the Spirit
of grace,' that is, to him as going about to work grace and holiness in the
heart.   The sin against the Holy Ghost, which is there described, not being
against the person of the Spirit, so much as against him in his workings ;
and that in his working grace and sanctifying, as in the words afore you
have it.   And as to grace in the general, as he is the author of every particular grace, so in the head himself, therefore much more in the members.
The prophet, speaking of the Messiah in Isa. xi. 1, ' The Spirit of the
Lord shall rest upon him,' and shall be in him, in respect of his effects upon
him, ' the Spirit of wisdom and understanding, the Spirit of knowledge, and
of the fear of the Lord.'   There is the like reason he should be denominated from every other grace.   He is in one chapter, John xiv., termed
' The Spirit of truth,' ver. 17, who reveals all truth to the understanding ;
' The Holy Spirit,' who sanctifies the will, the chief subject of holiness; ' The
Comforter,' who fills the heart with joy and peace in believing; which is
therefore usually styled ' joy in the Holy Ghost,' in multitudes of places;
that phrase speaking him not so much the object of it (which is rather
Christ, 1 Peter i. 8, ' In whom believing, ye rejoice with joy unspeakable
and glorious ;' and God, Rom. v. 11) as the author of it: Rom. xv. 13,
' Now the God of hope fill you with all joy and peace in believing, that ye
may abound in hope, through the power of the Holy Ghost.'

II. I shall now, secondly, give the reasons why this work is committed
to him, and is his lot.   These reasons are not of logical demonstration, but
harmonious, by comparing spiritual things with spiritual, and by the suiting
of one thing with another, in which the strength of divine reason lies ; for
divinity is a wisdom, not an art.

1. This operation of the Spirit is in a correspondency to the creation of
the first man, who was a type of what was to come : Job xxxiii. 4, ' The
Spirit of God hath made me, and the breath of the Almighty hath given me
life.'   It is evident he speaks of the new creation, in allusion to the old:
ver. 1–3, ' My word shall be of the uprightness of my heart, and my lips
shall utter knowledge thereby ;' and then adds, ' The Spirit of God hath
made me,' that is, hath given me a sincere heart, an illuminated mind, put
the words of life into me.   To have spoken of his first creation only, he
being a man fallen from it, had been a poor argument to persuade Job of
the truth of his heart, and the truths he went about to utter.   And yet,
too, he as evidently alludes to the first creation : Gen. ii. 7, ' The Lord
formed man of the dust of the ground, and breathed into his nostrils the
breath of life, and man became a living soul.'   Now, in this new creation,
we being dead in sins and trespasses, it is the Spirit of God that giveth
life, 2 Cor. iii. 6 ; who, as in respect of giving us this new life, is called
' the Spirit of the living God,' ver. 3 ; and in the Old Testament, Ezek.
xxxvii. 13, 14, ' I will bring you out of your graves, I will put my Spirit
in you, and you shall live,' which you find in the 36th chapter, ver. 27.
And it is observable that the first visible giving the Holy Ghost, which
was after Christ's resurrection, to enable them to be ' ministers, not of the
letter, but of the Spirit,' which should give life to them, and to others by

them, was the ceremony of breathing on them : ' And he said, Receive the Holy Ghost,' John xx. 22. We had his blood that ran in his veins first, and it is efficacious to wash away the guilt of sin. We have his breath next, which comes out of the inwards of him, which conveys his Spirit, which conveys himself into our inwards, as it is in the prophet, and gives us life. And as life comes with the breath of God breathed at first, and goes away with it, so doth spiritual life upon the going or coming of the Holy Ghost upon us.

2. It is the Spirit that converts and regenerates us, and forms the new creature in us, in a conformity to our head Christ. The Holy Ghost was, 1. The immediate former of the human nature of Christ in the womb ; 2. The uniter of that nature to the Son of God ; 3. The sanctifier thereof, with all graces dwelling therein above all measure.

(1.) He was the former of the human nature of Christ in the womb : Mat. i. 18, ' She was found with child of the Holy Ghost ; ' and ver. 20, ' that which is conceived in her is of the Holy Ghost ; ' which was in his forming and fitting that matter into a man, which the prolific virtue useth to do.

(2.) He was the uniter of it to the divine, and sanctifier of it with all graces, both which you have expressed in another place : Luke i. 35, ' And the angel answered and said to her, The Holy Ghost shall come upon thee, and the power of the Highest shall overshadow thee : therefore also that holy thing that shall be born of thee shall be called the Son of God.' Now, we being to be made as comformable to Christ as is possible, it was correspondent that the same person who was designed to form Christ's body for the Godhead to dwell in all its fulness should form Christ in us, that God and Christ may dwell in us : 1 Cor. iii. 16, ' Know ye not that ye are the temple of God, and that the Spirit of God dwelleth in you ? ' That same person that made that happy match, the personal union between Christ's human nature and the divine, the same person makes the union between Christ and our souls ; and so we become one spirit with the Lord, 1 Cor. vi. 17. The same person that made the man Christ partaker of the divine nature maketh us also. There is a higher correspondency yet. The Holy Ghost is *vinculum Trinitatis*, the union of the Father and the Son, as proceeding from both by way of love ; and who so meet to be the union of God and man in Christ, of Christ and men in us, as he that was the bond of union among themselves ?

(3.) In respect of sanctifying that human nature of Christ, it was the Holy Ghost who made him Christ, that anointed him with himself, and all his graces : Isa. xi. 2, ' The Spirit of the Lord shall rest upon him, the Spirit of knowledge and the fear of the Lord.' The graces of Christ, as man, are attributed to this Spirit, as the immediate author of them ; for although the Son of God dwelt personally in the human nature, and so advanced that nature above the ordinary rank of creatures, and raised it up to that dignity and worth, yet all his habitual graces, which even his soul was full of, were from the Holy Ghost. The Holy Spirit is therefore said to be ' given him without measure.' And this inhabitation of the Holy Ghost did in some sense and degree concur to constitute him Christ, which, as you know, is the anointed one of God : Acts iv. 27, ' Thy holy child Jesus, whom thou hast anointed.' Anointed with what ? Acts x. 38, ' God anointed Jesus with the Holy Ghost.' Now, then, if the Spirit made him Christ, and concurred in this respect to make him the anointed of God, much more is it he that makes us Christians.

3. Consider what this application of salvation unto us is. It is the revelation of the mind and love of God and Christ unto us, and the things of both. He that doth this must 'take of mine,' says Christ; and in doing so he must take of my Father's also, for all the Father hath or doth is Christ's. You have both in one place : John xvi. 14, 15, 'He shall glorify me : for he shall receive of mine, and shew it to you. All things that the Father hath are mine.' Great persons woo not by themselves, but employ ambassadors and ministers of state ; and so doth Christ. Now, who should do this but the Spirit, who knows the heart and mind of God ? 1 Cor. ii., 'We have received the Spirit who is of God, that we might know the things that are freely given us of God ;' that is, by our having him from God, who knows all that is in God, which is the reason there given ; ver. 10, 'God hath revealed them to us by his Spirit : for the Spirit searcheth all things, yea, the deep things of God ;' which he confirms and illustrates by a similitude fetched from our own bosoms : ver. 11, 'For what man,' that is, what other man, 'knows the things of a man' (that are in his own breast), 'save the spirit of a man that is in him ? Even so the things of God knows no man,' or angel, 'but the Spirit of God ;' who being the Spirit of counsel (Isa. xi. 2) even to Christ himself, helped him to all God's secrets ; and he also being privy and overhearing (as John xvi. 13), all that the Father and Christ have intended to us, and spoken about us, was only fit to reveal them unto us. And thus by him we come to have the very mind of God and Christ. The grace of Christ, and the love of God the Father, are revealed to us by the communion of the Holy Ghost, 2 Cor. xiii. 14.

CHAPTER VIII.

How the Holy Ghost is the gift of God the Father to us, in and by Jesus Christ.—That this inestimable gift is bestowed freely, by the pure mercy, grace, and love of God.

Not by works of righteousness which we have done, but according to his mercy he saved us, by the washing of regeneration, and renewing of the Holy Ghost ; which he shed on us abundantly through Jesus Christ our Saviour. —TIT. III. 5, 6.

We have seen, in a short but comprehensive view, the operations of the Holy Ghost in the great work of our salvation. The next prospect of him is, as he is the gift of God, conferred on us for this end and purpose. To open this to our sight, I offer these following considerations.

1. That it is God the Father who is the donor, or the bestower of him on us. This is plainly expressed by the words of the text, which declares that he sheds the Spirit on us. 2. This gift of the Spirit is in and through Jesus Christ, our Saviour and mediator. 3. This gift of the Spirit is bestowed, not according to the covenant of works, but of grace and free love. For those words, 'not according to works,' and the other words of the text, which speak of the appearance of the love and kindness of God, refer as well to this rich shedding forth the Holy Ghost upon us as unto saving us through regeneration, and renewing us. 4. The condition of the persons to whom he is given is altogether unworthy. When we were in our disobedience, serving our lusts, the Holy Ghost was poured out, and renewed us.

1. The donor or bestower of the Holy Ghost is God the Father through Christ. As the Father is the original of the persons in the Trinity, so of this great gift. Therefore Christ (John xv. 26) when he speaks of 'sending the Spirit from the Father,' adds, as the reason why he should be sent from the Father, that 'he proceeds from the Father' (his subsistence doth), naming him as the fountain both of himself and the Spirit also. He is termed the Spirit of God, τοῦ Θεοῦ, 1 Cor. ii. 11, in the same sense that we say the spirit of a man (as in the same verse); for as God is a Spirit, Isa. xlviii. 16, 'The Lord God and his Spirit,' says the prophet there; but the apostle further adds, ver. 12, the Spirit, ἐκ τοῦ Θεοῦ, who personally is from God, whom therefore we have and receive from God: 1 Cor. vi. 19, 'The Holy Ghost which we have,' ἀπὸ Θεοῦ. This gift is therefore especially attributed to the Father, and termed by Christ 'the promise of the Father,' Acts iv., Luke xxiv. 49, 'the Spirit of the Father,' Mat. x. 20, from whom Christ, as God-man, received the Spirit first. The Holy Ghost was sent down by the Father upon Christ as a dove in his baptism: 'God anointed Jesus with the Holy Ghost,' Acts x. 38. And when Christ ascended into heaven he received him from the Father, Acts ii. 33, and so he shed him forth on us. And therefore Christ also, as mediator, was to pray the Father to give the Spirit, John xiv. 16: 'I will pray the Father, and he shall give you another Comforter,' &c.

Yet so as, 2dly, even the Father himself sends him not, but in and through Christ: John xiv. 26, 'The Holy Ghost, whom the Father will send in my name.' 'Through Christ our Saviour,' says the apostle, Tit. iii. 6. Which imports not barely the Son's concurrence, as second person, in sending him as well as the Father, even as his person proceeded from both (as John xv. 26, 'whom I will send unto you'); but further, that Christ, as a redeemer, had a virtual meritorious influence or hand herein; so as for his sake, and through his purchase and intercession, the Father sends him. Christ purchased not only all the graces of the Spirit for us, but the Spirit himself (whom we had forfeited) to dwell in us. We have an express scripture, Gal. iii. 13, 14, 'Christ hath redeemed us from the curse of the law, being made a curse for us: for it is written, Cursed is every one that hangeth on a tree: That the blessing of Abraham might come on the Gentiles through Jesus Christ; that we may receive the promise of the Spirit through faith.' Where there are two ends adequately and alike made of Christ's being made a curse for us: 1. That we might receive the blessing of Abraham; 2. That we might receive the promise of the Spirit. And, forasmuch as the gift of the Spirit comes under a promise, as well as other blessings, it must needs come under the purchase of Christ's blood, which confirmed all the promises; and this, as all the rest of the promises are, 'yea and amen in him.' And to this end it is observable, that he breathed not the Spirit until after his resurrection; but then he did, John xx. 22, 'And when he had said this, he breathed on them, and saith unto them, Receive ye the Holy Ghost.' He had not shed his blood until now, and therefore breathed not the Holy Ghost until now. But Christ having died, and having, as the Lamb slain, purchased the Spirit, and being ascended up to the throne of God, he, as the Lamb, now sheds forth the Spirit: John vii. 38, 39, 'He that believeth on me, as the scripture hath said, out of his belly shall flow rivers of living water. But this spake he of the Spirit, which they that believe on him should receive; for the Holy Ghost was not yet given, because Jesus was not yet glorified.' He compares the Spirit, as communicated to us, to a spring of living water.

But not as then broke forth, as afterwards it should, because Christ had not died, and so entered into glory. Now compare with it Rev. xxii. 1: 'And he shewed me a pure river of water of life, clear as crystal, proceeding out of the throne of God and of the Lamb.' This water of life issues, you see, from the throne of the Lamb, who in the 5th chap., ver. 6, appeared at the throne of God as the Lamb slain, and redeeming us with his blood, and as such doth shed forth the Spirit upon us ; and is even there also said to have all the fulness of the Spirit on him, 'who hath the seven Spirits ;' that is, the Holy Ghost in all the varieties of his gifts and graces, called seven from perfection. For that the seven Spirits are taken metonymically for the Holy Ghost, is evident by chap. i., ver. 4: 'John to the seven churches of Asia: Grace be unto you, and peace, from him which is, and which was, and which is to come ; and from the seven Spirits which are before his throne.' Hence also when we receive the cup in the Lord's supper, which is termed the communion of Christ's blood, 1 Cor. x., we are yet said to 'drink into one Spirit ;' for that blood is *vehiculum Spiritus*, the Spirit runs in and with this blood. We therefore know whom we are beholden unto for the Spirit ; and whom to go unto for the Spirit, even to the Father, and to Christ, and to his blood ; and to the Father through Christ, who gives commission to the Spirit to work such and such measures of grace, at such times to fall upon us, and at such and such times to withdraw.

Hence, 3dly, the Spirit is given us from mere grace and love, and not according to works ; so in the text those words, 'who not according to works, but mercy,' &c., refer as well to this shedding forth the Holy Ghost, as to his saving us by regeneration. You may therefore observe, 2 Cor. xiii. 14, that the grace of the Lord Jesus, and the love of God the Father, are put before communion of the Holy Ghost, as that which proceeds from both. 'The grace of the Lord Jesus Christ, and the love of God, and the communion of the Holy Ghost, be with you all. Amen.' Therefore, in scriptures, both the law, the preaching of it, and the works of it, are in express words excluded and shut out from having any influence to convey the Spirit to us, that we may never so much as think to obtain the Spirit thereby: Jer. xxxi. 32, 'I will make a new covenant, not according to the covenant I made with their fathers ; but this shall be my covenant, I will write my law in their inward parts.' Which, compared with Ezek. xxxvi. 26, 27, is renewed with this addition, 'I will give you a new heart, and put my Spirit within you.' And you may compare with both, 2 Cor. iii. 3: 'Ye are manifestly declared to be the epistle of Christ, ministered by us, written not with ink, but with the Spirit of the living God ; not in tables of stone, but in fleshly tables of the heart ;' which clears both. Yea, so far forth as they in the Old Testament had the Spirit (as they had, Neh. ix. 20, 'Thou gavest them thy good Spirit to instruct them ;' and Hag. ii. 5, 'According to the word I covenanted with you when ye came out of Egypt, so my Spirit remaineth with you') ; so much gospel was even then mingled with it, and running in the veins of it. It was *fœdus mixtum*, and so in the virtue thereof the Spirit was (though in a lesser measure) given. Therefore, when the gospel came to take place, then the preaching of the law, or ceremonies of it, did not convey the Spirit: to shew that it was purely upon the covenant of grace that the Spirit is given, 2 Cor. iii. 6–8, 'Who also hath made us able ministers of the New Testament, not of the letter, but of the Spirit: for the letter killeth, but the Spirit giveth life. But if the ministration of death, written and engraven in stone, was glorious, so that the children of Israel could not stedfastly behold the face of Moses for the glory of his countenance, which glory was to be done away, how shall not the ministration of the Spirit be rather glorious?' You see that the old covenant is the ministration of the letter, and of death; and the New Testament, in exclusion of that Old, hath alone obtained this more excellent name, ' the ministration of the Spirit.'

As not the preaching of the law gave the Spirit, so, nor can any works of the law obtain the Spirit at God's hands. The text is as express for this as for the other: Gal. iii. 2, ' This only would I learn of you, Received ye the Spirit by the works of the law, or by the hearing of faith?' Paul useth that as *argumentum palmarium* against the law, as alone sufficient evidence. ' This one thing' (says he) ' I would learn of you,' and let that decide it, ' Received ye the Spirit by the works of the law, or by the hearing of faith?' By *Spirit* he here means the Spirit of regeneration and sanctification; for, ver. 5, he speaks of extraordinary gifts afterwards, and ver. 2, he speaks of that receiving which was general to all believing Galatians, even common to all saints, to whose universal experience he appeals, if ever any one of them had received him upon their doing. Now extraordinary gifts were not common to all saints, no, not in those days. And by ' the hearing of faith,' he means the doctrine of faith, the gospel; and ver 14–17, he asserts the Spirit to be given freely by the covenant of grace, which God afore the law did establish with Abraham, and in him together with Isaac (as the type) with Christ: Gal. iii. 14–17, ' That the blessing of Abraham might come on the Gentiles through Jesus Christ; that we might receive the promise of the Spirit through faith. Brethren, I speak after the manner of men : Though it be but a man's covenant, yet if it be confirmed, no man disannulleth or addeth thereto. Now to Abraham and his seed were the promises made. He saith not, And to seeds, as of many; but as of one, And to thy seed, which is Christ. And this I say, that the covenant, which was confirmed before of God in Christ, the law, which was four hundred and thirty years after, cannot disannul, that it should make the promise of none effect.' Yea (to end this), he makes it an evidence of not being under the law, if a man hath received the Spirit, and be led by him : Gal. v. 18, ' But if ye be led by the Spirit, ye are not under the law.' And for this also it is, that he is called ' the Spirit of grace,' Heb. x. 29, because given freely. He is ' the gift of grace,' Eph. iii. 7, and so given upon the terms of the covenant of grace.

Hence, from both these, appears the difference between Adam's having the Spirit in that estate of holiness, and the saints under the state of grace. Adam had the Spirit as well as we, and the Holy Ghost was at the making of him, and wrote the image of God upon his heart : for where holiness was, we may be sure the Spirit was too. The Holy Ghost was at that consultation,—' Let us make man,'—and one of the *us* spoken unto. Yea, and that Spirit that ' moved upon the waters,' who also is sent forth to ' renew the face of the earth' (Ps. civ.), the same Spirit was in Adam's heart to assist his graces, and cause them to flow and bring forth, and to move him to live according to those principles of life given him. But there is this difference between that his having the Spirit, and ours, apparent from what hath already been said.

1. That he concurred with Adam, merely as the third person, who joined in all works, and so upon no further account than as he concurred in assisting all creatures else in their kind, to cause the earth to bring forth fruits according to their kind; and, indeed, he must necessarily have a

hand in all works of creation and providence. Whereas we have the Spirit upon Christ's account, in his name, purchased by him, as whom he had first received, also purchased as the head of his church. And therefore it is ordinary in Scripture to term this Spirit as now dwelling in us, ' the Spirit of Christ,' Rom. viii. 9; ' the Spirit of the Son,' Gal. iv. 6.

And, 2. Hence Adam retained the Spirit according to the tenor of the covenant of works (which is but that equal law of creation between God and the creature), whereby he held a continuance of the privileges given him at the creation, even as he did life in God's sight, upon works of obedience : ' Do this and live.'

And as by one act of disobedience he forfeited life (' Cursed is he that continueth not in all things'), and so in like manner the Spirit was forfeitable by him upon the same terms. Even as in a man that comes from Adam, one mortal stab causeth the soul to depart, so here, one act of sin‧ning caused the soul* to depart ; for the bond of the union ceased. But as it would not be so in a man risen from the dead, and by the power of the second Adam, made a quickening Spirit ; no wounds would be mortal to such an one ; so here the gift of the Spirit to us is by promise, as Gal. iii. 14-17, the apostle argues. The gift of the Spirit, to a truly converted soul, is an absolute gift, and not upon conditions on our parts, but to work and maintain in us what God requires of us. The gift of the Spirit is not founded upon qualifications in us, to continue so long as we preserve grace in our souls, and do not sin it away. I will give you my Spirit to preserve you, and prevent your departing from me, Ezek. xxxvi. 26, 27. 'I will give you a new heart,' but you would soon make it an old one, as bad as ever ; to prevent this, it follows, ' And I will put my Spirit within you, and cause you to walk in my statutes, and ye shall keep my judgments, and do them.' And so it is said in Jer. xxxii. 40, ' Ye shall not depart from me.' He comes by virtue of election on us, as he did on Christ, Isa. xlii. 1, ' Behold my elect in whom my soul delights, I have put my Spirit upon him.' Gal. iv. 6, ' Because ye are sons' (by election, namely, as it is said, Eph. i. 5, God ' having predestinated us to the adoption of children'), ' God hath sent forth the Spirit of his Son into your hearts.' And Mat. x. 20, ' The Spirit of your Father is in you ;' that is, God having taken on him the relation of your Father, thereupon bestoweth his Spirit on you. And therefore it is that so few of many that hear the same sermons receive the Holy Ghost; for he comes on men by the grace of election, and so the Spirit picks and chooses (as God hath done), and rests on this soul, and not on that ; and so (as Isaiah says, Isa. xxvii. 12) they are gathered one by one. It goes as it were by lot, as it is (Acts viii. 21), spoken to Simon Magus, in relation to the Holy Ghost, v. 19. It hath the appearance of chance, because this man is taken, and not that ; when yet it is the eternal good pleasure of God that puts the difference. And the Spirit, that knows God's mind, seizeth on men accordingly ; and is said to be as the wind, that ' blows where it lists,' which is spoken of regeneration, John iii. 8.

Hence it is that he is given to us for ever, and not to depart from us ; the reason is, because his person is given without conditions, and to work all conditions, he is so in us as to be with us for ever ; John xiv. 16, 17, 'I will pray the Father, and he shall give you another Comforter, that he may abide with you for ever : even the Spirit of truth, whom the world cannot receive, because it seeth him not, neither knoweth him ; but ye know him, for he dwelleth with you, and shall be in you.' He came in

* Qu. ' Spirit' ?—ED.

Christ the head, to make his abode in him: John i. 33, ' And I knew him not: but he that sent me to baptize with water, the same said unto me, Upon whom thou shalt see the Spirit descending, and remaining on him, the same is he which baptizeth with the Holy Ghost.' Which was a fulfilling of that piece of the prophecy, Isa. xi. 2, ' The Spirit of the Lord shall rest upon him.' To which Peter alludes, speaking also of us, 1 Peter iv. 14, ' The Spirit of God resteth on you;' and to signify this, when visibly he came upon the apostles, Acts ii. 3, ' it sat upon each of them.' Christ's abode among us is compared to the dwelling in a tabernacle: John xiv., ἐσκήνωσεν, ' He dwelt as in a tabernacle amongst us,' for he soon removed to heaven. But the Spirit dwells in us as in the temple, which was, instead of that moveable habitation, a more fixed settled abode: 1 Cor. vi. 19, ' Ye are the temple of the Holy Ghost.' I go and come, says Christ, John xiv. 18, 19, but he shall be with you, and in you, v. 17, for ever. And therefore he is not only given as the earnest of our inheritance (Eph. i. 14, and 2 Cor. v. 5), a certain pawn that we shall have heaven; but he becomes also from that time a spring in us never to be dammed up, a living fountain of water, springing up into eternal life, as Christ himself speaks, comparing John iv. 14 with John vii. 38, 39. Now we do not say the spring shall continue whilst water is in the stream; but water shall continue in the stream, and bubble up whilst there is a spring. If indeed the spring could fail, the waters might fail. Now the Holy Ghost is given to become a perpetual spring, both of grace and glory. And accordingly also, 1 Peter i. 23, the Holy Ghost is said to be ' the incorruptible seed, of which we are begotten,' which some have understood to be meant of the word; but that is put in besides, as the instrumental cause, in the words following, ' by the word of God.' Nor is it the new creature which is there meant, for that is the thing begotten in us. But the principal cause of whom we are begotten is the Holy Spirit, John iii. 6, ' That which is begotten of the Spirit.' Now he is called the ' incorruptible seed,' because he is cast into the soul with the word, as the prolific virtue in the word; which is the seed *materially*, but the Spirit *virtually*. And this also shews the difference between this giving the Spirit by virtue of election, and that communication of him to temporary believers that fall away, who are said, Heb. vi., to be ' partakers of the Holy Ghost;' as Saul—' The Spirit of the Lord came on Saul,' 1 Sam. x. 10,—but so as to depart away again, 1 Sam. xvi. 14; thus on Balaam he did, Num. xxiv. 2. 2. and opened his eyes. The fundamental difference lies in the differing terms of the gift of the Spirit, insinuated here in the text: that many receive the Spirit, not from God as a Father, by virtue of election, or through Christ as a Saviour; they receive not, as children, the Spirit of God as from a Father; as Rom. viii. 14, 15; as also Mat. x. 20; and as Christ's speech also (in John 14th and 15th chapters, ' I will pray the Father,' &c.), doth import; but they receive him from God out of dominion and sovereignty, and from Christ as a Lord, who hath brought* even wicked men to serve him, 2 Peter ii. 1. This distinction of this double receiving the Spirit, the apostle insinuates both in that Rom. viii. and Gal. vi. 7, 8. In that Rom. viii. 15, he speaks of a ' Spirit of bondage,' which, as servants, they in some measure or other had formerly received from God. Look in what state men stand to God, they answerably more or less have a portion of his Spirit on them. If they are only in the state of servants, they have a ' Spirit of bondage' working legally that fear of death which is in all men: Heb. ii. 15, ' And

* Qu. ' bought '?—ED.

deliver them who, through fear of death, were all their lifetime subject to bondage.' The one place interprets the other. Those stirrings of guilt and condemnations which are in all men's hearts, are from workings of the Spirit in all men. The same Spirit that moved upon the waters, Gen. i., moves upon all men's hearts. Now if men live under the preaching of the law and gospel, then the same Spirit falls with higher works upon the spirits of men unrenewed, yet still but upon the same account that is mentioned : Gen. vi. 3, ' My Spirit shall not always strive with man, for that he also is but flesh.' He had spoken of the sons of God (ver. 2), that were the professors of that age, who lived under Noah's ministry, ' a preacher of righteousness,' Heb. xi. 7. And he went with his ministry in a way of striving with and opposing men's corruptions in their hearts ; of which Peter, (1 Peter iii. 18), having said that Christ was ' quickened or raised by the Spirit,' he adds (ver. 19), ' by which Spirit also he went and preached unto the spirits in prison, which sometimes were disobedient, when once the longsuffering of God waited in the days of Noah, while the ark was a preparing, when few, that is, eight souls, were saved by water.' These men were corrupt, and remained flesh, and yet received the Spirit, striving with them from God, as the Lord and Judge of the world, who to men fallen gives his Spirit, as at first he did to Adam, with a new stock of gifts and motions, but deals with them therein but upon a covenant of works. It is a favour indeed to give him, as all outward gifts of the Spirit are, but their persons being under the covenant of works, and servants, their retaining this Spirit is according to the terms thereof ; and so it proves in the issue, and their improving that gift is managed according to the dispensation of such a covenant. And so they, by opposing and resisting such strivings of the Spirit, God withdraws him. For he says, ' My Spirit shall not always strive.' He deals with them as with servants that are untoward and rebellious : John viii. 35, ' The servant abides not in the house for ever ;' but as Hagar was turned out of doors, and inherited not, so it is here. ' But' (says Christ) ' a son abides for ever in the house,' and therefore they, as children, receive ' the Spirit of adoption to cry, Abba, Father.' And the Spirit of Christ, as their head, remains in them, and they are overcome and led by the Spirit of God. These are sons ; and that they may abide in the house for ever, this Spirit abides in them for ever. You have the very same distinction of men receiving the Spirit as servants and as sons : Gal. iv. 6, 7, ' Because ye are sons, God hath sent forth the Spirit of his Son into your hearts, crying, Abba, Father. Wherefore thou art no more a servant, but a Son, an heir of God through Christ.' The meaning is, they receive the Spirit as sons, not as servants, as others do. To which add ver. 22, 23, &c., where Hagar and Ishmael, and Sarah and Isaac, are made the types of these two conditions of men living in the church, as they did in Abraham's family ; and Christ, John viii., alluded evidently unto it in that speech fore-quoted, verses 33, 34, 35, ' They answered him, We be Abraham's seed, and were never in bondage to any man ; how sayest thou, Ye shall be made free ? Jesus answered them, Verily, verily, I say unto you, Whosoever committeth sin is the servant of sin. And the servant abideth not in the house for ever, but the son abideth ever.' Both these, living under the means, had dealings with God : Gen. xxi. verses 17–20, ' And the angel of God called to Hagar out of heaven, and said unto her, What aileth thee, Hagar ? Fear not ; for God hath heard the voice of the lad, where he is. Arise, lift up the lad, and hold him in thine hand ; for I will make him a great nation. And God was with the lad,' &c. But yet this was but according to the covenant of works, whereof they were types. And their spirits used all gifts, motions, visions, &c., in such a way, and so at last the Spirit was withdrawn from them.

And therefore let not that deceive you, that men that fall away are said to be ' partakers of the Holy Ghost,' &c., for they may be so when yet they are not sons. The Holy Ghost comes to some as a wayfaring man, for a night. But do you not feel that though he may withdraw many effects, yet still his person is in you, and works, even amidst your sinnings, to reduce you again to God, and suffers you not to be finally overcome, but frames your hearts so as you give yourselves up to be led by him, and you treat with God of his abode in you, and of your salvation, not upon a covenant of works, but grace. Look to your tenure, by which God guides your hearts to seek the Spirit and salvation. Every man's heart and spirit (as a pen in his hand) is guided to write his own deeds and terms he holds salvation on. Dost thou treat with God, as a son, upon mere terms of free grace, renouncing Ishmael's covenant and tenure, not daring to treat with God upon these terms, If I walk thus and thus, God will give and continue his Spirit to me ? No ; but thou sayest as David, ' Lord, give me thy constant Spirit,' to work all in me, to cause me to walk in thy statutes. Ps. li. 10, 11, ' Create in me a clean heart, O God ; and renew a right spirit within me. Cast me not away from thy presence ; and take not thy Holy Spirit from me.' In the margin it is, ' a constant spirit within me ;' and if this is thy dependence and thy salvation, and if upon these terms thou holdest and retainest the Spirit, thou art a son. You esteem it in lands as a matter of great moment the tenure, whether it be freehold or copyhold. My brethren, know there is a freehold of the Spirit, and a copyhold ; and go over but thy prayers and the workings of thy spirit with God, and thou wilt easily see thy tenure.

CHAPTER IX.

That we not only partake of the effects of the Holy Spirit's operations in us, but also of his person dwelling in us.

There is a gift of his person, first and chiefly, or primarily ; but secondarily of his graces, to be wrought in us by him. And in this gift of his person doth consist the greatness, the richness of the gift. This is expressed in those words, ' Whom he shed on us richly,' Titus iii. 6. This, I say, is intended of his person first, and simply, and then of his graces and effects, as in the second place intended to us, as those which accompany the gift of his person, and as handmaids upon it, and do flow from and depend upon the bestowing and gift of himself. Thus there is the gift of the person of Christ to us and for us ; and there is the gift of all those benefits which he hath purchased ; but the gift of his person is, of the two, greater infinitely than that of his benefits, as the person is more worth than the dowry. And thus you are to look at the gift of the person of the Spirit more than all his χαρίσματα, or gifts. Let us hear how the Scripture speaks to this great point, and sets a value and indigitation upon it as in distinction from his graces : Rom. v. 5, ' The love of God is shed abroad in our hearts, by the Holy Ghost which is given to us.' Here you may observe a set distinction made between this one effect of the Spirit in us, viz., ' the shedding abroad the love of God in our hearts,' and the gift of the person of the Spirit; and how there is brought in a manifest super-addition of the gift of his person over and above that effect of shedding God's love : ' by the Spirit,' says he, ' which he hath given us.' Thus he speaks of the gift of the person himself singly and apart, distinct from the other ; yea, and as being the foundation of it. Take this instance and comparison. God having given a wife to a man, by whom he hath had such and such children, such and such an estate, benefits, and privileges ; when mention is made of any one of those good things that accrued by her, she, to heighten the mercy of the gifts, by the consideration of the person by means of whom the man hath them, might say, All these things are by the wife which God hath given thee. The same import you have in other such appendixes and additional clauses to the like purpose. Acts v. 32, ' And we ' (that is, apostles) ' are his witnesses,' (that is, Christ's) ' of these things ; and so is also the Holy Ghost,' (which manifestly refers to his person). The apostle adds, ' Whom God hath given to them that obey him ;' thus notably holding up unto their view the greatness of this gift. And indeed the pouring forth the Holy Ghost is all the discourse of the first ten chapters of the Acts. And therefore it is elsewhere called the ' gift of the Holy Ghost, Acts x. 45. It is not χαρίσματα (spoken of 1 Cor. xii.), gifts, in the plural, as speaking of his graces, but it is ' the gift,' as one absolute, full, and entire gift, once given for all ; his person containing virtually all other parcels and particular gifts, which he after works. The like addition to signify this you may observe, 1 Cor. vi. 19, ' Your bodies are temples of the Holy Ghost, which is in you, whom ye have of God.' This refers also manifestly to his person, as I shall have occasion further to shew ; and it comes in to mind them of the greatness of the gift, and the special favour of the donor, ' whom ye have of God.' Again you have it, 1 Cor. ii. 12, ' We have received the Spirit which is of God, that we may know the free gift of God to us.' Here is a double gift, and both from God, distinguished, 1, The grace or gifts of God and his Spirit bestowed on us, τα χαρισθέντα or χαρίσματα ; and 2, The gift of the person of the Spirit distinct from these, whom we receive (says he) as given by God first, and so received by us. And he is given (as to other ends) so that we may know these things he gives us, or works in us, the gift of which is distinct from that of his person, which is set out further by this τὸ πνεῦμα τοῦ Θεοῦ. The Spirit is out of God himself, and proceeding from him, and he is in God, as the spirit of a man in a man, ver. 11.

The reason of this is, because the Spirit is given us by the covenant of grace, which covenant makes freely over all that is in God unto us, and for our good ; all, both attributes and persons in him, the donation thereof running thus, ' I will be thy God, and thou shalt be my people.' I use to say that the covenant of grace is in all the transactions a covenant of persons. Consider that of election in the Father's hand ; he pitched not on qualifications, but persons, afore they had done good or evil, Rom ix. 13. And therefore so long as the persons remain, his love remains ; and thence he works that in the person which may make him comely : Eph. i. 4, ' He hath chosen us in him, before the foundation of the world, that we should be holy, and without blame before him in love.' And Christ, when he comes, he gives his person, ' He gave himself,' as everywhere it is said, both to us and for us ; and he died not for abstracted propositions, but persons. ' I lay down my life for my sheep, and I know them by name.' And when he applies his blood to us, he gives us himself, and the soul in the end see his person also, as Paul did, Phil. iii. 8. Thus answerably, in the third person, the gift of the Holy Ghost is the gift of his person to dwell in us.

The next thing to be considered is his coming upon us, and his dwelling in us. I have two assertions to add concerning this.

1. Concerning his coming upon us, and God's shedding him forth, my assertion is, that the first coming of the Holy Ghost is immediately upon us, as we are in our natural condition, in our uncleanness and pollution, without any preparation to make way for his coming upon us, or into us. He doth not work grace first, and then come into a man; but he comes first and seizeth on a man, then works grace in him. And this the text in Tit. iii. 6 insinuates; when weighing the mercy thereof, the apostle says, 'He shed his Spirit upon us.' On us; how qualified? The fourth verse tells us, 'Us, when disobedient, serving divers lusts and pleasures.' And he then sent him to renew us, ver. 5. Such were the vessels when this precious liquor was first poured into them, and upon them. And his coming first thus on men when in their natural state, is exemplified in the Corinthians; yea, and pressed on them as a great point, which the apostle would have them seriously to mind and consider, to the end they might ascribe unto the Holy Ghost his due glory: 1 Cor. xii. 1–3, 'Now concerning spiritual gifts, brethren, I would not have you ignorant. Ye know that ye were Gentiles, carried away unto those dumb idols, even as ye were led. Wherefore I will give you to understand, that no man speaking by the Spirit of God calleth Jesus accursed: and that no man can say that Jesus is the Lord, but by the Holy Ghost.' Being to treat of spiritual gifts infused into the people of God, he prefaceth this, I would have you (says he) know and consider these things about them. 1st, That the author of them is wholly and entirely the Spirit of God. 'No man can say,' or confess out of conviction of judgment, 'that Jesus is the Lord, but by the Holy Ghost.' And the embracing of this foundation of Christian religion was before any further spiritual gift was communicated unto you, but was indeed the foundation of bestowing it, 'for no man, speaking by the Spirit, calleth Jesus an execration.' Then, 2d, says he, I would have you remember the condition you were in when the Spirit of God began first to teach you this: you were all idolaters, led away as brute beasts after dumb idols, when also you execrated and abominated our Jesus (as to this day the Jews and heathens do), when it was certain, therefore, that you had not the Spirit of God in you; 'for no man that hath the Spirit calleth Christ accursed,' as ye then did. So then, who was the first beginner of this great change and alteration but the Spirit of God? And 3d, If this were your condition (as it was), what did or could the Spirit find in you, as preparatory and inviting of him thereunto? Absolutely nothing at all. The lowest and first step which can be supposed to be out of heathenism into Christianity, viz., the thoughts and profession that our Jesus is the Lord and Christ; even this first thought, which is the introduction to all, you, says the apostle, had from the Spirit of God first, as well as you have been enlightened by him since. 4th, He would have them further consider that they, when they were thus idolatrous, were acted and possessed by another greater spirit than their own, who invisibly was in them, and yet effectually wrought in them, and had possession of their minds, fancies, and affections (which unless he had been in them he could not have), 'Even Satan, that evil spirit, the god of this world,' who (as it is said, 2 Cor. iv. 4) blinded these heathens. This he clearly insinuates to them (and puts it in, as in opposition to their now having the Spirit of God) in these words, 'Ye were led after dumb idols.' Led, even as brute beasts are at the pleasure of them that possess them; and led by some other spirit than their own. It had

been impossible else that so many wise heathens should have worshipped dumb idols (as on purpose he terms them), themselves having reasonable souls, that thought and spake, which those idols, that had eyes and saw not, wanted. Now then the apostle would have them to consider that ere their judgments could be led to own Christ as Lord, this evil spirit must be dispossessed; and another spirit, even the Spirit of God, come in his room, and possess their hearts, and so lead them into all the truth they then possessed; without which they had never embraced the first element or principle of Christian verity. From which instance and experiment in the Corinthians, I infer, that the Spirit of God, when he converts men to things spiritual, comes upon a man when a heathen, suppose, as then the world went, or on us, when unregenerate. And it is confirmed by this, that the Holy Ghost reveals not any truth, or works any saving good, but a man first hath him sent down into his heart. He is first sent and shed upon us, ere we are led into all or into any truth; as the 14th, 15th, 16th chapters of John shew. We receive him as an unction first, ere he savingly teacheth us any truth. 1 John ii. 20, 'Ye have an unction from the holy One' (which is the Spirit, Acts x. 30), 'and ye know all things,' first and last. All that ye know in spirituals, it is from him, yea, and by having him first. And as from having him first it is that we begin to know, so, that we continue to know and acknowledge spiritual things savingly, is from his abiding in us. He in his person is first said to abide, and so to go on to teach us. So ver. 27 of that chapter, ' But the anointing which ye have received of him abides in you: but as the same anointing teacheth you of all things, and is truth, and is no lie, and even as it hath taught you, ye shall abide in him.' So then these idolatrous Corinthians, when they were converted to God, had first the Spirit communicated to them, casting out that evil spirit, and possessing his room in them, ere they could be taught the first letter in this school. Which agrees with what Christ says of the casting out Satan, in order to men's conversions (unto which Christ's scope extends): Mat. xii. 27, 28, 'If I by Beelzebub cast out devils, by whom do your children cast them out? therefore they shall be your judges. But if I cast out devils by the Spirit of God, then the kingdom of God is come unto you;' with which compare Luke xi. 20–22, &c. It is said by Matthew that it is the *Spirit*, by Luke, the *finger* of God, by whom Christ professeth to cast out devils, in men to be converted, as well as out of men possessed. This Spirit he compares there to a stronger than Satan, that comes upon him immediately as he is in his house or place,* binds him, and overcomes him; and so himself enters in, as Matthew's and Mark's phrase is. For it is entry and possession the Holy Ghost aims at; and it is the first thing he doth, after he hath pulled forth Satan, that was in possession, and bound him; and then, being entered, he throws out his goods and weapons, mortifies corruptions, and sanctifies the heart, and leads the soul into saving truths. And this is it which Paul insinuates, that he came upon these Corinthians, cast out the spirit that led them into error, entered himself, and led them into truth. And it was as necessary he should first come on them, ere they could spiritually assent to the first or least truth, as it is necessary he comes on us, and abides in us, to lead us into all truth else. And therefore it evidently follows, both, *first*, that the shedding forth, or entering in of the Holy Spirit is the first foundation to all wrought in us; and *secondly*, that therefore this his coming upon us and entering into us is immediately, without any preparation, when men are unregenerate.

* Qu. ' palace ' ?—Ed.

When Christ indeed comes to dwell in our hearts by faith, as Eph. iii. 17, there need be preparation in our hearts for that his coming, and there is a preparing the way of the Lord.   For he is to be received by our faith as a Saviour and Redeemer, and therefore we cannot receive him as supposed to be such until we see ourselves sinners.   But our receiving the Spirit is not *objectivè*, as we receive an object into our understandings or hearts, and so needs no preparation on our parts; for he himself must first come to work all apprehensions and affections in us, from first to last: Gal. iv. 6, ' He sends his Spirit into our hearts, crying, Abba, Father;' and he cries as he comes along.

There are two or three objections which I will answer.

Obj. 1. Can we imagine that the Spirit of God, who is so holy a Spirit, will come and enter into and possess himself of an unclean, filthy, and defiled heart, in the fulness and spring-tide of its filth and uncleanness ? Doth he not rather first make the heart holy, and then by that holiness dwell therein, seating himself in the new creature which he first creates ?   Thus indeed some have evangelised, and thereupon distinguished between his coming upon us, as at first, and his dwelling in us.

But I answer.

Ans. 1. That if the Spirit could be defiled in so doing, he would not do it ; but this earth muds not the water that gets into it to become a spring, no more than the sunbeams are by shining into a dunghill.

Ans. 2. The substance of the soul (which he comes to) is his own, and he comes to make it clean, which he cannot do, unless he gets within it.   It is well for us he is so holy, for no other water but of this preciousness would have virtue and power to cleanse us.   And this is no more absurdity than to say, that pure water is poured first into a vessel to take away the filth of it ; or that fire gets into and fills the pores of metals in the ore, whilst full of dross, to burn out, and consume, and separate it from them. Now these are the comparisons the Scripture useth: Ezek. xxxvi. 25, ' I will sprinkle clean water upon you.'   And is not that pity, you will say, that not only water, but clean water, should be poured upon defiled hearts, utterly defiled ?   God prevents the objection, in telling us that he thinks not much at this cost.   The cleanest, sweetest water that heaven affords, he chooseth, viz., his own Holy Spirit.   But the water is so clean, as it receives no tincture whilst it runs through you, and cleanseth you ; as it there follows, ' And ye shall be clean; from all your filthiness, and from all your idols, will I cleanse you ; and a new heart will I give you.'   And this is interpreted to be the Spirit: ver. 27, ' I will put my Spirit within you;' not *upon* you only : that will not serve to cleanse ; he therefore puts him first *into* you.   And what is this but what you read, 1 Cor. vi. 11, ' Such were some of you, but ye are washed :' there is the *genus*, or in common the Spirit's work ; the particulars follow : ' But ye are sanctified, but ye are justified, in the name of the Lord Jesus, and by the Spirit of our God.' The Spirit must do both,   And it is no strange thing ye should receive the Spirit, and he come into you to do all these, ere ever you are sanctified or justified.   That other comparison of fire, I need not insist on.   You have it, Isa. iv. 4, ' When the Lord shall have purged the blood of Jerusalem by the Spirit of burning.'   You know how the Holy Ghost in this respect is compared to fire up and down the New Testament.   Now what is it to the fire to enter into what is drossy and defiled, to eat it out and consume it ? Such fuel is proper for it to seize on, and shew its power upon.   And what is it to this rushing wind to enter into the middle of a rotten house (the old man) and blow it down, and rear up a new one in the room of it? And what is it for this strong man to enter into Satan's house, whilst he is in it, and throw him out, and spoil and rifle all his goods, and throw them out after him? He will not stand without doors to do it, as Christ also tells us.

Obj. 2. A second objection is out of John xiv. 17, where Christ, speaking of the Spirit, says, 'Whom the world' (or men unregenerate) 'cannot receive, because they see him not, neither know him : but ye know him ; for he dwelleth with you,' &c.

Ans. The answer is clear. That promise of the Spirit there is meant of him as a comforter and assurer of salvation; so ver. 16, ' I will pray the Father, and he will give you another Comforter, that he may abide with you for ever.' Now, as such, he can never come first on an unregenerate man, but he must be a Spirit of bondage first to him, and (as chap. xvi. ver. 8) ' convince the world of sin.' And therefore they in that condition are not capable of the Spirit as a sealer ; for they must have regeneration first, and faith first wrought: Eph. i. 13, ' After ye believed, ye were sealed with the Spirit of promise.' So as Christ's plain meaning is this : you that are already believers, and have already experimentally felt the workings of this Spirit in you, ' you know him' (says he), and to you, and to others that know him, by having been already wrought upon, I will send him as a Comforter, to fill your hearts with joy in believing, unspeakable and glorious. But unregenerate men are utterly incapable of this privilege, for they know him not in these first effects of regeneration and change of heart, and therefore as a comforter they see not nor know him. He must be a regenerator ere a comforter. Receive him they may to convert them, but not thus to assure them, until he hath wrought regeneration in them, as he hath done on you.

I shall now discourse about the indwelling or inbeing of the Spirit in us after he is thus come. Concerning which my assertion is this,

That the indwelling of the Spirit also is of his person primarily and immediately, and by his graces secondarily. And although it be *with* his graces, yet it is not primarily *by* his graces ; but his person is given to dwell in us immediately and for ever, and his graces secondarily. Our persons (bodies and souls) are the temples of his person immediately ; his graces are the hangings, the furniture, that he may dwell like himself, *ut habitet decorè,* that he may dwell handsomely. He is a holy Spirit, and ' holiness becomes his house,' as the psalmist speaks ; and so, though he comes first into bare walls, yet he afterwards adorns them. You have a parallel made in the Scriptures of this point of his indwelling with that former, of the gift of him : that as his person hath been shewed to be the great gift, and his graces the secondary gift, so his indwelling is primarily added to his person, and to his graces secondarily. Because sometimes in Scripture the Spirit is used to express his graces, the cause being put for the effect, therefore it hath been generally almost asserted that he dwells no otherwise in us than by having wrought such and such graces. But my position is, that as the person of the Spirit is primarily given, so his person doth primarily dwell in us, and his graces secondarily. And this I hope to make clear by parallel scriptures to those other.

I. That text in 1 Cor. vi. 19 (which I said I should have recourse to again), shews it: ' Your bodies' (and therefore much more your souls) ' are the temples of the Holy Ghost, who is in you.' It was not sufficient for him to say they were as his temples, for him to be worshipped in, by and through the graces he puts in them, but he adds, ' Who is in you, whom ye have of God.' Besides what afore was said, it appears further thus ; for as he heightens their sin of fornication, in the former verse, that it is against the person of Christ, in respect of their relation to him as a husband, so in like manner in this verse, that it is against the person of the Holy Ghost, an indweller in them : ' Ye are the temples of the Holy Ghost, who is in you.' It is therefore made a distinctive property of the Holy Ghost as in relation to the saints (even as procession is proper to him in relation to the Father), that he is the indweller in us : 2 Tim. i. 14, ' That good thing which was committed unto thee keep by the Holy Ghost which dwelleth in us.' You may observe that in the place before cited, how still there came in this superadditional clause, ' By the Holy Ghost which is given in us ;' so in like manner that other clause, ' the Holy Ghost which dwells in us,' where the person of the Holy Ghost, as thus dwelling in us, is spoken of as abstracted and severed from his grace by two characters: *First*, That he exhorts Timothy to keep the truth in faith and love ; ver. 13, as also ver. 14, that whole frame both of grace and form of truth, which he calls ' that good thing committed to him by the Holy Ghost.' For evidently severing the Holy Ghost's person, as the conservator of faith, and love of the truth, and of all that is good within us, or committed to us. He distinguisheth him (I say) from these graces as the things that are to be preserved by him. For else he should exhort to keep these graces by these graces themselves, if he meant that they were these graces by which the Holy Ghost doth only dwell within us. *Secondly*, his exhortation to Timothy runs not thus, ' By the Holy Ghost who dwells in thee,' which yet had been more proper if he had intended the indwelling of those graces in him ; but he speaks generally ' by the Holy Ghost who dwells in thee and us,' all in common.

II. It may be observed, that whereas both God and Christ, those other two persons, are also in Scripture said to be in us, and to dwell in us, yet this indwelling is more special, and *immediationi suppositi*, attributed to the Holy Ghost ; which, as it serves to give him an honour peculiar to him, so when set in such a comparison, even with them, must be meant and understood of his person immediately, and not by his graces only. Yea, the other two persons are said to dwell in us, and the Godhead itself, because the Holy Ghost dwells in us, he being the person that makes entry, and takes possession first, in the name and for the use of the other two, and so bringeth them in. I shall but name the place which looks this way : Eph. ii. 22, ' Ye are an habitation unto God by the Spirit ;' 1 Cor. iii. 16, ' Know ye not that ye are the temple of God ? ' namely, the Father, or (if ye will) the Godhead itself. And it follows by a special addition, ' And that the Spirit of God dwells in you.' So giving the original foundation or ground how we came to be tempies of God, because the Spirit of God dwells there. Or, as afterwards, chap. vi., ' The Spirit which ye have of God.' Likewise, 1 John iii. 24, ' He that keepeth his commandments dwelleth in him, and he in him.' Take it either of God the Father or the Son, for he had spoken of either : ver. 23, ' And hereby we know that he abideth in us, by the Spirit which he hath given us,' whom we feel dwelling and working in our hearts. And therefore our divines have generally affirmed it, that Christ is said to dwell in us, because first his Spirit dwells in us, from Rom. viii. 9, 10, compared. Now to me it were strange to interpret such speeches that God and Christ dwell in us, because their Spirit dwells in us, and then by the Spirit mean only his grace, or the Spirit only by his grace ; for the Spirit of God being a third person, must needs be acknow-

ledged an indweller as well as the other two ; yea, and to come in between
them and his own grace, seeing their dwelling in us is attributed to his.
The truth is, that it is in this union of ours with God, as in that of Christ;
that look, as in the union of the man Jesus unto the Son of God, and in
the indwelling of the Son of God in that human nature, the Son of God first
and originally dwells there, and he dwelling therein, the Father is in the man,
and the Spirit is in him, and he in the Father; so is it here in this subordinate union of ours that the third person comes as the first inmate in us, and
he taking possession, the other two come in and take up their abode also.

Or, if you will, you may view it in the Spirit's comforting of us, which
holds parallel to this.   Christ first promiseth to send the Spirit, as our comforter, into us: ' And when he is come ' (says he, John xiv. 15, 17), ' I will
pray the Father, and he shall give you another Comforter, that he may
abide with you for ever ; even the Spirit of truth, whom the world cannot
receive, because it seeth him not, neither knoweth him: but ye know him ;
for he dwelleth with you, and shall be in you.'   ' And in that day ' (ver. 20)
' ye shall know that I am in my Father, and you in me, and I in you.'   ' If
any man love me ' (ver. 23), ' my Father will love him, and we will come to
him, and make our abode with him.'   So the Spirit comes first.   And thus
it is even in their indwelling also ; so as indeed it may be rightly urged to
the point in hand, that if it be thus, that God and Christ dwell in us, because his Spirit dwells in us, that then much more it must be granted that
his graces are said to be and to dwell in our hearts, because the Spirit first
and primarily, who is the author of them, doth so ; as the beams do therefore dwell in this visible world, or the heavens, because the sun doth first
and originally dwell there, whose emanations and flowings forth they are.
I might bring an invincible argument from this, that he first comes ere he
works grace, but I refer it to the next head.

I observe that gifts and graces are called the manifestation of the Spirit,
1 Cor. xii. 7, that is, an outward demonstration or manifestation in men of
that Spirit that dwells and abides within the heart, and is invisible.   The
seeing of the eye, the hearing of the ear, the acting of the fancy, and speech
in the tongue, are the manifestation of the soul that dwells in the body, and
dwells not there *by* these, but *with* these ; and in order, the soul itself is
that ἐγελέχια,* that *actus primus* of these, as *actus secundi*.   And such is the
Spirit to our souls, and his grace, he dwelling first in us himself.   And
therefore, as *animalis homo* is a man that hath no more but a soul in him,
that informs him, and acts him, without the Spirit of God, so oppositely
he is a spiritual man (you have the opposition, 2 Cor. ii. 15) that hath
received into his heart the Spirit of God (read all the verses afore), that he
might know the things of God.

The objection which hath diverted men from this assertion is, that the
person of the Holy Ghost is everywhere: Ps. cxxxix. 7, ' Whither shall I go
from thy Spirit ? or whither shall I fly from thy presence?   If I ascend up
into heaven, thou art there,' &c.   And in that respect, his person is as
much in a worm as in the saints, and in all alike ; therefore, how can his
person be said to dwell more in the saints than elsewhere, otherwise than
by his effects and graces ?

1. According to the severity of this reason, the second person, the Son of
God, should not be said to dwell otherwise in the human nature of Christ
than by effects and graces, which, Col. ii. 9, he is said to do: ' For in him

* Qu. ''εντελέχεια ' ?—Ed.

dwelleth all the fulness of the Godhead bodily,' in distinction from saints and angels. For essentially, as he is God, he is also in the meanest creature; and yet the person of the Son, and the Godhead itself, dwells personally in that nature, and not the graces only. Now, what is it makes that indwelling to be more than by graces and effects, and so puts that vast difference? All acknowledge that it is because he takes up that human nature into a nearer relation to his person, so as to be one person with it immediately; and such an union graces alone work not, nor gives foundation unto. And so he dwells in him upon that account.

Well then, 2dly, it is true that into so near and high a relation the saints are not taken up. They are not made one with the Spirit, nor doth the Spirit dwell in them upon that account. The Spirit dwelling in a saint is not said to be 'made flesh,' as the Word is, John i. 14; for then, what good or evil the saints do would personally be accounted the Holy Ghost's; our prayers his, subjectively; yea, and our sins his; as the blood and obedience of that man Jesus was the blood and obedience of God, and the Son of God. Therefore our relation to the Holy Ghost's person is not so near by God's ordination. Yet,

3dly (as to the point in hand), We are capable and are made partakers, by the like ordination and free gift of God, of a relation, or propriety rather, to the very person of the Holy Ghost, which, though it be lower than that of the Son of God to human nature in Christ God-man, yet it is not founded upon graces, but is beyond them, and before them, even by God's free and absolute gift and donation of his person to us, in order to such graces, and the working of them in us. So as that this person should indeed dwell in us, in reference to graces as the final cause, but not the instrument at all, or means of his indwelling. It is *unio personarum*, an union of two persons immediately, us and him remaining two persons still, as that of marriage is of two persons immediately, in order to such and such ends. And it is not *unio personalis*, to become one person, as that of the two natures of Christ, the human and the divine, which is *unio duarum naturarum*, but not *unio naturalis*, of two natures, but not into one nature, but one person. And this difference was exemplified in Christ himself, our head, in the man Christ Jesus, in whom the Spirit of God dwells, not personally, for then Christ would be one person with the Holy Ghost as well as with the Son of God; nor doth the Father dwell personally in Christ, for then all three persons should have been said to be incarnate. And yet I suppose none will say that the person of the Spirit, nor of the Son, dwells in the man Jesus only by means of his graces. But further, the person of the Spirit first rests on the man Christ, which person he hath a right unto, that he should dwell in him, because that man Christ Jesus is now united to the second person personally, and so to his graces secondarily. So as if we ask whether in order of nature the person of the Spirit dwells in him first, or the Spirit by its graces, we may without any hesitation answer, the person of the Spirit primarily, and then his graces. Unto which seems to me to accord that in Isa. xi. 12, where it is first said, 'The Spirit of the Lord shall rest upon him;' namely, the person of the Holy Ghost, simply and absolutely considered; then relatively, as in order to endowing him with such and such particular graces, viz., 'The Spirit of wisdom and understanding, the Spirit of counsel and might, the Spirit of knowledge, and of the fear of the Lord.'

Now for the manner of the indwelling of the Holy Ghost's person; it is no error to affirm that it is the same in us and the man Christ Jesus. Sure we are capable of it, and therefore shall have it, we being to be conformed to his image and likeness (as he to ours) in all that is possible, as he was to us, sin only excepted; so we to him, the personal union and the privilege of it excepted. Only, indeed, we differ herein from him in two things. 1. In the measure; for he hath the Spirit given him 'without measure' in his effects. 2. In the right to this indwelling of his person in us, and in him. He holds it as a royalty, and one of the greatest, from his personal union with the Son of God. We hold it in his right, and by virtue of the covenant of grace, and free donation; for because we are sons adopted in him, 'he hath sent the Spirit of his Son into our hearts,' Gal. iv. 6. But the *modus*, the manner of the indwelling, is one and the same.

These things long since satisfied me in this great point, and I submit them to judgment.

CHAPTER X.

The uses of the foregoing doctrine.

Use 1. Let us view with admiration the riches of this gift of the person of the Holy Ghost. It is the word which the apostle useth here in the text, 'whom he shed upon us,' πλουσίως, 'richly.' Let us value him accordingly. You value the things (every one of them) which God hath given us; then value the Spirit much more, who is the author of the most, and discoverer of them all. Take the most precious of graces, 'like precious faith' (as Peter calls it), assurance of the love of God, which is the earnest of glory; the gift of the Spirit that works this faith, and the shedder abroad of this love, is infinitely greater. And therefore, in Rom. v. 5, after the enumeration of faith, and all the fruits of it, peace with God, rejoicing in hope of glory, patience, experience, shedding abroad the love of God in our hearts, it is super-added, as more than all these, being the root, the spring of all, 'the Spirit which he hath given us.' Yea, and as in ver. 6, 7, 8, he sets out the greatness of the love of God, that gave Christ to die for us; so, in those verses aforesaid, he would in like manner insinuate the greatness of that love that gave us this Holy Spirit to work all these graces in us, and reveal the love which God hath so commended. Insomuch as this hath been started as matter of debate, and most serious consideration, by some divines; whether *Filius datus* (Isa. ix.), 'To us a Son is given,' or *Spiritus datus*, 'The Spirit given' (Rom. v.), be the richer favour? Whether the incarnation, 'God manifest in the flesh,' or the diffusion, or 'pouring forth of the Spirit upon all flesh,' be the greater mercy? From heaven they both came down, the Spirit as well as the Son, 1 Pet. i. 2, and from the bosom of the Father both. They are both of them pawns, and earnests, and witnesses alike, of one and the same love. It is also a dispute among interpreters, whether the gift of God, which, Κατ' ἐξοχήν (as it is called), is predicated so much, and held at so high a rate, John iv. 10, be Christ, or the Spirit, 'Jesus answered and said unto her, If thou knewest the gift of God, and who it is that saith to thee, Give me to drink; thou wouldst have asked of him, and he would have given thee living water.' It is questioned whether, as the sole sufficient satisfying object of our desires, is the gift of the Son or the gift of the Spirit? Whether Christ means himself, or the Holy Ghost, as given to us? Many carry it to Christ, but the context more clearly carries it to the Spirit. For, 1, the gift of God (as there)

seems to be distinguished from, rather than explained by, that which follows. ' Who it is that saith to thee,' and ' give me drink,' seem as two
things, not one and the same.   And, 2, that gift is clearly that living water
which God and Christ give, and that is the Spirit, ver. 14 being compared
with John vii. 38, 39.   In the Old Testament you hear of it, as more than
all the mercies of giving the law, or bringing out of Egypt.   ' Thou gavest
them thy good Spirit to instruct them.'   So Neh. ix. 20, 80, it is twice
expressed, as also Isa. lxiii., when he professeth to mention ' the loving-
kindness of the Lord, according to all he hath bestowed upon us,' ver. 7.
Where you may see how he heaps up and multiplies words to set out the
riches of God's mercies by.   And this he reckons the greatest of their sins,
that ' they rebelled and vexed his Holy Spirit,' as the greatest mercy of all,
' and therefore he fought against them,' ver. 10.   And then himself remembers what his kindness of old had been, and how doth he express the height
of it?   ver. 11, ' Where is he that put his Holy Spirit within him ?'   And
when the temple was built again, and they delivered out of Babylon, what
is the greatest promise God could make, till Christ should come and give a
greater measure of his Spirit?   You have it, Hag. ii. 5, ' According to the
word I covenanted with you, when I came out of Egypt, so my Spirit
remains among you,' as the greatest pledge and pawn of my favour, ' fear
you not.'   But in the New Testament, there you hear of it again and again;
as in the Old, ' Thou gavest them thy good Spirit ;' so in the New, ' He
hath given his Holy Spirit,' is written almost in every epistle.   It is almost
all the talk, and fills their mouths throughout all the book of the Acts ;
especially the first fifteen chapters, it was all their talk and speech.   The
first question they asked, when they met any that professed Christ, was (as
Acts xix. 1, 2), ' Have ye received the Holy Ghost,' yea or no ?   So transcendent a privilege is it, that it is recorded as the emulation of the Jews
against the Gentiles.   The Jews had wont to make Messiah their glory (as
Simeon hath it, Luke ii. 32, ' The glory of thy people Israel').   But when
they had received the Holy Ghost (Acts ii.) they would have run away with
it alone, as the richest prize, till God confuted them, by pouring forth the
same Spirit equally, and as much upon the Gentiles, thereby giving both
sorts his children an equal portion in him, as being the whole of his estate
now left to bestow, having given his Son afore: Acts xi. 17, ' Forasmuch
as God gave them' (says Peter) ' the like gift of the Holy Ghost, as he did
unto us,' which argued the utmost of his favour to the one as well as the
other ; as that of the prophet also shews, Ezek. xxxix. 29, ' Neither will I
hide my face any more from them, for I have poured forth my Spirit upon
them, saith the Lord.'   Nay then (say the Jews there), let them take all,
as well as we.   God hath withheld nothing from them, ' for then hath God
granted the Gentiles repentance unto life' ver. 18, and estated them in
all promises, in all privileges of life, for he hath given them his Spirit.
Who dares deny to baptize them ?   Who dares to shut them out from any
privileges ?   ' For they have received the Holy Ghost as well as we,' says
Peter, Acts x. 41.   And in that hot dispute in Acts xv., about the Gentiles'
salvation, Peter silences all with this (ver. 8, 9), ' God, who knows their
hearts, hath given them witness, giving them the Holy Ghost, as he did to
us, and put no difference between them and us' (so ver. 11).   They and we
are heirs alike of the same salvation; and God (saith Paul an apostle, and a
Jew, unto the Gentile Corinthians) hath established us with you, and you
with us, ' hath anointed us,' and ' sealed us,' and ' given us the earnest of
his Spirit in our hearts,' 2 Cor. i. 21, 22.   That as the apostle argues,

'If he hath given us his Son, how shall he not with him give us all things?' so the sum of these agitations is, that if God hath given us his Spirit, how shall he not give us, I do not say, *with* him only, but *in* him, even in that one gift of him, give us all things? In this one gift of the Holy Ghost (as it is termed, Acts x. 47, and often elsewhere)—not gifts, as of many, but gift, as of one—is contained all the whole, both of grace and glory; *tanquam in fonte, tanquam in semine ;* as in the seed and fountain of both.

Use 2. Is the gift of the Spirit that great and rich gift which God vouchsafes to the sons of men ? Then how miserable are they that have not this Spirit in them, nor have had any workings from him in order to their salvation, to this very day! that live a life of sensual pleasures, in enjoying meat, drink, marriage, beauty, great houses, riches, fine clothes; and then say (as in Revelations iii. 17), 'I am rich, and have need of nothing; and knowest not that thou art wretched, and miserable, and poor, and blind, and naked;' for why, thou wantest the Spirit. When Jude would express the misery of these sensual wretches, his words are, ver. 19, 'not having the Spirit.' And indeed (Rom. viii. 5, 6), 'they that are after the flesh do mind the things of the flesh; but they that are after the Spirit the things of the Spirit. For to be carnally minded is death; but to be spiritually minded is life and peace.'

Use. 3. Let me instruct your hearts accordingly to direct your prayers hereafter with answerable intentions and vehemency, for the gift of the Spirit himself. You pray in the Spirit, and you bless in the Spirit ; let me exhort you to pray for the Spirit above all, and to bless God for this Holy Spirit, as one of the greatest blessings of all. When the apostle saw the Corinthians eager after spiritual gifts, his care and skill v as to pitch their aims and desires upon what was most excellent : 1 Cor. xii. 21, 'Covet the best gifts ; and yet I shew you a more excellent way.' Thou seekest after particular mercies, and some one particular grace thou at present findest thou needest, to be humbled for sin, to be emptied of thine own righteousness, to have the right way and art of believing particularly discovered to thy heart, or to have power against such a lust, &c. And thou dost well, for thou art to branch thy prayers into all particular wants. But yet let me shew thee a more excellent way. Pray for the Spirit himself to be given thee ; and whilst thou seekest for the stream, forget not the fountain. For when God gives thee him more and more to dwell in thee, and fill thee and mingle with thine heart, he brings with himself all these unto thee. Is thine heart hard? If God pour this water on thee, it will soak into it, and soften it. Wouldst thou see thy sinfulness, the most spiritual wickedness of unbelief, &c., in thee ? 'When he is come, he will convince of sin, because they believe not in me,' saith Christ. He that searcheth the deepest things of God, is much more able to search and discover the shallows of thy heart. Wouldst thou have no confidence in the flesh, but be purely carried out of thyself to seek the righteousness of Christ alone, and be found therein ? Read Gal. v. 5, 'We through the Spirit wait for the righteousness of faith.' Wouldst thou have joy and peace in believing, joy unspeakable and glorious, the love of God shed abroad in thine heart ? Pray for the Spirit: Rom. xv. 13, 'Now the God of hope fill you with all joy and peace in believing, that ye may abound in hope, through the power of the Holy Ghost.' Wouldst thou have thy lusts mortified ? 'We through the Spirit mortify the deeds of the flesh,' Rom. viii. 13. 'And ye through the Spirit have purified your hearts,' 1 Peter i. 22.

Our Saviour Christ, both in his own practice and direction to us, hath guided us to this, as the great request. 1. By his own example; for what is made the greatest and most professed subject of the flower of the most raised prayers that our great high priest eternally puts up for us ? Yea, and upon what occasion did he first promise that he would pray for us ? It is even this : 'I will pray the Father to give you another Comforter, even the Holy Ghost,' John xiv. 16, 26. You may judge what things your own or others' judgments and apprehensions are raised up to as most excellent, by what your prayers and desires therein reach forward to, as the mark of your eye. Therefore in Christ's judgment, that knows best what is to be prayed for, this is the most excellent. Yea, and you may take this further estimate of it, that he promiseth to spend his prayers now in heaven (and if ever his heart is wound up to the highest strains, it is there), yea, his prayers and intercessions there are spent most upon this subject. And though he may be supposed to pray for other things we stand in need of, yet I am sure this in particular is mentioned, and perhaps the first and chiefest.

And as his own practice, so his direction pitcheth us upon this also. And he cites his father's judgment also of this to be the best request we can put up ; that if ever we were confined to ask but some one thing, he would advise us to ask this. In the 11th of Luke, Christ himself had been praying, and was upon that occasion desired to teach them to pray, ver. 1 ; and he gives them many particulars in that we call *the Lord's Prayer*, and then makes a parable to provoke them to importunity, ver. 5, 6, 7 ; and bids them 'Ask,' and 'seek,' and 'knock,' all being several degrees of more urgency, vehemency, and importunity, so ver. 9 ; with promise that such shall in the end receive, ver. 10. But then what is the most eminent thing, the best, he would direct you to pray for ? Though he had given the particulars in the Lord's Prayer, he singleth out this of the Spirit : ver. 13, ' If ye then, being evil, know how to give good gifts unto your children ; how much more shall your heavenly Father give the Holy Spirit to them that ask him ?' He wraps up this direction in a promise, and delivers it by way of promise for their greater encouragement, and he calls in his Father's judgment to prove that this is the best and greatest request : ' If you, that are evil, know how to give good things to your children.' According to your judgment you use to give the best, and use to exercise your best judgment therein ; then take your heavenly Father's judgment, which is most excellent and desirable, even ' his Spirit.' And therefore, Mat. vii. 11 expresseth it thus : ' How much more shall your Father in heaven give good things,' even all good things (for such the Spirit summarily is), ' to them that ask him ?' This is the Father's judgment, you see, and it is Christ's, and you may be sure it is the Spirit's. You cannot honour him more than to pray most for him, that makes all your prayers ; and he takes it kindly to see himself most desired by you, that is the author of all your desires. You may observe also how Christ pitcheth our thirstings upon this great sea and ocean of goodness, able to supply us with whatever we desire. He had taught them (Mat. v.) to ' hunger and thirst after his righteousness,' and holiness therewith, with a promise of blessedness. But in the great day of the solemn feast, he makes this proclamation, John vii. 37-39, upon this last day of the feast he brings forth his best wine—' Be filled with the Spirit, and not with wine'—he proclaims his best commodity at the end of this assembly. And you may observe he says but in general, ' He that thirsteth,' he names not what ; because, let it be what good soever the mind of man could be supposed to stretch its desires to, that Spirit which he spake of, ver. 39, was a complete satisfaction to it, and so as they might thirst no more. And he directs them to two things; 1, to believe on himself, and come to him who was to give the Spirit; and then, 2dly, to come to his Spirit as given by him, whom we are also said to drink, 1 Cor. xii. 13. Our prayers are the most precious actings of our souls, and it is the greatest advantage that can be to us to have the aims of our prayers set to the best and highest marks. And upon all accounts you have seen this to be it, to pray for the Spirit. And therefore learn hereafter, in your prayers, not to deal or traffic in particular or small wares only, but put in for the whole stock of the Spirit, as wise merchants use to do, and as Christ himself (as you have heard) in his intercession doth. And observe it in experience, when the Holy Ghost comes upon you, and fills your hearts as another Spirit, sensibly mingling with yours, then if you go over all the promises and find them yours, you can then apply this or that, or any one. And why? Because you have the great promise, 'the Spirit of promise.' You may (let me say it with reverence) at such a time make use of the Spirit to anything whatsoever. You may fall upon your lusts by him, and do more at such a time for the destroying of them than in many prayers after. You may 'by the Spirit' then, at such a time, 'mortify the deeds of the flesh.' At such times improve your opportunity; for, having the Spirit, you have all good things, and you may ask what you will and have it. And yet even then ask still for more of himself.

Use 4. If the Holy Ghost be the great indweller in us, and graces but the manifestations of him, then let us shew forth the virtue of him that dwells in us, and be holy, as he is holy: as Cor. iiii. 16, 17, 'Know ye not that ye are the temple of God; and that the Spirit of God dwelleth in you? If any man defileth the temple of God, him shall God destroy; for the temple of God is holy; which temple ye are.' You see what a heinous thing it is to defile the heart or soul, because his temple. But elsewhere the apostle holds forth a stronger motive, even that the Spirit dwells in us, as the soul doth in the body, and the life we lead is his, not ours; as the life of the body is not of the body, but of the soul in the body. This is the purport of that Gal. v. 25, 'If we live in the Spirit, we walk in the Spirit.' The question first is (for opening of it), What is meant by that phrase, 'if ye live in the Spirit.' And how is it to be distinguished from 'walking in the Spirit'? If to live in the Spirit were meant to be active, lively, or striving in actions of spiritual life, to walk in the Spirit would be all one; it would be but *idem ex eodem;* for to live, in that sense, is to move and walk. But the genuine notion that interprets this is, that he intends a comparison:—

1. Between the soul's indwelling in our bodies as a principle of life, and the Spirit's like indwelling as the fountain of spiritual life; which that in the prophet also insinuates, Ezek. xxxvii. 14, 'I will put my Spirit into you, and ye shall live.' 2dly, That as walking or action of life spring from the soul's indwelling, so should an answerable walking from this of the Spirit's like indwelling. And so this expression, 'if ye live in the Spirit,' is a persuasion drawn from a common professed principle. His inference runs thus: Consider whom you have in you. The Spirit. And how? Even as a constant principle of spiritual life. And to that end he doth dwell and abide in you, as your reasonable soul doth in your bodies. If you profess this, then live, and act, and walk, and shew forth graces worthy and suitable to so great and holy a Spirit, that hath vouchsafed and condescended thus to dwell in you, and become a fountain of such a life in you and to you.

Every living thing acts according to that soul that is in it, according to the degree of vigour and activity, and kind of life communicated thereby. If you then profess to live in the Spirit, walk in the Spirit ; as if you should say to a sottish man (*Cui anima inservit tantum pro sale*), If you be a man, have a reasonable soul in you, act and carry yourself as a man, and be not not like a beast that perisheth.

The only inquest will be, Why, if he intend this similitude of the soul's indwelling (as it is evident he doth), he should express it thus : ' If you live in the Spirit '?

The answer is, It is true that we indeed, in common speech, rather use to say the soul lives in the body, than that the body lives in the soul ; though in reality it be true that the body rather lives in the soul, than the soul in the body, the soul being a principle of life unto the body, and not *e contra*. The apostle thereupon, to express perfect and real dependence of life spiritual upon this great Spirit, chooseth rather to say, ' Live you in the Spirit,' thereby importing this Spirit to be the same to us in respect of all grace and spiritual life communicated to us by union with, and indwelling in us, that the soul is to the body. And yet of Christ, Paul useth even that other phrase also (though only when he speaks of the activity of a Christian's life), that ' Christ lives in us,' Gal. ii. 20.

Use 5. Grieve not this Holy Spirit. That expression imports the highest motive. Superiors use to be offended, familiar friends grieved ; the Spirit, considered as a superior, therefore to resist him is termed rebellion, : Isa. lxiv., ' They rebelled against his Holy Spirit.' But because he vouchsafes also to become a familiar friend (as hath been declared), therefore he is also said to be grieved. And if you have love in you, that will move you more, when you think him you grieve is God, Isa. xxvii. 13. To grieve not man only, but God, is load enough ; more than to say you offend him. Grieve not the Holy Spirit of God, is comparatively guarded with a trinity of articles, τὸ πνεῦμα τοῦ Θεοῦ τὸ ἅγιον. They shew his greatness and his goodness : his greatness, that he is the Spirit of God ; his goodness (1.), the Holy Spirit in himself ; (2.) that he hath sealed you. We would not grieve a brother, Prov. xxiii. 19, much less a father. You would not grieve a minister that watcheth over men's souls, as a substitute under the Holy Ghost (Heb. xiii.), much less himself. If thou hast done so, there is no way but to be grieved too, and as fire best takes out fire, so thy grief that of the Spirit's.

I say no more but this to myself and you. There is a day a-coming in which you will need him and all his cordials ; therefore I speak to you in the words of Ecclesiasticus, which is the voice of that bodily self-love in us, and let it be of spiritual self-love also, ' Honour thy physician.' So treat this Holy Spirit, as thou wouldst one from whose prescription thou art in a continual course of physic, and none have skill but he. For when thou comest to die, his cordials must alone support, for none of any other's making will do thee any good. It is these, and these alone, must comfort, and carry thee to heaven.

‗ The chapter ends abruptly, and is probably incomplete. In the folio edition there is at the bottom of the page the catchword ' And,' and the following page is left blank in all the copies that we have been able to consult. In other cases we have found pages blank in one copy, but not in another of the same edition, the omission being manifestly caused by the carelessness of the printers. In this case, however, it is probable that the manuscript left by the author was unfinished.—Ed.

BOOK II.

That there are two states or conditions through which God carries the elect the state of nature, and the state of grace.—That the new birth is the passage between them, which evidenceth the necessity of the new birth, or regeneration.—The reasons why God hath so ordered it, that the generality of the elect, who live in riper years, should for some time remain in the state of nature before he renews them.—The uses of the doctrine.

*But after that the kindness and love of God our Saviour toward man appeared, not by works of righteousness which we have done, but according to his mercy he saved us, by the washing of regeneration, and renewing of the Holy Ghost; which he shed on us abundantly through Jesus Christ our Saviour; that being justified by his grace, we should be made heirs according to the hope of eternal life.—*TIT. III. 4–7.

CHAPTER I.

The words of the text explained; from which, and other scriptures, it is proved that the elect are in a state of sin and wrath before they are brought into a state of grace.

THIS text doth afford these heads to be treated on:

I. That there are two different states or conditions, which the elect of God, that are saved, pass through, between which regeneration is the pass.

1. The one is their first state in which they were born, a state of bondage to sin, and obnoxious to instant damnation whilst they remain in it. This is clear in the words, and is premised to celebrate the mercy of it; for having mentioned all men, in the very words afore, in exhorting to shew meekness to all men, it follows, for we ourselves, whom God hath now shewn mercy unto, and severed and called out from the rest of mankind, were also sometimes disobedient, serving divers lusts and pleasures. These words, 'we also sometimes,' both import, that as the rest of men remained in this woeful state, so themselves, though now saved, were once in the same state of bondage to sin, serving divers lusts, and thereby obnoxious to damnation.

2. The other state is of grace and salvation; therefore oppositely to that former state, he says, He hath saved us, justified us, and made us heirs of life. *Us,* who in the former estate had been heirs of hell, and children of wrath, as the opposition shews.

II. Hence it follows that the new birth is the *transitus,* or passage between those two states, and the necessity thereof from thence may be demonstrated.

III. And, thirdly, that God, to magnify his grace, mercy, love, kindness (for all these are named) the more, leaveth many, or most of those he saveth, to remain and continue, for some time, in the first estate, before he doth regenerate them.   For Paul, speaking of the commonalty and bulk of them in distinction from all other men, says, ' We ourselves were sometimes disobedient,' and so remained and continued in that condition as well as other men.   But at length, ' after the love of God appeared towards us' (says he), ' he saved us by regeneration,' and it all tends to shew as well the necessity as the mercy of it.

IV. Hence then it is evident, that the eminentest mercy that God doth, or which may be judged to be vouchsafed us in our whole lives, or to eternity, is the laying the foundation in his first renewing, and regenerating us by his Spirit, as being the *transitus*, or the passage between both, by which we become translated from the one, and actually admitted into the other, of salvation : ' According to his mercy he saved us, by the washing of regeneration, and renewing of the Holy Ghost, which he shed on us abundantly, through Jesus Christ our Saviour : that being justified by his grace, we should be made heirs according to the hope of eternal life.'

V. Further, to set forth the mercy of it, there is presented here as great a solemnity at this business, as ever was or shall be found in any work done for us, namely, a joint concurrence, and yet distinct appearance, in a set and solemn conjunction of all three persons, Father, Son, and Holy Ghost.   A happy constellation or conjunction of the planets falling out at the instant of the birth of some great prince (especially if you supposed it one of those greatest conjunctions, whereof but six have been since the creation) how wonderful a prognostic would this be accounted by astrologers, of great and glorious events to follow and accompany him so born, and thus honoured and marked forth at his birth.   But, lo ! a more glorious conjunction, of the three glorious persons in the heaven of heavens, of the three witnesses in heaven, as John terms them, solemnly meeting and appearing as witnesses at this great baptism, the only true baptism, the new birth of every believer ; called, therefore, ' the laver' or ' washing of regeneration, and renewing of the Holy Ghost.'   1. The Father is implied in the 4th verse.   After the love of our Saviour, he saved us by renewing us ; for God our Saviour, in the 4th verse, is clearly made a distinct person from Jesus Christ, our Saviour, ver. 6 ; so then the Father is meant. 2. The Holy Ghost is mentioned, for it is called ' the renewing of the Holy Ghost,' was then shed on us abundantly.   3. Jesus Christ is named in those words, ' through Jesus Christ our Saviour.'   All this displays the greatness of the mercy of our regeneration, which Peter had only in general words expressed (1 Pet. i. 3) ; but Paul, you see, doth it more particularly here, though Peter indeed doth also express the authors of this work ; for there is first God, as in opposition to all created causes : ' Blessed be God, who hath begotten us.'   In God all three persons are included, having a distinct and proper hand in it, though of all the three persons the Holy Ghost more eminently and specially.   His name is taken into its very denomination.   It is termed and denominated by the apostle, ' the renewing of the Holy Ghost,' as elsewhere the thing begotten : John iii., ' That which is born of the Spirit.'   Lastly, in Christ, who is κατ' ἐξοχὴν, our Saviour, of all transactions of his for our salvation, his resurrection hath the most eminent influence into our new birth, as the instrumental cause ; and for that I must have recourse unto Peter, and fetch it out of him, ' who hath begotten us again by the resurrection of Jesus Christ.'

Obs. That there are two vastly differing estates of sin and damnation, of grace and salvation, which the new birth is the passage between, and the *transitus* from the one to the other. This I must premise, as the apostle doth, in order to shew both the absolute necessity of regeneration, and greatness of the mercy of it. Not this scripture alone, but all the epistles, give eminent evidence to my assertion, and under several metaphors and expressions (wherein each delights in its variety) set forth maps and descriptions of these two estates, which argues this matter to have been, in the preachings of the apostles, a point of greatest moment. And this discrimination made is not to be understood as the setting out two sorts, or ranks, or destinies of men; as if the one sort consisted only of persons that were reprobate, the other of elect, or as if none but reprobate should be understood to be in the estate of nature, and the elect to be such as were always in no other estate but the estate of grace. It is true indeed that all elect, sooner or later, are in the end translated into the estate of grace, or they could not be saved. And on the contrary, those whom God passeth by are left to continue and persist in the state of sin and damnation to their deaths, and they die in their sins, as Christ speaks. But these two differences in mankind are to be looked upon as two estates or conditions, whereof the one hath salvation, the other damnation, actually belonging to them at the present; whilst any, either elect or they who are passed by, are respectively the subjects of either. And therefore we find this different condition exemplified in one and the same persons themselves of the elect, take them in several times of their lives, in that estate we usually call of nature; but afterwards, through being renewed, they are in the estate of grace. Only what the apostle speaks in another yet the like case, that by God's ordination holds in this, ' That is not first which is spiritual' (or the estate of grace), 1 Cor. xv. 46, ' but that is first which is natural; and afterwards that which is spiritual.' His reason (ver. 49) holding also in this, that we are to bear the image of the earthly, the first Adam first, and then the image of the heavenly. This almost every epistle to all the saints they wrote to, doth more or less indigitate: thus Rom. vi. 17, 18, ' But God be thanked, that ye were the servants of sin, but ye have obeyed from the heart that form of doctrine which was delivered you. Being then made free from sin, ye became the servants of righteousness.' And 1 Cor. vi. 11, ' Such were some of you: but ye are washed, but ye are sanctified, but ye are justified in the name of the Lord Jesus, and by the Spirit of our God.' And Gal. iv. 8, ' There was a time' (*then*) ' when ye knew not God,' and a *now* : ' After that now ye have known God, or rather are known of God.' And Eph. ii. 1, 2, ' And you hath he quickened, who were dead in sins and trespasses; wherein in time past ye walked,' &c., and so he goes on to describe their natural condition. And Col. i. 21, ' And you, that were sometimes enemies in your minds by wicked works, yet now hath he reconciled;' and chap. ii. 13, ' And you, being dead in your sins and the uncircumcision of your flesh, hath he quickened, having forgiven you all trespasses.' Neither do they exemplify this in the same persons of the Gentile converts, but in the Jewish also; who came in troops to John, to escape the wrath to come. And though himself was sanctified from the womb (Luke i. ver. 15) though conceived in the state of sin; ' for that which is born of the flesh is flesh;' yet the multitude of the rest of the elect lived in disobedience until riper years, ver. 16, 17, ' And many of the children of Israel shall he turn to the Lord their God. And he shall go before him in the spirit and power of Elias,' to turn them, namely through his ministry. And accordingly our Peter, writing to the Jews, that had lived in the bosom of that church, speaks of them as of those who before this their generation had a former estate, which he terms ' their vain conversation,' ver. 18, and (ver 14) calls that estate ' the former lusts of their ignorance ;' so terming their former estate, from the want of saving knowledge, when their lusts ruled, which now having escaped, they were made partakers of a divine nature : 1 Peter i. 4, having now ' purified their hearts, being born again of incorruptible seed,' ver. 22, 23. And more expressly he says of them (ii. 10), that they he thus wrote to (who were by outward character the people of God) ' in time past were not a people, but are now the people of God ; which had not obtained mercy, but have now obtained mercy.' It was a state wherein actually, and before God as a judge, or according to the judgment the Word pronounced of them (by which God will judge all the world,) they were not a people ; though before God, as God, they were elected, and his chosen people. The other is a state of grace and mercy, ' but now' (says he) ' have obtained mercy ;' and still regeneration or conversion is set out as the *passover*, as the equinoctial line to be passed, that divides between both climates, the one of darkness and the shadow of death ; the other a contrary climate of light and glory : so the words just afore intimate, ' who hath called us out of darkness into his marvellous light.' And as Peter speaks thus of the Jews as well as Gentiles, so Paul also having spoken (Eph. ii. 1) to the Gentiles (compare ver. 11) : ' You were dead in sins ; wherein in time past ye walked ;' he turns his speech from them to himself and his countrymen the Jews, and says of all the generality of the Jews then converted, ' Among whom also we all had our conversation in times past in the lusts of our flesh, fulfilling the desires of the flesh and of the mind ; and were by nature the children of wrath, even as others.' By those others he means the Gentiles, and he evidently speaks of what they had been in their conversation unto riper years.

Divines usually term the one the state of nature, as the other the state of grace ; and they give them these terms warrantably from the Scriptures.

1. For the terming a man's condition after regeneration the state of grace, the apostle doth it expressly : Rom. v. 2, ' By faith' (saith he) ' we have access into this grace wherein we stand ;' that is, into this station. It is a perpetual and standing condition of favour, when once we have admission or access into it, which by faith there, and by regeneration here in this text of Titus, we are said to have ; he speaks as we do, or rather we as he, calling it a state of grace. And so oppositely the other a state of nature, which you have as fully and as expressly mentioned, Eph. ii. For when he would sum up what was that estate of both Jews and Gentiles fore-spoken of, he, as in a general conclusion, speaks thus, ' We were by nature children of wrath, as well as others.' His meaning is not only that both were alike in such an estate when born, as restraining that phrase ' by nature,' merely unto what they had been by birth, and so only to their birth-sin (though that must be intended as the source or spring) ; but he speaks too of that race and whole time of their conversation, and course run, wherein they fulfilled the lusts they had by nature (as is evident) until quickened and saved. He termeth that whole stage they ran, and that scene of life, a condition of nature, as acting all that while according to the principles and swing of nature, and having nought but nature in them, afore grace came and wrought in them. And therefore, as Erasmus hath well observed, it is opposed to that which follows (ver. 5) ' By grace ye are

saved,' shewing in the former what naturally without grace, and until grace, their condition was, for sin and wrath. And this interpretation, that style of the apostle given to every man in that estate confirms, terming him, 1 Cor. ii. 14, ' a natural man,' in distinction from a spiritual, till made a spiritual man by regeneration : ' That which is born of the Spirit is spirit.' During all which time they remain (till new-born) ' children of wrath ;' that is, whose portion is wrath, and they exposed to it, during such their condition. And similarly to this sense, that this phrase ' by nature' should involve the whole time from the birth, as well as the sinfulness of our birth itself, do other scriptures speak when they would describe and set forth that natural condition : Ps. lviii. 3, ' They are gone astray from the womb.' And it is the natural condition afore and without grace the psalmist there speaks of. For he not only says they were corrupt in or by the womb, but all along from the womb, thereby expressing their whole state. The like you have Gen. vi., ' from their youth.'

Now when we say men's condition afore regeneration is all that while a state of sin and wrath, as that of grace is the contrary, I desire all men to consider what that imports. *Guilt* of sin is one thing (the best are guilty), but a *state* of sin is a further thing. *Corruption* of nature to be in a man is one thing, the *state* of nature is another : to be *worthy* of death is one thing, so every man in sinning is ; but to be in a *state* of death is another ; it is to be sentenced and adjudged to die, or as Christ speaks, condemned already : John iii. 18, ' He that believeth on him is not condemned : but he that believeth not is condemned already, because he hath not believed in the name of the only begotten Son of God ;' which is all one to say, He that hath not such a faith as renews the heart (for of regeneration Christ hath discoursed, ver. 3–5 of the chapter) is in a state of condemnation, so that he needs no other sentence. There wants nothing but execution ; for which how soon a writ will come out he knows not. As in the canon law for some transgressions a man stood excommunicated *ipso facto* upon the committing, as murder, &c., it depended not upon a new sentence. Here his state makes him instantly and immediately obnoxious to death. Every sin he sins not only deserves death, but it is ' unto death ;' not only the thing is worthy of it, but by reason of his state it redounds to the person, and binds him over to death, which is the true import of that phrase, ' A child of wrath by nature ;' as a man that stands sentenced and adjudged, condemned to die, is by a Jew termed a child of death : 2 Sam. xii. 5, ' This man is a child of death.' For David as a king did at that time pronounce it of him, as we translate it, that he should ' certainly die.' And Christ, on the contrary, is termed a ' Son of love,' Col. i. 13 ; we translate it ' his dear Son,' but it is υἱὸς ἀγάπης, noting forth a perpetuated state of grace and favour borne to him, which Christ calleth ' abiding in his Father' love,' John xv. 2 ; that is, he remains in a perpetual state of grace and favour ; and in the like sense these are termed ' children of wrath,' as abiding in it.

CHAPTER II.

That it is by the new birth that an elect soul is transplanted from a state of sin and wrath into a state of grace.—That it ought therefore to be our earnest inquiry, whether we are regenerated or no.—That though we are by nature the children of wrath, yet our case is not desperate, because this state is alterable.

I shall now evidence the assertion, that regeneration is the only alteration of this estate of death, and so make way for application.

A state is a permanent fixed condition, whether of good or evil, continued without cessation or interruption, until the legal terms of that condition be altered. This might be in many instances exemplified. I will only take such as the apostle, discoursing of these two states (Rom. vi. 7) hath illustrated them to us by, which do withal directly concern the doctrine in hand. The Romans they had servants, which were slaves to them, and some by birth, over whom they had the power of life and death. The condition of such was a permanent condition, and so is that of apprentice servants among us, till the terms of that condition are altered. If they ran away, yet their condition altered not, they might take them wherever they found them. The terms of that alteration were either manumission or expiration by death. Now, Paul professeth, by this instance of this outward condition among men, to set out those other we are now upon: ver. 19, 'I speak after the manner of men,' saith he; that is, I use this allusion to express the difference of those two states you once were and now are in; ver. 17, 18, 'You were the servants of sin, but now, made free from sin, ye become the servants of righteousness.' Now, then, to see how upon regeneration the terms of this state and condition are altered, the apostle tells us that their hearts having been new moulded, cast into that mould of doctrine of the gospel (τύπον διδαχῆς εἰς ὅν παρεδόθητε) into which they were delivered (so ver. 17), and they being ingrafted into Christ, and the likeness of his death and resurrection (ver. 3–5, &c., whereby they became dead to sin and were made men new risen again), therefore by the law of nations the terms of that condition were altered, 'and he that is dead,' saith the apostle, 'is freed' from his master; ver. 6, 7, 'Our old man being crucified with him, that the body of sin might be destroyed, that henceforth we should not serve sin. For he that is dead is freed from sin;' and we being new raised from the dead by Christ's resurrection. Look then, as if you could suppose a Roman slave had been killed and dead, and then raised again to a new life, the law must have freed him from that former state, for he was now a man of another world; so a man being freed from sin is also freed from a state of death, and he is said to pass from death to life, as it is expressed once by Christ: John v. 24, 'He that heareth my word, and believeth on him that sent me, hath everlasting life, and shall not come into condemnation; but is passed from death to life.' And as it is expressed by John, 1 John iii. 14, which is a second allusion to the state of a man adjudged to die in one kingdom, in which is absolute tyranny, and no pardon to be had, but certain death; wherein, whilst he remains, he is perpetually in a state of death, which every moment may befall him, and in the end certainly will. Now, what alters the terms of such a man's condition? Do but suppose there is another region, where grace and mercy only reigns, and which invites men

to come over to it, with promises of life and pardon; when he arrives there
his state is changed. These are the two estates (Rom. v. 21), 'That as
sin hath reigned unto death, even so might grace reign through righteousness unto eternal life by Jesus Christ our Lord.' Take a man that is a
servant to sin : sin is said to reign over him unto death, and whilst he remains in it he is a son of death, a subject of death; and that kingdom
shews no mercy. But regeneration, and such a faith as regenerateth, is a
bridge or ship to carry him over into another dominion of grace, 'where
grace reigns through righteousness unto eternal life,' and welcomes all that
will come into its dominions, and takes them for ever into its protection.
And if grace means to save a man, it prepares this ark for him, even 'the
washing of regeneration,' whereof baptism is the seal: 1 Pet. iii. 20, 21,
'As in the days of Noah, when the ark was preparing, wherein few, that
is, eight souls, were saved by water. So the like figure unto it, viz., baptism, doth now save us (not the putting away the filth of the flesh, but the
answer of a good conscience towards God), by the resurrection of Jesus
Christ.' It is not the outward but the inward baptism saves, and still by the
resurrection of Jesus Christ: 1 Cor. vi. 11, 'Ye are washed, ye are sanctified, ye are justified in the name of the Lord Jesus, and by the Spirit of
God.' Sanctified by the Spirit, and justified by the name of Christ, and
being thus wafted over to the other side of the shore, the devil, sin, and
hell, and death cannot reach you : 'You are not under the law,' the covenant of creation, by virtue of which sin and death reigns in the first estate
(for 'the strength of sin is the law'), 'but under grace;' that is, the
dominion of grace, Rom. vi. 14, where Christ also reigns, chap. v. 21.
The like you have Col. i. 12, 13, speaking of their conversion, and giving
thanks to God for it : 'Giving thanks' (says he) 'unto the Father, which
hath made us meet to be partakers of the inheritance of the saints in light :
Who hath delivered us from the power of darkness, and hath translated
us into the kingdom of his dear Son,' where we are safe for ever. And to
the same purpose he speaks, Rom. vi. 9–11, 'Knowing that Christ being
raised from the dead dieth no more; death hath no more dominion over
him. For in that he died, he died unto sin once : but in that he liveth,
he liveth unto God. Likewise reckon ye also yourselves to be dead indeed
unto sin, but alive unto God through Jesus Christ our Lord.' He would
have them reckon and account themselves, as for the permanency of that new
state, in that very same condition Christ is in, but then to take heed to
walk accordingly : ver. 12, 'Let not sin therefore reign in your mortal
bodies, that ye should obey it in the lusts thereof.' This is the natural,
supreme law in the hearts of the subjects of that kingdom, and which regeneration hath written therein.

There is another similitude, whereby the apostle sets out these two states
in their fore-mentioned fixed settledness, and this alteration from the one to
the other (chap vii.), and it is that of marriage, which with us, you know,
is a settled, fixed condition for life, till by death the terms of that condition
be altered. Now, what says the apostle ? Rom. vii. 2, 3, 'The woman who
hath an husband is bound by the law to her husband so long as he liveth ;
but if the husband be dead, she is loosed from the law of her husband. So
then if, while her husband liveth, she be married to another man, she shall
be called an adulteress : but if her husband be dead, she is free from that
law ; so that she is no adulteress, though she be married to another man.'
By the covenant of the first creation (under which a man for ever stands
till married to Christ), the heart of man was married to the law, and so

subjected to the power of it, as to its natural husband; as the wife by the law of creation is said to be to the husband (Gen. iii.), and among other things, to beget children according to his likeness on her.   Man falls from God, yet still the marriage holds, but through the disease of nature, and perverseness of the wife, children that are contrary to the holy law are brought forth by her, and no other, which, together with herself, are subjected to the punishment of that law, 'Thou shalt die the death.' But now, says he, if either we die or the law die, then we may marry another, and so the terms of that condition and estate of subjection alters; and thus, says he, it is here, ver. 4, 'Wherefore, my brethren, ye also are become dead to the law by the body of Christ; that ye should be married to another, even to him who is raised from the dead, that we should bring forth fruits unto God.'   So then regeneration, which consists in the mortification of lusts, and quickening us with Christ, and faith that marries us to him, makes the alteration; and the resurrection of Christ follows us still.

Let me, ere I go off from this point, apply it a little.   We are all here in the presence of God, and it is certain that we all stand under one of these estates before God this day.   We are all subjects belonging to one of these dominions, of death or life.   And it is as certain that we all once were in that condition of nature, and so of wrath, as sure as we are men.   And it is also sure that nothing doth or can make the alteration out of the one into the other but true regeneration, which alone, by God's ordination, alters the condition of sin and death, as it is a permanent estate.   For, to add this reason to the former, as the first birth alone was the foundation of that first estate, so this second birth alone is the entrance and access into this other estate of grace.

And now then, whether regeneration be savingly wrought in us or no, is a question the best man may ask his own soul; for God will not be mocked, or be put off with anything outward or inward that is below it.   As Rom. iii. 23, 'For we all have sinned, and come short of the glory of God.' And it is as certain, that if we die without obtaining of it, we are undone and lost for ever, and go to hell, as sure as we are now alive.

Use 1. Now then, first, for examination of our estates: consider that this being such a permanent condition, both that no change but into true holiness makes the alteration; and withal, corrupt nature will bear many elevations and refinements which are not the divine nature, it concerns us to make a very strict inquiry.   It is certain God tries in several degrees how far corrupt nature will be refined, and yet fall short of the glory of God.   You know what elevation Socrates was of among the heathens, and Paul among the Jews, by the addition of the light of the law, Phil. iii.; and how strict the young man in the gospel was in pharisaical observances; and how far advanced above these, those are among Christians who are enlightened and taste of the powers of the world to come, and yet fall short, Heb. vi. 4–6.   Now, suppose any one man should be by God gradually refined, and run through all such alterations as corrupt nature remaining still is capable of.   Suppose a profane epicure were turned first a Stoic or a Socrates, then, with all his heroic virtues, turned a Jew, and embraced that religion; yet Christ hath said it of the one and the other, 'Except your righteousness exceed the righteousness of the Pharisees, ye cannot go to heaven;' yea, *de facto*, many devout heathens did turn to the Jewish profession (in which was salvation then, John iv. 22, as in the Christian faith now), and yet of them Christ pronounceth (Mat. xxiii. 15) that they are twofold more the children of hell than before.   If, in like manner, the most devout and righteous Turk should now turn Christian merely in outward profession, and embrace all the articles of that profession, his condition would be but parallel to the former. Well, but then let this man be elevated further, let him receive the word with joy, as the stony ground; yea, let him cast off all outward evils, as the thorny ground did the tops of all its thorns that grew above ground, only the roots remaining not plucked up, let him escape τὰ μιάσματα, ' the gross defilements of the world,' 2 Peter ii. 20, 'through the knowledge of Christ;' let him ' escape the corruptions that are in the world through lust;' and in a word, let him further (as in Heb. vi. 4, 5) be ' enlightened, and taste of the heavenly gift, and be made partaker of the Holy Ghost, and taste the good word of God, and the powers of the world to come;' yet if he is not partaker of the divine nature (spoken of 2 Peter i. 4), whereby he mortifies the inward lusts themselves ; if he have not the divine image stamped on him, and made a nature in him, and child-like dispositions of love to God wrought, it is certain the terms of that condition he was born in are not altered. Like baser metals, corrupt nature will suffer many sublimations, and yet be base metal still; and until it comes to be turned into the true *elixir*, that changeth it into gold, the state of man is not changed. Men may run away from their master-sins (as servants from their masters) when their lusts are not crucified, their indentures not cancelled, and so long the terms of their estate is not altered, but sin fetcheth them again.   Men in prison may be taken out of the dungeon and put into more open rooms, and there have their bolts knocked off, and from thence be brought to the grate to look out abroad, and see the happiness of them at liberty, and have communion with them, and so not to be far from the kingdom of God (as Christ said to the scribe, Mark xii. 34).   Yea, in some prisons, as in the Tower, he may have liberty to walk abroad in the walks and open air, and yet still be a prisoner. Yea, suppose he makes an escape, yet still the terms of his estate, as prisoner, is not altered, till he have that to shew for it which gives him a discharge by him that is the supreme judge or creditor ; and so it is here in this case.   Again, take ice and melt it; when it is water, heat it; from thence boil it through fire or put hot irons into it ; yet still it is water, and retains its form in predominancy, and will return to its coldness again. So will corrupt nature, if the divine nature be not begotten in it.   But if thou findest the least spark of that divine nature struck out of thy heart, it will in the end enkindle the whole man, and convert all to its own nature, and Christ will never quench, but bring it forth to victory.

Use 2. Then in the second place consider, that even from a man's birth this estate of sin and death is a fixed, settled, continued estate, without interruption, until the change specified be wrought.   And go home and think how formidable a thing it is to be found therein, or continue in it but one night longer.   For ' thou fool ' (says Christ, Luke xii. 20), ' this night may thy soul be required of thee.'   And that it is such a permanent estate of sin and wrath, is that which, when a man's eyes are opened, strikes the terror into him ; and thus the apostles, in their writings, represent men's conditions to them.   They speak not to them only of the *guilt* of such and such sins, but of a *state* of sin and death ; which language the primitive Christians were most sensible of, as that which still roused and awakened them to consider their estates ; for the danger thereof was of common apprehension.   See how the apostle expresses it, 1 Cor. xv. 17, ' If so, then ye are yet in your sins.'   He speaks of it as of a fixed estate : you are *in* your sins ; and you are *yet* in them ; to this hour, as being a continued estate, and that wherein the extremity of all evil lies. It is as if you should say of a man tied to a stake in the midst of ten thousand barrels of gunpowder, He is in the fire (as Jude also speaks), and ready to be blown up every moment. And thus Christ also expresseth it, ' Ye shall die in your sins,' John viii. 21. Thus also Peter speaks to Simon Magus, Acts viii. 21, 23, ' I perceive ' (says he) ' that thou hast neither part nor lot in this matter ;' no interest in this ' common salvation,' whereof we profess ourselves partakers. ' I perceive that thou art in the bond of iniquity, and in the gall of bitterness ;' that is, thou remainest fixed in it, as in a permanent condition. And to the same purpose John speaks when he says, 1 John v. 19, ' The whole world lieth in wickedness,' as in its proper state and element. And (1 John iii. 14, and chap. ii. 9) his phrase expresseth a continuation or running on of it from the first : ' He that hates his brother is in darkness until now.' And ver. 11, ' He that hateth his brother is in darkness, and walketh in darkness, and knoweth not whither he goeth, because that darkness hath blinded his eyes.' That phrase, *until now*, is as if he had said, Let that man consider that he is not only in an estate of death and darkness at the present, that it is his present condition ; but that it hath been the condition he hath continued in, without interruption, all along the whole space of his life hitherto. And how dreadful must that be ! If there were a narrow bridge of ice made over the vast ocean, and no island or spot of dry ground all along, and a man from his birth had been set upon it, and had slid and furiously run upon it in the dark, and for twenty or thirty years made a continued journey on it even till now, and were now in the midst of it ; and at length light should rise and come upon him, to see how far he had advanced hitherto, and how he was in the height of continual danger of falling into the sea, either by the bridge's breaking under him, or through his own stepping aside : imagine what dread would strike that man ! And yet this is the case of many that hear me this day. Now John uttered that speech to strike their hearts who had been professors of the principles of the Christian religion in those times ; of which religion the most frequent and familiar principle was the infinite difference of these two estates of the sons of men. The sense and apprehension of which (he knew) they who were now apostatised, and hated those godly persons who continued to profess it, carried in their bosoms and consciences along with them ; insomuch as they had this abiding conviction, that if they were found to be in an unregenerate condition, they were, notwithstanding their profession, in the most desperate and deplorable estate, and darkness ' until now.' And however they were apt presumptuously to bear themselves up with this, that they once were enlightened, and had a saving work upon them when first they entered into this profession, and therefore must have so still, he plainly tells them they had remained in this darkness ' until now ;' for they never had a true work of regeneration to make an alteration of their condition, and so the dismal account of that estate had run on to this very day. And a great scripture this is with me, for its holding forth, that whoever is found in an unregenerate state *at any time* hath *ever* been in it ; and so consequently there is no intercision of grace, nor falling from it. Of such as fall away, the apostle professeth that they never had true grace ; but though enlightened, yet falling away, do shew that they have been, during all their time, unregenerate. To this also the 19th verse accords. ' They went out from us, but they were not of us ; for if they had been of us, they would no doubt have continued with us : but they went out, that they might be made manifest that they were not all of us.' As it is a true saying, If once in a state of grace, then ever so for the time to come; so it is as true, that this man who is in the state of nature and wrath hath ever been in it for times past, even until now. So as such a man (and let every man consider it), though he may have many changes in the time of his pilgrimage, and may take up himself, and commit fewer and smaller sins in his middle age than in his youth; or in his old age than in his old age* (for it is not necessary that to continue in that estate he should every day wax worse and worse); yet if he be not truly regenerate, he is still in one and the same hold, and so all the sins that he hath, or doth commit, or shall continue to commit every moment, they all shall centre in him, as being still in such an estate wherein an obligation stands in force against him for every sin he hath at any time put his hand unto. The power of corruption puts him on to sin, and then the guilt of sin binds him over to death. Every motion of sin from his cradle belongs to that estate. He is 'in the bond of iniquity,' go where he will, whether he sleeps or wakes; and all his sins are as fresh to God as if they had been this moment committed. Time wears not out the guilt of any, but rather helps to make up the treasure of wrath greater (as in debts time adds an increase), and all that time also the wrath of God abides upon him, and is ready to fall upon his head every moment; and God is angry with him all that time. ' He is angry with the wicked every day,' as the psalmist speaks, Ps. vii. 11. And this brings eternity upon a man; and all put together will amaze the stoutest heart that ever was. And yet who almost considers these things?

Use 3. And this may also discover some usual deceits, even of the wisest men. They flatter themselves that all are sinners, and they are only sinners as well as others. But they consider not a state of sin, which themselves and most of men are in. And if they hear the state of nature mentioned, they understand it only of that condition they were in when conceived or born, but they think that it is done away at baptism; and never imagine that it still runs on, *in omne volubilis œvum.* They also set themselves to repent, and turn from this or that sin, but seek not a change of state, a general and universal change. And so they think they may deal with mercy well enough for any particular sin they live in, acknowledging themselves worthy of death for it, as all are for the least sin; but consider not that they remain adjudged to death, and abide in death for every sin, and that damnation sleeps not, but is coming upon them. The great inquest at the latter day will be, What state thou wert found in? whether ' found' (as Paul's phrase is, Philip. iii. 9) ' in Christ,' or found in thy sins?

Use 4. The only comfort to the sons of men that find themselves in taht state is, that although it is a continuation of sin and wrath upon man whilst he is in it, yet it is alterable. It is not therefore said to be a state because it is unchangeable, as that of the devils is, ' who are kept in everlasting chains,' who ' abode not in the truth, but left their first estate ' (as Christ and Jude speak), and who are now in irrecoverable misery. No; there is grace and mercy in this text, Tit. iii. 4-6. There is also a Holy Spirit spoken of, that may yet renew thee, and alter this estate of thine. But know assuredly, nothing else will alter it.

There are two pleas upon which carnal men build the hopes of their salvation, though they go on in the sinfulness of their own hearts, and die without this work wrought in them.

* Qu. 'in his old age than in his middle age'?—ED.

1. They plead God's infinite grace and mercy. Who (say they) shall limit his mercy ? He may pardon me however, if he pleaseth.

2. They say Christ hath died, and perfectly wrought salvation for them ; and they cast themselves upon his death, to be saved by it.

Well but here are two things (in 1 Peter i. 3), that do answer both these deceitful reasonings of carnal hearts.

1. God is merciful, it is true ; yea more, the text tells you he is ' abundantly merciful ;' but withal it tells you, that when he shews mercy he begets a new nature (' who according to his abundant mercy hath begotten us'), so that if ever he means to shew thee mercy, he will shew it herein, and hereby, even in ' begetting thee anew,' that so he may shew thee mercy according to the wise counsel of his will. Thus also in Titus iii. 5, ' According to his mercy hath he saved us.' But how ? ' By the renewing of the Holy Ghost.' And in Jer. iii. 19, 20, God himself professeth how that else he cannot save them. Men think that for God to save them, is no more but only to put forth a prerogative act of pardon and shewing mercy ; as a king doth when he pardons a traitor ; but God always does more, for when he pardons any one, he makes a friend and favourite of him, a son and heir, in whom he may delight ; therefore, together with pardoning him, he also renews him.

2. And for Christ's death ; even that also will not save thee, without this new begetting ; and the text, 1 Peter i. 3, will warrant this too. For consider but this, that he rose again as well as died. Now as he died for the pardoning of your sins, so he rose again to regenerate and beget you again. Therefore says the text, 1 Peter i. 3, ' Who hath begotten us again by the resurrection of Jesus Christ.' If you will have the benefit of his death, you must find the power and virtue of his resurrection in sanctifying you, as Paul speaks, Phil. iii. 10. ' And you who are dead in sins and trespasses,' must be ' quickened with him,' unto a new life of grace, if ever you be saved. Both these you have in Eph. ii. 4–6, ' God, who is rich in mercy, hath quickened us together with Christ, even when we were dead in sins and trespasses, and hath raised us up together,' &c. And this new birth, or holiness, necessarily accompanies pardon, even as Christ's resurrection followed his death ; and his death extends to save no more than his resurrection puts forth a power to beget. As, if Christ had not personally risen, we had been still in our sins, so if Christ be not risen in thee, thou art still in thy sins, and wilt die in them : Rom. vi. 12–14, ' Let not sin therefore reign in your mortal body, that ye should obey it in the lust thereof : neither yield ye your members as instruments of unrighteousness unto sin : but yield yourselves unto God, as those that are alive from the dead, and your members as instruments of righteousness unto God. For sin shall not have dominion over you : for ye are not under the law, but under grace.' And chap. vii. 4, ' Wherefore, my brethren, ye also are become dead to the law by the body of Christ ; that ye should be married to another, even to him who is raised from the dead, that we should bring forth fruits unto God.' Which last place confirms that former reason given, that we being to be married to Christ, and he being to be risen from the dead, we must be made like him in a new resurrection.

CHAPTER III.

*That all God's elect do not indeed, before their regeneration, remain in that state of sin and wrath, as is evident in the case of infants.**

The great God, for holy and glorious ends, but more especially to give demonstration, or to make appear his love and kindness, his mercy and grace, hath ordered it so, that the generality of elect that live to riper years, should for some time remain in a condition of sin and wrath, and then he renews them, and turns them to himself. I have in the former chapters proved the matter of fact.

My present business is to consider the design of God herein, and to what ends and purposes, and for what reasons he hath thus appointed such their condition.

I must premise something by way of limitation, and explication, to prevent exceptions against this truth.

1. My meaning is not, that God regenerates none but such as are grown up to riper years. I should be injurious to multitudes of his elect, if I so asserted. But as infants are capable of all the essentials of regeneration, so, *de facto*, it is evident that he regenerates multitudes of them whilst such. For in the Old Testament the promise being indefinitely uttered for time or age as well as person—' I will be the God of thee and thy seed,' Gen. xvii. 7 ; 'And I will circumcise thy heart, and the hearts of thy seed,' Deut. xxx. 6—and circumcision (which has the sign and seal of that circumcision of the heart mentioned in the promise, and so the seal of that promise itself, and of the performance), being by God's command applied to infants, whereof multitudes whilst such died, necessarily imports that there are some of that age, whom God had in his eye, whom he inwardly circumcised ; or else the promise and seal to them had been in vain. And if it had took place in none but those that lived until they grew up to riper years, then circumcision would have been deferred unto that age, as that wherein God's ordination had only been to regenerate mankind, namely, all when come to such or such an age, grown up, and not before. And circumcision is the seal of that righteousness, the same righteousness which believers grown up have imputed to them (as Rom. iv. 11, the apostle, instancing in Abraham, says), ' He received the sign of circumcision, a seal of the righteousness of faith ;' which words do not assert circumcision to have been a seal of faith or righteousness only unto them that actually do believe, but the purpose of them was to signify and exemplify what righteousness it was that circumcision was the seal of, which he exemplifies in Abraham, saying that it was the same that Abraham the father had imputed to him, and which believers lay hold on, which is called the righteousness of faith ; because revealed from faith to faith, and so apprehended and made known to us that are of riper years by faith. And so hereby he gives us to understand that elect infants circumcised, the seed of Abraham, dying, had and might have the very same righteousness which we and Abraham had by faith, and which circumcision did seal up to his faith, even as well as they have the actual application of that outward seal as much as Abraham had. And indeed the half of mankind dying whilst infants, it may be well supposed that as great a portion, at least for number, are found amongst the seed that die, as experience shewed was found among them that lived, and so were inwardly circumcised. And those promises, ' I will

* This does not appear to be a correct summary.—Ed.

be the God of thee and thy seed ;' and ' I will circumcise the heart of thy seed ;' being spoken (as they are apparently) indefinitely of any age, one as well as another, who shall dare to limit them to years of understanding only ? And if indefinitely for age, then it may as well be supposed, that there is no time, or age, in the whole series of man's life, but there will be found instances of some of Abraham's seed that were therein regenerated, some in one, some in another ; even as there is not the least moment in the thread of man's life, but some or other have expired therein. And again, shall we limit it to infants of eight days old, to exclude all infants dying before eight days ? Surely no. The real intent was otherwise. As women were not excluded from the promise, though not circumcised personally ; to whom yet the promise held, as well as unto males ; and the female sex were representatively circumcised in the males ; so infants (take it still indefinitely of what age, yea, of what moment's standing you will, from their conception), were represented in the circumcision of those infants of eight days old. This deferring and staying of it then, and this representative circumcision at eight days old of some, was ordained typically to hold forth that representation of all the elect which that גבר, that strong male child Christ, the first-born of them, was to bear of all the seed, he standing in their stead.

And it is to no purpose to say, that circumcision sealed up to them only the promise of Canaan ; for beside that the promise to Abraham and his seed was one and the same, also infants that died (as half of mankind die when infants) enjoyed so little, some not at all, the benefit of that promise, ' that thy days may be long in the land which the Lord thy God hath given thee,' as it were ridiculous to assert circumcision was applied to them to seal up that promise only.

In the New Testament, we find that grace and all the privileges thereof are now more extendible, as to nations (' Go teach all nations,' not the Jews only) so in like manner unto all sorts of persons, more than these to whom the grace and dispensations of grace in the Old Testament could be supposed to extend ; and therefore if to infants then, so now. And it is observable that the first in the catalogue of the New Testament (both according to Christ's account, Mat. xi. 11, and also that of Zacharias) was John, who, as the first-fruits to sanctify in a more special manner the lump of infants, was filled with the Holy Ghost in his mother's womb, Luke i. 15.

Christ himself, who sanctified our nature, to the end that we might be sanctified (John xvii. 19, Heb. ii. 11), representatively sanctified every age of man he went through, as well as those ages or years of man's life he fell short of. Now therefore he was sanctified in the womb, to sanctify some infants in the womb. He was holy when born, even because some infants when first born might be then sanctified. And the same Lord Jesus pronounceth of infants, that ' Of such is the kingdom of God.'

Nor can it be supposed that he sanctifies only such infants that in his decrees he had appointed to die when infants ; for when Christ spake that last fore-cited speech, it was upon occasion of such infants being brought to him, who might be supposed to have lived up to riper years, and it being intended a direction to the apostles as ministers, with respect to infants coming or being brought to them, to be sure they were not first to judge who were to live and who were to die, and to regard the latter only, therefore Christ speaks indefinitely. And add to this, John Baptist, who lived to riper years, was yet when an infant sanctified.

And if we take a great lump of Christians that are grown up, some few will be found sanctified from their infancy, insomuch as they dare not say but they had workings of grace on them ever since they can remember, and that they had gracious dispositions (though proportioned to that age) mingled with the dawnings and springings of reason in them. This experience shews, and therefore you must not take this doctrine universally true, that of these that live to years of discretion, none are sanctified when infants.

Yet in the text it is more generally and ordinarily true concerning those elect who live, that God (in whose hands are the times and seasons of regenerating men, as well as of all things else, Acts xvii.) hath appointed and ordered their month (as the prophet speaks) or times of bringing forth to be, when grown up to years of discretion. And besides instances out of the apostles' epistles, many passages in the Old and New Testament evidence that thus it was even in those that lived in Zion, and were well educated in the church of God, and yet needed regeneration, and were regenerated when of years of discretion, or grown up.

In the Old Testament, David (Ps. li. 12) desires God 'restore to him the joy of his salvation, that he might teach sinners God's ways' (not heathens only, but sinners among whom he lived), 'and that they might be converted unto him,' ver. 13. And though men scoff to hear of converts in the church, yet Isaiah tells us of 'converts in Sion,' Isa. i. 27.

In the New Testament we have the example of Timothy, who though brought up by good parents, and taught the faith by his grandmother and mother (2 Tim. i. 5), and who, though he was one who knew the Scriptures from a child, yet for all this his conversion was afterwards by Paul's ministry; who therefore calls Timothy his own son (1 Tim. i. 2), not only as nourished up by him in the words of truth (as 1 Tim. iv. 6), but as truly begotten (in respect of regeneration), as ever any other was of whose conversion he was an instrument; and therefore elsewhere also he still calls him his son, 2 Tim. i. 2, 1 Cor. iv. 17, upon the same account that he calls Onesimus his son, Philem. 10, 'My son Onesimus :' and he gives the reason why he styles him so, ' whom I begat' (says he) ' in my bonds.' And accordingly elsewhere, he distinguisheth between spiritual fathers and instructors in the same, 1 Cor. iv. 15, ' Though you have,' says he—that is, might be supposed to have—' ten thousand instructors, yet not many fathers,' that is, that converted you ; none was an instrument thereof but I : ' For in Christ Jesus I have begotten you through the gospel.' And (Acts xviii.) he shews he was the converter of those saints at Corinth ; and as of them, so of Timothy, whom, in the very next words, he terms his son (which always speaketh relation to a father), and he having thus, in the words afore, distinguished between a father and an instructor, and having styled himself a father to them, for his having begotten them, that he should style Timothy his son, with the same breath, must necessarily be understood in one and the same sense. And when he says, 1 Cor. iv. 17, ' for this cause I have sent unto you Timothy, who is my beloved son ;' there was something of an argument in it to move them to receive Timothy, as sent them by him, being their natural brother, as it were, begotten by the same hand they had been. So then Timothy, though a towardly child, and well educated as any can be supposed to be, yet after he was come to years of discretion, it was that he was converted. And truly the additions of that word, ' begotten you through the gospel,' God having appointed as then, so now, the gospel, and that as preached, to be the ordinary standing means (though not with exclusion of other means) for begetting men to Christ, as well as building men up, argues God's secret ordination of those elect that live to riper years; and yet because a great part of his elect die when young, he hath appointed baptism as a net for them (as he did circumcision of old) and for the other that live, he hath reserved the word to catch them : Rom. x. 17, ' Faith comes by hearing, and hearing by the word.' That is the ordinance of God to that end, as it is also milk to nourish : 1 Pet. ii. 2, ' As new-born babes, desire the sincere milk of the word, that ye may grow thereby.' It is seed to beget them, 1 Pet. i. 23, even the same word which is preached to them, ver. 25. And therefore one of the first encomiums David gives the word (Ps. xix. 7) is this, ' The law of God is perfect, converting the soul.' And God appointed the tribe of Levi in the church of the Jews to this end, Mal. ii. 6. Though they had circumcision then, as we have baptism now, yet Levi was appointed to convert, and that many, which is the same speech that is spoken of John Baptist's ministry, Luke i. 76, 77, &c, And now God hath ordained pastors and teachers, as for the building up, so for the jointing in of the saints, that is, for the conversion of them, Eph. iv. 16.

CHAPTER IV.

The reasons why God suffers his elect, grown into riper years, to continue for some time in a state of sin.—The glory of God's mercy and free grace is the more illustrated by this dispensation.

This explication and caution premised, I come now to give the reasons why it hath pleased God so to order it, that the generality of his elect, who live up to riper years, should for some time remain in a state of sin and wrath.

You meet with a strange thanksgiving, Rom. vi. 17, ' God be thanked that ye were the servants of sin.' Had the apostle ended here, you would have deemed it blasphemy. But he thanks God, not simply for their having been the servants of sin; yea, not merely for this, that now they were converted (which follows, ' that ye have obeyed from the heart that form of doctrine which was delivered you,' that is, become men holy, both in heart and life), but he blesseth God complexly with respect to both, namely, for this change wrought in them, as it is set forth and illustrated by their having been the servants of sin formerly. No man likes or commends the shadow in a picture, if you take that alone; but it is the likeness thereof unto the life itself which makes both the piece and the workman to be esteemed and praised. And yet the shadow sets off the picture, and gives a liveliness unto it. He in the next words shews how the image of God had been faintly stamped upon their hearts, as this similitude of being cast into a mould, there used, imports. And that is the main thing he blesseth God for ; yet withal he admires and extols God's workmanship and art in taking the advantage of so great and dark a shadow as an estate of sinning is (which themselves had first drawn) to be a foil to this bright image of his holiness. God had let them alone a long while to draw the dark part (for sin was their work, and not God's work), who is only the Father of lights, and with him there is no shadow (as James speaks) and no darkness at all (as John hath it); and they had many years been apprentices at this work (' ye were the servants of sin '), and God all this while having had his work in his eye, he suffered them to go on unto a full measure (for the sins of elect men have a fulness before God converts them, as well as wicked men before God destroys them), and then God fell to work. And he that brings light out of darkness made that chaos and abyss of darkness which they had been so long a-creating, the groundwork whereby to set out his new world and workmanship of grace, more than if at first he had made all perfect, and begun it by sanctifying them in the womb. And therefore, says the apostle, ' God be blessed that ye were the servants of sin,' which you are to take together with that which follows: ' But ye have obeyed from the heart,' &c. For sin, or an estate of sinning, cannot in itself alone be made the matter of God's praise, but yet it may serve the more to ' commend the grace of God unto us.' So says the apostle, Rom. iii. 5, ' If our unrighteousness commend the righteousness of God, what shall we say ? Is God unrighteous ? ' If God, who is the judge of all the world (as ver. 6), will suffer the creature to go on in sin which it was justly born in, and for which he damneth millions of souls, and is not unrighteous in taking such a vengeance (as follows, ver. 5), then if also he will suffer an elect son of his to go long on in sin, even unto a fulness, and then, instead of damning him, converts him, justifies him, and sanctifies him (' Such were some of you,' says the apostle, 1 Cor. vi. 11, ' but ye are sanctified, but ye are justified,' &c.), he cannot be said to be unrighteous.

In a word, this is such a phrase of speech as in the like case is usual in the Scripture; so in Luke xv. 23, 24, says the father of the prodigal, ' Let us eat, and be merry: for this my son was dead, and is alive again ; was lost, and is found,' &c. Merry they were, not simply for that he was dead and lost, but that, having been lost and dead, he was now found and alive ; the mercy of his finding and life being heightened by this, that once he was dead and lost, and therefore it enlarged their joy that he was now found and alive, and that (as that parable shews) more than if he had never played the prodigal. Now nothing is more the object of thanks and praise to God than what proceeds from love and mercy.

And so I come to that which at first I propounded to shew, the ends God hath in this dispensation of his ; to give an illustration and demonstration of,

1. His love or kindness.
2. His mercy.
3. His grace. All distinctly mentioned in the text.

I shall first, in a word, distinguish these three.

1. Love is the foundation of mercy, whereby God peremptorily and unalterably pitched upon some men, and set himself to love them in all estates and conditions whatsoever. ' Who shall separate us from the love of God in Christ ? ' Now I join kindness and love together in one, for they differ but thus, that kindness is when love strives to express itself in the most taking way, and to set a lustre upon what it doth.

2. Mercy is a continuing to love them when they are in misery, for mercy properly respects misery.

3. Grace imports the freeness of both these, his loving freely, and shewing mercy freely, founded upon no respects in the creature moving him thereunto.

Now that which I am to speak to is not simply that God hath put forth all these his attributes towards his children in their salvation in general, but particularly that he eminently doth it in this dispensation of his, when having left them to an estate of sinning, he yet at length quickens and saves them.

Again, 2. By way of general premise to this discourse about all these three, whether God first pitch his love upon us simply considered as creatures, or *creabiles in massá purá*, in that pure mass, without the consideration of our being sinners, I will not dispute; for in relation to this point it comes all to one. For if he first set not his love upon men considered as fallen into sin, but purely as creatures, yet his wise counsels pitched on this course, that we should be left to this condition only of having sin in us (as in the mixed estate of sin and grace after regeneration), but also to an estate of sin and death, to the end he might shew the more love; that it might appear he took up so great a love, that though we were sinners it continued the same; and not only so, but stirred up mercy to pity us therein; and thus all our sinfulness comes to magnify his love. And although God might have communicated himself to us without letting us have fallen into sin, though he might have communicated (I say) himself to us, as he will heaven, immediately and directly, when the world shall be at an end, when sin shall be remembered no more, when God shall be all in all, as he is to Christ, and he might have in this estate yet made us apprehensive of mercy in this respect, that when he might have left us tò sin, and to such a condition of sinning, yet he in mercy would preserve us from it; thus he shews love and mercy to the elect angels. But because the creatures are apt to receive the stronger impression by sense and real experience, and his end was to take our hearts in a rational and most taking way, suited to our apprehensions; and then it is the understanding of man is taken and struck with admiration, when one contrary is set against or brought forth of another, which exceedingly serves to illustrate it; and also because God would suit his way of acting to the experience of man (by which Christ himself learned obedience), and in common experience what a man really falls into, and is then delivered out of, this affects more than what is altogether prevented; therefore God ordained this course, rather so to commend his love and mercy to us.

1. His love. The apostle John doth in this argument make a great matter of this one consideration, that we do not begin to love God, but he loved us first. 'Herein is the love of God,' says he, 1 John iv. 19, 'not that we loved God, but that he loved us,' and, as in ver. 19, 'loved us first.' And thus it may be greatened as to angels. But Paul goes farther, and, upon the consideration of this our unregenerate estate, winds this argument of God's love up to a higher pin, not only by the negative, that we loved not him first, but by aggravation positive, that we hated him, we were enemies to him; so in Rom. v., 'God commended his love, when we were sinners,' ver. 8, yea, 'when enemies,' ver. 10, 'Christ died for us.' And to set out his love herein, he makes four degrees of misery we were in, two negatives and two positives.

(1.) He describes us to be 'without strength,' ver. 6, unable to help ourselves; yea, dead, and utterly dead; for so of the body the same word is used; when it is dead, it is said to be 'sown in weakness,' 1 Cor. xv. The word is the same word that here he describes us to be.

A good-natured man is moved to pity a poor weak child or beast without strength, but it must then have life in it; but we were dead. This you have (Ezek. xvi. 5–7) set forth to the end to greaten God's love unto us. He compares that estate of ours afore to that of a dead child, still-born, cast forth on a dunghill, all in gore blood, its menstruous blood, and none eye pitied thee. Then says God, 'I passed by thee, and said unto thee, Live.' I therefore say, a dead child, because the mercy shewn was to bid it live, so putting life into it. Not only so, but ungodly.

(2.) 'Ungodly,' ver. 5, and empty of that goodness he at first saw in us, so as what by the law of creation might more move him, was lost and forfeited : as salt, when the savour, the goodness is lost, is fit for nothing but the dunghill. Yet in that case now he is moved to pity. But, further, there are two positives added.

(1.) We are said to be 'sinners,' ver, 8; that is, that had dishonoured God, and transgressed his law. But yet that might be pardoned if it were not out of malice and inbred enmity.

Therefore (2.) he heightens it by this also, 'even when we were enemies.' A love, by all these circumstances manifested to be such and so great that much water cannot quench it (as Solomon speaks), is love to the height of admiration.

And as hereby the greatness of his love, so the unchangeableness of his love, and peremptoriness thereof, is declared and made conspicuous.

Is it not an unheard-of wonder, that so strong a stream of infinite love should run under ground for so many years, and that so many rebellions all that while should not dam it up, but that it should hold on its course uninterrupted, and work out all that had so long obstructed the current of it, and at last bubble up at a time designed, and save, and wash, and purify the wretched defiled creature? Doth the earth bring forth such a wonder? Have mothers love enough to hold out thus? Other things may manifest other properties of his love, as the giving of his Son shews the greatness of it, and yet even that, too, is set out by our natural estate. But nothing more argues the peremptoriness and unalterable resolution of God's love, than its holding out against all the provoking oppositions in us, against all the sins committed before he had broke his mind, and declared his love unto us, or any open way engaged it: Jer. iii. from ver. 1 to the end of the chapter. It is usual with you (says God there), and according to the principles you walk by, that though yourselves cast a wife off, and not she you, yet if she becomes another man's (as then she may), you will then never own her more. Ay, but (says God to his betrothed spouse, his church), 'Thou hast voluntarily played the harlot, and run after other lovers.' 'And' (ver. 5), 'thou hast done as evil as thou couldst,' hast sinned, as it were to the utmost, and yet I cannot part with thee, and 'yet return thou unto me,' says he. He still loves her and allures her unto him; and why is it? He gives the reason at the 14th verse, 'For I am married unto you,' &c. There was knit so fast a love-knot between God and them, a secret pre-contract on his part, though unknown to them, made by himself, even from all eternity, that no whoredoms, no continued sins whatever of hers, could untie. Well therefore might the apostle say, 'Who shall separate us from the love of God' in Jesus Christ? Yea, and challenge angels, devils, afflictions, and all creatures else to do it, Rom. viii. 34–39. For surely if a continued course of sinning could not dissolve it, then nothing else can.

II. The second thing which God eminently manifesteth hereby is mercy. And though God's mercy be absolutely in God, or in his nature, and he had been merciful, although we nor any creature had ever been, or never had been miserable, yet the manifestation of that his mercy hath respect unto misery, whereof sin and death being the greatest that can befall the creature, the freeing it therefore from an estate of both must needs be the fullest manifestation of that his mercy and pity towards them. Thus, Rom.

xi. 32, the apostle says, ' God hath shut up' (or concluded) ' all under unbelief, that he might have mercy upon all,' both of Jews and Gentiles, of whom, in the 30th and 31st verses, he had discoursed how, in their several vicissitudes, first the Gentiles, then the Jews, had been shut up under unbelief, and locked up; they both were under the surest lock and key that could be, unbelief, and whereof God alone keeps the key; who openeth, and no man shuts, who shutteth, and no man openeth. The key of the door of faith (as Acts xiii. it is called) is in God's hand alone, for it is the gift of God. And unbelief is as a gravestone rolled over men, when already dead in sin, to keep them in that estate. Now unto those that have lain longest under it the greater mercy is shewn. God hath locked up the Jews under unbelief for sixteen hundred years, since Christ's death, as he had done the Gentiles for above two thousand years before Christ. And the design in this dispensation unto either was that he might have mercy upon both, who between them make up the all of mankind, for these two divided the world. Now this which he doth unto these two bulks and bodies of mankind, the more in the end to illustrate his mercy unto them, the like he doth to the particular persons of his elect. He shuts them up a long time under unbelief, that in the end he may have the more mercy on them. Whom likewise doth the apostle call ' vessels of mercy,' Rom. ix. 23, but those who once were not his people ? As appears by verses 25 and 26, vessels of mercy they could not be, till they had first been filled up with sin and misery. And that some of them are greater, and of a larger size than others, this comes to pass by how much they have been fuller filled with sin. Even as a bladder is more capable, and will hold more of a precious liquor, by how much at the first it hath been distended with wind; so these are enlarged to contain the more mercy, by how much they have, like a wild ass's colt, ' snuffed up the wind' (as the prophet speaks), and have walked on ' in the vanity of their minds,' as Paul says, and ' in a vain conversation,' as Peter's words are. God's children, as well as reprobates, have a measure of iniquity, and a stint of sinning; which, when they are once arrived to, and have filled their measure, God begins to empty them, and to fill them up again with mercy.

III. The third attribute, the glory whereof God doth hereby advance, is his applying grace, which is the grace he here speaks of, and which superadds to his love and mercy a freeness, as being extended to us upon no motives or incentives in us, but *ex proprio suo motu*. So Rom. iii. 24, ' Being justified freely by his grace.' Now nothing can be supposed to illustrate the fulness thereof more than this kind of dispensation. For there can be supposed fewest motives for God to shew mercy to those who have done nothing but offended and provoked him in a continued course of sinning. After we are regenerate once, though we continue to offend him, yet then he is engaged to be reconciled to us. And therefore, Rom. v. 10, it is made a greater matter to reconcile us to himself at first when we were enemies, than to keep us friends being once reconciled. For to the upholding of our friendship many motives may fall in, from which at least God may take an occasion to back one kindness with another. But in this case there are none at all. Now both the riches of his justifying grace, and also of his sanctifying grace, are illustrated by this dispensation. And I mention both, and upon this very occasion you have both these distinctly mentioned, 1 Cor. vi. 11, where the apostle, having spoken of their condition before they were converted, he says, ' Such sinners were some of you; but now you are justified, now you are sanctified.'

1. God's justifying grace is hereby (1.) Cleared; and (2.) Exalted; and that more than any other way.

(1.) Hereby is cleared to us that our justification is wholly of and by grace. Now, in the point of justification, the great competition is between grace and works. Grace looks upon works as its only enemy and compeer herein, which are therefore always set in a direct opposition throughout the epistles. This is in the text, and this dispensation it is the strongest conviction that could have been that works are no ingredients to the justification of us. Take for proof of this the course the apostle holds in the Epistle to the Romans to clear this to them. After in the two first chapters he had proved that both Jew and Gentile were in the like natural corrupt estate, he says, chap. iii. 9, 'We have proved both Jews and Gentiles, that they are all under sin;' not sinners only, but under sin, that is, the dominion of it. And this natural condition, and the corruption of it, he describeth from the 10th verse to the 19th; and then at the 20th infers this as a corollary from it, 'Therefore by the deeds of the law shall no flesh be justified in his sight;' and, ver. 23, repeats his reason, 'for all have sinned, and come short of the glory of God;' and therefore he concludes (in ver. 28), 'that a man is justified by faith without the deeds of the law.' This is so strong an eviction of this saving truth, that the papists themselves (to do Bellarmine and their doctrine itself this right) do acknowledge that works done afore regeneration, though never so outwardly righteous, are excluded from that first justification (as they by distinction call it); yea, he confesseth that justification then is therefore only in and through Christ's blood. But then after conversion, they say, there is a second justification, whereby a man is judged worthy of eternal glory, and such and such degrees of it; and this they attribute to good works after conversion, dipped in Christ's blood. A man in and by regeneration being made inherently righteous, and set up anew, begins with a new stock, and so trades for eternal life. And that is their error. But yet, even to convince that works are excluded from that their second justification as well as from the first, the consideration of a man's unregenerate estate doth most aptly serve. The total corruption of that estate hath spoiled and disabled all the righteousness that shall anew be bestowed for ever being fit to justify us. And this not simply because it hath defiled the person, and made him a traitor to God, and so nothing can ever, as from him (as in himself considered), be accepted. Nor is it the cause why works after conversion cannot justify us, because they are imperfect, and stained as a menstruous cloth (though that is a reason *ex abundanti*); but if we could suppose them as undefiled as after the resurrection they shall be, as perfect as in heaven they shall be, and if God should upon the first moment of conversion make any one so perfectly holy, yet they would not then serve to justify: 'If I know nothing by myself,' says Paul, 'yet I am not thereby justified.' And what is the true and utmost reason of this *yet?* Because he had known so much by himself in his former unregenerate estate. This you shall find to have been the apostle's scope and way of reasoning (in the 8th to 11th verses of the second chapter to the Ephesians), why salvation is of grace, and not of ourselves, nor of works, neither afore nor after: 'For by grace are ye saved through faith; and that not of yourselves: it is the gift of God: not of works, lest any man should boast. For we are his workmanship, created in Christ Jesus unto good works, which God hath before ordained that we should walk in them.' That is, these very works are given by grace, of which this your former condition enough convinceth you; for then you were nothing but sin, dead in sins and trespasses, not able to think a good thought, so as God was out of his grace to give you a new frame of heart on purpose created, or you had never come to have had the least good work. And if so, then you are not saved by these good works wrought by you, through this new workmanship in you, no more than by those afore; for they all are the mere free gift of God, and of his grace; and that righteousness that comes of grace, and holds of that tenure, can never come to justify. For the works that must justify must some way challenge that justification by debt or a due, not merited indeed (for so even Adam could not), yet by a natural due through that first covenant of nature, Rom. iv. 12.

(2.) As the doctrine of justification is hereby cleared to be by grace, so his grace in justification is hereby advanced and extolled, and that in two properties thereof.

[1.] The freeness of grace.

[2.] The exceeding riches thereof.

You have the one, Rom. iii. 24; the other, Eph. ii. 7, 8, &c.

[1.] The freeness of grace is hereby exalted; for if you observe it, upon what occasion is the mention of the freeness of grace in justifying brought in in Rom. iii. 24, but only upon his having said before, ver. 22, 23, that they all had sinned, and there was no difference; that is, all were alike in a state or condition of sinning. For those that are not justified are and remain in such an estate; now, says the apostle, so do all those whom he means to justify; he justifies them freely by his grace. For then it is apparent it is grace, out of its own mere motion, doth it, and so puts a difference, and that a vast one: 'Who caused thee to differ from another?' says the apostle, 1 Cor. iv. 7.

[2.] The exceeding riches of grace in justifying is hereby advanced; for when a man by sinning hath gone on to treasure up wrath, adding every moment to the heap for so long a time, it requires a vast sum of mercy treasured up by God to discharge and buy out (as it were) that other. And it is certain, when after so long and so lavish an expense of sinning, as falls out in a man's unregenerate condition, he comes first to God in the sight of all his sins, though afore he lightly took it for granted God was merciful, &c., yet now he stands aghast at it, and wonders where there should be riches of mercy enough to forgive so many millions of talents of sinning. And it is infinite mercy (God having such sums ready and lying by him) to forgive a man all after all, upon one single act of faith. It is infinite mercy in God to suffer such a poor and mean ticket to take up upon pure trust so much riches, whenas yet God hath no experience neither of our good behaviour. I will not now dispute whether then, at the first justification, God pardons all a man's sins to come as well as past. For whether the one or the other be asserted, yet this must be reckoned the great act and time of justifying, and of expending the riches of grace upon us, even when he first saved us by faith, as Eph. ii. 7–9. And if then all sins to come as well as past are pardoned, yet not till then; and then after so long a forbearance, God at once doth it. Well might the apostle triumph upon such an experiment, and say, 'Who shall lay anything to the charge of God's elect? It is God that justifies.' Shall sin, that a man was born in, that lay as an old debt from the womb? The apostle cuts that off with an easy answer, 'Not as the offence, so is the grace;' it abounds much more, Rom. v. 15, 16. Though sins, continued in with full consent, every one of which had made the corruption of nature of a deep dye, have abounded; nay, throw on heaps of actual transgressions as high as heaven, as Daniel speaks, and these reaching also as low as hell, let Manasses come with his fifty years' continued rebellion, and Paul with his, although these abound, yet grace much more. Yea (verse 20 of that chapter), the apostle is bold to make the utmost supposition, that where sin hath abounded, grace hath abounded much more; and in the next verse compares it to a mighty monarch that rejoices in the conquest of so many enemies: 'grace reigns through righteousness.' And the glory thereof lies (as of other potentates, as Solomon says) in the multitude of these its subjects.

2. This conduceth to shew forth the power of sanctifying grace, or that renewing grace. In the text, Eph. i. 19, the apostle Paul attributes to this the greatest power that ever God did or will put forth in any work, unless in that of raising Christ from that low estate the human nature was in unto the highest estate of glory. And how comes it that so great a power appears? He tells us, Eph. ii. 1, where he goes to prosecute it, 'You who were dead in sins and trespasses hath he quickened'; dead in the sin of nature, dead by transgressions actual, whereof each gives a fresh stab; not only twice dead (as Jude speaks), but a thousand times dead. And though in nature there is but one measure of death, one man that is dead of one stab is as dead as he that hath ten thousand; yet if you were to raise a man to life, it would require a greater power to raise a man to life that hath a thousand stabs in vital parts; for every stab must be cured, or he will be dead still. Or rather, to exemplify it thus: to raise a man rotten in the grave is a matter of greater power than to raise a man newly dead. Mary thought that Christ might have kept Lazarus from dying whilst any spark of life had been in him (so twice it is said, John xi. 21, 32, 'If thou hadst been here, my brother had not died'). But now (says Martha, ver. 39), 'he is not only dead, but stinketh.' He hath been dead four days, ver. 39; and indeed Christ had stayed away on purpose to shew forth the glory of God; ver. 5, 6, compared with the 40th. In like manner thus Christ defers and suffers his own children to be in a state of death. He defers his own not only four days, but many years, and before he raiseth them up, lets them stink in their sins. The virtue of Christ's death and resurrection is a sovereign remedy for any sore, and God is a skilful physician, that intends to shew the virtue of it, and often drives so long, till, as the prophet says, the wound is otherwise incurable, and then applies and cures them.

CHAPTER V.

Other reasons why God suffers his elect, who are adult, to continue for some time in a state of sin.—That this dispensation turns to their benefit and advantage in the event.—That it serves for the conviction and judgment of wicked men, and greater confusion of Satan.

Unto those ends of God's suffering his elect to remain for some time in a state of sin, which are the principal and more immediate, I may add others which are but additional, yet ingredients, into this his wise and gracious dispensation. And as the ends before mentioned related to himself, so these other regard all sorts of intelligible* natures, both men and angels, and all sorts of either, good or bad.

I. They regard good men.

1. The persons themselves whom he after such a state converteth. He

* That is, 'intelligent,' or, 'capable of understanding.'—ED.

disposeth of a state of sinning afore conversion for their good, as all things else to work together for good; namely, for the increase of their most precious graces afterwards. This Paul, in telling that story of his conversion which so much delighted him, holds forth: 1 Tim. i. 14, 'The grace of our Lord Jesus was exceeding abundant, with faith and love which is in Christ Jesus.' The sum of which is this:

(1.) He had shewn how much the contrary sins had abounded. 'I was a blasphemer' (says he), 'a persecutor;' I did it in unbelief.

(2.) How infinitely God's grace in pardoning him had much more super-abounded, ὑπερεπλεόνασε.

(3.) He had shewn how thereupon, when converted, the contrary graces and gifts abounded in him, instancing in faith and love. As on God's part, and in God's heart, pardoning and accepting grace abounded, so on his part also, and in his heart, faith and love abounded also. 'The grace of the Lord was abundant with faith and love;' that is, with those effects of it, in some proportionable correspondency to the grace shewn him; and in these returns to God again his heart was answerably affected to the comparative measure of his former sinfulness and God's grace. These were the reverberations, the reboundings and reflections, rising out of both. And it is observable that he carries his discourse so as to shew how, when he was converted, the graces particularly contrary to those very sins he had most exceeded in afore were wrought in him, and so that therein the abundance of God's grace was to be observed. The sins which he instanced in are three. [1.] Unbelief; 'I did it' (says he) 'in unbelief,' ver. 12. Oppositely, the grace of faith was afterwards abundant. [2.] 'I was a persecutor' (says he), 'and injurious;' but now grace was abundant in the love to God and all his saints, and his love rose higher than ever any one's but Christ's; he could have wished himself accursed for them, Rom. ix. 1. [3.] 'I was' (says he) 'a blasphemer,' the foulest throat that ever opened itself against God and his tabernacle, and the saints that were on earth. He had been a wicked Saul, breathing out threatenings and slaughters against the disciples, Acts ix. 1; but now Christ counted him faithful, and put him into the ministry, and he proved the best preacher that Christ ever had. 'He now preaches the faith he once destroyed,' was the bruit and character went forth of him, Gal. i. 24. And how he laboured more than all the other apostles, himself also reports.

2. It proves an advantage also to other saints, and that many ways.

(1.) It gives an occasion of glorifying God, in the conversion of some notorious sinner, throughout all the churches. So those that never had seen Paul's face—Gal. ii. 22, 23, 'I was unknown by face to the churches in Judea'—and who had heard only, that he which persecuted them in times past now preached the faith, glorified God.

(2.) It gives them occasion also of shewing forth the disposition of grace, which of all other is most noble and natural to the new creature, and that is a zeal for, desires to, prayers, and endeavours after the conversion of others, which, as in nature, so in grace, is the most natural work. Which that they may have opportunity to exercise, God affords them through this dispensation, matter in their several relations, and this not only to ministers, but to all sorts of private Christians. God, in his providence, marries a wife (that after proves a believer) to a husband that continues an unbeliever long after; 'And what knowest thou,' 1 Cor. vii. 16, 'O wife, whether thou shalt save thy husband?' So then, as God ordained it thus, to shew forth his own love and mercy the more, so withal he designed it, that we might give demonstration of our love and pity to the souls of men as he hath in his divine providence left the most of mankind in poverty or necessitous, to give occasion of that grace of charity which he so delights in, as being the likeness of himself. To save souls was the tempting argument to Christ himself (Isa. xlix. throughout, and Isa. liii.). Now Christ having paid the price, and so having perfected for ever them that were to be sanctified, he went to heaven on purpose to leave the actual conversion of souls unto us his brethren. He would not do it himself instrumentally, because he would not take that work out of our hands that believe. He knew they had the same graces and desires for saving souls himself had, and he would leave them matter for the specifying of it. He withal knew how great a joy it would be to a father to win his child, a wife to convert her husband, which often falls out, as the apostle insinuates, 1 Cor. vii. 16, ' What knowest thou ? ' He knew that he could not use a higher and greater motive to endure much (as they did) from heathen husbands. The like he says, 1 Peter iii. 1. So that, as the apostle says, he fulfilled the after-sufferings of Christ, that is, what he left for us after his example to bear ; so I may say he hath left us this as the after-work, which was properly his, and should have been his, even to save men's souls from death (James v. 20), but that he would have us have the honour of it. Neither doth he employ his angels (who are ministering spirits in all other the greatest affairs in this world) in this work, but reserves it wholly for us men. He gave the law by them, but not the gospel. He knew there was no greater joy, next to joy in God himself, can befall a Christian, than to convert a sinner. That which satisfied Christ himself, and for which he thought himself well a-payed for all his sufferings, was, that he saw the travail of his soul. Isa. liii. 10, ' He shall see his seed, and the work of the Lord shall prosper in his hands. He shall see the travail of his soul, and be satisfied.' And he knew that to see the like in converting souls, would, in our proportion, of all things else most rejoice us. 3 John, verse 4, ' I have no greater joy than to hear that my children walk in truth.' First, to see those he might call his children : ' My children,' saith he (as Isaiah speaks in Christ's person, ' Lo, here am I, and the children thou hast given me '), and then to hear they walk in truth.

II. This dispensation regards bad men, and such as God means to cast away. God hath a design upon them also in this dispensation of his. God in this world as well makes way and prepares evidence against the day of judgment, as for the salvation of his own. This, as one great work to be done at the day of judgment, Enoch held forth to the then ungodly world : Jude 14, 15, ' And Enoch also, the seventh from Adam, prophesied of these, saying, Behold, the Lord cometh with ten thousand of his saints, to execute judgment upon all, and to convince all that are ungodly among them of all their ungodly deeds which they have ungodly committed, and of all their hard speeches which ungodly sinners have spoken against him.' As to execute judgment, so to convince ; and I observe it is said, ' all ungodly among them,' that is, that have lived among the saints in this world ; and of what in a more especial manner are they to be convicted ? Even of their hard speeches spoken against him, that is, against Christ, as appearing in the saints. Thus Paul was convicted by that speech from heaven, ' Why persecutest thou me ? ' Now there is nothing of all passages of God's dispensations that falls out in this world, that hath more of conviction in it, than to see those that lived once according to the course of this world, and in the same lusts with themselves, to turn unto God, and become new men. Neither yet doth anything usually more provoke them to hard speeches, even against that conviction, than such strange accidents when they do fall out. Nothing hath more of conviction in it, and is therefore used as a most effectual means of gaining men, even when the word will not, nor the doctrine of it. 'If any obey not the word, they may without the word be won by their conversation,' 1 Peter iii. 1. It sets home the word, as an example of judgment doth a threatening against such and such a sin. Hence Isaiah says (Isa. xxix. 23, 24) 'When Israel' (speaking of the nation) 'shall see his children, the work of mine hands' (answerably to Eph. ii. 10, 'You are his workmanship, created,' &c.), 'in the midst of him; they that erred in spirit shall come to understanding, and they that murmured' (that were opposers of religion) 'shall learn doctrine.' Such an example sets home many sermons. They see the word verified; whilst men shall see and hear, as Christ speaks, ὅτι πτωχοὶ εὐαγγελίζονται, that the poor are evangelised, are gospelised, turned into a living gospel, the word of God taking hold of them, and they becoming an ingrafted word, as James speaks. What the word says and speaks of conversion, is made true and good, and exemplified in them in their conversion. Christ speaks it not of the bare preaching of it to the poor, for so it was to all as well as the poor; but thereby expresseth the effect of it upon them, reckoning it among the miracles that accompanied the preaching of it; 'The blind see,' &c. And therefore Christ there brings it in as a visible object : 'Tell John the Baptist' (says he) 'what you have seen and heard;' namely, these miracles accompanying the preaching of the gospel, and poor souls converted by it, the greatest of all the rest. And these Christ allegeth as a full conviction that he was that Messiah to come into the world. For that was the message, ver. 19, 20,* John sent them about, to the end they might ocularly be convinced of it. So then, my brethren let me say this to you, This hath the reality and power of conviction in it, that miracles were ordained for. Now though all other miracles are ceased, yet God continues this standing miracle. Men are apt to think with themselves, If I had lived in those times, when all those miracles were wrought, I should surely have believed. O adulterous generation, do ye seek a sign ? No other sign shall be given you, but that afore your very faces, your companions in evil, your children, or wives, that once lived in sin as you do, in that estate you continue in, are converted afore your eyes, and turn from their evil ways, professing damnation to have been in that estate which they lived in before. And if you will not believe by this, if one were raised from the dead you would not believe, for a greater resurrection is here. And therefore such a real conviction shall be brought against thee at latter day (if thou also turn not) with greater evidence than the multitudes of sermons thou hast heard. And though the word of God must judge us, yet this will much more. And yet when men do thus turn to God, and see converts live among them, they are enraged to speak evil of them, which serves to make up the full measure of that sinfulness and vengeance Jude speaks of. The apostle Peter (1 Peter iv. 1) gives a definition of a primitive convert; (1.) He is one, says he, that 'hath suffered in the flesh.' He and his lusts have been on the cross with Christ, and it hath had this effect, that he ceaseth from the common practice of known sins—'He hath ceased from sin'—and hath utterly left them for the salvation of his soul, and this for ever : 'That he no longer should live the rest of his time in the flesh, to the lusts of men, but to the will of God.' To the lusts of men,

* Of Luke vii.—ED.

that is the same lusts the most of men live in. This is his bent, this is his profession, and this is the work begun upon him. There was a time indeed, ' a time past in our lives' (says Peter in the next verse, ver. 3) 'in which we wrought the will of the Gentiles' (for whilst men live in the same lusts with others they please them, they are as they would have them), ' when we walked in lasciviousness, lusts, excess of wine, revellings, banquetings, and abominable idolatries.' Well, but now they had turned to God, what do the Gentiles among them think and speak of it ?   ' They think it strange,' that is, it is a wonder to them, for it is as a kind of miracle, they cannot tell what in reason or nature to ascribe it to.   And they yet ' speak evil of them,' and though they are convinced by nothing more, yet they are provoked to speak evil of them upon no occasion more, for it brings their consciences upon them, it publicly declares that the courses and state they still remain in are evil and wicked, and the way to destruction ; and this makes them put the cause of this alteration upon ten thousand other pretences or grounds, as hypocrisy, &c.   Well, but says Peter, all this makes but work for the day of judgment, and prepares evidences of conviction for to help Christ to clear his sentence of condemnation of them ; for so it follows, ' Who shall give an account to him that is ready to judge the quick and the dead.'   So then, this is one of those ends which God hath in his dispensation.   And surely for a wicked man to see another that walked in the same way with him begin to turn head on a sudden, run contrary ways so cross to flesh and blood, and which tends to reproach, and perhaps ruin in this world : this must needs amaze and awaken his companion.

III. This dispensation hath its influence also upon angels, both good and bad, and produceth as great effects, conjunct with God's glory, as any other dispensation of God's providence whatever.

1. In the good angels it proves the occasion of as great a joy as any we read of, that fills the hearts of those great spirits. They are the most curious spectators of God's works of wonder ; and themselves are employed by Christ in the greatest transactions that belong to this world, in wars and making peace, &c., and in what belongs to the preservation of God's elect ; and this is an inferior work for them.   But they are said in a more special manner to joy and rejoice in what themselves have no hand at all, not the least, viz., to see and behold sinners and lost sheep converted unto God. Christ says expressly, ' There is joy in heaven at the conversion of one sinner ;' and as it would seem, this joy befalls them in a great part of a reward and recompence for their other so cheerful undergoing those other employments and services in this world, which are below them ; which yet, as it were by the by, God entertains them with, as the Roman emperor did the people with their *spectacula*, sights and shows to please and to delight them. Sure I am, we read of this to be matter of joy to them, who have God so much to rejoice in, and not those other employments of theirs ; because this of all other is so meet to, and more conjunct with the glory of God, which they have made their happiness.   Thus also the glorious sufferings of apostles and martyrs are made a spectacle for angels to feast their eyes withal, 1 Cor. iv. 9.   So the preaching the gospel, the sending down the Spirit, the sufferings of Christ, the glory that followed, are rehearsed as things the angels do pry into, 1 Peter i. 11, 12 ; and also that which was the end of Christ's death, and of sending down the Holy Ghost, and of preaching the gospel, namely the conversion of souls.

2. This dispensation of God hath a design upon bad angels.   I observe

it, that next to man's salvation, Satan's confusion is that which God on Christ's behalf purposes with most vehemency and edge of spirit, to contrive how at once to save men, and together confound Satan in the most exquisite and artificial way. You may read and observe it, how God gave forth that first and great promise of Christ, the promised seed, and of man's salvation by him, not first and directly to Adam and Eve themselves (whose salvation yet it concerned), but in his speech unto, and in his cursing of the devil : Gen. iii. 5, ' I will put enmity between thee and the woman, her seed and thy seed. It shall break thy head,' &c. It was spoken in their hearing indeed, but immediately directed to the devil, and the point of it levelled point blank at his breast. He gave it, I say, with a vengeance, uttered with the highest indignation, it answerably being matter of pleasure and delight to him to disappoint that enemy. Now of all contrivements which God in his wisdom, sharpened with revenge, hath sought out, even next to the sending his Son in the world (*Non macies* invenit tormentum), God hath not invented a more exquisite rack and torment to that evil spirit, than that an elect child of God's, having continued many years in a state and course of sin, and in the devil's full possession, should be pulled forth of his clutches, and converted unto God after so long a time. And that he was in his possession, is the thing that vexeth the devil. Had a man been regenerated in the womb, it had been far less vexation to him. It is the usual description of conversion in the New Testament, that it is the turning of a man from the power of Satan unto God, Acts xxvi. 18, a delivering us from the power of darkness (which is Satan's), and translating us into the kingdom of his Son, Col. i. 13. It is certain that, afore conversion, the devil rules and reigns as fully in one that is elect, as any other man, and finds no difference, Eph. ii. 2. Now consider what a confusion it must needs be to the devil, that when for ten or twenty years he hath possessed a man in peace (as in the parable Christ tells us, Luke xi. 21), and like a strong man hath fortified his house round, insomuch as he is in peace and security, that he is his own, and that he shall have him to hell with him (he is called his proper goods and chattels, in that Luke xi. 21), that when he hath fortified his understanding, the tower of the soul, 2 Cor. x. 4, 5, with strongholds and high imaginations, when he hath cast up mounts and bulwarks, and environed and moated the ill ground again and again with corrupt affections, that there is no access to move it ; insomuch as he glories in the possession of a man (as Nebuchadnezzar did in his palace : and to shew the devil's like boast and vain account herein, Christ useth the very word in that Luke xi. 21, εἰς τὴν αὐλὴν ἑαυτοῦ, he termeth the man's soul his court, his palace), that when the devil is walking up and down, and in the midst of glorying, Is not this the man I have possessed so long ? ' Is not this the Babel which I have built for the glory of my majesty ?' In an instant a word comes from heaven, ' Thy kingdom is departed from thee,' and the Holy Ghost seizeth upon all, and none of Satan's fortifications can keep the wind of the Spirit out, which blows where he listeth, as Christ says John iii. ; and the Holy Ghost binds this strong man (as Christ speaks), in an hour, throws down, and in a great measure flights all the works which this spirit had been a-rearing all that man's lifetime hitherto. Oh, how must this needs still that enemy and avenger, when he hath had a man so long as it were in a string, 2 Tim. ii. 26, taking him captive at his will. He knew how and where to lay traps and gins for him, and take him as the fowler doth the silly birds. To have this poor forlorn man pulled out

* Qu. ' *majus* ' ?—ED.

of his jaws, when he had in his thoughts drunk him up (as Peter speaks), and in peace possessed him : what an infinite confusion must this be to him ?   Insomuch as Christ concludes of him, that being thus cast out he walks in dry places, like one banished, that is melancholy, and seeks solitariness, an heath, or a wilderness, as being ashamed to shew his head.

Thus you have seen all creatures reasonable, and of all sorts of them, affected with the thoughts of God's dispensation to his elect, all having an interest in it.   That as at Christ's birth all the city of Jerusalem is said to have been moved at it ; so are all sorts, both in heaven and in hell, at the new birth of one that hath been a lost sinner, which is that which putteth the notice upon it ; whereas the regeneration of elect infants passeth silently : they are still-born, and no such noise made of it.

CHAPTER VI.

The uses of the foregoing doctrine.—That they who are brought into a state of grace should always bear in their minds a remembrance of their former state of sin and misery.—That it will have an influence to promote and strengthen their faith.

You have seen God's ends and designs in his disposition toward the elect ; and they are great and holy ends, and of as large an extent in their tendency, as in any other dispensation of God to us.

I come now to the uses to be made hereof on our part, which must be such as may answer those ends on God's part.   And withal what uses may be made of such a time spent in sinning afore regeneration, may also fitly be turned upon the spirits of those that have had great fits of sinnings in any kind after regeneration.   They will serve for both, but I will speak more directly as in relation to the first.

You have run out many years in great sins, or few years in many ; look back, and now learn to make an improvement of that waste time in your lives.   Men are apt to think that there is no use to be made thereof, especially of so long a time as that of unregeneracy was, in which we all lay. Now the apostle, he would never have exhorted the Ephesians (as you see he doth, Eph. ii. 2), to remember what once they were, if there were not many most fruitful and profitable improvements of the consideration of that condition.   It is called our ' vain conversation' (so Peter calls it, 1 Peter i. 18).   And the apostle Paul saith, Rom. vi. 21, ' What fruit had you in those things whereof ye are now ashamed ?'   But, my brethren, assure yourselves of this, that God would not have left many, yea, most of his children, to so long a time of sinning against him, in which they brought forth no fruit unto him, if that after they were turned unto him there were no ways whereby they should improve, and improve with interest and advantage, all the experiences they had of their sinfulness in that condition.   God could have saved you cheaper than by letting you fall into sin at all ; it was not for his profit, in a proper and direct way, that those whom he went to save should continue in sin, though but for one moment.   He could have saved us, as he did the angels, a cheaper way.   He loves his children so well that he would never have it said, that they had so and so dishonoured him, if he had not meant to have more honour (in an indirect way, in the event and issue, when all is summed up), by all that condition of sinning, in which formerly they had lain.

This general exhortation, which is as a foundation to the rest, is to bear all your days in remembrance your sins, and the condition of sin in which you sometimes were. In Eph. ii., the apostle had at large discoursed of the state and nature they had been in, and the close and conclusion he makes of all is, ' Wherefore remember that ye were sometimes Gentiles in the flesh,' &c. There are two things which in the New Testament we are called upon in an especial manner to remember; 1st, The death of our Lord and Saviour Christ, which the sacrament calleth upon us to remember, ' Do this in remembrance of me.' And the 2d is, ' Remember what once ye were,' what your estate and condition was, and forget it not. There is a third, which is, That thou shouldst ' remember whence thou art fallen, and repent,' which is coincident with this second. Remember, it had need be urged, for we are apt to forget it; yet it is a duty lies upon us : Ezek. xvi. 22, He had discoursed there, in the former part of the chapter, what their condition was before God took them to be his people. ' Thy birth and thy nativity is of the land of Canaan ; thy father was an Amorite, and thy mother an Hittite,' ver. 3 ; and so he goes on to mind them of their abominations, ' When thou wast' (saith he) ' in thy blood, I said unto thee, Live.' Now, after he had took them to be his people, when they had gone a-whoring from him, what is it he lays to their charge, especially at ver. 22, that in all their abominations and whoredoms they had not remembered ? ' In all thine abominations and whoredoms thou hast not remembered the days of thy youth, when thou wast naked and bare, and wast polluted,' &c. And the not remembering of this, as it is made a great sin, so it is made a special reason why they had fallen from God so much, and so often, after they were his people ; even because they remembered not. Every place thou comest in, where thou hast lived before, may put thee in mind of some sin or other, Jer. iii. 2, 13. Every member of thy body hath sin written on it. The tongue is a ' world of evil,' thy feet have been swift to carry thee to vanity. The whole body is not able to contain the story of it. As of Christ's holy active life it was said, that all books in the world could not contain the history of them, so the same may be said of thy sins.

But in making the use, or application, I shall chiefly confine myself unto those ends which God had, as in relation to us, in this dispensation. I instanced in two eminent graces in Paul's example, 1 Tim. i. ; I shall now present them particularly.

I. The consideration and remembrance thereof may help and further thy faith. It is true, the guilt of many and great sins is in a direct way an opposite and hinderer of faith : it strikes the hand off, and discourageth from laying hold on Christ; yet by God's dispensation, that turns darkness into light, this may prove a provocative thereto, and an enlarger of it many ways.

1. Unfeigned faith of the operation of God is founded upon self-emptiness and poverty of spirit. If I would seek to move and stir my heart to kindly godly sorrow, I would take into consideration my sinning after conversion, as being committed against so much love, not only borne towards me, but either brought home to my heart, or on which my soul depends alone for its salvation ; also against the blood of so gracious a Saviour, not shed only, but relied on, and to which I have daily recourse to have it sprinkled on my conscience ; also against that Holy Spirit that dwells in me, and bears with me an unwearied patience. But if I would work my soul up to self-emptiness, I would, with the help of the Spirit, consider my natural condition, and that in two respects.

(1.) There I am sure to find a perfect emptiness of works of righteousness, for it afforded none ; no, not in any imperfection. This (when the sinfulness of such an estate is fully discovered) the heart needs not be taught, it is so apparent. These words, Tit. iii. 5, 'Not by works of righteousness which we had done,' come in not here only, but elsewhere, upon this occasion, as taken for granted by all believers that had any insight into that estate, of which the apostle hath pronounced this conclusive sentence : ' So then, they that are in the flesh cannot please God,' Rom. viii. 8.

(2.) A man looking back thereon may see the vileness of his nature to the full, for it was then that the power of sin remained in its full strength (or to use Paul's phrase, Rom. vii. 5), 'had force,' its full force in his members to bring forth fruit to death, which force is now in part broken and slain. A man then laid the reins upon his lust's neck. A man then committed uncleanness with greediness, πλεονεξία, such as he could never have enough of. And it is the greediness, the unsatisfiedness, and eagerness of a man's lusts in sinning, humbles more than the outward action. A man may, by the course he then held, see what a dragon that serpent would have proved ; but now Christ hath trodden on his head, to keep him from ever growing again.

(3.) A man consulting that, may be convinced of his utter inability to help himself, and of his want of power to believe. Take any man, and he will easily be brought to acknowledge that he hath so much guilt of sin, as needs a mediator to God for him ; and that it is necessary that he go to him, if he will have benefit by him. But yet still he flatters his heart with this, that he hath power to believe and lay hold on him ; otherwise men would not dare to defer to believe and repent, if they took not this for granted, and were not encouraged by such an opinion. But when a man comes to see his natural condition, he sees himself without strength, plunged into misery, and unable for ever to help himself, and that there is not only need that God would graciously provide a mediator, a sacrifice for him (as Abraham said, Gen. xxii. 8), but that God must as well give him faith to go unto Christ, as give Christ himself, and must find him hands to lay hold of him withal. And this also the apostle regards as a granted principle in believers' hearts, from a sight of their natural condition, Eph. ii. For having said they had been by nature dead in sins, he concludes, ver. 8, ' By grace ye are saved, through faith, and that not of yourselves ; it is the gift of God.' After conversion, a man finds himself quickened, through the Spirit and the new creature stirring in him ; but he was afore utterly dead in sins and trespasses. There is nothing gives a more perfect experience of this inability than that estate. Let the soul remember but that, and he must needs remember he wanted all ability to any good.

(4.) This, and this alone, teacheth a man one lesson (and it is one of the highest in faith's school) which but for the experiences hereof, a man would hardly, if ever, learn ; and that is, that whenever a man puts forth an act of faith for justification, and comes to Christ for it, he should look upon himself as an ungodly person, and to be so in himself for ever. This is made the very *genius*, and the spirit of faith : Rom. iv. 5, ' But to him that worketh not, but believeth on him that justifieth the ungodly, his faith is counted for righteousness,' and no other. Now after a man is once converted to God, although he is a sinful man in many respects, yet in that state he is not an ungodly, but really and truly a godly man. Doth the apostle then intend this speech of the first act of faith, which a man puts forth when he first believed only, that then indeed this acting faith was such as wherein looking upon himself as an ungodly person, in respect of all his former condition, he then came to Christ and God under such apprehensions of himself to be justified notwithstanding, looking on himself as a person utterly ungodly? Now, suppose the apostle had spoken it in respect of that first act of faith only, a man could not have had an experimental sense of his being, or having been ungodly, but by means of having lived in such an estate, wherein he had been both a sinner and also ungodly. But further, the apostle here speaks of the faith of a believer, which he continues to put forth from first to last; and his scope is to describe the whole of that faith all along, which in point of justification a believer lives by: which is evident, both

[1.] By the instance he is alleging for his proof, which is the instance of Abraham. Abraham was not justified by works (ver. 2), therefore not we. ' For what saith the Scripture? Abraham believed God, and it was counted to him for righteousness,' ver. 4, 5, as shewing and expounding what manner of act of faith that was which Abraham our father put forth. It was clearly this: he believed on him, or on God as justifying the ungodly, and so in believing looked upon himself under the consideration of an ungodly person. Now if indeed this act of faith in Abraham, which the apostle hath recourse to, had been that which at his first calling and conversion he put forth, then this speech of the apostle concerning this faith must have been limited to that first act of faith. But if it prove that that act of faith the apostle quotes of Abraham was that faith he put forth many years after he had first believed, then it must necessarily be understood that Abraham, after he was converted, in believing for righteousness looked upon himself as ungodly. He had no eye to works no more than at the very first. Now it proves to be thus indeed; for it is in the 15th of Genesis that you find this first said of Abraham's faith, whereas Abraham had been converted and a believer many years before; for Gen. xii. 1–3, you read of Abraham's call out of his own country, when yet he believed: Heb. xi. 8, ' By faith Abraham, when he was called to go out into a place he after received, obeyed.' So then Abraham, in believing, for ever looked on himself as ungodly.

[2.] The apostle's scope all along is, to assert the doctrine of justification by faith only, as well after conversion as in conversion, and how that in believing a man looks not at work or at himself as working, but eyes God under this consideration, as one that justifies a person, though ungodly; and upon those terms cometh to God for justification. And therefore justification (says he) is not by works, for they are a contradiction to the very *formalis subjectum,** or that *formalis ratio* of a person to be justified, which true faith hath in its eye; for it both considers the person to be justified as not working, yea, as ungodly. And the formal consideration it hath of God, or under which it eyeth him, is, that he is a God justifying the ungodly. Now if this be the nature, the tendency of faith as justifying, then, says the apostle, it is impossible to be justified at all by works; but if we are justified, it must be by faith. For by this faith excludes works in the very *formalis ratio* of the subject to be justified, who is one that worketh not, and in the *formalis ratio* of the object it eyes, the person justifying, God justifying the ungodly. And therefore we may be said to be justified by faith all along, after conversion as well as before we are; ' for the just live by faith,' and the righteousness of God is still revealed from faith to faith, as he had shewn

* Qu. ' *ratio subjecti* ' ?—ED.

in the beginning of his discourse: chap. i. ver. 17, 'For therein is the righteousness of God revealed from faith to faith; as it is written, The just shall live by faith.' Then it must be after conversion as well as before that the faith of a believer doth in some true and real perspective or other look upon himself as ungodly, and as having no works at all; and for every apprehension of faith the believer must look on himself as ungodly. Faith and truth are the nearest of kin of all things else; therefore that which God would have me believe must have the greatest and clearest truth in it. Therefore this must remain a certain and irrefragable truth, that after conversion a man may be said to be an ungodly person. And how can this be? Why, it is no way solvable but by this, that a man having once been an ungodly person, and in such an estate he is to look upon himself, as in himself, for ever as such, when he comes to be justified. In the 2 Cor. xii. 5, you have Paul distinguishing concerning himself: 'I knew a man in Christ: of him I will glory, yet of myself I will not glory;' yet this man was himself, that same one individual Paul. So then Paul in Christ is differing in his own eye from Paul in himself. Thus here a believer is taught this strange distinction, to acknowledge himself as in Christ to be a new creature, a person godly, but yet to turn the other end of the prospective, and view himself as in himself to be an ungodly person, utterly ungodly. And if he will at any time present himself afore God's throne for justification, he must plead *sub formâ impii*, as our law says in another case, *sub formâ pauperis*. He must appear in his unregenerate rags, or rather nakedness, as a person abominable, cast out, and weltering in all his blood; for God as justifying regards nothing at all that difference, which yet himself hath made, of godly and ungodly,—godly since regeneration, and ungodly afore,—but looks upon the man as environed with the guilt of both estates, and so having been once godly;* as one that is in that court to be adjudged, reckoned so still. It is not a man's new godliness takes away the guilt of his ungodliness, but it is only God's imputing a righteousness to him that is none of his own. Now look how God, as justifying, looks upon things; so will God have faith, as justifying, to view things also. And therefore when faith comes afore a justifying God, it must lay aside the thoughts of its own works; though it have never so many to plead in its own court, yet it must fall down and acknowledge (as they at the altar did), 'A Syrian ready to perish was my father;' and an ungodly person I was once, and am still, as in the guilt thereof ready to perish, and as in thy sight (O Lord) I present myself afore thee as such; and I cast myself upon thee to justify me, not as now godly and converted, but as ungodly, for so I was once, and am ever so to be reckoned, in myself considered. And this is clearly the faith we first brought to God when we first believed; this is the faith we live by, and this is the faith we are to die in. And so as justification in God is one uniform act, *actus individuus*, as divines speak, so hereby it comes to pass that faith (take it as it justifies) is also an act of one kind, uniform, constant, and like itself, both at first, at last, and all along; it is 'A believing on God, that justifies the ungodly,'

Now faith would not have a ground for such an apprehension, unless a man had been sometimes in such a condition wherein he was utterly ungodly; and experience of that estate, by having passed some time of a man's life therein, helpeth faith to think, yea, formeth in the heart the thought of this condition. Take John Baptist, sanctified in the womb, who grew up to actual faith after, yet he apprehended, though not by experience, yet

* Qu. 'ungodly'?—ED.

from the word, as David also did, that in his conception he was utterly ungodly, nothing but flesh.   But if a man hath found himself to live in such an estate some years, and hath been convinced of it, then experience helps faith, and teacheth it this so hard lesson, than which there is none harder in the school of Christ.   And this Abraham was taught by occasion, that himself had lived in such a condition afore his call, having been brought up in idolatry in his father's house : ' for they served other gods,' saith the Holy Ghost, Josh. xxiv. 2, speaking conjunctively of Terah, Nahor, and Abraham.   And therefore in God's call of him the words run thus : Gen. xii. 1, ' Get thee from thy father's house ; ' that is, leave their sins and ways, as Ps. xlv., in God's speaking to the church, that phrase is in like manner included.   Now hence it was that Abraham ever after, when he came to believe, first looked upon himself as in the guilt of this estate. I was an idolater, might Abraham say, and would have been so still ; therefore I believe on thee, O Lord, who justifiest not Abraham *as religious*, but Abraham *the idolater*.   I reckon not myself by what through thy grace I am, but what but for thy grace I should have been.   Paul speaks of himself, ' I was a blasphemer once,' and I reckon myself so still ; and all the sermons I have made, it was not I, but the grace of God in me.   Take the *I*, and put nothing but blasphemy, persecution, and all concupiscence to it, for this *I* consisteth of nothing else.   And the sense of this caused Paul to say, ' I know nothing by myself, yet I am not hereby justified,' 1 Cor. iv. 4 ; that is, suppose I did know nothing by myself since conversion, yet I know so much by myself before as it would never justify me.   But as to that point, the faith I live by is to believe on him that justifies the ungodly.   So then the experience of such a former estate of sin helps that part of faith which consists of self-emptiness.

2. As this dispensation of God layeth a foundation for that private part of faith, self-emptiness, so it is sanctified by God as a help and promoter of faith in its positive acts.

(1.) Faith, as ye know, lies in a confidence (as the apostle expresseth it) in an adventuring to cast my soul on Christ for salvation.   Now if a man hath adventured upon some uncouth doubtful way, and found success and issue therein, he is emboldened to attempt the like with more resolution, especially in some special desperate case ; he made such or such an attempt, and it succeeded.   Now, when thou at first conversion sawest thyself (I speak especially to such) as to the time past of thy life to have continued in a lost and undone condition, and foundest thyself hopeless and helpless in respect of any power or qualification in thyself that might stand thee in any stead, tell me, was it not a bold adventure to begin first to believe ?   It is certain the first act of faith that any man doth put forth (and every man had a beginning) was the boldest adventure in the world ; that thus thou, a soul guilty of nothing but ungodliness, and so much ungodliness for time past, shouldst stretch forth thy impure hand (perhaps trembling when thou didst it) to touch him that is the Holy One of God ; to dare so much as to think with thyself, he may yet love me, pardon me, and be my husband, was the boldest adventure which thou couldst make.   And yet God drew, and persuaded thy heart to come to him with such a purpose and aim of spirit, which venturous act of thine he seconded with easing, quieting, and pacifying thy heart ; stilling and commanding the waves, that were coming in upon thy soul, to be quiet for the present ; yea, perhaps owning thy soul with leaving some impressions and intimations of his love and grace inclining towards thee.   Now then, here is the improvement of this experience.   I would have thee (the greatest venture being already borne) be bold to reiterate the same act of faith continually, which thou mayest now do with more steadiness and freedom of spirit than when thou didst first believe. It is a phrase peculiar in the Epistle to the Hebrews, chap. iii. 14, ' To hold fast the beginning of our confidence stedfast to the end ;' as if he had said, your first onset and attempt, your beginning to venture upon Christ, was an act of daring ; do but hold fast and renew the same, which you have greater encouragement to do, if by no other, even by this, that you know what it is to begin. Consider, thy faith at first act of believing had no experience of its own to hearten it, as Adam and Eve had not when the promised seed was first preached ; but now faith hath had some experience, if never so small, at one time or other ; then believe again and again, and hold fast thy confidence unto the end.

(2.) Yea, the consideration of this may help thee in the worst and highest temptation that can befall thee, for usually the devil's worst, or the worst he is permitted to speak of thee to thyself, is to terrify thee with this, that thou art still an ungodly creature in thy natural condition ; and he well knows how terrible the fear of that is to a poor believing soul. Well, but yet such a desperate plunge is not usual with thee ; if thou wouldst speak truth, thou art seldom brought so low, thus to conclude, or to sit down so persuaded of thyself, though full of doubts and suspicions. Yet usually when thou hast cast up all, thou darest not say God hath wrought nothing yet saving on thy heart. Well, but suppose Satan hath overthrown thee in all suits and pleas, and thou art reduced to this, I am yet after all this an ungodly person ; do thou but yet strengthen thy weak knees, and if thou canst not walk, creep to Jesus Christ and say, What I was bold to do at first, I will do still ; if I be driven back to that point from whence I launched forth into the vast ocean of free grace at first, having neither sail nor compass, I will to sea again ; and as I ventured then, I will do so still. And though I have missed hitherto, yet there was a time when ungodly Abraham, ungodly Paul, &c., began first to believe, and to believe on God, as one that justifies persons ungodly. It is not disproportions of greater or lesser ungodliness that makes any difference. If thou wert more ungodly than thou wast at first (which yet thou art not), it matters not with God.

(3.) In the temptation about fears of perseverance or falling away, the consideration hereof may help thee. Thou hast corruptions break forth within thee, and thou fearest they one day will undo thee, and are apt to think, Will God bear with me to the end ? Well, but remember how disobedient thou once wert, committing sin with greediness, which now thou canst not do, a seed of God remaining in thee, which God upholds in thy heart, as a spark in the sea, that thou canst not sin as thou wert wont. It is certain thou art not worse in that respect than thou wert in that estate of ungodliness once ; then reason thus with thyself, If God then loved me so, and loves his people so whilst in that condition, as he in the end pulled me forth of that estate, will not this his love more easily be induced to preserve and keep me in this estate I yet stand in ? Yes surely, Rom. v. 10, ' For if, when we were enemies, we were reconciled to God by the death of his Son ; much more, being reconciled, we shall be saved by his life.' Do thou now then but make the comparison between the one estate and the other. Thou never camest at him then, nor didst anything for him, and yet he received thee, but now thou comest every day to him, and he reduceth, and brings thee back again. And consider further, that God, during all the time of thy unregeneracy, had all that while thou wert running on in sin, a time in his eye, in which he would bring thee home unto himself, and relieved himself (as it were) with this, Well, let him now take his swing, I shall have him shortly on his knees for all this, and he shall come home by 'weeping cross,' and seek unto me for grace and holiness, with the same eagerness he now pursues his pleasures. So now consider, though thy spirit by fits runs out into bold evils against him, and corruptions break forth in thee, that yet God doth, and can much more easily relieve himself about thee now, than he did before. He says with himself, Well, there is a time a-coming shortly, in which I shall take him up to myself, and sanctify him fully, and present him without spot and wrinkle afore myself, Eph. v. 27; it is but bearing with these trifling miscarriages and breakings forth a little space, I did forbear him much more afore when he did nothing but sin, and never sought to me in earnest or seriously, nor had I one jot of service from him all that while; but now, though he thus sins, yet I get now and then a lively broken prayer of him, I see his heart is with me notwithstanding, and he is never quiet till he comes to me again, and but half his heart and consent is in the sinning, and my free grace is honoured in him in pardoning of him; and though I honour not myself so much in keeping him altogether free, yet he never comes to be as bad as afore conversion in respect of the frame of his heart in sinning. Surely then, says God, as I bore with him then, and said his day of conversion is a-coming; so I will bear with him now, as a father doth with his son that serves him, for I see a day of his being made perfectly holy is a-drawing near, and it is but my waiting till that change shall come. Do thou relieve thyself with these thoughts too, and help thy faith with this also, that he that gave at first so great and fatal a blow to thy corruptions, and so sensibly deaded all thy desires to the world and the pleasures of sin, that thou foundest them as dead drink to thy stomach which had lost its spirit, and wrought so great a change in thee then, the same God will at the day of thy death (which is the next great day when thy change shall come) give all thy sins a final blow, and an eternal death's wound. Thou hast found the one in part, and trust him thou shalt find the other. 'Wait' (as Job says) 'till this great change shall come,' whereof that other was a beginning and a pledge, and of the two the greater.

(4.) Lastly, the remembrance and consideration of such an estate may serve, and is sanctified by God, to quicken a believer, and to take the faster hold of Jesus Christ. And although the strength with which we believe is wholly and entirely from the Spirit, and put into the soul by him who is said to 'strengthen us in the inner man,' Eph. iii. 16, yet he useth apt, and suitable, and fit motives by and with which he conveys it, and conveys it answerably to the fitness, strength, and force that is in such motives to work upon an intelligent nature. Now, among all the considerations that are like to thrust and push on a man's soul to take hold on Christ with violence, and that may quicken him in his way to the city of refuge, even when his knees would else grow feeble, that which is very powerful is the view and prospect of an unregenerate condition, and the sins thereof, like an army sent out to attach him, to course him, and to make him throw and plunge himself into the water-brook, as the hunted hart more furiously, when standing still and lifting up his ears, he winds, and hears the cries of all his sins that trace his blood. When a man shall see and consider, If I be not found in Christ, then not only all the sins I have committed since I knew God, but all the bold and bloody transgressions of my youth, the sins which I have vomited up, shall call me owner and author of them, and I am then still the miserable subject of them; the vast and thorough prospect of all this, ever and anon taken in, drives the soul with the more eager vehemence upon Christ. Or as a man hanging upon a high tree or pinnacle, having underneath him a gulf of all miseries, as suppose heaps of toads, and serpents, or ravenous beasts, that lie gaping in a deep pit, ready to prey upon him, and devour him, if he should let go his hold and fall down again amongst them (of which he is sensible, having lately scrambled forth of it, and got up upon that tree of life and preservation); the frightful view and prospect will cause him to make as sure hold as possibly he can, and to renew his hold again and again, and not to hold with one hand, but with both, entwining his arms and legs and his whole body about that tree, embracing it for preservation, as well as for the pleasant fruit that grows upon it; so it is here in this case too.

CHAPTER VII.

The second use we should make of the review of that wretched, sinful state out of which God removes us by the work of his grace, is to have our hearts affected with the sense of God's extraordinary love manifested herein, and to excite and heighten our love to God by the consideration of this his great love to us.

II. A second main improvement of the remembrance of thy former condition is to intend and heighten thy love to God. This is that second particular which Paul instanceth in 1 Tim. i. as the redound and consequent of having been injurious in his former condition. Grace was abundant in love (says he); that is, grace made this advantage thereof, to cause me to love God the more. And this is also the spirit of that saying, 'Mary loved much, because much was forgiven her,' Luke vii. 47. Christ founds his reasoning upon two things.

1. God's usual dispensation, which is, that where he leaves one to many sins, and long to continue in them, when he converts him, he works in him more love to himself; and on the contrary, where fewer sins have been, there is less love. For to assert the truth of this, Christ turns it both ways; for it follows, 'To whom little is forgiven, the same loveth little.'

2. Christ founds his reason upon this, that where God shews more love, he works and draws forth more love to himself again. God chose us to be 'holy afore him in love.' It was the end of his choice, and the aim of his love. And as he makes it an agreement that he loved us first, so he will not bate the least grain, degree, or proportion of love, but he will have use for it; and those whom he loves most, he will cause their hearts to love him more in the end. Now God shews love in this life in no dispensation more —(I do not say only, or most by this, yet in none more)—for, as I shewed you, his end in it was to set forth grace, mercy, and love. And therefore, when he hath effectually wrought upon a soul that had lain in such an estate, he makes the heart sensible of more love from himself, and so draws love forth out of the heart again. *Est magnes magni magnus amoris amor:* 'Love is the loadstone of love,' and draws according to the measure of the virtue and spirit that is in it. When did Christ ask Peter, 'Lovest thou me?' John xxi. 17, &c., but then, when he had denied him, when he first met with him after it. And it is observed, that as Peter had denied him thrice, so Christ asked him thrice, 'Peter, dost thou love me?' Christ

expects a proportion of love from Peter to his own love shewn in pardoning of him. And as for this converting love of God, when fully considered, whom indeed would not such a love move ? Think how, during thy unregenerate condition, God lay in ambushment for thee, to environ thee about, and then overcame thy heart with loving-kindness. Think how during all that time thou hadst not one good thought of God (Ps. x., ' God was not in all thy thoughts '), that yet God's heart and thoughts continually have been upon thee, thinking nothing but thoughts of peace to thee, and not of evil, Jer. xxix. 11. Thou wert written upon his heart and the palm of his hands all that time thou didst nothing else but write and score up sins against him. You may observe (for it is worth it), how out of this disposition of heart in God, the Holy Ghost cannot forbear bringing in the mention of Saul in the history of his life and actions, again and again before his conversion, as one he had his eye upon whilst he was a persecutor: Acts vii. 58, ' The witnesses,' knowing his zeal, ' laid their clothes down at a young man's feet called Saul,' who was consulting Stephen's death, Acts xxii. 20; his hand was in the murder of the first martyr. I saw thee then, said God to him when he converted him ; and if he tells us of it, he told himself much more. And again, you have it again repeated in ver. 3 of that chapter, ' As for Saul ' (he stood in God's eye more, and God all that while took more notice of what he did than of all other men), ' he made havoc of the church, entering into every house, and haling men and women, committed them to prison.' And as he said of Sennacherib, 2 Kings xix. 27, ' I have known thy abode, thy going out, and coming in, and thy rage against me ; ' so he shews he did take notice of Saul all that while, but with a differing intention. As he relieved himself against Sennacherib's rage and tumult, that he would put a hook in his nose, and a bridle in his lips (' And I will turn thee back by the way which thou camest,' ver. 29), so God did all that while please himself with the thoughts of his purposes towards this Saul ; that the time would shortly come, that he should have him come in as fast, and with as much holy violence, to seek mercy from God, as ever he had gone forth against him ; that he should see him in the pulpit preaching the doctrine he now destroyed ; that he should have a hook, a cord of love to strike into his heart and draw him back again ; and that he had appointed the instant moment when he would throw it at him, just when he was going to Damascus. And God, out of his love, pleased himself as much with the thought of this aforehand, nay more, than he did at the thought of his turning back Sennacherib, whom, you may perceive, that God makes sport at. And as God is said to laugh at the wicked, seeing his day a-coming, Ps. xxxvii. 13, God pleaseth himself with this thought concerning an elect soul: Well, let him play on the line, the day of his conversion is at hand, and then I shall have him. Well, this time draws near, and to shew how much God's thoughts were on it, as ours use to be on some great occurrence, for which a set time is appointed, God is speaking of it a third time: Acts ix. 1, ' And Saul, yet breathing out threatenings,' &c. You see the Holy Ghost puts in a *yet*, as if God began now to think the time long, or was then thinking with himself, his time is but short which I have allotted him to continue in sin, it is almost out, he *yet* breathes out threatenings, but his threatenings now shall breathe out their last. Now, the same heart and affection God had all that while towards thee whilst in thy natural condition, and when thou wert committing such and such a sin, God saw thee ere thou didst him (as Christ told Nathanael, ' I saw thee under the fig-tree ') loving thee all that while with the same love with which he loves thee now, though then concealed, as Joseph was to his brethren. And as he had appointed a fulness of time for the coming of his Son into the world, so he had appointed ' a set time ' to have mercy on thee, as the psalmist speaks, Ps. cii. 13.   And Oh, how did God long all that while until that time should come ; as Jer. xiii. 27, ' When shall it once be ? ' And when that day was come, you may see how his heart rejoiced in the parable of the prodigal : Luke xv. 20, ' When he was yet a great way off, his father saw him.'   It expresseth his longing, how he looked out aforehand ; his love sending forth his eyes, as messengers, to feed him with that news he so delighted in.   And after thou begannest but to utter thy heart to him, he could not hold long, but fell upon thy neck and kissed thee ; so ver. 20. He broke up that treasure of mercy he had from everlasting laid by for thee under lock and key of his everlasting purposes, and which he had reserved and kept for thee as thy portion.   Though millions in all ages had passed afore him, and might have been heirs of it, yet he reserved the rich robe for thee, and fetched it out for thee, Luke xv. 22.   And when thou begannest to melt towards him for having offended him, and to bemoan thyself (as, Jer. xxxi. 18, the phrase is) more out of love to thyself, and sense of thine own misery, than love to him, yet he fell a-weeping too as fast as thou, and his bowels were stirred for thee ; what, says he, ' Is Ephraim, my pleasant child,' come home to me ?   And is Ephraim, the wickedest of all the tribes, become pleasant to me ?   God speaks it wonderingly, as indeed admiring at his own affections, how enlarged they were, how his love was gushed forth, and therefore well mayest thou.   What heart is there that proves the subject of these glorious, yet true occurrences, that will not, is not moved at the remembrance or the rehearsal of them ?   They so took Paul's heart, that the love manifested therein would never out of his mind : ' I was ' (says he) ' a blasphemer, but I obtained mercy.'   If we had been in Paul's heart to have discerned the mixtures of the strange affections which met when he put these two together, *I* and *mercy*, who ever would have thought that these two should meet, that were as distant as hell and heaven ?   Who would not (thought Paul) have made a *but* of exception at me ?   Who would not have entered a *caveat* against my ever having mercy, of all men else, if there had been no more in the world ?   Ananias puts in a demur, Acts ix. 13, when Christ did but speak of him ; ' Lord, I have heard by many, how much evil he hath done to the saints at Jerusalem.'   And it is said, ver. 21, that ' all that heard him were amazed.'   But yet this Saul obtained mercy, and so hast thou.   Oh let this grace of our Lord be abundant with love in thy heart towards him again, as it was in Paul's.   Paul could never think of these passages, but a sea of love broke into his heart and overflowed it.

CHAPTER VIII.

That the thoughts of God's excellent love in bringing us out of this woful state of sin into a state of grace, should enkindle in us sacred zeal and fervency of spirit to live in all holy obedience to him.—And what a dreadful condition they are in who make an ill use of the doctrine of grace, by abusing it to an encouragement of carelessness, negligence, or licentiousness.

III. As the considerations of God's love in changing our state may thus inflame love, so they may enlarge obedience, which springs from love, and may excite thee to fruitfulness, and abounding in the work of the Lord, and to be willing to do or suffer any for him. It inflamed Paul's zeal, insomuch as none of the apostles laboured so much as he. His spirit was never at rest; he thought he could never do enough. Peter denies his Master, it is true, and he did it thrice; and you know how Christ came upon him for it, with a higher care of work and labour from him : 'Feed my lambs.' He says it thrice too in the forementioned John xxi. So as indeed Christ in that place, to which I have recourse again, would have Peter make these three commensurable : 1. That as Christ had loved him more, in pardoning more than to the rest; so, 2, he expected that he should love him more; and, 3, that proportionably to that love, he should give demonstration of it in his care over his lambs. To move Peter the more to be willing to do and suffer for him to the last of his days, Christ gives him a little touch, as I understand it, of some wildness and youthfulness that had been in Peter's spirit afore Christ had to do with him : ver. 18 of that chapter, 'Verily, I say unto thee, When thou wast young, thou girdedst thyself, and walkedst whither thou wouldest : but when thou shalt be old, thou shalt stretch forth thine hands, and another shall gird thee, and carry thee whither thou wouldest not.' Peter had had his vagaries, and lived as he listed; and further, as may seem, had given an instance lately of what kind of activities (as I may call them) his youth had delighted in (as many young men do in bodily exercises, and shewing their strength and vigour that way, with too much excess of delight and pride in them), in the 7th and 8th verses. He being in a ship (ver. 7, 8), and spying Christ, girds his fisher's coat about him, and makes no more ado but casts himself into the sea. The other disciples were of a more sober spirit, and came into the ship by land,* which he might have done as well as they, being not far off land; but as it would seem, he gloried in such feats and active pranks, and would shew his Master one, who was now risen from the dead, and was not taken with such things; and yet there was some love mingled with this. That which moves me to think Christ had a purpose to mind Peter of the way of his spirit wherein he had so much delighted, is that he seems to speak of the whole course of his youth, wherein he had taken liberty to do what he listed : 'When thou wert young, thou wentest whither thou wouldest,' that is, didst live to thine own lusts; which Peter, in his Epistle, involving himself with others, acknowledgeth : he was as a loose unruly heifer. And indeed many such things, in themselves innocent and lawful, young men are addicted unto; yet when there is a pride, vanity, vain glory, excess of delight, with expense of time, they are in God's eye great sins. As also is the vanity of those scholars who adore learning too much, and too inordinately love it, from a desire to gain reputation and esteem. This was Lipsius his confession on a great fit of sickness : I have not been (said he) covetous nor vicious, *Sola mihi placuit dulcis pellacia musæ;* only the harlotry of learning took his heart. Christ, you see, makes this use to Peter of his former wanderings, to move him to be the more willing to be carried whither God would have him, even to the cross, as that whereby God ordained to glorify himself in him. And seeing he had delighted himself in such activities, as a man of mettle and courage, God therefore would serve himself of this spirit of resolution in him in a way of trial contrary to the way of his spirit. He was to be hung up by the heels upon a cross (the worst of crucifyings), to be bound to his good behaviour thereon. And Peter (says Christ), see that thou, remembering

* Qu. 'in the ship to land'?—ED.

what thou wert when young, shew thy valour, thy resolution, when thou comest to that conflict; and Peter remembered it, and was moved by it, 2 Pet. i. 14. If this conjecture should not hold, sure I am I find Peter himself in his epistles urging this as a most provoking argument to quicken to future obedience. And he puts himself in among the number of those that had so walked in vanity and sin, for which the popish commentators would find excuses. He speaking of the genius and spirit of a Christian, he says, 1 Pet. iv. 3, he is one whose heart this principle hath taken hold of and prevails upon him, that he no longer should live the rest of his time in the flesh to the lusts of men, but to the will of God : ' For the time past of our lives may suffice us to have wrought the will of the Gentiles.' The strength of this persuasive lies in these two things :

1. They had a long time of their lives already lived in the sins of such an estate. They had served their lusts, and done nothing for God all that while ; and there is but a remaining remnant of it left, τὸν ἐπίλοιπον ἐν σαρκί, which is as a brand plucked out of the fire. Oh ! bestow that wholly upon God, with grief and sorrow that so much is spent and burned out in sinning! Do as much for God as ever you did for the devil. ' As you have yielded your members servants to uncleanness, to iniquity unto iniquity,' adding one iniquity to another, and thinking you had never done enough for your lusts, and growing worse and worse, so now yield your members servants to righteousness unto holiness. And if there were anything higher than holiness, they should reach at that too. And, 2, He edgeth it with this, ' that the time past might suffice to have served their lusts,' if they could suppose it to be lawful for any space of time to neglect God's service, and please and indulge their lusts ; yet those lusts had had sufficient time of their lives already, and indeed too great a share, and therefore it may well suffice. If a lust of thy former ignorance tempt thee, is it not an answer, a sufficient answer, You have been served already, you have your time out, and too much ? And if it urgeth thee to take a little pleasure for a moment, and then to serve God again, yield not, no, not for a moment, as Paul speaks, Gal. ii. Your lusts have had too many moments spent upon them, and your whole time was due to God, and he hath too little left. For as the apostle reasons, Rom. viii. 12, ' We owe nothing to the flesh, to live after the flesh,' we have no reason to do the least kindness for it, nor to give it a crumb, though it were to save a lust's life ; so nor to afford it one moment of our time, but to give the whole unto God. Now, therefore, it behoves you to redeem the time remaining to the utmost, to live much in a little, to do all for God, from a holy grudging that Satan hath had so much. The apostle Paul makes this of itself an argument to more holiness, that by how much less of a man's time is left in the flesh, he should be the more holy: Heb. x. 25, ' So much the more, as he sees the day approaching.' And Peter adds this to it, by how much of the time past hath been lost to God, we ought to take our measure, that the more of what is to come be consecrated to him. And in 1 Pet. i. 15, 18, his scope being to exhort to holiness (as that is the main drift and errand of his epistles), he sets together in opposition and in view their vain conversation (ver. 18) with that holiness of conversation which God now expected : ver. 15, ' Be holy in all manner of conversation, for ye are redeemed from a vain conversation.' He sets *conversation* to *conversation*, and *holy* to *vain*. Be holy in all manner of conversation, for you have been altogether vain in your former conversation ; let the total corruption that was in the one therefore provoke to a total sanctification in the other. And indeed such

grounds as have lain long fallow, you expect the greater crop from them.

IV. The last advantage which we may have by occasion of such an estate of sinning, is to remember it, to keep our spirits low and humble for ever, after conversion wrought; and the like use ought to be made of any great fit of sinning. You shall therefore find that the apostle Paul, who had as high manifestations of God as ever man had, for no man ever since or before him had the like (our Lord and Saviour Christ himself, though he was transfigured upon the mount, yet he had never been rapt up to paradise, nor into the third heaven, as Paul was, but lived by faith as we do), yet that which kept him low all his days, was the remembrance of what he had been. You find two expressions to this purpose. The one in 1 Cor. xv. 9, 'I am,' saith he, 'the least of the apostles, that am not worthy to be called an apostle,' though he doth profess elsewhere, that he laboured more than they all. But if you look into Eph. iii. 8, which is the next text, he goes lower : 'To me,' says he, 'who am less than the least of all saints.' The one phrase (viz., that which he useth in the Corinthians) is a diminutive expression, ἐλάχιστος, the least of the apostles, and yet there he compareth himself with apostles. But in that place of the Ephesians he compares himself with saints, and useth a more diminutive expression,* if there be anything 'lower than the least,' he humbleth himself to it ; and that not in relation to apostles, but in relation to saints. Now what was it that kept Paul, that had all his grace in him, and all the cause in the world to be rapt up above the rest of saints and apostles in privileges vouchsafed to him ? You shall find it in that 1 Cor. xv. 9 (that which I quoted even now), where having said, 'I am the least of all the apostles, that am not worthy to be called an apostle ;' in what follows, you find it was the remembrance of his former condition, and of what he had been, persecuting the church of God, that moved him to such humble thoughts and words. You know when he speaks of his unregenerate estate in 1 Tim. i. 11, 'I was a persecutor,' saith he, 'and injurious,' &c. This was it he bore the scars of, in his own spirit, to his dying day. And you may observe how he did grow up into this humility and into this lowness in his own eyes. When he wrote that Epistle to the Ephesians, he was an aged man : he styles himself there 'Paul the aged ;' he had written to the Corinthians long afore. You see he grows to a deeper sense ; he was the least of the apostles then, but now the least of all saints. And what was it that did make him thus low, and that he did grow up into a daily sensibleness, the more God loved him and revealed himself to him ? Even his own vileness, the consideration of what once he had been. 'Because' (saith he) 'I have persecuted the churches.' Why Paul, he had thought of that sin a thousand times, but still the older he did grow, the more it did sink into his spirit, and humble him the more. Hast thou had any manifestations of God to thy spirit ? Hast thou prayed well to-day ? And art thou proud of it ? Hath God lifted thee above others in spiritual privileges ? Come, take but a turn in thy unregenerate condition. Let me bring to thy remembrance thy old walks ; what wert thou ten, twenty, or thirty years ago ? And what wert thou doing of then ? Dost thou not remember ? Suppose a man had lived with Nebuchadnezzar after he had come out of the wilderness from amongst beasts, and should have heard him talk as presumptuously as before, 'Is not this great Babel I have built ?' If one should

* Namely, ἐλαχιστοτέρῳ.—Ed.

but have minded him, and bade him go to the wilderness where he was two or three years ago, it would have pricked his bladders and let out the wind; so it will have the same effect in thee.

I have made many uses, you see, of this great point for you ; there is one use more (it is a bad one), which I am afraid some of you will make for yourselves ; it was Paul's fear, also his fear to prevent it ; and that is, that seeing a man who hath lived in a a state of sinning often hath, and may have, this event, to be converted at last, I will even continue in sin, that grace may abound, or at least I will presume still to continue as I am.

1. I will give the apostle's answer, Rom. iii. 8, ' Let us do evil that good may come ; whose damnation is just.'   He throws hell-fire back again upon them, and that is all the answer ; that if God, upon such an arguing of thine, should pronounce such a sentence on thee, and swear against thee in his wrath, thy damnation were just ; and this God often doth against many. For in thus arguing, besides thy abuse of the sweetest attribute of mercy, thou assumest to thyself God's highest sovereignty and prerogative, which, if ever in anything, lies in this, that he can bring so great a good out of so much evil ; and yet in so doing he barely permits the creature to go on, leaving them to their own ways.   But thou art active in all thine, and by this proclaimest thyself, *ipso facto*, the greatest rebel that God hath on earth. You know that great and terrible place, Deut. xxix. 18–20.   God was tendering that day the covenant of grace, as is clear by Paul's application of that sermon, Rom. x., and by the first verse of that chapter.   And he bids them take heed, lest there be a root of bitterness, an evil heart in one, that says, ' I shall have peace, though I walk on in the imagination of my heart, and add drunkenness to thirst,' that is, to satisfy my lusts.   ' The Lord will not spare that man,' but then (even whilst he is thinking such a cursed thought), ' the anger of the Lord shall smoke against that man, and all the curses in this book shall lie upon him, and the Lord shall separate him unto evil, single him forth of all the tribes,' &c.

But shall I close with thee now at last ?   Dost thou begin to be sensible thou hast gone on in such a condition to this hour ?   Go home and tell God of it ; there is no remaining in it, no, not for an hour, for the wrath of God abides upon thee.   Yet say not there is no hope (as they in Jer. ii.), for you have heard, it is one of God's greatest designs to exalt grace, love, and mercy upon men, by and in that way.   Let all that is in God encourage thee.   Thy way out of it hath been made plain before thee ; it is regeneration, that passage from death to life.   Oh, begin to seek to obtain it ; if thou hast a mind to Christ, assure thyself he hath much more mind to thee.   Art thou wambling ?   Art thou whimpering ?   I assure thee he is gone forth to find thee ; Luke xv. 4.   He goes out to seek that which is lost, long before he finds it.   He will meet thee half way (as you have it in the same 15th chapter of Luke, verse 20).   Only let me persuade thee to turn now to him.   Thou art not only perhaps undone else, but if ever thou dost hereafter turn, thou wilt repent thou didst it no sooner.   Yea, thou wilt repent for nothing more, than that sin had so much more time after God had moved thee.   It is the ingenuity of true grace (which is love to God) so to work.   Come, it may be a match between Christ and thee before midnight yet ; it was so to the jailor, Acts xvi., in a less space. Come !   I have spoke thy heart, and have hold of it.   I will not let thee go. What thou and God will alone together make out of it, I know not ; there may be but an inch between thee and eternal glory ; wilt thou defer ?   Oh, unkind !   If thou hopest to go to heaven, shall God have no glory out of thee, in amends to what is past ? Shall thy 'no longer to live to the lusts of men,' be thy 'no longer to live'? Tell me how many years hast thou lived in sin ? What is thirty or forty years ? May not that suffice to an enemy that will destroy thee ? In a word, I have told you a long story of God's design in suffering the bulk of his elect to go on to years of discretion, ere he converts them; and that his design therein is glory to himself. But it is meet for me withal to tell you, yea, indeed end in telling you it, that as God's design is to shew love in it, so wisdom also. And therefore ordinarily his design is so to convert, after such a time of sinning, as providently to have such a time in thy years remaining, as to have a glory out of thee in thy fruitfulness and obedience. There are but few instances of late repentance. All the epistles of the apostles speak of men that had formerly been in such a condition of sin, but they were yet written to them, whilst alive, and now turned, and as remaining surviving subjects of exhortations to all holiness, and left to give demonstration thereof. My brethren, God is so wise, as he will compass and grasp both ends. As he will leave a time in which you may have experience of such an estate, so he will ordinarily so convert, or not at all, as there may be a time to shew forth the contrary graces for his glory, which is made the end of conversion 1 Peter ii. 9. And of the two, you may well give God leave to project the latter for the longer time, for a little of the other sufficeth. I observe it in this epistle to Titus, that this grace and love (which Paul says appeared to us who were sometime disobedient, in this third chapter), is in chap. ii. 12 said so to appear, as that men may afterwards give demonstration of their living soberly, righteously, and godly, according to that grace, even in this present world : for otherwise, whilst they are in the world, God would lose his design.

BOOK III.

The necessity of regeneration demonstrated by this argument, that all that God and Christ have done towards their reconciliation to us will profit us nothing, unless we be reconciled to God.—And how conversion is set forth under the notion of reconciliation as on our part.

And all things are of God, who hath reconciled us to himself by Jesus Christ, and hath given unto us the ministry of reconciliation; to wit, that God was in Christ, reconciling the world unto himself, not imputing their trespasses unto them; and hath committed unto us the word of reconciliation. Now then we are ambassadors for Christ, as though God did beseech you by us: we pray you in Christ's stead, be ye reconciled to God.—2 Cor. V. 18–20.

CHAPTER I.

That notwithstanding what God and Christ have done for their reconciliation to us, it is, by God's ordination, necessary that we be reconciled to God, if ever we be saved.—This proved from God's design in his reconciliation to us, to glorify his holiness, &c.

Our apostle professeth to declare in these, and the foregoing words, the whole substance of the ministry of the gospel, which he and his fellow apostles were entrusted to deliver to us: ver. 18, 'God hath committed to us the ministry of reconciliation;' which message or ministry consists of two parts.

1. A reconciliation wrought on God's part towards us, in the effecting of which Christ was concurrent with him; for 'God was, in Christ, reconciling the world to himself.'

2. The other business is a reconciliation on our parts, enforced from what God and Christ had done; and this is equally necessary unto man's salvation, as that reconciliation on God's and Christ's part is: ver. 20, 'Now then we are ambassadors for Christ, as though God did beseech you by us: we pray you in Christ's stead, be ye reconciled to God.' Now as these are the two parts of the 'ministry of reconciliation,' that is, of the gospel, so they must be understood to be two essential requisites, to make our salvation complete, and both alike essentially necessary thereunto, and without which we shall never be saved, as those obliging words of God and Christ, 'beseeching us,' ver. 20, shew. Now under the notion of our being reconciled to God, he intends, and involveth both, the whole of what is requisite on our parts from first to last, both that work of reconciliation effected in our regeneration, whereby we enter into that estate, and which is required of those to whom this gospel comes, to estate them into salva-

tion, and also a daily proceeding to perfect that reconciliation (after it hath been begun) by faith and repentance towards God and Christ.

For he applies this doctrine to the Corinthians, that had been reconciled already. And yet (says he), ' be ye reconciled.'

Obs. Notwithstanding what God and Christ have done towards our reconciliation on their part (which is the first of the message), there is a necessity, by God's ordination, of our being reconciled to God, if we be partakers of salvation. For the apostle, having distinctly declared both God's care in it and Christ's, he from thence presseth this on our part; as that without which the other would be in vain, to the attainment of God's intention and aim in both, which is our effectual salvation. And to impress this the more effectually upon the spirits of men, the apostle tells them that himself and other apostles and ministers to whom this ministry is committed, are ordained ambassadors of God, not only to proclaim and declare to us this fore part of the message, ' That God was in Christ reconciling the world unto himself,' and that Christ ' was made sin for us ;' but that himself and the other apostles were ambassadors of God and Christ, to beseech us to be reconciled : ver. 20, ' Now then we are ambassadors for Christ, as though God did beseech you by us : we pray you in Christ's stead, be ye reconciled to God.' Which beseechment denotes not only their gracious condescension, or mere desire to us, but loudly speaks the absolute necessity of our being reconciled by God's appointment ; as without which, if not performed by us, God should lose what he had wrought towards it, and Christ should lose his labour and reward ; and the design of his having been made sin for us. And that this is God's resolved ordination, he further enforceth from the end of God's having set up and established such a ministry of his apostles and their successors in the world, whose office is an embassage from the great God by preaching, and then by writing their epistles, to reduce and bring in the elect fallen into a rebellion against him. Which reconciliation of them, if it had not been necessary, this great institution of God had been in vain and to no purpose. I might say of this matter what the same apostle on behalf of the resurrection argues : 1 Cor. xv. 14, ' If Christ be not risen, then our preaching is in vain.' Thus I might say concerning your reconciliation, If what God and Christ have done had alone perfected it, and no more had been to be done in us, then is our preaching the Scriptures of the New Testament vain: Rom. x. 13–17, ' For whosoever shall call upon the name of the Lord shall be saved. How then shall they call on him in whom they have not believed ? and how shall they believe in him of whom they have not heard ? and how shall they hear without a preacher ? And how shall they preach, except they be sent ? as it is written, How beautiful are the feet of them that preach the gospel of peace, and bring glad tidings of good things ! So then faith cometh by hearing, and hearing by the word of God.' The word of God is God's ordination and appointment, without which none of us of years shall be saved. Here the necessity lies, it was God's pleasure so to order it ; if therefore our apostle makes a necessity of his preaching the gospel to men (' A necessity,' says he, 1 Cor. ix. 16, ' is laid upon me to preach the gospel), then there is a greater necessity that those that hear the message of it should obey it, if ever they be saved. For the necessity of his preaching the gospel was the foundation of the necessity that is laid upon all other ambassadors like to him. All this is farther illustrated by Rom. x., verses 13 and 17 compared. Let us now consider how God hath threatened (2 Thess. i. 8, 9) finally to destroy them who obeyed not the gospel, who came not in to him, and entertained not this infinite love and grace with all acceptation, in humbling themselves, believing on him and his Son, and turning unto him. And it will be manifest that God is more engaged to punish those his enemies for their refusal of his entreaty, by his ambassadors, who are in his stead, than the greatest kings on earth are, or can be thought, obliged to avenge an affront offered to their ambassadors. Read the parable of the vineyard, Luke xx.

Let us next consider the interest which God the Father and Christ his Son have, and the part which they act in this our reconciliation. God the Father's part was to contrive the whole of our salvation, Christ's part was to purchase it. ' God was in Christ reconciling the world to himself,' &c. I have elsewhere discoursed of God the Father's original transaction with Christ about this,* which I will not repeat, only I cast in the single consideration of it in the text to enforce the thing in hand. In the 28th verse, his preface to all this is, ' All things are of God, who hath reconciled us to himself by Jesus Christ:' the spirit of which connection I extract into this, that the great God, of whom all things else are, hath made this his masterpiece, and his heart was in it above all other things (and therefore he sets it against all things else), and his wisdom and all his other attributes were especially at work about this, ' who works all things according to the counsel of his own will.' As the same apostle says upon the same occasion, Eph. i. He therefore hath been most consultive about the effecting of this, and for the bringing it to its performance according to his own desire. And therefore he who hath contrived to effect all things else in such a manner wherein they shall be most for his own glory (' All things are of him and for him,' Rom. xi. 36), hath above all others contrived this business of man's salvation. And therefore we may be sure he was most regardful and heedful that it should be effected upon such terms as should be for his own high honour and glory, as well as our salvation; that he might have glory by it, as well as we have peace. When that great proclamation of peace and goodwill to men was made by the angels at the birth of our Lord (which contains the whole of reconciliation on God's part), it runs thus : ' Glory be to God on high,' that is first ; and then it follows, ' Peace on earth ; good will towards men.' This was to shew that he had so ordered it, that our peace and his glory should run along together. Now if we should have peace and pardon from him on account of what Christ hath done, and we should remain unreconciled to him both in heart and life, then here were dishonour to God the Most High, and a violation of peace on earth too. But surely he hath disposed matters so, that as he would shew himself a friend to you, and manifest good will to men, so withal he would appear a friend to himself, and true to his own interest, which is his glory. This is indeed but a general, and yet it comprehends all his attributes ; all and each of which are his glory. I shall instance particularly in the glory but of one or two of them.

1. As to his holiness, when I discoursed of those transactions of the Father with Christ, I shewed that God, merely to give satisfaction to *justice*, ordained the sacrificing his Son. And it was (as we have it, Rom. iii. 26), ' that he might be just, and the justifier of him that believes in Jesus.' Now if, to be true to that attribute, ' he spared not his own Son,' so then here he having another attribute as near and dear unto him, viz., *holiness*, that must be complied withal to vindicate its honour. And therefore, as

* In the Discourse of Christ the Mediator. Vol. III. of his Works. [Vol. V. o this Edition.—ED.]

God will be *just* in saving, which cost Christ his blood, so he will be *holy* in saving us too. Therefore, ' as he that called you is holy, so you must be holy,' and ' called with an holy calling,' 2 Tim. i. 9. It is not his purpose of grace towards you in Christ Jesus will serve the turn. Because it is written, ' Be ye holy, for I am holy,' 1 Pet. i. 15, 16. He is resolved on it, and therefore ' without holiness no man shall see God,' Heb. xii. Certainly he abated not his Son the least point that justice demanded. If he would not that the cup should pass at his then so earnest entreaty, then if it were possible to suppose Christ would supplicate him now, to let regeneration or reconciliation pass off without effect in saving any of you, God would not.

2. A second attribute he intended the glory of in the matter of reconciliation between him and us, was principally the glory of his grace. He designed to set forth his love so as to attain the ends of loving. It is not to give forth peace only, but to manifest good will and kindness, as that speech of the angel shews, Luke ii. 14. Yea, the ground of his shewing mercy is his love : Eph. ii. 4, ' God who is rich in mercy, for the great love wherewith he loved us.' And although on our part our love and friendship to God is not the ground of his, yet it is the end or aim of his. Though he did not love us because we loved him first, yet he loved us that we might love him again, for ' He chose us that we should be holy in love,' Eph. i. 4. Therefore in those he saves, if there were not wrought an inward principle of love and friendship, and good will mutual again to him, that might answer this his love, his love would not have its end ; and would be finally cast away. For so we reckon love to be given away in loss when it is not answered in its kind ; that is, with a true love again. God would have his love valued and esteemed by those he saves ; for love is the dearest thing that any one hath to bestow, because whosoever hath a man's love hath all he hath, for it commands all. And therefore God, who is love (1 John iv. 8), will not cast away his love, especially not such a love as this. And yet this love were lost if not esteemed by us, and if esteemed by us it will work holiness in us, and we shall be ' holy before him in love,' Eph. i. 4. These arguments, to prove the necessity of our being reconciled to God, have been drawn from the part which God the Father hath in our reconciliation.

CHAPTER II.

The necessity of our being reconciled to God evinced from Christ's design in his work of reconciliation.

The next argument shall be fetched from Christ and his part in reconciliation, of whom it is here said, ' God was in Christ reconciling,' &c. Christ's interest was considered by God, and Christ's concernment is such in this matter that I may without any scruple of diffidence pronounce, that Christ would rather lose all he hath on his part done or suffered for us, than that we should be saved without being reconciled to God by a true work of regeneration.

In the foresaid transaction of God with Christ about the reconcilement of us, I shewed there was a covenant made between God and Christ in our behalf. And therein God the Father meant not to put such upon Christ as

should continue wholly averse in disposition towards him ; for Christ by
covenant was to be a husband as well as a redeemer from sin, and the
agreement between him and his Father was (as Jacob's with Laban), to purchase his wife to himself : Eph. v. 25–27, ' Husbands, love your wives,
even as Christ also loved the church, and gave himself for it; that he might
sanctify and cleanse it with the washing of water by the word, that he
might present it to himself a glorious church, not having spot, or wrinkle,
or any such thing ; but that it should be holy and without blemish.' It is
but reason then, and what he deserved, that he should have such for his
spouse as should love him again.   This covenant between God the Father
and the Son is rehearsed in Ps. cx., ' The Lord said to my Lord,' &c.   And
he took an oath to it, that ' he should be a priest,' ver. 4, which was a
great word ; God the Father therein expressing the call he gave him.   But
then withal his Father engageth and promiseth that ' his people should be
willing in the day of his power.'   Thus the Father acts in his part of the
covenant with Christ.   And then Christ on his part resolved and agreed to
see those he would save, to become ' his seed,' and to be born of him, or
he would never have been satisfied : Isa. liii., ' He shall see his seed, and
be satisfied.'   He resolved that they should come to him, as his Father
promised they should, as that speech of his shews : John vi., ' All that the
Father hath given me shall come to me.'   The Father not simply gave
them to Christ to save them, but promised withal that they should come to
Christ ; and coming be subject to him in all things, Eph. v., as the law of
the marriage covenant requires.   And there is a promise on Christ's part,
to ' raise them up at the last day.'   And to that end he ceaseth not till he
presents them to himself, ' a glorious church, without spot or wrinkle,'
Eph. v. 26, 27.   Yea, I may not stick to say, that Christ otherwise would
be content to lose all he now hath done, rather than that any one should be
saved and not reconciled to God his Father.   And the reason is manifest;
for otherwise he should be the minister of sin, which he abhors.   Thus the
apostle argues, Gal. ii. 17.   And it is the full and direct scope of the
apostle there.   For, treating of the doctrine of free justification or salvation
in that epistle, which the adversaries thereof branded for a doctrine of licentiousness, the apostle abhors it with the greatest indignation, in saying
that this were indeed to make Christ the minister of sin, if he should have
died to procure the justification of any that are not sanctified.   And from
heaven Christ himself declared to Saul, that ' He sent him to open the eyes
of the Gentiles, to turn them from darkness to light, from the power of
Satan unto God, that they may receive forgiveness of sins, and an inheritance among them which are sanctified by faith that is in me,' Acts xxvi. 18 ;
that is, to be a means of their regeneration.   And otherwise he should but
have tied God's hands from hurting us or destroying us, whilst we should
have a licence left us to provoke him and continue in sin.   No ; Christ is
more tender of his Father's glory than so ; and though he is a ' Saviour
perfect,' yet he becomes the ' Author of eternal salvation,' but ' unto those
who obey him,' Heb. v. 8, 9, which none will do until born again.

Lastly, The demonstration is drawn both from God the Father and Son
jointly.   This great design of their reconciling sinners, as agreed on by
them, became matter of the greatest delight to them ; and which, when
concluded, their hearts were infinitely taken up with ; as in Prov. viii.
Wisdom, that is, Christ, exults in the remembrance of it, as it was in his
own and Father's heart afore the world.   Yea, and God's end in loving us,
and Christ's end in dying, was to delight in our persons ; as Zeph. iii. 17,

' He will rejoice over those he saves, and will rest in his love towards them,'
as thinking his love well bestowed, and being abundantly satisfied and contented in it. And he promiseth Christ that he should greatly delight in
the beauty of his queen, Ps. xlv. And Christ accordingly in that love-song
declares his infinite delight in his spouse, and Cant. vii. 6, ' How fair and
pleasant art thou, O love, for delights !' It is Christ's speech. Now if to
delight in those he saves were one great end of both in their counsels about
us; then of necessity there must be wrought a reconciliation in us unto them,
as well as a reconciliation for us by them : there is no way for them to
attain delights in us, unless our hearts were won to them, to love and delight
in them again. It is true, God loved us when we were enemies, Rom. v.;
yet delight in us he could not, unless we be made friends to him. All the
sweetness of love lies in the reciprocation. There is nothing more grievous,
more hateful, than to love and not to be beloved. As out of his own heart
and experience he expresseth it, 2 Cor. xii. 15. *Dulce est amare et amari.*
At least otherwise there is no *rest* in one's love, no contentedness or satisfaction in it. If God's end in saving us, indeed, were principally to pardon
us, then he need do no more than kings do when they pardon traitors : pass
such an act upon the party, and there is an end. But God is also to make
friends and favourites of them whom he pardons, and so to delight in them,
and to have communion with them, graciously to accept of them, as well
as pardon them : Eph. i. 6, 7, ' To the praise of the glory of his grace,
wherein he hath made us accepted in the beloved ;' over and above that
' in him we have also redemption through his blood, the forgiveness of sins,
according to the riches of his grace.' And therefore he changeth the in
ward frame of men's hearts, and makes of enemies friends of them to himself. Otherwise he could not rejoice in them. For can a man delight in a
toad or a serpent (between which creatures and us God hath put an
enmity) ? What fellowship and communion can light and darkness have ?

The conclusion of this matter discoursed is, that although God the Father
hath transacted all these things from eternity, and that Jesus Christ hath
long since performed all that which might pacify and reconcile his Father,
and procure our atonement with his Father, according to the command and
request of his Father ; yet it was withal agreed mutually then by them,
that not a man, no, not an elect man, should have benefit by either, until
they come in to be reconciled. And that state of this affair I explain by
this instance or similitude grounded upon Scripture, that suppose one oweth
a great sum, and the creditor to whom he oweth it is willing to forgive it
unto this debtor, upon payment made by another whom the creditor doth
under-hand himself procure to pay it, at his request ; yet withal unknown
as yet unto the debtor ; but with this compact of the surety and creditor,
that when this transaction shall come to be made known by them to the
debtor of what they have secretly done, he, upon effectual notice thereof,
shall come in and acknowledge the debt, seeking the remitting of it unto
him, and acquitment of him, with professed subjection to them both for
ever. Until this be performed by him, the bond, though by agreement cancelled, as in respect of any other payment, yet is still to lie and be kept in
the creditor's hands, who obligeth himself not to give a discharge or release
to the debtor, or deliver in his bond as cancelled, until he makes his
address, and humbly acknowledgeth the debt ; seeks for an acquittance,
yea, and gets the party who paid it to go along with him to the creditor,
to mediate and plead for him his satisfaction given him ; and sue forth the
acceptation of that payment of his for him in particular, undertaking the

party's heartiest and sincerest engagement of future love and service to both for ever. And thus does Christ's righteousness and our debt lie both in God the Father's hands, the creditor, until the sinner for whom the payment was made shall thus come in. And if we could suppose that Christ had died ten thousand deaths (which was but one sacrifice once offered) for one man, yet both Father and Son have and are resolved that this man should never be the better for it till he comes in.

And in expression similar unto this management and ordering of this matter, you shall find the Scriptures speaking in both the Old and New Testament, compared. There is to this purpose a passage in Job xxxiii. 22–26, ' His soul draweth near to the grave, and his life to the destroyers. If there be a messenger with him, an interpreter, one among a thousand, to shew unto man his uprightness : then he is gracious, and saith, Deliver him from going down into the pit : I have found a ransom. His flesh shall be fresher than a child's : he shall return to the days of his youth : he shall pray unto God, and he will be favourable to him : and he shall see his face with joy : for he will render unto man his righteousness.' They are the words of Elihu, which, taken together with the foregoing, from ver. 15, and then with those which follow after, do set out a fair pattern or draught of the workings of saving conversion, at the rate they went in those ancient times, collected by the observations of Elihu upon divers persons in his view, and set afore Job, to provoke him to conform himself unto them (as his only course to take), with encouragements of mercy from God, that in like manner God will be gracious to him, to restore him to his favour, and that he shall come to ' see his face with joy,' ver. 26. And together with the works or operations, he sets forth the means, which God then often did use to work upon men's hearts. As first, visions and dreams, ver. 15–17 (for there this his discourse of conversion begins), ' In a dream, in a vision of the night, when deep sleep falleth upon men, in slumbering upon the bed ; then he openeth the ears of men, and sealeth their instruction, that he may withdraw man from his purpose, and hide pride from man.' And this dispensation was the more ordinary means in those times (although to us now extraordinary). Then secondly, another means were great sicknesses, even unto death : ver. 19, ' He is chastened also with pain upon his bed, and the multitude of his bones with strong pain.' And thirdly, the awakenings thereby are followed by the ' seasonable instructions ' and ' directions of a teacher,' one skilled in soul-saving work ; ' an interpreter ' of God's mind, to shew what that is for which God saves man, as also what a sinner is to do, ver. 23, &c.

And that such a saving work of true conversion is intended, the whole sense of his discourse, from the aforesaid ver. 15, doth plainly manifest. And first, this his discourse at the entrance shews, at the 16th and 17th verses : ' Then he openeth the ears of men, and sealeth their instruction, that he may withdraw man from his purpose,' his resolved course of sinning, ' and hide pride from man ;' that is, truly to humble him, and break the staff of the pride of his heart. 2. His more full and special instance he gives in the middle of his narration ; the sick man's case, in the verses afore : taken together with this inference he draws from it for instruction unto all men, ver. 27, 28, ' He looketh upon men, and if any say, I have sinned, and perverted that which was right, and it profited me not ; he will deliver his soul from going into the pit, and his life shall see the light.' And 3. The conclusion of all, in the 29th and 30th verses, as much doth declare, where Elihu sets a remark upon it : ' Lo, all these things God

worketh oftentimes' (twice or thrice) 'with man: to bring back his soul
from the pit, and to enlighten him with the light of the living:' that is, with
the saving light of life; as John viii. 12 speaks of them that ' live by faith.'
And this speech is the general close unto these instances foregone, and
gathers in all he had said, from the 15th verse downwards; and signifies
all the outward ways and means, with many other the like, which God had
then a-foot, to work savingly upon men; as also all those particular inward
operations which had been instanced in, and which might be drawn forth
out of one or the other of these passages.

And those particulars are, 1. Conviction and confession of sin, with
brokenness of heart: ver. 27, ' If any man say I have sinned, and perverted that which was right,' &c. 2. A laying hold by faith on Christ's
righteousness and ransom for his own righteousness and redemption, when
he is affected with that sense of his sin, and own un-uprightness, which
was and is the greatest point which that interpreter shewed or discovered
to him; instructing him where and in whom the true and perfect righteousness of fallen man doth lie, which this humbled soul desires, prays, and
seeks for, and to be made his; and God to be gracious to him, and accept
him therein; which God accordingly delivers and renders to him. These
are summarily in verses 23, 24, and 26. And this is accompanied with
turning from sin, in uprightness of heart and holiness of life, for time to
come; in a course utterly opposite to his former perverting that which was
right, which, ver. 27, he confessed he had run into. And there is a most
comfortable issue of all these upon this man; which begins at ver. 24,
' Then he is gracious, and says, Deliver him.' *Then*, namely, when the
interpreter's instructions (whereof some are implied, others expressed) have
had their due course and effects, in all such gracious workings specified,
in the man's heart, answerable to the matter of his message; which shewed
this man what is man's uprightness; which in a summary contains directions unto all these; and which being impressed on his soul as the wax is
with the seal; for it is with a sealing the instructions (as the word afore
was, ver. 16) he must necessarily be supposed to have had these proper
prints conformable thereunto. Now the issues or consequential privileges
hereof are two.

1. That God doth then, or thereupon, out of his grace, absolve and pronounce the justification of him. ' The Lord is gracious, and says, Deliver
him.' The word *deliver* signifies *redeem* him, that is, from the guilt of his
sin, and hell, or God's wrath. Thus forgiveness of sins is styled, Eph. i.
7, ' In whom you have redemption through his blood, the forgiveness of
sins, through the riches of his grace.' The word *deliver* him, here signifies
redeem him. And he, that is, God, says it within himself. For justification is an immanent act, in God's breast and heart, and that is that justification we call *in foro cœli*, in the court of heaven. He says it before and
unto Christ the mediator. He pronounceth the sentence as in heaven, as
the supreme Lawgiver, ' able to save and to destroy.' Yea, he often says
it and applies it to the man's own conscience, and by a word of his messengers declares it. And then he adds the ground for and through which
he doth it; for (says he) ' I have found a ransom;' and thus he applies it
to this particular sinner. And then,

2. God further causeth this justified soul to ' see his face with joy,' ver.
26; God lifting up the light of his countenance, and causing his favour to
shine upon his soul, with joy greater than when corn and oil increase.
Which dispensation, after great humblings, deep repentings, long and mu ch

seeking of his face, God is wont to gratify sincere new converts with Rom. iv. 5–7, and Rom. v. 1, 2, 3, 5, and 11.

And 2dly. That initial conversion wrought at first, which is called regeneration, is specially intended, and that the words are not meant only of men renewed or converted already, but declined—though they are indeed included—the words of those 27th and 28th verses evidence, ' He looketh upon men; and if any say, I have sinned, and perverted that which was right, and it profited me not; he will deliver his soul from going into the pit, and his life shall see the light.' He lays two things together: 1. That they are a general invitation and encouragement given to all men who shall in like manner come in and apply themselves to him; that God will be likewise gracious, and pardon and receive any of them into grace and favour, and ' deliver his soul from going down into the pit,' as he had done this sick convert : and so general and indefinite a declaration, must necessarily respect and take in men unregenerate. The bulk of mankind shall hear this; who mostly lie in unregeneracy in all times, especially did in those. Thus John saith of his times, 1 John v. 19; hence therefore that exhortation and encouragement to repentance, ' If any man say I have sinned,' &c., must in a special manner intend the first work of regeneration, and initial repentance.

The second thing is, that this general proclamation is brought in as a corollary or inference from the example of this sick convert; and comes in upon it, as Elihu's deduction out of it. And therefore the case of that sick man proposed, must involve and extend to a first conversion, which we call regeneration. And it is not to be limited only to such as had been converted already. And truly the tenor of those words, ' To shew to this man his uprightness,' doth argue him to have been one ignorant afore, of what course to take for him to be saved, till taught by this instructor.

But lastly, The final conclusion of all puts it out of exception : ver. 29, ' Lo, all these things worketh God oftentimes with man ;' and it is a general one too, comprehending these, and all the blessed operations or effects that God doth work upon any, to save any of the sons of men (who at any time are saved) from hell; and not to be limited to restoring of those patients that are sick, from bodily sickness, or of men who had had a work of regeneration already, and had gone astray; but speaks to all, of all sorts, and to the unregenerate in a special manner.

CHAPTER III.

That we may be reconciled to God, it is necessary for us to be convinced that we are enemies to God.—That our estate is dangerous.—That yet God is appeasable; that there is a mediator by whom the soul may come to God ; that we must also seek God and his favour in Christ; and seek him with confession of, and mourning for, sin.

The particular passages which a true and sincere reconcilement doth require, are either such as prepare the heart to be willing to be reconciled, or such wherein the substance or nature of reconciliation itself, or wherein the frame of a heart reconciled, doth consist.

1. For the preparing us to be reconciled it is necessary that we be convinced that we are enemies to God, and that he accounts us such; and that so long as we remain in that estate, he is also an enemy to us, and can

he no other. This what God in Christ hath done, gives demonstration f. He would not save us upon Christ's bare entreaty, but he would have satisfaction, and have Christ feel what it was to stand in the room of sinners. Yea, one end why God saved us by way of satisfaction to his justice, was that sinners pardoned might, in what Christ suffered, see and thoroughly apprehend what sin had deserved. And is it not then requisite that they should at least lay to heart and be sensible of their own treasons and rebellions, and that God and they are at odds? Traitors must be convicted and condemned ere they are capable of a legal pardon; as sentence must be pronounced ere a legal appeal can be made. It is so in man's courts, and it is so in God's proceedings also. Neither indeed will men be brought to sue out for his favour and prize his love till then; for it was never heard any man did heartily sue to one for pardon and peace, with whom he did not first apprehend himself at variance.

2. It is necessary also that men apprehend the danger of going on in this estate; for though one should know another and himself to be enemies, if he thought his enemy were either careless or weak, he would slight reconciliation with him, and though sought unto would not seek it. He who is mentioned, Luke xiv. 31, 32, sat down and considered if he were able to go out and meet his enemy, else he would never have sought conditions of peace. So the soul, until it apprehends and considers (finding God and itself enemies) what a sore enemy he is, and what a fearful thing it is to fall into his hands (Heb. x. 30, 31), will not till then care to seek out to him.

3. If one apprehended God implacable, not inclinable to peace, or hard to be entreated, he would never come at him neither. Thus David, when Saul and he were at odds, suborned Jonathan secretly to observe what mind Saul bare towards him, 1 Sam. xx., and when, at the 33d verse, he found him bent to kill him, David came not at him. So the Jews came away from God, as a wild ass from its owner, Jer. ii., because 'there was no hope.'

4. The soul comes to be persuaded better things of God, and things that accompany reconciliation, and conceives hopes that reconciliation is to be had, and had for it. And therefore in all whom God means to reconcile to himself, after he hath humbled them he fixeth a secret persuasion on their hearts that he is ready to be reconciled to them, if they will be reconciled to him. God gives them a secret hint of his intended good will to them. He reveals what a gracious God he is, and how freely he pardons. And because that all acquaintance begins with knowledge, and is the ground of it, therefore God, when he brings any into this covenant, the first thing he doth is, 'He teacheth them to know him,' Jer. xxxi. 34, and 'gives them a new spirit,' that they may be able to know him after another manner than ever before. He teacheth them to know him, especially in his mercy, in those vast thoughts of mercy laid up in him, Jer. ix. 24; to know him to be 'a God that ever hath loving-kindness in the earth:' though not in hell to devils, yet in earth to men, and that therein he delighteth. He enableth him also to see what happiness is to be had in communion with him, by reason of those glorious excellencies which are in him, and makes such representations of himself to the soul as allures the heart, Hosea ii. 14; God draws the heart, John vi. 44, for in the 45th verse it follows, 'They shall all be taught of God,' referring to these places of Isaiah and Jeremiah; for says Christ, 'It is written in the prophets, they shall be taught of God.' And the lesson is (as hath been said) to know God; and God doth this in a peculiar manner, working another kind of knowledge of himself than a man had before, or than other men have; for it is a knowledge that

enamours their hearts with him, and allures them with his good will. And (says Christ) every man that hath thus heard and learnt cometh to God. Though all hear the same message of reconciliation, yet God whispers something to a man's heart that he doth not to every man. The same God who from everlasting spake unto his Son, and wooed him for us, doth speak likewise secretly to a man's heart, to allure and woo him to come in to him.

5. And yet, fifthly, if the soul should look upon God alone, as he is in himself, a God just as well as merciful, he would thereby be discouraged to come alone into his presence, who is a consuming fire. The glory of God's justice would dash him and confound him. And as Adam trembled, so would he, and could do no otherwise. It is the instinct of nature (witness the heathen sacrifices and lesser gods, as mediators to the great God) to seek out ' a daysman,' Job. ix. 33. Yea, it is the way of man seeking friendship with another to use the mediation of some other that is great with him that is wronged. Therefore God teacheth such a one, to whom he means to be reconciled, to know his Son also, whom he hath sent as his beloved Son, in whom he is well pleased with others too. God holds and sets forth him as a propitiation, ' that in his blood he may both be just, and the justifier of us,' Rom. iii. 25. And he causeth his glory to shine, and appear ' in the face of Jesus Christ,' and secretly points and directs the heart with an instinct to go to Christ : ' Every man that hath heard and learnt of the Father, cometh to me,' John vi. 45, as the beasts were taught to go to the ark. And we thus coming to Christ by faith, and taking hold of him by the hand thereof, Christ then leads us by the hand to God, Eph. iii. 18. We have προσαγωγήν, conduct, and entrance, and access to God, having such a person with us, and his interest in God to plead for us, and whose blood and satisfaction we may plead ; we have free liberty of speech παρρησίαν, to plead his righteousness and satisfaction, and that with barefacedness and boldness, as the word signifies ; not to stand as condemned prisoners with our faces covered, but as persons acquitted in Christ, pleading pardon and confidence. And this is necessary, for as God intended to shew us no favour without satisfaction, so no more can we apprehend that his favour, but in and through Christ's alone satisfaction : Rom. iii. 25, ' God hath therefore set forth Christ a propitiation by faith in his blood, that he might be both just, and a justifier of him that believeth in Jesus.' And how God should be just, and a justifier of a sinner, no man could ever apprehend till he bottoms his faith on Christ's righteousness alone, which only can stand before justice, and break through it unto God.

6. And yet, sixthly, when all this is done, the man must be set a-work to seek, as a condemned man, God and his favour in Christ, and peace and reconciliation through him for life, Job. xxxiii. 24, ' He shall pray to him, and he will be gracious, and say, Deliver him, I have found a ransom.' God himself first sought to Christ, and sought him with all earnestness and vehemency to become a mediator to him for us, and therefore reason it is that he should stand upon it to be sought unto, ere we obtain peace with him. Yea, and though his own Son hath performed it, and he covenanted with him that he should see his seed, yet God expected that his Son should seek to him for the acceptation of his mediation, who yet hath merited it, and who undertook it at his request. And therefore you see what a long prayer he puts up, John xvii. ; though he says at the 4th and 9th verses, he hath ' finished the work he gave him to do,' yet he prays for the persons redeemed, and the acceptation of the redemption wrought, throughout that chapter. God hath told him, Ps. ii. 28, he must ' ask the heathen for his

inheritance ;' and though they were his inheritance, as he was his Son, and whom besides he had purchased and bought with his blood, yet he must ask them. Yea, that glory which was his own before the world was, he seeks to his Father for, ver. 5. And if it were thus between God and his Son in the business of reconciliation for us, and that in what he might challenge as his own, then surely much more it must be so between God and us, whom this reconciliation most concerns. He therefore pours upon a man a spirit of grace and supplication, Zech. xii. 10, that is, a spirit to supplicate for grace.

And the same is evident from the nature of the thing itself. God is the party superior, and it is fit the inferior should seek to the superior. And also he is the person wronged ; and though he be willing and desirous to be reconciled more than ever, yet he will have his favour prized. David longed to be reconciled to Absalom, yet he would be sought unto, for he would have his favour prized to the utmost, and not cast away.

Yea, and to be in favour with God being better than life, God will be sought to with more earnestness, contention, and constancy, than a condemned man seeks for life : Jer. xxix. 13, ' They shall find me when they seek and search for me with their whole heart.' And Mat. xi. 12, ' The violent take it by force.' Though God be most willing to part with this great blessing, yet that it may be prized and sought, indeed he doth as it were hold it fast in his hand, and will have it wrung from him by force, as it were : Mat. xi. 12, ' And from the days of John the Baptist, until now, the kingdom of heaven suffereth violence, and the violent take it by force.' And in Luke xiii. 24, ' Strive ' (saith he), ' for many seek.' The word in the original signifies an eager violent contention and wrestling of mind. And there is reason, from what God did in Christ for us, for this also ; for how earnestly did God seek to his Son for us ! He expressed all the earnestness that might be, laying his command upon him, and he added an oath to it, &c. And doth he not expect earnestness at our hands ? Yea, how did Christ also, in the days of his flesh, put up an atonement, seeking to his Father with strong cries and tears ! And shall we think to be heard with dull and faint cries ? Nay, look, as God himself was more earnest in this matter of reconciling us than ever in anything else, so he will have us seek to him with more earnestness and contention than ever we sought anything, even life itself. And surely, if God hath bidden us seek peace with men, yea, and to ensue it (as in Ps. xxxiv. 14, 1 Peter iii. 11), that is, though it fly away, yet to follow it, much more are we then to seek peace with God himself ; and though he seem to reject us, yet to follow him, and press upon him as it were from one room to another, that is, from one performance to another, and so to ' follow hard after him,' as David says, Ps. lxiii. 1, 2, 3, to verse the 8th, ' My soul followeth hard after thee : Thy right hand upholdeth me.'

7. He will be sought unto with confession of, and mourning for, offending him. For being in bitterness, Zech. xii. 10, and mourning, is joined with supplication for grace.

And this is necessary to reconciliation, because an acknowledgment is to be made, Jer. ii. 13. God would be sought humbly unto by us, as those that are traitors and rebels. And God will have men know when he pardons, that he knows what he pardons, and therefore will have them acknowledge what they deserve, ' that every mouth might be stopped, and become guilty,' and obnoxious in their own acknowledgment before him, Rom. iii. 19. As if a man will become wise, he must become a fool ; so a man that will become a friend to God, must turn enemy against himself, and judge himself worthy of destruction.　And God will have the freeness and glory of his grace acknowledged in pardoning ; and therefore will have us confess our evil ways and deservedness of destruction.　In the 36th of Ezekiel, when at the 31st verse he says, ' that when he pardoned them they should remember their evil ways, and acknowledge themselves worthy to be destroyed ;' the reason follows in the next verse : ' Be it known to you, I pardon it not for your sakes ;' I do it freely : and that ye may know so much, remember your evil ways ; be ashamed and confounded for your ways.

And there is good reason also that mourning should be joined to all this, from what God did in Christ when he reconciled us to himself.

1. For, first, was not Christ, who never knew the pleasure of sin, put to grief ?　Yea, all the sorrow and smart was his : Isa. liii. 4, ' Surely he hath borne our griefs,' was ' a man of sorrow,' &c.　Which sorrows were put upon him by his Father also : ver. 10, ' He put him to grief;' and therein indeed put himself to grief.　And if they both were thus put to grief and afflicted, for our reconciliation and peace, then surely the least that we, who have tasted of, and enjoyed the pleasures of sin, can do, is to grieve also, for that thing which made both Father and Son to grieve.　God required of Christ to bear our sorrows.　Now the sorrows of death, and of his wrath, God exacts not of thee ; but the sorrow of a friend, the sorrow of kindness, which causeth not death as other sorrows do, but peace and joy in the very performance of it, ' repentance never to be repented of.' He requires thee only to mourn kindly for thy sins that pierced him ; and such a mourning the nature of reconciliation requires.　For,

2. Secondly, Where mourning for offending God is wanting, there is no sign of any good will yet wrought in the heart to God, nor of love to him, without which God will never accept a man.　' For the least thing wherein good will towards a friend whom we have injured can be shewn, is to mourn and be sorry for it : as the least requital for a kindness is to be thankful. And this all that have affections in them do, when they can in no way else make amends.

3. Else there is no hope of amendment.　God will not pardon till he sees hopes of amendment.　Now, until a man confess his sin, and that with bitterness, it is a sign he loves it, Job xx. 12–14.　Whilst he hides it, spares it, and forsakes it not, it is sweet in his mouth ; and therefore till he confess it, and mourn for it, it is a sign it is not bitter to him, and so he will not forsake it.　A man will never leave sin till he finds bitterness in it ; and, if so, then he will be in bitterness for it, Zech. xii. 10 ; and ' godly sorrow works repentance,' 2 Cor. vii. 10.

CHAPTER IV.

How our reconciliation to God consists in renouncing all friendship and interests which stand in competition with his ; and in choosing him for our alone friend and portion ; in resigning all to him ; in having a disposition and nature like to God ; and also in all our addresses to God proceeding from an inward principle of pure good will unto God.

8. Eighthly ; He that will be reconciled to God must part with, and forsake, all other friends and lovers ; renounce and break off all interests and

correspondences with them, and choose God for his sole friend and portion. And he must choose God for ever, to cleave to him with full purpose of heart.

(1.) He must renounce all other friendships : James iv. 4, ' Ye adulterers and adulteresses, know ye not that the friendship of the world is enmity with God ? Whosoever therefore shall be a friend of the world is the enemy of God.' As God will not have us serve other masters, so not to have other friends : ' Whosoever doth not forsake father, mother,', &c., ' is unworthy of me,' says Christ, Luke xiv. 26. And still what God hath done in Christ for reconciling us, will persuade to it.

[1.] First, God was content to part with his Son, a friend, an old friend, and a bosom friend, brought up with him ; and yet he was content for a time to forsake him. Witness that speech, ' My God, my God, why hast thou forsaken me ?' And Christ was content to part with and leave his Father for a time. That speech, ' For this cause a man shall forsake father and mother,' is, in Eph. v. 31, applied to Christ, in his giving himself to the church, as the context shews.

And he came down from heaven for to make such friends. And thus each of them parted with their old friends to get new. So do you, and be content to forsake the dearest you have delighted in, and have been brought up with. The church forsook her father's house.

[2.] The nature of reconciliation requires it ; for friendship with anything else is enmity with God, James iv. 4. A friendship not only with proclaimed enemies, open sins, but with all the things the world hath, is vanity * with God. A believer may have a lordship over them, but not friendship with them. He may use them as strangers and servants, but not as friends ; so they must not have his heart. ' He that hates not father and mother is unworthy of me,' says Christ, that is, not worthy of my friendship, and such a friend as I am and mean to be.

[3.] Choose him alone for your God, to betake yourselves unto him for ever. Friendship is entered into by choice. Kindred indeed is not, for I chose not who was to be my father ; who shall be the son of my mother is not in my choice : but friendship goes by choice. So Jonathan chose David : 1 Sam. xx. 30, ' Thou hast chosen the son of Jesse' (saith Saul). So the church : Hos. ii. 7, ' She shall follow after lovers, but she shall not overtake them ; and she shall seek them, but shall not find them : then shall she say, I will go and return to my first husband ; for then was it better with me than now.' She forsakes all other lovers, and betakes herself to God ; and what says God ? Verse 23, ' I will say, They are my people' ; and they shall answer my love again, and ' say, Thou art my God,' ver. 23. Which place shews the reason whence it may be enforced. For God, you heard, chose you, and gave you to Christ before you were, and he chose Christ for you to be your mediator, and said concerning him, ' Thou art a priest,' and that he would not repent his choice. Now, in like manner as God did choose you, so must you also choose him. As God chooseth you ' freely,' Hos. xiv. 14, out of good will, and pitcheth his choice upon your persons, so must you choose him freely, and choose him, as Jonathan chose David to be his friend, though to the loss of a kingdom, as Saul told him, 1 Sam. xx. 30. So do thou choose God, though to thy undoing in the world ; and as he chose you for ever, never to cast you off, making an everlasting covenant with Christ for you, giving him a charge to save you, choosing you out of an everlasting love : so you are to

* Qu. 'enmity'?—ED.

choose him to be your God for ever.   And, as Jonathan's heart cleaving to
David, he sware to him, and entered into covenant with him, so must you
do with God.   'I have sworn' (says David), 'and I will perform it,'
Ps. cxix.   And as no difficulty could put God by from his purpose he had
took up towards you, as you heard, so strong was he in it, so bent and
set upon it; so let nothing that can fall out in your way, losses or
crosses, that you meet with for him, alter your purpose towards him.
As nothing can separate you from his love, so let nothing separate him
from yours.

9. Ninthly, let thy heart resign up itself, and all that it hath, and devote
it all unto God for ever, to be commanded and used by him.   Thus friends
use to do, and thus God did for you.   For if he 'spared not his own Son,
how shall he not with him give you all things else?'   Let all you have be
God's; giving up yourselves first unto the Lord, as they in 2 Cor. viii. 5.
Let God have all thy understanding, will, affections, and whatever else.
Let all be his, to command in anything as he pleaseth, and study how to
set all a-work for him ; for he set the infinite depths of his wisdom a-work
to find out a way to be friends with you, and chose that which would shew
most love; and so do you choose the things that will most please him:
Isa. lvi. 4 and xliv 5, 'Subscribe with your hands to the Lord, and say, I
am his,' even as friends use to say, *Yours to command*, and *All I have is at
your service*.   God wrote with his own hand your names in heaven (Heb.
xii. 23), in the heart of Christ; and he wrote it down in the books of his
decrees, and made Christ subscribe to it that he should be a priest.   And
so subscribe you, that you will be for ever his to command and use.

10. And tenthly, ὁμόνοια, or likeness of disposition, is the only sure
lasting ground and foundation of friendship, and is the soul of it, so as it is
impossible two should long be friends, unless they agree in their minds and
affections, loving and liking the same things ; 'Can two walk together and
not agree?' Amos iii. 3.   Therefore, you must get stamped upon your
hearts a likeness to God in holiness, whereby to hate where God hates, and
to love where he loves, so as to become an enemy to his enemies, and a
friend to his friends.   And in this respect David is called a man after God's
own heart; that is, whose mind and disposition was fashioned to the Lord's
in all things.   So Ps. cxix. 127, 128, 'I hate every false way; but thy law
I esteem aright concerning all things.'   So do you love and approve holiness in all things : in the abstract and concrete, in the word as it is delivered, and in men's lives and hearts as it is practised and appears.   And
so the believer also hates sin in himself and others, and counts God's enemies as his own.   Thus David did, Ps. cxix. 21–23.   And this in Scripture
is termed a true heart, Heb. x. 22 ; true as a man to his friend, as to his
own self.   True and faithful, as a spouse to her husband ; true and loyal,
as subjects to their native prince.   Job xxii. 21, 22, 'Acquaint thyself with
him' (there is an exhortation to friendship with God), 'and be at peace.
Receive, I pray thee, the law at his mouth.'

11. Eleventhly, Accordingly, a man that is thus reconciled, must endeavour to walk and behave himself as unto a friend.   The nature of reconciliation requires it: Prov. xviii. 24, 'He that hath friends must carry himself friendly.'   And Christ hath said, 'If ye be my friends, then keep my
commandments,' John xv. 14.   Therefore you must endeavour so to do,
and to do it upon that motive chiefly ; and to walk with God, as Enoch
did, observing all God's carriages to you, and yours to God-ward ; as one
that is reconciled observes him in all his dealings, interprets all in love,

depends on him, trusts on him, &c. And also, watch over yourselves in all your ways, and be fearful to displease him and his goodness, Hosea. iii. 5.

12. Only, in the last place, all these addresses tending to reconciliation must proceed from an inward principle of pure good will unto God, which is the soul of reconciliation, and which, therefore, God regards and requires above all things else, not only in respect of his own greatness and sovereignty (which exacts all in the creature to be for him, Rom. xi. 36, and to be wholly referred unto him), but also in a way of ingenuity. He is the superior, yea sovereign, in this friendship. The nature of true reconciliation requires it, especially with respect to such an one, who, being so infinitely above us, doth condescend to this relation of friendship with us; yea, and subjects himself to all, even the lowest laws and expressions of love and friendship, which any, the meanest friend on earth, can be supposed to do. Aristotle indeed denies that the true law of friendship can hold between one too much superior and inferior; for the interest of one riseth so high to sovereignty as excludeth pure good will; and in the inferior, it falls so low to subjection, as it admits too great a mixture of by-ends; and so true friendship is excluded on either hand. But this philosopher never knew our God, nor yet the power of the divine nature in us. He could not have imagined that God, who is so great, could be so good, and stoop unto such low carriages and terms towards us as (to instance in one out of the text) to 'beseech us to be reconciled.'

But above all, this is expected by him whose friendship is wholly free. The title of it is free grace, merely out of pure good will, 'The good pleasure of his will,' and can have no other ends. And all, without such sincere observance of God, is but plain flattery. And God, who also is so wise as not to be mocked, accounts it so; for so he judgeth and pronounceth of those that yet earnestly sought him; Ps. lxxviii. 34–37, 'They sought him, and sought him early;' that is, diligently. 'When he slew them, they sought him; and they returned and inquired early after God. And they remembered that God was their Rock, and the high God their Redeemer. Nevertheless they did flatter him with their mouth, and they lied unto him with their tongues. For their heart was not right with him, neither were they stedfast in his covenant.' But God is not mocked; for though men cannot see and discover thus much often in those they deal with, yet God doth, who searcheth the heart, takes notice of it, you see, and deals with men accordingly. Now flatterers are distinguished from friends by this: that a flatterer is one who seeketh indeed friendship, and abounds in offices of friendship for his own ends, and chiefly out of by-respects; but a true friend is one who, besides by-respects, doth things out of good will to the party. God doth indeed give those who seek reconciliation with him leave to have a respect to themselves, their own safety, and recompence of reward, for else he were not a true friend to them, if he did not suffer them to look to their own good, which as he subordinately professeth to have aimed at in their reconciliation to himself, though contrived chiefly for his own glory, so may they; and therefore, says Christ, Luke xii. 4, 5, 'I say to you, my friends' (to speak in the language of the text), 'fear him that can kill body and soul.' So as to fear God, as one who is able to cast us into hell, may stand with friendship. 'I say to you, my friends,' there is the fear of hell allowed those who are in communion with him, and also hopes of heaven. So God said to Abraham, whom he calls his friend, 'I am thy exceeding great reward.' And one eye he had thereto: Heb. xi. 16, 'But now they desire a better country, that is, an heavenly: wherefore God is not ashamed to be called their God; for he hath prepared for them a city.' And Moses too, ver. 26, 'esteemed the reproach of Christ greater riches than the treasures in Egypt: for he had respect unto the recompence of the reward.' And this Moses God treated as a man doth his friend: Exod. xxxiii. 11, 'And the Lord spake unto Moses face to face, as a man speaketh unto his friend.' But yet, if there be no further principle of good will predominate, it is but flattery; and though I confess that happily in one newly scared out of his natural estate, this principle is not so soon and so easily discerned, yet after a while it may; which, because it is the main and soul of all the former acts, I will therefore a little more enlarge upon it. And herein I will not attempt to affix a different character of friendship and flattery upon each and every of those particular acts and passages of reconciliation formerly mentioned, nor keep punctually unto all those acts specified in the 78th Psalm, though this is seizable, and might be done; as, for example, it is here said, 'When he slew them, then they remembered he was their Rock and Redeemer.' A traveller in fair weather passeth by a rock, minds and regards it not; but in a storm, he runs for shelter to it, but yet dwells not there. But one truly wrought on, though he first run to God in his distress, and after often doth so, yet ever after he makes him his house and dwelling-place, Ps. xc. 1. It is the voice of the whole church, age after age, 'Lord, thou hast been our dwelling-place in all generations.' And in the next Psalm xci., ver 1, 'He that dwells in the secret place of the Most High, shall abide under the shadow of the Almighty.' I observe,

1. That it is the description of a man truly godly to be one that dwells in God, yea, and in the secret place, the heart, the bosom of God, and hath intimate communion with him. He affects that room, and if he cannot get in, is still knocking at it, takes it up for his constant abode. And 2. A shelter in it, and from it, comes in it secondarily as to his aim, for it is the promise made upon it. 'He shall abide under the shadow,' that is, the protection, 'of the Almighty.' It is the love of God he principally aims to dwell in; 1 John iv. 16, 'God is love; and he that dwells in love dwells in God, and God in him.'

2. I might, secondly, observe the like upon that other passage, 'They flattered him,' in running then to him, but only as a Redeemer. The Holy Ghost is exactly punctual in expressing the bottom differences of their flattery. A man is like to die: he sends to the physician, but as a physician only; he never did, nor doth now, regard the friendship of the man. Pharaoh sends in all haste (it is said) for Moses and Aaron, Exod. x. 16, when he never cared more to have seen them: so ver. 28, 'See my face no more.' But yet in his distress he says unto them, 'I have sinned; forgive, and entreat the Lord your God to take away this death only.' What need was there for him to put in this exclusive, *this death only?* He was an ignorant heathen, and so speaks out his heart plainly. He knew not how to flatter this God; for God was a strange God, whom he professed not; he still styles him *your* God. He speaks as indeed it was, he professeth to care for God no further. But those very men (of whom the psalmist here speaks) that were brought out of Egypt from under this Pharaoh, professed God to be their God, and to have been their redeemer out of Egypt. And they, in their speeches, when they return to God, carry it otherwise, yet their hearts at the bottom were the very same; and therefore of them it is said, they flattered him with their tongues. And thus men professing Christ in the church do not say unto God, when they

pray to him, or unto men when in distress of conscience, sickness, &c.,
Take away this hell only. They do not say it; but God, that knows the
mind of their spirit in them, knows it is all, and the whole they would
have with him; yet they give good words, conceal this to be all, or the
main, of their intentions; yea, themselves, out of self-flattery, discern it
not. But yet still they think and mean the very same, though Pharaoh
only spake it out. And therefore they are said to flatter him. But what
doth a godly man's heart say in his distress? He runs to God indeed as
a redeemer; but coming to him, he finds, *Est aliquid in Christo formosius
salvatore.* 'The Lord is my portion,' says the soul, Lam. iii. 24. And
it was spoken as in deep distress, as every soul was in, as is apparent from
the chapter. What saith David, from the very bottom of his heart, in his
sickness? Not, Take away this death only. No; but David being sick,
first comforts himself with this promise, Ps. xli. 3, 'The Lord will strengthen him upon his bed of languishing, and make his bed in his sickness;'
and then adds, ver. 4, 'I said, Lord, be merciful to me, and heal my
soul;' that is, Destroy my lusts, which are the diseases of my soul, Lord;
and heal my soul, and renew life and communion with thee, which is the
health and strength of my soul. Do not take this sickness and death only
away; but this sin away, that hath dishonoured thee, hath separated between me and thee: 'Heal my soul, for I have sinned against thee.'

I need not so punctually pursue the rest of these instances of their flattery,
that follow in the 78th Psalm. I choose rather to single forth some of the
eminent acts contrary to the fore-mentioned particulars, in which I shewed
reconciliation to God to consist; and I must instance but in a few of them,
and in them make forth the difference between flattery and true friendship
and good will.

1. The first is that of seeking God (which I have been large upon before),
and even that also is mentioned in the psalmist: Ps. lxxviii. 34, 'When
he slew them, then they sought him, and inquired early after God,' that is,
diligently; as what a man riseth betimes to do, he may be said to do with
earnestness and diligence. 'They sought him,' but still as a redeemer
only, as was observed. Now, let us bring it to the business of reconciliation, which is the point in hand, and the difference will appear, what seeking of God is only out of flattery, what also out of friendship.

First, then, There are two things in reconciliation which the gospel propounds, Luke ii. 14, peace and good will. First, peace, quiet of conscience
in regard of the pardon of sin. Secondly, God's favour and acceptation, so
that God receives us, loves and delights in us. Now, to seek peace only,
and to aim at peace alone in seeking God, may be in a flatterer, as in those
(Ps. lxxviii. 34) who sought him whilst he was a-slaying them; who were
earnest that God would be pacified towards them; but that was all. Enemies to a prince may earnestly seek peace, and their pardon, who yet care
not whether ever they see the king's face any more, and whether they live
in his presence and serve him, and attend him all their days. But now
one that hath good will to God in him, though he will seek peace also, yet
that alone doth not content him; for he seeks as a favourite seeks to his
prince, as a lover or mover to one he is in love withal, whom nothing
but love and good will again will satisfy: Jer. ii. 2, 'I remember,' says
God, 'the kindness of thy youth, the love of thy espousals, when thou
wentest after me in the wilderness.' They went after him, and wooed
him, as a fond lover doth. So doth he that seeks aright: he seeks to God
for favour, as a friend doth to a friend, to be answered with love, and to

live in his sight and presence for ever. To such a one therefore, who thus seeks God, and hath such an aim in seeking him, if half the news were brought to him, that God would pardon him indeed, and not throw him into hell, but let him enjoy the world, but yet that he can never love or delight in him again, this would grieve him more than the other would rejoice him. That which Absalom but feigned, they can do and say in truth, 2 Sam. xiv. 32, ' Let God kill me, rather than not suffer me to see his face,' for it is his face they seek. And so the generation of them who seek the Lord is distinguished, Ps. xxiv. 6.

Secondly, It will appear whether good will be in your seeking God, from the issue and event of it, for either God withholdeth his face from a man in seeking him, and seemeth to reject his suit, keeping him so in suspense, as he knows not whether he will save him or no ; or he gives him some evidence and assurance of it. One of these two cases will fall out, and in either of them will pure good will to God discover itself, when a man seeks aright.

First, If God withholds himself and his face from a sincere soul, yet still that soul is enabled to cast himself upon him and his free grace, and to refer himself and his case to his mere good will and good pleasure. He can still put himself into his hands, as David did : 2 Sam. xv. 26, ' Here I am; if he hath not pleasure in me, let him do what seemeth good in his eyes.' Thus Job also did : Job xiii. 15, ' If he kill me, yet will I trust in him.' If he dies, he resolves to die seeking at his feet. And it is the good will he beareth unto God which causeth him to do thus, because he cannot leave God. But one whose heart is not right with God in seeking him, when he hath sought a while, and seeking amiss, obtains not, he leaves off his suit, and withdraws himself, and will not trust his soul with him ; this seems express by comparing that speech of the apostle, Heb. x., with what you find in Habakkuk, whence it is cited. The words of Paul are, Heb. x. 36–39, ' For ye have need of patience, that after ye have done the will of God, ye might receive the promise. For yet a little while, and he that shall come will come, and will not tarry. Now the just shall live by faith : but if any man draw back, my soul shall have no pleasure in him. But we are not of them who draw back unto perdition ; but of them that believe to the saving of the soul.' Patience in waiting and believing is made the character of a true believer, and withdrawing is the character of impatience in one whose heart is not upright within him : Hab. ii. 3, 4, ' For the vision is yet for an appointed time, but at the end it shall speak, and not lie : though it tarry, wait for it ; because it will surely come, it will not tarry. Behold, his soul which is lifted up is not upright in him : but the just shall live by his faith.'

Secondly, One that seeks out of good will, when he obtaineth any glimpse of God's favour, he rejoiceth in it, and in God, more than in life and the hope of heaven, Rom. v. 2 and 11 verses compared. The apostle, you may perceive, proceeds by way of gradation in the effects of faith in a good and sound heart. He hath first peace, ver. 1 ; then, 2dly, he rejoiceth in hope of glory, ver. 2 ; then, 3dly, not only so, but (ver. 3) ' we glory ' (says he) ' in tribulation,' and not only so, but (says he, ver. 11) ' we joy in God,' even in God himself. To rejoice in hope of glory, speaks something of good will, as hope imports. But it is a strain yet purer and higher to rejoice in God himself. And therefore if the soul hath not outward things, yet God is enough ; and if he hath them, he rejoiceth more in them as they are love-tokens of his God, than in the things themselves. And he is more fearful to displease him out of fear of his goodness, Hos. iii. 5. When God speaks peace he returns no more to folly, Ps. lxxxv. 8. It works more strength, hatred, and loathing of sin. But the insincere soul, if he conceives any hope (as often they do feed themselves with ungrounded hopes and shadows of assurances), grows the more securely presumptuous, turns that grace into wantonness, as self-love is apt to do ; Jer. iii. 4, 5, 'Thou callest me Father, and yet doest as evil as thou couldst.' But when God truly works, he says in opposition to that former, 'Thou shalt call me Father, and shalt not turn away from me.' Even as Absalom sought to be in favour with his father, but rebelled the more, so it proves in the issue with a soul insincere ; for though the assurance of God's love is the surest motive to work upon a principle of love and pure good will unto God in the heart—'the love of Christ constrains me,' saith the apostle—yet when there is nothing but self-love in the heart, it abuseth that grace it seeks for, and thinketh it hath attained, for it hath not ingenuity in it to God.

2. The second particular I would instance is, confession of sin with mourning, which I instanced in, as one eminent ingredient into reconciliation with God. This flatterers also may seem seriously to do. So Ahab mourned and went softly ; and (Isa. lviii. 5) they are said to 'hang down their heads like bulrushes.' But if the mourning be out of good will, then,

First, A man's heart will not only mourn for sin, as having brought misery upon him, or as that which hath cast him out from God, which whilst a man doth, he indeed lamenteth but himself ; as a traitor at the gallows lamenteth that he should come to such a miserable end, and deserve such a death ; as Cain mourned when he cried out, 'My punishment is greater than I can bear.' It was the punishment pinched him. Thus to mourn for sin in relation to misery, though we do it thus before God, is not mourning but howling, Hos. vii. 14, or, as David terms it, roaring, Ps. xxxii. 3. But in true mourning, which comes out of goodwill, they are said (Zech. xii. 10) to 'mourn for him whom they had pierced, as a mother for her only son.' In which two things are observable for our purpose (which is to distinguish mourning), first, that they are said to mourn, not so much for sin, much less their misery, as for *him*, that is, for sin in relation to him, as it is an injury, provoking, wronging, and piercing him. As David in confession, Ps. li., sets this accent upon his sinning, in saying, 'Against thee, against thee have I sinned.' In the verse afore he says, his sins were ever before him, as that which is a man's greatest and heaviest affliction useth to be. David had other things enough to have had afore him, as the shame, &c. But these things, though when sin fell light, they were heavy, yet now are vanished and disappear ; and the sin, the sin is ever afore him. And what was it in the sin ? Even this, that against God he had sinned. Wherein I observe, 1. That he considers it not only as done in God's sight, in his presence, and afore him only, and he looking on, though he aggravates it by that ; but chiefly, that the sin was committed against him as the object. And, 2dly, he repeats that twice, as in sorrow we use to do what most deeply affects us ; as David on another occasion cried out, 'O Absalom, my son, my son ;' so here he says twice, 'Against thee, against thee,' &c. And, 3dly, as not content with this, he adds *only* ('against thee only'), as the only consideration that at present moved him, though he had sinned against Bathsheba and Uriah too, and all the people of God. And hence, because God is the object, the *terminus* of such sorrow, it hath therefore its denomination from God, and is called 'sorrow according to God,' 2 Cor.

vii. 9, 10, *κατὰ Θεὸν λύπη*, as acts are denominated from their tendency. And,

Secondly. The comparison the prophet useth, Zech. xii. 10, argues it sprang from pure good will. For his words are, ' as a mother mourneth for her only son.' What else moveth a mother to mourn for the loss of a son, especially of an infant, but goodwill to it? You know how David took on for his son Absalom. Children are in dependence upon their parents, and may mourn out of self-love, because when they are gone, they are left orphans and helpless. If therefore he had instanced in the mourning of a child, self-love might at least have been supposed the principal motive ; but when he says, ' as a mother for her child,' he can mean nothing more than that out of love they do it. It is one thing to come and mourn for sin before God, and bemoan ourselves to him, and another to mourn for him, and for sin, as done against him. A flatterer may do the one, but an ingenious friend only the latter: Ezek. vi. 9, ' They that escape of you shall remember me among the nations whither they shall be carried captives, because I am broken with their whorish heart, which hath departed from me, and with their eyes, which go a whoring after their idols : and they shall loathe themselves for the evils which they have committed in all their abominations.' This also is spoken of the true and kindly sorrow of heart wherewith the godly come unto God.

Now as afore you heard, they mourned for him: so here, says God, ' they shall remember me.' And upon the thought of him, whom they have so sinned against, shall loathe themselves. Now that which must cause self to hate itself, must be pure good will to God above a man's self. To remember God is to think of him with the deepest affection of love, as the words of Christ in the institution of the sacrament import, ' Do this in remembrance of me.'

3. What is it concerning God in sin that makes them loathe themselves? Even this, that it hath broken God's heart. The godly look upon sin as God doth, see that to be the evil in sin which God doth ; yea, they look upon it also with God's heart, and what affects God in it affects them. It is said (Num. xi. 10) God was angry, and Moses was displeased also. Yea, they mourn for it, because it affects God's heart, as true friends, that have but one heart and one soul : ' Thy friend' (Deut. xiii. 6) ' that is as thine own soul.' So God and the saints have as it were one heart, which consists in pure good will. And therefore God, that knows the temper of true hearts to him, propounds this as the object of their sorrow, that the thought that his heart was broken, was the chief thing that breaks theirs. And this motive no principle in man but love can apprehend and take in. A sincere soul considers this as the eminent evil in his sinning, that God's heart is broken with the unkindness of it, as a husband for the departure of a wife whorishly from him (to which that place alludes), and so mourn for it.

4. The last words (in Ezek. vi. 9) do import some such thing, for they run thus : ' That they should loathe themselves for the evils committed in their abominations.' Not for their abominations simply, in the grossness of them, for wicked men mourn for their abominations when outwardly gross. But this expression imports there were certain special evils in their abominations (the greatest of the evils therein) which they spied out to mourn for, as their unkindness to God, falseness in them to God, &c.

Thirdly, The sincerity of this mourning will appear in the issue and event, in the cases fore-mentioned. For,

1. If God forbear to speak peace and pardon to him, and rather seems to be an enemy, and to fight against him (Isa. lxiii. 10), in that case he joins with God in self-revenge. Thus, 2 Cor. vii. 11, ' Godly sorrow ' (among other things) ' worketh revenge ' on one's self (as they had done on a church member, of which it is principally spoken), so as he hates and loathes himself, and turns enemy against himself : Ezek. xxxvi. 31, ' Judgeth himself worthy to be destroyed.' So the old translation renders it. He finds it in his heart now that at the latter day his heart would of itself step out the first, before ever it were accused, and say, Here am I, that have deserved thy utmost destruction. And if he thought he should be destroyed, he finds some little relief in this, that God is avenged on one of his enemies.

2. If he hath assurance that God will pardon him, then the more assurance or hopes (that rise to any greatness) he hath of pardon, the more he mourneth. Assurance broacheth godly sorrow, sets it a-working, and giveth vent to it. Ezek. xvi. 61, ' Thou shalt remember thy evil ways, and thy doings, which were not good.' And remembering them, ver. 63, ' shalt be confounded and never open thy mouth any more, because of thy shame, when I am pacified towards thee for all that thou hast done.' Then cometh in the greatest confusion, shame and grief overcoming the heart most, when God is pacified. God overcomes when he pardons as well as when he judgeth, and hath a greater victory over the soul whom he pardons than over the damned in hell. And there is in such a soul as true a confusion of face, though of another kind, that so no flesh may glory in his presence. But the more hope an insincere soul, who seeks out of self-love, and mourns only out of self-love, hath, the less he mourns ; like a traitor, that when he hath got what he would have, and is in hope to obtain his pardon, his eyes are dry.

Fourthly ; There must be good will in acts of obedience also, and in choosing the things that please God. You know what Christ says, John xv. 14, ' If you be my friends, do what I command you.' Now if there be goodwill in the heart it will appear. A man may discover it one time or other by the dispositions of his heart, either, 1. Sometimes before the obedience performed. 2. In the performance. 3. After the performance, or the doing anything for God.

1. Before the performance by two things.

(1.) Inasmuch as the chiefest aim of his heart in it will be to shew forth and express his good will to God. As he does it as a friend, by way of requital to a friend, whose utmost end is to shew his love to the party, so the chiefest thing he desires is, that God would but accept it for such, and take it in good part, and take notice of his love in it ; which love of his is more than the thing, though he grieves it should be so little. And therefore a godly man's obedience is termed thankfulness. When Mary came and bestowed that cost upon Christ, and washed his feet with tears, her utmost end was but to shew her love, which therefore Christ took notice of, and speaks of, and accepts of above all else : ' She loved much, because much is forgiven her,' says Christ ; as if he had said, All this is but to testify her love and godly sorrow, which I take notice of, and will therefore have recorded to the end of the world. Therefore it is called, Heb. vi. 10, ' The labour of love.' And hence oftentimes (perhaps not always) the greatest and strongest motives that can be used before to persuade and prevail with the heart to obedience, is taken from love's topics, from God's love, as appeareth by Christ's dealing with Peter, whom when he would effectually persuade to feed his church, he telleth him not of livings and preferments by it, nor of the woe if he preached not, but he useth a motive of another kind, stronger than all these. 'Peter, Lovest thou me?' I am persuaded it broke Peter's heart to hear Christ thus questioning with him, and to think that he had given him occasion, by his denial, to make a question of it. He modestly replies, 'Lord' (saith he), 'thou knowest that,' though I have dealt unthankfully and falsely with thee, that yet 'I love thee,' and am willing to do anything for thee. Whereas another performs his duty, but at best as a servant doth a business for a master, and so he may do it even because he is commanded; but yet his utmost aim is not as a friend to shew his love. But what says Christ, 'If ye do whatever I command you,' that is, out of love, then 'henceforth I shall call you friends, not servants,' John xv. 15. Or else the man doth his duty as a bribe to a judge to buy off his punishment : Micah vi. 6, 'Wherewithal shall I appear before the Lord?' What shall I give him? His manner of speaking bewrays he did it to bribe the Lord, to get his pardon. An enemy, being in an enemy's lurch, may do as much for his enemy, and for one he regardeth not.

(2.) Secondly, The good will that is in the heart will appear before the performance of any divine service, in a readiness to do it. As if a man truly loves a friend, his love to him is a preparation in his heart, and makes it ready to do anything before he asketh it. And therefore (1 Peter v. 2) they are said to do what they do (if they do it as they ought) 'out of a ready mind.' And though they cannot do always what they would, as Paul complaineth, Rom. vii., yet (says he) at the 18th verse, 'To will is present with me.' And therefore it comes off willingly, frankly, and freely, 1 Chron. xxix. 14. ; whereas another, though he goes about it, yet it is out of constraint, as Peter speaks, 1 Peter v. 2. And that is not only when worldly and by-ends move a man, but when conscience also pricks a man on to it by legal motives only. And when the heart is put upon it, it is sorry, and wincheth, it is sorry that it is propounded so, as when it is propounded and urged by motives drawn from God ; that of all love between him and us we would do such a duty, as ever we would do him a kindness, or shew our love to him ; as ever we have received mercy from him, or look for communion with him as a friend, we should obey him in this or that particular; yet the heart stirs not for all these, comes not off, until self-respects strike in. God in this case thinks himself denied.

2. Good will appeareth in the doing of the service to God, 1 John v. 3. This is the effect of love to God, that his commandments are not grievous, and a man goes about his work as about a friend's business, as Jacob went about Laban's business ; when love to Rachel set him on work, it was not grievous to him ; he thought not the time long because he loved her. So anything we do for God, love sweeteneth to us, 1 Chron. xxix. David offered, and he offered willingly, and rejoiced with great joy in the doing of it : ver. 14, 'And who am I,' says he, 'that I should do it?' He thought it a mercy God would use him, and accept it.

3. It will appear after the performance by two dispositions. First, thou wilt think everything too little that thou dost, as when a friend sends presents to one who is a friend indeed, still he thinks that they are not good enough, and wisheth they were better for his sake. There are two companies of men who seem to have done much for Christ, who shall appear before him at the latter day : the one thought they had done so much, that they speak of it themselves, 'Have we not prophesied,' &c. ; but the other,

that had done much more, and out of love to him, were silent, and not only so, but when Christ took notice of their love they were modest, wondered at it, were ashamed, as it were, that such poor services should be spoken of, as not worth the owning. And the reason is, because he that hath good will in his heart to God, still his heart exceeds his actions ; he doth them out of the abundance of his heart, as Christ speaks. As the woman that gave her mite emptied her purse, but not her heart, being (as it is likely) sorry she had no more to give. And such a one also, doing it out of love, and that of answering and requiting an infinite love, measuring what is done by both, finds it infinitely too little ; not big enough to express his own love, but much less to answer God's ; and so he is sorry and ashamed it is no better ; whereas, one that doth not do things out of good will, thinks everything enough that he thinks will but save him. His heart is less than his actions, and though by reason of convictions of what he ought to do, he cannot think it too much, knowing it to be his duty, yet when he doth it, and afterward, his heart thinks it much, and grudgeth it.

Fiftly; Lastly, In case of trial, when in temptation poor souls think all they have done is in vain, this goodwill will appear, in that they repent not of what they have done ; 2 Cor. vii. 9, 10, it is therefore called ' repentance never to be repented of.' There can no case befall them, wherein they do repent, or are sorry for what they have done ; but still wish it had been much better for God's sake. If he hath any glory by it, and if they should be damned, and not rewarded, they are contented to give him so much in. Whereas the other, as suitors when they are out of hope, send for all their tokens again, though they pretended much love ; so they did in the prophet : ' It is in vain,' say they, ' to serve God ; and wherefore have we fasted, and thou seest it not ?'

CHAPTER V.

The application or uses of the foregoing doctrine.

I shall now shut up this discourse with what is the apostle's chief scope in the text, 2 Cor. v. 18–20, viz., an use of exhortation, to ' beseech men to be reconciled to God ;' because reconciliation imports an having been formerly enemies ; and in that case, it is (as I shewed), necessary for men to apprehend themselves in a state of enmity with God, ere they will ever seek unto God for peace and reconciliation, or listen to the true terms of it.

1. I shall therefore, in the first place, earnestly beseech all men to consider whether yet such a work of reconciliation be wrought in them, yea or no ? And this is a question the best and greatest man living may, without offence, be entreated to ask his own heart ; and it concerns every man that will have reconciliation with God to do it. To this end I beseech you to consider that we were once enemies, that is, in a state of enmity, and it is not Christ's having died that altereth that state. You see that the text supposeth God's having been in Christ reconciling the world, when yet the world remaineth unreconciled to God ; for upon that supposition he foundeth this exhortation. It is true, Christ died for us, when we were enemies, and therein his love was shewn ; Rom. v. 8, ' God commendeth his love to us, that while we were yet sinners' (and enemies, as it follows), ' Christ died for us.' Yet withal it is as true that we remain notwithstanding in that state, until a work of reconciliation to God is wrought in us, through Christ's death : Col. i. 22, ' And you that were sometime enemies, yet now

hath he reconciled.' Nothing is more sure than that we were all once such; and it were well if we had good reasons to be as sure that now we are not. And the apostle everywhere stands upon the important *now* of every man's condition, as putting every man upon the examining his present condition.

2. And, secondly, consider, that this enmity is seated in your minds and natures. You are ' enemies in your minds,' Rom. v. 8. Whence therefore it must be acknowledged that there must needs be some great alteration wrought in your minds, if God and you be friends. And thence consider that therefore it is not education, or outward privileges, or deportment in the church, that either doth alter, or argues your condition altered. As take a wolf, a cub, that is newly fallen from the dam, which is, as we know, in its nature an enemy to a lamb, though you put it into a lamb's skin, and bring it up with the sheep in the same fold, and feed it with the same food, yet still it will remain a wolf, and an enemy to a lamb:—such is our woful case, being born in our natures enemies to God, though immediately when we fell from the womb, we had a Christian's ear-mark given us, were trained up in a Christian profession, and have been ever since fed with the same word, &c., yet we are enemies still, if there be no more alteration in us. It was the case of Simon Magus, Acts viii. 23, ' I perceive thou art still in the gall of bitterness.' And ver. 21, ' Thou hast neither lot nor part in this matter,' though he had been baptized, &c. And though an innocent and harmless carriage in the world be added to this, yet this will not argue your estates to be altered, for a wolf may be so tamed, that it shall not do much hurt; for every beast hath and may be tamed, as James saith, James iii. 7, ' Every kind of beasts and of birds, and of serpents, and things in the sea, is tamed, and hath been tamed of mankind.' And if mankind can tame beasts, their inward natural disposition remaining, but restrained, God can do the like, and much more, to the hearts and spirits of men, without changing of them. Thou mayest be a tame wolf, be chained up from ranging and devouring, and yet still remain an enemy. For remember that this enmity is seated in thy mind and nature. That your hearts are not filled with so much gall, as to carry you on to evil works, doth not argue you friends and reconciled, if withal they be not seasoned with so much good will to God, as to make you ' zealous of good works,' Titus ii. 14. Mere neuters (if you could be such) are no friends. God accounts them enemies; Mat. xxi. 30. ' He that is not with me is against me,' says Christ, our supreme judge.

3. Neither, thirdly, is it a forward profession of what is outwardly good, added to your inward carriage, which will argue you to be friends; for flatterers may abound in outward kindnesses, as well as friends, Isa. lviii. 2. You see a company there to mention kindnesses to God, whom God regards not. For it is with God herein as with great men, who have many flatterers, but few friends, as Solomon expresseth it, Prov. xix. 6, ' Many entreat the favour of the prince,' &c., because of gifts, ' and will be friends' (that is, seem to be), ' to him that giveth gifts.' And thus also God, having great gifts in his hand to give away, heaven, &c., and the keys of death and hell at his girdle; he hath many who do seek and earnestly entreat his favour, out of such respects and ends; and apprehensions strongly set on upon their hearts, who yet do but flatter him. Therefore trust to none of these, but love to have such a work of true reconciliation wrought in you as hath been spoken of. Which, if there be, the before mentioned dispositions of pure good will will be sooner or later bubbling up in your hearts.

In brief, therefore, take the help and benefit of all those particulars to examine your estates by, and try whether such a work hath been wrought in you.

(1.) Consider, whether thou, having first apprehended thy enmity against God, thou' wert therewithal brought to know God anew, and his Son; and knowing him, didst fall in love with him (and all that ever yet have known him, have loved him) not with such a love only as we bear to some hero, that doth great and noble things; or to our dead founders, whom we speak well of, and commend their doings, although we never knew them but by tradition (and such at best is the common love to God and Christ which men bear to them); but so to know and love him, as to be enamoured with him, as one in love useth to be with the person he sets his affections on. Doth thy heart burn after him, when thou seest a glimpse of him but passing by thee? Or, to use the phrase in Job, 'Art acquainted with him?' Job xxii. 21. Hath he imparted any secrets to thee, as to his friends he doth? John xv. 15. Hath he shewed and manifested himself to thee, John xiv. 20, if not in assurance of his love to thee, yet in the goodness that is in himself? Though thou hast seen him but as through the lattice (as the church did, Cant. v.), yet canst thou never be at quiet till thou seest him again? Hath thy heart been divorced from all other lovers upon acquaintance with him? Hast thou chosen him, and dost thou seek him for ever? And for what hast thou chosen him, and why dost thou seek him? Good will looks especially at the person, not the fortunes (as you call them); 'I seek not yours, but you,' is the language of a friend. Alexander had two friends: the one he called Φιλοβασίλευς, a lover of the king; the other, Φιλαλέξανδρὸς, a lover of Alexander, as being a lover of his person and dispositions. So many profess to love Christ, yet do it only as he is a saviour, and their judge, and king of heaven and hell. They love him not as Christ, not for that which God chiefly loves him for, namely, because he is his natural Son, his image, the express image of his person. Nor do they love him as Christ, that is, as anointed with the Spirit, and all the graces thereof, full of grace and truth above measure. For which yet the virgins are said to love him: Cant. i. 3, 'Because of the savour of thy ointments, they love thee;' and that, as virgins, with a pure and chaste affection to himself, with a savour of his graces, sweetness, and perfumes thereof. Is it the holiness, the amiableness, the love, the goodness, that is in him, which draws thy heart unto him? What says Paul? Phil. iii. 7–9, 'But what things were gain to me, those I counted loss for Christ. Yea doubtless, and I count all things but loss for the excellency of the knowledge of Christ Jesus my Lord: for whom I have suffered the loss of all things, and do count them but dung, that I may win Christ, and be found in him, not having mine own righteousness, which is of the law, but that which is through the faith of Christ, the righteousness which is of God by faith.' Observe it, he had suffered the loss of all for the excellency of the knowledge of Christ Jesus his Lord; and counted them dross in comparison of the knowledge of him. And his great desire was, that he might win Christ and be found in him, his person first; and then to be found in him, not having his own righteousness.

(2.) Again; Of all the things which he hath to bestow, or that is in him, what is the thing thou especially seekest for, and shalt never rest satisfied or contented without it? Is it his love, his favour, to have his heart towards thee, his delight set upon thee, to enjoy his presence, his face, to live with him for ever? And desirest thou to be happy thyself, that he may greatly delight in thy beauty ; and that thereby thou mightest be suited to him, and so mightest come to delight in him ; and this in such a manner as nothing else will satisfy thee, neither pardon, nor Christ's death, with addition of all the world, if it could be separated from the favour of God, would not content thee ?

(3.) Again ; Dost thou choose the things that please him ? And what pleaseth him most, dost thou choose most ? As a man useth to do his friend, whom he affects to please. As because thou hearest faith pleaseth him, Heb. xi., because a broken heart pleaseth him, Ps. li., glorifying him more than thousands of rams, Ps. l., because private prayer pleaseth him (as himself declared, ' Let me hear thy voice ; it is pleasant,' Cant. ii. 14). Because thanksgiving pleaseth him more than thousands of rams, Ps. lxix. 31. Do all these things therefore delight thy soul ? Because the Sabbath is his delight, and honourable to him, that is, for his honour, is it therefore thy delight, and dost thou call it honourable ? Isa. lviii. 13, 14. Because the saints please him, and are his delight, are they therefore thine ? Ps. xvi. 2. In a word, take all ordinances, dost thou use them as backdoors to let Christ thy private friend in, to the end to speak with him, and to enjoy communion with him ? Doth thy heart upon that account value the word thou readest or hearest, as a private letter sent from a dearest friend ? Dost thou think of going to the sacrament, as of going to a friend's house to supper ? Rev. iii. 20. In like manner, dost thou regard private prayer as an opportunity of speaking privately and alone with a friend in secret ?

(4.) And again, in thy doing what pleaseth him, what is it setteth thee in thy constant course a-work ? Is it his love that sets thee a-work, and ' constrains thee ? ' 2 Cor. v. 14. Or if not the sense of that, yet is it a desire to please him ? And when thou dost it for him, dost go about it as about a friend's business, not coldly, but so as to do it to purpose with all thy might, serving him with all thy strength ? Grudgest thou if thy lusts or corrupt affections do get any of thy spirits, so that they are not spent for him, and upon him ? Thinkest thou all this to be no trouble to thee ? Art glad when thou canst do him a kindness, that is, anything which he may be pleased to accept ? Thinkest thou that day best spent wherein thou canst do him a service ? Yea, most of all, thankest him that thou hast a heart to do it ? as David did, 1 Chron. xxix. 14. And when thou hast done, thou yet still fallest down as an ' unprofitable servant' and unuseful friend. Thinkest thou that it is all too little, and confessest still, this and that is not good enough, so as thou couldst find in thy heart to do over all again ? Wast never yet (and that out of love, not conviction only) satisfied with the best prayer that ever thou madest ? Art ashamed of the performance in any kind ? Yet because it is thy best he hath enabled thee to do, thou desirest him to take it in good part ; but not at, or in thine own name, because of thine unworthiness, but for his Son's, thy Christ's sake. Dost thou not find that thou hatest also, where he hateth ? whether it be sinners, or persons as clothed with sins. Dost thou hate those that hate God ? Ps. cxxxix. 21, 22, ' Do not I hate them, O Lord, that hate thee ? And am I not grieved with those that rise up against thee ? I hate them with perfect hatred. I count them mine enemies.' And as for sins, canst thou say (as David), ' I hate every false way' ? And that (as he says there) out of prizing ' all God's precepts in all things to be right,' Ps. cxix. 127, 128. And when it falls out that thou dost sin against him that is so good, canst thou yet in truth say, ' I do what I hate' ? Rom. vii. And then what is it in sin thou hatest most ? Is it because thou feelest thy heart turned (as it were) within thee ? saying, as 2 Sam. xvi. 17, ' Is this thy kindness to thy friend ?' Shall I do my God, my friend, this wrong ? Shall or should I so evilly or unthankfully requite God ? Or dost thou hate sin, because it breaks communion betwixt God and thee ? And when thou hast thus sinned, art thou never quiet till thou hast returned, and God and thou art friends again ? And returnest thou again to him, not as healed* by conscience into his presence ; and so stayest not till an arrest come forth for thee, or be served upon thee, and until thou art fetched in by terrors or afflictions only (though sometimes these are needful) but returnest thou out of a longing and lingering after him ; as one without whom thou canst no longer live, no, not in this world, where thou hast so many things to comfort thee ? From whom to be estranged, is it bitter as death to thee ? So that during all that space of distance from him, when thou but hearest or thinkest of him, thy heart glows within thee, burns after him, and in the end thou resolvedly comest to say, I can no longer bear this life, I must return to him again whom my soul loves, for then ' it was better with me than now,' Hos. ii. 7. I never enjoyed good hour since I wickedly and foolishly forsook him. And then when thou comest again into his presence, what is it broacheth thy heart, and makes it gush ? Is it thy unkindness to him ? Doth that dissolve and melt thy heart, confound and overcome thee, stop thy mouth, so at first thou canst do nothing but sit in silence with thy mouth in the dust, laying that most to heart which God lays most to heart ? ' If it had been an enemy he could have borne it.' But that thou, his friend, καὶ σὺ τέκνον, dost it, is intolerable. Thou who wast once a perfect and utter enemy unto him as ever was, and yet seeing the misery and danger of that condition, and having heard of his loving-kindness, grace, and mercy, wast sweetly drawn in, won, and allured, by himself too, to seek his favour and friendship more than life. And he as graciously also condescended to entertain a treaty with thee about it; gave thee many hopes and evidences of his favour, which thou hast prized more than life ; and thou wast even then, when this unhappy lust betrayed thee, and carried thee captive, upon the very point of obtaining the assurance of his love from him. Or suppose (I speak to one who hath obtained assurance from him) that thou wentest, as Saul, seeking after asses, a world of vanities, and yet even then hast found thyself in the ambushment of an infinite and everlasting love, surrounding thee without the possibility of escape from it. That thou who hast received all this, should use God thus, what base ingratitude is it ! Well, and yet further, when thou hast come unto him again and again (for this is not the first or second time that thou didst serve him so), and when thou didst expect nothing but frowns, if not rejection by him, lo, he hath fallen upon thy neck ere thou hast spoke out thy requests to him with trembling heart and lips ; and lo, he fell upon thy neck and kissed thee, and wept love, eternal love, and the blood of his dearest love, into thy bosom, faster than thou couldst pour tears into his. And instantly he bid fetch the best robe in all his wardrobe, that never yet was put upon angels' backs, woven by his Son, and appointed by himself, and told thee he had reserved it by him for thee from everlasting, and that all were friends again, and it would be so for ever. And he left only this kind sting behind, that he told thee that thou wouldst yet sin again as thou hadst done before ; and so thou hast. And hath not, doth not this yet more melt thee, and cause the tide of godly

* Qu. ' hauled'?—ED.

sorrow to swell yet higher, as it did in Peter ?   A good look of Christ made him ' go out, and weep bitterly.'   And when God hath used thee thus kindly, only bid thee take heed of returning to folly any more, didst thou, after that, fear his goodness more than ever thou didst his anger ?   Weepest thou if others do see thee, or thou seest others sin ?   Do, or have ' rivers of tears fallen down thine eyes, because men keep not his law ?' as David speaks, Ps. cxix.   But how remote are such dispositions as these from the hearts of the most of men, even of those who yet profess themselves as great and good friends to God as any ?   And if for want of such or like dispositions to these, so many will be found enemies (for Christ hath said it, ' He that is not with me is against me'), where shall you that are opposers of God and goodness, and mockers of holiness ; you that are secret maintainers and flatterers of bosom-sins, of uncleanness and worldliness in your own hearts, strangers from God and the life of God ; not sub-ject to the law of God, and to the multitude of duties he requireth ; not calling upon God (as the psalmist speaks), where will you appear ?   I have ransacked your hearts ; let me now prosecute my begun exhortation afresh.   I beseech, therefore, all those that shall have the least beam of light darted into their hearts by these considerations, to consider with themselves what to do.

For consider how nearly it concerns you to be reconciled to God. For know that ' he is angry with you every day,' Ps. vii. 11, though he says nothing.   And if thou turn not ' he will whet his sword, and prepare instruments of death.'   Unheard of tortures are a-preparing ; therefore it behoves us to inquire in what terms we stand with God.   That king in the parable, Luke xiv. 31, hearing that a foreign prince, provoked, was making war against him, sat down and considered whether he were able to encounter him.   And I beseech you so to do.   Who ever went on against him and prospered ?   ' Do we provoke the Lord to jealousy ?   are we stronger than he ?' 1 Cor. x. 22.   ' If I speak of strength.' saith Job, ' there is no deal-ing with him,' submitting to him, for he is strong, Job ix. 19.   ' What is weakness in God is stronger than the strength of men,' 1 Cor. i. 25.   What is weaker than a man's breath, which can scarce blow away a straw ?   And yet ' by the breath of his countenance we are consumed,' Job iv. 9.   It was but a word, but a breath, that made the world ; and we are but as the dust of the balance, Isa. xl. 15, soon blown away.   He is wise and also strong; so Job saith.   And therefore consider withal, that there is no way of escaping, but by sending out for conditions of peace.   So in the parable, Luke xiv. 32.   That was the issue of that king's consultations, that when he found that his enemy had prepared against him, and would be too hard for him, he sends out his conditions of peace.   And withal let me tell you this for your comfort, have any of you a mind to make peace with him ? Then be assured he will be at peace with you.   The text, 2 Cor. v. 18, brings the news of it : ' God was in Christ' (hath made it his business) ' re-conciling the world.'   And contrary to the use and custom, sends em-bassages to us to be reconciled unto him.   And lo, his earnestness : ' All things are of God, who hath reconciled us to himself.'   If ever God was earnest or serious in all or anything, he is in this : Isa. xxvii. 4, 5, ' Fury is not in me : who would set the briars and thorns against me in battle ? I would go through them, I would burn them together.   Or let him take hold of my strength, that he may make peace with me ; and he shall make peace with me.'   Though he be strong, yet as it is there, let a man take hold of his strength.   Take hold of that arm which is lifted up in fury, all the whole creation cannot stay or rule it. 'And he shall make peace with me,' says God. Yea, all the power which is in him shall be turned for you, and shewn in pardoning you. Only let the briars and thorns, Heb. vi., sinners that go on in their sins, and set themselves in battle array against him, let them look to themselves, for 'I will go through them' (says God), 'and burn them together,' ver. 4.

And therefore take Amos his counsel, Amos. iv. 12, that seeing he will surely do thus unto thee unless thou turn, 'prepare to meet thy God,' as that king did in the parable, and as Abigail did when she heard that David was coming on in fury. Throw away your weapons, 'cast away your transgressions,' 'why will you die?' Do as Shimei to David: seeing he will overcome, go forth to meet him, and put yourselves into his hands: 2 Sam. xix. 20, 'Thy servant knows' (saith he) 'that I have sinned; so I am come to meet the lord my king.' This overcame David, though egged on by servants for to kill him. David was overcome by it, being an ingenuous man; much more it will prevail with God, a God of all mercy. The truth is, he desires but to be acknowledged to be God both in damning and saving; to overcome and to be justified, when he is judged, which he is when he is submitted unto. 'Do I not know that I am king this day?' saith David, giving a reason why he pardoned him, ver. 20. Thus also, when Ben-hadad was in Ahab's power, 1 Kings xx., his servants advised him to send messengers unto him with ropes about their necks, and to put on sack-cloth, thereby to acknowledge he might hang them up if he pleased, for they and their king were in his power, if so it pleased him to deal with them. Only they knew the kings of Israel were merciful kings, and so they came and put themselves into his hands, and humbly sought him, running by his chariot-side, waiting if any word of hope and encourage-ment might fall from him. And thus they obtain, not of a David, but of an Ahab, a hard-hearted Ahab. And if this king of Israel (the worst of them) were thus merciful, what is the God of Israel? 'the God and Father of mercies!'

Go home therefore, and fall down upon thy knees, and with a heart broken and dissolved to water, acknowledge thy treasons, rebellions, and injuries against him who never did thee hurt; yea, who hath never ceased to do thee good; yea, who hath striven with an unwearied patience to soften and overcome this strong and stout rebellion. Lay open all thy sins, and spread all thy bold and bloody transgressions as a scroll before him; set over each their accents and aggravations. Point every confession with tears and sighs; rip up thy heart and life; say it is thou who hast polluted the earth, sinned against heaven and him that sits therein, and art alto-gether unworthy of the name, much more of the privilege, of a son; that thou hast forfeited thy creation, and deservest not to be called a creature. Acknowledge thy crime, with self-loathing and self-condemnation, as with a rope put about, and ready fitted to thy neck by thine own hand, as Benhadad's servants did. Say to God, that if he will destroy thee he may; and if he doth he shall need no other judge to condemn thee but thyself; no other indictment than this thy free confession, made of thine own accord. And to shew that he needeth not to send for thee, and hale thee to execu-tion, say, Thou freely presentest thyself to him. And referring thyself to him, say, as David did, 2 Sam. xv. 26, 'If thou hast not pleasure in me, do with me as seemeth good to thee.' Yet withal, bemoan thyself to him, as Ephraim is said to do, Jer. xxxi. Confess thou hast 'perverted that which is right,' and it hath not profited thee at all; that thou hast wearied thyself in the ways of sin, and last run away from him days without number, who is thy fountain of life ; and that it was never well with thee since thou didst forsake him. Yea, that thou hast destroyed thyself to do him injury, in whom alone thy help is to be found. And falling down yet lower, tell him that now thy life depends upon his breath, that he is that lawgiver who alone is able to save thee or condemn thee. A word of his saves thee, and it may condemn thee. And above all, get thy heart to melt for thy unkindness to him. Say, that though thou hadst never been the better for the goodness that is in him, or shouldst never hope to be, yet to wrong him, who is a God that is so great, and yet withal so good, that hath infinite glory joined with holiness, riches of grace, mercy with so much power, that is so able to destroy, and so willing to forgive, is that most grieves thee. That thou shouldst kick against him in whom thou livest, and movest, and hast thy being ; at whose expense and charges it hath been that thou hast hitherto been maintained ; and yet to no other end but to sin against him ; say to him, that it is this thought which wounds thy soul. Acknowledge that thou hast already spent him millions of riches of patience and long-suffering, and all to no other fruit or purpose but to offend him ; and of all which thou canst give him no other account but millions of sins and injuries returned against him. And besides this vast expense of the common stock of mercy, common to others with thee, thou hast neglected and despised the offer of as much mercy as were sufficient to save all the devils (if they were capable of it) ; and if he yet pardon thee, thou must cost him yet much more than thou hast already spent him, the mercies of eternity, the soul-blood of his Son, which blood and mercy is what thou art now a-suing for. And after all this thou must be beholden to that free grace thou hast all this while been sinning against and despising, or thou art undone. And none but everlasting, unchangeable, and sure mercies will serve thy turn. Thy transgressions, and rebellions, and corruptions are of that extent, that less mercy will not reach or hold out to pardon thee, but fall short of what thou owest ; which mercies, if yet thou obtainest not, it is not for want of good will in God, but from hardness of heart in thee to him, yea, to thyself. And let this consideration further make thy heart to gush and bleed, and strike thee down into the deepest confusion, never to look up again but with shame and sorrow; but yet tell him, that if thou couldst yet find in thy heart truly to turn to him, he can find enough and enough (to an overflowing) in his heart to be at peace with thee.

Thus ' go and take words unto thyself,' as he himself directs thee in Hosea xiv. 2. He will be sought to, and he loves to be entreated. It is melody in his ears to hear a poor soul bemoan itself unto him. Soft words pacify wrath, Prov. xv. 1, much more stirs bowels of mercy. His heart cannot hold out against such volleys of tears and cries from a heart that is broken. Turn all thou hast heard or read about reconciliation on his part into motives and arguments to move him to shew mercy unto thee. Tell him it is true, it is in his power to shew his justice on thee if he will, and that thou art freely come to present thy naked breast to him as a butt that deserves to be shot at, and he might spend his arrows on thy hateful soul, or sheath his sword in it ; only desire him to remember, before he doth it, that it is the same sword which he once thrust into his Son's bowels, when it pleased him to ' put him to grief, and make his soul an offering for sin.' And when thou hast said it, shut thine eyes and trust him. And oh ! wash, bathe, and plunge thy soul in that fountain which he then opened. Beseech him to consider that he himself found out a way to pacify himself for sin, such a way as thou and all the angels should have trembled to have thought of, and couldst not have believed, but that himself hath done it and revealed it; yea, and that he himself, unbespoken to by thee, or any of us of mankind, sough', to his Son to be mediator, when thou hadst no being. And say to him, Lord, wilt thou not now accept it, when he hath performed it at thine own request, and when it is sought for at thy hands? Further tell him, that as the motion came first from himself to his Son, so from himself first to thee; that thou shouldst never have had the face, or heart, or will, to have sought him thus; but that he first set thee a-work, spake to thy hard heart, won and allured thy soul to trust, by what thou hearest of his love, which hath so taken thy heart, that now thou canst never part with it. He doth beseech thee by us to be reconciled to him, and though he doth it by us, yet he would have come himself, but that he is to appear in heaven to intercede. Urge him that there are but a few in the world that do seek to be reconciled to him, and if he should turn any away that do, he would have fewer. Who would fear him, if there were not mercy in him, and plenteous redemption? And thou mayest wax yet bolder, according to what you heard out of Job xxxiii. and other scriptures. Thou hast heard by his messengers, those who have been sent to thee by himself, of an infinite and all-sufficient righteousness in his Son, laid up in him also by his own procurement, and betrusted with him for the bestowing of it upon those that should come to him for it. Whereupon he hath said, ver. 26, ' I will render to man his righteousness.' Put this in suit, for it is but as in trust committed to him, and plead that he received it to that very end to give it forth to them that sue for it. And he hath therefore said that when any one soul draws nigh unto the grave (as thine doth now) and a messenger from him shews to him, and gives him this righteousness, Job xxxiii. 23, and that thereupon if he pray unto him, he will be favourable, and he shall see his face with joy; and that he will say, Deliver him, I have found a ransom; for he will render to man his righteousness, ver. 26. Go sue for it therefore as thine; pray, and plead thou thus, and he cannot deny thee.

But if it be objected against thee, that it is true these things are in him, but thou art a sinner, an enemy; say thou then that if this objection stand good, his Son must be in heaven alone, and none of mankind must be there with him; no man must stand in his sight. Say, Thou hast heard that to take away sins was the main design of the covenant of grace, and had it not been that he meant to save sinners, he needed not have pitched on the course of saving men by his Son, for he might have created new friends cheaper; but that he knew the saving an enemy would shew more love. If the greatness of thy sins be urged upon thy conscience, say, All fulness dwells in his Son; a fulness, and all fulness of merit above what thy sins can reach to. If that these sins have been continued in by thee these many years, urge that this fulness dwells in his Son, and hath done so, longer than sin hath done in thee. But if he say, Yea, but those I do save, believed and repented; ask him, Who gave them that repentance and that faith? Didst not thou, O Lord? ' By grace ye are saved, through faith,' Eph. ii. 8. And that faith is not of ourselves neither, ' it is the gift of God;' which beseech him therefore to work in thee.

Come thus with a true heart to him, for thou must draw near to him, as with confidence of being accepted, so with a true heart, for both are joined together, Heb. x. 22. Wherefore I take the meaning to be (in opposition to a false, disloyal, and traitorous heart) to signify such a heart as for the future resolves to be true to him, even as one friend would or ought to be to another, or as thou wouldst be to thyself; a heart truly loving him, resolving to keep thyself chaste and true to him alone. Even as the spouse that had played the whore with many lovers in former times, and now returns wooing and suing to her husband, not only for to pardon her, but to love her, and to receive her again with a conjugal love, and to let her enjoy communion and fellowship with him, as a wife doth with a husband, from whom she had been so long time estranged. Do thou seriously and truly resolve to let go all whorish and carnal friendship, with other lovers, as the world and all things therein, which hath enticed thy heart away from God. Come also with a true heart, resolving to be loyal and faithful to him, as a subject to a lawful prince; submitting to all his laws for ever, hating and standing out against every sin as an utter enemy; being for him and for his glory; having respect to him in all your actions (as you would have such a regard to one you love more dearly than yourselves, whom it grieves you to displease, and in comparison of holding whose friendship you count not your life precious or dear unto you); fully submitting to his commanding and condemning will; standing out in nothing, resolving to give up thyself in the deepest services of doing or suffering whatsoever he shall set thee about; resolving to be nothing for thyself, but to be all to him, and true to him as thou wouldst be to thyself. All this, I take it, is meant by a true heart; and this it is to be reconciled. Now sue thus, and continue suing, and all the saints in heaven must yet be condemned if ever thou art, for they came thither no other way than thus. But without this, though not for this (for God accepts freely), an husband would never accept his adulterous wife (though she slubbered never so much) except he saw she resolved to live now true and chaste to him. No more will God receive, except he sees in thee such holy resolutions. And though man may be deceived, yet God searcheth the hearts, and cannot be deceived.

Only in the last place, as the conclusion of all, see thou dost this presently, and not defer it a whit; and this the nature of reconciliation requires of thee. For that reconciliation which shall be accepted must proceed out of good will to God, as hath been spoken. So as when a man returns, he mourns that he hath stood out, and been an enemy so long, and that he came in no sooner. And therefore if thou sayest now, after all this urging, that thou wilt reconcile thyself hereafter, it argues thou intendest not to do it in truth of heart, so as God should accept thee. For if thou afterwards comest out of necessity, though thou suest (as Esau did) with tears, yet thou shalt not be accepted, as he was not. If a bare submission would serve thy turn, though unfeigned, thou mightst defer and make thy peace afterwards; but it being to be reconciliation, it requires absolutely the present time. No time so fit as now; deferring argues enmity. An enemy will submit to an enemy when he is cast into a strait, as Shimei did, but a friend will return of himself.

And besides, secondly, let this thought move you, Shall God and Christ have busied themselves about your reconciliation from everlasting, and spent an eternity of thoughts upon it; and will you defer to think of it till the hour of death or sickness? Hath God made this his first work and master-piece? And do you make repentance to be your refuse work, to be done at your castaway leisure? Hath it took up the delights of the great God, hath he been so forward in it; and must you be haled and forced to it? And if that will not move you, consider the danger of delays.

'Agree with thine adversary' (says Christ) 'while thou art in the way.' God now in this life offers to deal with thee upon terms of friendship, but if once thou comest before the judge (as Christ says), and so before God as a judge, will he regard any ransom? Will he then come to any composition? No; he will not rest content (as Solomon saith) though thou givest him many gifts. Or if thou shouldst then obtain thy peace, yet it would be upon harder conditions than now ten thousand times. Learn wisdom of him in the parable, Luke xiv. 31, who when he saw he was not able to encounter with his enemy, he sent to him for conditions of peace, 'whilst he was yet afar off' (the text says); for he knew that if he deferred till the enemy came nigher, with his armies of thy sins and his wrath, and sat down before the walls, he would hardly be brought to remove his siege; and if so, yet upon harder conditions, if at all. Now his coming against thee may be nigher than thou art aware. 'This night' (it may be): 'The judge stands at the door,' says James. Yet suppose judgment be deferred and the judge to be afar off, yet it is the safest way to send out speedily, and to sue for conditions of peace. For when God's wrath hath begirt thee round about at the day of death or sickness, it would be more difficult by far, if at all thou dost obtain it.

God may shoot at thee suddenly, and at one shoot, at one blow, kill thee as he did the sons of Eli, and cut thee off ere thou hast time even to do that which thou thinkest will serve the turn, which yet will not. For it is not bare submission, but reconciliation; not necessitated, but free and voluntary, proceeding out of good will, that must be the condition of thy peace. Observe Shimei's policy, and follow his example; who, when he heard that David was settled in his kingdom, and so knew he had power to crush him, he being conscious of his rebellion, came in voluntarily, and was the first of the rebels that submitted, and soon got his peace. So do thou; do it now, and be glad and thankful if God will yet, after this long time of rebellion, accept thee again.

BOOK IV.

Of the work which the Holy Spirit effecteth in us, as it is expressed under the notion of our being begotten unto God, and of a new birth; from which the necessity of regeneration is farther demonstrated.—Of the nature of the thing begotten in us, as it is set forth under the notion of spirit, John iii. 6.

CHAPTER I.

The necessity of the new birth demonstrated, and the nature of it described, from the notion of our being begotten unto God, 1 Pet. i. 3–5.

*Blessed be the God and Father of our Lord Jesus Christ, which, according to his abundant mercy, hath begotten us again unto a lively hope, by the resurrection of Jesus Christ from the dead, to an inheritance incorruptible, undefiled, and that fadeth not away, reserved in heaven for you, who are kept by the power of God through faith unto salvation, ready to be revealed in the last time.—*1 Pet. I. 3–5.

THE believers whom Peter wrote to were stranger Jews, cast out and dispersed from their own land and inheritances (as ver. 1 insinuates); and he being the apostle of the circumcision, and so the Jews being committed to him as his proper flock (as Paul was the apostle of the Gentiles or uncircumcision, Gal. ii. 7), to comfort them against this their dispersion, he puts them in mind of another and greater inheritance, which also by a birth higher and diviner than that of theirs from Abraham, who gave them right to the other inheritance in Canaan, was estated on them. 'Who' (*i. e.*, God, saith he) 'hath begotten us to an inheritance,' &c. The carnal Jew boasted of his birth from Abraham, as that whereby also they challenged God to be their Father, John viii., from the 33d to the 45th. And when they had occasion to bless God for any eminent mercy, their form of blessing was, 'Blessed be the Lord God, the God of Israel,' &c., Ps. lxxii. 18. But Peter, under the New Testament, instructs them that, instead of glorying they had Abraham to their father, they should rejoice and glory in this, that they were begotten again of God, and of the 'incorruptible seed,' the Spirit of God, ver. 23. And so John Baptist, the son of that Zacharias, in the early times of the gospel, taught them, John i. 12, 13, compared with Luke iii. 8; and by that birth they became a 'choice generation' indeed, as our Peter speaks in his second chapter.

Again; instead of entitling God by the name of 'God of Israel,' Peter in the New Testament teacheth them to enstyle and bless him now as the 'God and Father of Jesus Christ,' and to view him upon that account as become a God and Father unto them. And lastly, instead of boasting of their Canaan, their so ancient inheritance, from which these saints of that nation were now cast out, and the whole nation was to follow them soon after his death, he instructs them to solace themselves with a lively hope of an inheritance far better seated and conditioned : ' An inheritance incorruptible, and undefiled, and that fadeth not away, reserved in heaven for you ;' which their new birth had given them right unto.   And this is the more special aspect and coherence of those words.

I have no further design upon this text in the opening of it, than what it offers to us concerning regeneration ; which done, I shall leave it, and pass to another that speaks of other things about it.   This text will put us upon the consideration of two things concerning it.

I. Why it is termed or called a begetting, as elsewhere a being born again, and what that metaphor eminently imports, and instructs in it about it.

II. The necessity of it, as without which God shews us no mercy ; we can have no hopes or title to this inheritance.

I. Why is it called birth, or being begotten ?   I shall not prosecute the metaphor, but chiefly insist on it to shew the nature of the thing begotten.

1. It is called a being born again, to shew that it conveys an image, or likeness of the begetter.   Men are said to *make* many things which are not like themselves, as artificers do ; but they are not said to *beget* anything which bears not in species their own likeness.   The first Adam had an image to convey to his seed : therefore, Gen. v. 3, it is said Adam begat Seth after his own image and likeness.   So Christ, the second Adam, hath also an image to convey unto them that are his, 1 Cor. xv. 49 : therefore the way of conveying it is called a birth, and he a Father : Col. iii. 10, ' The new man is renewed after the image of him that created him,' namely, at first, it being for substance the same, which (as it follows) is to be like God and Christ in those gracious dispositions which he shews to be in himself in his dealings towards us.   So, ver. 12, 13, ' Put on therefore, as the elect of God, bowels of mercies, kindness, humbleness of mind, meekness, long-suffering ; forbearing one another, and forgiving one another, if any man have a quarrel against any : even as Christ forgave you, so also do ye.'   As if he had said : As the elect of God, and chosen of God to be his children, be like unto him and Christ ; ' so also be you :' or (as our Peter expresseth it, 1 Pet. i. 15, 16), ' Be holy, as he is holy.'   Now God's holiness lieth in two things : 1. In the things he willeth and commandeth us. 2. In making his own glory his own end.   Therefore the image of God in us must lie in these two things.

(1.) A conformity or frame of spirit suited unto the things he commands or willeth, as the piece is to the pattern : 1 Thess. iv. 2, 3, ' For ye know what commandments we gave you by the Lord Jesus.   For this is the will of God, even your sanctification ;' that is, your sanctification lies in a conformity to his will, and that will of his as expressed in his commands.

(2.) In having God's glory set up in our hearts as our own utmost end, and as the square and measure of all our affections and actions, &c. (as self-love was before in us), and the one to be made as co-natural to us as self-love once was.   This is holiness, and it can be no other or further thing, even as in God himself it is not ; it being that in him which forms, orders, disposeth, guides, directs, acts all for himself, and swallows up all into himself.   Now, in the creature, holiness is the likeness of what is in himself, and so it is a disposition to be for God, even as God is for himself. Therefore whatever is good or excellent in the creature, of what kind soever of gifts of righteousness, it falling short of the glory of God, it becomes sin. So saith the apostle (Rom. iii. 23), setting forth in a summary conclusion the sinfulness of man's nature as fallen from God, to which he had spoken, ver. 10, 11, ' As it is written, There is none righteous, no, not one : there is none that understandeth, there is none that seeketh after God ;' that is, there is none that aimeth at or setteth up God as his chiefest end, or seeks after him as his chiefest good ; and so they fall short of the glory of God, and his image, in which at first they were created. To be born again and to become a Christian is to make God's interest my own for ever. It is the fundamental law of regeneration, and the first enacted in the heart, and is general to all believers that are truly such ; so Paul says, Rom. xiv. 7, 8, ' For none of us liveth unto himself, and no man dieth unto himself. For whether we live, we live unto the Lord ; and whether we die, we die unto the Lord : whether we live therefore, or die, we are the Lord's.' *None of us*, that is, *of us* that are true Christians, though other men are guided by other principles. Yea, and observe his inference, it is therefore that we are the Lord's, because we are in both life and death for the Lord. Thus it is the image of God that is begotten, and although the new creature may have many other workings and stirrings of heart divers ways, in humblings for sin, sight of a man's natural condition, which are as the films in which the new creature is enwrapped, yet this is the birth, the substance of what is begotten, and all the other tend unto it. It is the image of God's holiness, limb for limb.

II. This work of grace, and the image of God wrought in us, is termed a beginning, to shew that it is made a nature in us, as that image stamped on us by birth is said to be, and as all dispositions which we have by birth are said to be natural. To have a thing by birth and by nature is all one in phrase of speech ; so to be blind by nature signifies that which is so by birth. Hence this work, which in the scriptures cited hath been termed the image of God, is by our Peter termed ' the divine nature,' 2 Peter i. 4. *Nature*, for its manner of inherency, as natural dispositions use to be inherent in us ; *divine*, for its tendency and quality, as that which bears a likeness to God's nature, and which carries the soul up to him, as nature doth us unto what is suitable thereto. And that by *divine nature*, which some would raise up to a higher sublimation of participation of the essence of God, there is meant such divine, holy dispositions wrought in us, is clear by its opposite there mentioned by Peter in those words, ' Having escaped the corruption that is in the rest of the world through lust.' Corruption through lust is that which is destroyed. And as you usually say, that *corruptio unius est generatio alterius*, so here, the corruption of this corruption is the production of the new creature. Now, the corruption that is in all mankind through lust, is the corrupt dispositions and inclinations to evil, which are natural unto us ; this is corrupt nature, as we use to say. The divine nature is the contrary hereto, which, because freely given, is indeed called grace, but yet becomes a new nature to a man begotten ; and according as the Spirits acts it, it puts forth itself in dispositions in manner like to those which are natural, as will appear by bringing James's words to Peter, chap. iv. 5, 6, ' The spirit that is in us lusteth to envy, but God giveth more grace.' That is, whereas the natural spirit that is in us puts forth itself in lustings and dispositions to envy, and it doth it naturally, God gives grace or holiness to lust after meekness, humility ; and the one, after a man is regenerated, is as natural as the other afore. And accordingly, as the flesh or corrupt nature is said to have its lusting to evil things, so the spirit of regeneration is said to have its answerable lustings to things holy, Gal. v. 17, so as a man may come to understand, and withal take an estimate, whether he have the spirit of regeneration or no. Every man knows by experience what it is to have lustings to evil, dispositions to envy, ambition, uncleanness, pride, and finds they are his nature. Hast thou found the like dispositions of love, ingenuity to God, to seek his glory, to love the communion of saints, &c. ? 'I need not write to you : ye are taught of God to love one another,' says Paul, 1 Thes. iv. 9. The opposition shews he speaks of it as such an impression as by nature God puts into the creatures, and so they are said to be taught of him ; such is this divine new nature. Therefore, measure that good that is in thee by the evil ; I say not for the degree (thou mayest find corruption working more strongly), but for the kind, the one works as naturally, as to the innateness of workings, as the other.

Use 1. We read much in Scripture of men greatly enlightened, receiving the word with joy, made partakers of the Holy Ghost, that yet fall away ; yet among all the great and glorious things said of them, you have it nowhere said that they are begotten again, or born again, as likewise nowhere that they are justified. And the reason is evident ; 1. Because justification is the act of God towards his, pardoning and accepting of them to life. And therefore if God doth it at all, he doth it truly and really, or not at all ; it can have no counterfeit. So in like manner, to be begotten again notes a state of sonship, a being truly made a child ; for if God begets, he begets genuinely, it proves always a true child of his begetting ; and whoever is born of God hath his image, his nature, or, as the apostle speaks, true holiness: Eph. iv. 24, 'And that you put on the new man, which after God is created in righteousness and true holiness.' They are said to be sanctified, Heb. x. (for that may have a counterfeit), namely, a setting apart to outward service by gifts and enlightenments ; but to shew it is not true sanctification, or after God in true holiness, they are never said to be born of God. They as servants live in the family, are put into offices and services, and to that end do receive gifts and graces to lay out as talents, Mat. xxv., which not improved, they lose ; but being not made children, therefore it is they abide not always in the house ; as Christ speaks, John viii. 35, 'And the servant abideth not in the house for ever, but the son abideth ever.' They are hired servants, not begotten children. They have gifts from him as a lord, but not his image as from a father, and so are never said to be begotten. Now, take then the poorest soul, whose heart hath childlike dispositions running in his heart to God, good nature, ingenuities ; for grace is but good nature to God, and works toward God, as good nature doth to them we love. Take a soul whose heart is taught of God to apply itself unto God in all his dealings, so as still his heart works good naturally and like a child towards him, if he frowns or smiles, loves or chides, whips or gives favours. He fears his goodness more than his wrath, finds the glory of God in some degree naturalized in his soul as the supremest law, as set once next in him before. And though perhaps his faith cannot call God Father, or challenge him as such, yet his heart utters it, his love cries it. He finds love to God and his people working as kindly in a measure, as he hath found self-love working to and for himself ; his affections of fear, joy, desires, hatred, rising and falling according as the glory of God is interested. The least of these are better and surer evidences than many of those glorious incomes you hear spoken of, that come and visit men's souls at times, as flashes of lightning do a house, transiently and away ; whereas it is a new nature, a holy frame of heart, that is constant, a seed of God abiding, that makes man said to be born again. This is regeneration, and without this all other will come to nothing. After the apostle had spoken such glorious things of men that fall away, Heb. vi., a man then reading ver. 9 that there are better things than these that accompany salvation, would expect some seraphical manifestations, exceeding all these, to be those better things. But the apostle instances in love to the name and glory of God, and his truth and children, as one of those things that exceeds all these, which is a childlike disposition of one begotten and born of God.

Use 2. The second thing to be considered is the necessity hereof to salvation, which is demonstrated out of the text thus : All do and will acknowledge that without God's being merciful to a man, there can be no salvation. But God's mercy (suppose it is as abundant, as it is, as you are able to conceive of it) can nor never will save any man without regeneration ; for it is clear in the text, that herein it is that God shews the abundancy of his mercy, even to beget again those he means to save, as without which he could not save. This is clear also from Tit. iii. 5, ' According to his mercy hath he saved us ;' so then we are saved by mercy only, as the moving cause, but yet how doth mercy save whom it will have mercy upon? It is ' by the renewing of the Holy Ghost.' Yea, in ver. 4 herein is made the great appearance or manifestation of the love and kindness of God borne to any soul, that he renews it : ' After that the kindness and love of God appeared, not by works of righteousness which we have done, but according to his mercy he saved us, by the washing of regeneration, and renewing of the Holy Ghost.' So then if God means to manifest love and mercy in the salvation of any, he doth it in and by this, or which is all one, if he loves any it appears in this. Herein is the love of God manifested, as John upon another occasion speaks. Now, for the demonstration of this, take such reasons as are congenial to the text.

(1.) Without regeneration God bears not the actual relation of nor becomes a Father to us. God owns no children but such as are like him, and begotten of him after his image. If you call on him as your Father, says Peter in the same chapter, ver. 17, then as obedient children you must be holy as he is holy, ver. 14–16, not fashioning yourselves according to your former lusts ; that is, you must be new cast, new fashioned, and so become holy, as he who called you is holy. All are ready to challenge God to be their Father, as the Jews (John viii. 40) did with a bold and impudent forehead challenge God to be their Father, when yet they were full of envy and malice towards Christ and his disciples. No, says Christ, ' Ye are of your father the devil,' and his image you bear, ' and his lusts you will do,' ver. 44. In Jeremiah iii. God, as Christ doth in John, upbraideth the impenitent Jews for the like impudence : ' Wilt thou not from this time,' he speaks what had been their wont from time to time, come and ' cry to me, My Father ?' whenas it follows, ver. 5, ' thou hast done evil things as thou couldst,' and thinkest to call me thy Father, or that I as a Father will ever own such. But seeing God will become a Father even to such sinners, how comes it to pass that in the 19th verse God is brought in as consulting with himself how to save these rebels, and how to come to own them for his children ? And he brings it in by way of objection : ' But I said' (God makes a stand at it), ' How shall I put thee among the children ?' come to enroll thee into the catalogue whom I will own as such ? And it is an objection God himself can never well answer, without turning and regenerating them, and causing them not to depart from him. So it follows, 'Thou shalt call me, My Father; and shalt not turn away from me.' There is the answer, and the only answer can be given to it. So then God is no Father, nor owns any among his children, without it.

(2.) Without this work wrought in us, Christ becomes not our Lord and husband. When Adam was to be married, God looked over all the beasts of the field, and finding never a fit match for him among them, he made one like him of his own rib, and in the same image with him. Now, if thou hast the same image wherein thou wast born, thou art a more unfit match for Christ than beasts for Adam. Would any of you be content to have no other wife but a beast, a cow, or a sow, or a devil *succubus?* God would not have Christ unequally yoked: 'Now what fellowship can light have with darkness, Christ with Belial?' 2 Cor. vi. 14. He speaks it to us in the name and person of Christ, that we should not be unequally yoked, and therefore he would not have Christ much more. God would have his Son have a wife that should please him, and have a beauty suitable to his mind. Christ loves beauty as well as you, as you may see Ps. xlv. 11, where Christ is set forth as one who hateth iniquity and loveth righteousness, ver. 7, 8, and therefore God gives his daughter, the church, commandment to forsake the sins she was born and brought up in: 'Hearken, O daughter, and consider, incline thine ear,' that is, to my Son's commandments, 'and forget thy father's house; so shall the king (Christ) greatly desire thy beauty.'

(3.) Without this we can have no title to, no hope of enjoyment or possession of, that inheritance, 1 Pet. v. 5. We can have,

[1.] No title. Heaven is an inheritance, and as inheritances go by birth, so doth it also: 'Who hath begotten us again,' saith the text, 'to an inheritance incorruptible.' If no son, no heir; and if no new birth, no son. Kingdoms upon earth have two ways of succession: first, by choice or election; secondly, by birth; and this latter, for a monarchy, is held the best way of succession. Now God (who takes into his dispensations all the rules that men go by), hath ordained to settle and establish heaven, to all that shall be saved, by both these titles. 1. By election, but that is secret to himself: 'The Lord only knows who are his.' Therefore, 2, to declare it to men themselves, and to others, he hath ordained a heavenly birth openly and actually to entitle them to it: 'Whom he hath predestinated, them also hath he called,' Rom. viii. 30. As God gave the earth and all things in it unto Adam, and all that should be born of him, so hath he given heaven and all the promises unto Christ, and unto all that should be born of him also. And as such as was the earthly man, such are the earthly men; so such as was the heavenly man Christ, such are all his to become even heavenly as he is.

[2.] Without being converted there is no hope of this inheritance. Thou mayest have a dead hope, a false hope, that will deceive thee, but not a 'lively hope.' Is any man so fond as to hope for a crown that was not born to it? How then can we hope for heaven, if we have not the new birth, God's image, to shew for it?

[3.] We cannot otherwise possess it. If a reasonable soul, so created by God, would come into this world, and possess the good things in it, it must necessarily be put in a body, and clothed with flesh, which is to be had from Adam by a fleshly generation (it could else never come to see the light of this sun, it could else never see this world, nor possess anything in it), so nor can men's souls ever come to set a foot into the other world, the kingdom of heaven, if they be not clothed with God's image, and so born of Christ. In 2 Cor. v. 3, there is a parenthesis which bears this sense: 'If so be that being clothed we be not found naked.' He is a-speaking of the soul's being clothed with a house from heaven when separate from the body; and discoursing thereof he casts in this as a caution for all Christians, that they look to it their souls be clothed upon with the new man, which is the begotten of Christ; for if they be found devoid thereof, and naked, they cannot expect the enjoyment or possession of the house that is above. This is Calvin's interpretation, and it is a true one. And hereof Christ himself useth this expression, that 'unless a man be born again, he cannot' (so much as) 'see the kingdom of God,' nor peep into it; and much less can he enter into it, or set a foot in it.

[4.] I may add, fourthly, though he could enter, yet he could not enjoy it. Heaven would not be heaven to him. Heaven is an inheritance of light, says the apostle, Col. i. 12, and therefore we that are naturally sin and darkness must be made meet for it: 'Who hath made us meet to be partakers of the inheritance of the saints in light: having delivered us from the power of darkness,' ver. 13. Heaven is 'an inheritance incorruptible,' 1 Pet. i. 4. Now, if flesh and blood (that is, frail mortal flesh) cannot inherit the kingdom of God, nor corruption incorruption, as, 1 Cor. xv. 50, the apostle speaks, then much more not flesh, that is, that sinful defilement which we were born in. If the body must be changed ere it can be glorified, then much more the soul; for this glory in heaven is an inheritance undefiled, and no unclean thing can enter in, Rev. xxi. 27. Without holiness no man can see God; that is, so see him as to be happy in him. Blessed are the pure in heart, for they shall see God, and so be blessed in the sight of him.

Let us see and make* this necessity of the new birth. We are fallen into times in which the thing and doctrine of it is forgotten and laid aside, in which there are multitudes of professors, but few converts, many that seem to walk in the way to life, that never came in at the strait gate. There is a zeal amongst us to advance this or that reformation in religion, and it hath been all the cry. But, my brethren, where is regeneration called for or regarded? We have seen the greatest outward alterations that ever were in any age, kingdoms turned and converted into commonwealths, the power of heaven and earth shaken; but men, although they turn this way and that, from this or that way, from this opinion to that, yet their hearts generally turn upon the same hinges they were hung on when they came into the world. In this University of Oxford we have had puttings out and puttings in, but where is putting off the old nature and putting on the new? Where do we hear (as we had wont) of souls carrying home the Holy Ghost from sermons, of their being changed and altered, and made new, and of students running home weeping to their studies, crying out, 'What shall I do to be saved?' This was heretofore a wonted cry. Conversion is the only standing miracle in the church, but I may truly say these miracles are well nigh ceased; we hear of few of them.

With whatever advances in religion and incomes from God, or purity of reformation, we may flatter ourselves, I am sure that regeneration and conversion is it that must make Christians in this age, as in all the ages afore us. As take the whole generation of mankind, though mankind in one age hath grown up in stature, and in duration of years of life (as afore the flood),

* Qu. 'mark'?—Ed.

more than in another, and may be more civilised in manners, more raised in parts and abilities in one above another ; yet the propagation of the race of men on earth is one and the same in all, by being born, begotten, formed in the womb, in all substantials of being. If they be men they must be born. So in the church : of whatever progress in truths or holiness one age may excel in above another, yet if regeneration, the thing itself, and the doctrine of it, goes not on, the church is not increased, nor is there a multiplication of inhabitants of the other world.

CHAPTER II.

That by spirit, John iii. 5, is not meant the indwelling of the Spirit.—Nor that, in the new birth, the Holy Ghost produceth in us the same nature which himself hath.

That which is born of the Spirit is spirit.—JOHN III. 6.

You have here the thing begotten in us by the Spirit of God at the new birth, set forth in the whole and the general nature of it, expressing what is most sublime in it.   It is spirit, which denotes the supremest kind of being. I say in the whole nature of it, that which is born of the Spirit is spirit. It is all, and the whole of it, spiritual, and this gives us a general nature common to all the parts of the new birth.   All, and every grace, though diversified by the special objects they are exercised about, yet agree in this common and general nature that they are spirit, or spiritual graces.   Sorrow for sin, and humiliation, is such a sight and sense of sin as is spiritual. And thus justifying faith is a spiritual faith in all the acts of it.

1. Let us inquire what is meant by *spirit* here, by considering what it is not.

(1.) It is not the communication of the Holy Spirit himself which is here meant, for though, indeed, he himself is given to us as the author of our regeneration, and though himself dwelleth in us immediately, and not by his graces only (as I have before proved), yet the giving of and the indwelling of the Holy Ghost in us, is in no wise to be termed our being born o' the Spirit, nor is it anywhere in Scripture so styled.   Our being born of the Spirit notes out an effect or work of the Spirit in us, as that which is born of another is, and as the conception of the human nature of Christ is said to be of the Holy Ghost, Mat. i. 18, 19.

(2.) It is not the begetting of a nature or being, the same that the Spirit himself is of.   It is not a communication of the Godhead to us, making us ' God of God' (as some have blasphemed), nor ' Spirit of Spirit' ; in which sense Christ's Godhead is termed *Spirit* (Heb. ix. 14), and ' very God of very God.'   But this spiritual nature in us is not a spark of the divine nature struck or shot forth unto our souls.   But it is, for the kind of it, a creature which is for ever distinct from the Deity, as the apostle severs them, Rom. ix. 5, when he speaks of God as ' blessed for evermore.'   And indeed the Godhead in the indivisible whole of it is eternal, Rom. i. 20, but this spirit, or spiritual nature (of which we are now speaking), is born in time, for it is produced after a man's having been first born flesh.   And besides, it is not only styled a creature, but the new creature ; and therefore if it were the divine nature, or God, there would be as many new gods as there are men regenerate.

2. We are now to consider what this spirit, which is born of the Spirit, is. One way and a sure one is to conceive of it by the opposite to it, and which is set by it on purpose to explain it : ' That which is born of the flesh is flesh,' saith Christ.

Now, what is flesh in Scripture sense, as it is opposed unto the new creature ? It is plainly not the substance of a man's nature, or any other substance a man is transformed into, but the corruption, the natural sinfulness and defilement of man's nature. And therefore ' the spirit,' or that which is born of the Spirit, is in its kind and proportion to be understood in like manner. I shall not name many places, but only one which is apposite : in Gal. v. 17, ' The flesh lusteth against the spirit, and the spirit against the flesh : and these are contrary the one to the other : so as you cannot do the things you would.' That by flesh here, he means not the essence or substance of man's nature, much less as created by God, is evident ; because, in ver. 19–21, he says, ' The works of the flesh are manifest ; adultery, fornication, uncleanness, wantonness, idolatry, witchcraft, hatred, and such like : whereof I tell you,' says he, ' that they which do such things shall not inherit the kingdom of God.' What is meant therefore, is man's corrupt, degenerate nature : the ' old man' which is said to be ' corrupt through deceitful lusts,' Eph. iv. 22. And as all men are born flesh, they are in the flesh (Rom. viii. 8) until born again.

Now together with this he represents the contrary principle of spirit in a regenerate man, whereof the one lusting after the spirit, the other after the contrary, even before the consent of man's will, they distract the will of a man, so as he ' cannot do what he would.' Now then hereby two inherent principles in a regenerate man's nature must necessarily be denoted.

(1.) For as the flesh (which all acknowledge to be man's nature by birth) ' lusts against the spirit ; ' so the spirit is in like manner said to ' lust against the flesh.' And this naturally, for it is before a consent of the will one way or other, as well as after such consent. Now to lust (one way or other) is the proper and immediate product of the inward inclinations of a man's heart and nature. And from these principles, as inherent in our nature, each of these lustings draw the will several, yea, contrary ways. They work a contrariety of will in us also : ' You cannot do what you would.' And therefore *spirit* must be understood to be a principle in man's nature, as well as flesh or corruption is.

Neither must it be said that the Holy Ghost is that spirit that lusts in us, in the like manner as the flesh doth lust against the spirit. He may be said to work in us indeed this lusting against the flesh, as he is said to make intercession for us in stirring up groans in us, &c., Rom. viii. 27, yet so as we are said to groan and pray. So here to lust against the flesh is our act, and not the Holy Ghost's ; and therefore is from a principle opposite to flesh in our souls, and inherent in us as flesh is, and so made a contrary nature in us unto that flesh.

(2.) These two are said to be contrary, and therefore are as two contrary qualities in man's nature. For qualities only, not substances, are contrary. And if then flesh be such that lusts after evil, then spirit is also such that lusteth after good. These are as heat and cold, sickness and health, in the same subject, stirring and acting one against the other.

(3.) They are to this purpose compared unto two roots or seminal principles seated in the soul, producing contrary effects and fruits. For he says, ver. 22, ' But the fruit of the Spirit' (mark that allusion) ' is love, peace, joy, long-suffering, gentleness, goodness, faith, meekness, temperance;' whenas he says on the contrary, 'The works of the flesh,' the fruits of the flesh, 'are envyings, murders, wrath, strife,' &c. And this place alone is sufficient to confute those that would have the Holy Ghost's indwelling only, without his working, an inherent root or principle of grace, by which all acts of holiness should become properly ours subjectively, as well as his sufficiently,* as he alone acteth that grace in us to bring forth every good work.

Obj. Those of the forementioned high-flown persuasion will interpose here, that flesh in Scripture is put for the whole of man's nature, substance, and excellencies of any kind ; yea, and the whole creation is denominated flesh, and so even man's pure nature, as it was at first created in Adam, and all the glories of it are termed flesh. He was a fleshly, earthly man. And therefore not only corrupt nature, but all those holy qualities created in Adam at first, or that is of the like created nature or rank, though never so excellent above them, are here to be understood by *spirit.* For else that which you call *spirit* (say they) is still indeed but flesh, as the whole creation, whether new or old, is to be accounted.

I thus answer the objection.

Ans. 1. Be it so, that *flesh* imports in some scriptures all created excellencies in their utmost perfection; yet in this text, and multitudes of others throughout the New Testament, it is taken not in that general notion, but strictly for the degeneration of man's nature by the fall, conveyed by generation fleshly; out of which, if man's nature be not restored by a new birth spiritual, he is eternally lost. Well then in this place, and the other places now cited, *flesh* is strictly taken for that corruption of man's nature, and *spirit* likewise oppositely for the principle restored in it, contrary thereunto. For it is that flesh that is destroyed by this spirit, as it is contrary.

Ans. 2. It is true that the best and highest excellencies of Adam's nature were but flesh, taken as compared with the nature of God himself. I can give you scriptures that even the human nature of Christ, which was the glory, the head, the sum of the whole creation, old and new, is but flesh, with all its prerogatives ; yea, and profits nothing, as in opposition to the Godhead in him. What else is the meaning of John vi. 63, 'The flesh profiteth nothing, it is the Spirit that quickeneth'? And further, that in respect of glorying in God's presence, all the grace in a renewed man, termed *spirit* here, is but *flesh* in that respect, and comes within the compass of that saying, 1 Cor. i. 29, 'That no flesh should glory in his presence.' For when he adds, 'For of him are ye in Christ Jesus, who is made wisdom, righteousness, sanctification, redemption,' he there instancing not only in all the glorious graces that are wrought in us, as wisdom and sanctification, but also all the benefits bestowed upon us, as justification and the glory of heaven itself, expressed by redemption, he doth thereby plainly call all these flesh, as in themselves considered, and as they are excellencies for us to glory in ; the glory of which God hath in that respect robbed them of and deflowered, forasmuch as God hath made Christ all these to us, which otherwise in themselves would be but flesh in us, as the old creation at first was. And God doth this that so we might in all these glory in the Lord only, and not so much in them thus given us.

Our souls, by Christ's restauration of them, do remain created substances still. He doth not transubstantiate them into the being of the divine nature. And when it is said, 'He brings things that are unto nought,' or nothing, his meaning is not that God destroys them in respect of their being or

* Qu. 'efficiently'?—ED.

existence; they must have that still. For if by flesh were meant all that is created by God, differing from himself, then the substance of the soul, yea, the whole of the man, would be destroyed by grace, so there would be no subject left capable of having this spirit begotten in it; no, nor would salvation be the salvation of our souls. If they say there is some new thing created in the room thereof, which they would call spirit, yet still concerning that new thing I ask (1.), Either it is a creature made by God, and distinct from him, and then I urge upon them it is flesh, even as well as the former soul; for in comparison unto God, so it is, and still within the same sphere and rank of beings that are created. Or (2.) it is God and the Godhead. If that be their meaning, let them but say so; but then I will not argue it, but rend my garments. And the truth is, they can mean no other thing, if they will speak otherwise, of these things than we do.

Ans. 3. The third answer to the objection made is this. I grant that this new spirit, begotten of the Spirit, is of a more divine temper, genius, and aspirement than the image of God in Adam was, which though holy, yet but in a natural way; in knowing God in and by the creatures, and by the covenant of works, and so only according unto what is naturally due unto a creature reasonable, as he first falls out of the hands of his maker. And I should not only grant that this new divine nature, born of the Spirit, is supernatural, in comparison to corrupt nature and the dispositions thereof, but also in comparison of pure nature. Insomuch as Adam was but an earthly, natural man, comparatively to that which is born of the Spirit, which is the image of the heavenly, and is ordained in the end to see God in himself, and will be raised up thereto; and at present hath such a way of knowing and enjoying God, and such objects spiritual suited to it, as Adam's state was not capable of. Now therefore, although all the old and new creation are flesh to God, as was said, yet the new being of our highest aspirement may be termed spirit in comparison of its fellow-creatures; and so this new creature, in regeneration wrought, may perhaps be styled, in comparison of Adam's image.

The *use* of all in brief is this, that men should take heed of being seduced and drawn into opinions, under the pretence and allurement of still more spiritualness, and spiritualising still all that the Scripture says, or can be said of true spiritualness, till they lose all spiritualness. It may be truly said that many that seemed to begin soberly in the Spirit, whilst they have affected to go still a note higher than the gospel allots unto the creature, as the portion of it, intruding into things they have not seen, they have in the end come round, and ended in the flesh, even where they were before they did begin. You must not think to spiritualise the soul of man beyond what can consist with its being a creature, and beyond what, in a lower rank of union with God, than Christ hath, it can bear. The nature of things must not be destroyed, God must alone be God, and that eternal Spirit. The soul must be the soul, enjoying God as such, remaining distinct from him; then attribute what spiritualness you can, lower than what Christ and the eternal Spirit is said to have, as being God, and the Son of God. And also withal stay but a while to have that addition of grace and glory, which our doctrine gives and proclaims to spirits made perfect in heaven, where God is all in all; and yet still he and the creature are distinct, though the glorified creature enjoys a fulness and immediateness of knowledge in him, as in himself, face to face, and in a love raised up and proportioned thereto. These distances being kept, let men urge what spiritualness they can, and our doctrine will rise as high as they can do; yea (which is the glory of our doctrine), they cannot speak beyond it, but are forced to cant their own wild notes in our expressions. If men will go higher, it falls out here as with chemists, going about to seek further spirits out of spirits already extracted, out of wine or metals sublimated as much as the things will bear. In seeking to sublimate them yet further, in the end they all vanish, and all ends in smoke.

So then, that which is spirit here, is metaphrased elsewhere by Paul 1 Cor. ii. 15, and is all one as to say, 'That which is born of the Spirit is spirit,' and that the soul of a man born again is spiritualised ὁ πνευματικὸς, that is, a spiritual man, and thereby fitted to receive and take in (as the word v. 14 is), τὰ πνευματικὰ, spiritual things, πνευματικῶς, spiritually, or as spiritual.

CHAPTER III.

That by ' spirit,' John iii. 6, is meant all those gracious dispositions in the soul, which do suit it unto things spiritual, as spiritual.

I now come to the explanation of the thing itself, in the general nature of it, what is meant by *spirit*.

I give this distinction of it. *Spirit* is all those gracious and heavenly dispositions and habiliments wrought in the whole soul, especially the spirit of the mind, which do elevate and raise it, fit and suit it unto things spiritual, as spiritual. I shall give you an account of this definition, as it is extracted and drawn out of the import of the very word *spirit* : and then come to the examination of it in several particulars.

1. In the general common nature of it, I term it a new *disposition* or temper of spirit. The acceptation and use of the word in the general in Scripture, warrants the word *spirit* being put to import a disposition or temper of a man's heart, whether it be applied to what is good or bad therein. 'The spirit that dwells in us,' saith James, ' lusteth to envy,' James iv. 5. He termeth the very inclination and disposition to envy, that is natural in us, the *spirit* that is in us ; although again, in respect of its corruption, it be flesh and fleshly. So Luke ix. 55, Christ rebuking James and John for their zealous wishing that fire might devour those of that city that did not receive Christ, speaks thus, ' You know not what spirit you are of ;' that is, what fiery disposition is in your hearts, which you have declared by this wish. Thus too an inclination to whoredom is termed ' a spirit of whoredom,' Hosea iv. 12 ; a jealous disposition, ' a spirit of jealousy,' Num. v. 14. On the contrary, dispositions unto what is good are in like manner termed spirit, ' the spirit of meekness,' Gal. vi. 1 ; ' the spirit of love and fear,' 2 Tim. i. 7. As also any habiliment that elevates and enables the understanding to discern the difference of things spiritual (as acquired habits, by reason of use, are said to do, Heb. v. 14), is denominated spirit, Isa. xi. 2, 3, ' The spirit of wisdom and of the fear of the Lord shall rest upon him, and make him quick of understanding in the fear of the Lord.' So as if you would run over all graces particularly, they are heavenly and divine principles put into the soul, and each faculty of it carrying it forth to such and such spiritual actings towards such or such spiritual objects, Zech. xii. 10. A ' spirit of prayer, of supplication, and of grace,' that is, to seek after grace and the favour of God ; and the same may be said of all other graces whatever.

2. I add, *gracious dispositions*, to distinguish this work of the Spirit from

gifts ; which though common to reprobates, yet we find them called spiritual gifts, 1 Cor. xiv. 1 ; which in the 12th and 13th chapters he distinguisheth from graces, true love to God and the saints, &c. Thus also when the apostle James (James iv. 9, 10), had said, ' The spirit that is in us lusteth after envy,' he adds these words, ' but God gives more grace,' *i. e.*, a contrary spirit of grace to overcome it. It is there termed in the opposition grace ; it is therefore a gracious disposition. The abilities of mind are termed gifts, χαρίσματα, because freely given ; and spiritual, because they empower the mind to take in the notion of spiritual truths, so far as to do good to others, but not to a man's own soul savingly, which grace doth. True knowledge hath *vim plasticam* in it, a formative virtue. Neither do these gifts raise up the mind to things spiritual, as spiritual, which is the great difference to be attended in this matter.

3. I call it *heavenly*, that is, which is wholly divine, and carries the soul up to, and fits it for things heavenly. Adam, 1 Cor. xv. 47, 48, is in his best estate termed an earthly man. It is evident by the saying, which the apostle cites out of Genesis, that he speaks of him and his graces when first create l But God hath fitted and prepared for this spiritual man (of whom we speak), things heavenly, far above the reach of Adam's estate. I observe, Eph. i. 3, that the apostle, when he speaks of the whole lump of blessings with which in Christ we are blessed, termeth all and the whole of them ' spiritual blessings in heavenly things,' say I, and not ' places' only ; and such Adam's were not. And the reason is, because these are all blessings in Christ, who alone is that heavenly man, the Lord from heaven, 1 Cor. xv. 47, 48 ; but Adam but an earthly man ; and so Christ alone is the founder of spiritual blessings in heavenly things ; and therefore this spirit coming from him, the quickening Spirit (as Christ is there termed, in opposition to Adam's being but a living soul, ver. 45), is wholly heaven-born, is an optic glass, set to the eye to see into things heavenly, which Adam's sight fell short of. *Spirit* here, is the foundation and beginning of all those glorious enjoyments of God in the other world, and shall be raised up thereto. And in this life the spiritual man hath an aspirement thereunto, and could never be satisfied without it. And in this life, where this spiritual and heavenly temper completes no degrees, as Adam's primitive holiness of nature was, it would raise a man up to infinitely higher proportions of communion with God and active holiness than Adam's state was capable of. But, alas ! our life here is hid with Christ in God, through our imperfection and the like. And indeed this very word *spirit*,—' That which is born of the Spirit is spirit,'—speaks a sublimated work, the most refined and most raised work that man's heart in this life is capable of. For the extract, the quintessence of things (leaving the gross parts behind them as severed), you still call spirits. I need not give you chemical instances. Also in the creation, those things which are of the highest rank, strength, and excellency, and nearest God himself in their natures, are termed spirits : —' Who maketh his angels spirits,' Heb. i. 7.—And the substance of his own pure nature is set out by this, ' God is a Spirit,' John iv. 24. Yea, take an estimate from hell: the height, the quintessence of all wickedness, is, as you know, found in the devils ; and how is it expressed ? It is named ' spiritual wickedness,' Eph. vi. 12. And they are elsewhere termed ' wicked spirits,' Mat. xii. 45, because the substance of their nature or being is spirit, and they are filled with wickedness. But here the wickedness they are filled with is further termed spiritual ; that is, it is a wickedness of the highest kind, which exerciseth itself in opposing and contra-

dicting things heavenly, as it follows there about things heavenly, which are the things this spirit (in the text John iii.), is raised unto, and contends for, and aspires after ; and therefore as their wickedness is termed spiritual, so the nature of this is termed spirit or spiritual, as pursuing after those very things heavenly, which their wickedness sets itself against.

4. These heavenly dispositions have for their seat the spirit of a man. This is the immediate subject in which it resides, in which it was chiefly and first implanted, and from thence diffused to the whole man, and so is justly denominated spirit from its subject, the very spirit, quintessence, and centre of the soul: Eph. iv. 22, 23, ' Be renewed in the spirit of your minds,' by infusing into it spiritual principles of heavenly light and dis-positions. The new man is there said to be put on. And to the same purpose speaks the apostle, 1 Thess. v. 23, ' The God of peace sanctify you throughout,' or wholly, ' your whole spirit, soul, and body.' Body is the exterior part, and soul is the inward part, of senses, affections, &c. But spirit is the top, the highest region of the mind, which is capable of a higher intuition of things spiritual ; and this is sanctified first and chiefly, and therefore first named, and the sanctification hereof is termed spirit. The seat of the powerful workings of sin, and of the first suggestion usually thereunto, is the lower faculties, which entice and allure, and propound the pleasures of themselves to the will and affections ; which, being corrupt, and knowing no better, yield, and approve them suitable to the outward man ; and therefore it is termed the law of the members. But the work-ings of grace are perfectly contrary. The seat of grace and its chief dominion is the spirit of the mind, termed therefore ' the inner man,' ' the hidden man,' ' the law of the mind ;' which, giving forth laws and impres-sions to the outward, rules and commands it. And because the strength that must sway the man lies there, therefore it meets with more difficulties than the dominion of sin doth, for it hath all the affections to subdue by spiritual light and fresh comings in from heaven.

CHAPTER IV.

What it is to have the heart elevated and suited to all things spiritual, as spiritual.

But the last and main thing in this definition to be most attended unto is, what it is to have the heart elevated and suited unto all things spiritual, as spiritual.

There are three things to be inquired into for the explanation hereof.

1. What those things are which are spiritual.

2. What it is to have the heart suited to these spiritual things.

3. An account why this should be added, ' To spiritual things *as spiri-tual.*'

1. What are things spiritual ? It needs not long be insisted on. The particulars are become known to us all, if we have hearts unto them : they are the things of God, which the Spirit reveals, ' the deep things of God,' 1 Cor. ii. 10, 14, and Rom. viii. 7. They are things of the Spirit, Rom. viii. 5. They are another world or system of things, opposed to things of the flesh, which flesh, or corrupt nature, is suited unto, which are mani-festly fruits of the flesh, Gal. v. 19, downright sins, or things of this world, abused by our lusts, 1 John ii. 16.

(1.) First and primarily, God himself and Christ are the chiefest spiritual things and blessings. They are the first original of all things spiritual, and so are the most spiritual, and have all and only true spiritualness in them. 'God is a Spirit;' it is his pure nature so to be, and therefore he is to be worshipped in spirit by us. Even as it is said, 'God is holy, therefore be ye holy;' so God is Spirit, therefore be ye spiritual. And therefore all things else are spiritual as they refer unto him. As God only is good (as Christ says), so God only is Spirit; and as the sun only is light, so God only is the Father of all light that is truly heavenly; God is the measure, the standard of all things spiritual. And thus also Christ, who is styled 'The Lord,' is also said to be 'that Spirit' (2 Cor. iii. 17) who puts all the spiritualness that is in the gospel into our minds.

(2.) There are things that are spiritual derivatively from God and Christ, which are the things of God, and which are not otherwise, no, nor further spiritual, than as they relate unto God and Christ, and partake of them, and redound to their glory, who is the measure of them. And of this distinction we shall have great use in the sequel; for in all the benefits bestowed in our salvation, there is no further a spiritualness to be found than as God shines in them, and his excellence and glory are illustrious. And that, and that alone puts every other thing into the being and rank of things spiritual.

[1.] All blessings, adoption, forgiveness, redemption, fellowship with God, and heaven itself, are termed spiritual blessings, Eph. i. 3, 'Blessed be the God and Father of our Lord Jesus Christ, who hath blessed us with all spiritual blessings in heavenly places in Christ;' and these blessings consist not in houses, lands, &c., but in things heavenly.

[2.] Thus all graces of the Spirit are also spiritual. Col. i. 9, true saving knowledge is styled σύνεσις πνευματική, 'spiritual understanding.'

[3.] All the immediate duties of God's worship, when God is worshipped in spirit in them, are termed spiritual. Prayer, hearing, &c., all are termed 'spiritual sacrifices,' 1 Pet. ii. 5, which become such, so far as God is sanctified and closed withal in them and by them.

[4.] Every duty of the moral law, as it is directed unto God, is a service in spirit, Rom. vii. 6. And the whole moral law, and every particle of it, in this right tendency, is spiritual, Rom. vii. 14, 'The law is spiritual.'

2. What is it to have the heart made suitable to these spiritual things?

You all know, by analogy from nature, what it is to have the soul, in the powers and faculties of it, suited unto the object of it; as the eye is suited and fitted to colour, and the ear unto sounds. I shall give you some philosophical instances which the Scripture makes, Eccles. xi. 7, 'Truly the light' (saith Solomon) 'is sweet, and a pleasant thing it is to behold the sun.' Here is a heavenly outward object, and the visive or seeing faculty, declared suited or fitted one to the other. The apostle Paul also (1 Cor. vi. 13) speaking of the present condition of the bodies of men, 'The belly' (says he) 'is for meats, and meats for the belly;' that is, they are by God suited and fitted one for another in this present state. And consider the purpose of his mentioning this. It is to illustrate how in a proportionable manner, and in a spiritual way, even the bodies of men after the resurrection, when they shall be made spiritual, 1 Cor. xv., shall then be suited unto Christ, so it follows, ver. 14, 'And God hath both raised up the Lord, and will also raise us up by his own power.' And it is said too, in ver. 17, 'He that is joined to the Lord is one spirit.' Now then to make up the analogy, as he will suit spiritual senses to spiritual things after the resurrection, so he doth suit men's souls and spirits aforehand in this life unto the spiritual things manifested in the word, afore the resurrection of body and soul into a greater glory. And this the Scriptures also speak as expressly to this point of regeneration or grace, as it doth to that other point of nature : 1 Cor. ii. 9, ' Eye hath not seen, nor ear heard, nor hath it entered into the heart of man, the things which God hath prepared for them that love him.' The things prepared, &c., are manifestly here the things of the gospel in this life revealed, and not only those in the world to come, as by the context hath been long since observed. And the only use at present I make lies in these words, ' Prepared for those that love him ;' that is, aforehand suited and fitted by God unto the new creature, or unto those into whose hearts he puts his love. And if it be not an allusion intended by the apostle, yet it may well be represented by the correspond-ency that is between the story of the first creation and the new creature, which the apostle intends by those who love God. The apostle in those words of his, ' As it is written,' refers us to Isa. lxiv. 4, ' Since the beginning of the world, men have not heard, neither perceived by the ear, neither hath the eye seen,' &c. Now consult the story of man's first crea-tion, to which this is a manifest allusion, and it stood thus. God made and prepared a world consisting of, and filled with, variety of creatures, the making of which cost him six days' work. There were delicacies of fruits for the taste, an entertainment for the eye in all sorts of colours, light, ornaments, and tapestry, which heaven and earth affordeth to this day. There was a brave world, and richly furnished, as the apostle speaks of it, 1 Tim. vi. The angels stood by, and wondered all the while for whom all this should be prepared, for they had not senses to be affected with them. God after all, at the latter end of this his work, brings in man, and sets Adam down in the centre of this world ; and lo, he had at the first of his creation an eye to see and to be taken with all the beauties God had scattered up and down throughout the whole. He had an ear to hear all the music which the melodies of birds singing, or the murmurings and warblings of rivulets, could afford. He had a taste and belly suited to take pleasure in all these varieties of fruits, or whatever else God had provided as a banquet for him ; insomuch as there was not any one thing God had made but he had some sense, inward or outward, to take in a pleasure from it, or some faculty in his mind to close with and make use of it. Whence it was apparent unto himself and the angels, the spectators, that God had first prepared and set out all these for the man, and then created the man, in like manner prepared and fitted for all these things. He had an ear and an eye (as both the prophet's and apostle's words are) to receive and take in what was thus made for him. Thus the apostle tells us it falls out in this new creation, God hath been from everlasting contriving and ordaining, and in the fulness of time preparing, all those glorious truths and things which the apostle (to whom was committed the news and tidings of this world to come, Heb. ii. 5) by the Holy Ghost, have given us in their writ-ings a full discovery of. And whenever God regenerateth any man, and constitutes him a new creature, lo, the man hath a new eye to see, an ear to hear, and all sorts of new senses to take in all sorts of spiritual things, as the Spirit shall be pleased to reveal them to him. He no sooner opens an eye but he finds himself to be come into a new world, and to be environed with new objects. Thus they are prepared for him, and he for them ; and hence it comes to pass that he hath an eye to see, and an ear to hear, and a heart to understand, such things as never from the beginning of this world entered into the heart of man, no, not of Adam in his first creation. Now the principle by which he is enabled to this, is called *spirit*.

If you will have another scripture that speaks this suitableness between this spiritual man and these ' spiritual things,' look into Rom. viii. 5, ' Those that are after the flesh, do mind the things of the flesh ; but they that are after the Spirit, the things of the Spirit.' You have here the suitableness between spiritual things and a spiritual man illustrated by its contrary, namely, the like of a carnal heart towards carnal things, that so all men, whether carnal or spiritual, might be equal and just judges out of experience, whether they had as yet flesh only, or further, spirit, begun in them ; for all mankind have experience what it is to mind, to favour, and find a heart suited to things fleshly and outward. We feel every day how our bowels work, and our affections are inflamed after things fleshly, as beauty, pleasure, &c. Now, says he, descend into your hearts, and be righteous judges ; if ye be after the Spirit, if that supernatural frame of heart be in you and predominant, you will in like manner be taken with the things of the Spirit, for both stand upon like just and equal reason ; for as flesh is suited unto things fleshly, so Spirit is suited unto things spiritual, even as it is here, John iii., ' That which is born of the flesh is flesh,' so ' that which is born of the Spirit is spirit.'

CHAPTER V.

That this suitableness of the mind to spiritual things, is the great distinguish-
ing character of one that is ' born of the Spirit,' John iii. 5, from others
who are not so.

3. I shall now give an account why I put in this restriction, ' a suitableness of the heart unto spiritual things, *as spiritual*.' The truth is, herein lies the spirit, or the formal constitution and difference of that which is here termed spirit. The meaning whereof is, that spiritual things are to be considered barely and merely as they are in themselves and their own nature, abstracted from all other considerations and concomitants adherent to them, and abstracted from such benefits as are accidental, external, and foreign to them. Spiritual things may indeed be viewed as wrapt up in worldly conveniences, the avoidance of punishment, or the obtaining something which a man apprehends good to him, which occurs by them or with them. But spiritual things, as spiritual, are the things themselves, which are represented in their own real nature, in their native hue and proper colours to a spiritual man.

(1.) In other things, the formal reason of any objects is that which puts the difference between sciences and arts, yea, and the senses. Bodies natural are the subjects of a multitude of arts and sciences; but take it as a natural body, and simply so considered, it is the proper subject of philosophy, and makes an essential difference between that and other knowledge. So it is here ; spiritual things are the proper objects of that true, genuine, heaven-born spirit, begotten by regeneration.

(2.) The apostle is my warrant for putting in this distinction; for he sets this fatal and eternal difference between a natural man and a spiritual man : 1 Cor. ii. 14, 15, ' But the natural man receiveth not the things of the Spirit of God : for they are foolishness unto him : neither can he know

them, because they are spiritually discerned.   But he that is spiritual judgeth all things, yet he himself is judged of no man.'   To say, 'because they
are spiritually discerned,' and to give this as the reason why a natural man
cannot therefore receive them, is all one as to say, that if they be rightly
discerned, they must be discerned in their spirituality ; that is, as they are in
themselves spiritual, *as spiritual*.   Thus the soul, whilst in the body, cannot
see or discern the angels that daily attend us, nor the devils that hourly
tempt us.   Why ?   Because they are spirits, and are spiritually to be discerned, and so can be viewed only by naked spirits like themselves.   They
may be seen if they will thicken and condensate the air, or take a shape,
enclose themselves in a body : but still as spirits, and in their own substance and nature, they are discerned by none but those of their kind.   And
(as he here speaks of a spiritual man, ver. 15) they can see all we do, but
themselves are not discerned by us ; we see not their motion nor their actings.   I know this similitude, as none other, will hold in all ; for our soul,
stripped of our flesh, would thus see angels ; but not so an unregenerate
man, he would not discern spiritual things though he were stripped of flesh,
if he was not also spiritualised.   And by this natural man is not barely
understood a sensual man, sensual for lusts and bodily pleasures, but a
man endowed with the greatest gifts of knowledge and wisdom, such as
were the scribes and pharisees, and the disputers of this world, 1 Cor. i.
7, 8, 20.   And for the discerning of these things spiritually, a man must
not simply have the Spirit of God to reveal them objectively (vers. 10–12),
but he must subjectively be made by that Spirit a spiritual man, and have
spiritual senses given him, else, though the Spirit should reveal them, he
could not receive them.   ' The natural man receives not the things of the
Spirit of God ;' for *quicquid recipitur, recipitur ad modum recipientis*.   As
a blind eye receives not the light of the sun, ' neither can he know them ' ;
which words speak an impotency or an incapacity in the subject ; for there
is a disproportion between the objects, take them in their spiritual nature,
and the subject.   ' For,' says he, ' they are spiritually discerned ;' and
therefore the man must be made spiritual, or he cannot take them in ; as
a beast must be made rational, ere he can understand or take in the things
of a man.   That look, as now this natural body of ours (as, 1 Cor. xv., the
apostle calls it), cannot discern an angel or spirit, as he is a spirit ; but
when God shall make his natural body a spiritual body (which how he will
do it, we know not), then we shall see angels and spirits, even as we are
seen of them ; but a spiritual body it must be made first.   So it is, a man
must be spiritual before he can see spiritual things.

   (3.) A third ground why I say that a spiritual man must discern spiritual
things as spiritual, is, because he otherwise receives not the things at all,
which the apostle hints.   This is a great truth, that if the soul of a man
does not arrive at, and close with, and embrace the things themselves, as
they are in themselves and in their own nature, it knows them not, it receives them not at all ; but only ideas and notions, shadows and clouds,
instead of them.   God will be known as God, and glorified as God (Rom.
i. 21), or he accounts it no knowledge.   Then we know and affect things
as they are, when our knowledge and affections towards them are such as
the nature of the things requires.   If the knowledge of Christ in my heart
be not answerable, similar to what is in the thing itself, I do not know it ;
as I am not said to know a man, if I know him but by hearsay, or have
seen but his picture.   And therefore the apostle distinguisheth as I do ;
Eph. iv. 21, ' If you have been taught as the truth is in Jesus ;' that is,

to know Christ in himself, and the truths about him, which are beams of him, as they are in their true and naked hue. Thus also affections to any thing or person is not true love, or a genuine affection, if it be not suited and carried out to the thing and the person itself; you call it harlotry love else; lust, not love. And therefore, of necessity, if our knowledge of spiritual things be true, and such as it ought to be, if our affections unto them be genuine, our hearts must be suited to the thing as spiritual. Yea, otherwise the things, whatever they are in themselves, do become to us but ' things of the flesh,' as the law was to the carnal Jew, and all spiritual privileges are to an unregenerate professor.

4. This is the great difference or constitutive distinction of men regene-rate from the unregenerate, though never so much enlightened, elevated to the tasting of the powers of the world to come. Those that are truly re-newed are made spirit, or spiritual in all things ; so not the other. Al-though raised up and elevated to be exercised about things spiritual, yet not about the spirituality of the things, and to be carried out to them as such. This will appear in the particulars of the work of grace all along. There is a carnality about spiritual objects, else the apostle would never have termed the Corinthians carnal, in comparison of other Christians, and not spiritual, 1 Cor. iii. 1. Now that which was in a great measure re-maining in them, is predominantly in temporary believers. It is in them as that which constitutes their estate, without any genuine principle of spirit at all. It is nowhere said of any temporary believer, or person that fell away, that he was born again, nor is it anywhere said of any such that they are spiritual men, or begotten of the Spirit.

The main *use* I intend is of examination of our estates, whether we are savingly regenerate or not ? Consider what the frame, the posture, the vergency, your spirits are of unto things that are spiritual, as spiritual. I speak now only unto men that are or have been some way or other affected with things spiritual ; for as for such as are not, but live wholly in things earthly and sensual, such need not a jury to pass upon them to condemn them. Towards our help in this examination, let us take these two things.

1. Take instances of several particulars of spiritual things, and search-ing out wherein the spiritualness of them lies, bring them and your hearts together, to put you upon considering how your hearts and they agree and suit each other.

(1.) Learn to understand in your own hearts what these two things mean, and what a vast difference is between them. 1. To have heavenly natural dispositions and inclination suiting the heart to things spiritual, as spiritual ; and, 2d, To have accidental and forced elevations or stirrings of heart towards things spiritual, and those but upon considerations that are but accidental to the things, or are but appurtenances of them, attendants and hang-byes to them, and are not of the nature of the things themselves.

You will ask me, What do you account but accidental affections in men's hearts to things spiritual ; and what is it that is accidental in the things themselves ?

[1.] That is but an accidental affection in the heart itself, which is forced and strained in respect of what the whole stream of thy heart other-wise doth naturally carry thee forth unto ; whereas that which is born of the flesh doth wholly and naturally mind and savour nothing but what is earthly, worldly, &c., Rom. viii. 5, and the whole propension and *pondus* thereof would of itself for ever run that way ; yet so as look, as streams that naturally run but one way, yet are capable of a turn, and to be diverted a contrary way by winds, or stoppage, or the overflowings of waters, &c., without having a new and natural spring or fountain to feed and carry it on that contrary current: so the natural mind may sometime flow in another current than that in which its own inclinations carry it. But now the apostle Peter, speaking of the hearts of men regenerate, expresseth it thus, 1 Pet. v. 2 : that what they did was ' not out of constraint, but willingly, and out of a ready mind.' The great and predominant principle in us is self-love; it is the spirit, the quintessence, of original sin. Now this spring or fountain of all lusts in us naturally cuts forth a channel to itself only towards things earthly; and the poise of it (as it is the predominant principle in man's nature, as by nature it is) doth lie clean another way than to fall in at all with any of the things which are spiritual, or to have anything to do with them; but it secretly and closely enjoys itself in cleaving and adhering unto things earthly and sinful; yet so as if it be stormed with the noise and conviction of the things of the other world, as with what is the dreadful consequent of sin, viz., wrath and destruction, and of what is the deliverance out of it, even to leave sin, to seek after pardon, &c., the enlightenings of these things coming powerfully in upon self-love in men, that other natural stream and current to things earthly may be stopped, yea, and (as is said of Jordan) turned backwards, and the affections run that way; and yet all this be but accidental and violent, in respect unto the natural tendency thereof, which remains still one and the same.

[2.] There are answerably also accidental or consequential respects or considerations that are but appendixes to things which in themselves are the most spiritual, which are foreign and extrinsecal to the things, and yet are revealed in the word together with those things, with the apprehension of which a natural man, that hath nothing in him but only self-love, may be stirred, moved, and affected. As take sin for one instance : there is the evil of sin as sin; that is, the spiritual evil in it as spiritual, and as it is contrary to God; and there is the wrath of God, &c., which is the consequent of sin, that is an accidental evil to it, as it is sin. As there is the charcoal in its foulness, and there is the fire in the coal, likewise there is Christ's righteousness as it is a satisfaction to God for sin, and the glorious way of saving sinners by it, above all ways else, this is the spiritualness of it; and there is the freedom from that wrath thereby; the one is the thing in itself, the other is the consequent or accidental appendix of it. Now (you know) like will still find out its like, suit and consort with it. Hence my exhortation is, that you would, in searching yourselves, narrowly observe what your spirit doth match withal; that is, what it is in spiritual things which your hearts are taken with in them, whether with what is accidental chiefly, or chiefly with what is truly spiritual. The apostle hath an expression, 1 Cor. ii. 13, which may allusively help me to convey my meaning, ' comparing' (saith he) ' spiritual things with spiritual.' He speaks there indeed of the delivery of spiritual things to be preached of by us; and it is as if he had said (comparing the words afore and these together), if you be to make orations about things civil, politic, scholastical, then use all your flowers of rhetoric and art to set them out with; for fleshly worldly matters are best dressed up in clothings and ornaments that are suitable to them; but if you be to make sermons, take and seek such words and expressions as may be savoury and spiritual, and so suited to the matter. In like manner (say I, in allusion to it as to the point in hand), if you be to examine your hearts, compare spiritual things with spiritual, or else accidental with accidental; lay things of a sort together; that is, observe what kind of affections in thy heart are stirred, and to what sort or kind of things, and upon what considerations. If, therefore, thy case be such, that only transient and accidental affections are in thy heart (accidental I say to the natural whole current of thy heart), finding out and consorting with the like accidental considerations in things spiritual; here is no genuine true spiritual regeneration, here are but plainly two bastards married, two slips of each family, accidental affections, to accidentals in things spiritual; and their brood will be answerable, they will not inherit with the sons of the free woman, that is, *spirit* here. But, on the contrary, if there be a new spring and fountain set open in thy heart, that works forth itself a natural current and channel contrary to that other, whose poise was to each,* which doth withal find out that in spiritual things which are truly spiritual, suits and complies with the things themselves as in themselves, and pours out its streams upon them and runs into them, here is a noble match between two offsprings of two heaven-born families, which will never be parted, but, as a noble plant, will bring forth fruit unto God, and unto everlasting life.

Another consideration I would premise, as both useful to prevent a mistake in examination of ourselves hereby, and which also ariseth from, and is the natural corollary of this part of my definition, ' suiting the heart to spiritual things.' The premise is this, that the spiritualness of our affecting of spiritual things lies not in a total opposition or exclusion of what suiteth self-love in us, or aiming at our own good; but if it be rightly stated, it takes it in the most naturally that can be. Some good souls, when they hear of such doctrines as these, that spiritual things are to be affected for themselves, and as spiritual, have presently made this interpretation of it, that if the heart be truly spiritual, then it must affect them in opposition to themselves altogether, and to their own good: and that, therefore, they must wholly renounce and cashier all thoughts of a man's self therein, thinking that if they at all intermix them, they do unspiritualise all the rest.

Or when they hear that there is an accidental goodness in spiritual things, which will take self-love in a carnal heart, they then presently judge that therefore true spiritualness lies in this, in having no affection of self-love working or stirring at all to anything in things spiritual. These are both mistakes: and the very terms of this latter part of the definition I have given, duly understood, clears and states this great case, and is preventive of these mistakes. Mark it: it suiteth the heart unto the things; now if the heart be made suitable to the very things themselves, it is certain that a man must and doth at once affect both the things for themselves, and for his own good also. For why? Let the thing be the most spiritual that ever were revealed, wherein doth a man's own good lie, but in the enjoyment of what is comfortable to him, and which he most desires? And what is it that is most comfortable, and yields most content to any man, but the things that are suited to him, and he unto them? If, therefore, the being and end of grace lie in this, to suit the mind to spiritual things themselves, and for themselves, then it must needs most happily fall out and come to pass, that at once in affecting the things in themselves, the believer pursues his own good and happiness.

The general truth of this assertion, that men's comforts, and so that which they account their chiefest good, do lie in the suitableness or frame of their minds as it stands unto the things, is so evident in experience, as I need not insist on it. What is the reason that *trahit sua quemque voluptas,*

* Qu. ' earth '?—ED.

one man is pleased with one thing, another with other things? It lies in the several humours and suitableness of dispositions to such or such things. You use to say, that which is one man's heaven is another man's hell; what otherwise is the reason that carnal men mind the things of the flesh, or earthly things, naturally, but because they are suited to them? Else they have a light within them which tells them they are not the best things. You see in nature it is not every stone, though good and precious, that will draw iron after it, or unto which iron will greedily run or clasp with, but with the loadstone it will; and again, no other metal but that will close with a loadstone. What is the reason? There is a suitableness. Now then, take a carnal heart, and change the inward radical disposition of it, make and render it suitable to God, and Christ, and all other spiritual things as they are in themselves (and the power and efficacy of saving grace must lie in this, or differs not from flesh), and instantly that soul is taught, and hath an instinct for its own good, and greedily and naturally (according to the measure of grace given) runs out unto and after these spiritual things as spiritual, and placeth its happiness and good in them, as truly as ever it did in the other.

You will say, wherein then is the difference between a carnal man's affecting these things, and a spiritual man's doing so? For it is out of self-love in both.

I answer, out of the principles already delivered.

1. That the fundamental and original difference lies not in this, as if that were a carnal heart, that, with respect to its own good, or with love to itself, did affect spiritual things; and on the contrary, he only were truly a spiritual man that did not at all out of self-love affect them. No, God forbid; but that which puts the difference is, what that goodness is, which in spiritual things the heart of a man doth thus affect, and find his good to lie in. If it is only that which is the accident of all goodness, and but the consequent of the other, as ease of conscience, freedom from wrath, judgment, &c., and the man not affected with the things as in themselves, there being no suitableness at all to the things if they could be nakedly represented to him, and in their spiritual hue; this heart is a carnal heart, and thou that wearest it art not a spiritual, but a mere outward and accidental Christian; for, as a man affects, so he is. The usual comparison I give to express the difference between these two is this: take two men, whereof the one is in perfect health and vigour, and as hungry as Esau was when he came out of the field, and take another who is heart-sick; set meat or drink before these two, the one falls to eat it (and that as it is meat) out of appetite and suitableness to the thing in itself; for God hath ordained ' the belly for meats, and meats for the belly.' The other's stomach nauseates the thing simply in itself considered, and the native scent overcomes him. But yet rather than he will die, he will take down something, and yet by his good will he takes that only when it is so sauced as the natural scent is not discerned. So it is here. If God, and Christ, and his righteousness, and the graces of his Spirit, could be represented in their native naked hue, a natural man could not receive them, as the apostle speaks; but take them as dipped and sauced with ease of conscience, hopes of freedom from wrath, &c., carnal men take them down. In a word, they make use of them as physic, not as meat. Here, in this case, a man affects not the thing, hath no mind or suitableness to the thing itself, but to the consequent of it, and a mere accident belonging to it, which is freedom from pains, &c.

2. Another difference is, where only thus the accidental goodness of

spiritual things affects a man, there is self only, or love to a man's self only, that is the root of such affections ; yea, and such a carnal self as of itself would pour out its affections to other things much rather, to which only it hath an inbred suitableness. The whole heart of itself would run that way, and no other, by its good will. But being overpowered by the power of the world to come, there is a stop put to such affections, and the current of them turned another way. But, take a spiritual man, who is in his inward man suited to things spiritual, and spiritually naturalized, or naturally spiritualized to them, and though the accidental considerations might have first moved him (for, alas, at first a man hath no other principle but self-love to be wooed and courted), and in their rank lawfully continue still ; yet he now, being come unto them, and himself spiritualised, he closeth with the things themselves as in themselves, and as best and most excellent, Phil. i. 10. He finds so much in the things themselves, that he wisheth no greater good, yea, no other good, than what ariseth from the things, and from communion with them and enjoyment of them. He finds his good lies in them, which (as was said) ariseth out of a suitableness. So that now the state of the case is not whether thou affectest them out of self-love or for thine own good, yea or no, but whether the things themselves have been made suitable to that inward man, and so withal unto that self in thee. The root of all that which we call hypocrisy, or counterfeit grace, though* wrought by the Spirit, doth lie in this defect, the man hath not a heart to the things, but chiefly to the appurtenances of them, and so is said in Scripture to have ' a heart and a heart,'† and to be a double-minded man, because he pursues not the things for themselves, but for what accompanies them, when all the while, as to the things themselves, he hath a heart against them, if they were represented in their true spiritualness. And this is the true meaning of that phrase ; for otherwise it were far more proper to say of a regenerate man, that he hath had a heart and a heart in him, for he hath really two principles, flesh and spirit : two men, two springs and fountains in him ; of flesh, suited to things fleshly ; of spirit, suited to things spiritual. But yet because his heart is truly suited unto these spirituals, therefore he is said to affect them with his whole heart, and not to have ' a heart and a heart.' But the other in their most overflowing affections, that seem as a land-flood to carry the whole stream that way, as in the people's hearts when the law was given, ' We will ' (say they) ' obey the voice of the Lord.' ' Oh ' (says God), ' that there were such a heart in them ! '

As a corollary from what hath been spoken, I shall a little further enlarge on this question, whether a regenerate man, as such, may and doth affect spiritual things for his own good, and how far ? Briefly,

1. Take self-love, as it is a natural principle, and annexed to being or entity itself, if grace will have a subject to reside in, it must have this for part of it, for it is the adjunct of being. If you think to spiritualise your affections so far as nothing of love to yourselves should remain, then you must destroy the subject of those affections. If you cut off this nail entirely, you cut off the finger too. Pare it you may, and must, as to the inordinacy of it ; thus to the captive woman taken to wife was done by the law, Deut. xxi. 11, 12.

2. If grace sanctifies us throughout, and every faculty and principle in us, 1 Thes. v. 23, then it sanctifies self-love in us ; for of all things in us it is most a part in ourselves. And if there be a sanctified self-love, then

* Qu. 'not'?—Ed.   † 1 Chron. xii. 33. Marginal rendering.—Ed.

part even of our holiness must lie in loving ourselves. But then withal observe, that this sanctification of self-love is eminently seen in this, that the heart being made spiritual, and suitable to spiritual things, it is enabled and made so truly happy, as to find its own greatest good in those things, and is carried forth towards them with the greatest contentment to itself. And so it comes to pass that when a man's soul is perfectly sanctified, he loves these spiritual things with a stronger love to himself, than any carnal man can do, or ever did, carnal things. And hence these two make but one stream : I at once love myself, and spiritual things themselves, and all comes to be reconciled by this, that the heart is made suitable to them. Yea, upon this ground I will go yet higher. The more I judge God, Christ, and all other spiritual things, to be the best and chiefest good for my soul (and this when considered in the highest spiritualness that can be supposed to be revealed by the Spirit, and discerned and apprehended by me), when they rise up in the most spiritual spirituality, the Holy Ghost himself can or doth represent them, then for my soul to be most able to say, ' These are the best for me,' and to have spiritual affections rise up as these other apprehensions of the spirituality of the things do rise, this argues still that my heart hath the greater degree of grace. And the reason of it is clear from this principle, that grace suits the soul to spiritual things ; and therefore those actings of my heart argue it still to be the more spiritual, as being so suited that still I find my highest good to lie in the highest and utmost spiritualness of them ; even as the more a man's stomach affecteth and relisheth meat, the stronger meats, yea, and the more sweetness it finds therein, the better stomach it is. David's heart hath in a great degree decided this in few words : Ps. lxxiii. 28, ' It is good for me to draw near to God.' He found communion with him, out of suitableness, to be his greatest good.

CHAPTER VI.

How we may discern, value, and love spiritual things, purely as spiritual, and yet view them as blessings to us; and regard and affect our own interest and benefit in them.

If any do yet understand me so as to have this objection still in their thoughts (putting it by way of supposition), that if any man should love spiritual things as spiritual, chiefly for his own good, would not this be hypocrisy, and he be a carnal man ?

I answer, Yes. And even this will also follow from that principle I have insisted upon. For if a man's heart be carried out suitably to the things, that is to God and Christ, &c., as they are in themselves, then he cannot but prize, adore, value, and love them above himself. For if his heart be not suited to the things, as they are proportionally in their own worth, his knowledge and love of them is not such as the things require, and so are not suited to them. And (as I said) it is a false and a counterfeit knowledge of, and affection to them, as was afore observed, so that it is a contradiction to say a man's heart is suited to the things, and to say that he affects them as such chiefly for himself. For if he knows God as God or Christ, as the truth is in Jesus, then (as John says in another case) he finds these to be infinitely greater than himself, and himself to be but as a mote flying in the beams of the sun. And if he did not accordingly prize and affect them and their glory, his affections would not be suitable to these things; therefore self falls down, and gives up itself most to exalt the things above itself, when it finds them most suitable to it. Yet still notwithstanding, this on the other side falls on with the highest consistency, that a man never loves himself more, yea, and never finds he doth it more, than when he finds he loves them above himself, and not for himself chiefly.

If you ask me how far these two may stand together? I answer, they are consistent in a due subordination of self unto God, and the things of God. All men must acknowledge this, that true grace is the image of God's holiness, Col. iii. 10. And it so long continues to be his image, as it keeps a due and answerable proportion unto that holiness that is in himself, the great and only architype and master-pattern of all true holiness. Therefore it is consistent with so loving God and ourselves, in such a subordination as God loveth himself and us. Now if we consider God, he as God loves himself above all, and works all things for his own glory, and therein lies his holiness in choosing his elect unto salvation, for he did it for his own glory: Eph. i. 5, 6, ' Having predestinated us unto the adoption of children by Jesus Christ to himself, according to the good pleasure of his will, to the praise and glory of his grace, wherein he hath made us accepted in the beloved.' And yet everywhere the Scripture also doth ascribe God's electing us and redeeming us to his infinite love borne unto our persons (' God so loved the world,' &c.); and that not comparatively only as to others (' Esau have I hated'), but simply as he bore an affection to our persons: Deut. x. 15, ' Only the Lord thy God had a delight in thy fathers to love them.' You see then, that in God's heart our salvation and his own glory, love to himself above all, and infinitely above any respect to us, had a great place, and yet a true, real, and special love and affection borne unto us, did sweetly meet together and run in one channel subordinately to the other. And this hath been to many a great help and inducement to their believing God's real intention and heartiness to save sinners and themselves, that it is a design which falls in with the utmost manifestation of his own glory. Yea, and God in effecting it, or bringing it about, hath contrived all the means of salvation, so as to represent at once to us an intermixture of transcendent love to us, and a prerogative respect of his own glory. Look one way, and you think he loved us as if he regarded nothing else; look on the other side, and the glory of his grace doth so appear that we seem to be forgotten, and God's glory alone shines in it. Are these two then so reconciled in God's heart, love to us and himself? Come we now then to the heart of a man saved and regenerated spiritually, and certainly they may consist also there. And the ' saving faith' of both these respects and affections had by God to his own glory, to us, and our salvation, may also work both ways in our hearts. And, indeed, God in commanding us to love him above all things, yea ourselves, hath withal given leave to us to love ourselves, in so doing, in an answerableness to his own loving us, whilst yet he aimed so eminently at his own glory as if nothing concerning us had moved him. For grace in us is the image of what is in himself. And all this (say I still) may justly be enforced by this assertion, that grace in the heart is a principle that elevates and suits the soul unto the spiritualness of things spiritual. Now the glory of God above our salvation, being the most spiritual of spiritual things (it is spiritual *in summo gradu*), then if the heart be suited to the thing, it must in the end exalt and set this up, as it is in this its spiritualness, and so set it in this its high throne above itself; it were not grace else, nor suited to this object. And because it is a principle that suits the heart thereto, therefore it withal must have the greatest delight when it finds it can do so, therefore the greater happiness consists therein, and therefore the believer enjoys his own good most in being so affected. Grace is the strongest creature and principle that ever God did, or shall make. It comes upon the heart when it is an utter stranger unto God, and when it is full of self-love, and is as contrary to God as any one thing can be to another; and yet it comes and begets an instinct in that soul to make its own highest good to lie in the good and happiness of that God aimed at and delighted in above its own. I will end this. This love to God ariseth not out of self-love (though it is so in a carnal man) but it may more properly be said to be joined with it, self-love to take it into itself.

3. When we say that *spirit* here, in John iii. 6, is a suiting the heart to spiritual things themselves, the meaning is not that the closing with God himself, and with the person of Christ abstractly considered, is all and the whole of true spiritualness, or which are the only objects of a spiritual heart; but there are many benefits by Christ, and that come within the soul's cleaving to God, which are spiritual also, and so are truly and spiritually the objects of the affections of a regenerate man as spiritual. This I add, to prevent a mistake also.

Many, when they hear of such a doctrine as this, that spiritual things are to be affected as spiritual, take it in thus, that therefore all affections to anything but to God, and to the person of Christ, simply for themselves, and not at all for any benefit or blessing with them, are affections of a heart that is carnal.

It is true indeed that those before-mentioned dispositions are in a spiritual heart raised up unto an intense degree (for these only are spirituals *in summo gradu*, as we use to speak of other things, as of heat in fire, &c.), yet withal the benefits that flow from adhesion to the persons of God and Christ, are in their degree spiritual also. Thus you have it expressly pronounced, Eph. i. 3, 'Blessed be the God and Father of our Lord Jesus Christ, who hath blessed us with all spiritual blessings in heavenly places in Christ.' Here you have mentioned the persons of God the author, and of Christ the conveyer, distinguished from the blessings; and yet the blessings themselves are termed spiritual, as well as God and Christ elsewhere are. And adoption (ver. 5), and redemption through his blood, and forgiveness of sins through the riches of his grace (ver. 7) are ranged among the number of them. So that even in these blessings themselves there is a spiritualness to be found, and spiritual considerations about them, for which a regenerate heart spiritually affects them, and seeks them. The eye that loves to behold the sun's light, and to behold the beams of the sun, doth certainly love the sun itself, the fountain; for those beams are high and heavenly, as well as the sun itself is a heavenly body. And thus it is with respect to all spiritual blessings. Justifying faith, which is as spiritual a grace as any, hath not immediately the person of Christ in its eye, abstracted from his righteousness or forgiveness, but as arrayed with them. There is therefore a spiritualness in Christ's righteousness to be found, for which we must value it, and to close with it as truly spiritualness, as to close immediately with the person of Christ. Paul desires, Philip. iii. 9, 'to be found in Christ, not having his own righteousness,' &c. So is it in all graces, they are spiritual things. Only I add this, that all these are spiritual, but derivatively, and as they relate to God and Christ, and unto their glory. If you cut them off from that relation, and value not their worth, as in that relation they lose their spiritualness. As the sun's beams have a glory in them, why ? Because they are beams of the sun, as rooted in it, flowing from it; which if you would cut off, they would lose. Now carnal hearts, in valuing and affecting these benefits, cut them off from God and Christ. A dark cloud of self interposes, and they do not most value them on the account of their relation to the persons of God and Christ.

This also is farther to be considered, that many believers, especially when young in grace, may not have those principles and gracious dispositions, so far stirred and acted (although the things are in them) as to be able eminently to discern that high suitableness to God and Christ in its true spirituality, with difference from what is from carnal self. That is, they may not presently find that love to the things themselves for themselves, budding and shooting up so as to overtop that other remaining principle of regard unto their own selves.

(1.) It is therefore to be considered, that believers at first, having carnal self stirred towards spiritual things (even as temporary believers have), as well as spiritual self, they are in respect of this mixture termed carnal rather than spiritual, because that principle is, if not predominant in acting, yet so vigorously, and perhaps more sensibly, acting in them than the spiritual part, purely as such, is found to be. When Paul wrote to that church at Corinth, he wrote to saints, yet professeth he wrote not to them as to spiritual, but as to carnal, 1 Cor. iii. 1 ; that is, as to babes in Christ, whose workings are to sense more carnal than spiritual, though they afterward do grow up to be more spiritual. Thus in the first birth a child, first lives the life of a plant, then of a beast or sensitive creature, and last of all springs up reason ; and yet the reasonable soul was the root of all these, and so was the principle of them there from the first. So it is in the new birth often. Therefore let none be discouraged though the present actings of their spirit have been low, and not risen up eminently above carnal self (as to their sense); for true grace or spirit may be in them carried out with the mixture of the other, and that genuinely (as to the thing itself) unto what is spiritual.

(2.) In the main and whole ordinary course of a Christian, these two streams run together in one channel, and have no occasion of parting ; but they find that loving their own selves, and their affecting spiritual things for themselves, do concur, insomuch as whether they affect themselves most, out of love to themselves, or most affect the things themselves, they cannot discern : as when all the bells strike at once, it is hard to discern distinctly the sound of the loudest above the rest. So as although a man's heart truly affects the things most, yet so much of self, carnal self, is mingled with it, that which is most eminent is not perceived. Only this they find, that their affections are still carried on one way or other to things that are spiritual ; and in this case the constancy of the stream (though at some passage of a man's life more shallow than at another) is that which doth best evidence the Holy Ghost to be the spring of all, and that a fountain of spiritualness is sprung up in that heart, which feeds it thus to eternal life. The truest issue therefore which, in examining ourselves, we are to bring our souls unto, is ultimately to search, taking the help of those cautions given along with us, and not to rest satisfied till we have found some dispositions in our souls naturally matching with, and suited unto, what is spiritually good in things that are spiritual. And although in the meanwhile, till this is some way discerned, the soul may support itself with the thoughts that those affections that have been drawn forth to things spiritual revealed in the word, perhaps in present sense, only out of self-love, may yet in the issue prove to have true strains of spiritualness running along with them. But yet still thou canst not have an undoubted or infallible evidence of thy regeneration, till thou findest thy heart carried forth to and closing with what is truly spiritual in those blessings.

CHAPTER VII.

That the blessings which we have by Christ are purely spiritual, proved by an enumeration of them.—How a spiritual heart considers and affects them in their pure spirituality.

I come now to reduce this inquisition into particular instances; that is, to view over some things spiritual, and to single forth in them what is truly spiritual, severed from what is accidental, and so to bring them and your hearts together, and to see how they will and do match and agree.

I will begin first with such things as may seem less spiritual, because suited unto what is in ourselves. Such are the benefits that come by Christ. Now, in each of these there is something that is purely and truly spiritual, towards which for the heart to be suitably carried forth, argues spiritualness in the heart. Now, to clear our understandings in this, take this for a true and certain general rule, that all the spiritualness that is in every such spiritual benefit consists in its relation and reference unto God himself, who is that great Spirit, and the fountain and measure of whatever is spiritual. Neither grace, nor any spiritual benefit, is further spiritual than as it is a tenant of his, and holds of him; and both issues and flows from him, and returns again unto him, as redounding to his glory. So as it is the shine, the lustre, the reflection of his glory on these blessings, some way or other, which alone makes them spiritual, as they are stream- ings down of God upon us, and are redounds and reverberations of glory back again to him; which is more eminent in those blessings, and their being benefits unto us. And without this aspect unto and conjunction with God, they, if simply considered as benefits, would lose their spiritual- ness. So as although, because they are truly benefits, and for our good, and do make us happy, therefore self-love is admitted to partake of, yea, and to embrace them, for its own good (for they were also ordained there- to), yet unless that self-love be taken with what is of God, and tends unto God in them, so as really to find its own good to lie therein, it would not be spiritual love.

And the truth of this notion (that you may not think it a mere imagina- tion) discovers itself in things that are human, and in the professions of men, concerning things that are found amongst men.

1. A great king, in bestowing his benefits, puts the worth of them upon what is from himself, and redounds to himself. That story of Alexander illustrates it. You know the great king Alexander, when he thought fit to give a gift, he professes to give as a king, and so gave a city as a reward for a mean service; justifying it thus, 'I give as a king' (as the scripture phrase also is, 2 Sam. xxiv. 23), as becomes a king to give, and not as becomes the man to receive. So as in that gift or benefit there shined more of honour and glory to Alexander, than there did of good and benefit to the person on whom it was bestowed. The same strain was in Ahasuerus, 'Thus shall it be done to the man whom the king delighteth to honour.'

Thus it is in the spiritual benefits we have from God; God hath set them out unto us infinitely more by what is in them of benefit to us, and would have us accordingly entertain and embrace them; and when the heart is answerably thus affected, then it is spiritual.

2. The heart of an ingenuous man, though carnal, may understand how it is in this respect with a regenerate man's heart, so as to be convinced of it by what they feel, at least often pretend unto, in human affections. If a person be far your superior, or a friend very dear, and you are either suitors to him for a gift, or place, by reason of which you shall be near to him; or if you be to return thanks and obligations, or if you have a token given in remembrance of a near friend, your hearts prompt you, or your wits, at least, counterfeit such strains as these, *Non tam dono (lector) quam abs te dato*, I rejoice not so much in the gift, as because it is by so noble a hand and so noble a mind. And what you must profess to regard is, that he who gave it would cast an eye upon you, or that you might come thereby to have a nearer approximation to him. For instance, will you take one of Paul's realities (I must not term them compliments) in Phil. iv. 14, 17. He celebrates and magnifies their gift (ver. 14–16) more than any, from any church; and concludes (ver. 17), 'This I speak, not that I desire a gift, but that fruit may redound to your account.' He considered the benefit as it was to himself apart, and also as in its tendency it redounded unto the givers again, whom he valued. Thus also you value a medal, or a piece of gold, or the picture of a friend, not by its worth or weight, but as it relates to him, a thousand times above the value of it in itself. Now bring but the analogy of such things as these on to God, and his benefits or graces bestowed on you, and judge righteous judgment; and ask your hearts this question, For what it is you do affect them, and what is in them takes your hearts?

Run over those particular benefits celebrated (Eph. i.), all which the apostle pronounceth to be 'spiritual blessings' (ver. 3). And particularly observe wherein the lustre of their spiritualness lies.

1. What greater benefit or honour can be to us than to be the sons of God? ver. 5. Is it a small matter to be a son-in-law to a king? Oh, what honour is it to be a son to God! There you see is the benefit; well, but see what are the beams of spiritualness that irradiate this, and shine every way through it?

(1.) That the original of it was the good pleasure of his will.

(2.) That this is bestowed by Jesus Christ.

(3.) That it is bestowed to the praise of the glory of his grace. Take this benefit, as it is thus spiritualised, and there is no heart that can truly prize and affect it, as thus considered and circumstantiated, but it must be a spiritual heart.

(1.) That heart is spiritual which values it in respect of its original, viz., The good pleasure of his will. This took Christ's heart in God's saving of his people (which Christ is personally interested in as much as we) more than the salvation itself of them: Mat. xi. 25, 'Father, I thank thee. Even so, Father: it seemed good in thy sight.' Christ sets his seal, his own concurrency of will with God's, as that which above all pleased him also in it, namely, that 'so it seemed good in his sight.' What is it the beloved disciple in like manner calls up believers to behold and value their sonship by? Even this original of it, the love of God: 1 John iii. 1, 'Behold what manner of love the Father hath bestowed upon us, that we should be called the sons of God.' Herein lies the spiritualness of their value for the love of God, in respect of its fountain in God's heart; his love therein is valued more than the thing.

(2.) That heart is spiritual which values the privilege of sonship on the account of its being bestowed by Jesus Christ, and that it is possessed by virtue of a relation to him. This also holds forth spiritualness above what our sonship is otherwise in itself. Adam was a son of God's by creation, Luke iii. 38. But to be a son of God by Christ, this is a higher thing, and puts the spiritualness upon it which a holy heart values. For it is to be a son-in-law by marriage unto, and union with, the natural Son of God. So then the spirituality of our sonship lies in that relation it hath unto Christ. Now bring a spiritual heart unto it, and though it cannot but infinitely rejoice that it is become a son of God, yet that this should be such a sonship as is founded upon relation to Jesus Christ as a husband, this makes his joy greater. To which of all the angels hath he said, My Son is thy husband, and thou art his spouse, and so thereby becomest my son ? ' To as many as received him, he gave power to be the sons of God,' John i. 13. This infinitely adds more unto it in a spiritual heart's esteem.

(3.) A spiritual heart rejoiceth that this should tend ' to the praise of the glory of his grace :' that God should take sons, who at best were such but by creation, and then by 'the fall were made sons of wrath, children of hell, sons of Satan, and make some persons sons, and sons by Christ. And this rebound that it hath unto the praise of the glory of his grace, is the spiritualness of this benefit, the apostle being judge. How hath or doth thy soul close with it ?

2. Then take the second benefit, instanced in ver. 6, which is, to be ' graciously accepted ;' and still it holds of God and of Jesus Christ. Therein lies the spiritualness of it. First, There was mention of the free grace of God in it just afore, and then follows, ' wherein he hath graciously accepted us.' This David valued above all, when he said ' Thy favour is better than life ;' yea, even above the life he had by it, or through it, whether spiritual or temporal. God's grace and love ought to be more valued than the benefit that occurs thereby.

3. A spiritual heart considers that this acceptation is ' in the beloved.' If God would profess to love one man immediately, as he is considered in himself alone (as some say he doth still the angels, or to be sure, as he did Adam at first), and to love another man in Christ, who is the *primum amabile*, his first and naturally beloved, his only begotten Son ; Oh, how would the heart of a third man standing by, that is spiritual, say, O Lord, love me in the beloved with that love thou lovest thy Son ! John xvii. 23. What love is it that Paul values and triumphs in ? When, Rom. viii. 37, 39, he had first said, ' In all these things we are more than conquerors through him that loved us ;' what love was it he had in his eye, that he thus valued, and which caused him to triumph ? He tells us, ver. 39, that it was ' the love of God which is in Jesus Christ our Lord.' Take this away, and all other love is but a common love, a providential love. But herein lieth the gospel spiritualness of God's love, that the favour of God is transmitted through Christ, who first hath contracted all the beams of God's love into himself, and so diffuseth them unto us. This takes and inflames the heart more than if in common, and immediately, the divine love was cast down upon us ; as in a burning glass you see the beams of the sun to be more contracted and strengthened.

4. A spiritual heart considers the other benefit, ver. 7, ' redemption and forgiveness of sins.' This all men will readily and greedily listen after.

Well, but a spiritual heart takes it in those rays of spiritualness Paul hath set it in. (1.) In whom we have it, namely, Christ. (2.) Through his blood. (3.) According to the riches of his grace. Justification and pardon of sin through Christ's righteousness is the glory of our religion. And take it in all that doth surround it, it is as spiritual a point as any other. And indeed it is too spiritual, not for papists only, but for many in these times, to cleave to. There are those among us who begin to be weary of it, though formerly, out of reverence to the Reformation of religion, even carnal hearts entertained it. But take it in its true spiritualness, and then to be sure only spiritualised souls will value it.

A spiritual heart regards justification by Christ's righteousness as it relates unto God's glory, that is, the glory of his grace. If ever God contrived anything for his glory, he did this. Inherent grace in us justified us once, but though it was the love of God the creator, and the due of innocent nature, yet God had no great liking to it; for as, Rom. iv. 2, 4, man had thereby whereof to glory; and the greatest reward was, by that way, reckoned of debt and not of grace; so man falling, God was willing to take that escheat and forfeiture, and for ever to despoil inherent grace (though he meant to bestow such grace still out of grace anew) of its first ancient privilege, and hath pronounced his sentence against it, that whatever it might avail and serve for in man's primitive innocent state, to be sure it should never justify him that hath it more. The glory of his own grace entered upon this, and hath sequestered it as his own prerogative for ever, to the glory of his grace. And he valued this one thing so much, as he hath given it away, and entitled his own Son to it, on purpose to magnify his blood, that this might be his eminent title, 'Jehovah, the Lord our righteousness.' And he hath put him into the possession of this honour, as won by his sword and his bow; as Jacob said of a plat of ground he gave to Joseph.

Use. Now to bring this home to our hearts by application. The news of forgiveness, justification, redemption, all men run away with. But, I beseech you, consider wherein the spiritualness of this benefit lies, and whether ever your hearts have been taken at all with it. Indeed, they should be most taken with it.

1. We ought to adore this way of our salvation, as it brings in so great a glory to God's grace, and to Jesus Christ; so as, were we to choose, we would have this way. This was the disposition of the heart of Abraham our father, as appears in Rom. iv. Compare but the beginning and the conclusion of the apostle's discourse about our father Abraham. Whereas, ver. 2, it is said, that 'if Abraham had been justified by works, he had whereof to glory' (which was contrary to God's design), and whereas he made Abraham's faith the subject of his discourse in the residue of that chapter, at last he concludes, ver. 20, that 'he staggered not at the promise through unbelief, but was strong in faith, and gave glory to God,' and '*therefore,*' ver. 23, 'it was imputed to him for righteousness.' This his giving glory to God (though withal he commends the strength of his faith he did it with) hath a respect to ver. 2. Where, in opposition to Abraham's glorying (if he had been justified by works) he had had whereof to glory, but not afore God. So then, by comparing each, the meaning is, that Abraham fell down afore God upon the revelation of this way of justification, which he perceived much to tend to glorify God and his grace, that willingly upon that account he gave up all his own works (a greater sacrifice than that which he intended, namely, the sacrifice of his son, which is

celebrated as a noble work proceeding from faith, James ii.), and laid them upon the altar of God's glory. And he was glad that his heart had light upon such a way as did so highly glorify God by the Spirit, being the more strengthened (as it is said) to seek salvation by this way, because it gave all to God, and nothing to man. Hath this in justification taken thy heart, which took our father Abraham's? Perhaps thou wouldst serve thyself on God, and take the benefit of this his pardon ; but hath it ever been done with giving the glory to him and to his grace ?

2. Thus also when thou comest to have recourse to Christ's blood and righteousness for justification (which is the second thing Paul puts in to spiritualise this benefit unto us), is it the glorious relation to, and the influence that Christ and his blood hath upon justification, that causeth thee to value it, looking upon it not only as a thing thou must have or thou art lost and damned, but Oh ! dost thou desire to be clothed with it, to be found in it ? For what doth a spiritual heart value it ? What ! is it only because their own righteousness is as filthy rags, therefore they throw it away ? No. But that if it had the righteousness of Adam, yea, that which all the angels had at first, yea, all the inherent grace and glory which both angels and saints have now in heaven, it would gladly take the occasion to throw it away, and make a trophy and spoil of it to glorify this righteousness of Christ. It was the apostle's desire ' to be found in Christ, not having his own righteousness.' He speaks like a man afraid of being taken tardy in that place of residence, and runs away from it as far as ever he could. ' Unto me' (says Christ, Isa. xlv. 23, for it is spoken in his name, as appears by the apostle's citation, Rom. xiv. 11, Phil. ii. 10) ' shall every knee bow.' And what special glory is it that the saints shall give to him ? The 24th verse tells us, ' Surely one shall say' (as the greatest thing they could say, and they say it with the greatest asseveration, as if they were to utter but one thing they would say this), ' In the Lord (Christ) have I righteousness.' Ah, how feelingly is it spoken ! And they give it to him as a matter of glory, for so it follows, ver. 24, ' In the Lord shall all the seed of Israel be justified, and shall glory.' And truly the conjunction of these two in that place, ' In the Lord I have righteousness' for justification (as it is interpreted, ver. 25), and ' in the Lord have I strength' for sanctification, makes me consider Augustine's interpretation of that passage in Ps. lxxi. 16, which an hundred times he celebrates to this very sense (though our reformed interpreters reject it), ' I will go in the strength of the Lord God, I will make mention of thy righteousness, even of thine only.'

This relation that forgiveness of sins hath unto Christ's blood as the price, how doth it raise the price of it unto a holy heart ! How do the apostles speak of it, and thereby teach believers how to esteem it, and the benefit by it, as it is by his blood, and that as having a relation to his person, that gives the value to it ! ' We are redeemed ' (says Peter), ' not by gold or silver, &c., but by the precious blood of Christ,' 1 Pet. i. 18, 19. Oh, value your redemption by this great price of it. And to this Paul also directs us when he speaks, Acts xx. 28, of the church which God ' hath purchased with his own blood.' Mark it, the blood is valued as it hath relation to the person whose own it is. And again John speaks to the same purpose, Rev. i. 5, 6, ' From Jesus Christ, who hath loved us, and washed us from our sins in his own blood ; to him be glory and dominion for ever and ever ! ' How was the thought of forgiveness of sins (as it is a mere benefit to us) swallowed up into an adoring and giving glory to him who shed his blood for that benefit! When the apostles speak but of faith as in this its relation to Christ's person, Oh! how do they singularly term that grace above all others precious in that respect, and call upon all generations to call it blessed, because it is that grace which thus adores, glorifies, and magnifies the blood and the righteousness of God and of our Saviour Jesus Christ: 2 Pet. i. 1, 'To all that have received like precious faith,' ἐν δικαιοσύνῃ, 'on the righteousness of God and our Saviour Jesus Christ.' Faith may have a thousand other virtues and properties in it; but the glory it gives to Christ and his righteousness in point of justification is that which makes it precious faith indeed. This stone set in it, serving to make the lustre of this righteousness to shine forth, is that which makes the ring so rich and precious. I shall name one general conclusive place more, in 1 Cor. i. 29–31, 'That no flesh should glory in his presence. But of him are ye in Christ Jesus, who of God is made unto us wisdom, and righteousness, and sanctification, and redemption; that, according as it is written, Let him that glorieth glory in the Lord.' The thing I quote this now for is, that it is not justification or redemption, alone and singly taken, nor Christ's being made righteousness and justification to us, and our sanctification, being accepted in him, which the heart should alone glory in, but the heart should rejoice in the honour which Christ hath by all his, or it is not truly spiritual.

CHAPTER VIII.

That a spiritual heart desires heaven, as it is a spiritual happiness; desires and prizes inherent graces as spiritual ornaments of the soul, and a divine likeness, in which God is pleased; takes pleasure in holy duties, on the account of his having converse and communion with God in them.

You have hitherto seen how all the benefits reckoned, Eph. i., are spiritualised.

Now take heaven itself, which he there also mentions, ver. 11, 'In whom we have obtained an inheritance,' &c. If any benefit seems to be desired and affected by the generality of men, it is heaven; because it is conceived to be the ultimate happiness that will fill up the natural desire of the soul to the full. Yet if men did take in true and genuine notions of it, what that happiness is, and wherein it lies, in the spiritualness of it, and we could suppose their hearts remained still carnal, nothing would be more unsuited to them. If (as Christ says to the sons of Zebedee) you knew what you asked, or knew what it is to be there, none but a heart truly, yea, sublimately spiritual, can find in its heart to desire it. The apostle Paul, Eph. i. 17, 18, prays for these Ephesians, that they might have a spiritual knowledge of the God of our Lord Jesus Christ, in these words, 'That the God of our Lord Jesus Christ, the Father of glory, may give unto you the spirit of wisdom and revelation in the knowledge of him: the eyes of your understanding being enlightened; that ye may know what is the hope of his calling, and what the riches of the glory of his inheritance in the saints.' Elsewhere it is called an inheritance of the saints, Col. i. 12, as the possessors of it: here (in Eph. i. 18) he speaks otherwise of it, as an inheritance, αὐτοῦ, of him. It is translated, 'his inheritance in the saints.' The signification of it is, that it is what the saints have by inheriting himself. I would but ask who or what in heaven is the inheritance of the man Jesus?

It is said, Rom. viii. 17, that we are 'heirs of God, joint heirs with Christ.' Now what is Christ's inheritance? It is God himself: Ps. xvi. 5, 'Thou art the lot of mine inheritance.' It is Christ's speech. It is not a happiness only from God as the author, but it is in God himself, who is there to be enjoyed. In heaven, God is set afore us to pick all happiness out of; and so all that happiness must arise from suitableness of heart to him. And therefore the saints are said, Col. i. 18, to be 'made meet to be partakers of it.' And here in this place of Eph. i. 11 it is added, ' in the saints ;' for none else can take comfort or joy in God, Rom. v. 11. Come now, canst thou say, and say it heartily, out of a taste how good the Lord is, 'Whom have I in heaven but thee?' Canst thou out of a taste (I say) declare there is nothing on earth which thou hast enjoyed in comparison of him ; so as thy soul saith with itself, If God be in heaven, and if all hold good which the word says of him, and I have him there, though I should have nothing but him, I find I should be happy enough? Canst thou say this ? It is a sign thy heart is spiritual.

5. Take grace inherent in us, what is it draws out thy heart to desire it but the spiritualness of it ?

(1.) It is certain that grace hath the greatest dowry that any creature, whether in heaven or earth, hath. ' Godliness is profitable to all things,' 1 Tim. iv. 8, 'having the promise of this life, and a better belonging to it ;' but these simply are but additionals unto it ; and it may be thy heart is only willing to match with so rich an heiress.

(2.) Virtue hath an ornament in it, as it adorns the soul, and is the perfection of it. And so the philosophers, Plato, Hercules, and others, judged it. But wherein doth the excellency, the spiritualness of grace, lie ? 1. That it is the image of God and Christ, and so is allied to him, of kin to him, as being divine nature. 2. That it fits thee for, and carrieth forth thy heart unto communion and fellowship with God, and is a principle that enableth thee to sanctify him in thy heart. 3. That it makes thee in these respects beautiful, amiable, yea, glorious in God's eyes and esteem, whose favour thou valuest above life. It makes thee such that Christ greatly delights in thy beauty, Ps. xlv. Doth God there move the church to get much of grace, Eph. v. 26, 27, that he might sanctify and cleanse it, and present it glorious to himself; that is, for his own delight and rejoicing in her as his spouse ? And doth godliness thus alone considered, or (as the apostle's own phrase is, 1 Tim. vi. 6) in its own self-sufficiency, μετὰ αὐταρκείας, take thy heart to seek it as great gain ? Here is spiritualness.

6. Take duties of obedience, as prayer, reading the word, partaking of the holy ordinances of God : there is a spiritual part in all these ; which is, to meet with God in them, to sanctify him in the heart whilst we are conversant in them. The law of these duties is to have to do with God ; and if with God, then to glorify him as God in our hearts and affections; that is the spirit of them. And therefore, 1 Tim. iv. 8, godliness is opposed unto bodily exercise, that is, the outward performance only, for godliness is the spirit of obedience ; which is,

(1.) When God is sanctified as the end of thy duties.

(2.) When he is regarded as the object matter of them, and as one with whom we converse in them, then they are spiritual duties ; when God is sanctified in the heart ; and then God is sanctified, when either the motives for duties are fetched from considerations of God, and he is made the matter of them, and the converse we have with him is from some suitableness of heart unto him. But that which causeth carnal hearts (or any heart so far as carnal), to neglect them, or to be weary of them, or wish they were over and done, is, that the law of them is to have to do with God all that while, who to a carnal heart is burdensome company. And so carnal men perform these duties to him, as complimenters do visits to persons whose company they regard not. ' Will the hypocrite pray always ?' says Job. And why will he not ? Because ' he will not delight himself in the Almighty,' Job xxvii. 10. That is the law of the duty, and he cannot consort with God, but overly, and so his prayers grow overly, and in the end he gives over. To pray, or read, to ease thy conscience, and to keep all quiet there, what is it ? That is not the essential part of the duty. Paul considered the law and duties of it in its spiritual nature, Rom. vii. 14. The law is spiritual and good, and, verse 22, he tells us that he delighted in the law of God *in the inner man*, and in every duty of it. Now delight is out of suitableness, and why ? Because his inner man, that delighted itself in God, was assimilated to God, Rom. viii. 7. The carnal mind is said to be enmity against God, first, and therefore not subject to the law ; and so the reason men delight not in these duties of the law, whose tendency is to carry the soul up to God, is because they delight not in God. But the state of the case is quite contrary in a godly man : Ps. cxliii. 10, ' Teach me to do,' says David, ' thy will, for thou art my God ; thy Spirit is good, lead me into the land of uprightness.' None but a spiritual heart could experimentally and feelingly have moved God with this, as being first moved thereby itself. He had found the Spirit of God coming upon him in duties, teaching and leading, acting and quickening him, verse 8, and was so good to him, that he loved these inward influences and effluxes of his heart to God therein ; and they were so good to him, so suited, that he prays for more, and could not be content without it. Oh ! (says David) thy Spirit is good ! Oh, therefore, give me him, act me by him in all that I do.

7. To mention no more ; take God, and Christ, and the Holy Spirit, which are (as I said) *prima spiritualia*, the first and chiefest spirituals. What suitableness hast thou had unto these, abstractly considered in themselves, cutting off what accidental goodness is annexed to them as represented in the word ? Doth thy soul say at times, yea, at any time, ' The Lord is my portion ?' Lam. iii. Doth thy naked soul say it of the naked Lord, and say it heartily from the soul ? Lovest thou him by all thou hast heard of him, or knowest of him by his attributes, laws, decrees, and dispensations ? Thus also for Christ, dost thou love him for himself, and not only as a Redeemer ? Though to love him as such, he doth allow thee ; for therein he hath shewn and manifested infinite love unto thee. But yet there is *aliquid in Christo formosius Salvatore*, there is that in Christ that is far more amiable than his being a Saviour. Dost thou love him as thy head and husband, more than as thy Saviour ? So a wife unto a physician, if she loves him, will really do all for him, although she be never so diseased and needs his help (both these relations of head and Saviour in Christ, are distinctly insisted on, Eph. v.). Or dost thou love him for what God most loveth him (and that is, that he is his only begotten, and therefore beloved, Son, and because he pleased his Father in all things), as well as because out of love he did work thy righteousness ? God therefore loved and exalted him, because he was obedient to death, Phil. iii., because he loved righteousness and hated iniquity, Ps. xlv., therefore God exalted him, and anointed him with the oil of gladness. There are and have been souls that have found their hearts drawn forth in love to Christ, chiefly because in

doing (though for themselves), he expressed so much obedience to his Father, and thereby shewed he loved them,* John xiv. 31, having that in his eye more than their salvation. And dost thou reckon withal this as thy chiefest good, and desire of thy soul, to be and live for ever with him? Oh, to be with Christ is best of all, says Paul. Dost thou value the indwelling of the Spirit? Canst thou say to God, ' Thy Spirit is good,' who helps me to all that sweet communion with thyself, and takes of Christ, and gives it to my soul. ' Oh, take not thy Spirit from me,' for ' thy Spirit is good,' &c.

Obj. You will say, these are but notions, and such as are invented to express in the abstract spiritualness by.

Ans. I answer, they are such notions as will distinguish one day all your souls into heaven, or into hell; and they are such real notions, as holy and happy souls feel them and live upon them. Paul, you see, writing to them that were spiritual, spiritualiseth all these things in this manner as I have now done, and thus sets out these things, as taking it for granted they (as so represented) would take with spiritual hearts, as suited to them. And therefore he provoketh these Ephesians to bless God for them as spiritual benefits, spiritual in these respects, as he had set them forth ; so he writ, so he preached, and so were their hearts suited to them. I conclude (as the apostle doth, 1 Cor. xiv. 37), ' If any man think himself to be spiritual, let him acknowledge ' these things to be spiritual, and then see how they (as such considered) and his heart do agree.

Use. You learn hence what is the true measure of judging of our spiritual growth. It is to grow up in what is true spiritualness, which is a raising up all in the soul unto things spiritual, in their spiritualness. It is not a growth in respect of bulk, either of duties, or knowledge of, or affections unto, things spiritual, but still they must be discerned and loved in their spiritualness. And by this character is growth in grace, with difference from younger Christians, still expressed. Gal. vi. 1, ' If any be overtaken in a fault, you that are spiritual, restore such an one :' that is, you that profess to have more grace, and are more deeply acquainted with temptations, as in the next words insinuated. Thus also the apostle speaks, 1 Cor. iii. 1. ' I could not write unto you as unto spiritual, but as unto carnal, even babes in Christ.' Spiritual men he opposeth to babes, and therefore understandeth by those spiritual persons, grown Christians ; that are raised up to discern of things that differ, and to approve the things that are excellent.

---

* Qu. ' him '?—ED.

BOOK V.

*Of the work of the Holy Ghost in us, as it is represented to us under the notion
of a new creature.—That besides the Holy Spirit's indwelling in us, and his
motions and actings of our spirits, there are permanent or abiding principles
wrought in our souls, which dispose them for holy actions, and give spiritual
abilities for the performance of them.—That this new creature is a change
of the heart.—That it is a conformity to the image of our Lord Jesus
Christ.*

CHAPTER I.

*That exciting and moving grace is not all that the Spirit doth for us, to enable
us to the performance of holy actions. But he works grace inherent, which
is an abiding principle in us. The opinions of the popish doctors, of the
Arminians, and of some enthusiastics, considered.*

That which is born of the Spirit, is spirit.—John III. 6.

I have proved from this text of Scripture that the thing wrought in us
by the Spirit is spirit, and makes us spiritual. I now resume the same
text, to demonstrate from it this assertion or doctrine.

Doct. That over and above exciting, and moving, and aiding grace unto
acts, there are inwrought and infused in the soul at regeneration, inherent
and abiding principles of spiritual life, by which the soul is inwardly fitted,
capacitated, inclined, and quickened unto the operations of a spiritual life.

I shall first consider, and refute some opinions that are contrary to this
assertion. Though the papists very much speak of habitual grace as a
principle by which the soul acts, yet they assert that the first and only grace
that actually turns the soul is no more than exciting and adjuvant grace;
and that so to conversion it is sufficient that we be aided and assisted by
divine grace, without receiving a new principle of life from it. But yet
they say when a man hath turned to God out of free will, excited by an
internal motion of grace at first, then God infuseth a habit of grace as a
root, or a radical principle of good works. But then observe the reason,
and to what end they thus state it, and affirm how that then, and not before,
the soul's first turning to God, the habits of grace are infused by God.

1. Because, in plain terms, according to their doctrine, sanctification,
or inherent grace, or the infusion of a new principle of life, is justification,
or that for which God adopts and accepts a man to eternal life, as that
which renders a man amiable and acceptable to God, and constitutes him
righteous.

And 2. They assert that a man being at present made righteous, or
justified thereby, then those habits infused further becoming the roots and

principles of good works, these good works come accepted in order to the meriting eternal life, and are habitual graces given as the foundation of merit, but so as still the first acts of turning to God are carried on by exciting grace ; and therefore they say the understanding and will are but as of a man in the dark, that can see imperfectly, or of a man fettered or sick, that can stir if helped. And they therefore call all these acts of turning to God by the names of attrition and contrition, and the like, as pre-dispositions of the soul to the infusion of this form or principle of grace, even as fire or flame is introduced into the wood when it hath been heated and hath smoked. This is the papist's doctrine. See *Bellarmin, de gratiâ, lib.* 6, *cap.* 15, *per totum.* And so Bishop Davenant in his *Determinations, Quest.* 9, and in Perkins his *Reformed Catholick,* do state their opinion and refute it.

And though I know many of them say that to every supernatural act of exciting grace, a habit at least, or an inherent disposition infused is required; yet I retort this as a contradiction in their doctrine, which is that justification after a man is so turned to God in the infusion of habits, which therefore they must necessarily thereby deny to be afore conversion ; or else why is not the man justified thereby, or else acceptable afore ? Bishop Davenant also, in that before-cited *Determination* of his, retorts it further thus upon them : ' Some papists (says he, citing Suarez) overcome by force of argument, do yield, that unto the bringing forth of spiritual acts, there is always infused by God a quality which supplies that which a habit serves for. Yet to solve that other principle, they withal say that it differeth from a habit only in this, that it is not permanent, but passeth away together with the act, when that ceaseth. To what end (saith he) are these evasions ? Why do they not acknowledge these kind of infusions into the powers of men's souls to be the vivification of them, and that to continue as permanent and to be increased.' *

Others, who are not papists, putting our justification upon faith in Christ alone, and not upon habitual grace at all, yet withal falling in with the popish doctrine of free will and exciting grace as sufficient to the first conversion, they professedly and utterly deny any infusion of habits or principles abiding in the soul necessary to conversion, but that it consists altogether in acts stirred up by supernatural motions, by which the will is strengthened to accept or refuse. And so all of our conversion, according to this Arminian opinion, lieth in such acts of our parts, excited by extrinsecal motions and enlightenings on God's part. Hereby it comes to pass (as they would have it) that the whole of conversion is parted between the will, nakedly considered, and the adjuvant grace of God, assisting or elevating the will by way of motion and persuasion, without any working or infusion of a new heart and spirit unto us ; for they being not necessitated to embrace such habits for justification, as the papists do, and yet falling in with the freedom of man's will and supernatural exciting grace only, as the papists do, they reject all such infusion of habits, and wholly deny any part of regeneration to lie therein, and say it is *figmentum scholasticum*, an invention of the schoolmen. Only indeed this they own, that the soul being thus once turned to God by exciting grace, by its multiplying such acts, though that grace acquires a habit or facility to act graciously, as by the often repeating of other acts men use to do in arts or faculties acquired (as in playing on the lute, &c.), which indeed supposeth (as their principles

* How Alvarez states it out of the writings of many modern papists, you may read in his book De Auxiliis, lib. 7, Disp. 66, Nu. 1, whom yet he opposeth, as we do see also Suarez, lib. 8, de Gratia, cap. 5, 6, 7, 8, 11, 12, 13, 14, &c.

do) an imperfect inchoate power already in man's will to act graciously, which through assisting grace, stirred up by crebrous and frequent acts, grows up into a habit or facility of working.   But the doctrine of regeneration which we profess is differing from both.   We detest that doctrine of infusion of habits for justification, or as a foundation of works, to make them meritorious.   But we say they are simply required for man's acting holily, and for the pleasing of God by good works, which good works declare and assert withal that in our regeneration, from the first acts to the last, and so throughout our lives, there are infused supernatural principles of life and grace, which remain and are inherent in us ; and so the works thereof, nay, the workings of grace in us, are not merely from motions and excitations of the Holy Spirit in us, which is the full scope of the apostle : Eph. ii. 10, 'We are saved' (that is, justified and made heirs of life) 'through faith ; not of works ; for we are his workmanship, created unto good works, which God hath before ordained that we should walk in them.'   Here are good works as the fruit, and here is a workmanship created in us as the principle whence works proceed ; ' we are his workmanship, created to good works,' and there are no good works without it.   But yet instead of good works being ordained to justify us, he* is the adequate and full end and ordination of God's workmanship in us unto good works, which is only that we should walk in them.

There is another opinion of some high-flown people, who reject and despise all habits and effects of grace, esteeming such a participation of the divine nature (and of which the apostle speaks, 2 Peter i. 4) to be merely by accidents and qualities, which they contemn.   This notion is too low for them, and therefore they boldly assert that they are partakers of the divine nature by being transubstantiated into God, and that though they be no more than creatures in appearance, yet the being of God is in reality the substance of their being.   And though this opinion is veiled under the notion only of higher union with God, yet it is demonstrable out of their writings, that they, rejecting all that our divines say of our blessed state in heaven itself, and of God's being all in all, as to the communications of himself to us there ; and rejecting also the hypostatical union of the human nature to the person of the Son of God, they cannot feign any higher union above those than that which consists in this, that the saints shall become God.   And their believing themselves to be God, though in appearance creatures, is the fundamental in which all their religion centres, and indeed they need no more.   So then as God said, upon occasion of the fall of man, ' Man is become as one of us ;' so say they of man restored, that he becomes God.   And therefore they professedly cry out against two things especially in our divinity, because they lie in the way of this high imaginary preferment of the new creature, to which they profess to advance it.   One truth decried by them is the personal union of our nature with the divine in Jesus Christ, which, though it be the highest advancement any creature is capable of, yet falling lower than this which they aspire unto, they despise it, as not nigh enough for them, all the saints being (as they say) raised up to the form of God, and transformed unto God.

Among many other grounds of this bold assertion, there is one more plausible, which is this, that by our opinion we make all our communion with God to be but accidental, by virtue of accidents, or qualities in the soul, and not real or substantial.

But I answer, It is true, that as the soul itself, and its faculties of under-

* Qu. ' here ' ?—ED.

standing and will, are but creatures, so graces are but qualities in it, and that knowledge and love which remain in heaven, are no more than qualities. But yet if they will allow the substantial soul of man to be a mere creature, and to remain a creature for ever, distinct from that divine essence and being, then it cannot otherwise be partaker of the Godhead than by such communion with him as our * person with another person, who never become one in nature and essence, but continue two several beings. The communications therefore of God to us, and our communion with him, are transacted no otherwise than by our knowing God, loving him, and enjoying him for ever. A created understanding and will in a creature, not united to one of the persons hypostatically, can come no otherwise to be capable of communion and intercourse with God. And yet to say that this is but an accidental enjoyment of God, or the divine nature, is utterly false. For as we acknowledge and profess that it is God himself, and all the blessedness of him *objectively*, that is both known and loved of us, so we profess to enjoy as our happiness the divine nature as it is in itself; for such will our enjoyment of him be in heaven, where these inherent principles of communion with him, viz., the knowledge of God, and the love of God, will continue, and be perfected. And withal we affirm, that the soul is swallowed up into the enjoyment of God, as its all in all. But as for essential participation, viz., so to enjoy him as to be made one being with him, that can never be. The manner of the enjoyment is by means of accidents indeed, but the thing enjoyed is the divine nature made known to us, and beloved of us, as most blessed in himself. But withal we say that if the soul had not these faculties of understanding and will, which are but accidents, though essential properties of it, and likewise if it had not those infused qualities of grace and holiness superadded, it could not have this participation of God. Look, as the eye, when it beholds the sun, hath an immediate communion with the sun ; yet if it had not a visive faculty, a power of seeing, and were but a mere ball of flesh (such flesh as other parts of the body are), the eye could not be a receptive of the sun ; so it is here. The understanding could not see or know him as God, nor the will glorify him or love him as God, if it were not inspired and endowed with those new principles for which we are contending. Much less would it be capable of taking in the glory of God (as in heaven it doth) to be itself glorified thereby. And look, as when the eye beholds the sun, it reflects not on itself, it thinks not of, nor regards to boast of this, that it hath such a power of seeing in aspect, but it is wholly taken up with the glory of the sun itself, which is all in all in such a view ; so is it in heaven, when God is all in all to the blessed souls there. Only if there were not a new eye given to the soul to see with, and a heart to love him, or a divine nature like unto God's, it could never have to do with him, nor were it capable of it, nor meet for it. Take lead, yea, gold itself, and the loadstone will not draw it, nor will it follow the loadstone nor cleave unto it ; but let the divine power turn that gold into iron, which hath qualities like to and assimilated to the loadstone, and then you shall see the new-made iron in motion, as the loadstone moves to it ; yea, if the loadstone doth touch a piece of metal, it infuseth a magnetic virtue to draw needles unto it, and yet that virtue is but a new quality, or accident. So it is here with souls ; it is not the best or largest or most refined soul for the substance of it, with all its essential faculties, nor the largest or greatest understanding faculty in any such soul, that is fitted for this communion with God. But take the dullest soul and

* Qu. ' one ?'—ED.

meanest among all the number of souls, and let God infuse his likeness unto it, that is, give it a divine qualified understanding to know him and a disposed heart to love him, and instantly it runs after him, and doth it naturally and suitably.

CHAPTER II.

That the Holy Ghost, when he makes us new creatures, works in us fixed and abiding principles of a spiritual life, proved : 1. *Because it is a new birth, which supposeth a principle of life given ;* 2. *Because this new creature is called spirit ;* 3. *Because it is called so in opposition to flesh ;* 4. *Because the apostle speaks of our being born of God, and so having received a seed of divine life which cannot sin ;* 5. *Because he speaks of eternal life abiding in us ;* 6. *Because, 2 Pet. i. 3, we are said to be partakers of a divine nature, and this is something which is continually growing in us ;* 7. *The same is proved from the parable of the sower and his seed, Mark iv. 17, and of the ten virgins, Mat. xxv.*

I have in the foregoing chapter given an account of those opinions which allow no other work of the Holy Spirit, than to move and excite us to holy actions, and which deny his influence to produce in us living and abiding principles, from which, when regenerated, we have some inherent abilities (though in dependence still on his renewed enlivening us, both to ' will and to do,' Phil. ii. 13) to perform them.

I shall now prove the doctrine which I propounded in the beginning of that chapter, which is this :

Doct. That the Holy Ghost doth not only move and stir us up to all good actions which we do, but that in the work of conversion, he produceth in us living and lasting principles of a constant holy life.

I. First, I shall first explain this doctrine.

II. Second, I shall prove it, by several arguments.

I. For the explication of the doctrine. All men may understand the difference between an inherent power in the soul, or principle wherewith to act, and the act, or operation itself, be it inward or outward, proceeding from it as the effect thereof. In the body we see a hearing ear (to which that speech of Christ's concerning spiritual hearing alludes, ' He that hath an ear to hear, let him hear'), which is made by God, and endowed with a ready disposition and ability to hear sounds ; and this power is inherent in the ear, and is ordained for hearing as the act. The same we may understand of the eye ; there is a visive power residing in it, and enabling it actually to see colours when laid afore it, which are the objects ordained and fitted by God unto it. The necessity of which permanent power in either we see by experience, and is mainly understood by the example of those whom Christ cured (that were born blind and deaf), if we consider the different condition of the persons afore and after the cure ; as also that there was an almighty power put forth, first, to give an inherent power to their ears and eyes to hear and see, ere their soul could put forth the acts of hearing or seeing. And of both these, the blind young man cured was so sensible that he proclaims it to Christ's praise : John ix. 25, ' One thing I know, that, whereas I was blind, now I see ;' and he knew too that it was extraordinary, and a work of omnipotency ; ver. 32, ' Since the world began, was it not heard that any man opened the eyes of one that was born blind.'

And however there were a capacity and remote radical power in his soul, yet it could never have produced an act of seeing anything in this world, which it was in the midst of, without a new bodily eye, or a new endowment of it with a new power of seeing.

Now there is in the case of a man unregenerate and regenerate, a further distinction to be made : 1. Of a natural faculty in the souls of each ; 2. Of a principle in the said faculty in order to act; 3. Of the acts both are ordained for.

Take the soul of a man unregenerate : it hath naturally and essentially an understanding faculty in it (he were not of mankind else), and that understanding hath a capableness and a remote faculty to have spiritual objects taken in by it, and so to act towards them. For when it shall once come to know them in a spiritual manner, it must be said that it is the understanding faculty which is essential to the man that doth understand them. Indeed, before a spiritual light induced into it, it still remains as one born blind as to those spiritual objects ; ' and it cannot receive them, for they are spiritually discerned,' 1 Cor. ii., but must be super-endowed with a new ability and principle infused into it by a new birth, or it cannot spiritually eye, nor at all understand, them as they are in themselves ; and although through adjutories of light, &c., men may see them in the painted glass and literal notion of them, yet not as they are in themselves in their true spiritual nature ; no, no more than our bodily eyes can see angels, that are of that other invisible world, a higher world than ours, unless they do assume visible shapes, or we see them painted with earthly colours. Answerably Christ says, John iii. 3, ' Jesus answered and said unto him, Verily, verily, I say unto thee, Except a man be born again, he cannot see the kingdom of God.' They cannot see them. And thus also God pronounceth of the Jews in the wilderness, after forty years' experience of God's wonders and giving the law, Deut. xxix. 3, 4, ' Yet the Lord hath not given you a heart to perceive, and eyes to see, and ears to hear, unto this day.' Eyes they had, and understandings they had, as men, but not as spiritual men ; and so had not the true sight of spiritual things to affect their hearts towards them in their spiritual nature, without which God regards not any other apprehension of them.

Now though this new spiritual visive power with which the understanding is endowed, be for the kind of its being but a quality, and a super-additional accident introduced into the understanding, and not a faculty, as the understanding is essentially inherent in the soul ; yet as it is planted in the soul in order to receive and take in things spiritual (which are of a higher order of beings unto our natural understandings, and are infinitely transcending things natural and worldly, which are the objects of our natural understandings, and by which, or like terms, the apostle distinguisheth those two differing, both objects and powers of a regenerate and unregenerate man), so this new divine and heaven-born power, elevating and empowering the soul to discern them, hath justly the name of being enstyled a ' new understanding:' 1 John v. 20, ' And we know that the Son of God is come, and hath given us an understanding, that we may know him that is true,' that is, truly to understand him that is true.

Thus the bodily eye of man after the resurrection, elevated to see angels (which now are invisible unto it), may be enstyled a new eye, yea, and a spiritual eye, even as the whole body then shall be ' a spiritual body' (as it is called, 1 Cor. xv.) ; and yet that change will be but the superinduction of new spiritual qualities, suiting the eye and whole body unto such spiritual objects, as angels, &c., are; the substance both of those eyes and of those bodies remaining the same that now. And yet those new spiritual habilities then are said to constitute their bodies spiritual, and transform and raise them into bodies of a higher rank and order like to angels, as Christ says; and he speaks it of what manner of persons, in respect of our bodies, we shall then be. In like manner, the whole of a man new born, so endowed with this divine quality of spirit (though it be but a quality), is styled a ' new man,' a ' spiritual man.' It gives a new name to the whole man, and doth as truly constitute him such in that sphere of spirituality, and deserves to be so styled, being the principle of this new spiritual life, as much as the soul with its natural faculties, simply considered, hath the name of, and constitutes the man, to whose body it is joined, in the rank of a living soul. For though grace be but an accident, yet it is such as is worth all men's souls in the substance of them devoid of it.

And further, If the soul were not, by the infusion of this new spiritual quality, elevated and admitted into that order of spiritual agents, having spiritual life, it would want that essential property (in common to all sorts of living agents in their kinds) to act from within itself ; but must be acted merely by a principle extrinsecal to itself.

And further, The necessity of such a new spiritual hability to be infused into our souls, to constitute them spiritual, and agents of that kind, is, that both act and principle may be of one and the same kind and nature ; a spiritual acting, proceeding suitably from a spiritual principle ; which had first constituted the man, in whom it is, a spiritual man, as good fruit is from a tree first ' made good,' as Christ says, without which it cannot bring forth good fruit.

And as the bodily eye, at the resurrection, cannot exert the least spiritual act to those spiritual objects specified, nor those bodies put forth any one exercise that is proper unto spiritual bodies, until at the resurrection the body be constituted a spiritual body ; so is it here.

And lastly, This endowed spiritual principle in the soul is abiding, and permanently inherent in the soul, when those spiritual actings cease ; as the exercise of our present senses do in sleep, or when they are disturbed and hindered.

II. Having thus explained the doctrine, I come now to prove it, by these following arguments :

1. In the words of my text, John iii. 6, the work of the Spirit in us is expressed to be a being, or thing born, which implies principles of life given it, in order to acting and operations, or works of life. All other births do this. They give a natural being; and so this gives a spiritual one ; and both according to their kind. In Scripture it is not the acts of faith or love that are said to be born of God, or a man to be born of God through those actings; but, on the contrary, they are made signs of a man's being born of God, as effects are of their proper cause. As a child's crying, which is an act of life, is in law made a sign of a child's being born alive, so faith is made a sign of a man's being born again : 1 John v. 1, ' Whosoever believeth that Jesus is the Son of God is born of God.' And this our regeneration doth contain in it many more graces besides faith. And this expression, ' to be born of God,' signified in the language of the primitive church a fundamental common general character, denoting a Christian truly and savingly wrought upon by God. Of which new birth, this one act of believing Christ to be the Son of God was an evidence. *Deus possuit in corde fundamentum fidei*, says Prosper : God puts

in a foundation of faith into the heart, and then draws forth the acts of faith. So John i. 12, 13, They 'who believed in his name,' which were 'born not of blood, nor of the will of the flesh, nor of the will of man, but of the will of God.' They were born first. The like is spoken of the act of love: 1 John iv. 7, 'Every one that loveth is born of God, and knoweth God.' The act of loving God is alleged as the effect and the note of a man's being born of God. That which is added, 'and knoweth God,' shews that act of loving God dependeth likewise on an act of knowledge and of acquaintance with God persuading it, but both of them depend on our being born again. The act of the understanding in knowing God depends upon being born of God as the foundation of it, as well as the act of loving. 'Unless a man be born again, he cannot see the kingdom of God,' says Christ, John iii. 5, nor know anything belonging to it. The Scripture, speaking suitably to this allusion, compares these new powers and abilities unto natural faculties and powers, themselves in the soul, which are the principles of acting; such as is the faculty and instrument of seeing, where seeing denotes the act. And the Scripture speaks of giving eyes to see, ears to hear, and a heart to understand: Deut. xxix. 4, 'Yet the Lord hath not given you an heart to perceive, and eyes to see, and ears to hear, unto this day.' Now that which is properly said to be given by one's birth is the natural faculty and ability of any thing to act so and so, according to its kind. So then, like as the natural birth brings a man forth with all the powers of sight, hearing, &c., so doth the new birth the like. The child exerciseth not these in the womb at the first, yet hath them all in the principle. It is Basil's comparison :* As the power of seeing in a sound eye; as art in him who hath acquired it; such is the grace of the Spirit in him who receives it; always indeed present, but not perpetually operating.

2. A second argument to prove the doctrine is, that the work of the Holy Ghost is termed spirit here in John iii. 6, and a spiritual man, 1 Cor. ii. 14, 15, and that in order to discerning spiritual things. This argument will be farther strengthened, if the analogy be considered between this new birth of the soul, and the resurrection of the body (which is called the regeneration). Of the resurrection of the body it is said, 1 Cor. xv. 44, 45, &c., that 'the body is sown a natural body, but it is raised a spiritual body.' I would ask what is that new spiritualising of the body, but an endowing it with such new qualities and abilities as shall fit the body unto a spiritual condition and actings? It shall be endowed with such new qualities, namely, as incorruption, glory, agility, &c., and perhaps with new senses, which we cannot now guess at, which are differing from, yet answering unto these natural qualities and powers our bodies now, as natural bodies, have; unto which the character of these spiritual bodies is opposed. The change then is not barely of new acts, but of new powers and endowments enabling us to act. Therefore, verse 50, he speaks of our present bodies as those that are incapable of the objects and acts we shall have then: 'Flesh and blood cannot inherit the kingdom of God.' They want powers to bear and sustain the objects of spiritual glory, and they want qualifications to take them in. And, therefore, it is said of those that do not then die, that they 'shall be changed,' ver. 52, and these 'vile bodies shall be changed and fashioned like to Christ's glorious body,' Phil. iii. 21, which is spoken in respect of new inherent powers and endowments, which are qualities, and are styled the 'image of the heavenly man :' 1 Cor. xv. 48,

* De Spiritu Sancto, cap. 26.

'As is the earthy, such are the earthy,' viz., Adam and his sons in their bodies ; for so endowed are ours from him.   'And as is the heavenly,' namely, Christ as risen, and in heaven, such shall our bodies be.   All import likeness in qualifications, &c.   Now then look, as the body is at and by the resurrection made spiritual in those respects, in like sense it is that the soul is made spiritual by regeneration, which is termed a resurrection to the soul, as the other is the regeneration of the body ; as commonly in Scripture they are interchanged.   The resurrection is termed a regeneration, Matt. xix. 28 ; Col. i. 18, where Christ is called ' the first-born from the dead.'   And ' this day' (says God, Acts xiii. 33), ' have I begotten thee.'   And so regeneration is termed a resurrection : Eph. ii. 5, 6, ' Even when we were dead in sins, hath quickened us together with Christ (by grace ye are saved), and hath raised us up together.'   And Christ is as powerful, yea, and a greater benefactor to our souls now, than he will be then to our bodies.   He will therefore be ' a quickening Spirit' to both. And, therefore, in making our souls spiritual, he doth as much for them, and works the like things, viz., new powers in the soul to ' see the kingdom of God' (as the phrase is in this third of John), as well as he will work new qualifications in the glorified body, that it may ' inherit the kingdom of God.'   To give our bodies such eyes as shall see angels, who are spirits, and are not otherwise the objects of our senses, is but in analogy what is done to our souls in giving them eyes to see, and an understanding to know, God and Jesus Christ, as they are in themselves.

3. A third argument from what is in the text for this, is the opposition (in John iii. 6) between *flesh* and *spirit*.   *Flesh* is evidently evil dispositions and inclinations unto evil which dwell in a man, and which as a root hath fruits.   And pursuing that similitude, the apostle, enumerating the ' works of the flesh,' which ' are manifest,' termeth them the 'fruits of the flesh,' Gal. v. ; and in opposition thereto spirit, in the 17th verse, is used in like sense.   And when Paul, Rom. vii., speaks of that sin that dwells in him, he expresseth it to be a sin that, by occasion of the law, ' wrought all concupiscence,' ver. 8.   Mark that word *wrought*.   It was a sin which was distinct from the works of sin, and therefore it was an active disposition and inclination, distinct from those acts, as the cause of them ; which sin is also called an indwelling sin in the man, and so notes out what is permanent.   And in this sense doth the apostle up and down in Rom. vii. speak of it, terming it flesh, as ver. 5, and himself, in respect of this sin, carnal, ver. 14 ; and ' in my flesh,' says he, ' dwells no good thing.'   And in that very speech of his there, which he speaks by way of explanation or limitation, ' In me, that is,' says he, ' in my flesh, dwells no good thing,' he implies that he had another self, or *me*, wherein all good did dwell (even as in himself, as he was flesh, no good thing did dwell), and wherein the contrary good did dwell ; that is, an inclination to what was truly good and spiritual.   And therefore it follows, ' to will is present with me.'   To will what ?   Anything that is good, which yet he was not able to perform ; as it follows, ' but how to perform that which is good I find not ;' as if he had said, Yea, but yet I have so much of good, too, continually dwelling in me, opposite to this flesh, as is ready to put forth, and doth put forth, though but an imperfect act or will (for the principle is but imperfect, and *læsa principia habent læsas operationes*) unto what is good, when it is presented to it.   Now, what is an inward readiness and preparedness to good, and that spiritual good, as the law is, but a habitual principle indwelling ? And therefore as of that wicked man it is said, he was ready to all evil,

Acts xiii. 10, so of a godly man it is in like manner said, he is ready to every good work, Tit. ii. 14, meet and prepared as a vessel is for his master's use, both by its habitual fashion and make, as we say, which are inward dispositions that fit it, by the cleanness of it from defilement, as 2 Tim. ii. 21.

4. A fourth argument is drawn from what the apostle John says, 1 John iii. 9, ' Whosoever is born of God doth not commit sin ; for his seed remaineth in him : and he cannot sin, because he is born of God.' He speaks of our being born of God, and that there is a suitable nature, a seed of divine life in us which cannot sin or be touched with evil, for it cannot act contrary to its own nature and being ; as fire being preserved cannot act contrary to its nature. It may indeed be put out by subtraction of fuel, yet if it be kept up, and remain fire, it cannot either moisten or cool. This in analogy is the force of the apostle's reasoning, that every believer by his new birth receives such a seed of spiritual life, such a heavenly nature, which cannot sin ; for to do so would be to act contrary to itself. It is the soul itself which is endowed with the seed of life, and is the subject and intrinsecal principle of action. The Holy Spirit, though he is in us, and dwelleth in us, yet is not this seed of God here mentioned by the apostle, for he is extrinsecal to the soul herself, as to the actions which she doth. Now, it is the property of all things that have life to have, in their several kinds of life, a principle by which they bring forth actions of that life. And thus free and intelligent agents, in their kind, have a principle of life and action, besides that first and supreme Mover of all, ' in whom we live, and move, and have our being,' who, though he be in us, and acts us, yet he is but extrinsecal to the act. For we ourselves, being endowed with principles of action, are moved by him ; and therefore the actions which we perform, as praying, &c., are not attributed to the Holy Ghost as the subject of them, but only as the efficient. We must not say that they are the Holy Ghost's prayers subjectively, but only efficiently. He makes them in us and for us, and helps our infirmities in praying, Rom. viii. ; but that which constitutes us in the ranks of spiritual actors in the duty, and the subjects of it, is a principle of a spiritual life inherent and seated in the mind and will, and quickening us thereunto. And this is the seed conveyed in the new birth, and communicated from God, who hath life in himself. And that a man, thus born again, becomes thereby an agent from a new vital principle within him, is evident from a parallel scripture in the same epistle of John : 1 John v. 18, ' We know that whosoever is born of God sinneth not ; but he that is begotten of God keepeth himself, and that wicked one toucheth him not.' He speaks it indeed of the unpardonable sin unto death. But when he adds, ' he that is born of God keepeth himself,' he means that the regenerate man is an agent in the business, and acts from what is within himself. And his saying that he is born of God, implies that he hath received and doth retain the seed of God within him.

That the Holy Ghost is not the seed meant in these two places, 1 John iii. 9 and 1 John v. 18, is evident, as by what hath been said, so by this farther reason, because it would be improper to say that therefore the man born of God cannot sin, because the Spirit of God in him cannot sin. This were utterly improper ; but to say (as aforesaid) that the man who is born of God, and hath his seed, cannot sin, is a speech which is consonant to the voice of nature. It implies the voice of an inward disposition, which causeth a man to say he cannot do thus or thus, contrary to his nature, so remaining. It is nature speaks, but the Holy Ghost himself becomes not the new nature in or unto any soul.

And that other speech, ' he who is born of God keepeth himself,' doth most properly shew, that though the Holy Ghost in us be the great conservator, and keeper, and actor of us, yet by means of our being born of God, and receiving a seed of God within us, our understandings and wills do act, though actuated by him. So that the holy actions, though the Spirit excites and stirs us up to them, are our own, and we are the intrinsecal agent of them, and constituted to be so by virtue of a divine seed, conveyed to us in our spiritual birth. And the metaphor of seed remaining is (as Thomas Aquinas* out of Augustine explains it) an allusion to what God doth to his other creatures, bearing seed according to their kind. He hath communicated to every such creature a seminal principle, ordained to increase and grow up to such and such effects of bringing forth fruits, as we see in trees, &c. And so in the second creation, God in like manner puts in a seminal virtue, which, as the seed of mustard, the least of seeds, as Christ says, is yet to grow up to a tree, the greatest of all other. And therefore look, what proportion and ordination that natural seed, with its virtue sown in the ground, hath unto natural fruits and effects, the like hath this seed of God, sown in the soul† of the heart, unto supernatural acts. Seed is the communication of a principle of life from things that live, ordained to grow up and act according to its kind. And in a similar manner this here is the seed of all that holiness which after follows in our lives, and which springs from it; yea, and it is the seed of glory itself.

Nor is this seed merely the word of God heard or read by us, and remaining in our minds and memory, as what we have heard our minds are said to retain. It is true, if the word heard become ἔμφυτος, an ingrafted word in the heart, changing that stock into its own nature, then indeed it is all one with this seed of the new birth; as the apostle speaks, James i. 18, ' Of his own will begat he us with the word of truth, that we should be a kind of first-fruits of his creatures.' Wherefore, says he, ver. 21, ' Wherefore lay apart all filthiness and superfluity of naughtiness, and receive with meekness the ingrafted word, which is able to save your souls.' This ingrafting of the word is in substance the same with regeneration itself, being a similitude to illustrate it. But though the word be sown, the mere sowing it is not regeneration, if it doth not take root in a good and honest heart, Matt. xiii. 18, &c., and therefore the mere receiving the good seed of the word, as the stony and thorny ground did, regenerateth no man. For if it be so, that the letter of the word falls either carelessly into men's ears, so that the understanding is not so much as possessed with a notion of divine truth, it is no more than seed laid up in the hard-trodden highway ground. Or if it falls into the understanding, yet so as not to affect the heart, the devil soon takes it away, as the fowls pick up loose seed which hath not taken root in the ground. Or if it works so as to stir the affections, yet still if it wants depth of earth to take root, it is not the inherent abiding principle of regeneration which we treat of, and indeed such a bare receiving of the seed regenerateth no man.

That therefore which is meant by the ingrafted word is the law of God written in the heart (as God hath promised in his new covenant to do it), utterly differing from the work of the law in the letter of it, which the heathens had, Rom. ii. For it is such a writing of the law as God had written in Christ's heart : Ps. xl. 8, ' I delight to do thy will, O my God :

* Summa Theolog. Par. i. Quest. 62, Art. 3.   † Qu. ' soil '?—ED.

yea, thy law is within my heart.' It is this ingrafted word, the word or law written by the Holy Ghost, 2 Cor. iii. 3, and therefore is distinct from that Holy Spirit himself, that is the abiding principle wrought in us by regeneration. And as Christ had this law written in his heart, Ps. xl. 8, so we hereby are conformed unto Christ's image, Rom. vi. For what is that but an inwrought strong disposition in the soul, conforming and inclining it to what the word and will of God directs unto? Grace is the word of God concocted and digested into the heart, and made one nature with it. In which sense, and for which cause the word is said to abide for ever in the souls of men converted, 1 Pet. i. 2, 3. And that phrase, of writing the law in the hearts, imports no less than such an abiding principle. Words spoken are transient, and vanish into air ; but *litera scripta manet*, what is written abides, and is extant to be seen and read.

5. I draw a fifth argument, to prove that the Holy Ghost in regenerating us works an inherent permanent principle of a spiritual life, from what the apostle John farther says of eternal life abiding in us. It is not only that eternal life abides *upon* us (as it is said, John iii. 36, that the wrath of God abides upon him who believes not), but it is said to abide *in* us. Eternal life must have a beginning as well as accomplishment. And we all say that the life of grace is the beginning of a life that is eternal, and will be perfected in glory, and abides in the mean time in him that hath obtained a right unto the life of glory to come. It is not only said that a man hath eternal life, in that sense as a man is said to have an estate, an inheritance he hath right unto ; but a regenerate man's condition is expressed by this, that he 'hath eternal life abiding in him ;' as an unregenerate man's condition is expressed by the contrary : 1 John iii. 15, 'He that loves not his brother hath not eternal life abiding in him ;' that is, in short, he hath not grace. It was a phrase in those times to express a man's spiritual state by that character, that he was one that had eternal life abiding in him, which phrase I urge. Now, says the apostle, I hope you will all grant that a murderer, whose heart and spirit is full of blood* to the saints, as Cain's was to Abel (in whom the apostle had instanced), such a man cannot have eternal life abiding in him, as not being consistent with such a heart and inward disposition which his soul is filled withal. He argues from the same topic and principle that he had done, ver. 9, that inherent grace, that is, eternal life, that abides in the soul, cannot consist with such a frame of heart as to hate the saints as such, and to seek their death and ruin. The act of murder, and that of a saint (as it may seem Uriah was) may with a right to eternal life consist in David, but a heart at enmity with the saints (which is John's scope) cannot, for it is a contradiction to that principle of eternal life which is begun in him and abides in him. You heard afore that grace is called a seed, because it is the seed and beginning of eternal life ; and this place confirms it, these both in like manner being said to be abiding in a Christian, and the apostle alike arguing from both.

6. Further to prove my assertion, that by regeneration an inherent and abiding principle of life is wrought, I argue from 2 Pet. i. 3, 'According as his divine power hath given unto us all things that pertain unto life and godliness, through the knowledge of him that hath called us to glory and virtue.' He speaks not of those external privileges and benefits by justification and adoption, &c., which are given us, which is evident by two arguments. (1.) Because they are such things as are wrought in us

* Qu. ' hatred ' ?—ED.

by power. The giving justification and adoption is ascribed to his grace, &c., towards us ; and so works done upon us, and out of us, and yet bestowed on us, are usually said to be ' to the glory of his grace,' Eph. i. But what are done in us are the proper objects of power.

(2.) Again, secondly ; It is added that God, or Christ, in giving us these, is considered as he that hath called us to glory and virtue. Now you know the true maxim is, that God's calling any person unto any employment or dignity is joined with the giving him abilities, and a heart suited with principles answerable. So then his meaning is, that God having by regeneration and faith called us unto a possession of glory hereafter, and the prelibation of it here, and in order thereunto the exercise of virtue and holiness in this life; he hath answerably, by the working of his almighty power in us, given us a spirit fitted thereunto ; that is, ready furnished with all things that are the beginnings of, and preparations to that life (which you heard termed ' eternal life abiding'), as also to all the duties of godliness, which we are to walk in here. He hath fitted us in some measure for that calling. And you see that he speaks in the time past, that his power hath (in time past and already) given us all and the whole of them, as to the several virtues, seeds, and principles of them.

7. Add to this, seventhly, as another argument, What is that divine nature which is spoken of there in the fourth verse ? Not the divine being of God ; for that cannot be made common between God and us, or divided. It is therefore inherent grace, which is opposed to lusts in the words following, ' Having escaped the corruption that is in the world through lust.' Nature is an abiding, permanent principle, carrying on the things which it is to act accordingly. We are not partakers of God's nature essentially, therefore not as a nature ; otherwise than by having his likeness or image in divine qualities stamped on us, and so becoming like to him, to be holy as he is holy, which makes us fit to have fellowship with him, and so to take in his glory, and to be made happy by it, which, unless we agree in a holy nature, and holy dispositions with him, we cannot do. And this new nature denotes a stable and permanent being in the soul ; as also a principle of working, or it were not truly a nature. Dionysius has rightly expressed it, Nothing can come to work or act till it hath received a nature and a being as the principle thereof ; so nor to act divinely or supernaturally till it hath a being of such a supernatural nature given to it; and this is still the same with the seed of God, and eternal life abiding in us. We have by the new birth a supernatural being, as by the first a natural.

8. It is a seed, a nature, a life, &c., for it is said to grow up in us ; or else what is meant by ' growing in grace,' and ' renewing the inner man,' and the like ? How can this be meant, but that as a seed, which is an imperfect communication of life, grows up to a stalk, and blade, and ear, so this of grace in us ? It is such as all other growths are, and subsists therefore by the increasing of those permanent qualities and virtues. A living man is not said to grow as such, or as a living man, otherwise than as he adds one act of life to another. A man is said to grow rich by adding to a heap, but a living man grows in strength and bulk answerably to the principle of life at first received.

Learn what is meant by those distinguishing characters in the parable of the four grounds, and in that of the wise and foolish virgins. The stony ground's defect was this, ' they had no root in themselves,' Mark iv. 17. Which speaks the very language of inherent grace, which is that which is properly in a man's self inbred and implanted. And Job calls it ' the root of the matter,' Job xix. 28.   The foolish virgins wanted oil in their vessels, when that they had oil in their lamps.   The wise, on the contrary, had oil in their vessels, when yet their lamps were out, as in Mat. xxv. you read. Let any give a more rational interpretation than this, that the oil in the lamps is such assistances by motions and enablings as serve to hold forth an outward profession, and to perform the same duties, and to give the same light to others, which the foolish virgins had, but they had not grace in the heart, oil in the vessel, as a stock or treasury abiding in them, when that in the lamp might be out.   But the wise virgins had that abiding in them when themselves were asleep, and their lamps clean out.   It uses to be made an argument in this case or point, that if there were not abiding principles of grace, that then, when a believer is asleep, he ceaseth to be a holy man or a believer.   If life lay only in the actings and stirrings of life, then when they cease there would be no* intercision of life; and so eternal life, as such, should not abide in a man, as you have heard.   And the argument is strong as to the point.   But it is more strengthened by this scripture, Mat. xxv., speaking the same, or the like to it.   There are Christians not only asleep, as they are men, but even as Christians also, and their lamps go out, their profession and actings in a great measure ceasing; and yet they have oil in their vessels, grace in their hearts, ready to be drawn up into the lamp, and to become matter of a new shining forth in good works.

It is also urged, that if it were not for such inherent principles abiding, a holy man could not be denominated holy, but when he acts holily; as a man's countenance is not denominated ruddy for blushings or flushings, but from the constant constitution and complexion.   And here you see a confirmation of the foregoing argument also, for they are denominated wise virgins, when yet their actings ceasing, they were as fools and not wise; even as Solomon says of himself, that in the midst of his decay, his wisdom, that is, his grace, remained with him, Eccles. ii. 9.

Yea, this oil in their vessels or hearts did they carry with them into glory with the bridegroom, and were made vessels of glory, as you read there. Yea, and it is said that our souls are thereby made meet for glory, Col. i. 12, and 'prepared for glory,' Rom. ix. 23; even as well as thereby they are 'prepared for every good work,' as vessels meet for our master's use, 2 Tim. ii. 21.   And when we die, not only our 'works do follow' us, Rev. xiv. 13, as a man's treasure, which he hath wrought and gotten; but also the soul itself is wrought by God here for this very purpose, to be made capable of a further degree of glory, as it brings grace with it into the other world: 2 Cor. v. 5, 'Now he that hath wrought us for the self-same thing is God.'   Not only have we actively wrought, but we ourselves are here passively wrought by God, having our fruit the increase of inherent holiness, Rom. vi., 'and the end everlasting life.'   And therefore, 2 Cor. v. 3, he had said we shall be clothed with glory 'if we be not found naked;' that is, devoid of the image of God, but clothed upon with it, as the apostle elsewhere also speaks.

* Qu. 'an'?—ED.

CHAPTER III.

That the Holy Ghost, in regenerating us, works in us an abiding principle of a spiritual life, demonstrated by other arguments deduced from the nature of the work wrought in us.

I have thus far proved, by direct scriptures, that by regeneration we receive an inward principle of life. I shall now use other demonstrations of it.

1. If in regeneration there be a mortification of that flesh in part, which (as we heard) is an inherent corruption, then there is an habitual principle of grace, that cometh in the room of that inherent corruption that was destroyed. That in regeneration there is a mortification of an inherent corruption, is evident, because the subject of mortification is that flesh that dwells in us ; for if there be such a ' body of sin ' in us, it must be ' destroyed,' Rom. vi. 6. And therefore the subject hereof is called the old man, the body of sin, the earthly members, throughout the Scriptures. And also it appears by this, that if mortification were but a deading the soul to a present act of sinning, then it were no more but restraining grace. Well then, if this mortification be a destruction of an inherent corruption, then there is also an habitual principle of grace comes in the room of it. This is evident ;

(1.) Because vivification, or quickening, is of as large an extent as mortification can be supposed ; for they are commensurable. The spirit of life that comes into us is proportioned, and is as large and ample as the death of sin, and God's work in quickening is no less than what is seen in mortifying.

(2.) And secondly ; If it were otherwise, this also would follow, that so much of the soul in which sin was afore, and in which sin is now mortified, should remain (as the apostle speaks) naked and unclothed upon with grace, and have neither grace nor corruption in it. And so, whereas still a part of the soul remains corrupt habitually, this other part would remain unsanctified habitually. The state and condition of the soul would have this disadvantage in it, that unto evil it hath a bias, a poise, or (as the apostle expresseth it) a weight continually to pull it down, but it would have no inherent quality of grace to carry it God-ward, in that other part in which corruption is destroyed, but remain naked, and neutral, and volatile, to be tossed with the very* wind. And yet (according to those men's opinions that held the contrary to ours) this man must be said to be regenerate forsooth, in as true a sense as the part remaining corrupt in him is said to be corrupt. Which indeed is in effect all one as to affirm that a man is as truly alive that hath not a soul remaining in him, as he is dead whose soul is not only gone out of him, but expelled.

(3.) Yea, thirdly ; this would necessarily follow, that so much of the soul as had a corrupt habit expelled, and not a new contrary habit introduced, would be just in that condition which the papists feign to have been due to man in innocency, even in pure naturals, without supernatural grace, which they say was added but as a bridle unto nature or sin. I speak this to those that know this opinion which our divines detest, viz., that the restoring of us is but to such a condition, and that this is all our gospel regeneration. And yet this will follow upon the assertion that natural corruption only is mortified, and not habitual grace restored.

* Qu. ' every ' ?—Ed.

(4.) Add to all these a fourth argument. If grace wrought in us be the perfect curing and healing of corruption, then if flesh be a corrupt principle inherent, so must grace likewise be an inherent principle. There is a habitual aversion from God and a conversion to the creature, a frame of heart set and inclined that way; and it is not exciting grace will proportionately cure an habitual distemper, for as in the bodily, so in soul diseases, contraries are cured but by contraries. If therefore Christ comes with full healing in his wings, and sanctifies throughout, he doth cure habitual corruption with habitual impressions on the mind and will.

2. A second demonstration is taken from the parallel of the new creature to the image of God, which at and with man's first creation was given to him, and which he hath now left. It is evident it consisted not in bare acts of holiness, for he is said to be created in it. It was therefore as well produced by creation as the soul of man, and concreated therewith. And he is said to be created in it, before he put forth any act of knowledge, or righteousness; and yet he lost it by sinning. What can that be but something that is distinguished from the soul and the faculties of it, for it was lost; and distinct also from all acts of the soul, or actings upon him, for an image notes a thing permanent and inherent. I say what could this be but habitual inclinations and dispositions unto whatsoever was holy and good, insomuch as all holiness radically dwelt in him? The apostle informs us, that the image of God at first was ' in righteousness and true holiness,' Eph. iv. 24, and Col. iii. 10. Now the same holiness and righteousness is required of us, when we are called to turn to God. God calls for his old debt; yea, and it is as expressly said that this new image is created after God, in answerableness unto God's creating that image at first. And surely to confirm this I may add, 1. That if original righteousness be still required in us, then habitual holiness; else the want of it would be no sin. Again, secondly; Christ, in being a quickening Spirit, doth as much for us in respect of God's image as Adam should have done if he had not fallen. Adam would have conveyed it to his children long before they could have put forth any act; therefore sure in quickening us Christ must convey at least the same, if not higher; else God doth not so much for us in restoring his image, as he did at our first creation. Yea Adam had in conveying it, if he had stood, done more than Christ doth for us. Yea, and therefore when the creation of this image is spoken of, it is not only in one place said to be, εἰς ἐπίγνωσιν, for knowledge, that is, to enable to know; and therefore notes a new created power, but it is expressly termed a workmanship ' created to good works,' Eph. ii. 10. It is a whole frame of new powers, to enable a man to act that for which good works are ordained.

Yea, further, if the new creature be truly the image of God's holiness, then there is a permanent holiness of nature, or divine nature, as it is called. For God is first holy in his nature and in himself, and then is holy and righteous in all his ways and works ad extra. He is good, and so doth good, Ps. cxix. 68, and the thing is undeniable as to his transient actings; for if God had never made or done any good to the creatures, or given his law, or sent his Son, yet he had been as good in his nature, and was so from everlasting. Yea, some attributes which yet were in him, as power, mercy, &c., had never put forth acts, &c., had there not been creatures.

3. A third demonstration of it is drawn from what is said of some infants, when it is expressly said of such, that they are sanctified in the womb. So it is said of John the Baptist, Luke i. 15, that ' he was filled with the Holy Ghost,' as sanctifying of him even from the womb. He puts that in

emphatically. And to be filled with the Spirit hath a respect to that great measure of the fruits of the Spirit wrought in him then ; they were not actings holily, therefore habitual holiness. And because there was that in him which was born a spirit of the Spirit, in relation thereunto it is said of him, ver. 80, that ' he grew and was strengthened in spirit,' that is, in that inner man begotten at first, which now grew up and was actually strengthened and enlarged. And there is this further confirmation of this, that there is in infants a capacity of this habitual holiness.

For *first ;* In the state of innocency they should have had that image of God (spoken of afore) conveyed by birth, which Adam had by creation, for he was to beget in his likeness.

Secondly ; They have, now man is fallen, the image of inherent corruption conveyed. And they should not have been capable of sin inherent upon Adam's fall, if by the law of nature they had not been capable of having inherent holiness conveyed by birth. For sin and the evil is conveyed but upon the equity of that law, that the contrary good should have been conveyed, if Adam had stood. And it is withal as certain, that so far as they are capable of sin, whilst infants, they are so far capable of the contrary holiness ; and therefore of habitual holiness, as well as of habitual sin, the venom of which we all feel in our bowels from the womb.

CHAPTER IV.

That it is necessary, and congruous to the nature of things, that such inward permanent principles should be wrought in us by the Holy Ghost, to enable us to live holily.

I shall now give the reasons for this, both from the congruity and necessity of the thing.

1. It was meet and congruous, if not necessary, that God should proceed by the same law in the work of his new creation, that he doth in his first creation. Now take the law that is common unto the whole creation of God, and it will be found true upon a particular survey, that all acts or workings of any kind, in any creature, have an inbred principle, suiting and enabling the creature that acts or works thereunto. God moves all his creatures to their ends by inbred principles put into them. God in the whole creation (*qui disponit omnia suaviter*) not only or barely assists or concurs with his creatures, by a moving of them unto all their actions, but furnisheth them with powers and virtues inbred, that are the principles of such motions, by which they are inclined to such and such things, that so their actions may be connatural to them. If a stone moves downward, it hath a natural poise : if the soul understand, it is not barely by light shot into it, but there is an understanding power, faculty, or ability inbred, which beasts want ; of whom it is said they have no understanding. If the soul joined to the body sees, it is by an eye endowed with a visive faculty ; and so it is in hearing too. Again, in other creatures, you see an inherent instinct put into them, guiding and swaying them to such or such a particular action ; as you see in bees in framing their combs, and in birds building their nests, and bearing love to their young ; by which also (as the prophet says) ' the stork knows its appointed time.' It is something inbred and interwoven with their nature. Even in arts and sciences acquired, there are imperfect abilities in nature, perfected by use, yet still so as there

are principles, though imperfect, which are the foundations of them. He that invented painting first, or that hath attained the art of it, had images in the fancy, disposing him to begin to draw the pictures. And this also is the reason that some are excellent in one trade more than in another. In like manner, if a natural man performs any action morally good, he hath an inbred principle of light of conscience, impressions of moral virtues, and the law written in his heart, that moves and instigates him thereunto ; and it is an abiding principle in him : Rom. ii. 14, 15, ' Men do by nature the things of the law, which shew the effect or substance of the law written in their hearts.' Now it might be shewn that the new habiliments of the new creation are assimilated unto all these, the Holy Ghost having regulated and reduced the new creature to this common law.

1. It is like to the natural powers of seeing and understanding.

2. It is like to an instinct put into irrational creatures, who are taught of God to love their young. ' As concerning brotherly love, I shall not need to write unto you,' says the apostle, 1 Thes. iv. 9, ' for you yourselves are taught of God to love one another.' It is opposed to external teachings, and referred to the rank of instincts or endowments. As when God teacheth a brother to love his brother, the mother to love the child, or as God is said to teach the ploughman discretion and skill, Isa. xxviii. 26, in like manner all that come to Christ are said to be taught of God, John vi. 44. 45, by an impression on their spirits, such as the beasts had that came to the ark. He parallels it also with the law written in the heart by nature, yea, makes it infinitely the greater work, when he says, ' I will write my law in their hearts, and put it into their inward parts,' Jer. xxxi. 33, 34.

But although these are of themselves arguments, yet they are remoter confirmations unto that which I intend to make forth, viz., that the reason of the congruity or necessity is the same in the new creature as in the old. Yea, that there is a greater necessity in this than in the other, and that the soul should be no less enabled and furnished to spiritual things than all other creatures are unto their actings, which generally and universally is by having an internal principle enabling them so to act.

1. There is as much reason and necessity it should be thus in the new creation, as in the old.

(1.) Because this rule holds both in the second creation and in the first, that everything that acts should act according to its kind ; and they are differing inbred principles that put the difference of kind between one creature and another. Every creature hath a proper, special nature, that doth constitute its kind, and then the fruits and effects are answerable thereto. You have this law, Gen. i. 21 and 24, concerning fishes, and beasts, and plants ; trees bring forth differing fruits because of differing kinds given them, and that depends upon inbred principles, which are existent in them, even in winter, when they do not bring forth. Our Saviour Christ bringeth this very law of the first creation into the second, and urgeth it upon the Pharisees : Mat. vii. 17, 18, ' Every good tree bringeth forth good fruit, but a corrupt tree bringeth forth evil fruit. A good tree cannot bring forth evil fruit, neither can a corrupt tree bring forth good fruit.' And then in Matthew xii. 33 Christ says, ' Either make the tree good, and its fruit good, or else make the tree corrupt, and his fruit corrupt ; for the tree is known by his fruit.' Wherein (although Christ urgeth not regeneration, but conviction) ' make the tree,' &c., that is, acknowledge yourselves to be bad when your fruits are bad, and so on the contrary ; yet the ground of his conviction lies invincibly in this truth, that ere a man can bring forth a good work he must be made inwardly and radically good, for acts follow nature. Also in another place he says, 'Can you gather grapes of thorns, or figs of thistles? Can you that are evil speak good things?'

(2.) It is so, because to have inbred principles of actings maketh the creature to act connaturally and sweetly. Thus though a mother, as a woman, hath love in her, yet to act the more naturally in the loving her child, a special instinct is requisite. The sun rejoiceth to run his race, and so all creatures rejoice to keep God's ordinances to this ,day, Ps. cxix., because God hath put inbred principles in them so to do. Now of all actings of his creatures, God would have it so that this of souls in gracious actings should be most connatural, and done with the greatest alacrity, and that 'his people should be a willing people,' Ps. cx., and be acted by a free spirit, Ps. li., not by constraint, but of a willing mind. God would have the new creature so to move itself in its actings as to be the inward formal principle of that work, that it might in that respect be termed its own. And therefore as all other creatures have to their actings inbred principles to enable them unto their actings, so it was most meet that the soul of man, and especially the will, should have a bias clapped on it, a poise, an inclination, or (as the apostle's phrase is) 'a readiness,' whereof God accepts more than of the deed, 2 Cor. viii. 10–12.

2. There is a far greater necessity for the soul to have new principles, abilities given to act holily and spiritually, than at the first creation to act naturally. And the reason is far more strong, because the acts are spiritual and supernatural, and so are the objects. God and Christ, as they are revealed in the gospel, are supernatural unto the natural powers and faculties of the soul, and there is no proportion between them. There is not only such a disproportion as the bat's eye hath unto the sun, but as a blind man's eye is to the sun. In man's corrupt state, yea, and at man's best estate in innocency, though God, as revealed in the creature, and in outward effects, was the natural object of man's understanding, that is, which was naturally ordained for it by the due of creation, yet God, as in himself to be revealed, had that disproportion unto that estate, that a spirit or an angel, not appearing in some outward effect, hath to the eye of a seeing man. The most quick-sighted in that case must have a new eye, a spiritual eye made, or the same eye endowed with new spiritual power. And therefore the Scripture speaks of this as giving a new visive power, as 'eyes to see, and ears to hear,' and 1 John v. 20 it is said, 'He hath given an understanding to know him that is true,' speaking both of God and Christ. It is not merely to relieve the weakness of natural sight, as when one is to see an object far distant by the help of an optic; or as when Stephen was enabled to see and behold Christ's body in heaven, which of itself is visible, as the sun is, though disproportioned in excellency; but it is spiritual sight given wholly to enable the eye to see the spiritual objects, and to take them in. And therefore the phrase which the Scripture everywhere useth is, that else men cannot see them, nor know them, nor receive them, as hath been said. And therefore there is a necessity of infusion of such spiritual abilities, for there are no principles in man for him to begin with, by which they should be acquired.

But here a further question hath been made: Whether the necessity of such inherent principles as these is such, that God by his absolute power might not raise up, and draw forth out of the soul supernatural spiritual acts, without infusing such new principles as powers into the soul first ? Whether God's motions and excitations, and actings upon the understanding and will, might not elevate them unto such acts as Stephen's eye, without a new power of seeing, was elevated and raised up to see Christ's body in heaven ?

I answer this ; that it is not for the understanding of us poor creatures to forge shackles, or set limits to the absolute power of God, or to say he can work this and not that. Yet I think this may in the first place safely be said, that,

1. As to the privative part, there must at least be a destruction of that habit of sin in respect of the strength and the impression which it had in the soul afore. For if the soul be naturally full, and all over possessed with nothing but flesh, according to what is in John iii. 6, ' That which is born of the flesh is flesh ;' then whilst it doth so remain it can never be brought to act the contrary, no, not in the least spiritual act, for there is something within that hinders. Whilst the mind inwardly remains fleshly, it cannot be ' subject to the law of God,' Rom viii. 7. That word speaks the common language of nature, that whilst such a form remains, and fully possesseth the mind, it cannot be brought to act the contrary. God indeed can change fire into water in an instant, and so that which was fire shall moisten ; but whilst it remains fire, and is continued to be such, we may say that it cannot do so. Indeed, it may be kept from acting as fire, as the fire of Nebuchadnezzar's furnace was, but it cannot be brought to do the contrary. And thus the Scripture pronounceth of the fleshly mind, remaining such, that it cannot be subject to God, and that ' those who are in the flesh cannot please God,' Rom. viii. 7, 8. Yea, even of a regenerate man, so far as flesh is in him, so far as he is still possessed with flesh, the apostle says he cannot will or do good, Gal. v. 17. It is not only that he wants an ability, but he hath an habitual contrariety, an enmity, as one contrary form hath to another ; and that contrariety therefore must necessarily be destroyed and expelled, that the soul, being so far freed from it, may be capable to act holily. So then at least we may say, that that part of regeneration we call mortification, or (as it is expressed in Ezekiel) the ' taking away the heart of stone,' is an habitual permanent work absolutely necessary.

If it be said (as it is by some) that if Adam's soul, being wholly filled with holiness, fell into an act of sin without a principle of sinning first in it, therefore a soul, possessed with nothing but flesh and enmity to God, may be elevated to a supernatural act.

I reply, *first*, That when Adam's soul fell into that act of sinning, the holiness that was in him was that very moment expelled ; and so then the parallel here must be, that at the same instant the soul is raised to holiness, the contrary corruption must be so far expelled also. And as, in the act of sin, Adam's soul slipped the collar of its habitual grace, and so ran away from God, so must the heart, as it is acted holy, slip from so much of its inbred corruption at the same instant. But if you will suppose that corruption doth remain in its full strength and possession, it is such an uncircumcision as keeps the soul in an impotency to any such act.

But, *secondly*, The fuller answer is this, that there is not the same reason of raising up man to act holy, as there is of his falling into sin. For the possibility of his falling into sin lies in his deficiency and mutability as he was a creature, and in his aptness to fall, which his will was subject to, merely as it is a creature made out of nothing, and so its habit of grace doth perish by that deficiency when it falls out. *Solum liberum arbitrium sufficiebat ad malum* was Augustine's constant cry, the deficient will of man need no innate principle to sin, its frailty was sufficient, or rather, insufficient to it.   But it is not so in the power to do good, as it is in the transgression ; as in another like case the apostle speaks.   To sin, the soul need not be first made sinful, to constitute it formally an intrinsecal agent in it, for this may arise from a defect ; but if man will become a supernatural worker, and as an intrinsecal agent formally produce a good work, he must have such a divine form, or nature, first infused in him, or it will not be natural in him and genuine, nor is he capable to do it.

2. As to the positive part, viz., the necessity of the infusion of a new principle.   There are many that deny that any more than a help and a supernatural assistance is absolute needful, because the almighty power of God can and doth (say they) supply the room of such an inward principle, and so raise up and actuate the understanding or will without it.   For (say they) in the soul God finds a faculty of understanding, capable of that spiritual knowledge of him ; and the habit, or the new principle you call for (say they), serves but to enable or elevate that understanding to take into it God in a spiritual manner.   Now that which your supposed habit contributes hereto, why may not (say they) the power of God supply by a mere acting of that understanding, and raising it up to such acts by an almighty motion of his joining with it and overpowering the soul to it ? There is this difference (say they) between the necessity of an understanding faculty and of this new spiritual principle ; that if we suppose that first wanting, then all must say the power of God doth not supply the room of it.   God doth not understand for us, but man understands only with his own understanding, nor without an understanding can he understand, as a beast, remaining a beast, cannot.   But now for that other case of a habit, that being (say they) but a help to the understanding, may be supplied ; for what help a second cause affordeth, that the power of God alone can, if he please, supply without it.

But if the Scripture itself, and the Spirit that wrote it, and also works all grace in the heart, and knows best the proportion of things, do speak of this new inward principle of habitual grace, in the same language that it doth of this power of the natural understanding itself, or as it doth of the visive faculty whereby we see, terming it an eye to see, an ear to hear, a heart to understand, terming it also an understanding given, that we may know : then even that also is to be judged to be to the soul, in understanding supernatural things, of the same nature and necessity, that an understanding itself is to know natural things.   Yea, if it be a principle of life unto the soul of one that is dead, as a new life to a dead eye, as in Scripture it is termed (Eph. ii. 1, 5, compared), and if it is expressly termed eternal life itself inherent in a man, 1 John iii. 15, which doth constitute him formally a living man, in respect of that kind of life which is spiritual and supernatural : if this be so, then upon the same necessity, that an understanding faculty is required to a natural act, this new understanding, power, or spirit (as my text calls it), this new heart and new spirit to understanding things supernatural withal, is as absolutely required.   All grant this, that though God can give to this stone an understanding, yet he cannot be supposed to make a stone to understand without an understanding faculty.   Now in order unto an act of understanding spiritual things, this new principle infused is so styled, and is really in its proportion such, so as without it the soul is said to have no understanding, but to be blind, yea dead, as to these things that are spiritual.   God can and did take a body of red earth, and breathed into it the breath of life, and caused it to live ; but it was not possible to have made and constituted it a living soul, as the Scripture terms Adam, without having a living soul put into it, and united to it, for a thing cannot be caused to live without a spirit of life. Now so it is here, as those scriptures clearly shew. We must not call these new principles, powers, or faculties in the soul, in the same respect, or sense, that the understanding is in and to the soul. For the understanding is one and the same understanding faculty, and so is the subject of that spiritual act, after regeneration, that it was afore ; and it is the same understanding that understood other things afore, or that doth now understand other things besides spiritual things after regeneration. But by analogy it is affirmed to be a new power and a new understanding, in this respect, because the soul, which hath but one and the same faculty of understanding, must be enlivened with this grace as another life to it, ere it can spiritually understand. That grace puts a new ability into the understanding, as necessary as the understanding itself is to understand withal, as all the scriptures shew.

If indeed such principles as acquired habits do serve to give only facility or easiness in working, or serve but as spectacles to an eye that can see already, only to help it to see better and more clearly, or to see what else at such a distance it could not see, then the work might be supplied only with God's external actings. But these principles of grace do give *potentiam simpliciter*, as some schoolmen speak, power simply and absolutely. Yea, and say I, it is not only analogous to a new power, but it is to the soul more than a new power, and of a sublimer nature, and greater worth than all men's understandings devoid of it. It is ' spirit' (says the text), which is more than a power. It is ' a divine nature,' which is more than a natural power. It is indeed as the soul is to a dead eye, when it comes to enliven and inform it, which is more than to give an eye simply or barely organised, and fitted to see. Or at least it is, if not as the soul, yet as the life itself, by which, as diffused from the soul, the eye is made a living eye, and so immediately capable of that vital or living act of seeing ; and by reason of which it is a seeing eye, a living eye, when yet it ceaseth to behold anything, as when closed, and in sleep. It is the seed of God, which (as the seed of any other thing) hath the virtue of that which it cometh from in such a manner as the soul itself hath not, though it cometh from God.

That which hath much conduced to misguide the schoolmen* in this great point, hath been,

1. Their addictedness to the natural power of man's will and understanding, that in supernatural acts it should share with the grace of God. They have therefore easily been led to judge that these natural principles, strongly assisted, and only extrinsecally acted by God as an efficient and mover with

---

* Aquinas distinguisheth the necessity of a principle of grace, and that of ordinary habit thus : of the first, *ut intellectus fiat potens ;* of the other, *ut intellectus fiat potentior,* 1 par. quæst. 12, artic. 5.

Suarez, when he comes to the decision of this, treads upon ice ; and is loath to deny these principles of grace to be *potentiæ,* because they give new power to the soul ; and yet he must have the natural power of the soul itself to be a sharer with them in their motion, supernaturally, and therefore concludes it thus. *Quod si quis, de nomine magis quam de re contendens, dicat hos habitus, quatenus dant potestatem agendi, vocandos esse potentias ; respondebimus saltem non esse potentias integras seu completas ; imo nec dare inchoationem, ut sic dicam, et radicalem potestatem : at dare quasi complementum potestatis.*—Lib. 6. de grat. C. 5. Num. 12.

them, might produce such acts: and that such divine habits as grace are only required to make them more natural to the powers of the soul.

2. The schoolmen's mistake in this point ariseth from their opinion, that the natural understanding and will in the soul are the root or principle of whatever life or act, either spiritual or natural, the soul produceth as a living agent. So that it is the natural understanding, and other faculties in the soul, which (as they speak), are the sole *principium vitale*, that is, the living principle, or seat and subject of all life. The soul, and the active faculties and powers thereof, are those that live and have that life in them, and so live this supernatural life. And this is proper to that which lives, that it intrinsecally moves itself; for so you know all living things do, and not from an extrinsecal force or power acting them, as stones are moved.

And therefore (say they), the soul and its powers having an inward principle of self-motion, there is nothing more required than that God should move and act them. But if they consulted the Scriptures they would find, that that which is termed the vital or life-principle of this kind of life spiritual and eternal in the soul, is not the natural powers of the soul; but that all the life-principle the soul hath in understanding or willing, is naturally deadness unto this life; and that the grace infused is called eternal life, &c. It is true, indeed, the subject or root upon which this new principle, or power of spiritual life is engrafted, is the soul, and thereby it is diffused to the faculties of it, and so the natural soul is in that respect absolutely necessary as the subject of this new spiritual life (of which a beast, remaining a beast, is not capable), and so the natural soul and its faculties are as the root and foundation, or as the stock that the other new principle of life is engrafted upon. But still that which is the formal next complete principle or power of active life spiritual, as such, is that grace which God engrafts upon that stock, yea, and the whole of the soul's principle of spiritual life doth lie and consist therein: though still if this grace were not in such a subject, viz., a reasonable soul, that spiritual principle of life would not be a life at all. Thus far indeed the natural powers do contribute unto it. So then in producing these supernatural acts of knowing or loving God, there are three principles to be considered.

(1.) *Principium quod*, the principle which; that is, which is the seat and subject of all; and that is the soul, and its natural faculties, as they have a natural life in them.

(2.) There is *principium quo*, the principle of life by which the soul acts, and from which, as it acts spiritually, it hath a spiritual life; and that, say we, is grace infused, which is termed eternal life in a man.

(3.) There is God, who is the fountain and efficient cause and worker both of that principle of life in the soul, and then of all the acts from it, by his motions, influences, and helps, and elevations, and raisings up of that life to act according to its kind; which actings, notwithstanding this infused life in us, do depend upon God's power to work them in us, Phil. ii. 13, as much as the infusion of life itself doth.

This being thus explained, herein lies to me the necessity of such an inward principle of spiritual life to be infused (besides what life of understanding or willing the soul hath of itself, as also besides God's assisting motions and strengthenings), that if any soul be ever brought to put forth any act of spiritual supernatural life, that soul must be constituted or made first a supernatural living agent or worker: it must be put into that order or rank of agents or workers, and thereby so be fitted to move from, and within itself, as a supernatural living agent or worker, that so all such acts of life as proceed from it may come to be denominated, or called its own, as acts of a creature that now lives such a supernatural kind of life, and so that every holy action may be termed the act of its own life, when it so works. And the reason is clear from the analogy or like proportion of any other living agent in any kind. For if any act of any living creature be accounted a living act, or a life-act, that creature must first be a living creature, endued with that kind of life which the act itself is of, which it doth put forth. If it be an act of natural or sensitive life (as to see, hear, &c.), as in a beast, necessarily the beast must be a living beast, or creature; living, I say, within itself that kind of life it putteth forth in that act, or that action cannot be a living action. Now then, by the same reason and proportion (for such as the act is, such is and must be the principle that works it, which holds in this and other kinds of life whatever), if the soul come ever to produce a supernatural-life-act (as I may call it), it is absolutely necessary it be constituted and put into the rank of a supernatural-life-agent, to have a principle of supernatural life wholly anew communicated unto it, over and above its being in the order or rank of nature's catalogue a life-agent. And though men talk that the soul, with its faculties, is a living principle, yet still it is not a living principle supernaturally, otherwise than life, eternal life; and the soul, with all its faculties, remaining purely natural, is dead in respect to that life.

Another thing that deceived many of the schoolmen is, that they take the similitude of acquired habits, and make the measure by which to judge of these infused habits, and so imagine that the natural faculties are the immediate subjects of the infused principles of grace, and not the soul itself, even as those natural faculties are of such acquired habits; and so they thought these infused habits of grace should be no otherwise required, in order unto working, than those other acquired. Now it is certain and granted, that God's power extraordinary can in an instant supply the defect of such kind of habits, only by assisting acts, without infusing any new principle. Thus whereas man's tongue is apt to learn, and acquire by pains and use, any tongue or language in use, yet God in the primitive times did, without infusing the settled permanent habit of speaking such and such a tongue, assist a man's mind for that present, whilst the Spirit acted him, to speak or interpret that language, as if he had learned it by use. Thus some spake with tongues who did not understand the tongue, and some interpreted a tongue that were not able to speak it; as might seem by some passages in 1 Cor. xiv. Now, indeed, if those supernatural principles we speak of, were, at the highest supposition, but the infusion of such abilities as these, that might be otherwise acquired in time, by the natural powers of the soul by use, then indeed the opposite assertion might pass, that God could (by his assisting power alone) supply without such a principle, what the infusion of the principle served for; because the natural soul, as such, did hold a proportion to such acts, if it were acted and assisted by God; for as it is a natural soul, it might acquire them of itself. But it is not so in the principles of grace, for they belong wholly to another rank, and order, and kind of life, as hath been said. They are not such superficiary, washy tinctures, or additional impressions on the soul, such as those other habits which are seated but finger deep (as when a man's fingers, fancy, and memory have acquired a skill to play on musical instruments, musical tunes, which have no deeper subject than the finger, fancy, and memory), but this heavenly tincture goes deeper. It is not as an ordi-

nary accident seated immediately in an accident, that is, the immediate
subject of graces are not the faculties of the understanding and will, as they
are powers and accidents themselves in the soul; but this heaven-born
image and likeness of God (which is more worth than all men's souls), is
immediately by God diffused into the soul itself; and the soul is as immediately the subject of it as of those powers themselves. It is not in the
soul only as paint or white in a wall, in the outward superficies of it; but
as light in the body of the sun, and as the glory that is in the spiritual
bodies of men at the resurrection. 'The God of peace sanctify you
throughout' (says the apostle) 'in body, soul, and spirit;' yea, it seizeth
on 'the spirit of the mind itself,' Eph. iv. 23, that is, if there be anything
pure, the soul is throughout immediately steeped and dyed in it; it hath it
by infusion (as the school word is), or it is shed abroad in the heart, as the
Scripture saith. It is in the soul as a new soul or life to it, and it then
diffuseth itself to those powers that are therein : and in the understanding
it becomes a spiritual understanding, and the light of life : in the will it
becomes love, an infusion of love to that God above itself, whose image it
is. And so it is indeed a thing (which I have all this while pleaded it to
be) that deserves as much to be styled a new power, and life in the soul,
as those natural faculties themselves are said to be. Neither is it beholden
to them for its interest and station in the soul, but can vie with them for
immediateness of inherency. Yea, it inspiriteth and teacheth them, and
actuates them with new powers of an endless life, which they had not
afore. And so by this means, this new principle of grace becomes an ear
to hear, an eye to see, an understanding to know spiritual things, as spiritual, in as real a manner as these other natural powers of understanding
and will are, in their kind of life, able to perceive natural things.

CHAPTER V.

That the new creature wrought in us by the Spirit of God is a change of heart.

*A new heart also will I give you, and a new spirit will I put within you ; and
I will take away the stony heart out of your flesh, and I will give you a heart
of flesh.   And I will put my Spirit within you, and cause you to walk in my
statutes, and ye shall keep my judgments, and do them.*—Ezek. XXXVI.
26, 27.

The glory of God's grace in the application of salvation unto us in this
life, and the commitment of it to the Holy Ghost, you find it put together
in this one scripture. Here is,

1. A creating and issuing new abilities, and vivific principles of spiritual
life, whereby the soul is quickened and enabled to act as a supernatural
agent, or worker of all sorts of spiritual works and operations, which is here
in Ezekiel said to be the giving a new heart and a new spirit, together with
taking away the heart of stone, which is as truly a work of omnipotency as
to turn a stone into flesh, into living flesh, or to transform stones into bread
(upon doing which the devil himself would have believed Christ to be the
Son of God); or of stones to raise up children to Abraham, whereby John
the Baptist celebrateth God's omnipotent power.

2. Here is set forth the Holy Ghost's effectual drawing forth, and efficaciously working every such spiritual act, causing us to walk in his ways,

both by his giving Τὸ θελεῖν, 'to will and to do of his good pleasure,' Philip. ii. 13.

3. Here is the giving this person of the Holy Ghost unto our persons; to dwell in us for ever, as the author of both of these, which is expressed in those words, 'I will put my Spirit within you,' which comes in between the former two. It is he who gives us the new heart at first; and having predisposed and prepared us thereby, causeth us to ' walk,' and do; that is, draws forth that new heart into act.

The words of my text, Ezek. xxxvi. 26, 27, are promises of the covenant of grace concerning all that is wrought in us by God, from first to last, unto salvation, summed up to two heads: 1. The giving a new heart, &c.; 2. The intent of that gift, viz., to enable us to do, and to walk, which is a continuation of doing. The first is the principle of doing, placed first in order, and accordingly given first, as the foundation of subsequent doing and walking ever after. There is also the Spirit of God, over and besides that new spirit promised, given to them, to cause them to act and do, when once the new heart and spirit is given. And although the Holy Spirit of God is promised, to cause them to do, as without whom the new heart alone would not produce those new actions, yet so as withal the Spirit himself doth not cause us to do without a new heart first given; and unless the old heart, the heart of stone (the principle of the former contrary walking and doing), be removed and taken away, as being that contrary principle that letteth, and would let for ever, if it continued in its old full being and strength. The Holy Ghost is the extrinsecal cause of the operation therefore said to be put; but the new heart is the intrinsecal cause of our doing, though as acted by the Holy Ghost.

And these things are consonant to reason and scriptures.

1. The heart doth, in the language of nature, speak the primary intrinsecal cause of motion and action, being the first seat and forge of all the vital spirits by which we act and move. And so in the soul there is that answers to it, which is the spring; and actions are the streams that issue from thence : ' Above all keeping keep thy heart, for out of it are the issues of life,' that is, the course and actings of a man's life, which are as issues from the heart as a fountain. The walking and doing here are not the new heart itself, for that (as was noted) is a new gift and benefit distinct therefrom. Nor is the Spirit's acting our natural faculties and principles already in our hearts, the whole or sole work on God's part in us. Nor consists it only in actings (which the promise of the 27th verse is wholly spent upon), but that verse before, the 26th, is taken up as much with the promise of giving a new heart and removing the old, and is a promise of as much grace as this latter in verse 27.

2. It is true that the natural faculties of the mind, and will, and affections, are in Scriptures termed the heart, or connotated at least when the heart is spoken of; and therefore they must be taken in and supposed here, for they are the subject and intrinsecal principle of all the actings of a man in doing whatever is done, be it good or evil. And this is common to all men, whether regenerate or unregenerate, in their doing good or evil, to do it with their hearts. And therefore Solomon admonisheth, Prov. iv. 23, ' Keep thy heart, for out of it are the issues of life,' which reason in general concerns all men, that such as the heart is, such is the course of life. He compares the heart to the fountain, and the actions to the streams that issue out from it: ' A good man,' says Christ, Mat. xii. 35, ' out of the good treasure of the heart bringeth forth good things: and an evil

man out of the evil treasure bringeth forth evil things.'   So as a heart to do is ascribed to either of them.

3. I shall confirm this by other scriptures.   You have a workmanship said to be created unto good works : Eph. ii. 10, 'For we are his workmanship, created in Christ Jesus unto good works, which God hath before ordained that we should walk in them,'   Here is a whole frame or ποίημα created and wrought in us, in order unto our working or acting, God having ordained the one for the other, viz., those works for us to walk in (as it follows), and this workmanship to bring forth those works.   You read in like manner of the image of God created, εἰς ἐπίγνωσιν, 'unto knowledge,' for it is wrought to that end.   And it is more expressly said, 1 John v. 20, 'He hath given us an understanding, that we may know him that is true.'

Another scripture is that passage in 1 John iii. 9, 'Whosoever is born of God doth not commit sin ; for his seed remaineth in him : and he cannot sin, because he is born of God.'   The words I lay hold on for my purpose are what that seed of God that remains in a man born of God should be.   I might annex this argument, to be drawn from the interpretation of these passages, unto the first argument I drew before from John iii. 6, that it is a *birth*, a thing *born*.   And this which I shall now urge, you may well put to that, for it seconds it ; and they do mutually confirm each other.

The scope is, to set out the difference between an unregenerate man and a regenerate (under the dominion of grace), in point of sinning.   Yea, and it may be extended to the differing case of Adam in his first sinning.   He mentions indeed only the case of a regenerate man, but asserts concerning him : 1. That a man born of God commits not sin ; that is, persists not in any constant track or course of sinning ; for committing sin here is meant in the same sense as that in the words afore, 'He that doth righteousness is righteous,' is meant, which position is further amplified that 'he cannot sin.'   2. The reason of which is resolved into this, 'because he is born of God,' he hath by and from that his birth, a seed of and from God remaining in him ; that is, he hath a new principle of holiness, a divine nature, and *indoles*, which God that begat him, and formed anew for himself, maintains in his heart, out of his gracious favour towards that grace, so as to continue the station and residence of the substance and matter of it in the heart, whilst yet its activity may be, or is weakened and abated by the prevailing of the contrary corruption (that is in the soul) through the will's indulging to it.   And yet so far as that seed and principle in the solid substance of it thus remains, this corrupt will, nor all a man's own lust that tempts him, cannot employ or draw this seed to close with that sin, but it stands off, and is averse, and co-operates not—'It is not I, but sin that dwelleth in me '—yea, more or less it lusteth against it.   But it is not thus with an unregenerate man's will, nor was it thus with Adam in his first sinning.   But all his principles and concreated habits of holiness inherent, were by one single act of sinning, through the mere mutability and vertibility of his will (suppose his sin had been the least sin), utterly driven out of his heart and destroyed at once.   The reason whereof lay in this : the terms of his state then being the covenant of works, the curse of that law in threatening—'In that day thou sinnest thou diest the death '—took hold of his soul, and began to have its full process and execution against all that spiritual life that was in him, and raised out the whole of what was holy in him, which was the best of his lives, to whose keeping the whole stock of his grace was committed and betrusted ; and he was no more able (when he sinned) to keep the least mite thereof to remain still in him, than a man that is stabbed to the heart is able to keep his soul in his body. But a stronger law is now, under grace, in force over men that are born of God, who are 'not under the law, but under grace;' which law is, that the strength of this inherent grace is the gospel of grace, which preserves this seed in the heart in the midst of sinning, so as that grace in the soul is not wholly expelled upon every sin the will consents to, as it is acknowledged by all. And who can set or put the limits of the difference, that in some sins to which the will yet consents, sin should not totally expel that seed for that present; and in other sinnings, perpetrated by the will's allowance and consent,·grace should be destroyed for that present? Now the preservation of this seed is because it remains upon that gospel-account specified in such a man, and that is the τὸ κατέχον, the thing that lets, or hinders, that he cannot sin with fulness of consent. And whilst this seed upon this account remains, so much of it as remains and hath possession and residence in the heart cannot be made use of, or be drawn to a party with its contrary, or to act the same thing which its contrary doth act. Nor will we grant that the activity of that principle, though preserved in being, may be retunded so as to put forth no acting; for the apostle affirms (Gal. v. 17) that it is never so but in some degree it makes a resistance, though so weak as it is not discernible by his heart in whom it is, as there is some motion of the pulse, though not felt, whilst there is life. This that holds invincibly true, that whilst this seed of life remains in the will at all (and that it remains is the apostle's word and assertion), it, to be sure, cannot sin, no more than sin, whilst it remains in the heart, can act holily. Sin and corruption, so far as it remains, cannot become an actor of true holiness; you may much safelier affirm that fire, as fire, may cool and moisten. It is true God may, and once we read of did, retund the activity of fire whilst it remained fire, so as not to burn, or so much as singe, as was seen in Nebuchadnezzar's fiery furnace; but that fire, remaining fire, should cool and moisten, this were utterly contrary to its nature. And the truth of this maxim the apostle confirmeth, and applies it to this very case of sin and holiness in us, bottoming it upon this very reason; viz., that a thing contrary in its nature, whilst it remains contrary, cannot be brought to co-operate in the same act with that which is contrary to itself. Gal. v. 17, 'For the flesh lusteth against the Spirit, and the Spirit against the flesh: and these are contrary the one to the other; so that ye cannot do the things that ye would.' And the same is the bottom ground of that other assertion of his in Rom. viii. 7, 8, 'The carnal mind is enmity against God; for it is not subject to the law of God, neither indeed can be. So then they that are in the flesh cannot please God.' And let no man say it is in the power of the will to cause it so to do; the apostle says the contrary, 'So as ye cannot do what you would,' neither in sinning with your whole will, nor in doing good with your whole hearts and whole souls. And although corruption that is in us may so far prevail over the will, against the active power of grace in the will, as often exert for the outward act to commit a sin, yet still, so far as a principle of grace exists, and God causeth it to continue and abide, and whilst God upholds it so to do in the soul and will, that part of the soul and will cannot be prevailed with by the corrupt part to join with it in sinning, for they are contrary. Our apostle John, in this his first epistle, expressly says that it doth remain. And how should that be if God did not maintain it by his grace? For that sin is stronger than created holiness, take it in its own efficacy, and as in itself, we have found by Adam sinning. And it is in effect said, in that verse, that it is God that causeth it to remain, even 'because it is born of God;' and is therefore so beloved of God, that he says, 'Destroy it not, there is a blessing in it.'

And what is the thing that doth remain, but a seed; and as all must grant, distinct from fruit? Now, every fruit must have a root to grow upon. And therefore, gracious actings proceed from a seed let in by a birth, and that birth is from our being born of God, whose seed it is called. Which fully makes good the assertion, that in regeneration, not merely our actions are altered, but there is a change of heart.

Use 1. We see then, that one fundamental difference between them that fall away, and others that persevere in grace, is, that in the first, there is not a change of heart nor a new principle, a seed from God that remains. Many glorious things are spoken of temporary believers, but it is nowhere said in all the Scripture (that I can find), that they are born again. This assigned difference is congruous to the works that are wrought on them. In the one, there is a stirring, an elevating what is in nature, as of virtuous dispositions and self-love, by such motives as suit self, laid down in the gospel; which motives, when they cease, those actings in their hearts, which men take for grace, do cease also. It was the case of the stony ground, who 'received the word with joy, but immediately' (as the word is, Mark iv. 17) they fall off from it, whereas in the other, it becomes new; new acts towards new objects, so new principles: 2 Cor. v. 17, 'Old things pass away, and all things become new.' And though operations may cease, or be weakened and overborne with the contrary corruption, so far as to prevail unto the outward acts of sin, yet there is a constant abiding principle which lusts unto the contrary. And this difference is found by experience in the one sort and the other. And you find also this difference in Scripture, in that parable of the sower, of the stony ground; Mat. xiii. 21, Mark iv. 17, it is said, 'they have no root in themselves,' which phrase expresseth the proper language of inherent grace habitually seated in the heart. There might be, and was, a springing up, from an external principle moving them, as the Holy Ghost stirred them by the word, but they had no root in themselves. And thus Job expresseth the difference between himself and the hypocrites, in the number of which his friends went about to persuade him that he was; Job xix. 28, 'The root of the matter' (says he) 'is in me;' that is, truth and sincerity of heart towards God, whence my profession hath risen. And the apostle (Gal. v.) alludes to the same comparison, where he calls adultery, fornication, and so forth, 'works of the flesh;' 'but the fruits' (says he) 'of the Spirit' (the new creature in us, to which flesh is opposed; as also in that text, John iii.) 'are love, joy,' &c. And in this sense they are opposed in the 17th verse of that chapter, 'The flesh lusteth against the Spirit, and the Spirit against the flesh: and these are contrary the one to the other.' By *spirit* he means not the Holy Ghost in us, for it must not be said that the Holy Ghost lusteth against the flesh, but it is that spirit which he begets, and then acteth, which is contrary to the corruption in us, as two contrary qualities use to be. And that metaphor of 'fruits of the spirit,' and 'works of the flesh' doth congruously argue this spirit to be a root, whence these fruits arise.

The like difference I observed from the parable, in Mat. xxv., between the wise virgins and the foolish. The foolish had oil in their lamps, for a profession. They had present assistance for what they did, by motions and the like. They had heat, and warmth from rubbing, and stirrage, but tney had not oil in the vessel, which remained, as principles of grace do when men are asleep, as these were. They had not warmth and heat from a principle of life.

Use 2. Let us therefore examine ourselves. Acts and motions will not save us, without a spiritual new frame of heart, which is acted and wrought upon; whereas when these other motions are off, men's hearts remain as bad as ever, Heb. xii. 28. The apostle useth this argument, that 'seeing,' by the state of grace in which we are, 'we have a kingdom that cannot be shaken,' perpetual and abiding, 'we should have grace' correspondent and answerable; let us therefore have a fixed and abiding principle thereof within us, 'that we may serve God acceptably,' seek unto God to work this in you, as well as the act and deed. 'Turn me, O Lord' (saith the convert Ephraim, Jer. xxxi. 18), 'and I shall be turned.'

Use 3. When a lust stirs and ariseth in thee, either from Satan's temptation or from thine own heart, and the mass of corruption that is in thee, seek thou unto God to give thee the contrary grace, and to act that grace in thee, that it may lust against that corruption and overcome it: James iv. 6, 'The spirit that is in us lusteth after envy; but he gives more grace. Wherefore he saith, He giveth grace to the humble.' And for this especially the apostle frames his prayer for the Thessalonians : 1 Thes. v. 23, 'And the very God of peace sanctify you throughout; and I pray God your whole spirit and soul and body be preserved blameless unto the coming of our Lord Jesus Christ.' And bless God if thou dost find such an abiding principle so wrought in thee, a seed of God, that thou canst not sin or do what thou wouldst, in the sense before explained. Bless God for it, for this is a great work ; as in Adam at first there was the image of God, as a principle concreated with him, which was the foundation of all.

Use 4. And then again, rest not in having sleeping habits. The wise were saved, having oil in their vessel; but being asleep, they were frightened out of that sleep, or they had not been saved neither, Matt. xxv. And therefore endeavour to exercise every grace upon every occasion it is ordained to act in, and that is the end of it. 'Let patience have her perfect work.' Patience as the grace given habitually, let it have its perfect work that it is ordained for. And so do as to every grace else, that every grace may be able to say at your death, 'I have done the work thou gavest me to do.'

The apostle, 2 Pet. i., having exhorted to add grace to grace, as to faith, virtue, &c., both by increasing the principle and acting accordingly, he concludes, ver. 8, 'If these be in you, and abound' (the root of them in bringing forth fruit), 'they make you that you shall not be barren nor unfruitful in the knowledge of Jesus Christ.' As thou mayest have every sin in thee, though yet thou hast not acted it; so thou hast every grace in thee, in the root, which thou hast not yet experience of. And therefore (as Paul saith) as in other graces, so 'see you abound in this grace also,' for grace is ordained to act. It is the image of God, and as God is pure act, so grace, in imitation of him, should be.

CHAPTER VI.

The new creature in us is a conformity to the image of Christ.

But we all, with open face beholding as in a glass the glory of the Lord, are changed into the same image, from glory to glory, by the Spirit of the Lord. —2 Cor. III. 18.

That you may know the scope and coherence of these words, our apostle in this chapter throughout sets forth the excellency of the gospel of Jesus Christ, whereof he was made a minister; though, as he himself says at the beginning, he needed not to have done it unto them, because they had sufficient experience of the power and glorious efficacy of it, even in their own hearts, God having used his ministry as a pen to draw forth even his own image, and the image of his Son in their hearts, by the power of the Spirit accompanying it. I need (says he, ver. 3) no letters of recommendation, ' for you are made manifest to be the epistle of Christ, ministered,' or written ' by us, not with ink, but the Spirit of the living God; not in tables of stone, but in fleshly tables of the heart.' And from thence he falls upon a set and large commendation of this ministry, to the end of the chapter, and for that purpose makes a comparison between the law and the gospel, the ministry of Moses and of Jesus Christ. The sum of which is this: The law indeed (says he) had glory in it, for it revealed the glorious will of God, setting before men's eyes that image wherein they were created ; for the law was the copy of it. Which glory was shadowed out by the shining of Moses's face when he came off the mount. But yet, alas! it was but the ministry of death (as it is called at that 7th verse), to the hearers and beholders of it; for though they beheld it, yet it changed not their hearts into the image of it ; nay, it dazzled their eyes so that Moses was fain to put a veil over his face, in token that his ministry did not change men's hearts or open their eyes, but a veil lay over all men's hearts in the rending* of it ; but now the ministry of the gospel doth exceed every way in glory, ver. 9.

1. It is as the glass or mirror, which represents unto us a far more excellent glory, even the glory of the Lord Jesus Christ, he being (Gal. iii. 1) pictured, described, and set forth therein to men's eyes in all his glorious properties of life and death, being crucified before men's eyes. So that the gospel sets forth the image of Christ, who is the image of his Father, and the brightness of his glory, Heb. i. 3. So that in the face of Jesus Christ, revealed in the glass, doth shine the glorious image of God the Father, and that more clearly than it did in the law, or in man at his first creation, 2 Cor. iv. 6.

2. There is not only a brighter discovery of the glory of Christ in the gospel, but believers have a clearer view of it in the dispensation of the gospel than they had who lived under that of the law : ' We behold with open face ' (says the apostle) ' the glory of the Lord,' not veiled and obscured, but in the clearest light.

3. We do not barely behold it and view it, but it changeth us into the same image. The law was a dead letter, and though it shewed us the will of God, yet it changed us not into the image of it ; but the gospel reveals the glorious image of Jesus Christ to true believers, and changeth them

* Qu. ' reading ' ?—Ed.

into the same image, yet so as by degrees, from one degree of glory to another, this glorious image being perfected by little and little, till we come to the full stature of Christ.

4. Then lastly is shewn the ground and true reason why the gospel thus changeth those that look into it by faith, because (ver. 6, 7, 8) the gospel is the ministration of the Spirit ; but the law is a dead letter. The Spirit accompanieth the ministration of the gospel, and we are changed into Christ's image, by the Spirit of the Lord.

Obs. In all true believers, that have their eyes opened to see Jesus Christ in the gospel by true faith, there is a most blessed change wrought in them into the same image of Jesus Christ, as he is revealed in that gospel.

1. I say *all believers*, for ' we all ' (says the apostle) that do ' behold Christ ' by faith are thus changed. He doth not speak only of ministers and apostles, but all true Christians ; for the comparison stands between true believers and the people or children of Israel, who could not behold the glory of Moses's ministry. But they are believers that in that gospel with open face behold the glory of the Lord. Compare the 13th, 14th, and 15th verses with the 18th verse.

2. They are changed thus in this life, for it is by beholding Christ in the mirror ; but after this life is ended, the glass shall be taken away, and we shall see him as he is.

3. They are changed into that image of Christ which is revealed in the gospel ; for being changed by beholding him therein, therefore so far as they behold of Christ in the gospel, so far are they changed. The doctrine having so good ground in the text, so as you cannot look on the text but it presents itself to your consideration, I will omit other Scriptures that be alleged for it, and give you some reasons of it, and so come to the uses. I shall give only one place. In this chapter, 2 Cor. iii. 3, the apostle affirms of the Corinthians, to whom he wrote, that they were made manifest to be the epistle of Christ, which was written in their hearts. What doth he mean there by the ' epistle of Christ,' but copies written out by the Spirit, even word for word, line for line, so that in their hearts and lives might be read the grace of Jesus Christ in some measure, and the likeness of his death and resurrection ? They were his epistle, but Christ's image was the matter of it.

The first *reason* of the doctrine is drawn from that special and ultimate end that God hath predestinated us to. I do not say the end he chose us for, but that which he did predestinate us to. For that is the difference between election and predestination ; the one is *for* an end, his own glory ; the other is *to* an end, that is, what he means to do with his children and chosen ones. Now if you look into Rom. viii. 29, 30, you shall find the apostle says there, that ' those whom he foreknew, he also, or withal, did predestinate'; that is, appoint to this especial end ! What ? ' To be conformed to the image of his Son.' The apostle adds withal the reason, ' that he might be the first-born among many brethren.' The scope of the apostle, why he brings the general proposition there, is to arm believers against afflictions, for it was Christ's portion before us, and God hath predestinated us to the same image, and yet not only to afflictions, for an image implies a conformity in every part ; it is not otherwise an image or likeness. And so he brings in this general proposition for their comfort, that as they are like to Christ in suffering, so shall they be in all things else. He brings it in for their comfort, that God had ordained them in all things to be like unto his Son, and to be conformed to the same image, both of grace, sufferings, and at last of glory, thereby to arm them against these afflictions, that so they might be content to be like unto Christ in this as well as in the rest, as knowing assuredly they should be like him in glory, as well as in suffering conformed to the same image. It is a general proposition, brought to this particular purpose ; and as an image is not an image of another, unless it be conformable in every part, so we are not conformed to Christ's image unless we be made like him in all things.

1. It is the end to which we are predestinated, containing the full purpose and intention of God in his decree, that we should in all things be made like to Christ, in this life, like to him in grace and afflictions, in our measure, and after in glory.

2. There is the reason and measure of this conformity, ' That he might be the firstborn among many brethren.'

(1.) Forasmuch as all are said to be his brethren, it implies it. God had many children to bring to glory, and he would have them all alike as brethren, all to resemble him and one another ; and therefore conformed them all to the image of his eldest son. God set up Christ as the masterpiece, first pattern, and draught of his decree, predestinating all his to be like unto him ; that what graces and glory he had, they in their measure should have also. And as, Heb. ii. 11, the reason why he took our nature on him (being made like unto us by taking the similitude of sinful flesh) is given, that he might call us brethren, so also that we might be able to call him brother. He conforms us in all things like unto himself, that he might be the first-born of many brethren. And this too in respect of the sanctification of our nature, that ' he who sanctifieth and they who are sanctified might be all of one ;' yet still so as he might be the first-born among all those brethren, were they never so many. In the old law, the elder brother had the pre-eminency ; and therefore, though we should be made like to him in grace and glory, yet he would have the dignity, the priority, and the pre-eminence in all those things wherein we were made like him, both in grace, and glory, and also in sufferings. There are none equal to him ; they are but like him. So that out of this place you see, that howsoever God created us in his own image at the first immediately, yet his intent was to restore it by another way. He, having a Son that was the image of himself, resolved that he should take our nature upon him, that he might be therein made like to us, that so, filling his nature with all grace and with all glory, he might conform us again unto the image of that his Son, that we might all be brethren, all alike conformed unto him. The same apostle tells us, Col. i. 19, that ' it pleased the Father that in him should all fulness dwell ;' and God ordained him as the store-house and treasury of all that grace and glory which he means to bestow on his children. Adam lost all, and all is now in Christ, the second Adam, that ever the elect sons of men shall have ; and this fulness dwells in him, Col. ii. 9, that we might be made complete in him. It is principally there meant in regard of sanctification, as appears by what follows there. Now, how are we therein said to be complete in him, but when we do partake of that his fulness in a completeness suiting with our measure, and conformity unto him, so as no part of likeness to him is wanting, as the word *complete* implies? And therefore the apostle, in the 11th, 12th, 13th, and 14th verses, shews wherein it consists, viz., in being circumcised as he was, and in being buried as he was, and in being raised up as he was. Therefore all fulness is in him, and therefore also he is called the Sun of righteousness, because as all light is gathered up into the body of the sun, and dwells there in the fulness of it, and of it the moon and other stars do partake; and the sun, shining on them, makes them in their measure light as the sun itself is, so is it here. God hath appointed Jesus Christ as the person in whom should remain, in the fulness of it, the glorious image of God, and all believers upon whom he shines are transformed into the same image; and the nearer they come to him, the more they are transformed. This you see is the decree of God concerning all his: to be conformed to the image of Christ; and it contains fully all that can be said of what we were ordained to.

2. A second reason of the doctrine is this: when God doth call any man, then he begins to execute that his decree, and so to renew the image of Christ in him. For 'whom he hath predestinated, them also he hath called;' and calling is nothing but the conforming us to his image in this life, in regard of grace; and therefore, says Paul, Gal. i. 15, 16, 'When it pleased God to call me, and to reveal his Son in me;' that is, when he began to manifest this image of Christ in my poor soul. What then is the new birth, but the forming and fashioning the image of Christ in us? 'I travail in birth again,' says Paul, Gal. iv. 19, 'until Christ be formed in you.' What is the meaning that Christ should be formed in them, but that the lively and real image of Christ should be imprinted on their hearts? And in the word *formed* there is a metaphor taken from the shaping of a child in the womb; that look, as the natural parents communicating matter of their own bodies, it is framed and shaped by the spirits into the lively likeness of themselves, limb for limb, answerable to themselves, so likewise is Christ appointed by God as a 'second Adam,' as it is in 1 Cor. xv. 45–48, and an 'everlasting Father,' Isa. ix. 6, who communicates to us the seed of his word, 1 Pet. i. 23, to be shed into our hearts, and the Spirit of Christ enlivening it, frames it and fashions it in every limb like unto himself; and as the first Adam begat a child in his likeness, Gen. v., so doth this second Adam in his likeness. And though indeed the full conformity to him shall be in heaven, yet so far as Christ is revealed, so far are we made like him; we see him but as he was upon earth, revealed in the gospel, and unto that image are we conformed here in the new birth. As we see him in the mirror, we are made like to that image in it; but when we see him as he is, we shall also be like him in glory, 1 John iii. 1, 2. And therefore, Isa. liii. 10, we are called his seed, which do prolong his days upon the earth; for though he be ascended up to heaven, yet he begets daily those that are like to him as he was on the earth; so like him, as they are said to prolong his days on earth; as you use to say of a child, like his parent, that so long as he lives, his father will never die, he is so like unto him. So the resemblance of Christ in us doth prolong his days on earth; and therefore Christ is said to prolong his days on earth. Christ is said to be 'in us,' 2 Cor. xiii. 5, to 'live in us,' Gal. ii. 20. And we are said to put on Christ, even in regard of sanctification, Rom. xiii. 14; that is, we clothe our hearts and lives with his image, fashioning ourselves to him. Will you have all in a word? The church, the body, the members of Christ are called, 1 Cor. xii. 12, *Christ:* if you read the whole verse, and consider it well, you will find it so; and that both in regard of union to him, and communion with him in his image and likeness, and therefore also have the same common name with him, as brethren and members use to have. For the name Christ signifies *Anointed;* and he is indeed anointed first, as our head, with the Spirit and the grace of it above measure, even above his fellows; but yet so that as from Aaron's head that oil ran down and anointed his clothing and all his body, so do the grace and virtue of all that

Christ did or suffered descend to them that 'receive the anointing' of him, 1 John ii. 27.

Use 1. The first use may be a use of trial or examination, whether we yet belong to Christ or no. Let us examine whether we have his image renewed in us. We are predestinated (as you have heard) to be conformed thereunto. And in our calling also, God begins to renew this his decree on us. If that therefore we would make our calling and election sure (as the apostle speaks, 2 Peter i. 10), we should labour to try and examine whether Christ his image be in us or no. Let me therefore exhort you in the words of the apostle, 2 Cor. xiii. 5, to try and examine yourselves, whether Christ's image be in you. 'Know ye not your own selves, how that Christ is in you, unless you be reprobates?' that is, in the same state with them; for those that are predestinate are predestinate to be conformed to the image of his Son, which if it be not in you, ye are as reprobates. My brethren, we profess ourselves Christians; whence is it that we have our name, but from our conformity unto Christ, as you heard out of 1 Cor. xii. 12? And therefore, those that have not the image of Christ in them begun in some measure, are but bastard Christians. We plead we are baptized, and by it made members of Christ; and did not we read that those that are baptized truly into Christ have put on Christ, his graces, his image, in sanctification as well as justification, as you heard out of the 12th of the Romans, and the last verse? We profess ourselves also such as Christ hath died for, and in the persuasion of this we labour to soothe up ourselves daily. Well; if he hath died for us, he hath died in us; if he hath lived for us, he also lives in us, by his grace and by his Spirit. Thus Paul, when (Gal. ii. 20) he says, 'Jesus Christ gave himself for him,' put this before it, 'I am crucified with Christ, and Christ lives in me.' We all also profess ourselves to be the children of God, and call God Father, and Christ brother; and have you not heard out of the 8th of the Romans, that God predestinates his to be conformed to the image of his Son, that he may call them brethren? And if you do not in some measure resemble your elder brother Christ, you are none of the children of his Father. Have you not also heard that Christ begets them in his image? How will you be able to ask your inheritance at his hands, unless you be his son? And, my brethren, howsoever we may pass current here for good Christians, and think ourselves so, yet God at the latter day, and day of death, when your souls are brought to him, either to own, or to refuse, the very first things that he will inquire into will be, as Christ did when he saw the penny, whose image is it? And as he said, 'What is Cæsar's to Cæsar, and what is God's to God,' so will God say; if it hath the image of Christ on it, give it to Christ, for it belongs to him; if of the devil (for one of these you must have), then give it to him, for it belongs to him. Nothing will pass current coin with God, but what hath the image of Christ on it; none will be taken for his sheep, but those that have his mark; and then he will raise it up at the last day, as he himself speaketh. All this, my brethren, I press upon you to stir you up seriously to lay your hearts to what shall be spoken, by way of trial: for to help you therein, my intent is to shew you the particulars wherein the image of Christ doth consist, to which we are conformed in this life. And these take along with you. *First*, that it is not perfection, but truth therein, that God accepts. For the best are but imperfectly changed into this image, for it is from glory to glory, that is, from one degree to another; if therefore you canst discern the prints of his image, and superscription on thy heart, though they be but as rude and imperfect stamps, and thy evidence be but as the prints in a blurred sixpence, yet if thou beest sure thou findest them there, thou mayest have comfort ; God will not deny any such imperfect coins.

Now this image consisteth especially of two parts : first, in a conformity to his graces ; secondly, to his example. I speak of that image which in this life we are changed to ; there is also the image of glory, which in the life to come we shall be conformed to, and that of suffering, which is here in this life, neither of which are pertinent to this text. For only that image of him as here on earth is revealed to us in the gospel ; we see him not as glorious in the heavens ; but his grace, his work, his death, his restoration, and other parts of his mediation, which are the objects of faith, unto these here must we be conformed ; for as the apostle says, 1 John iv. 17, ' Even as he is, so are we in this world.'

1. The image of Christ in us is a conformity to all his graces. The like graces in us must be renewed that were in him : John i. 16, ' Of his fulness we have all received, grace for grace.' Christ was said to be full of grace in the former verses, and of his fulness do all we (says the apostle), that believe in him, receive grace ; and that grace for grace ; as you ought to say when you copy out one thing out of another, that it is done word for word, so do we of Christ (says John) receive grace for grace, that is, look, what graces are in Christ are derived to us, grace for grace, and therefore, John xv. 5, he is compared to the vine, and we to the branches, because he conveys the same kind of sap of grace to us, that is in himself, so as we bear the like fruit unto that he did, pleasing through him unto the Father. John xvii. 19, ' For their sakes sanctify I myself, that they' (even all that thou hast given me) ' may be sanctified through the truth.' Christ sanctified our nature, that by it he might be made sanctification to us ; and the place here implies, that to that end he received the graces of sanctification, that he might sanctify us with the same kind, receiving it to that end, and therefore there is no grace in Christ but is renewed in his children ; otherwise that grace in Christ were in vain, for he received all as a fountain to convey his store to us. And why else is it that believers are exhorted to be holy for he is holy, 1 Peter i. 16, who are said to be righteous as he is righteous, that is in the same kind ? not measure, 1 John iii. 7. Why are we called to shew forth the virtues of Christ, 1 Peter ii. 9, if we had not received them ? My brethren, let us be exhorted to examine ourselves by this. It is not enough to have gifts from Christ (as reprobates had, Judas and others), an abundance of swimming knowledge, common enlightening, natural wisdom, learning, abilities to express a man's self ; all which I confess came from Christ ; but yet are not part of that his image, but are endowments which flow from him to the sons of men. For he is thus the light that enlighteneth every man that comes into the world, John i. 8. And as the sun in the heavens, so the Sun of righteousness, with his common gifts, shines both on good and bad. But his image is his graces, and those not civil virtues only ; for they are but common gifts ; but Christ was not only a civil man ; no, he called for more righteousness than the Pharisee had. ' Except your righteousness,' says he, to his disciples, ' exceeds that of the Scribes and Pharisees, you cannot enter into the kingdom of God ;' and yet they were civil men, and lived soberly and justly, were no adulterers. And yet who greater opposites to Christ than these were ?

Truly methinks the consideration of this truth should amaze all civil justiciaries in the world, and deliver them from resting in their glittering sins. Mark but of what strain Christ was, look into the state, mark and observe his steps in the story of him.   He made the duties of holiness his chief trade, he lived not only civilly but holily ; it were blasphemy to say the contrary.   And if that men were begotten of him, in his image, those virtues they would shew forth most.   Christ, you heard, is our father, we his seed, begotten by him, and he formed in us.   Now as in a father those limbs that are greater, are proportionably so in the child, or else it were a monster, so all these graces which were most in Christ, would be most in us if we were his children.   Whenas a man makes a great show of all kind of civil virtues, of sobriety, chastity, and the like, but none of holiness, it is a sign he is a monster, and Christ begets no such.   Let men but consider that these virtues are found in those that never heard of the name of Christ, as the ancient heathen and the Turks at this day, who are not Christians, not so much as in name ; and therefore those that go no further deserve the name less than they.   Wild trees do bring forth blossoms, that grow in wildernesses, as well as those in gardens.   But those that are ingrafted with Christ do bring forth fruit also according unto its kind, and the root they are ingrafted on.   But what are moral virtues only but blossoms ? And though indeed it is true, that even those were in Christ, and ought to be in Christians, yea, and are ; yet, if you would make them signs of a good estate, you must discern them as growing from union with Christ, and then they will be of another kind than mere moral virtues are ; differing as much as sweet marjorum from wild, the one a weed, the other an herb.   Your meekness will proceed, not from softness of nature, but from a heart humbled, tamed, sweetened with the apprehension of thy injuries done to Christ, which now thou findest forgiven, and from this ground thy spirit is calmed and subdued.   In the 11th of Matthew, ' Learn of me ' (says Christ), ' for I am lowly and meek ;' the civilest, the meekest men by nature must learn of Christ to be meek and humble.   And so also that love, sweetness, and ingenuousness of nature, would reach higher than it doth or can do in civil men, it would extend itself to thy enemies ; for so Christ loved thee when thou wert an enemy : ' If you love them that love you, the Gentiles do so,' says Christ ; there is but one good turn for another. Good nature and love in a gracious heart will also burst out and be seen, especially to the saints and those that excel in virtue.   Indeed when Christ met with that young man, that was but a civil man, it is said he looked on him and loved him ; but when he spoke to his sheep, to his poor disciples, to Mary Magdalene and others, he opened himself to them, expressed bowels of his love unto them, countenanced them, cherished them, comforted them !   And when they told him of his brother, and sister, and mother, he shewed that they that were spiritually akin to him were dearer to him.

Also our mercy and pity would shew itself to the souls of men especially ; he was good to their bodies, for he healed many, fed five thousand out of his compassion ; but it was to pluck their souls out of the jaws of death, that was his chiefest aim ; stronger it was in him than hunger to convert a soul ; for whenas he came an hungry to Samaria, and they went to buy victuals, he met with the woman of Samaria and forgot his dinner ; it was meat to him to convert herself ; and therefore, wheresoever he came, he went up and down instructing of men ; prayed for his enemies' salvation, even at the last gasp ; wept over Jerusalem when he went to be crucified in it ; and if we had any of his compassion, our bowels would yearn within us to see men lie in the fire, and would move us to labour to pluck them out ; for, alas ! that is men's greatest misery.

And so our humility would not be that proud humility the world is so full of. When his kinsfolk came to him (in John vii. 3–5) and spurred him on to go shew himself—' If thou dost these things, go shew thyself to the world'—alas, he suppressed it, shewed it no further than it might be for the salvation of his chosen, and that they might believe in him, John v. 34, 44, denied himself, emptied himself of the glory that was due to him (as from the beginning of the world), regarding it not if his Father might be glorified. And when it came to that dismal hour of crucifying, and encountering with his wrath, ' Not my will' (says he), ' but thy will be done.' How content was he to bear any condition of hunger, nakedness, the taunts, reproaches of his most base enemies ; ' and when he was reviled, reviled not again.' How did he express his contempt of the world, in having an eye to that glory which was set before him, that though he had all the world offered him at once, yet he refused it all ? What zeal and courage did he express in his Father's cause, whipping the profane out of the temple, withstanding the corruptions of those times ; opposing the Pharisees, calling them hypocrites to their very faces ; what hatred and detestation did he express against their sins !

Use 2. By this we may learn how much the image of God in us is advanced and improved above what was in the heart of Adam in innocency, as also above that which the image of God is, in respect of conformity to the law and will of God. For though holiness in all states is one and the same, the same for substance ; for holiness is to aim at God's glory, and that runs through all states, both in innocency, and in the state of grace, and in heaven ; yet that holiness which Christ works in us under the gospel, and by which we know God and Jesus Christ, and God in him, hath far more elevated strains, of a more excellent genius, and far higher, nobler, and heavenlier, than what was in Adam's heart, or his heart ever knew. For instance, I will go over but some graces which are all but Christ in us.

First, Adam had humility ; he must needs have it, as he was a creature. The angels they have humility in them, for they cover their faces when they behold the glory of God ; they have wings on purpose to do it. But the humility that Adam had, whence did it spring ? Why, by seeing himself to be a creature, made out of nothing, and that there was an infinite distance between God, that was the Creator, and himself. But now take that grace of humility that is in the heart of a believer, and it is of another make, and springs from another and more noble rise ; for was Adam so humble as to be laid so low as to see himself a creature and God the Creator ? Why, sin lays a believer lower, far lower ; and humility in a believer riseth thence. It riseth likewise from this, that he that was God himself was humbled, and therefore shall man be proud ? Had Adam such motives to humility ? That humility and self-emptiness that is in a believer makes him not value his own graces ; they are all as nothing to him, and Jesus Christ is all in all to him. It lays him not only low, seeing himself nothing as a creature, but it makes him account himself worse than nothing, a creature deserving hell itself. Adam, though he was humbled as a creature, and knew his distance, yet he could stand upon terms, terms of creation, with God ; he might challenge a justification that was due to him, for so the covenant of works doth, which he was created under. Look into Rom. iv. 4, and see what the apostle saith there : ' Now to him that worketh is the reward not reckoned of grace, but of debt ;' and verse 2, ' If Abraham were justified by works, he hath whereof to glory ;' but Abraham had not whereof to glory before God, therefore he was not justified by works; that is the apostle's argument. He clearly in that place holds forth the difference between the covenant of works and the covenant of grace: the one, he saith, is κατὰ τὸ ὀφείλημα, it is according to debt or due; but the other is κατὰ χάριν, according to grace. Now, is it not a strange speech, that he that should have been justified by works (as Adam should have been) had whereof to glory, had something that was a debt, which in some respect he might have challenged, and have stood upon terms with God about it? Here now is the humility of this Adam, that he knew himself to be a creature, made out of nothing, and that God might annihilate him when he would, though being under the covenant of works, while he did continue so there was a justification that was his due, that was his natural due, that God should account him and pronounce him righteous. I confess I have often wondered at the expression of the apostle in that Rom. iv; for we read in Rom. xi. 35, 'Who hath first given to the Lord, and it shall be recompensed unto him again?' Therefore that is not the apostle's meaning, as if Adam could have given anything to God, and therefore he might challenge a recompence from God; but the meaning is only this, that in the way of a dueness and of a natural justness, such as is between the Creator and the creature, whilst the creature remaineth holy, God should according to that law justify him according to his works, and so he had whereof to glory. It is not a debt of retribution (that is the distinction), it is not *debitum restitutionis*, as if he could in a mercenary way procure anything of God, yet it was *debitum conveniente*,* it was meet that if he wrought, and remained holy, God should justify him. So that Adam's humility was joined with what was a natural due, which he might have challenged if he had continued holy. But what is our humility we have from Christ? Why, instead of standing upon terms, 'the wages of sin is death.' The reward, saith he, is reckoned of debt, and he receives it as wages; but all the wages we have now, it is but the wages of sin, and that is death. And the heart of a believer acknowledgeth it, and doth not only submit himself to the sovereignty of God, as he is a creature,—so Adam must do,—but he lays his neck upon the block, tells God that hell and destruction are his due, puts his mouth in the dust, and walketh humbly with God; and if God gives him life, Oh! it is the free gift of God! 'The wages of sin is death, but the gift of God is eternal life.'

Secondly, Consider the justification that Adam had, and that which we have by Christ. The justification of Adam was natural. It was plainly this: if he did continue righteous, which righteousness was preserved and conserved by working according to the rule and the principles in his own heart, he thus obeying God, and remaining righteous, it was a natural due to him, a meet thing for God upon this to approve him and pronounce him righteous, because he did act and continue as God had made him, and he walked according to the law of a creature toward his Creator. Now, what was it for God to give him this approbation, and so to justify him? It was only this, that he pronounced him to be good in his kind, even as he pronounced all the other creatures to be so in their kind, Gen. i. 31. God viewed all in the creatures that he had made, and said they were very good; he viewed Adam so too, for this was before Adam fell, and he pronounced him good, as he did the rest; only good in his kind, which was the goodness of righteousness, holiness, and integrity which he yet stood in. So that indeed the justification of Adam, according to the covenant of works, it was but an approbation of him, that he continued good, that he

* Qu. '*è conveniente*'?—ED.

walked uprightly, &c., as he pronounceth of the heavens that keep their ordinances to this day, that they are good; so he would have done of man, if he had kept his ordinances according to the law of creation. But, alas! all this goodness and righteousness he had would not have stood out against the least sin; if he had but sinned, all this had been forfeited, all gone, utterly lost. But now what manner of righteousness is it that we have by Christ revealed in the gospel? Why, we are justified freely by grace, we are justified by a righteousness which is sin-proof, by a righteousness which, when it hath made a purchase of the forgiveness of all our sins, gives us in heaven too, by a righteousness which believers never can, never shall, out-spend, by a righteousness that pardons all a man's sins, pays all his debts, the very first hour that he believes and lays hold upon it, and which continues to everlasting, and would continue to everlasting, to justify him, though he should remain in a mixed condition of sinning against God, as we are in this life, by a righteousness which breaks through God's justice to God's throne of grace, and makes the soul do so with a world of confidence.

Thirdly, Let us compare the love that was in Adam's heart to God, and the love which Christ works in us. Adam loved God, it is true, because he was a good God to him, and his creator; but he so loved him as that Adam withal knew that if he did but trip, did but sin, God would instantly hate him more than ever he loved him, and his wrath would fall upon him, and he must die the death; so that, indeed, the term of love between God and man, then, what was it? I love you, while you love me. God had, out of love, made Adam holy, and given him power to love; but then so long as he continued to love God thus, and to love God at such a height, so long God continued to love him; so that indeed it was but a temporary love, as I may express it, that is, a love which might fail, and did fail as such. It is a saying that Seneca hath, and it is a true one, ' To love one so as a man thinks with himself it may fall out so one day that this man may hate me; this is the bane of friendship.' There cannot be a perfect love where this is. ' Perfect love doth cast out' all such ' fear.' But yet this was the state and condition of Adam. It is true, he knew that so long as he loved God and obeyed him, God would love him; but yet so as he knew withal, that if he sinned (and he knew not how soon he might sin, for he was but a creature), God would then presently hate him. This was clearly and truly the friendship and love that was between God and Adam. But now what is the love, what kindleth the love now that is in the heart of a believer of a more noble flame? It is a love that is free, a love that is not fixed upon us while we love God, or because we love him, but was eternally, before we had done either good or evil, as the phrase is, Rom. ix. 11. ' Not for your sakes, but for my own name's sake, do I this,' saith God, Ezek. xxxvi. 32. Indeed he hath chosen us in Christ, that we should be holy in love; but he hath not chosen us because we loved him, nor doth he continue his choice therefore. Is it a love which may prove but temporary? No; it is a love from everlasting to everlasting; it is a love that is pitched upon our persons; I love such a person, saith God, be he sinful or holy; and if sinful, I will make him holy. The love pitched upon Adam was in relation to his graces, and the love that God bare to Adam was but single to him, as to his creature; but the love that is in God's heart now is through Christ his Son, professing to love us with the same love he loveth him. That love he bare Adam was such as he bare to any creature, be they what they be, so long as they remained holy and kept in their first state; but the love that a believer takes in, it is a peculiar love, it is a love with difference : ' I will shew mercy to whom I will shew mercy,' that is all the reason of it : ' Jacob have I loved, and Esau have I hated ;' and he gives no reason of it. The love that Adam had in his condition was such, that sin took away all God's love, and turned it into hatred ; but here is a love now that, though we be sinful, we are not children of wrath when we are believers ; a love which much water cannot quench ; a love which, when we were sinners and enemies, it was the more desirous to manifest itself, because it should have more opportunity by giving Christ to shew the more love, by how much the more we were sinners. Now all this love doth the heart of a believer take in under the gospel, and doth Christ work in us, therefore raiseth up this love to a height, to a nobleness, to a generosity, to a heavenliness, such as never Adam's heart was capable of. ' Perfect love casteth out fear ;' he knows God so loves him as he will never hate him, nor never can do it ; a love which is not mercenary, doth not serve for reward ; a love which (when the gospel once hath kindled it) will cleave to God though a man's heart knows not whether God love him or no ; a love which will not only make a man submit to the will of God, but makes a man's soul willing, if it were the will of God, to be lost for him. So it was with Paul.

Fourthly, Take self-denial in a Christian, which is a new grace. ' Not my will, but thy will,' was Christ's motto. Alas ! Adam was put to live, he was to keep within his bounds which God created him in, and it was fit he should be kept in them. But we are put to deny ourselves, yea, sometimes when it comes in opposition to God, to deny friends, father, mother, life, yea, a man's own graces. No such self-denial was Adam put to, which is the most great and glorious grace of all the rest.

Fifthly, Go take all motives to obedience, and they are far more noble in a Christian than ever was in Adam ; as in 1 John ii. 7, love is called not only an old commandment, but a new. And why a new one ? Because when the gospel cometh, it brings new motives, and urgeth the commandment of love to our brethren and fellow-creatures upon such grounds as the law and the covenant of works never did. We have higher motives to the smallest duty than ever Adam could have or his heart was capable of. Are we to be kind to our fellow-creatures ? Saith the apostle, ' Put on kindness.' But how ? How doth he move it ? ' As the elect of God, holy and beloved,' Col. iii. 12, as those whom God hath chosen with an everlasting love in Jesus Christ, ' forbearing one another and forgiving one another.' And so you have the like in Eph. iv. 32, ' Be ye kind one to another, tender hearted, forgiving one another, even as God for Christ's sake hath forgiven you.' And so in Eph. v. 24, the obedience of wives to their husbands, and the love of husbands to their wives, is urged upon such a ground as Adam should never have had such a motive run through his heart : ' Let wives' (saith he) ' be subject to their husbands in everything, as the church is subject unto Christ. And let husbands love their wives, even as Christ also loved the church.' Such motives as these, in these common relations, doth the gospel give us. These old commandments Adam had, of duties to his fellow-creatures, and of love to his wife, and the like ; but they were upon lower motives, infinitely lower than what the gospel holds forth. He had no such example as we have in Christ for every duty, no such motives as we have from him.

Lastly, The assistance which we have from Christ is of a higher kind than that which Adam had. How did God assist Adam in all the works of the law that he was to perform ? What was the promise of assistance ?

No other than to assist him in his kind (God having created him holy) as he doth assist other creatures in their kind. I say his assistance was but the concurrence of a common providence, so as to other creatures; only it was applied to Adam in his kind, as a creature that was holy. But now the assistance that we have under the gospel, for every work we do, is of a higher nature, for Jesus Christ is our covenant, he hath undertaken to fulfil all in us and for us; all that God would have us to do, he hath undertaken to work it in us, so far forth as to save us, or to bring us to that degree of glory he hath appointed us unto. He works in us both to will and to do according to his good pleasure : 'I am able to do all things' (saith Paul) ' through Christ that strengtheneth me ;' so that ' it is not I' (saith he), ' but the grace of God that is in me,' the grace of God acting me, falling upon me, and overpowering my spirit. A believer he is in the Spirit, and so he walketh in the Spirit. But this was not the law of assisting Adam, which was only the law of common providence.

2. The second thing which we are conformed to is Christ's example ; and so the author to the Hebrews calls him ' the Captain of our salvation,' Heb. ii. 10, because like a valiant general he hath set us a pattern, and ' left us an example to follow his steps,' 1 Pet. ii. 21 ; and therefore the same apostle Peter, following the same metaphor, 1 Pet. iv. 1, says, ' Arm yourselves with the same mind.' Nay, lay but aside the works of his divinity, as healing, fasting, &c., and of his mediation, and the like ; and it is a sure rule, that whatsoever Christ did *for* a Christian he doth *in* him also, there being a likeness and proportion, and an assimilation in his works of grace in us and for us. He is conceived, formed, born again in us, as you heard out of the Galatians :* ' We circumcised with him, with the circumcision made without hands, are dead, buried, raised up again with him,' as it is Col. ii. 11–13. So that the conversion of a sinner is but the acting over again of Christ's part. Now though I might go over many, yet I will insist, this time, only in these which are mentioned, Rom. vi. 5–9 ; the sum of which is in the 5th verse, that ' we are planted with him into the likeness of his death and resurrection.' For those two being the chiefest parts of his mediation, the work of sanctification in us is assimilated and likened unto them. Mortification, or the killing of sin, and vivification, or quickening us unto newness of life, are assimilated to his death and resurrection ; and that not only because they are wrought by the power of them (though that be true, as appears by Phil. iii. 10), but also in regard of a likeness that there is between the one and the other, and so we are said to be planted with him into the similitude of his resurrection. I desire you to consider Rom. vi. 3–7, &c., because I will ground the rest on what is there. In the 6th verse, you may observe how the apostle puts upon the mass of corruption and sin that is in us, the name of a body, calling it ' the body of sin,' not only because that it is compact and made up of innumerable lusts in us as members of it (as it is Col. iii. 3–5), which, like members, are knit together ; but chiefly in respect of this, that he might shew us the likeness between Christ's dying, and our dying to sin, that as he had a body was crucified, so we have a body of sin to be destroyed ; yea, and in the same manner crucified as his was. Such is his phrase in the 6th verse, ' that our old man,' or body of sin, ' might be crucified with him' and destroyed. Yea, and the apostle Peter, in 1st Epistle chap. iv., useth the two parts of Christ's crucifying to express this.

1. Christ was condemned, and had sentence of death passed on him ;

* Qu. ' Colossians' ?—Ed.

so are our sins condemned, for we having resolved to leave and forsake them, to cherish them no longer, have passed the sentence of death on them; and so a Christian hath vowed the death of his sins, as of his known enemies ; and though a man loved his lusts never so well, though they have been his old bosom friends, he hath formerly had so much solace in, yet now when he hath discovered their treason out, and apprehends how they are his enemies, enemies to God, to Christ, and that he must now either kill or be killed, that they fight against his soul (as Peter speaks), he seeks the death of them by all means, accuseth, arraigneth them, by confession, and pleading guilty ; his own mouth condemns them daily, hales and drags them before the judgment-seat of God ; and because he cannot execute them, he cries, Lord, thou art able to give this lust a stab, and its deadly wound, which is ready ever and anon to overcome and kill me.   And how glad is he when he hears the sentence of death pronounced against it in the word ; lays his heart open to the ministry of it, the reproof of his sin, and suffers the sword of the Spirit to have its full blow at it.   Oh, my brethren, examine your own hearts : who among you have gone thus far in the mortification of his lusts ?   Who is at enmity, and daggers drawing at them daily ?   Who is he that stands in terms with them, as with an enemy, nay, rather, doth not cherish them as dearest friends, keeping them under their tongues as sweet bits ?   How many are there that never made prayer against any one sin, that storm at the word when it condemns them ?

2. As Christ, after he was condemned, was brought to the cross, and there executed, crucified, so also the Sprit of God in true Christians comes with the power of Christ, naileth his lusts to the cross of Christ, Gal. vi. 14 ; and so, 1 Pet. iv. 1, we are said to suffer in the flesh, as Christ did ; and the apostle Paul, Rom. vi. 6, useth the same word of crucifying to express the one and the other, both of Christ's and ours.   As Christ's body, in crucifying, was in every member and part put to pain, which in no death scarce but that falls out ; not a vein, not a sinew, but was stretched ; so also is every member of the body of sin crucified, it reaching to every lust, great and small, Gal. v. 24, they all now stretch for it.   And oh, my brethren, who knows the pains in parting with lusts, but they that have done it, and in truth ?   And though some have stronger hearts than others to endure more pain, yet every lust being as the strings of a man's heart, as dear as his life, therefore the parting with these, the crucifying of these, must needs be as the breaking of the heart-strings, and making the vital sinews crack.   Examine yourselves, how many are there of you that never parted in earnest with one lust yet, much less with all.

And then, 3dly, as Jesus Christ being thus crucified gave up the ghost, so also doth the Spirit of Christ, in likeness unto this, take away the life and power of sin ; at the first stab it hath a deadly wound given it at the heart ; and therefore the apostle, in Rom. vi. 2, 3, affirms that believers are dead to sin, baptized into the death of Christ, it having a deadly blow given it ; and how shall we that are dead live therein ?   He argues it is absurd and impossible ; how can it be ?   Can a man that is dead, or deadly-wounded, live ? that is, perform the actions of life with delight constantly, for that is to live.   Why, he cannot ; no more can we (says the apostle) live in sin ; that is, we cannot with delight, and in the life of comfort, continue in the practice of any of our former sins in a full career, that is, continue with delight in the actions of it.   For to live in sin, in the 2d verse, is all one as to continue in sin, in the 4th verse.   My brethren, let us all examine ourselves hereby; we came all into the world sinners, and with lusts all as lively as ourselves; and every man, also till that he hath the power of Christ's death thus conveyed to him, lives the life of his lusts as well as that of his natural life; performs the actions whereby he satisfies them with as much life and delight as he can do those of his natural life, Col. iii. 7. Now therefore examine yourselves, whether that you have felt a thorough work ever wrought in you or no, by which this power and life of sin was killed, and thy sins had and hath a deadly wound given them, which will go with them to their graves, and which they could never since recover. Try this in thy master lust. Doth a lust live in thy heart still? live, and is as brisk as ever when it is put in, or stirred up in thee, even as a fish in its own proper element? Then thou art not mortified. But dost thou find a deadness and stiffness to those sinful delights wherein formerly the comfort of thy life consisted, so as that they are all as dead drink to the stomach, or as a stone put into a dead man's mouth, and thou cannot find the relish that savours, the sweetness and fulness of contentment in them that formerly thou hast done, so that thou art crucified to the world, and the world to thee? This proceedeth from union with Christ's dying unto sin, which is likened to his dying for sin. But especially try it in regard of thy course, for the apostle says, if that we be dead to sin, how shall we live therein? If a man were crucified or dead with Christ, he could not live in his old courses: 1 Pet. iv. 1, 'He that hath suffered in the flesh,' that is, whose sinful corruption of nature is killed by the power of Christ's death, 'hath ceased from sin;' that is, the course and practice of any known sin, for that is the most capable interpretation can be given of it. My brethren, pray consider, either that is not the word of God, or this is not the meaning of it, or else any one that lives in the practice of any known bosom sin is not a Christian. How can then those that live in the lusts of the Gentiles, as they are termed there, in ver. 4, 5, 'in wantonness, chamberings, drunkenness, uncleanness,' and the like excess of riot, be termed Christians? In 1 John iii. 5–8, speaking of our conformity unto Christ, among the rest he makes this as one, that as Christ had no sin in him, so he that abides in him continues not in sin; for so the word must be interpreted, for says he, ver. 8, 'Christ appeared to dissolve the works of the devil;' that is, in those that are his, to put an end to the work or devilish trade of sin in themselves. If therefore we be dead with Christ, how shall we continue in sin? When a thief is hanged, doth he not leave the practice of his thievery? And so should we break off our course in sinning if we ourselves had ever been on the cross with Christ, and crucified with him. Well, my brethren, this know, that none shall have the benefit of his death for the forgiveness of sin, that hath not a likeness to it in the death of it in himself. And lest it should be thought that sin is not thus truly killed with Christ, the apostle goes farther, in Rom. vi. 4, and says that 'we are buried also with Christ.' There is also a conformity to his burial, whereby is shewn that sin is truly dead. A living man would not suffer himself to be buried; and by the conformity to his burial he means the progress of a Christian in the further and daily mortifying of his lusts; that as a body being laid in the grave rots away and consumes, till at length it be destroyed, so doth the body of sin (as it is at ver. 6), being crucified, it is destroyed also, and that is not till the day of death; and therein indeed it differs from Christ's body, which remained unconsumed in the grave, saw no corruption, and remains now glorified in heaven. And therefore examine whether sin moulders and decays in thee or no.

BOOK VI.

That the work of grace, wrought in us by the Spirit of God in regeneration, is a different and higher principle than natural conscience in its greatest elevation of light.—The deficiency of natural conscience shewed, and the mistakes of men about it detected.

CHAPTER I.

That all men being under a covenant of works, or a covenant of grace, there are two principles of actions, viz., conscience alone in its natural light in the one, and supernatural grace with its light in the hearts of the other, who are regenerate.—The two texts, Rom. ii. 14, 15, and Jer. xxxi. 31–33, explained.—That the principle by which the law of God reigns over men is conscience.—What notions the philosophers among the heathens had of it.

*For when the Gentiles, which have not the law, do by nature the things contained in the law, these, having not the law, are a law unto themselves : which shew the work of the law written in their hearts, their conscience also bearing witness, and their thoughts the mean while accusing or else excusing one another.—*ROM. II. 14, 15.

*Behold, the days come, saith the Lord, that I will make a new covenant with the house of Israel, and with the house of Judah ; not according to the covenant that I made with their fathers, in the day that I took them by the hand, to bring them out of the land of Egypt (which my covenant they brake, although I was an husband unto them, saith the Lord) ; but this shall be the covenant that I will make with the house of Israel : After those days, saith the Lord, I will put my law in their inward parts, and write it in their hearts ; and I will be their God, and they shall be my people.—*JER. XXXI. 31–33.

HAVING opened the nature of the true work of grace, I shall now, for the fuller and larger illustration hereof, subjoin the discovery of its counterfeit, which is the work of the law written in the heart by nature, or the powerful effects which a natural and enlightened conscience hath in the hearts of men remaining unregenerate ; which men in all professions of religion do ordinarily mistake in themselves for true and inherent holiness. The use and necessity of this discourse is to shew more clearly the nature of true sanctification, by the detection of its counterfeit. For things come to be distinctly known, as well by discovering the difference of what usually pretends to be, or is commonly and generally taken, and goes for current among men, to be such or such a thing, when it is not, as by defining positively what the thing itself is, in the genuine nature of it. We learn truths with an advantage (especially spiritual truths) when we compare them with the appearance of errors, and sever them from, and extract them as spirits out of that dross, and mixture of a deceiving likeness that cleaveth to them.   It will also serve to remove practical mistakes about regeneration, which are of infinite moment, and yet generally incident unto men.

Now as the sum of our religion is reduced by the apostle to these two, ' Faith, and a good conscience,' 1 Tim. i. 19, *faith*, which is *principium credendorum*, the principle of things to be believed ; and *conscience*, which is *principium agendorum*, the principle of things to be done by us ; for as the object matter of all religion is reduced to *credenda* and *agenda*, so the principles within us are answerably thus generally expressed by these two, faith and conscience.   Faith looks upward to the things of the gospel, and takes in all supernatural truths, with application to a man's soul.   Conscience looks both inward, to our own actings within ; and outward, to the law or rule which is to guide us.   And it also is the spring to all the wheels, and the mover in all provocations to duties, or avocations from sins.   Now as these two are the two principles (when true and good) of all true religion ; so all the imperfect works and counterfeits of the true, which are to be found in unregenerate men's hearts and lives, must be reduced unto these two also, both as to the principles thereof in their hearts, and to the effects of them all in their lives.   As there is a false common faith, which men do generally mistake for true (and therefore the apostle distinguisheth, terming the true, ' unfeigned faith,' 1 Tim. i. 5), so there is a ' pure heart,' and a ' good conscience' in the same place also opened.   It is a conscience good, with such a goodness as qualifies the heart, and this by way of distinction and difference from conscience, which is but natural, and the low effects thereof in men unregenerate, which they ordinarily do in little matters mistake for sanctification.   So then all counterfeit religion (I speak of such as is any way serious, and not grossly and merely hypocritical) are either, 1. The effects and workings of conscience, as it is a natural principle, and though still remaining defiled in a heart unregenerated, yet elevated and enlightened by the word and Spirit ; or, 2. The effects of supernatural light in matters of faith joined therewith, and shining into an unrenewed understanding, and affecting self-love, with what is suitable to it in the things that are revealed.

Again, all men's conditions falling to be either under the covenant of works, or the covenant of grace, hence all that are enlightened and carried on with any powerful effects in the profession of religion, are either acted therein by conscience, as the predominant principle, which is the seat of the dominion of the law and covenant of works ; or by faith, which is the inlet or receptive of the dominion of grace.

That all men are under one of these covenants is evident by the whole current of the apostle's writings,* who still distinguisheth between works and grace as the only two possibly to be supposed ways men take unto salvation, ' Not of works (says he), ' but according to grace ;' and ' you are not under the law, but under grace,' Rom. vii.   He makes this distinction as that which takes in and divides the whole of mankind.   And the reason is evident from Rom. vii. 1, 4, 6.   For every man having been born under the law and covenant of works, the law continues to have dominion over him, either in commanding or inciting, yea, often in acting and carrying him on unto what is commanded thereby, or else binding him over unto condemnation.   And no man is freed from this until he is married to Christ, and so come to have a new nature, together with the privilege of

* 2 Thess. i. 9 ; Eph. ii. ; Rom. ix., x., xi.

being a subject of grace. And therefore he continues under it so long as he lives in that first estate, for the law's right over him was not forfeited by the fall. Now suitably, that every man might come to be subject to and sensible of this several dominion over him, according as his condition is, there are two principles planted within man, by God suited hereunto, and suscipient of each of these. The one is in every man by nature (since every man's condition is to be under the law), and that is conscience. The other is a supernatural grace, and that is faith. Eph. ii. 8, 'By grace ye are saved through faith.' Now Jews and heathens were under the dominion (as explained) of both these,* and also ignorant Christians. But if man that remains unregenerate be enlightened by the gospel and the knowledge of the grace of God, although it may be a while doubtful unto himself or others unto which covenant or dominion he belongs or is the subject of, yet in the issue and event his spirit doth fall, and will act or be acted according as his condition is, and he will lean either to the one or the other as his lord and sovereign. If a man that is under the covenant of works takes in the present over-powering light of the doctrine of grace, and the truth thereof, which hath good and blessed news for every man to listen to, yet in the issue and event he will fall into one of these two cases or conditions. He will either come to abuse the grace of God to wantonness through self-love, which remaining unsubdued to the dominion of grace, makes use of the knowledge of grace underhand to back and strengthen that corruption in him, in which the power of sin doth lie, and so self-love, in a way of presumption (which hath the appearance of the strength of faith in that man), eats out the active power of conscience in him, and so he comes to fall under the dominion or stroke of the covenant of works more strongly than ever; and the law comes to bind him over to a deeper condemnation when conscience shall come again to be awakened; and even the gospel itself, which he knew, will be turned into a sorer avenger than the law of itself would have been. And this is the case of such as swallow down the gospel whole, and so make shipwreck of conscience through their presumption on the principles about the doctrine or application of it to themselves.

Or 2. The case of one that is enlightened will be, that his conscience being enlightened and awakened by the law, continues to act and provoke him unto doing in religion in a legal strain and way, and carries on duties upon the wheels of legal motives, and so the law becomes the predominant principle, to over-top and over-sway evangelical faith. And that it doth so is but suitable to the state of the man; for as he is still under the covenant of works (self not being broken, nor Christ having slain the law to him) so answerably the best and most active swaying principle in him is that which is the seat and throne of the law's dominion, namely conscience; and so the best of that man's religion is but the actings of a legal conscience. And how he compounds with the gospel, and subordinates his apprehensions of it, is too long here to insert.

So then (that I may set out that subject I mean to treat of), it is not my purpose here to treat of temporary faith, the counterfeit of true saving faith, but singly and simply an enlightened natural conscience and the effects thereof, as they are or may be mistaken for true sanctification, and the effects of it. And the eminent distinction and difference between these two is, by these two texts, Rom. ii. 14, 15, and Jer. xxxi. 31–33 compared, clearly held forth, both for the ὅτι and the διότι thereof; the one speaking

* That is, 'the law and conscience.'—ED.

of the effect of the law written in the heart by nature (thus, Rom. ii.), the other (Jer. xxxi.) of the writing the law in the inward parts, as the eminent and proper fruit of the covenant of grace, and that in distinction from the other.

The first text, Rom ii., gives instance in the Gentiles (whom all acknowledge under wrath and unregeneracy), and their having the effects of the law written by nature. And above all other effects of the law, he instanceth in conscience accusing and excusing, as that which of all other argues the law written there; yea, and his scope in bringing in this example of the Gentiles is in the coherence of it to convince the carnal Jews, whom he had taken to task to convince them in this chapter that they were unregenerate and in their natural condition, as he had done in the former, who rested in the law, and the effects thereof upon them for their justification and acceptation with God, thereupon 'making their boast of God,' ver. 17. Having proved the Gentiles to be under wrath, chap. i., he then comes upon the Jew therewith, and improves their example as a special engine to unsettle and overthrow the Jew in his carnal boast, by giving him to consider,—

1. That even the Gentiles, whom they accounted unholy, though they had not the law delivered by revelation from God to them (for God dealt not so with any nation, &c.), yet had the effect or substance of the outward precepts of the law written in their hearts.

2. Those letters of the law were so powerful and prevailing in many of them, that the prints of them were published and stamped in fair characters in their lives; that is, they acted according to it: ver. 14, 'They do by nature the things contained in the law;' and, ver. 15, 'shew' or give demonstration that the effect of the 'law is written there.'

And 3. The eminent principle or seat of this effect of the law he makes to be their consciences, ver. 15. For he gives that as the eminent instance of the law written in their hearts, that it did μεταξὺ ἀλλήλων, excuse and accuse; that is, by course and alteration* between themselves singly or in their own breast (as the margin also hath it), it did some while excuse and approve, pronounce a sentence of absolution and justification, both to their actions and persons, when they do well; as also when they do ill, it again at other times accuseth.

4. Now from this instance of the Gentiles he would have the carnal Jews themselves reflect that they had indeed the advantage of having the law and word of God outwardly revealed to them, over and above the bare light of nature, and so more fully and clearly than the Gentiles had; and had also the 'more excellent things' thereof: ver. 18, 'Thou approvest the things that are more excellent, being instructed out of the law.' All which came to pass, because they had the same principle of conscience, he had spoken of, which the Gentiles had; which principle was apprehensive of the righteousness of the law, revealed to them of God, and so approved of it, and received it from God, and was apprehensive of its subjection thereunto, and thereupon had set them a-work to act according to that eternal word. But yet in all this (says he) thou that art a Jew actest, at the best, but in the same sphere, and upon the same foundation in nature, that is found in the heathens by nature. And though thy conscience comes to know more excellent things by revelation from the word, and so to act outwardly more gloriously from thence, yet the inward principle is one and the same in thy heart that is in the others, namely, natural conscience enlightened, for

* Qu. 'alternation'?—ED.

magis et minus non variant speciem. These are but further degrees within the same kind, and internally and ultimately it is but the nature in both that all is resolved into.

Yea, and 5thly, he urgeth them from the 21st verse, Thou that art a Jew (says he) in thine obedience and conformity to that law given thee, fallest more short, according to the compass of thy principles and light of conscience, than the Gentiles do, according to what they know by the light of mere nature in their sphere. Yea, and oftentimes some things (which their consciences keep them from) thou sinnest against thy light therein. Now then his conclusion is, Be thine own judge : ver. 26, 27, 'Therefore if the uncircumcision keep the righteousness of the law' (that is within his compass of light, so far as he knows, as really and as conscientiously from a principle within him, as thou canst be supposed to do thy law, whilst but from the same principle), shall not he, by the analogy and proportion of that rule by which thou dost judge of thy estate before God, ' be also justi-fied ?' And ' shall not his uncircumcision be counted circumcision,' and so in his measure and proportion be accepted of by God as well as thou ? It is not that Paul affirms this, as if a heathen should be saved ; but he useth and urgeth it as a conviction to the Jews, according to the principles they judged of themselves by, leaving it to them to judge of themselves by analogous reason. And therefore his last conclusion and resolution is, ver. 29, that it is none of these principles mentioned that is true holiness, but regeneration or circumcision of the heart, as the apostle elsewhere termeth conversion : Col. ii. 11, ' In whom also ye are circumcised with the circumcision made without hands, in putting off the body of the sins of the flesh by the circumcision of Christ.' And ' he is a Jew' (says he) ' that is one inwardly : and circumcision is that of the heart in the spirit,' which is a principle beyond both natural conscience in the heathen, or enlightened conscience in the Jew, and all the works or effects thereof in either. And this, says Paul, you will find all true (as the 16th verse hath it, which comes after that parenthesis of verses 13–15), ' In that day when God shall judge the secrets of men by Jesus Christ,' who by discovering the secrets of all hearts, will make a full discovery of these things, and the practical differences between them, and thereupon difference in men's estates.

2. The other place, Jer. xxxi., is most adequate to this general scope of mine ; for the full direct and professed intent thereof is to hold forth this very distinction and broad difference that is between the entertainment of the law in the heart of a carnal Jew, with the effects thence ensuing, and the writing the law in the heart by grace. And you may observe that he contents not himself nakedly with setting forth the effects of the covenant of grace, that it is a writing the law in the heart ; but sets by it, for illus-tration thereof, the consideration and remembrance of the former covenant by Moses in giving the law, with the effects thereof, ver. 32. Yea, he brings it in by express distinction from this other, ' Not according' (says he) ' to the covenant I made with their fathers in the day that I took them by the hand to bring them out of the land of Egypt.' Now the effects of that covenant upon the most, or on the generality of the Jews (though secretly the new covenant, which was conveyed with it in the types, did then work in many of the elect), you have lively deciphered at the very first giving the law, unto which very transaction Jeremiah most aptly refers, and sends us to understand this difference. You have it, Deut. v. (where the story of giving the law is rehearsed from ver. 5), at verses 24–27, &c., you

find how their consciences made them sensible of the greatness and glory of God who gave the law: ver, 24, 25, ' And they said, Behold, the Lord our God hath shewed us his glory and his greatness, and we have heard his voice out of the midst of the fire. We have seen this day that he doth talk with man, and he liveth. Now, therefore, why should we die ? For this great fire will consume us : if we hear the voice of the Lord our God any more, then we shall die.' And these apprehensions of theirs did work up unto resolutions to ' do whatever God should say.' ' I have heard' (says God thereupon, ver. 28), ' the voice of the words of this people, which they have spoken unto thee : they have well said all that they have spoken.' And yet, at ver. 29, you read how the main was wanting, ' Oh that there were such an heart in them, that they would fear me, and keep all my commandments always, that it might be well with them, and with their children for ever !' Now the thing that was wanting was the law written in the heart (as Jeremiah discovers it to be), as that which, with respect to the more general and more apparent and professed workings of it in men, was reserved for the days of the New Testament, as the fruit of the covenant of grace. Now this writing the law in the heart, spoken of by Jeremiah, the apostle (Heb. x. 16) doth genuinely interpret of the work of saving sanctification, as it is distinct from that of justification, and is peculiar to them that are justified.

So then upon all accounts these texts do fully warrant, and give bottom to the proposed subject; namely, the distinction of the effects of the law in natural conscience, from the writing of the law in the heart by regeneration. The main and more substantial difference it holds forth to be this, that God, in giving the old covenant, came upon and took man's natural old heart without renewing it, and gave the law thereunto, and tried how it would work upon it ; but in this new covenant he gives a new heart and a new spirit, writing the law in the very inwards, and makes it the groundwork of all his other workings.

Further, ere I come unto these particular heads which are to fill up the bulk of this intended discourse, I must premise one thing as introductory to what follows.

That which I premise is this assertion. That principle or faculty in the heart of man, which is the seat, throne, or sceptre, by which the law of God comes to rule over and to have these effects in the hearts of men, is conscience, by means of which it is said, that ' the law hath dominion over a man as long as he lives '; that is, whilst he lives in his natural condition, Rom. vii. 1 compared with ver. 4. This faculty is the Zion or Tower of David in the soul, from whence the law goes forth to the outmost ends thereof. To this purpose, you may observe how the apostle here, when he speaketh of the law written in the Gentiles' hearts, maketh especial, yea, only mention of this, and of no other faculty, because this faculty of conscience is that first and most immediate seat or subject of this writing of the law by nature, and is also the great officer of state, betrusted with the executive power of that law, to see it done and performed. Which accordingly both urgeth the heart of man thereto, as well as after that actions are done, it hath the office of a witness, under the great judge, to accuse, or excuse, and to serve his writs upon a man.

You that are versed in the writings of the wisest philosophers for morality, viz., Plato and the Stoics, Seneca, Epictetus, Hierocles, and Marcus Antoninus, &c., you find them still to cry up and magnify in man as his supreme guide and judge, ὀρθὸς λόγος, *recta ratio*, *right reason*, which they term a branch of God, and σκῆπτρον τοῦ Θεοῦ, the *Sceptre of God*, yea, *God in a man*, and many such eulogies they give forth of it. Now by right reason they meant primarily that practical part of reason in the mind, which guides a man in his actions according to the eternal law of God (as they speak) or the mind of God, which they termed the principal and primary law. So Tully* expressly speaks in his second book *De Legibus*, in the name of all the wisest philosophers. And Hierocles upon Pythagoras his verses speak answerably ὁ λογισμὸς τοὺς Θείους νόμους ὑποδεξάμενος. It is reason taking in the divine laws of God; and so it is δικαστὴς ἄγρυπνος ἑαυτῷ γίνεται. It becomes the most vigilant judge to a man's self.† And although these heathens sometimes used the word conscience even as we Christians do, yet more sparingly; and when they did, it was usually intended by them of one part of its office, viz., that after actions are done by us, it doth accordingly torture and disquiet, or refresh and rejoice a man, as he doth good or evil. Thus Tully‡ deciphers his sense of *recta ratio*, or right reason, to be a true and certain law within us, which calls upon us to what is our duty, and pricks us on to do well by commanding us, and restrains from evil by forbidding us with terrors; which, said he, the wisest of the heathen took to be the mind of God himself, who by that reason in men did order men by commands or restraint, as by a supreme or sovereign law.

Hence therefore, in their usual language, to *obey God*, and to live *according to right reason*, were all one; which they also termed living according to nature, as they accounted right reason to be. And what is all this, but as the learned Selden § makes the interpretation of these and the like speeches (citing of them) but that which in other terms themselves, and we Christians do call conscience. And Chrysostom afore him, ' When God formed man at first,' saith he, ' he put into him a natural law; and what that law of nature is, conscience hath explained it unto us, and of itself hath made manifest to us the cognisance both of things honest and that are otherwise.' Conscience is that only principle in a man, under whose cognisance comes all that hath the notion of what is morally good or evil, and which with one and the same eye vieweth a rule or law forbidding evil or commanding good; and together therewith do we take a glance of God, as the supreme judge, giving that law, and backing it with threatenings or promises of rewards. And this the etymology of the name denotes, *Conscientia, quasi cum alio sciens*, viz., with God, and from this knowledge of God, which it carries about with it, together with its being a rule or law, it is that that obligation, power, or force of it doth arise which binds a man, though no creature doth look on to be a witness of his sin, and so he becomes ' a law unto himself.' And conformably to this, as being the truth, the apostle

---

* Hanc video sapientissimorum fuisse sententiam ; legem esse æternum quiddam, quod universum mundum regeret. Ita principem legem illam et ultimam mentem dicebant, omnia ratione aut cogentis aut vetantis Dei.—*Cic. De Legibus*, lib. 2.

† Lex vera atque princeps apta ad jubendum et ad vetandum ratio est recta summi Jovis.—*Ibid*.

‡ Est quidem vera lex recta ratio, constans, sempiterna, quæ vocat ad officium jubendo, a fraude deterret.—De Rep., lib. 3, apud Lactant., cap. 8. And in his book De Legibus, lib. 2 : Ad recte faciendum impellens ; et hanc video sapientissimam fuisse sententiam, illam principem mentem dicebant aut cogentis aut vetantis Dei. λόγω δὲ ορθῷ πείθεσθαι και Θεῷ ταυτόν ἐστι.—*Hierocles in Pythag. Car.*

§ Quibus verbis id quod ipsis philosophis a paganis aliis non raro, τό συνειδός, in vitæ peragendæ ratione, seu Conscientia dicitur, optime designatur.—*Selden, de Jure Naturali*, &c. lib. 1 cap. 8.

speaks, ' Be subject for conscience sake,' Rom. xiii. 5, which is elsewhere rendered, to obey God. And hence also Paul termeth the leading of a good and regular life a ' living in all good conscience before God,' Acts xxiii. 1. The having done which Paul doth attribute to himself, even whilst he was under his pharisaism, and he terms it living in good conscience, because this conscience was that principle which took in the law from God, and so did provoke him to act outwardly according to it, which hath a goodness in its kind, and therefore is termed good. And it is said to be living in a good conscience, because no man doth make conscience of anything at any time, but it is with an eye to a deity more or less, as he is enlightened, be he a Jew or Gentile, or a professor of Christianity. And in all these it is conscience, whether truly sanctified or not, which is that τὸ ἡγουμόνικον, which, as Hierocles' * word is, is the suscipient of the divine laws. It is that province of reason, which lies open unto light from God to come in at, and to urge and enforce obedience, and which is capable and apprehensive of what God shall in that kind speak. It is the judge of good and evil moral, not only of right and wrong between man and man, as Gallio spake, but of things honest and wicked. It is *communis intelligentia, qua non solum jus et injuria dijudicantur, sed omnino omnia honesta et turpia*, as Cicero speaks. And it judgeth of them with application to all particular actions, to direct, provoke, restrain, or if the action be done, to excuse or accuse according to its judgment, and that in the name of a deity or god. Insomuch as I may apply here what Paul says in another though like case, ' What things soever the law says, it saith to them that are under the law,' Rom. iii. 9. I may add, whatever the law saith without us, is a conscience within us, the principle capable, according to the light received from thence, to urge it upon the rest of the faculties, so as these phrases are equivalent, to be under the law, and to be under conscience : to be ' concerning the law blameless,' and to ' live in all good conscience.' And the goodness of conscience there spoken of by Paul, is but a conformity of his outward conversation to the light of the law in his conscience.

And by the way, let me add this, that those that say there is no use of the moral law to a Christian, may as well say that there is no more use of that faculty of conscience in the soul of a Christian. Put out that faculty out of man's heart, if you tear out that other, namely, the obliging part of the law. Even as if God would annul colours and light, he must also take away and close up the sense of sight.

CHAPTER II.

That the natural light of conscience in unregenerate men hath a great influence on their actions.

Now these things being premised, there are three parts which fill up the body of that discourse which I intend.

I. That in men whom the Scriptures pronounce unregenerate, this principle of conscience hath had great and powerful effects upon their hearts.

* Ἐξ ἀρχῆς πλαττῶν ὁ Θεὸς τον ἄνθρωπον νόμον αὑτῷ ὑσικον ἐγκατέθηκε, καὶ τι ποτε ἐστι νόμος φυσικος ; τὸ συνείδος ἡμῖν διήρθωσε καὶ αὐτοδίδακτον ἐποίησε τὴν γνῶσιν τῶν καλῶν καὶ τῶν ου τοιουτῶν. ὁ ὑποδεξάμενος τοὺς θείους νόμους λογισμὸς.—*Hierocles in aurea carmina Pythagoræ.* [It is only the last sentence of this extract that is from Hierocles. The rest is from Chrysostom. *Orat.* xii. *ad Pop. Ant.*]—ED.

II. That these effects men of all professions, Jews, heathens, or nominal Christians, are apt to mistake, in the judgments which they pass, concerning their own state and condition, when they think that an observance of the dictates of conscience will make them acceptable to God. Yea, and if they be professors of Christianity (that are unregenerate), and so here of grace and regeneration, they take this to be true holiness, or sanctification. I shall also herewith give the reasons and grounds of this mistake.

III. I shall make a discovery of this great counterfeit, and of its deficiency, and of its falling short of grace, in the light of it, and in the effects of it, together with a detection and conviction of those mistakes.

I. In discoursing of the first head, there are two things to be treated of.

1. I shall prove that in men whom the Scripture pronounceth unregenerate, there are such powerful effects of conscience to be found.

2. I shall shew what those effects particularly are.

1. To prove that, in unregenerate men, there are powerful effects of conscience, I shall give instance in three sorts of men, in whom God hath given demonstration thereof, how far, and how high, this principle of conscience may and hath been elevated, and what effects it may have, and yet fall short of the glory of God, thereby more to magnify his sanctifying grace.

(1.) The first instance is of heathens under mere nature, which the writings of the heathens are records of, and which are indeed the truest comments upon this treatise of Rom. ii.

(2.) The second instance is of Jews under the law, whereof the Pharisees, and the carnal Jews under the Old Testament, are evidences. All the Scribes and Pharisees (whatever some of them might be) were not gross hypocrites, but many were serious in what they did, and their consciences being greatly enlightened in the law, they acted according unto conscience. We have an instance, both of that young man, who said he had kept the commandments from his youth, and also of the scribe : Mark xii. 32–34, ' And the scribe said unto him, Well, Master, thou hast said the truth : for there is one God ; and there is none other but he : and to love him with all thy heart, and with all thy understanding, and with all thy soul, and with all thy strength, and to love his neighbour as himself, is more than all whole burnt-offerings and sacrifices. And when Jesus saw that he answered discreetly, he said unto him, Thou art not far from the kingdom of God.' He had in his light pitched upon the first commandment of duties to be directed immediately to God himself, and his conscience rested not in outward performances, sacrifices and burnt-offerings, but the light in it had dictated to him further, although it was not able to mould his heart thereunto. For he says expressly, that ' to love God with all the heart, and with all the understanding, and with all the soul, and with all the strength, and to love his neighbour as himself, is more than all whole burnt-offerings and sacrifices.' And Christ, that discerned his heart, gives him this approbation of him : ' Thou art not far from the kingdom of God ;' which for that mere notion, if this scribe had been in his life a gross hypocrite, Christ would never have given. But yet this man, wanting that love to God whereof his conscience had the light (for conscience, never so much enlightened, will never work love to God), he fell short (as the word elsewhere is), for otherwise there is not any that thus truly love God, who is far from the kingdom of God, 1 Cor. ii. 9. Paul also giveth this record of many of the Jews his countrymen : Rom. x. 2, ' I bear them record, they have a zeal of God ;' that is, a study and care to please God in keeping of the law (of the works and righteousness whereof he there speaks, and had spoken, chap ix., the last foregoing verses), which zeal in their affections conscience had provoked and stirred up.

But the eminentest instance of all other in that kind is Paul himself, whom God did set up, before conversion, as the highest pattern in the Jewish religion; as after conversion, in the Christian. Paul speaking of himself, whilst a pharisee still, tells us how zealous his religion made him, as to the persecuting the opposite party, so to the observation of that righteousness of the law, Gal. i. 14, and Phil. iii. 6, ' Concerning zeal, persecuting the church; touching the righteousness which is in the law, blameless:' that is, I was so truly zealous for the law, that I persecuted what way was opposite to it. Now, what made him so? It was conscience, Acts xxvi. 9, he ' verily thought that he ought' to do so. Now that principle in us which convinceth that we ought to do a thing, is conscience, Acts xxiii. 1. That apology which Paul, being set before the council, was about to make, but was broke off by the high priest, and the tumult, runs thus, ' Men and brethren, I have lived in all good conscience before God until this day.' Many of you are not ignorant how most interpreters do understand this speech as relating to, and taking in the whole of his life, not of Christianity only, but even in Judaism also, for he doth not by any express word date it from his conversion. He doth not say, since I turned Christian, or was converted to the faith; but only says, ' until this day,' which indefinitely includes the whole of his life till then. And his manner was, in telling the story of his conversion, to begin with his exactness in observing the law before his conversion (which he was about to relate, but that he is interrupted here), which outward obedience, because of its conformity to the principle of it, is frequently termed a good conscience, that is, a good or regular life conformed to and springing from conscience. And that which Paul here intendeth in reference to that part of his life under pharisaism, is all one and the same with what elsewhere he saith, Phil. iii. 6, ' touching the righteousness which is in the law, blameless.'

But there were a third sort, in whom conscience enlightened may be supposed yet further improved in the effect of it, when yet it fell short of grace. There were those who were supernaturally enlightened by the gospel, of whom Paul, Heb. vi., and Christ's parables speak. Such light the understanding of man, not renewed, is capable of, and it lies exposed for God to shoot into it, without infusing a new habit, or spiritualising that faculty. It lies exposed also unto influences and effects of the promises of the gospel, working upon self-love in the will and affections, with tastings of the powers of the world to come. Now when the light of the gospel is added to the light of the law, and when a supernatural light of things revealed in the gospel is added to that of conscience in the law, conscience cometh to have its dominions enlarged, and is more strengthened and backed hereby. Now in such, so wrought on by the gospel, and also the law, and in whose hearts both these meet, the effects must needs be supposed more powerful and vigorous, because there is brought in a stronger light of God himself, in the efficacy of knowing whom, more or less, the obligation and power of conscience lies. An instance that mentions the conjunction of both these in express words is hard perhaps to meet withal; although, where such supernatural enlightening in things of the gospel falls out to be in such as have fallen away, it must necessarily be supposed that there is a more vigorous actuating and stirring that light and principle of conscience that doth accompany the same; especially considering that the workings of the law upon conscience is that which prepares men's hearts (both that are saved or otherwise fall away) for their listening after, and so receiving in, the supernatural truths of the gospel. Howsoever, thus much is evident to the thing in hand, that these Jews, of all other, who were of the sect of the Pharisees, that made conscience of the law, when they came to be enlightened by the gospel, became the raisers and fomenters of that great opposition to the gospel which was the ruin of many professors in those primitive times. Of these Pharisees mention is made, Acts xv. 5, ' There rose up certain of the sect of the Pharisees who believed' (and some, as in charity we are to think, savingly, who yet were the defenders of that great error), ' saying, It was needful to circumcise men that believed, and to teach them to keep the law of Moses ;' that is, the whole of it, which circumcision did oblige unto. As these men had faith superadded, so I may say of them, as Paul of some Gentiles, they had a ' conscience of that idol,' the law, to that day ; and their conscience having been inured to that yoke, knew not how to discharge itself so soon of that subjection (I speak as to that sense mentioned), and so by that addition of faith, conscience was more provoked to be zealous for the law, and to observe it, that they might keep in with God.

Now, what the estate of these particular persons there mentioned was, we know not, nor the issue of them as to God ; yet this we are sure of, that many of the followers of that doctrine, which these there first did broach, and who had embraced the faith upon a supernatural light (for else none in those times would easily have professed it) did out of the same principle of conscience urge and profess obedience to that whole law of Moses, and set out therein with the same zeal in both (for the reality of it) that these Pharisees, that were the first authors of that opinion, did. It was the profession of making conscience, and of their obligation to God's command, which was the ground of that zeal ; and yet we are sure that many of them are branded to have been apostates to the faith in the end. And I observe that when Paul twice speaks of this kind of professors (as he vouchsafes to name them, Tit. i. 16), who thus urged the observation of the law as well as faith in the gospel, he still makes mention withal of faith and conscience. For the latter was that which these so much pretended ; for the obligation of the law (they contended for) did principally respect conscience as the seal of it, and as subject to it, and over which it had dominion in men. Thus Paul writes, 1 Tim. i., concerning some at Ephesus who pressed the law in the sense these Pharisees had done, as well as they pressed faith, as appears by ver. 7, 8. And because they did urge this upon pretence of conscience, therefore, in opposition to that religion of theirs, which they made up both of law and gospel in an untoward mixture, Paul professeth the true religion (or that part of it which relateth to the commandments) to be this, ver. 5–7, ' Now the end of the commandment is charity, out of a pure heart, and of a good conscience, and of faith unfeigned : from which some having swerved, have turned aside unto vain jangling ; desiring to be teachers of the law ; understanding neither what they say, nor whereof they affirm.' He by these cords* intimates to us, that though these men did profess the same faith in Christ, yet their zeal to the law, for which they pretended conscience, was the cause of their swerving from both, they never having had the true genuine or saving principle of either. And therefore, in his enumeration of the saving principles of faith and a good conscience, he upon occasion of them is forced to distinguish upon these

* Qu. ' words '?—Ed.

principles, as is evident by those cords,* 'The end of the commandment is charity, out of a pure heart, of a good conscience, and faith unfeigned.' And why is it he should use this distinction there, when he had occasion to speak of these men, but to put the difference between faith, and such a conscience, and principle of zeal in religion, which is defiled? In distinction unto which he calls the principle of true holiness, a good conscience, as he had characterised true and saving faith with this of her† 'unfeigned faith,' and a 'pure heart' as the effect of both these; for a purified heart is expressly made the effect of faith, Acts xv. 9. So then there is a conscience zealous of religion, that is joined with a pure heart, and there is a conscience that is joined with a defiled heart, and that in men enlightened in religion, which Paul, in his Epistle to Titus, thus expresseth, in words near akin to those he useth in Timothy of the same sort of professors: 'Unto the pure are all things pure: but unto them that are defiled and unbelieving,' that have a faith that purifies not the heart, but leaves it still in its natural defilements, and so as good as no faith, and therefore he terms them unbelievers still, 'even in their mind and conscience,' which yet are the supremest and purest part in them, even these 'remain defiled,' however enlightened, and whatever conscience of the law they do pretend. Now, therefore, if their consciences remain defiled, saith he, no wonder if in the end of their profession their lives prove also such, ver. 16; for as Christ says, 'If the light be darkness, how great is that darkness! But if the eye be single, the whole body is full of light.' And in these two discourses compared, Paul discovers and rips up the inwards of true profession and false. In the practice of religion mentioned in the one, viz., that of Titus, he resolves apostasy and falling away into its true causes. And in this other, to Timothy, speaking of the contrary, sincere obedience, that holds out to the end, he resolves his perseverance unto its true causes also. In the one he tells us that their consciences, which having been enlightened, had been the groundwork of their zeal for the law, and of obedience to it, had yet continued and remained defiled notwithstanding all that light. In the other he tells us that they have obtained such a 'good conscience' and 'faith unfeigned,' as had 'purified the heart.' Neither is his scope in his Epistle to Titus only to shew what at present their consciences were become through sinning, but to resolve things into their causes (as in that of Timothy he had done), shewing that this defect had been in their profession from the first of it, in that their consciences and minds had remained in their natural defilement. And thence all their best actions, as well as their outward legal observations, had become defiled to them, and in the end had wrought out that light and goodness that had any impression upon them.

2. I come now to shew what effects a natural conscience may and doth produce in men unregenerate. The instances I give of these effects shall be only such as have been found in heathens and Jews, of whom it must needs be acknowledged that they were not renewed. And such effects, even in professors of Christianity who are not savingly regenerated, are still but of the same kind, only are more heightened by the addition of gospel light, more clearly revealing God; and also perhaps in such persons these effects are extended objectively unto more duties than came to the cognizance of either Jew or Gentile. The reason why this addition of gospel and supernatural light must needs increase the same effects more powerfully, is because (as I said) conscience hath in all men two things

* Qu 'words'?—Ed.   Qu. 'other'?—Ed.

still in its eye : 1. The law, or rule ; 2. God as the judge giving that law ; and from its eyeing, more or less, God as the judge, doth arise that authority that is in the dictates of conscience. And hence, as the conscience doth more clearly and fully take in light from God, and is thereby convinced of him and his greatness, and that the rules given are from him, proportionably must these effects of conscience become more powerful, and work more strongly upon the heart ; yet so as still this light, and these effects, are but of the same kind with those that are found in heathens or Jews.

(1.) I shall give instances of these effects in respect of what is good.

[1.] Conscience in a natural and unregenerate man may and doth often pass an act, both of assent and approbation, to what is a good and holy duty, and to what the law says, or to the duties and commands thereof, that they are good, and just, and right ; otherwise it could not accuse a man for what is evil, unless it secretly approved of what is good. *Video meliora proboque*, says Medea in Ovid : I see what is better, and approve of it, though I choose and pursue the worse. Seneca* also, speaking of the worst of men, says that virtue hath that amiableness in it that it is ingrafted in those that are most wicked, to approve the things that are good and best. They are heathens that speak these things ; and as for the Jews, Paul expressly says, Rom. ii. 18, ' Thou approvest the things that are more excellent,' which is a phrase suitable to the other, *Probo meliora*. And this is one respect for which they are said to be under the law, and the law to have power or dominion over a man, as Rom. vii. 1, 2, even because men have a principle in them capable of its love, and naturally subjected thereunto, which maketh them acknowledge and own it for their lord. Now, it could no way bring men under that subjection and bondage but by this, that there is something in this principle of conscience unto which this law approves its equity and justness ; or, to use the apostle's phrase, 2 Cor. iv. 2, ' commendeth itself to every man's conscience.' And thus the law, held forth in a godly man's life, in the concrete, approves itself to a wicked man. Saul could not but acknowledge of David, ' Thou art more righteous than I.' And in the abstract it doth it much more. In the story of the Acts, the apostle appeals to their consciences (as Socrates before had done to his heathen judges), whether it were not better to obey God than men ; for their natural consciences could not but so adjudge it.

[2.] Natural conscience not only assents to what the law commands as good, but it commends it to a man as his duty, and lays it as an injunction upon him to do it. So says Paul, ' I verily thought with myself that I ought to do many things,' &c., Acts xxvi. 9. Therefore it is called *conscientia* by some, because it lays an obligation upon a man ; and so it is *quasi concludens scientia*, which binds him to his good behaviour.

[3.] It provoketh, yea, prevails, with men to do what it shews them to be good, and their particular duty. It is not a sleeping, idle principle, but active ; for so says the apostle of the heathens, Rom. ii. 14, ' They did by nature the things of the law,' as instigated thereto by conscience. For he renders that as the ground of it, that ' they were a law unto themselves.' So Herod, as you know, ' *did* many things' which John the Baptist urged upon his conscience out of the word.

[4.] In these their acting what is good, the workings of conscience are the main engines which set them to work, and not simply outward respects.

* Adeo gratiosa est virtus ut insitum etiam malis sit probare meliora.—*Seneca*, Ep. i.

Thus Paul resolves what he did in his unregeneracy unto this principle: 'I verily thought I ought to do it,' says he; and so did what he did, Acts ix. 15. It also appears in this, that a man will go against all outward respects merely to satisfy his conscience, as Judas did, when he confessed and restored the money for which he had betrayed Christ; wherein he did an act cross to the dearest lusts in him, his credit and his covetousness. *Conscientiæ satisfaciamus*, says Seneca, *nihil in famam laboremus:* Let us satisfy conscience, no matter for credit.

[5.] Hence also natural conscience may in these actions have a real respect to God, to whom (as was said) conscience looks, and from whom it fetcheth its binding power; so as the man takes his command in, as a consideration that moves him: John xvi. 2, 'He that killeth you shall think he doth God good service,' that is, he shall look upon it as a service done to God, and have some respect to him in it. And though this is spoken of such actions as materially in themselves were not service to God, but the contrary, yet the inward motive it proceeded from was, that they judged it a service unto God. And therefore when it falls to be in itself a duty, conscience presseth it much more, and urgeth it upon this motive, Rom. x. 1. The carnal Jew is said to have a zeal of God, or for God. Thus also we read of carnal and wicked men who out of awe, and fear, and respect to him do forbear some sins: 'It is in my power,' says Laban to Jacob, Gen. xxxi. 29: 'but the God of your father spake to me, saying, Take heed thou speak to Jacob neither good nor evil.' God commanded Balaam also that he should not curse the Israelites; and Balaam kept to that command, and durst not go outwardly cross to it, although inwardly he desired leave to have done it, that so he might be rewarded by Balak. Yea, he therefore durst not do it, because of the word of the Lord, Num. xxii. 18. So Cyrus says of Ezra, Ezra i. 2, that 'the God of heaven had charged him to build a house for him.'

[6.] When a man hath done what conscience, and God in his conscience, have commanded, he hath much peace in it, for it excuseth him, as the text, Rom. ii. 15, says. Thus a heathen also could say, *Recte fecisse merx est;* it is reward enough to do well. Therefore Paul's heart was kept alive, Rom. vii., in joy and peace, by doing what the law required; so also a man will be exceeding glad when such a sin is avoided, or if a sin take not full effect, as Darius was glad when Daniel was alive, Dan. vi. 23.

(2.) I shall give instances of the workings of conscience, in relation unto evil, either sins of commission, or omission of duties.

[1.] Conscience in natural men causeth a reluctancy and a commotion of affections against a sin, before the commission of it, and a displacency in committing of it. Thus Darius, a heathen, Dan. vi. 14, was so displeased with himself, when he was put upon putting to death so just a man as his conscience told him that Daniel was. We may observe it in Herod also, Mark vi. 26: when John the Baptist's head was required of him, you read what a reluctancy he had, and sorrow against it; 'he was exceeding sorry,' ver. 26, and it was his conscience that wrought that in him, for, ver. 20, it is said that 'he observed John, because he was a just and an holy man;' yet, for his oath's and lust's sake, he murdered him, though to have parted with half his kingdom would not have troubled him so much.

[2.] Conscience excites in men an endeavour to avoid and decline evil. So Darius set his heart to deliver Daniel, and he laboured till evening, Dan. vi. 14; so Pilate did all he could, a great while, to free his hands of the guilt of Christ's death by saving of him.

[3.] It worketh much sorrow and repentance after sinning. So, of Darius we read, vi. 18, that he was troubled all night, could not eat his meat, and his sleep departed from him ; and thus the apostle, Rom. ii. 15, says of the heathens, that their consciences do accuse them. Thus Judas also, Mat. xxvii. 4, 5, says, ' I have sinned, in that I have betrayed the innocent blood. And he cast down the pieces of silver in the temple, and departed, and went and hanged himself.' And (by the way) here are all the parts and ingredients that the papists require in repentance : 1. Contrition : ' He repented himself.' 2. Confession: ' I have sinned in betraying innocent blood.' 3. Restitution and satisfaction : ' He cast down the silver pieces' that had betrayed him to that sin. 4. He purposes never to return to it, as Saul resolved not to kill David (his conscience was overcome with his righteousness), and as Pharaoh resolved to let the people go.

These things might be enlarged, and other instances given ; but I have given instances of such as all must needs acknowledge to have been unregenerate men.

CHAPTER III.

That men are apt to regard the natural light of conscience, and the influences of it, to be the effects of true grace.—The reasons of their mistake.

I come now to prove all sorts of men unregenerate, have been, and are, apt to mistake this light of conscience in them, and the powerful effects of it, to be true righteousness which makes them acceptable to God. And if they be professors of Christianity, they are ready to take it for sanctification and true holiness.

There are three things under this head to be spoken unto.

I. That, *de facto*, all sorts of professions have mistaken it.

II. The reasons of it.

III. Some grounds of the mistake.

I. All sorts have been apt to this.

1. Heathens have been so. It were infinite to reckon up the flesh-blown conceits of the heart of man in the instances of the heathens (as they may be authentically drawn out of their own writings), how they magnify and cry up in themselves that which they called right reason forementioned, as their Diana ; what divine eulogies they give it, and how they blessed themselves when they lived conformably unto it, and the decrees or dogmata of it, as Epictetus calls them.

1. For the light thereof itself they judged it holy, divine, heavenly ; yea, and nothing more divine or heavenly, not God himself ; it being (as they say) a part of the divine Spirit put and drenched into a human body. Thus Seneca speaks,* and he speaks it not of the soul itself, but of reason or conscience, for he speaks of that which he terms the rule and measure of virtues ; yea, and because it is right reason or conscience that lets in the light of a deity into the soul (as the word itself imports) as a judge ; therefore they called it not only a good angel, or *Daimon*, in a man (as frequently they do), but Seneca terms it *sacer spiritus*, a sacred or holy spirit. *Sacer*

* Una inducitur humanis virtutibus regula ; ratio recta simplexque : Nihil est divino divinius, cœlesti cœlestior. Ratio autem nihil aliud est quam in corpus humanum pars divini Spiritus mersa.—*Seneca*, Ep. 66.

intra nos spiritus sedet, malorum bonorumque nostrorum observator et custos. Hic prout a nobis tractatus est, ita nos ipse tractat. There is a sacred spirit that sits within us, which is the observer, and layer up, and keeper of all the good or evil things in us (that is, which we do or are found in us), who so deals with us as we deal with him. This eminently refers unto conscience, for that is that principle which lets God in upon us as a judge of our actions in our own hearts. And you see it is spoken of that in us which is the observer of all good and evil in us, yea, and the layer of it up and remembrancer of it for a long time after ; and which, as we follow the light and guidance of it, so it deals with us, accusing or excusing us, as here, in the text, conscience is said to do. All which are evidently properties of conscience (as in this text), unto which he (as from his own experience) attributed a deity ; as indeed himself in the very next words says, he knew not what god to call it, but a god it was (*Quis deus incertum est, habitat deus*), for his conscience still represented a deity unto him.

Yea, this light and principle in them they also accounted a thing equal unto God, calling it not only a branch of the divine nature (Antoninus, lib. v., *de vita sua*, chap. 6).[*] Epictetus also thus speaks, ' As for thy reason, O man ! thou art not less or inferior to the gods ; '[†] which they spake as concerning the nature of it ; so in respect of its ability to guide and bring us unto happiness, in this respect equal to the reason or divine light that is in God, though indeed in him it was infallible and supreme, by which he governed and managed himself and his affairs. Thus Seneca expressly makes no other difference between right reason within a man and God,[‡] than between two mariners that have like skill to steer and govern their vessels ; only the one, viz., reason, hath a less ship to guide, God a larger ship of the same fashion and make. Yet so as that right reason in a man is as supreme in his compass as God in his ; both had the same rules they steered by, and in that sense and intention they attend the usual speech, that in following reason they followed God. And so indeed I may in this respect make a parallel, that look, as the papists having set up the pope as the supreme universal judge of controversies, though in pretence as Christ's vicar, to increase his power, yet in the apostolical interpretation of it, 2 Thes. ii., they set him ' even above and against Christ, and all that is called God,' for that which they attribute to him doth really arise to so much ; so these heathens, and the wisest of them, did set up right reason in a man, though in pretence as God's vicegerent, yet really and in effect as equal unto God in a man, and as man's supreme guide or judge, only dictating the same rule or δόγματα, as Epictetus calls them, which God did. Yea, to make the parallel more full, they made it a universal rule and concern (as Euripides calls it§), that had so full a power over all their actions, as to constitute them good or evil. Thus they gave forth this maxim,|| *Ni tibi concessit ratio, digitum exere, peccas*, unless right reason gives commission, even to the putting forth a finger, it is a sinful action. They speak (you see) higher things hereof by far than the Scripture doth of the new creature, which yet is termed a participation of the divine nature.

---

* ἀποσπάσμα ἑαυτοῦ οὗτος δε ἐστιν ἑκαστοῦ νοῦς καὶ λόγος.—*Anto.* lib. 5. *de vitâ suâ,* cap. 6.

† κατὰ τί τὸν λόγον οὐδε χειρὼν τῶν Θεῶν οὐδε μικρότερος.—*Epict.*

‡ Quam inter duos quibus par scientia regendi gubernaculum est : meliorem dixeris, cui majus speciosiusque navigium.

§ κάνωνου τοῦ κάλλου.—*Euripides in Hecub.*

|| Persius, Satyr. 5

Secondly, And 2. For the fruit and effect of this principle upon their hearts and in their lives, they judge themselves therein according to that measure and esteem which, we have heard, they had of the principles of self. A good life they termed a harmonious, suitable living to the height and dictates of this light, as that wherein the happiness of a man lay. Now all that the apostles attribute to a true saint, or a holy man (in this respect), they attribute also to themselves *in terminis*.

1. They term it the image and likeness to God, ὁμοιώσιν τῷ Θεῷ, so Plato, yea, and he puts it into the same division; and in the same words the apostles express the parts thereof. Plato's words are these :* A likeness unto God consists in what is holy, and what is just or righteous, with wisdom and knowledge. The apostle's words are these : ' The image of God, which is in knowledge created after God in righteousness and true holiness,' Eph. iv. 24, compared with Col. iii. 10. Only, for distinction, the Holy Ghost adds *true* holiness, for theirs was not so.

2. Doth the Scripture call such a man a good man, a blessed man ? These are the ordinary titles which they also usurp, and that with distinction from others, ὁ ἀγαθὺς ὁ ἐνδαιμῶν, the good, the blessed man, and the like.

Yea, 3. Doth James call a man grown up in Christianity a perfect man ? And Paul use the same: ' I speak to those that are perfect ' ? So do they.†And as the apostles said that all graces go together, so they affirm of all virtues, and that else a man is not perfect. Yea, they go higher than the apostles did, for they assert that good men are impeccable, and cannot fall or transgress, and that a wicked man was one that had no virtue in him ; and they distinguish also of *proficients* and of perfect men. Do the apostles say that a godly man hath dominion‡ and fellowship with God (' Truly our fellowship is with the Father and the Son.' And Abraham was called the friend of God). They will needs say the same of their blessed man, Unto whose estate (says Seneca§) when thou hast attained, thou beginnest to be a companion with God himself. Another describes his wise man to be one who doth, *in mortali corpore agitare societatem Jovis*, in a mortal body pursue fellowship with God. Yea, and herein they are bold to vie with God himself. *Cum Diis*, says Seneca, *ex pari vivit:* He lives as blessed a life as God, and differs from him (say they) but in duration, passions, and mortality ; but I will not trouble you farther with their notions. I shall only add unto all these one scripture instance of a heathen, who though in these first times of the world we find more modest, yet standing upon his integrity and righteousness before God himself, he says, Gen. xx. 4, 5, ' Wilt thou also slay a righteous nation ? Said he not unto me, She was my sister ? and she, even herself said, He is my brother : in the integrity of my heart and innocency of my hands have I done this.' This man was a heathen, as also his people whom he was king over. The speech of Abraham, ver. 11, declares it upon the general observation of their manners. ' What didst thou see in us?' says Abimelech. I said, says Abraham, ' Surely the fear of God is not in this place;' that is, God is not worshipped by or amongst this people, or there is no religion amongst them. Parallel

---

* ὁμοίωσιν Θεῷ δίκαιον καὶ ὅσιον μετὰ φρονήσεως γινέσθαι.—*Plato in Philebo.*

† τὸν ἀγαθὸν ἀνδρὰ τελείον εἶναι λέγουσι. Nec virum perfectum qui non omnes virtutes habet, nec actionem quæ non fiat secundum omnes.—*Chrysippus.* ἀναμαρτήτους τους σόφους, τῷ ἀπεριπτώτους εἶναι ἀμαρτήματι.—*Laertius in Zenon.*

‡ Qu. ' communion '?—ED.

§ Incipis esse Deorum socius.—*Sen.*, Ep. 35. Epictetus, Seneca, Chrysippus.

to which is that speech of David's, Ps. xxxvi. 1, 'The transgression of the wicked says within my heart, there is no fear of God before his eyes.' It is so apparent and speaks so loud; yet this Abimelech, in the case of Sarah, having dealt there according to his knowledge, and the principles of his conscience commonly received amongst them, in that nation, says that for conscience' sake he would not have taken her, if he had known her to have been Abraham's wife : 'In the integrity,' says he, 'of my heart, and innocency of my hands, have I done this,' ver. 5.   And this he speaks not to Abraham (and so as what he could pretend to before men), but to God, of whom he had some knowledge, though a heathen, and whom he doth acknowledge to be judge over nations, and to judge righteous judgment.   In the words afore, ver. 4, he makes his appeal to God, the only judge of his conscience, professing not only in innocency of hands as to matter of outward fact, but of integrity of heart, as having been sincerely conformable therein to his conscience.   And he speaks herein the very language of a holy man, even of David, whom you hear, Ps. xviii. 24, thus pleading with God, 'According to my righteousness, according to the cleanness of my hands in his eyesight.'   Now, what he says of one action, that in all other (if conformable to his conscience) he would make the same plea.

2. That the Jews did so mistake the natural light of conscience, and the powerful effects thereof to be true righteousness, the Old and the New Testament are so abundant in known instances as I need not mention any. They 'rested in the law, and made their boast of God,' says the apostle, Rom. ii.   And the resting in the law was, by those that were the best of them, by reason of their conformity unto it ('These have I kept from my youth,' said that young man in Mat. xix.), for which, as they thought themselves righteous (as Christ speaks) so they judged it ordained unto life and justification, as Paul says, Rom. vii.   And thus they 'went about to establish their own righteousness,' Rom. x. 4.   And what is all this, but to take the effects of conscience for true holiness, yea, for justification ?   So (as was said) this as the principle was the suscipient of the law, and the cause of all that obedience in them.

3. Christians also are obnoxious to the same mistake.   What Pelagius did boldly and plainly in his doctrine utter, that in application do the most of Christian professors secretly rest upon for their own salvation, even what goodness is found to be in nature.   We have all *fibra Pelagiana* in us, we are naturally all Pelagians, and the great deceit of men's hearts is, that what opinions they doctrinally condemn in their speculative judgments, those they practically approve in their secret transactions with God for their salvation.   We generally declaim against Pelagianism, as extolling nature for grace, and yet as generally we take the fruits and effects of it in ourselves for grace.   And I may say, as the apostle doth, 'Blessed is the man that blesseth not himself in what he condemns.'

Now Pelagius in his doctrine professed conscience, and the light thereof, to be grace and holiness.   He hath a manifest saying * to this purpose : 'There is in our minds a certain natural holiness, which residing in the supreme part and tower of the mind, doth give forth and exerciseth the judgment of what is good and evil, which encourageth to and cherisheth honest acts in us, and condemns what are evil and wicked.'   Now what is this but that which we call conscience ?   And to this purpose he would

---

* Est in animis nostris naturalis quædam sanctitas, quæ velut in arce animi residens, exercet mali bonique judicium, honestis actibus fovet, et sinistra opera condemnat.

draw the very words (of Rom. ii. 14, 15) to be intended of Abel, Noah, and all just ones before the flood, and before the law was given, that by nature they did what was acceptable to God. *Et justas illas imagines*, says he, *quis nisi injustus prohibet a regno Dei?*

II. Secondly, The reasons of this aptness to mistake are these :

1. In general; It is conscience itself that is the judge ; yea, in a man's own heart, the highest and most supreme, and there is no higher principle to control it. Yea, and no more of the word prevails with a man than this takes in, and the proper office of it is to judge what makes a man acceptable to God, and what not. And next unto God (who is greater than our hearts) all appeals are made to this court ; and therefore no man doth imagine but that conscience doth direct him right ; and that if the dictates thereof were followed and obeyed, he should be a just and an upright man. Conscience being the supreme judge, hath this opinion of its own judgment, that if it were followed it would save a man ; and the rest of the faculties have that good opinion of it also, for else it would never be acknowledged as supreme. And there is no man that doth or will think himself so far off from grace as not to think he hath right opinions about it. If, therefore, conscience finds its judgment hath any sway or stroke in a man to overpower the heart, or the actions, it presently applauds both this its own power for grace, and also thinks well of the man, so far as he is conformable to its dictates ; and applauds him with a ' Well done, good and faithful servant !' And this, because it doth think well of itself, even as we are apt to think the better of ourselves, when we see ourselves respected, and entertain good opinions of those who do respect us.

2. Secondly, The main reason is, because all men are under the covenant of works, or the covenant of grace (Rom. vi. 14, ' Ye are not under the law, but under grace.' Compare it with Rom. vii. 1) ; and the one hath ever set up its righteousness against the other ; and now that man is fallen, yet corrupt nature is so conceited of itself, that it attempts to vie and outvie that righteousness that is of the spring of grace in us. The genius in that covenant is to trust in itself for righteousness. It is strange to see how contrary to the way of salvation by Christ, the way of nature is. Christ's way is to cause all men to distrust themselves, and be nothing in themselves, that ' he that glories might glory in the Lord.' But the greatest maxim of nature, among those of the heathen, that professed to live most righteously, was expressly, *Sibi fidere*, to trust in a man's self, and to what in and by nature he was able to do. And Paul hath insinuated the reason of it also in those words, Rom. x., ' They went about to establish their own righteousness ;' and they did so because it was their own.

III. Thirdly, The particular grounds of the mistake are,

1. Men find conscience to be an inward principle, as grace is, inherent, seated and rooted in themselves, as they hear grace is ; and therefore if it hath any power in a man, they easily take it for grace. Men would think otherwise, indeed, if that which carried them on against evil, and unto good, were only and merely outward, as Socrates his genius, &c. ; or if outward weights and enforcements of worldly respects hung on, only moved the wheels ; if only vainglory, or fear of superiors, or conformity to others, acted them. But men find something here within them, over and besides all these, which is real and serious for good, and against evil, and that such a spring should move, and have any stroke in them, as a part of themselves, this they easily think to be grace. Now such a principle is conscience, and the light of it in men ; for the effect of the law is

written in the heart, as the text says, and they are a law to themselves. It is not other respects only that moved them, but a law in themselves, and to themselves. Yea, and oftentimes, when a stream of outward respects would carry them against what is good, and unto what is evil, yet this inward principle, conscience, moves them contrary, to swim against that stream; as in Socrates, and Brutus, and Fabricius, whom no threats or entreats could divert; of whom it was said, that sooner might the sun be turned out of its course than Fabricius be swayed by respects. And we have an instance too in Balaam, whom ' an house full of gold and silver' (though himself was covetous) could not persuade, God having a hold upon his conscience within.

2. Again, 2dly, That which helps forward this good opinion is, that men find it a constant and incorrupt principle, and (as the schoolmen say) that it keeps itself a virgin. It dwells in them, as grace is said to be ' a seed that remains.' And it is incorrupt in this respect, that it will not let sin pass uncontrolled, nor be charmed to hold its tongue, but will talk and speak against it, whilst it hath a tongue, which, though it be imprisoned, will preach in prison. In keeping itself thus incorrupt, men are apt to think it is grace in them.

3. The fruits and effects are so like to those of true grace, that no wonder if men mistake them. The phrase used to express both are so nigh akin, as a man must criticise to observe the difference. Grace is ' the law written in the heart,' the light of conscience is the ' effect of the law written there.' The same outward duties which grace directs to, conscience enlightened doth urge unto, and speaks against the same sins. And at once to give you a clear demonstration, both that the effects are much alike, and thence men are apt to mistake : How comes it to pass, that the 7th chapter of the Romans, from the 14th verse to the end, should be so variously interpreted by men of great understandings, that one and the same draught and representation, which Paul there makes of that great fight between grace and corruption, the law of the members and the law of the mind should be drawn by Arminius and others as a representation of the effects and conflicts of natural conscience enlightened, and that he should carry on every phrase and particle therein, in all the particulars, with so much seeming appearance ? This argues the effects to be alike. Yea, which is yet stranger, Augustine himself (who knew the difference of the effects of grace and natural conscience ; yea, and in his *Confessions*, relates the experiments of that difference in himself to have been the first evidence of regeneration, or of that new work of grace upon him, in comparing the then frame of his heart, when new converted, with his former, in his unregenerate condition). After this work he interpreted that chapter of the effects of the natural conscience, though after he retracts it. We also hear carnal people, that apparently have no grace, yet allege out of that chapter, excuses for their grossest sinnings, that ' they do what they would not;' and ' it is not I, but sin.' That thus one and the same picture should seem two several pictures of two several men, argues there is a near resemblance. That the complexion and lineaments of natural conscience should seem to one to be pourtrayed in this chapter, and yet the resemblance of grace appears in it, to another that hath experience of what is grace, argues a great likeness, as indeed there is. But I will discourse of this more particularly.

1. The grounds why heathens were deceived in their high esteem of conscience, were these. They thought reason, and conscience in them, to

be the same that is in God himself. *Orta est simul cum mente divina ; et princeps lex est ratio recta summi Jovis,* says Tully.* And Hierocles† also says, that it is the same thing to obey right reason, and God ; such a mind enlightened differs not from the mind of God, but being intent on that divinity and brightness by which it is enlightened, it comes to do those things which it doth. And the heathens, knowing no higher illumination, and therefore thinking that it was thus adequate and correspondent unto the light that is in God, whom whilst they glimmeringly knew, they judged altogether such a one as themselves, and glorified him not as God in their knowledge of him ; they therefore knowing no higher, judged nothing could be higher. And so look, what pleased reason in them, they judged it must fully please God also, of whom it was the participation. And although they could not but acknowledge God as the supreme judge (for conscience still urged them with his authority), yet they did in their doctrines do what they could to persuade themselves and others that this right reason, or law in their consciences, was the supreme visible judge, to which a man himself only was to give an account, and receive his happiness or woe from it, according as he lived after its dictates.

2. The Jews receiving the law immediately from God himself, as a perfect copy of his mind, saw not the end of it, 2 Cor. iii., and considered not that the end and intent of God's giving it, was to discover to them now fallen, their weakness and contrariety to it, to drive them to Christ ; but they thought that God prescribed the law to them as the way to life, by which they might live in doing of it as they were able ; and so their consciences taking it from God, set them a-doing it in the letter of it, and this they judged must save them, because the primitive intent of the law to man at first was ordained to life. This Paul speaks as his thoughts, in the name of the rest, Rom. vii. 9. But that which deceived them was that man was not as at first, though the law, in itself, was what it was at first.

3. We Christians, that know the gospel, yet remaining unregenerate, do still verge in our spirits to the way of the covenant of works, for it is nature in us ; and so we set up conscience, and close with the dictates of it for religion, rather than the way of faith and rules of believing. And further, hearing religion expressed to us by such phrases as these, of a man's being a conscionable man, and the integrity of a man's actions being expressed by doing things ' for conscience sake,' Rom. xiii. 5 ; and having‡ all religion also to be reduced to those two, and so expressed to us, viz., ' faith and a good conscience,' (1 Tim. i. 19 ; faith being the principle of all things to be believed ; conscience, of things that are to be done. *Fides principium credendorum et conscientia agendorum*), therefore faith to be a common assent to what they are trained up in, and is delivered in the word ; so look what effects conscience hath upon their hearts, either for good or against evil, they think must needs be what the New Testament means by ' the new creature,' not dreaming that there is a ' defiled conscience,' which sets men a-work till faith and regeneration come with power and purify the heart.

* Lib. 3, de Repub. lib. 6, cap. 8.   See *Chrysippus* apud *Laertium.*
† Hierocles *Comment. in Carmin Pythagor.*
‡ Qu. ' hearing '?—Ed.

CHAPTER IV.

A discovery of the defects wherein natural conscience falls short of true grace.

The third and main head is to make discovery of this deficiency, as also of the grounds of those mistakes fore-specified.

1. I shall make inquisition or search into the principle of conscience itself, and into the light with which the consciences of natural men are endowed. And I shall inquire also into the nature, seat, condition, and goodness of that light ; and this in many assertions introductory unto what shall follow. For, to be sure, the goodness of the effects of conscience cannot rise higher than that of the cause.

2. I shall consider the grounds of those several mistakes forementioned, by which men unregenerate are induced to think the light of natural conscience to be holiness.

3. I shall particularly examine all those effects of natural conscience which have been enumerated, and the deficiency of them from that holiness which is in a man regenerate.

1. As to the inquiry concerning the principle of conscience itself. Suppose that you had some person that were counterfeit, that pretended to some great inheritance under examination, you would strictly inquire into his birth, original, place of abode, and residence, and the like. Let us take the same course here.

(1.) For its original, I acknowledge that the light thereof is from God, upon a new account ; but this will make nothing for the justification of the grand mistake, that therefore it is holiness. There are those who would have those sparks of moral light in conscience, as also of moral virtues and inclinations in the will and affections, found in corrupt nature, to be relics of the former image of God ; so that, by the stumps of stubble remaining on the ground, you might know what corn once grew upon that soil, viz., the heart of man, now laid waste and desolate. And indeed if the case was thus, this controversy were at an end, for then these remaining sparks of conscience must be of the same kind with that primitive holiness, as being the stumps thereof and so every man by nature would be in part regenerate, which is the highest perfection here. But that which I would assert is, that take these seeds of light, &c., abstracted from the natural faculties, and they are new plants rather in the heart of man, though of another kind (as herbs that are wild in wildernesses are from those in gardens), which God through Christ's general mediation for all mankind hath planted there, *de novo*, out of pity to the totally ruined condition of man's nature ; out of which by the curse, all stems were utterly rooted out and stubbed up ; the nature of man being left in the rigour and utmost extent of the curse, nothing but flesh, or as an *abrasa tabula*, devoid of all good (Rom. vii. 18), insomuch as it would not have had the shadow or appearance of what is good ; as Christ's curse upon the temple was, that not so much as a stone should be left upon a stone. Insomuch as in the execution of that curse, after that the Romans in Titus's time had razed and thrown down the upper parts and walls thereof, even unto the ground, God in Julian's time gave the earth a vomit by an earthquake, and it cast up the very foundations, that not a stone was left upon a stone. So it befell man's nature upon the fall, in respect of all moral good. And so though these sparks of light and κοιναὶ ἐννοίαι, common notions of God and goodness, are indeed the imperfect shadow of that former image created in true holiness (as by distinction from these Paul termeth that original primitive purity), yet they are no way the relics or remainders of it, but indeed are new donatives, over and above that birthright of nothing but sin, and natural faculties, the necessary subject thereof, which Adam, and the curse for his sin, left unto us.

For, 1, Christ himself hath designed and set out the pittance of that birthright portion to be this, ' That which is born of the flesh is flesh,' John iii. That is, there is not that thing which is born or derived to us by that birth, and the dues of it, but flesh ; and of that flesh Paul says, again and again, that it is ' enmity to God,' Rom. viii. ; and that ' no good thing dwells in it,' Rom. vii.

Neither, 2, had the curse for Adam's sin any eye to pity, or commission to spare some good, whilst it stretched out its sword to cut off all. It alike struck at root as well as branch, and its devouring jaws left no broken fragments. The threatening was, that ' that day thou sinnest thou diest.' Whatever good then is found, is from the mitigation of this curse on another account, viz., of riches of mercy, though but common mercy, such as the fourth verse of this Rom. ii. speaks of.

And truly, 3, the great inequality of the distribution of these moral lights, or goodness, which is found either in conscience or any other faculty, doth evidence this. Socrates had more thereof than Epicurus ; whereas the curse of itself would work in all a like deprivation of moral light. And this to me is unanswerable, that so far as any one man's conscience doth by nature prove more dim in light than others, even to the lowest degree of glimmerings, such as is found in the merest natural fool that ever was yet in the world, unto that degree at least (as it must be acknowledged) would the curse of itself work in all men to leave them to the same proportion. For even that small proportion (in comparison of what others have) is from the same curse ; which of itself in justice was to overflow to all, and as a sweeping rain would carry all away. And truly whilst we give the name of ' mere naturals' unto them who have the lowest degree of light, and are but a nice distinction between an elevated brute and a rational creature, we do thereby tacitly acknowledge that this least pittance is the whole dowry which mere nature, as accursed and corrupt, would have left to any man : so as utter darkness, blindness in things, is nature's legacy. ' Man is born' (says Elihu* in Job), ' as a wild ass-colt,' Job xi. 12. And thus, though conscience be a natural faculty, and there is the altar, yet the fire and the light of it, and what is morally good, even to every spark thereof, is not raked up in the ashes of our nature, as remainders of that holy light which was there before ; but as sparks struck into conscience, as the tinder fully capable and recipient of them. In Rom. ii., you have one phrase makes for this, and another that makes against it ; let us examine the force of either. Paul says it is the ' effect of the law written in their hearts.' Writing is *opus artificis*, and notes out characters imprinted by an exterior hand. Our consciences are the paper, that is all we bring, which the very renewal or revival by the law typified. God at first formed both by one immediate hand, in the state of innocency ; but after man had broken these tables, man finds the stone, but God the letters, and writing still. But then how is it said, verse 14, that ' by nature they do the things of the law' ? This on the other hand, seems to make against it. But the answer is easy ; nature is opposed to God's outward revelation of the law, as the

* Zophar.—ED.

context shews. The Gentiles that have not the law, that is, the outward knowledge of it by revelation, have yet a light derived with their births and nature (for the sparks of this must be acknowledged to be therewith derived), according to the purport of that expression, 'He enlighteneth every man that is born into the world;' and so it accompanies our birth, and more or less is made a dowry common to the nature of man, and made innate in man; yet it is still written there by an external hand. And all those other scriptures convince me of this, in that when speaking of this truth (whereof conscience is the seat) concerning God and righteousness, which, Rom. i. 18, he says, was 'withheld in unrighteousness' by the Gentiles; and which, verse 19, he calls 'that which may be known of God' which was 'manifest in them;' he is wary in a special manner to speak something of the sense or original of it, and how they being naturally (as we all are) so corrupt, came by it; 'For God' (says he) 'hath shewed it to them;' he by his secret instruction teaching them to spell those characters of his eternal power and godhead written in the creation, verse 20, which without his teaching, and shewing them, as one doth a child, they would never have understood. This they owed to God, and therefore this reflecting power in man 'that searcheth the inward chambers of the belly,' Prov. xx. 27, is called 'the candle of the Lord.' He speaks evidently of conscience, which is that light and faculty which pierceth by reflections upon all faculties, witnessing, accusing, excusing, discerning just or unjust, that is never so secretly done in any room of the soul. And why is it called the candle of the Lord? But because we are all in the dark, and should have so remained, if God had not brought in and set up de novo that candle within us, or at least lighted it and snuffed it. And as a candle is extrinsecal to the room, at least the light is extrinsecal, in respect of its original, to the candle, so here it is in this case. And this assertion, that there is light from God himself as the enlightener (especially in things moral, and which concern himself), even in man fallen, is no new opinion, even among both Jewish, heathenish, or Christian writers.* And by them it is judged to be that to the conscience or mind (which is the natural faculty itself), which an external sun or candle is to the eye of the body. There have been large collections out of all these, and references to them for the demonstration of it, made unto your hands. Now this light, though extrinsecally from God, comes to be defiled, and to have a tincture from the defilement of the mind, as the light of the sun shining on, or through a glass dyed green or red, useth to receive a tincture suitable, for *quicquid recipitur ad modum recipientis.* To which that of the apostle accords, 'To unbelievers all things are impure, because their minds and consciences are defiled, Titus i. 15.

I added, in the beginning of this assertion, that the light was vouchsafed thus to all, more or less, through the mediation of Christ. By which I understand such a mediation as he hath made for the upholding the whole creation, which the curse would else have pulled about Adam's ears. And truly that scripture seems to look that way; John i. 9, 'He is that light, which enlighteneth every man that comes into the world.' The analysis of that chapter might give light to this, if I could insist on it. The apostle shews, 1. What before the fall Christ was to all creatures, ver. 3. 2. What he was to man in innocency, verses 2, 4. 3. What he is to man fallen and become darkness: verse 5, 'And the light shineth in darkness, and the

* See the schoolmen on that question, in their tracts de Gratia. Also Seldenus de Jure Naturali, lib. i. cap. 9.

darkness comprehendeth it not;' which in this 9th verse he again en-
largeth on.   He is in himself that true light, from whom all men born into
the world have that light, which accompanies their nature.   He shews what
Christ was to the Jews in revealing the law and gospel, verse 11.   And 5,
What he is to believers whom he regenerates, verses 12, 13.   And it is
evident that part of John's scope is withal to distinguish this common
light vouchsafed to every man in the world, verses 5, 9, 10, from that of
faith and regeneration, of which he speaks, verses 12, 13.   That common
light turneth not the natural darkness or corruption of the heart into holiness ; ' the darkness comprehends it not.'   It changeth not the heart into
the same image ; even as the light of stars is such a light as serves to discover themselves, but they alter not the air into light, as the sun doth.   And
he speaks of that light specially shining into men's dark and corrupt hearts
as gives the knowledge of good or evil, and of God, because it is such a light
as the darkness of man's nature would avoid, and is some way contrary unto
it, for it avoids it, receives it not, so as to have its full effect on their hearts,
it discovering that darkness that is found in the chambers of the belly.
Now natural knowledge, in other things, man's darkness is not opposite
unto.   The drift then of what we have hitherto said hereof is, that this
light of conscience is not the remainder of the former image, and so no part
or spark of the former holiness, but a light *de novo*, brought in by God and
Christ, as, in common, a mediator for all mankind.
     There is, or may be supposed, a difference in the kinds or sorts of light,
and so there is a difference of this from what is holy and spiritual; although
all be derived from God, as the Father of lights, as James in the plural calls
them, when he insinuates a distinction of gifts perfect and imperfect, yet it
follows not that it should be holy, no more than other notions, in the
knowledge of things merely natural and philosophical truths are.   It falls
out in the lights of the mind, whereof God is the Father, as it doth in bodily
visible lights, which Paul speaks of upon occasion of the resurrection, and
in setting forth the difference of the qualities now and after the resurrection :
1 Cor. xv. 39, ' All flesh is not the same flesh, but there is one kind of flesh
of men, another flesh of beasts, another of fishes, and another of birds.'
And ver. 14, ' There is one glory of the sun, another of the moon, and
another of the stars.'   Now by their glory he means their differing light
that is in them and from them.   So say I of these lights vouchsafed by
God ; although they be from God, yet they differ both in their kind and
efficacy, and also according to the tincture of the subjects they are shed
into.   The light of the natural conscience is one kind of light, which is as that
of the stars ; the light given the Jew from the law, and the light of men
that fall away (spoken of Heb. vi.), are as that of the moon ; and the
light vouchsafed the saints in regeneration is as the sun.   Our Saviour
Christ therefore, in John, gives this note of distinction of it from all lights
else (though all be from God), in calling it ' the light of life.'   John viii. 12,
' He that followeth me ' (saith he) ' shall not walk in darkness, but shall
have the light of life,' viz., that which converts, saves, and only giveth life.
Which Elihu in Job speaking of (Job xxxiii. 30) names it a being enlightened with the light of the living, which brings back a man's soul from
the pit.   Which distinction the apostle John, that wrote the Gospel, confirms
(1 John ii. 4, 9, 11), when he says, ver. 4, ' He that says I know him,
and keeps not his commandments, is a liar, and the truth is not in him ;'
and, ver. 9, ' is in darkness even until now,' that is, in his dark condition,
devoid of light, and (ver. 11) ' walks in darkness.'   Now consider that the

apostle (Rom. i. 18) calls that natural light the heathen had ' the truth,' and (ver. 19) says it was ἐν ἑαυτοῖς, manifest in them. And these professors of Christianity which John speaks of were certainly enlightened with that light (Heb. vi.) which drew them in their profession to say that they knew God, without which in those times men had no encouragement, but all discouragements to profess him. How then doth he say that the truth is not in them, and that in saying they knew God they lied ? This could not have been unless there had been a knowledge, which is comparatively the only true genuine knowledge and light of God indeed, and in comparison of which the other are but as darkness. As the light of the sun is such a light, and so different from all other, that it alone bears the title of the true light, which only makes day, and in comparison of which all other is but darkness and night, though one night may be more light than another, as we see when the moon shines in its brightness, and some star-light nights are clearer than others ; yet still a man that knows the difference may say, These all are not the true light, not the light which makes day, for they overcome not the darkness when they shine, as the least beam of the sun doth. Now regenerate men are called day, as set in the daylight. And the state of unregeneracy is termed night and darkness. Now as suppose a man that had been kept in a close darkness all his days, and from seeing any light, yet had heard some talk in general of the light of the day, and the shining of light that makes day ; and bring this man into a room where a great and stately lamp or taper burns, ' Oh, this is the light I have heard so much of,' would he presently say ; and lo, this is day, and oh, how pleasant a thing would he affirm it to behold this light, in comparison to that darkness he had been condemned to. So if we could suppose any one of the sons of men brought up in those *meræ tenebræ*, mere darkness which were only nature's legacy, and on the sudden God should set up in the lantern of his brains the light of the greatest magnitude that Plato or Socrates ever had, how would this man bless himself (as much as we heard they did), magnify this as the only light, and the same which God himself hath, as they also did. Well, yet for illustration's sake, let us make a further supposition, and that is, that this man were told, Oh, but there is a further and higher light yet, that gives light to all the world : there is the sun, which is placed in the heavens, and not on a candlestick, to give light only to one house or one room. And then let this man be carried forth into the open sky, and let any one shew him a full moon, walking in her greatest brightness, as Job speaks, Oh, how would he kiss his hand to it, and passionately cry out, Oh, this is light, this is day indeed ; and what a miserable creature was I (would that poor man say within himself) that have hitherto lived in such darkness, and wanted this blessed light of the world ! Well, let this man a while enjoy his fancy, and keep him still in the open air awake, and anon when the day is approaching let him discover the twinkling stars to close up their lights and vanish, and the brightness to wash off by degrees from his so adored moon, which he verily took for the sun, and her face to grow pale and wan ; and a far differing, stronger light to steal in by degrees, and he looks about him, and discerns not from what cause it springs, nor can at first imagine, till at last casting his eye to that quarter of heaven which is brightest, he discerns the body of the sun beginning to peep up above the horizon—do but think with yourselves, upon the sight hereof, what this man would say. This is day indeed, this is light indeed, the only true light I have heard spoken of, and differs (though the other had the name and reality of light) as much from the former as any sorts of creatures that are the counterfeits of others that are genuine can be supposed to do. This man would acknowledge what John affixeth to natural men, enlightened not savingly, that he had been but in darkness, and walked in the night all this while until now; and that his boasts and brags that he knew day and had commerce with the sun were mistakes, and that the truth of life had neither been in him, nor in them which hitherto he had seen.

Let your own judgments and consciences make the application. For like mistakes there are about the light of life, and of eternal salvation. Neither is the difference of these several lights, but only in and by the effects, demonstrable to any man, but him that hath seen the true light of the sun shining on him. Other men will walk and abide in night and darkness, and yet will say they have the true light, and their error can never be discovered to them but by the arising of the true light. Only the saints can say (as John in their names there) with difference from all others, ' We know we know him,' 1 John ii. 3 ; and ' the darkness is past, and the true light now shineth,' ver. 8, and there can be no other.

The present drift of this discourse hath been to shew, that a difference is and may be supposed between the light that God vouchsafes regenerate and unregenerate men in kind as well as in degree. For if there be one glory of a torch or taper, which is a light on earth, another of the stars and moon, which is a light in and from heaven, and yet another of the sun, which alone deserves the name of being a true light, which difference God the Father of all lights hath set amongst them ; why should we not think that the same God can diversify and vary the lights that he causeth to fall and shine into men's hearts, and make them of a several kind ? Common light in heathens is but as a candle on earth ; light in Jews and Christians but as the light of the moon ; and though heavenly, yet not dispelling night. Although all these be light, and represent in many things the very same objects (though somewhat more imperfectly), as all these forementioned lights do, yet still the light of regeneration describes* only the name of the true light, the light of life, and the other in comparison are darkness, according to that of Solomon : Prov. ix. 10, ' The knowledge of the Holy is understanding,' and that only.

The third consideration is touching the seat of the power and dominion of the natural light of conscience.

1. The light of conscience hath a power over the rest of the faculties. 2. The seat of that power and dominion over the rest of the faculties is not the whole heart, but conscience, which is but one faculty. That a power and dominion it hath over a man's heart, the forementioned effects do shew; and Paul's discourse manifests it in his Epistle to the Romans, the 6th and 7th chapters. In the 6th chapter the apostle, treating of that sanctification which is in a man truly regenerate, in the 14th verse expresseth his state thus, ' Ye are not under the law, but under grace ;' wherein his state is both negatively and affirmatively set forth.

(1.) Negatively, it is being not under the law, which is on purpose inserted in opposition to the contrary state of men unregenerate, who are under the law ; and the law hath a dominion over such.

(2.) Affirmatively, it is set forth in those words, so as grace comes to have a dominion over a man's spirit when sanctified; and under these two conditions are all men cast.

Then in the 7th chapter, from the first verse, he sets out this dominion

* Qu. ' deserves' ?—ED.

that the law hath over an unregenerate man in more express terms : ' the law hath dominion over a man as long as he lives.' Where these words, ' as long as he lives,' respect not simply the term of a man's life in this world, but limitedly the time of his continuance in that estate wherein he was at first born into the world. For life there relates to the death mentioned ver. 4 and 6 : ' Ye are become dead to the law,' speaking of their regenerate condition, ' that being dead wherein ye were held.' Christ's body, which was crucified for us, in virtue of it works a dying to a man's former estate, by humiliation and mortification, whereof also he speaks, Gal. ii. 19, ' I through the law am dead to the law, that I might live unto God.' He speaks particularly with respect to the law, as a husband, that had power over a man before, as is evident from ver. 1, 2, ' You know, brethren, how the law hath dominion over a man as long as he lives. For the woman which hath an husband is bound by the law to her husband so long as he liveth ; but if the husband be dead, she is loosed from the law of her husband.' And suitably, in following this allegory, he expresseth the change of their condition in those that are wrought upon : ver. 4, ' Wherefore, brethren, ye are become dead to the law by the body of Christ ; that ye should be married to another, even to him who is raised from the dead.' So then it is clear from this, that as Christ and grace have a dominion over a man after regeneration, the law hath dominion over every man before conversion. And to set forth this the more, the apostle compares the unregenerate heart of man unto the wife, and the law unto the husband, who, according to the law of nature, hath dominion over the wife whilst both live. And that the law was once the natural husband of man's heart, and God by it, you may observe out of Jer. xxxi. 32. God there speaking of the old covenant, and expressing the tenor of that covenant of works, which was the same with that of man's creation, says, ' I was a husband to them.' And now that man is fallen, God still urgeth his right, and the obligation which is upon a man whilst under the mere covenant of his creation ; and the terms of his condition, by his fall, are no way altered. Now, further, it is the law, whether written by nature or given by revelation, which calls for this subjection to God, which it doth though men be departed and gone a-whoring from him ; and urgeth all sorts of duties conjugal upon the heart ; and the heart cannot deny but that it is her duty to be subject, for she is conscious of her primitive allegiance, which in that state of nature she can never shake off, but is an adulteress in every act of disobedience or rebellion.

2. The seat or proper throne of this dominion which the law hath, and from whence the exercise of it comes, is the conscience of a man. The case stands thus : the husband and wife are not wholly parted, although they live at odds, but the husband challengeth to live under the same roof with her ; and so although the heart would and hath for her part cast off God, yet God keeps possession in one corner of the house, by the light of his law, that he causeth to shine into conscience, which (as I have shewn) is the suscipient of God's law. Sin in the heart hath shut God out of all the rest, and keeps it to itself, and hath crowded him up into that narrow corner, and grudgeth him that too, and if it could possibly, would throw him out of all ; but God will so far keep and maintain his right and possession, as that the heart may know and acknowledge his ancient right over it, and its subjection to his law. Yea, and by means and virtue of its residence there, doth the law continually provoke the heart to her duties, and overrules her in many things, and tells her of her adulteries and de-

partments* from God, &c.   But all that the law speaks is contrary to the full bent and inclination of her heart : ' Her desire is not to her husband,' for the apostle, ver. 5, tells us that this husband begets nothing but motions of sins on her, through her perverseness.   I may otherwise express it under the similitude and metaphor of a kingdom, which the apostle also useth, Rom. v. 21 and chap. vi. 14.   All mankind had clean shook off the sweet and natural subjection of the heart to God and his law ; and sin and self were become absolute and supreme, and had got the power, and had entered upon God's rights and dominions.   And though in title sin be but a tyrant, yet in power and jurisdiction it is (now man is fallen) owned by the whole man as its natural lord and prince, giving forth laws, Rom. vii. 23 ; which laws being men's own lusts, are willingly and cheerfully obeyed, Rom. vi. 12.   But shall sin think to carry it thus from God, to enjoy a settled dominion quietly, so that God shall have no remedy, no law to take place ?   The truth is, God had beforehand made and placed over the soul of man one tower (for so conscience is termed by the ancients *arx animæ*), which is by the natural situation of it so unfortifiable by the utmost power of man, and lies so open and exposed immediately unto God, and beams of light from him, that let man revolt and become never so sinful and rebellious, yet he cannot keep God nor his forces out of it. Man can never stop that passage, but God can bring in what forces and what number he pleaseth, and all the power in man can never hinder it. The devil himself cannot keep God out thence, for ' they believe and tremble.'   This is the practic part of the understanding, viz., conscience. Yea, the truth is, that but for this principle, which is natural to men and devils, and can never be demolished by the wickedness of either, God could never come to punish for sin either of them in their spirits.   Yea, the devil would wholly have escaped, for he is not capable of bodily punishment in outward things.   It is conscience, which is a tender part, and which is such in man as God hath made in wild beasts to tame them by, as a snout in a bear and the mouth in an horse.   It is conscience that is only, or at least primarily, sensible of God's wrath, and hell fire could not take hold of the soul but at this corner.   And so God created it for all events and for all states, viz., to stop men's mouths when he indulgeth, to execute vengeance upon them when he punisheth in hell, and on earth to rule and cut short men's spirits, and restrain them from wickedness ; there being this difference between the state of wicked men and devils, that he doth not rule the devils by conscience.   It is not their conscience that keeps them from any evil, for they certainly make conscience of nothing. He punisheth them indeed by conscience, and at that channel lets in all the streams of the lake of fire and brimstone into these vessels of wrath. Conscience, the moderate effects of which men magnify so much, hath its fullest dominion in hell, and is in its height of power there.

But to return to the similitude.   God having thus aforehand taken order to erect in man's soul this out-work, this castle upon an impregnable rock, which can powerfully command the rebellious town and malignant inhabitants that dwell below it, plants his great ordnance there (namely, the awful knowledge of himself, of the works of the law, and of his wrath), hangs out his flags of summons, sends out proclamations with sound of trumpet from this mount Sinai (as in giving the law he did), often thunders down with fears, and horrors, and dreadful punishments, in and with which the law of God is ' revealed from heaven against all ungodliness and

* Qu. 'departures'?—ED.

unrighteousness of men, that withhold the truth in unrighteousness' (as of the very Gentiles the apostle prefaceth, Rom. i. 18); yet all this while the city, and the towns about, and adjacent parts of the heart of man, are perfect malignants, stand out in rebellion, having set up a contrary king and kingdom, which they obey in the lusts thereof, and will obey only. From this fort God now and then sends out parties that bring them to some contribution, that prevail to make them take many conditions, and bring them to much outward conformity, even to the laws of God; yet so as still the seat, the place of residence to all these foreign forces (as these are to the heart), is but this one faculty from whence God commands the rest, though they are not brought into a natural subjection. Whereas regenerating grace, where it comes, immediately plants itself in the whole man, takes up every faculty, one as well as another, for God, and ' brings every thought into subjection,' 2 Cor. x. 5. It wins the heart of every faculty, that had rebelled, unto itself and unto God, sets up a new kingdom in the midst of the soul, alters all the state and form of government, insomuch as the laws of that kingdom are made natural where grace reigns, Rom. v. 21. And the laws of God are become the law of a believer's mind, Rom. vii. 23, and if he were to choose, he would be governed by no other. But the condition of an unregenerate man is very different; for, as in a state or kingdom, a foreign power may have much quarter and many compliances, when yet the laws of that kingdom are still in force; so in an unregenerate man, though the law of God may, in the light of it, be said to be in his mind and prevail much there, yet it is not become the law of his mind, which hath still a contrary law and government that stands in force. The reason whereof is clear, for the power of it being but the power of the law, therefore it can never sanctify; and though it may come to have much power, stroke, and command amongst the subjects of this kingdom of sin, yet it can never pull down the power of sin, or put sin from its dominion. It is an apostolical maxim, resolutely delivered: Rom. vi. 14, ' Sin shall not have dominion over you, for ye are not under the law.' Therefore, whilst a man is in such an estate as he is still under the law, sin will retain its dominion. Indeed, the law by conscience may much interrupt and impede sin in its proceedings, and overrule a man unto much good; yet it must be something stronger than the law to alter the whole form of government and frame of the heart, and subdue it to God, and restore to him his kingdom again. Christ alone can do this. The law, as it can never justify, so nor sanctify, although indeed what is written in the heart in our sanctification is the matter of the law, as also in Christ the performance of the same law is the matter of our justification. Yet it is not by the power of the law that we are sanctified or justified. ' If there had been a law given which could have given life, verily righteousness had been by the law,' Gal. iii. 21. But the apostle hath informed us, Rom. viii. 3, that the law was ' weak through the flesh,' and could not free a man from ' the law of sin and death,' but the spirit and power that is in Jesus Christ must do this; Rom. viii. 2, 3, ' For the law of the spirit of life in Christ Jesus hath made us free from the law of sin and death. For what the law could not do, in that it was weak through the flesh, God sending his own Son in the likeness of sinful flesh, and for sin, condemned sin in the flesh.'

The *fourth* consideration or assertion is touching the exercise of this power, which the light of conscience hath in a man. Concerning which, I assert,

1. That the strength and force that is in all the workings of it, whether in motives to duty or restraint from sin, do lie in the law; and the weapons

of its warfare, whereby it works its chiefest effects, are all fetched out of that magazine. The great artillery thereof are charged both with powder and bullets of the law ; as it is said, ' the strength of sin is the law,' 1 Cor. xv. 56, viz., in respect of holding us under the guilt of it, so the strength of natural conscience is but that of the law, as to the motive part thereof. And the reason is clear from the apostle's forementioned maxim : ' Ye are not under the law, but grace ; therefore sin shall not have dominion,' Rom. vi. 14. Hence therefore, in whomsoever sin hath dominion, there the law is the most prevalent principle ; and so whatever hath the presence of goodness in them must have its rise chiefly from thence. Everything is in working as it is in being. Now the condition of the person is to be under the law, and he belongs to that dominion, and therefore the swaying principle of his actings must be from the power thereof. Insomuch as if an unregenerate man be enlightened, and duties of the gospel be urged upon him, as to mourn for sin, to believe in Christ, &c. ; yet the motives that prevail with that man are but such as are of the same kind with those of the law. As faith turns the commands of the law into gospel in a regenerate man's heart, so conscience, in an unregenerate man, turns the gospel into law. As faith writes the law in the heart, and urgeth the duties of it upon evangelical grounds and motives—as the love of Christ, conformity to him, union with him, and the free grace of God—so in a man unregenerate, gospel duties are turned into legal, through the sway and influence of conscience, and that dominion which the covenant of works hath over him. And if to such a man you use such motives as are drawn from Christ's love, God's free grace, &c., they are but as wooden cannons set upon the walls for show. But those that do execution, make dints and impressions on the heart, are at best in such cases but the threatenings of the law. Conscience, at best, is but a legal preacher. I call it so, because though the law lays down the doctrines and shews what is man's duty, yet conscience is that which makes the application, and as occasion serves, makes uses of direction and exhortation to good, or of comfort if a man doth well, or of reproof if he doth evil. And let the doctrine be what it will, yet the motives, with which it backs its uses, are still legal, and so it is but a legal preacher. And therefore, Gal. v. 18, ' to be led by the Spirit,' and to be ' under the law,' or conscience (its minister), are two different things, and two distinct principles of men's actions, regenerate or unregenerate.

2. My second assertion concerneth the kind or condition of this power, and the exercise of it, which is plainly this : It is a tyrannical and forced government which natural conscience exerciseth over the heart. Whereas, on the contrary, the government of the grace of regeneration in the soul is (so far as a man's heart is regenerated) sweet and intrinsecal, congenial and connatural to the heart, it being endowed with dispositions suitable, and changed into the image of that light, and so the subjection of the rest of the faculties is such as of subjects to their natural prince ; but, on the other case, it is a subjection as to a foreigner or invader. And this difference, as to that part of it, conscience, viz., its government, is clear from what hath been said. For if one faculty only rules over the rest, when their bent remains contrary to its laws, this government must needs be extrinsecal ; as also, if it be but a legal government in the main and fundamental constitution of it. I shewed (out of Rom. vii. 1–3) that the law in the conscience is compared to the husband, and the heart of man to the wife. Indeed, for his title over the heart, it is a natural jurisdiction, for it was once by nature. But take the condition of the heart of such a man,

now corrupt with sin, it is a cruel government. They are man and wife indeed; but so contrary, that there is a vexatious life between this couple. He offers to do his duty, and makes motions to this and unto that, but she is averse, and the motions to the contrary often become the stronger thereby: Rom. vii. 6, ' The motions of sin which were by the law,' that is, begotten on the heart as children by a husband, ' did work in our members to bring forth fruit unto death.' Conscience in unregenerate men finds all in the heart armed against it; but grace hath created an interest in the heart throughout, and made a party for itself, so as it fights not alone. Conscience in the end, as a severe governor, comes to be ' imprisoned,' Rom. i. 18, ' in unrighteousness;' for men are all weary of its yoke, and rise up against it, and are glad when it is stopped or seared.

CHAPTER V.

What goodness, and of what kind, is to be acknowledged to be in this light from God, vouchsafed to natural conscience, though it doth fall short of true grace.

That light which is in a natural conscience being from God, who is the Father of all lights, it must needs have a goodness in it. For as all that ever God made at first was good (Gen. i. 31, ' God saw all that he had made was good'), so all that ever God shall make must be good: 1 Tim. iv. 4, ' Every creature of God is good.' The very letters of the law, written on tables of stone, were good in this sense, much more the same, though but literally written on men's consciences. Let me say it: all the actings and stirrings of conscience of men in hell, as they are from God and the Spirit of bondage, they are good with this kind of goodness.

2. It hath that further goodness which the outward letter of the law, considered as distinct from the spiritual part thereof, may be said to have.

Four things are to be explained.

I. That there is a literal part of the law, and a spiritual part.

II. That it is the spiritual part that constitutes the law holy.

III. That the light of the law in an unregenerate man's conscience is but literal, not spiritual; and so is but the shadow and picture of true knowledge of the law, as it is spiritual.

IV. It will be necessary to explain what goodness is in the literal part severed from the spirit, above what is common to all other creatures.

The three first I shall intermingledly handle together, because they are in a great part the subject of that 7th chapter of the Romans, where he treats of the light and dominion of the law in and over a man unregenerate, and the difference of it from that which is in a regenerate man.

I. You may observe Paul putting this difference between the law, as dwelling in his heart or conscience, when an unregenerate Jew and Pharisee, and in himself when renewed and become a regenerate Christian: Rom. vii. 6, ' But now we are delivered from the law, that being dead wherein we were held; that we should serve in newness of spirit, and not in the oldness of the letter.' He sets forth the difference of the two states, and termeth the one, ' serving in the oldness of the letter,' but that of regeneracy is ' in the newness of the spirit.' The oldness of the letter is not simply the law of Moses in itself, as delivered to them of old (as some interpret it out of Mat. v. 23), but it is that knowledge and light of the law, and a frame of heart accompanying it in the old man, or in a man's unregenerate estate, which is called the state of old things, 2 Cor. v. 17, which passeth away. And the newness of the spirit is the light of the same law, for the substance of it, and that frame of heart accompanying it, as it is in the new man, which is created in good works.

II. You may observe the spirit, or spiritual part of the law, hath a more transcendent goodness than the bare letter of, if you will suppose the one severed from the other ; as in an unregenerate man's light they are actually severed. This will appear from Rom. vii. 12, ' The law is holy, and the commandment holy, just, and good.' Here you have a goodness of holiness ; the law is holy and good, that is, good with that kind of goodness. Now, what is it in the law that renders it good with this goodness of holiness ? It is the spiritualness, the spirit of it. Therefore, ver. 14, by way of application, this other epithet is added, ' The law is spiritual, but I am carnal, sold under sin.' Thus, in his regenerate estate, he discerned and discovered the difference of things. He in these words, comparing that spiritual light (which he now when a Christian had) with his own old frame of heart, and the remainder thereof in him in part ; and all the excellency, or the best goodness thereof, he now brings to the spiritual knowledge and light of the law, which as a Christian he now had obtained ; which therefore by way of emphasis and difference, he thus utters, ' We know the law :' that is, by the light which is spiritual. We now have found that former estate and frame of heart to be, and to have been, but flesh. And then he says in ver. 18, ' I know' (still he speaks in the style of that his new spiritual light he now had attained of the law) ' that in my flesh dwells no good thing,' whatever I have judged aforetime of what was in my flesh, in the state of unregeneracy. And whereas it might be said unto Paul, Yea, but was not, and is not now the natural light of the law in your conscience, and the impressions you have had from the law then, were they not good things, and are not the remainders of them such still ? Oh, but (says Paul) they all fell short of the goodness of holiness that ought to be in them, viz., of that goodness which the spirit of the law requires. The law is holy, spiritual, and good. But no such good thing was to be found in my flesh. And the reason of this is, because that even the letter of the law itself, as given by God (if you would suppose it severed from that wherein the spirit of the law, or wherein the holiness of it consists, and is as the soul thereof) commandeth many outward duties, as to pray, fast ; yet if the spiritual part were taken out and concealed, which is to perform them in a spiritual manner, with holy affections of love to God, joy in God, and with holy aims and ends for God and his glory, so as to sanctify him in the heart : in this case, even these very commandments alone, as so considered, could not be said to be good, with a goodness of holiness. Nay, so considered, they are but the carcass of the law. And as the body without the soul is dead, so would these commandments or duties, performed thus only according to the letter, be but the dead letter of the law ; for the spirit that should inspire them with that which is their proper life, would be still wanting. So that as we may say of the body, when dead, that it is good indeed with the goodness that is common to other creatures, but not with that goodness which is proper to a man, much less that is proper to a holy man (the proper and primary subject of which is the soul of a man, which is now gone and departed), so is it here. And in analogy to this notion, the works or actions of men, when they are conformed but to that outward part of the law, and the duties thereof, are termed in Scripture but the carcass of duties : 1 Tim. iv. 8, ' Bodily exercise profiteth nothing' (so here he compareth the outward performance), but the inward part, the spiritual part, in the words afore, he termeth ' godliness,' in opposition or distinction from the other godliness,* and as that which is the soul, the life, and form of holy duties, and constitutes them such. Yea, and in the like allusion he termeth such performances ' dead works,' which men use to perform from that old legal conscience; and for the taking away the guilt of which, and withal to inspire their consciences with a new principle to serve the living God, a man needs the blood of Christ : Heb. ix. 14, ' The blood of Christ shall purge your conscience from dead works, to serve the living God.'

You see what account the outward part of the law hath (severed from the spirit of it) in this supposition made. Now, it is certain, *de facto*, that that light which is in the consciences of men in their natural condition, though never so much raised, doth fall short of or is severed from the spirit, or spiritual genuine tincture, or shrine of the law (by the rule of this proposition), and so is not indeed the true, proper, real light of the law, and so can no more be called the law written in the heart, than, as I said, bodily exercise, or a carcass, can properly be termed a man, or a picture the man himself of whom it is the picture. This is evident from what Paul acknowledgeth of himself, whilst he was a legal illuminate, or a Pharisee, in that same chapter, Rom. vii. Is it not strange you should hear Paul say of himself that whilst he was a Pharisee he was without the law ? But so he expressly speaks : Rom. vii. 9, ' I was alive without the law once.' He speaks of his former estate under the light of the oldness of the letter, of which he had spoken, ver. 6. What ! is Paul without the law ? Why, his skill and knowledge therein was his greatest excellency; and if he were versed in anything, he was in the law. Yea, but, says Paul, it was not the law, it was but the carcass of it, which lay buried in my understanding. ' And when the commandment came,' says he—the commandment, that is, that which is only and properly the commandment, and which is the spirit of it, when it came—' sin revived, and I died.' It is a like phrase of speech as when it is said of a dead carcass raised from the dead, 1 Kings xvii. 22, ' that the soul of the child came in,' or that ' the spirit of life entered in,' Rev. xi. 11 ; so here a new spiritual light of the law came in, and informed that former light his conscience had in the oldness of the letter, and this he calls the commandment; and then he saw the difference to be such as hereupon he says now, and not afore, ' the commandment came,' and now, and not before, says he, ' I know the law is spiritual, but I am carnal,' and ' there dwells no good in my flesh,' as in the following verses he cries out.

III. The light of the law in an unregenerate man's conscience is but literal, the shadow, the carcass of the true knowledge of the law. This I touched on in the former assertions ; but further, my text here speaks correspondently to this. He doth not say here of the Gentiles, that the law is written in their hearts, but only the τὸ ἔργον τοῦ νόμου, the work, or rather the effect of the law; but it is not affirmed that the law is written there. It is but the carcass of the law and conscience ; whilst according to that light it urgeth the duty to be done, and yet by motives short of the spiritual end, it bringeth forth but a dead work, a dead child, something only of the law, as the text hath it. As itself, and the best light thereof, is but a dead letter of the law, so the work or birth thereof exceeds not the life or kind of the principle or work it came forth of, which the apostle, if not under this similitude, yet in the thing itself, holds forth in that foremen-

* Qu. ' bodily exercise' ?—ED.

tioned Heb. ix. 14, 'He shall purge your consciences from dead works, to serve the living God.' Where, 1, he conjoins these two, conscience and dead works. Conscience is the cause or principle, works are the effect; for conscience is the cause of all actions or works that pretend to any goodness in us. 2. He speaks of what our consciences are by nature, and in our natural condition, and of itself, and so it would ever be the producer of dead works, which the living God would not accept, as not suited or proportioned to him, as he is the living God. 3. Our consciences therefore need the blood of Christ to purge them, as well from that defilement that is in them (which causeth them still naturally to miscarry, and to bring forth none but dead works) as well as to purge away the guilt of sins, whereof it is the proper and only receptacle. 4. That the blood of Christ is thus applied, that conscience, being purged and renewed, may be enabled for time to come to bring forth living works, or fruit to the living God, as formerly; for so far as it remains unregenerate it brings forth none but dead works; conscience, whether good or bad, being in all states one eminent principle of either.

Now, to draw up what has been said, and so to join what is yet to follow to what hath gone before. As the outward precepts of the law itself, if in supposition severed from the spirit of the law, are not properly the law, but only the carcass and shadow of it, and so have not the proper genuine goodness of the law in them; so answerably the light of natural conscience in natural men, which directs only unto this carcass of bodily exercise, and wants that which is the life and spirit of the law, is but the shadow thereof. And therefore such are the works thence issuing, they are all but 'dead works,' and works of the flesh, performed in the 'oldness of the letter.'

Now, to draw forth this thread of analogy yet further, as the Scripture gives us the clue and line, you may find, Rom. ii. 20, that this light of conscience and knowledge in the law, which the highest in the form of that Pædagogy, or school of the Jews, attains to (that were unregenerate), was but μόρφωσις τῆς γνώσεος, 'a form of knowledge, and of the truth in the law.' I termed it even now the picture or shadow of the law; and this expression here answers for it, it being spoken as in opposition to the truth and real spiritual knowledge of the law, as the very letter of the words imports, μόρφωσιν τῆς ἀληθείας ἐν τῷ νόμῳ, the form or appearance of that which is the truth, reality, or spirit of the law. There are three things to be considered : 1. The truth of the law; 2. The knowledge of that truth; 3. That the light a carnal Jew had was but the form, or μόρφωσις, of the knowledge of the truth which is in the law. Some have understood this word, 'form of the knowledge,' to signify no more than that system or method of knowledge which the learned Jews had in the law drawn into a form, such as scholars have in other arts and sciences. And that which seemed to afford strength to this notion as the sole support of it, is that (2 Tim. i. 13) the sum or substance of that doctrine Paul had delivered to Timothy, as a teacher of others, is called 'a form of wholesome words.' And Paul here speaks of those that were teachers of the Jews, that boasted in that knowledge. But let it be considered,

1. That the word here is not the same with that used there: it is μόρφωσις here, it is ὑποτύπωσις there, which latter is an artificial draught or sampler, either serving for doctrine or practice, whereby to teach others or a man's self to work by. It is not drawn from painters' pictures only, but from patterns or examples, and things lively acted. And so interpreters make it

to be the subject of vehement exhortation in Paul to Timothy, to be both a real ' pattern in life,' as well as a teacher in doctrine, according as he had presented an example or platform of both unto him.

But 2. Moreover, then, Rom. ii., the word is μόρφωσις, the *vizor*, the *mask*, the *appearance*, the *outward form*, of what is the truth, reality, or substance, and so holds affinity with that phrase, 2 Tim. iii. 5, ' Having a form of godliness' (it is the same word), ' denying the power thereof;' and so it is opposed to the reality, power, or substance of godliness, whereof this is the shadow, the appearance.

3. Now, parallel these two places, and you will find that, as the words, so the scope is the same. His scope here is to unmask the best of the unregenerate Jews, in respect of what they most prided themselves in, viz., the knowledge and light their consciences had of the law. And he accordingly sets himself to speak by way of diminution or derogation, that the best of their knowledge, though such as had the system of the whole law in it, was but the shadow, the outward form, in respect of what was true knowledge, and the real truth of the law, the spiritualness and holiness that was in it; even as in Timothy he terms the outward profession of godliness in the lives of hypocrites, or the impressions of it on their wills, but a ' form of godliness,' severed from, and in opposition to, ' the powers' thereof. *Truth* and *form* are opposed in the one, *power* and *form* in the other. Now, if the light and knowledge, in the understandings and consciences of the best of the Jews, was but in this sense the form of knowledge, and the mere outward picture or shadow of the truth in the law, and so utterly differing from the spirituality of that law, then the dim light in the Gentiles (whom in the 13th and 14th verses he spake of) is so much more. And then this is the result of all, that the light both of the one and other, and so of all men unregenerate, doth fall short of that real goodness or holiness that is in the law, because it is but the shadow of the truth of it.

IV. I proceed now to the fourth proposition or query, namely, What further goodness this light of the law and word hath in natural men, more than is common to other creatures ?

1. It would seem to have more, because it is the picture of the law, which in every part thereof hath a transcendent goodness, above what is in other creatures.

2. So as to give the goodness it hath what title or term you please, essentially short of holiness, and that goodness that is in the law, as it is spiritual and good, there will be found a moral goodness in it, which, according to the rate or exchange of philosophy, is above that which is merely natural, or the common goodness of other creatures. Such we grant it to be; but add withal, that still men do but afford thereby an evidence to condemn themselves the more deeply for having abused it, and for having been unholy under it.

3. It is no dissonancy to truth to say that there is, if not a middle kind of goodness, yet an excellency above that which is natural or common to all creatures, and this other of holiness. As, for example, there is an image of God in man, in the substance and natural faculties of the soul, that it is a spirit, and hath his understanding, will, and sovereignty over the creatures. There is a likeness to God, which is not found in other creatures; which (as may be inferred from Gen. ix. 6) continues in a man now fallen, and for which God there puts that valuation upon the life of a man above that of a beast, or any other creature, and in comparison

of which the goodness that is in man's nature substantially (though now fallen) hath the peculiar honour to be called the 'image of God;' whereas other creatures are but *vestigia*, or footprints, and no way the image.   There is a transcendent goodness, which yet still is short and void of the image of God, which consists in true holiness, which man hath utterly lost, though he was at first created in it, Col. iii. 3 compared with Eph. iv. 24.   Now so it is with these impresses of the law on conscience.

Yea, 4. I shall acknowledge further, that these beams of light are a more excellent image of God than that natural or substantial image spoken of, and that because they are the shadows and impresses of his law and divine will, and so are more worth than all the substance or faculties of man's soul considered apart from them; yet still I may say comparatively of them, as Paul speaks of the old literal covenant, Heb. x. 1, ' They are but the shadow, and not the very image of the reality of the things' of the law.

And the light of that similitude which was struck out of Scripture will help to clear this farther goodness that is in it above that which is natural; and yet relieve no man in his thoughts that it is holiness, or any degree of it.   You have heard that it is the form or outward picture of the truth of the law.   Now, as in a picture, there may be considered a double truth and goodness, the one natural in the colours laid, which are the materials of it, especially when they are true and good colours of their kind; the other truth in the picture is artificial, as it is a true picture of that which it represents, which is by so much the more esteemed true and good, by how much it is more like unto him for whom it is the picture: so this form of knowledge, and of the truth in the law, hath a natural goodness in it, which is in all creatures.   It hath also a further goodness, it resembles the law, and shadows forth the things thereof, which yet is short, far short of that truth and goodness of holiness, or of the spirit that is in the law itself, or of that pure light thereof which is in the conscience of a man regenerate.   And it ordinarily falls out, that as pictures represent but the outwards, so this shadow of the law in natural conscience represents only the outwards of the law, the things to be done, the letter of the law (as the apostle, Rom. ii. 27, speaks), but there is a life, a spirit, a soul in the law written in the heart of a regenerate man, which this reacheth not, till God shall breathe it in, as he did a soul into Adam's body, which was formed first.   The holy word and law consists of letter and spirit (as was said), which letter severed from the spirit is not holy with that holiness which is proper to the law, for *Quicquid dicitur de toto, non dicitur de qualibet parte*, What is said of the whole law, take the spiritual part and literal part together, is not said of that one part, the letter only.   Or suppose (as you will object) that, in some men, light of conscience imitates to represent the inwards, and so instruct and direct to the right end; yet still, as the inwards of a man have in anatomy their pictures cut and drawn, as well as the outwards of a man, so there is a literal knowledge even of the real spiritual knowledge, which is seen in the effects, that it sanctifies not the heart, nor the conscience in which it is.   Some men's knowledge is more to the life (the Holy Ghost hath a curious pencil), and yet but μόρφωσις τῆς γνώσεως, the form of knowledge still, and wanting the light of life, as Christ calls it, John viii. 12.   These goodnesses I for my part shall ever acknowledge to be in the light of conscience and moral virtues; and I have the more amply insisted on it, that protestant doctrine may not be accounted so absurd, as to affirm that all in men unregenerate is esteemed by them so wholly sinful, as even the light of conscience, moral virtues and spiritual gifts, are in themselves sinfully corrupt; but only in the subject they do become such, and in respect of their hearts' management of them.

CHAPTER VI.

What is necessary to make conscience a good and holy conscience, which the Scripture describes to be only in persons regenerate.

The inquiry next will be what goodness it is in the light of conscience that riseth up to the goodness of holiness; or, which is all one, when it is that a man's conscience, in the balance and proper language of the Scripture, is termed 'a good conscience.' To make way for the resolution of this, and clear my way for it, I must premise two things.

1. That a regenerate man is said to have a good conscience in two respects. 1. In respect of this justification of his person, and sprinkling the blood of Christ on his conscience, to clear him from the guilt of his sins. And a man is said oppositely to have an evil conscience—thus, Heb. x. 22, the sprinkling from an evil conscience is termed—when his sins are not pardoned, but himself remains in an unjustified state, with the guilt of all his sins abiding on him, and in his conscience, the register of all. Look, as a bill is called a foul bill when it contains many heavy articles of sad crimes and accusations, so is conscience named too. It is also called a good or evil conscience, as the state of the man is good or bad, for it is the representer of that state unto him; even as the urine is said to be good when it shews a healthy and good state and habit of the body, or to be a bad water when it represents a bad Κράσις, or distemper. For conscience is the sink of all sins, as the urine is the drain of all humours. Now, this kind of goodness or evilness of conscience belongs not unto this subject, this is but a relative goodness or badness of it.

But 2dly. The goodness we seek after is that of holiness, or in respect of sanctification. It is this inherent goodness of it I seek to define.

I premise two things.

1. You know that God himself alone is the fountain of all goodness, and the measure and standard of it.

2. In discoursing of the inherent goodness of the conscience, I am not to shew at large wherein the holiness of all light that is in a believer's heart doth consist, but I shall, punctually to my subject, confine myself to this consideration, in what the holiness of the light of the law in a regenerate man's conscience, and as it is properly seated in that faculty, doth consist.

You know God himself alone is the fountain of goodness, and the measure and standard of it, 1 Kings xiv. 13. It is spoken of a child of Jeroboam, to express the truth of that grace that was in him, that 'in him only was found some good thing towards the Lord God of Israel.' That alone is goodness, which respecteth and is pointed unto him who is only good, Mat. xix. 17. And so the goodness in each faculty consists in what sets up God in it according to its kind. Now then, by the help of this general rule, let us proceed to the discovery of this goodness in conscience.

1. That light in conscience which sets up the knowledge of God, *as God*, is the light of life. This is certain; and it is common to the light in the conscience of all men, good or bad, that it hath a knowledge of, and an

eyeing God, and of a divinity ; for from thence ariseth the power, the oblig
ing or terrifying power, that conscience hath in any man.   The Gentiles,
so far as they had any conscience, so far did a glimmering of God rise up
in their hearts.   There is a holding the truth in unrighteousness which is
spoken of, Rom. i. 18, whereby is signified their sinning against light ;
and the next verse tells us that the truth so sinned against was the τὸ
γνωστὸν τοῦ Θεοῦ, something of God known, or manifest in them.   And yet it
is said of all these Gentiles, that they were 'without God in the world,'
Eph ii., even as of Paul you heard it said, that he was 'without the law.'
Wherein then did this light of theirs fall short ?   The apostle hath let fall
that reduplication I even now mentioned, Rom i. 21, on purpose to discover their deficiency, when 'they glorified him not as God.'   Their knowledge reached not unto that, but (as he says, Rom. iii. 23) 'fell short of
the glory of God.'   He speaks it on purpose to give a distinction in the
very case in hand.   That knowledge they had in their consciences did not
set God up, *as God*, in their knowledge, and so glorified him not therein.
It gave not that real knowledge of him that was worthy of him, answerable
or genuine to him, and to what he is in himself, and so glorified him not.
   Two things I urge with much vehemency.
   1. That all unregenerate men's practical light that works on them falls
short of the knowledge of God *as God*.   Carry it through the whole lump
of them, their light, their virtues, their graces, zeal of and for God, still
fall short in this, that though some of these may be terminated upon God
as an object of them, yet they rise not to glorify him *as God*.   You may
love and respect God, as you do your dead benefactors ; but if it be not *as
God*, that is, suitable to, worthy of, and as so great a God is to be loved
withal (I speak for the kind of it), it is not that which he regards ; and
thus it is also in the knowledge of God.   Yea, the cause of the defect why
they fall short in sanctifying God in their wills and affections, is because
they fall short, proportionably, in their knowledge of him, which therefore
directs them not to that spiritualness of love, joy, fear of God, that is suitable to his nature ; for all these are conformed to the apprehensions we
have of him.   The fundamental defect lies here: all men have low thoughts
of God, not only for the degree (so no creature can know him as he is), but
for the kind ; and this causeth the other defects in men's obedience.   There
were zealous men for sacrifices and the worship of the law (whom you read
of among the Jews, Ps. l. ; God spends that whole psalm upon them) that
professed they knew him sufficiently, and yet served him but formally, and
outwardly, and untowardly.   God discovers the bottom defect, ver. 21,
'Thou thoughtest I was altogether such an one as thyself,' and so thou
didst imagine that thou mightest put him off with outward obedience and
respects.   Men that live under the light and revelation of the word, yet have
but childish thoughts of God.   All the word can say, represents him not
as in himself genuinely (as they take the light thereof in), and so men come
to think they can easily please and serve him.   The apostle John throughout his Epistle resolves all the defects of loose profession and backsliders
into this, 'They know him not.'   He is peremptory in it ; and Paul in like
manner useth the same reduplication about knowing Christ which he had
used about knowing God : Rom. i., 'Knowing and glorifying God as God ;'
Eph. iv. 20, 21, 'If so be you have learned the truth as it is in Jesus :'
not the truth literally only, but of Christ, as Christ is in himself, which all
unregenerate men's thoughts fall short of.   Now then bring it to the point
in hand ; if natural conscience, whether by natural light, or from revelation,

still falls short of knowing God as God, then all the obedience and all the effects of it, though very powerful and great (because backed, urged with, and in the name and authority of a deity threatening wrath), yet rising not up to this knowledge of God as God, or of God, Heb. ix. 14, as ' the living God,' and as the truth is in God, make not a God of him in the heart, like himself in the heavens, but must needs all fall short of holiness, the spirit of which is to exalt God as God. You may observe it of the Jews, that their consciences were greatly awakened by reiterated sermons of Joshua's, which were very pungent, Josh. 23d and 24th chapters. And all the people, the multitude answered, chap. xxiv. 16, ' God forbid we should be such wretches as not to serve the Lord,' or to ' forsake him ;' ver. 18, ' We will serve the Lord, for he is our God,' say they ; but says Joshua to the unregenerate rabble of them, ver. 19, ' You speak you know not what.' You know not what a God you have to do withal, and therefore you utter this, and speak thus slightly of serving him. ' Ye cannot serve the Lord, for he is an holy God,' says he. He is holy, and his service must be answerably holy as he is ; and his holiness is to exalt himself as God, but you (poor souls) take him not in as God. Men think of him, though as of a supreme power above them, yet of one like themselves, their prince or lord, and so think they may please him and serve him as they do such a one. You are mistaken, says Joshua, ' He is an holy God.' Men run away with their natural notion of him, or with what is improved by the letter of the word, and so their conscience runs away with an under-obedience, below what is suitable to his nature, and due to him as God ; and conscience works in the strength of that light it hath of God himself, and no further. So as if it falls short, all falls short.

2. The second thing I urge is that when God means savingly to convert a man, he doth not only, or primarily, actuate, and awaken and snuff the candle of the Lord, which he hath set up in the heart, nor doth he only add more oil to make that light burn brighter. All the notions of God that can be had out of the letter of the word, added as oil to that old light, will never cause him to know God, *as God*, and in himself, though these may wonderfully enlarge it in its kind. All the candles or tapers in the world will not help you to see the sun ; but where God means to save he shines in with a new light of faith, superior to that which conscience had before. God himself riseth anew upon the heart with the light of himself ; and as the sun riseth with its own light, and is seen only by its own beams, so in God's light you see light. And therefore faith is still joined in (Paul's Epistle to Timothy) with a good conscience ; for it is the light which faith brings in that enlighteneth conscience with a new knowledge of God, which is holy and spiritual, as that which immediately cometh from, and so leadeth up to himself. It is a new and genuine light and knowledge, not *from* God only, but *of* God by faith. I speak not now of faith as justifying only, which is only terminated on Christ, and God's free grace as justifying, but I mean spiritual faith, which Paul, Heb. xi., treats of. Conscience then receiving, by the means of faith, this true knowledge of God, as God, (for conscience is not the first suscipient of this light, but faith, as Paul in Heb. xi. instructs us), and participating thus thereof, this light, as soon as it comes into conscience, instantly puts and brings that spirit we speak of with it, and adds it to that literal knowledge which conscience had of the law in the outwards of it, and is as a soul breathed anew into a body or dead carcass. It instructs the heart what kind of inward worship, what spiritual affections and motions suitable to this God, must fill and inspire every out-

ward duty; and it is content with no other but such in the service of God, for he knows now that none else will please that God whom he now clearly understands. It instructs the heart (without more ado) what love to, what zeal for God, what mourning, what sorrow for sin, what joy in, and fear to such a God is due, if he be exalted as God in the heart, and holy affections be stirred up by holy ends and motives; living affections for a living God; spiritual affections for God that is a Spirit, and will in spirit be worshipped. He sees now it is not all the sacrifices in the world (as he in the 50th Psalm thought) will please him. But he cries out (as the holy convert David, Ps. li.), 'If sacrifice would please thee, I would offer it; but thou requirest truth in the inward parts,' thou requirest a clean, upright, and renewed heart, for thou art a God of truth and holiness, and wilt be served in truth. And this is the true meaning of that passage also (which you have, Hosea vi. 6, and which our Saviour so pointed to for the legal Pharisee to learn), that 'God delights in the knowledge of God more than sacrifices.' Why are these thus opposed, but because those persons who have not the true knowledge of God (which they wanted) think to put God off with sacrifices and legal performances. And what satisfies their consciences, they think must needs satisfy God. But if once this genuine knowledge of God as God enters into their souls, it will call for the inwards of the soul to be offered up as a burnt-offering, and is not satisfied without it. This transforming of their minds will teach them to know that good and acceptable will of God, and to offer up themselves a holy, living, spiritual sacrifice unto God, as the apostle speaks, Rom. xii. 1, 2.

And that such a new knowledge of God himself is the foundation of writing the law in the inward parts (of which Jer. xxxi. 33 speaks), and of which knowledge the light of conscience falling short is not able to do, is evident by that very scripture, ver. 34, 'They shall all know me, from the least unto the greatest.' And so you have both texts of Paul and Jeremiah brought into a comparison. Look, as the defect in natural conscience in Jew and Gentile (spoken of, Rom. ii.) is by Paul attributed to their not knowing, and not glorifying God as God, Rom. i., though they did many things of the law, and were a law to themselves; so, on the contrary, the groundwork and foundation, the first thing taught, the first lesson written, when the law comes to be written in the heart, is to know God : 'They shall all know me, from the least to the greatest.' And this being first written in capital letters in the soul, then the whole law, not in the outward duties only, but that which is the spirit and the soul of all, is written there.

As when the sun riseth, a man looks on the world and all things in it, in a new hue, and sees all those things everywhere round about him, and on the face of the earth which he saw not till now; so is it in this case : what is it humbleth a man for sin, and convinceth him of it, but this new light of God shining upon, and actuating the knowledge of the law? It now sees sin as a spiritual evil in itself, contrary to this God; yea, he now sees that contrariety which hath been in all, and every motion of the heart unto God as holy, and falls down and cries out, I was before without the law. So also he is hereby convinced of judgment, that true holiness God as God requires in the spiritualness of it, and he sees the beauty that is in grace. Yea, by knowing God anew and aright he looks with a spiritual eye upon whatever relateth unto God any way.

So then it is not the natural light of conscience, nor that improved by the word, which converts any man to God (although this is the best spring of most men's practic part of religion), but it is faith bringing in a new light into conscience, and so conscience lighting its taper at that sun, which humbleth for sin in another manner, and drives men to Christ, sanctifieth, changeth, and writes the law in the heart.   And this you will find to be the state of difference between Augustine and the Pelagians, semi-Pelagians, which the whole stream and current of his writings against them hold forth. They would have had the light of natural conscience and the seeds oi virtues in men (as in philosophers, &c.) being improved and manured by the revelation of the word, to be that grace which the Scripture speaks of.   He proclaims all their virtues, and their use of natural light (as in them) to be sins, because deficient of holiness, and requires not only the revelation of the objects of faith, which else natural light could not find out, but a new light to see them withal.

2. The second thing upon which I state the holiness of the light of conscience, which is proper to that faculty, and which is the office of it, is, that in directing the heart unto what is its duty, or in urging the matter of obedience, it insists on God's interest and glory as the principal motive, and doth both frame and press such motives as are drawn from thence.   I take it for granted that true holiness in any or in all faculties lies in setting up God as our chiefest end.   All the faculties in their motions, like the stars in their courses, fight for this interest ; yet each according unto its kind in a way proper to it, which must be set out and the measure of it taken from what is by nature's appointment proper to each faculty; for grace is ingrafted on, and works according to the nature and kind of each faculty.   As in a man's body every part hath its proper office (as the apostle, 1 Cor. xii., speaks), so it is in the faculties of the soul.

1. Holiness ingrafted on the understanding works it towards God, and for God, according to what is its peculiar proper office, as to know God as God, and to admire him as God, &c.

2. Holiness in the will and affections influenceth them to love God and cleave to him.

Then 3. Answerably ; the conscience must act for him according unto its kind, and that which is proper to it is to be the mover to obedience, chiefly for God and his glory.   When the whole soul therefore by regeneration once hath received and admitted God as its supreme end, lord, and natural king, then the office of conscience as his attorney-general, or lord-chancellor, is to frame such pleas and motives on his behalf as shall sway the heart, and vigorously to press them.   That this is the proper office of conscience, both reason and Scripture shew.

(1.) Reason shews it ; for conscience is one part of practical reason; now the office assigned unto practical reason (which guides us in our actions in general of any kind) is to incite the heart to action, by motives drawn from what is a man's end.   As the speculative understanding reasons from truths, to prove or clear one truth from another, so the practical understanding guides us in our actions, and fetcheth arguments to move us.   Yet as this is but the office of practic reason in the general, so conscience being the top branch of practic reason, hath this more eminent office assigned to it, viz., to urge such motives upon us in our actions as are drawn from moral goodness or ends.   Conscience being the proper judge of all moral good or evil, and so the seat of moral ends, this is likewise the kind or office of conscience in general.   If then it be inquired what should be the holiness proper to it according to this kind, the resolution is easy by the former principles.

[1.] The former law of holiness comes upon it, namely, to set up God as a man's end in its kind, and according to its kind.

[2.] The next work is to draw motives for all our actings from God's interest as our chiefest end, and to press them on the heart naturally and fully; for no man's reason deliberates about what concerns his chiefest end.

(2.) The Scripture evidenceth the same : Rom. xiii. 5, when the apostle exhorts Christians to obey, he useth this phrase, ' for conscience sake.' He speaks there of a regenerate man's conscience, and of what should move a true Christian. It is ' for conscience sake' (says he), which is a like and parallel phrase, as when the Scripture says we are justified by faith, which is all one as to say, by Christ's righteousness, which is the object of that faith ; or which faith alone considers as that whereby a man is justified, and so faith is metonymically put for its object. So here, because to obey God as our chiefest end, is that which conscience, in moving obedience, ought to have in its eye, therefore to do a thing for conscience sake, and for God as a man's chief end, is all one ; which when conscience hath performed, and swayed the heart unto it, it is termed, ' the answer of a good conscience towards God,' so far as that speech relates unto sanctification (in 1 Peter iii. 21), it being God to whom conscience is to give its account, in which, when it hath been faithful to him as God, it is a good conscience, and can give an answer, a true and just one, as having discharged its trust on its* behalf. In like manner to be a ' servant of righteousness,' and a ' servant to God,' is in the apostle's language all one (Rom. vi. 18, 22, compared), for take God out of a man's end, and it is not righteousness. Thus here, to obey God, and to obey conscience, and to obey for conscience sake, and for God's sake, as our utmost end, are equivalent. Now in a man that remains unregenerate, this essential property of holiness (as it is to be in the conscience), hath not as yet taken place in his conscience, nor hath it become the natural supreme law thereof. And the reason is clear.

For, 1, until God himself hath been, by a work of regeneration on the whole heart, set up in the heart as a man's supreme end, and generally owned and proclaimed such in the heart, conscience (whose office is to argue from what really is a man's end), cannot heartily and naturally draw motives from it; for it would argue then from what is not, and so not have a foundation for its reasonings, such as to persuade the heart, and as should have power and force in them to prevail. And further, it is so because that, until regeneration comes, and makes this great alteration of a man's end, it is certain that self-love remaineth a man's supreme end, and the swaying principle in all. Self is the soul, the spirit of unregeneracy, that runs through, inspires, and leavens all the faculties. If therefore self be predominant in other faculties, then also in this. If self-love sways in the will, then self-respects, and motives must also be in the conscience ; and everything moves according to that which is in itself, to its own centre.

Now it is certain that conscience in men unregenerate remains unsanctified, for these two reasons.

1. That else a man unregenerate might be said, in respect of that one faculty, to be a man regenerate, whenas there is not any one thing born of the flesh, but is flesh.

And, 2, because else, in a regenerate man, that one faculty needed no renewing ; seeing, according to this supposition, it had the same light, as truly good for the kind of it, afore regeneration, as after ; whenas 1 Thes. v. ver. 23, the apostle prays, ' The very God of peace sanctify you wholly,

* Qu. 'his' ?—ED.

your whole man, spirit, soul, and body,' &c., so as all are sanctified anew, and therefore conscience also. And the same apostle says, Eph. iv. 23, ' Be renewed in the spirit,' in the very spirit, the purest part, ' of the mind.'

There is one query, or objection, the answer to which will further clear the meaning of this assertion. The query is this, Doth not natural conscience, in natural men, urge obedience to God, yea, and urge respect for God, as motives thereto ?

Ans. 1. If conscience had not some eye to God, or at least to moral good, it were not conscience. Conscience, as such, keeps to this as its own sphere or circle. To move for worldly outward ends or respects, pertains not unto conscience, as such, but is from lusts to such outward things ; or at best, 2 Cor. i. 12, it is worldly, ' fleshly wisdom,' as the apostle calls it.

Ans. 2. There are many respects which natural conscience hath unto God, as an object of its thoughts, whilst it presseth obedience on us, and under the consideration of which it urgeth it ; yet still if this one respect I insist on be wanting and left out, or not made the main of all other, then those other motives, which conscience useth, do not rise so high as to constitute the conscience holy. For though the subject, which in this case it is conversant about, be God, yet still it remains defective in what is proper to it, and truly constitutive of holiness, as it ought to be in conscience. For example, when conscience doth consider and present God to us as a supreme lawgiver and judge, who is ' able to save or to condemn,' as James iv. 12, when yet the heart hath not entertained this God as its natural Lord and liege-king : in this case, though obedience be urged indeed for God, and unto God, yet not for God, as the chief motive. So that, as speaking of the knowledge of God, I said, men might have large and great literal knowledge of God, yet if they knew not God as God in himself, they wanted a holy knowledge of him ; so say I in this case, though conscience may eye God in many respects, under which he is revealed unto us, as a judge, or a sovereign, yet if not under this, as he is set up as our chiefest end, the conscience is not holy in respect thereof.

3. For the clearing of this I add, that natural conscience being leavened with self-love, doth naturally and heartily urge only such motives on the heart as do concern self, and in such a way as self-interest is rather spoken for than God's. The meaning is, that when such motives only are urged, and professed, as are but fitted and suited to self, although those considerations be taken from God, yet in this case, not God's interest, but our own, is pleaded for. There are many considerations may be drawn from God as presented to us in Scripture, which alone considered are fitted but to move self-love in us, which is naturally our chiefest end. As for example, the consideration had of God as a lawgiver, a commander, a judge, able to save and to condemn, doth more properly speak for self than for God ; for they urge but what is in God, in relation unto self. And although God and his name be materially used, and objectively, yet finally, and so formally and really, self-love is more regarded and spoken to in them, than God's interest.

Obj. But you will yet say to me, May not, and doth not, natural conscience hold forth to men unregenerate, that God ought to be a man's utmost end, and that it is the duty of the heart to be moved with arguments drawn from thence ?

The *answer* in general is, that if the meaning be that such thoughts and considerations do materially come to mind, that is, that natural conscience hath such flying thoughts under its consideration at times, it cannot be denied, for it cannot indeed avoid them.   For if God himself be the enlightener of conscience, as hath been declared, then surely he will, to the end of leaving all men without excuse, cause at times such thoughts to pass through men's hearts, as flashes of lightning use to do through natural darkness.   And natural conscience is not only capable thereof, but cannot resist their being the matter of its thoughts.   But now in the acting and management of these, and such other considerations, darted in by God, is the goodness or holiness of conscience itself seen and discovered.   The apostle hath this saying, 1 Cor. i. 21, speaking of the heathen, that ' by the wisdom of God the world knew not God.'   Which implies two things : 1. That there were suggested to their thoughts, by God's Spirit, many divine considerations, leading on to, and tending to discover God unto them, which is therefore termed the wisdom of God, that is, which he suggested to their thoughts as object matter for their thoughts to work on.   But, 2, their spirits, which took in these notions of God, did make use thereof according to the predominant principles within itself, and not according to the tendency of the things themselves suggested by God unto them ; and so they through their own wisdom or corrupt principles knew not God ; no, not by those notions that God suggested unto them.   Here you see the wisdom suggested by God is received and made use of according to the qualification of the receivers.   Now what the apostle speaks there of natural wisdom, of the knowledge of God, I apply unto natural conscience in the thing in hand. It is true, natural conscience doth take in such suggests as these, that God ought to be a man's utmost end, and that it is the duty of the heart to set him up as such.   But still these are made use of but according to the temper and disposition of conscience itself (which is the receiver of these) which is poisoned with self; so that although these suggests, as to the matter of them, be good, yet the conscience itself, that is the suscipient of them, may be, and is, in the management thereof, deficient of holiness; yea, and the motives or motions themselves, which conscience maketh from hence, are (as they come from it) deficient of that holiness is proper thereto.   So then, if the conscience be holy, it must not only take in the matter of such considerations and suggest them to the heart, but it must urge and enforce them with that vigour and strength which is answerable unto the virtue, spirit, and power that is in them, and worthy of the motives themselves.

This deficiency of natural conscience herein is discovered by these particulars.

1. Inasmuch as conscience being prepossessed with self-love's interest, as its chiefest end, it thereby becomes weak and faint in the pressing and urging of God's interest as a man's chiefest end, for these two are inconsistent.   It gives not the due accent, puts not the weight, the emphasis thereon; it cries Shiboleth in the pronouncing, and so dishonours, spoils, enervates, and withers them in the propounding.   Conscience being weak through the flesh, miscarries with them whilst it conceives them, and hath not strength to bring forth.   Some motives perhaps drawn from God it may, and doth, with a powerful hand shoot up to the arrow-head, so as they pierce the soul through and through ; but these motives drawn from God as a man's utmost end (which in their own nature and ordination are, and should be the great artillery) natural conscience doth faintly and weakly pursue, lets them fall at the cannon's mouth, dischargeth them without powder, so as they make no impression or dint on the heart at all ; yea, they never reach it.

2. If it urgeth such considerations, yet not constantly in the course of a man's life. Alas! they come in but now and then, and but as God is pleased to convince the soul of its defects; but this principle is not made natural and inlaid therein. And if such considerations do come in, they come unseasonably, *post factum*, after miscarriages, and at times of God's reckonings and accountings with us (as the prophet Daniel urged upon Belshazzar, a profane, idolatrous heathen, that 'that God in whose hands were his breath and ways, him he had not glorified,' Dan. v. 23), so to continue* and condemn us. Whereas the right cure and season of such considerations (if the conscience were made holy) is before we act, or *inter agendum*, in the time of acting; otherwise they only come as witnesses against us in obedience.† And the reason of this is, because they are not natural to such a conscience, but come in forcibly.

3. By urging motives of so high concernment so faintly, instead of giving demonstration of any true holiness to be therein, it discovers the greater sinfulness, falseness, and hypocrisy towards God. For insomuch as it taketh in and suggesteth the matter of such considerations, it pretends to be for God, and to discharge its trust committed to it; when yet, like a false-hearted pleader at the bar, who is bribed by the adverse party (for such is self-love in a man unto God), it pretends to this and that, but urgeth nothing home, and his tongue falters whilst he seems to plead for him whose cause he hath undertaken. Now this is really and in truth the greatest dishonour that can be put upon God; as, in the like case, any sovereign prince would esteem it, if his agent or minister, that appears for his interest, should either urge any lower interests or properties than those of a king (as such which he stands upon), or urge his proper interest, as of a king, coldly and faintly. *Docet negare, dum urget timide.* His name, and the greatest glory due to it, is taken in vain, whilst it is mentioned to no higher or more efficacious purpose.

4. And, lastly, such motives so used deserve not the name of motives. They fall from that denomination, and they are receptions or motions rather made *in* conscience, than motives made *by* conscience. As imperfect wishings and wouldings in the will we term *velleities*, so proportionably are these in the conscience. Now no power or faculty in a man can be said to act for God as its utmost end, unless it acts with a strength some way suitably. It is an observable phrase, Col. iii. 23, 'Whatsoever you do, do it heartily, or with all your might, as to the Lord.' The import of which is this: that whatsoever is truly done to God, and for God, he being so great a God, and the nature of his service (as they say of a king), being such, as it falls short and is deficient of what deserves the name of service in respect to him, or by way of motive for him, if it be not performed with vigour and strength answerable; it is therefore not done to the Lord, unless it be heartily. And this is true of all the motions conscience makes for God; they are not for him, nor worthy of him, nor indeed motives as for God, unless prosecuted predominantly for him above all other ends.

So then two deficiencies, or fallings short of holiness, have been discovered to be in natural conscience.

1. That it falls short in an effectual direction to, or instruction in, the right manner of obedience to the law. It either not knows, or practises not, what are the inwards of duties, because it was never elevated to the knowledge of God as God in himself, and so is ignorant how to call for a worship or obedience suitable unto him, which consists in spirit and in truth.

* Qu. 'convict'?—ED.   † Qu. 'disobedience'?—ED.

2. It also falls short in that which is the eminent part and office of it, namely, faithfulness to God, to try vigorously on the heart such motives as are drawn from God's interest, set up therein as our utmost end. And these defects lie in the very light of conscience, and in conscience itself, besides what deficiency is discovered in the effects themselves, which are answerable to these defects in the cause itself.

3. I shall make this additional remark to complete this head, that this deficiency in the light itself, from conscience to true holiness, appears and manifests itself in the effect; namely, that the light that is in natural conscience maketh not the heart good, it sanctifieth not, and therefore itself is not good, with that goodness which is proper to that faculty. As that is a good tree which maketh the fruit good, so that is a good conscience which maketh the heart good. This is a certain truth, that the difference between saving light or knowledge, and common light raised up into a great blaze, are difficultly distinguished in themselves abstractly considered, compared with themselves, although the difference in itself is great, *consequently*, as by the fruits they are distinguished manifestly in the issue and event. Insomuch as the difficulty in distinguishing them thus in themselves hath occasioned a great divine* to say, *Non distinguuntur nisi consequenter, ad actum voluntatis*, that they are not distinguished unless consequently, to the act of the will. Which indeed holds true in respect of discerning that difference, but not in the real distinction of the lights themselves; for the difference must needs be in the light itself as the cause, or else one faculty in an unregenerate man needed not sanctification and regeneration. Now, that that only is a good conscience which maketh the heart good, appears both by Scripture and reason.

1. By Scripture. Paul therefore said he had a good conscience, because he desired to live honestly in all things, Heb. xiii. 18. For else, had he had never so much light, which had still directed him and instigated him to good, yet had not wrought in him a desire to live accordingly, he could not have termed his conscience good. And therefore, also, having a good conscience is put for a holy conversation (by the apostle Peter, 1 Peter iii. 16), as the cause for the effect; for so it follows, ' That speaking of you as evil doers, they may be ashamed, that accuse falsely your good conversation in Christ.' Therefore a good conscience makes the man good.

2. In reason it is evident. For when anything hath lost that special virtue, which once it had, to effect that which it was ordained for, we say of it that it is not good, which that familiar saying of Christ confirms in the general, ' Salt is good, but if it hath lost its savour ' (or virtue of its seasoning and diffusive virtue to season other things), ' it is good for nothing.' Compare Luke xiii. 34 with Mat. v. 13. Yea, if it might be supposed good for some other inferior purpose than what that native virtue once eminently served for, yet we use to say of a thing in such a case, that it is not good; that is, not answering its kind. Take any drug which hath a cordial virtue: if that virtue be gone, you use to say it is naught, though some weaker or lower effect it may still retain. Take wine when it is soured, or the spirits of it are gone : you say it is naught, that is, as it is wine ; it still may make good vinegar, or may serve some other use. A purging drug, when the purgative strength of it is gone, it is not good ; though it may have so much left as to stir the humours a little, yet if not enough to carry them away, it is not good, because it wants that virtue it was ordained for, although still a skilful apothecary knows how to make

* Amesii Medulla, lib. i. cap. 3, Thes. 4.

some use of it. Thus conscience, though it retain some weaker acts it had in man in innocency, and which now are common to a man regenerate and unregenerate, yet the special virtue and energy of those acts it then had, and which now in a regenerate man it hath in sanctifying and purifying, being lost and gone, the special proper goodness of it is gone and lost also. It may serve to stir the humours, both the guilt and power of corruption, and it may serve to drive corruption in, but its purging virtue is gone. And though God doth make use of those weak properties that remain, so as to discover sin, or to witness against the sinner, yet the native use is extinct, and so it is not a good conscience.

CHAPTER VII.

How a natural conscience, in its highest operations, is deficient in that which is necessary to make it really holy.

Now, to give a demonstration of the deficiency of conscience, in its operations on the heart in all particulars, might be too large; I shall do it but in some few, which shall be fitted to two cases or conditions of men unregenerate, under one of which all such men's conditions will fall, and in either of which it will appear that natural conscience sanctifies not the heart throughout, as regenerating grace doth.

The first case is, that in men unregenerate there are to be found, besides light of conscience, virtues, and impressions on their wills and affections inclining them to good, which the heathens called *semina virtutum*, seeds of virtues, inclining them unto what the light of conscience doth direct them unto ; and in this case will it not be said that it maketh the heart good, or that a goodness of heart doth accompany it ?

But 1. None had a universal goodness, no, not in that sphere of moral good, but were deficient in some virtues, whereunto the light of their conscience did direct them. God did never make light of conscience, and moral impressions to virtue, adequate or even in any man, that is, not of like extent, but left it so as in those who naturally or otherwise have had most of moral inclinations in them, yet their consciences have had strong convictions to such duties and actions unto which their wills and affections have had no inclinations stamped on them to correspond therewith, but the contrary inclinations have been left to their full strength. And this God doth to give a ground of discovery unto all men of their natural condition, by letting them see the strength of corrupt inclinations, and their emptiness of good, by some such particulars. This is exemplified both in heathens, Jews, and Christians. The heathens had dispersed among the bulk and multitude of them all seeds of virtues ; but so as all were not in each and every man, but one had justice, another abstinence from pleasures, a third continency. God withal left each of them in their dispositions naked and void in respect of some virtues or other. Thus Socrates was given to the love of boys ; and such vile affections is the very instance Paul gives of the wisest of their philosophers (Rom. i.), that so that fatal doom might with condition be pronounced of all and each, which the apostle there recordeth, 'They withheld the truth in unrighteousness.' Their corrupt hearts were too headstrong for their consciences to rule in some particular or other.

I confess, I have sometimes wondered at those high passages I before rehearsed, both concerning their crying up right reason, and also of their professing to live thereto; as being a seeming vindication of them from that which the apostle, Rom. i., chargeth them withal, viz., 'imprisoning the truth in unrighteousness' in some things. But in the end I perceived the juggle (for it was truly such); for whilst all cried up this right reason in the general as their rule, and professed to live by it, yet come to the particulars, therein each sect or person would judge this or that to be according to right reason (or nature, as they termed it) as they listed, and as agreed with their lusts. Diogenes accounted self-pollution, or (as the apostle terms it) 'defiling their bodies' (ἐν ἑαυτοῖς) 'committed alone by themselves,' to be lawful, and according to nature; which the apostle (Rom. i. 24) instanceth in, as one of their philosophical practices. Plato* (the divinest of them) held communion of wives. The like might be said of others. 'Though all men understand what is meant by iron, what by silver, as soon as they hear each named; yet' (says Plato) 'when we use the name of just or good, one is carried to one thing as just and good which another dislikes, and we differ therein amongst ourselves.' Thus he confesseth. And hence, under this general proclaiming the right rule, and magnifying right reason (as all did), so many sects arose amongst them, differing in their judgment of what was just or unjust, morally good or evil, lawful or unlawful, so as every one did surrender the judgment of his reason to his lusts; yea, and made many abominable vices things in their nature indifferent; *leges naturæ opiniones suas faciunt:*† each made his own opinion, and what they had a mind to, the law of nature and right reason. And then indeed they might well boast (as they did) they lived according to right reason; for wherein their virtues fell short, or their lusts overruled them, they would flatly argue for that to be lawful, or natural, or indifferent, and so blessed themselves in their own deceivings. And, if I mistake not, the apostle had this very thing in his eye when he says, 'They became vain in their reasonings' (διαλογισμοῖς), 'and their foolish heart was darkened,' Rom. i. 21; and 'professing themselves wise' (so each sect pretend), 'they became fools,' the vainest that ever were, corrupting themselves in what they knew naturally, and making use of corrupt reason in them to defend what natural reason condemned. And so I may make a parallel between the mystery of iniquity among the heathen and that in the popish religion. The pope cries up the Scriptures in general, and professeth to give us religion from thence; but then he, taking on him to be the supreme judge, can and doth give us out from thence what religion he pleaseth, and frameth opinions to his own lusts and ambition; and so did the philosophers, whilst they cried up reason.

2. Both the light of their consciences, and also their highest virtues, when they did most exactly fall on them, did carry them but to the letter, but not to the spiritual part of any virtue. At the best, they are said to do but the things contained in the law (τὰ τοῦ νόμου in the text), even wherein they were a law unto themselves. Observe it, they are not said to keep the law, neither to have the law written in their hearts; whereas of a believer both these are at once affirmed, John xiv. 21, 'He that hath my commandments, and keepeth them, is he that loves me.' *First*, he is said to have the law truly and genuinely stamped upon his soul; and *secondly*, out of that principle is said to keep it; whereas these have but the duties, the outward works of it written there, and accordingly do but 'the things of the law.' Or again, they may be said to have the effect of it, as brute

* De Repub., lib. v.   † Tertullian.

beasts are said to have the work or effect of reason, as bees in making their hives, &c. The works which they do are *operæ intelligentiæ*, as if reason had done them; but they do them not from a principle of reason. And this difference did Augustine long ago urge and insist on, in his answers to Pelagius, and Julianus, and the Massilienses, who urged this text, that the light of conscience, and virtues, and good works thence flowing were such as had a true and real goodness in them. But he* distinguished how that in the law commanding, and in every action to be done according to the law, there were *opus*, or (as from the Stoics he termed it) *officium quod faciendum est*, the duty that is to be done; *et finis, vel propter quod faciendum*, the end for which it is to be done. Which end he still asserts against them, to be not merely the good of any creature, though a public good to the whole world, but the chief end of a good action is God's glory, who himself is the chiefest good and the chiefest end. The *officia*, the duties, are not *the law*, but only τὰ τοῦ νόμου, *the things of the law; officia legis*, as Beza interprets it. But love to God is the end of the law, and the performance of it, 1 Tim. i. 5, and so it is the soul and spirit of it; and when it is not written as the supreme law and sovereign dictate in the conscience, it may be said the law is wanting there.

In heathens nature spoke out, and their highest pitch was to love virtue for virtue's sake, judging and valuing it to be the greatest ornament of their rational souls. They therefore decried all outward respects as unworthy, and too mean to be motives unto virtuous actions; but yet still all their admiration was raised no further but to virtue itself, and virtuous actions for themselves, as the supreme excellency. They never raised virtue to a tendency or subordination to God, and to glorify God, as God, by it; herein they fell short, and therefore short in holiness. For I may safely affirm, that if a Christian himself could thus love true grace, and prize it as a supreme excellency, and love goodness only as it is a habit in the soul which makes us good, this would not be holiness. For in so doing, a man would value it only as a particular good unto his own soul, which is but a small piece of the creation of God. And the mind, in so doing, would but glory and centre still in itself (as well as in valuing riches or honours), and not in the Lord; for there is the same reason in either.

The second case is this, that to the Jews and us Christians, there are, by the revelation of the law and will of God, many duties of God's worship (as prayers, meditation, holy conference, and reading the word) whereunto there are small, if any, moral inclinations stamped upon men's wills to assist them in them, or facilitate these unto them; and therefore conscience, calling upon the heart for such duties as these, is forced to raise the tax or levy of them, by calling in foreign assistance and aid. And for a supply of natural strength and inclination unto duties of this kind, it is reduced to such motives of the law as are fitted to stir self-love in the affections; as fear of hell, &c. And this is also the case of temporary believers under the gospel. Now in this case it doth yet more evidently appear that the light of natural conscience doth not sanctify the heart throughout, as grace in a regenerate man in some measure doth.

1. Natural conscience puts a necessity upon the performance of a duty, saith and urgeth that it ought and must be done; but it puts no inward freedom and willingness into the will to the performance of it, as grace doth. For grace makes a man willing, as conscience makes the duty necessary. It puts an inclination, ' a spirit of liberty and freedom; a free spirit, an ingenu-

* Lib. iv., contra Julian., cap. 13.

ous spirit,' as David calls it, Ps. li. 12. And therefore Paul opposeth (Gal. v. 18) the working of the spirit of the law, or of conscience by the law, in these words, ' If you be led by the Spirit, ye are not under the law,' and so è *contra*. Now, to be led by the Spirit is to have the will ready to follow God in everything ; to have the will easily carried on to a duty, for leading implies readiness of following : Isa. xi. 6, ' A child shall lead them ;' that is, a little thing may persuade them.

If it be *objected*, that conscience carried on the will to do duties, for else they would not be done,

I *answer ;* There is a willingness which is intrinsecal and direct, and *per se*, when a man hath a mind and will to a thing for itself ; and there is a made willingness, which is *per accidens*, which is a comparative willingness. There is no man so averse to anything but may be thus made willing, that is, comparatively, and *per accidens* willing. The most covetous man in the world, that loves money never so much, may be made willing to part with it, and glad to do so, if it concerns his life to do it ; or if a great necessity of bonds, or going to prison, be laid on him, which is indeed ' a constraint,' and so Peter terms it (1 Peter v. 2) and opposeth it to ' willingly.' But a godly man hath a ready mind to whatever is good, in the principle of his heart, and often good duties come off at the first motion, ' To will is present with me,' Rom. vii. 18. Or if flesh lie uppermost, and so there is an averseness in the entrance, yet when God and his heart have closed in the duty and grown familiar, he finds his whole heart to be in it.

Now, the reason of an unregenerate man's unwillingness unto such holy duties lies in this, that they are appointed, and the tendency of them is, to bring God and their hearts together, which indeed is to bring two enemies together, for such are their hearts and God. And the reason of a regenerate man's willingness is, that in the duty two friends meet together, God who hath from everlasting owned that soul, and the soul that hath chosen God to be his God.

2. Natural conscience gives light and enforcements from legal motives to the duty, but it gives no new inward strength. And the reason is clear ; for natural conscience carries a man on but upon the strength of the covenant of works. Now, ' the law is weak ' (says the apostle, Rom. viii.) as to any such effect. Urgency of conscience is but as if a man should come to one that is lame, and his joints frozen and stiff, with a light in one hand and a cudgel in the other, and waken him, and jog him, and tell him, Here is light for you to walk by, and there are blows if you will not. Or it is as if one should ride a tired horse ; there is a bridle to direct, and a spur to put him on, but the rider giveth no strength for the horse to travel with. Natural conscience in its government is tyrannical, and, like the taskmasters of Egypt, requires bricks to be made, and beats men if not, but gives them no straw. But grace adds another principle to conscience, and that is, faith and the new creature. Faith fetcheth life, and quickening, and strength from Christ, both habitual strength, which is called ' strength in the inward man,' and co-operating strength. ' I am able ' (says the apostle) ' to do all things, through Christ that strengtheneth me.' The spirit of adoption not only puts us on to pray, but ' helpeth our infirmities,' Rom. viii. 26, which is spoken in opposition to the spirit of bondage. The Holy Ghost comes and fills the soul with arguments and motions and inclinations to pray, insomuch as the soul is like a full breast till it be drawn, or a pregnant womb till it be delivered of what is formed in it. And the soul ests not till it hath gone alone, and poured forth itself to God. Conscience

indeed wakens the old man so, as he makes him bestir himself and his lazy
stiff joints, and so to mend his pace in duties, but still it gives no strength,
so as it is extrinsecal enforcement and instigation only, and not inward
strength, which conscience doth afford.

3. Natural conscience cannot sweeten the law to a man, and cause him
to 'delight in it,' and the duties of it, as a regenerate man is said to do
(Rom. vii.), for if it gives not suitable strength and will, it cannot give
delight; for delight follows these, whilst forced extrinsecal motives carry us
on, and there is a grievance in the motion, for fear is an affection which
hath grief in it (1 John iv. 18); and thus though they (Mal. i. 13) brought but
the lame and the lean sacrifices, yet they grudge at it, and said 'what
weariness is in it?' They were weary of doing anything for God, but love
sweetens all to a man: 'This is the love of God, that his commandments
are not grievous,' 1 John v. 3. Now it is a certain rule, that as natural
conscience works by fear, so faith works by love, and love sweetens the law
to a man. Conscience may bring a sick man meat, but it must be the
inward constitution of a sound mind that tastes the sweetness of meat.

4. Lastly, As thus its weakness is seen in holy duties, so in regard of sin
also, it is not able to condemn sin in the flesh. Of the law it is spoken,
Rom. viii. 3, that it discovers sin, but kills it not; it hath power to kill
the man for sin, and to condemn him, 2 Cor. iii. 6, but not to kill sin in
the man (as the phrase is, Rom. viii. 4). As the law came into the world,
that sin might be imputed, that is, known and discovered, but not destroyed,
so light of conscience hath no farther power. Like flashes of lightning, it
on the sudden discovers, but expels not the darkness, yea, often leaves the
soul the more in the dark; yea, which is more, it enrageth some lusts the
more, and that whilst it restrains the outward acts. So Paul, who had a
strong work of the law (through conscience) upon him, says (Rom. vii.)
that 'the law wrought all concupiscence in him.' As a horse that is reined
grows the more fierce; as the winds that go to blow out the fire spreads it
more; as the water in lime makes it burn within the more; so the light of
conscience makes lust inwardly the hotter and more violent: therefore those
are more eager in sinning that have most knowledge. It is true indeed,
violent terrors of conscience upon a man, when the guilt of sin in its turn
comes to take the dominion and to reign (which is but an after part of
the dominion of the law over a man), will restrain men from sinning; but
yet the ordinary light of it, though it restrains the acts, yet increaseth the
lust, and so doth more hurt one way than good another.

Use. Let us then mind the main and primary scope and extent of conscience's commission, and God's primary end in putting the light of it into
men, which is the same with that of the law, as the power of it and the
effect of it is the same. Now the law was sent that man's sinfulness might
be discovered, and he convinced of it, to see his weakness and the power of
sin, and his utter averseness to good and proneness to evil; that so men,
despairing of being saved by the effects of it, or their conformity to it, might
seek help in Christ, and work anew from him, Gal. iii. 15, 16, 17, 18.
And if this use be not made of it, then God hath ordained it for another
use, to convince and condemn men by it at the latter day, and leave them
without excuse; which use the apostle speaks of, Rom. i. And God will
make use of the light of natural conscience even to condemn the strictest
heathen.

What a great mistake is it then utterly to pervert this use and extent
both of God and it, and to deem this light of the law and of conscience,

and of the work of it, to be grace itself? Oh! that ever men should thus abuse the very witness God hath appointed to convince them they are not in a state of grace, and mistaking the intent of his speech and verdict in them, should judge it to be grace, and because it checks them for evil, and puts them on to good, think by conforming a little to it to be saved! Thus the Jews understood the law, and the effects of that in them; and because they had the law which God gave them, to see themselves out of his favour, they thought therefore they were in it (Rom. ii.), rested in the law, and thought if they conformed to it, because it called for obedience, they should be saved, Rom. x. Whereas if men would listen to it, it would shew them their inability to conform to it, and so begin to humble them, and to take them off from resting in their obedience. There is enough in the light of it to do this, for God means to judge them by it at the last day.

CHAPTER VIII.

The grounds of the mistake upon which men proceed, in judging the actings of natural conscience to be the workings of a principle of true grace, considered and detected.

I now come to examine those grounds of mistake which unregenerate men go upon in the judging this principle of conscience, and the workings thereof to grace and true goodness.

1. The first ground of mistake is, because men find it to be an inward principle, as grace is inherent and sealed in their inward parts, Jer. xxxi. 32. And the motions thereof unto good are not outward or external, but from within, nor are they outward respects by which it moves.

Ans. 1. Though it be a principle within a man, as in relation to its residence, yet as to the working of it upon the rest of the faculties it acts as if it were an extrinsecal and violent principle. It may be remembered to this purpose, how I have before proved that the motives it useth at best, to carry the rest of the heart on to obedience, are legal, and the government of it vigorous, whereas that of grace is sweet and natural, having the hearts of its subjects, so far as a man is renewed. There are three sorts of moving principles to be found distinct in men's spirits. 1st, Mere outward respects for things worldly and outward; such as are the motives which arise from our lusts as carried forth to outward objects. 2dly, There are the outward impulses by which natural conscience works. And 3dly, There are the kindly, sweet, and natural, gracious motions of grace and holiness in a regenerate heart. To exemplify these three by similitudes: take a clock or a watch, and observe the principles of each of their motions. A clock is moved by weights that hang without it; and such are outward worldly respects that pertain not to conscience, as vainglory, love of praise, filthy lucre, &c. But a watch hath a motion from what is within itself, a spring that sets all the wheels on work; and yet the motion of the watch is truly and indeed but an extrinsecal motion, in comparison with what is natural. And such is that of natural conscience in respect of those duties unto God which it enjoins; both the one as well as the other are external, in respect of a violence or a forcedness of their motion; for the wheels which move have not a natural poise to move of themselves. But take a bird that flies, there is truly and properly an internal principle of life and motion in the wings and all the limbs thereof, which moves the whole, and every member; and such a principle is grace in comparison of natural conscience.

Ans. 2. Though it be thus a principle within thee, yet it makes not up another self within thee, as grace doth. Though thy conscience is against a sin, before or after it is committed, yet thou canst not say, I am against the sin, which is thy beloved sin. No; thyself art for it, but conscience in thee is only against it. Hence thou canst not say with Paul, Rom. vii., ' It is not I, but sin,' for thy conscience only stood out against it, when thy heart was wholly for it. But this a regenerate man can and doth say; and this was it which moved Austin to fall off from that interpretation of Rom. vii.: that the passages thereof should be meant of an unregenerate man (of whom once he understood them), because he found that though the light of his conscience was against the sin, yet made not up another whole inward man, which a man might term himself. Yea, you may observe, that when conscience speaks against a sin, it speaks to the rest of the whole man as to a distinct person from itself, though it be seated in the man; for it speaks thus, Thus thou oughtest not to do, or this thou hast done. The language of conscience is as the language of another person, whose part it takes, even of God to a man, as Menander said, ἐν τὸις ἁπάσιν ἡ συνείδησις Θεός : Conscience is as God to all, and every mortal man. And therefore it acts the part of an advocate against a man's self. But the grace of sanctification hath won all the faculties in their courses to go the same way with itself. And therefore a regenerate man can say to conscience, that besides, and over and above thy checks (O conscience) I have a whole new man, an inner man within me, that had no hand in this sin, but is for God and his law, as well as thou, and serves him in the inner man, even whilst the law of the members doth prevail to the outward action.

Ans. 3. In respect of many actings of conscience in thee, thou art a patient, not active, or an agent. But, on the contrary, when it checks, restrains, and condemns for sin, or invites unto duties, thy whole heart is against it. It is true these are truly acts of a faculty within thee, for the apostle, Rom. ii. 15, calls them 'their thoughts' (when he speaks of their consciences accusing them), yet they are (if unregenerate) sufferers, endurers, and patients under them, because it is God (as I have shewed) is the author and actuater of them, puts a word into conscience's mouth, as once into Balaam's, so as it cannot but speak, nor can it say the contrary, when yet (as Balaam) the whole man is against that word, and follows after the ways of unrighteousness, and would not have the vision, so to speak. It is full sore against his will, and bent and grain of his spirit. In the text, Rom. ii., it is said, συμμαρτυρεῖν, its witness being joined with another's, namely, God's. Thus checks and terrors of conscience are acts upon a man, rather than of a man, and so men are endurers under them. And therefore men hate them, and would be rid of them, if they could, or knew how. They secretly say of it, as Ahab to Micaiah, ' Go, mine enemy, thou never prophesiest good to me.' The other faculties do look upon it as the Sodomites did upon Lot, and cried out, ' Shall this stranger judge us ? ' They would thrust it forth of their jurisdiction if they could, as none of their company. Men use mirth and jollitry to allay the checks of it, and give themselves a medicine to kill this worm. Speculative light men like, for it is pleasant; but light that is busy with them, and active in them, they like not to retain in their knowledge, Rom. i. 28 ; whereas a godly man writes up such knowledge in his heart, as one doth memorandums in his table-book : Prov. iii. 3, ' Write them,' says he, ' in the tables of thy heart;' having said before, ' My son, forget not thou my law.' He is as glad of new light that discovers to him a sin or corruption he saw not before, or a duty he knew not, as a man is of finding great spoil. It is David's comparison, Ps. cxix. 162; whereas another man looks upon every such discovery of sin or duty as men do now upon a new tax or levy, and hate the light of conscience as a task-master, as the Jews did a publican.

2. A second ground of mistake is, that conscience is a good and upright principle, contrary unto sin, and for what is good, and cannot be charmed to hold its peace.

Ans. 1. The goodness that is in the light of conscience riseth not up to the goodness of holiness, as hath been shewed. It is but the letter, not the spirit, of the law. Now, consider that the shadow, as of truth, so of goodness, sanctifies not.

Ans. 2. As for its contrariety and opposition unto sin, condemning, restraining, and coming in against it, I answer, there is a twofold contrariety, the one real and physical, as fire is contrary to water, which are destructive each of other, and are armed with power to expel the one the other. And thus in a regenerate man flesh and spirit are contrary : Gal. v. 17, ' The flesh lusteth against the spirit, and the spirit against the flesh ; and these are contrary the one to the other; so that ye cannot do the things that ye would.' They therefore cannot exist in a predominancy each in the same heart ; but if the spirit that is in man ' lusteth after envy, God gives grace ' to subdue it ; so as to be under the dominion of sin and grace cannot stand together, Rom. vi. 12, 14. Such a contrariety to sin as this is not in the light of an unregenerate man. But there is another sort of contrariety, viz., testimonial (for unto a witness the text compares it), which in appearance conscience bears to a sinner. But indeed it is contrary, only as a witness is to a bad man and a bad cause ; contrary only in this, because he comes in and gives testimony against him, and that not out of a contrariety or antipathy to the man, but as witness of the truth. Paul hath told us such a testimony is remote from enmity ; Gal. iv. 16, ' Am I therefore your enemy, because I tell you the truth ?' Or the contrariety is as that of a lawyer that pleads a cause against a man ; he is said to be contrary, only because he speaks against the man. And indeed in these testimonies conscience is rather contrary to the man that sins, than to the sin itself ; for it expels it not. It hath not a destructive virtue in it; but a beloved sin, notwithstanding light of conscience testifying against it, doth in a predominancy continue still in the heart. Or if you will, it is but a representative or demonstrative contrariety, not a natural. Light hath a natural contrariety to darkness, and expels it ; whereas the light of a glow-worm only discovers itself in the dark, but enlighteneth not the air round about it. And therefore, though thou hadst never so much light, that, directed to good, checked thee for evil upon all occasions, and continued to do so all thy days ; if this wrought not a desire to live well in all things, but thou goest against it, and imprisonest the light of it, this will aggravate thy sin. And however thou takest this for a good conscience (as if conscience had a peculiar abstract goodness in it), yet when the naughty man that lived against conscience goes to hell, what will become of this good conscience ? It will even go to hell with thee, and be thy executioner ; yea, and even conscience itself will be most punished there, for that is the part on which the wrath of God lights. It is the tunnel through which God fills the vessel with wrath; and that, both because it gave light only, but no power; as also because the man whose conscience it is was wicked, and his heart naught. And therefore though conscience was against the sin thou committedst, yet conscience itself will be reckoned as guilty, and to be an evil conscience, because it wanted power to hinder thee, which power it once had.

3. A third ground that helps forward the mistake is, that they find it a constant principle, which will not be charmed, nor hold its tongue. And as grace is said to be a ' seed that remains,' so is this.

Ans. 1. Consider that for that very cause it is not grace, but nature. Grace is in us not from the first, but only after that it is received; but this light of conscience, and these workings of it, have been always in thee for the time past.

Ans. 2. Though the faculty itself always remains, yet thou shalt find, if God turn thee not to him, sin winning ground of it, and weakening the exercise of it, till it hath put thy conscience past feeling. Whilst men are young, their consciences are tender; but as they grow old, they are hardened; and this is part of their growing in wickedness. So, Eph. iv. 19, it is said, ' after they are past feeling,' which implies that they had a sense once. It is the like phrase to that you use of a man dying, you say, He is past sense, past speaking. The allusion there is to palsy-benumbed members, which are come to such a pass that they feel no pain. Conscience having spoken often, when it sees it cannot prevail, ceaseth to speak; yea, 1 Tim. iv. 2, Paul speaks as if some men's consciences were in the end ' cut' (so the phrase by Beza is interpreted), ' seared off with a hot iron,' as a putrefied member, that is grown dead and senseless, useth to be; not that the faculty is cut off, but it is meant in regard of the acts of it, which are cut off, and men walk as if they had no consciences. The reason is, because (as I said) the exercise of it depending upon God's working on it, and in it more or less, therefore when he hath striven long with men, in and through the checks of their consciences, in the end ceaseth striving, and then conscience ceaseth to check any longer. And therefore God is said to give them up to a reprobate mind, that is, void of judgment, even in judging those things sins which are to the light of nature most abhorrent, and as the phrase in such case is, ' inconvenient' (which the apostle there useth, Rom. i. 28). Whereas David's smote him for numbering the people, when he was old (for that was towards the end of his reign), as well as, when he was young, it did so for his cutting off Saul's lap. And Paul when old, and the time of departure at hand (as he says in the Second Epistle to Timothy), yet then he continued to serve God ' with a pure conscience,' as in the 1st chapter of that epistle, ver. 3, himself speaks.

Or if this light in natural conscience be not, in the exercise of it, almost extinct, yet it will be quiet and suffer itself to be close prisoner, not striving to get out, as, Rom. i. 18, the phrase is; but any truth in a good conscience will make the prison too hot for it. The evil conscience will keep commissions and writs lying by it, and not so much as open them, much less put them into suit; like those lights in those Roman urns, that give light within, but never break forth, because they were made of such matter as had light only, and not heat; and such is the light of a natural conscience, till God joins his wrath with it. But on the contrary, in a godly man light against any sin, or for the doing any duty, like fire imprisoned and smothered, burns inwardly, and ceaseth not till the flame break forth, Jer. xx. 9. When Jeremiah, through fear and discouragement, was resolved to preach no more, but to live a quiet life with the world, when he knew it was his duty to do otherwise: ' In the end' (says he) ' it was fire in my bones, and I could not stay or forbear.' Men use a natural conscience as a dark lantern; they shut up as much of it as they please, and if it burn, let it shine inward, it shall not outward. Grace will not be soused or dealt with, but like the apostle (who spake it as led by this principle) in the end, it says, ' I cannot but speak the things I know,' Acts iv. 20.

4. A fourth main ground of mistake is, that religion is expressed unto us, by making conscience of what we do ; and uprightness is understood to consist in this, that we follow our consciences. A conscionable man, and a religious man, are equivalently put each for the other. Yea, did not Abimelech plead it, Gen. xx. 5, and did not God acknowledge this to be integrity, ver. 6, he having in that matter of Sarah gone according to the principles he was enlightened with. Had he known her to have been another man's wife, he would not have taken her, for he made conscience of committing adultery ; and this God takes for integrity, inasmuch as he went not against his conscience.

Ans. 1. I answer ; That all do and must acknowledge, that when a man doth so act according to an erroneous conscience (as to the matter of fact, taking that to be a duty or lawful which is a heinous sin, and which is incompatible with the state of grace for the present), though in this he principally acts out of and according to his conscience, yet therein he hath not that integrity which is required to salvation. For example, Paul thought verily he ought to persecute the church ; and what he did therein, he did out of conscience ; yet he was far enough off from sincerity or integrity, for the matter of fact could not stand with godliness. Now as conscience may thus, in the matter it directs, be damnably erroneous, unto the prejudice and certain hazard (as to the present) of man's salvation, so it may be, and is much rather and more usually defiled, and deficient, and false unto God, in respect of the manner of performance, and in respect of the end it moves for ; and even when yet it guides aright unto what is the right matter of the duty, yea, and is obeyed therein by the heart. Holiness and integrity do always essentially lie in urging to the right manner, and propounding right ends in duties, but it doth not always consist essentially in the matter, or outward duty to be performed. An action for matter mistaken may yet in respect of the ends of it be accepted, as in David's offering to build a temple; but not *è contra*. So that in these cases what thou dost is out of conscience, but far off from integrity. The bow may be a strong bow, and the arrow may be good, but if the eye that shoot it be a-squint, and aims not at the right mark, the shot miscarries ; so it is here.

Ans. 2. What is truly and properly integrity, but a conformity of a man's heart and actions unto the rule ? Even as truth is said to be an agreeableness unto that which is its rule ; as truth in a man's speeches is an agreeableness to what is in the things that a man speaks of; and truth in the things themselves is a conformity to those ideas or images of them which are in the mind of God, the fountain of truth. Now every man's conscience being every man's immediate rule and square, hence, when a man's actions are conformed unto the light that is therein, there may be said to be (as to that respect, and within that sphere) an integrity in the action which a man doth according to his light. But there is a higher rule above conscience (' there is a higher than they,' as Solomon speaks, and one ' greater than our consciences,' as John says) even the word of God, which consists of spirit as well as the letter, and so is ' a two-edged sword, dividing between the marrow and the bones, which is a judge and a discerner of the thoughts and intents of the heart,' Heb. iv. 12. And to this spiritual light conscience itself must be conformed, set, and turned, and by this light the goodness of conscience is alone to be measured ; and yet natural conscience utterly swerves from this light, even when it directs to the letter and outward action. Hence therefore those actions, so performed, according to this light and dictate of conscience, want that integrity which is the truth and soul of them; because they are not conformed to, nor agreeing with the supreme rule. It is a conscientious work, but not a work wrought in God ; because though it is a conscience, yet not a 'conscience of God' (as Peter speaks) in the man which doth it. For example, take a church-dial that is joined to a clock ; although the dial follows the clock never so truly, and so on its part there is a conformity to its next rule, yet if the clock be not set to the sun, that is the supreme moderator and keeper of time, it cannot be said to be a true dial, nor a true clock. For both the clock and it also are appointed to tell the true hour of the day, wherein if they fail, they swerve from their ordination they were (as such) made for. So when the dial of thy outward actions agrees with the clock of thy conscience, and thy hand turns as the clock moves it, yet if conscience itself be not set right, and made conformable to God's interest and ends, who is the supreme rule of goodness and integrity, both are false to him, and err in what he is most concerned. In a word, as truth is *conformitas rei cum archetypo summo*, so integrity of heart is conformity of conscience, and of all in the heart, to the highest rule. And yet when a man speaks as he thinks, and what he says is an untruth, though indeed it is not a lie, for there is some integrity in his speech, yet there is not an absolute integrity in relation to the thing that is spoken, for it is falsehood, and that which he ought not to speak. So it is here in this case.

Ans. 3. As for that allegation concerning Abimelech, that his following his light of conscience was acknowledged integrity by God himself, the answer is,

(1.) That that speech of God being in answer unto Abimelech's plea made, it is to be understood as spoken in the same sense that Abimelech himself meant it. God talked now with a heathen, and speaks not in the language of his sanctuary, nor in the dialect of that court he means to keep at the day of judgment, but, by way of concession, acknowledgeth such an integrity to have been therein, as Abimelech stood upon, viz., a moral integrity; which is, when the action that is outward agrees to the inward light that is in a man, and so is an integrity in its kind, but not an evangelical integrity, such as should be accepted to the salvation of a man's person. If you bring me a brass shilling, and plead that it is good brass, good metal, I should readily acknowledge it such ; but if you press me to take it for a shilling, or demand if it be good coin, I deny it. Thus, in Ezekiel also, God speaks in their language when he says, ' If a righteous man fall from his righteousness,' &c. And such also was that speech of Paul, when speaking of his unregenerate estate he says of himself, that ' as touching the righteousness which is in the law, he was blameless,' Phil. iii. 6, 7, which must be understood of that kind of righteousness whereof he was there treating, which was that righteousness which was current among his fellow-pharisees. So (says he, ver. 5), ' I was according to the law a Pharisee.' Yea (ver. 6), he reckons together with it, ' persecuting the church ;' and all this the Pharisees judged an excellency. And he speaks in all this but their language. And he doth the very same, being called

before a court of Pharisees (Acts xxiii. 1), where, being accused and brought
before them as guilty of high crimes, he makes his apology, and justifies
his whole cause in these words, ' I have lived in all good conscience before
God to this day.' He speaks this in their dialect, according to what they
who accused him, according to their principles, accounted a good conscience. And, besides that, it had been to no purpose to have alleged his
integrity as a regenerate Christian, unto them that were no way apprehensive of it : the 6th verse shews also that his purpose was to get off from
these his enemies by pleading their principles, and so in their sense he
might well say (as he doth), I have lived in all good conscience to this day.
For what they counted living in a good conscience (and was the truth in
him) that he had done all his life. He had followed his conscience in all
things according to their strictest principles. But if you had brought him
before God's court, and bidden him speak for himself, you should have
found him in another tone, as (in the same Phil. iii. 9) you hear him
uttering of himself, how for ten thousand worlds he would not be found in
that righteousness. ' That I may be found in Christ' (says he), ' not having
mine own righteousness, which is of the law.' Now then, as Paul, speaking before the Pharisees, to justify himself as in man's court, speaks in
their dialect; so God, speaking to a heathen (Abimelech), answers him
in his, when he acknowledgeth in that action integrity to have been
in him.

Or else (2.) It may be termed comparative integrity as to that particular, in comparison to other actions and carriages of his against conscience,
and acts of other men who sin against their consciences : as a judge, that
is free from bribes, and partiality, and injustice, is said to be a man of
integrity ; that is, he is comparatively such as a judge, though not in other
respects as a man personally. He may do justice out of vainglory or importunity, as that unjust judge did in the Gospel ; and this is comparative
integrity, because he is free from those common corruptions in judging that
others are subject to. And so compare the carriage of Abimelech's heart
in this, with the ways of other heathens, and it was integrity ; or with
other of his actions, and it was integrity : but it was not absolutely so.

CHAPTER IX.

*That the natural conscience may approve of the law, and commend the duties
enjoined, yet it is deficient in those acts.—A discovery of those defects.*

The next head belonging to this discovery, is a consideration of the
defects of natural conscience in all those effects fore-mentioned, which are
reduced into two generals.

I. A respect of what good the law requires.

II. A restraint of sin or evil.

I. As to a respect of what is good ; the two first effects are,

1. That the conscience approves of the law and duties thereof as good.

2. That it commends them as such to the heart, and binds the soul over
to the performance of them.

The query then is, whether these two be not the same with what are the
proper effects of grace (as to these two particulars) and what difference that
is specifical may be assigned thereto. For, Rom. vii. 16, this is recorded
by Paul in the name of men regenerate, and as the voice proper to them—

it is the voice of Jacob—to ' consent to the law that it is good.' And so, in Rom. xii. 2, to prove what is the good will of God, is a proper effect of the renewing of the mind : ' And be not conformed to this world, but be ye transformed by the renewing of your mind, that ye may prove what is that good, that acceptable, and perfect will of God.'

To which I answer,

Ans. 1. It is true there is a great seeming affinity and likeness between the approbation and the instigation of natural conscience and renewed conscience. For the same word, the very same, would not have been used to express the one and the other by the apostle, Rom. ii. 18, and Phil. i. 10. Of an unregenerate Jew he says in the one place, ' Thou knowest his will, and approvest the things that are excellent ;' that is, the things of the law as excellent and good ; and in the other, Phil. i. 10, praying for knowledge to be given to the Philippians (and if there were any knowledge better than this, surely he would wish them it), ' I pray,' &c., ' that ye may approve the things that are excellent.' The words are the very same, and δοκιμάζειν, the word there, is the same that is used, Rom. xii. 2, when the knowledge of a renewed mind is spoken of. And it is taken from a goldsmith, that both tries and allows of silver as good and current. And silver so tried is called δοκιμόν. So as indeed there must needs be a likeness.

Ans. 2. The difference or deficiency of natural conscience will be discovered by two things. An inquiry

(1.) Into the several grounds of the assent of regenerate and unregenerate men's consciences.

(2.) The differing manner of their assent. And the question in both is, what is that proper goodness or excellency, for which the one or the other doth approve of the law as good.

First, For unregenerate there are two grounds, and perhaps many other, which may help forward this assent.

[1.] Some for the wisdom and concordancy unto reason which appears in that law, and the commands thereof. As reason is man's excellency, so what agrees with reason it approves as most excellent. The heathens, as you heard, magnified the dictates of conscience under the notion of right reason, as the general title they gave thereto, and so was the ground of their assent and approbation. Now, the duties of the law agree with the common principles of right reason in men, and the deductions out of those common principles, and also the rules of it, have the greatest harmony and agreement in them, one with the other, that may be. And so far as reason doth apprehend this, so far doth natural knowledge and conscience acknowledge a goodness and an excellency therein. And to shew this was the ground of the assent to it, we have an express scripture, speaking of the Gentiles and their approbation of Moses's law, as it was given to the Jews. And Deut. iv. 6, ' This is your wisdom in the sight of all nations, which shall hear all these statutes, and shall say, This is a wise and an understanding people.' It is, you see, the wisdom, the harmony to reason, they are taken with, and unto which the law did super-eminently approve itself. This was Gallio's principle : Acts xviii. 14, ' And when Paul was now about to open his mouth, Gallio said unto the Jews, If it were a matter of wrong or wicked lewdness, O ye Jews, reason would that I shall bear with you.' He saw reason why wrong and wickedness should be punished, but for God's worship he saw none. If it were a matter of wrong and wickedness, reason would, says he, or as in the original, κατὰ λόγον, ' according to reason I would bear with you ;' that is, listen to you. But God's worship and Paul's doctrine he saw no reason for, and so it was out of his element; besides or above the rule he judged of things by, and he thought it a just excuse. You see, he made reason his professed rule, and as far as that gave him light for his particular light, so far he judged of things of this nature; and if others go further, yet still by the same rule. Thus men in the church, seeing no reason for the spiritual part of religion, and strictness in God's ways, therefore account the ways of God foolishness, 1 Cor. ii. 14. The reason is, because they see not the reason of them, for what we see no reason for we use to account folly.

[2.] A second ground which works on others to assent to the law, that it is good, is, that they see how the whole and the particular laws thereof do tend to the good of men, and many of the laws to a general and common good. God hath moulded and fitted the commandments to the condition of the reasonable creatures, and their good, according to their condition in this world, as well as for his own glory, and to sanctify himself: Deut. x. 13, 'which I command thee for thy good.' That consideration is put in as the motive to obedience, as being found in the law. Men see that the tendency of the duties of the first table are for the good of men's souls. Their consciences acknowledge there is a God; and if so, then he must be worshipped, or they cannot be quiet or happy. They have immortal souls, that must live in another world, and therefore it is meet to apply themselves to this God, according as he hath given command how he will be worshipped. Then for the commands of the second table, all may readily see how they manifestly tend unto the general good of men. As the fifth commandment, if there were not superiority and obedience, as to parents, magistrates, &c., the world would prey one upon another, and all fall into confusion; we should teach our children to despise us, when we come to be old and stand in need of their help. 'Thou shalt not murder,' it is a guard to the lives of all; 'Thou shalt not steal,' a fence and hedge to the goods of all men; 'Nor commit adultery,' this proved that their own children, and not strangers, should inherit men's estates. Such considerations as these are found in most of the commandments; and accordingly these, or whatever else like these, may cause them thus to approve them.

I come to the grounds whereupon a regenerate man doth further assent unto their goodness, upon which, to be sure, an unregenerate man doth not.

1. Not only because it accords with reason, but also because it is an expression of God's most blessed will, which is the supreme rule of goodness. And this especially commends it to a regenerate man also; yea, and this commends it to him enough as good, in some particulars wherein yet he sees no reason for it at present. David admires indeed the equity, the wisdom in the law, for which he terms them the 'wonderful things of the law.' But that which commends it most to him was, that it was 'the law of his mouth,' as his expression is, Ps. cxix.; his will, his command, who was the righteous and the holy God: Ps. cxix. 137, 138, 'Righteous thou art, O Lord, and upright are thy judgments; and thy testimonies that thou hast commanded are righteous and very faithful.' He assents to their goodness, because God commands them, Rom. xii. 1, 2. Though the service he is to perform to God be reasonable service (as some understand the word), yet the goodness that a renewed mind approves in it is, that it is 'the good and acceptable will of God.' And that is the goodness which the τὸ δοκιμάζειν, or the approbation of a renewed mind there spoken of, pitcheth upon more eminently. That it is that which God

commands, and that which God is pleased to accept when performed, this is it endears it to him, and for which he accounts it good. And therefore though he should see no reason, yet that it is God's will is enough to commend it to his conscience. So it was to Abraham, when God bade him sacrifice his son. So to Eli: ' It is the Lord' (says he, 1 Sam. iii. 18), ' let him do what seemeth to him good.' What God thought good, he should think so too. Which holds, as to endure God's suffering will, which was the case there, so to do his commanding will. There is the same reason for both. You may see this in Christ, Ps. xl. and Heb. x. compared, ' Thy law is in mine heart;' Ps. xl. 8, 'And I come to do thy will.' This principally commended the command of laying down his life, that it was his Father's will: ' Thy will be done;' and 'As my father hath given commandment, so do I,' John xiv. 31.

2. The most proper goodness for which a regenerate man assents to the law is, that in the spiritual part of it it is the image of God's holiness, and tends to set up God in the hearts and lives of men. We know ' the law is holy and good,' Rom. vii.; which, ver. 14, he speaks in respect of the spiritualness of it. Ps. cxix. 140, ' Thy law is pure,' says David, ' therefore thy servant loves it.' Purity is the holiness of it, as it is the image of God's purity: ' Blessed are the pure in heart,' that is, the holy in heart. And all holiness lies in setting God up. And the more of this he spies stamped upon any command, the more he assents to the commandment as good. To which purpose it is observable, Neh. ix. 13, 14, that having said that God gave them good laws and statutes, and so calling them good because God gave them, he instanceth in the following verse only that of the Sabbath: Oh! that commandment, it was a good commandment indeed! And why? But because it was to be kept holy to God; God is to be sanctified upon that day; and to that end it was appointed, and a whole day set apart to that end. This took his heart.

The second thing I mentioned to manifest this difference, was the differing manner of this assent of the one and the other. In an unregenerate man it is rather an assent of reverence than of free approbation.

There is a ' majesty of the Lord's,' which shines in the uprightness of his law, and in the lives of his saints, as they are conformed thereto, Isa. xxvi. 10. The life of this transcendental goodness of holiness shining in the law, lights upon the conscience, as the splendour of the sun doth upon a sore eye, and finding it hath a commanding brightness in it, it cannot but yield to be glorious. For if it should deny this, its own winking at it, and being dazzled with it, would confute itself. And this the apostle holds forth, 2 Cor. iii. 7, alleging concerning the law, that such was the glory that shined in Moses his countenance, who was the deliverer of it, that the people could not stedfastly behold it. It was so as they could not but acknowledge that there was a glory in it, which typified forth what their hearts did towards the law itself. But as I said before, this is rather a commanded, extorted, reverential assent the conscience gives to this its goodness, than free, and out of liking and ingenuous estimation of it. So as men's consciences rather say as those in Acts iv. 16, ' We cannot deny it,' than that we do freely like it. Look what kind of approbation their hearts give to the holiness and righteousness that shines in an upright man, the same and no other it doth or can give to the law itself. For the reason of both is the same ; holiness in a godly man being but the same law written in his life, that is given in the word. Now, then, observe what kind of approbation it is a wicked man gives unto the holiness of an upright man,

and the ground of it. Herod he was convinced of John's holiness and justness, it was an assent of fear and reverence : ' He knew,' says the text, ' he
was a just and an holy man,' Mark vi. 20. But withal it is said, ' Herod
feared John, knowing he was a just man, and an holy, and observed him.'
And thus it is that men assent to the law as holy. That part of it which
reveals the image and the glory of God in it, it commands an assent and a
subjection to it, rather than they freely give it; an assent of reverence, not
of love. So then it is rather assent in a wicked man, than consent, which
implies a willing yielding up the mind to it, and of all in a man. That
word used, Rom. vii. 16, συμφήμι τῷ νόμῳ, ' I consent to the law,' is empha-
tical. It Englished, is this, ' I say together with the law, that it is good :'
implying that it is free and ingenuous, and that all in a man together say
and join with the conscience, that it is a good law; there was a joint vote or
suffrage of all the faculties. Here is consent, not assent only. It is one
thing to ' receive the truth,' another thing to ' receive it in the love of it.'
Those in the Thessalonians received the truth, but not in the love of it ;
they *assented* to it, but they *consented* not to it. And therefore, if you
observe it in that place before quoted, Phil i. 10, though the same phrase
is used that is used, Rom. ii., of an unregenerated man, that the one is
said to ' approve things excellent,' as well as the other, yet there is this
added by way of difference, ' that your love may abound in knowledge, that
ye may approve the things that are excellent.' It is an approbation out
of knowledge, rooted in or joined with love.

And that wicked men's assent is but such as hath been described, appears
by this, that they wish there was no such law, no such duties to bind them.
As Balaam, though he assented to that word God gave him, and could
speak no other, yet wished for, and desired some other message, yea, the
contrary : so doth the conscience and heart of an unregenerate man. And
therefore, Jer. v. 5, their knowledge of the law is compared to bonds ; as
also, Ps. ii., to cords. For as they endeavour to imprison their light in
unrighteousness, so they account themselves as prisoners fettered with the
cords of it, which they would break or shake off. Whereas a regenerate
man looks on them as bracelets ;—(so Prov. vi. 21, 22, ' Bind them about
thine heart, and tie them about thy neck')—which a man puts voluntarily
upon him, and looks at as ornaments. For though they reverence the law,
yet they may wish it were not. Reverence is often severed from love. When
an austere holy tutor keeps a rakehell in awe, he may reverence his tutor
much, as a man that is good, and wisheth his good, and yet wish he were
from him, and out of his tuition.

The second effect mentioned was, that conscience commends the law
to the heart as good, and lays an injunction upon it, for the performance
of it.

There are two things in natural conscience makes it put two steps towards
this, but there is a third in which it fails, and makes a halt.

1. Conscience assents to the goodness of the duties of the law in the
general, that they are good to be done in such respects fore-mentioned.

And 2. It further also particularly tells the heart, that it ought now at
this time to do them ; yet it cannot bring the heart to assent, that the performance of these duties are particularly good to him, that is, that his good
lies in the performance of them.

Or thus ; there is, 1, An assent of reason, that in general it is good ;
2. An assent of his subjection to it, that he ought to do it out of a sense of
the majesty and superiority it hath over him ; but, 3. Not an assent of

suitableness, or sympathy, or mutual delight, that it is best for him ; which assent is in a godly man's judgment to be found. For as he is said to ' consent to the law that it is good,' so to delight in the law as good. And the word συνήδομαι, implies a joint delight, a concurrence of all in him in that delight. Even as that other word συμφήμι, imported a joint sufferage or consent, and both as between things suitable, both argued the commands as suited his whole man ; Ps. cxix. 70 sets forth and illustrates his sense and meaning herein by this opposite comparison, ' Their heart is as fat as grease, but I delight in thy law.' The comparison carries this with it, that the same natural delight which in outward things they found suiting with and nourishing their carnal hearts to a fatness and contentment, the same I find in thy law, as suiting all within my soul ; and verse 72, ' The law of thy mouth is better to me than thousands of gold and silver.' Not better in itself only, but better to me, says he. And this ariseth out of a suitableness and sweetness of taste, which ver. 66 holds forth, ' Teach me good judgment and knowledge.' That which is translated good judgment signifies good taste ; it being the same word that is used, Ps. xxxiv. 9, ' Taste and see how good the Lord is.' So David prayed there for two sorts of knowledge of the things of the law : 1. *Scientiam visûs*, which he calls knowledge, whereby men see the commandments to be good in the general ; and not this only, but also, 2dly, *Scientiam gustûs*, knowledge of taste, that is, that he might have a rectified palate to taste the goodness that is in the commandments and the keeping of them. And this will lead us to another note of difference, besides the former given upon that place Phil. i. 10 (where, when the same words are used of a regenerate man's approving that are used of an unregenerate man's, Rom. ii. 18, as was shewed ; and therefore we had need to take hold of what differences the place will give), and it is the same we are now upon, he prays they may abound in all knowledge and in all sense : πάσῃ αἰθήσει, a knowledge that had sense and taste joined with it, that so they might, namely, upon such a knowledge, ' approve the things that are excellent.' And so this prayer of Paul's accords fully with that of David, ' Give me good judgment, or sense of taste and knowledge ;' which two words Paul useth, and our translators have rendered, as the former, ' knowledge and judgment.' And accordingly ver. 68 of that psalm, we find the greatest good that David desired, was ' to know and keep these statutes ;' his words are these, ' Lord, thou art good, and dost good.' And what is the mind and meaning of these so deep concernments ? But this : ' Lord, as thou hast infinite goodness in thee, and as ever thou intendest to do me good, yea, and if ever thou wilt do any good for me, do this.' What ? ' Teach me thy statutes.' If God from heaven should have bidden him to ask one request that was most eminent in his heart and desires, it should have been this, ' Teach me thy statutes.' This is a preface to a petition which his heart must be in, in a peculiar and extraordinary manner affected with, that he should urge it upon the highest consideration that can be alleged. For he calls upon, and urgeth, all the goodness that is in God's nature, ' Thou art good ;' and also all those vast purposes of his doing us good, which is ' above all we are able to ask or think.'

Natural conscience is able to judge in the general, that the law is better than sin, and that to obey it is better. Therefore Peter appeals even to those wicked Pharisees, Acts iv. 19, ' Whether is it better to obey God or man, judge ye.' And Socrates had done the like even to the consciences of the heathen Athenians, in the same words well nigh ; so that, take it in the abstract proposal of it, and no man can deny it. But out of suitableness,

&c., to judge that it was better for them in particular; as David said, 'the law of thy mouth is better *to me*;' this particular assent out of experience, is joined with the taste which uregenerate men want. It is an assent, I say, out of experience of their goodness. For as they find a suitableness to them in themselves, and a taste of their goodness, so they find they do them good. So Micah ii. 7, 'Do not my words do good to them that are good?'

And whereas it will be objected, Doth not conscience tell men it would be better for them if they would obey, and that it will go worse with them if they do not, and so presents the duty as particularly best for them?

Therefore I add this third conclusion concerning their assent: That it is one thing to present a thing as good for me by consequent, another thing as good to me simply considered in itself such; as for example, a physician presents a potion to a patient, and bids him drink it, tells him that it is good for him, that is, by consequent good for him, because it will restore him and deliver him from death. But all the physicians in the world can never persuade him, that it is simply good, and of itself good for him; for his own smell, palate, and stomach tell him to his teeth the contrary, and are ready to rise up against it. And thus even when conscience tells a man such and such duties of the law are good for him, it can nor doth say no more in effect but that they are good by consequent, that the omission of them will be death to him. But not all the angels in heaven, nor ministers on earth, can never work an assent in him, that in themselves they are good for him, *per se*, simply good. No; for his corrupt heart and judgment tells him the contrary, and he finds no relish in them, in his knowledge of sense (spoken of), even his heart pronounceth the contrary. Thus indeed, and in this sense, a righteous man may look upon the greatest afflictions he ever had as good for him, that is, by consequent: 'It is good for me I was afflicted;' but not for themselves, no man rejoiceth in them. There is no affliction, but for the present, in itself, is grievous; yet by consequent he looks on it as good, that is, that will work for good: but at no hand as upon things which a man would have to choose, as wherein his happiness lies. But, lo! that you may discern upon what terms a godly man judgeth them good; afflictions (which are in themselves so grievous) David esteemed good, and profitable and comfortable unto him; for this reason, that God used them as means to teach him his statutes. Thus, Ps. cxix. 71, 'It was good for me that I was afflicted, that I might learn thy statutes.' That must needs be good simply and in itself to a man's esteem, which will sweeten and make afflictions, and the bitterest of afflictions, good in his esteem. Yet such are God's statutes to a holy heart. So that, to conclude, this natural conscience in such a man may tell him, that this or that duty is to be done, and that he had best do it, or that it is best to be done; but never that the very doing of it is best for him. Of the bitter potion, they may say it is best to be drunk by them: but that it should be judged and found best by a man in the present drinking of it, as food is, so it is not, nor can be. And yet the commandments were such to David; 'In keeping thy commandments there is great reward,' Ps. xix. This for the two first effects.

CHAPTER X.

Though natural conscience may prevail with men to do the duties required,
yet not for conscience sake, in the sense which the Scripture gives.

Natural conscience prevails with men to do that good which it enjoins ; and that not only out of outward respects or worldly motives, but upon principles and workings of conscience. But the main question or thing to be searched out in this is, what it is in Scripture sense truly and accept- ably to do a thing ' for conscience sake.' For discovery of which I must have recourse, *First*, in the general, unto what I have before premised as an undoubted and undeniable conclusion (by which all our actions shall be judged at the latter day), that in the balance and estimate of the Scripture, nothing is acceptably done for conscience sake, but what is principally done for God as our utmost end, and for conscience principally as respecting God as such. Which laid as a foundation (and it is the great foundation of the practic part of our religion), all under-pretences of doing things for conscience, with which men soothe up themselves, will presently vanish and come to nothing. When the apostle speaks of the actings of that affection of ' sorrow for sin,' 2 Cor. vii. 9, ' I rejoice not ' (says he) ' in that ye sorrowed, but in that ye sorrowed κατὰ Θεὸν, that is, for and accord- ing to God,' and as looking at God and his interest as the moving cause thereto. The rule there given concerning the acceptableness of that affec- tion of sorrow for sin, for its object, holds true and good of conscience and every faculty, and the workings of it. So that if you sorrow for sin com- mitted against God, yet if not κατὰ Θεὸν, respecting him chiefly therein, it is not, in Scripture sense, accounted godly sorrow. And so, if you do never so much, out of never so violent and efficacious impulses of con- science, yet if conscience doth not therein move in the virtue of respect to God chiefly, it is not to be accounted a good conscience. And this latter is founded upon the same equitable reason whereupon the former is founded. For there is the same measure of holiness in one faculty that is to be found in another. If sorrow for sin stirs upon under-respects, and not for God, it is not true sorrow, although sorrow for sin. So if conscience in thee stirs up any under-respects (which it is capable of), and not chiefly for God, it is not conscience for God, though conscionable respects may move thee.

So, then, here lies the spirit of the answer to these allegations of the effects of natural conscience, which pierce through and annul them all, that in Scripture sense, and in the sense of true religion, to do a thing for con- science sake is opposed to all such respects as conscience itself is capable of, if it fall short of this.

I alleged one scripture to this purpose, unto which I shall join another, and compare both together : Rom. xiii. 5, ' Wherefore ye must needs be subject, not only for wrath, but also for conscience sake.' He had used, in the words afore, this motive for obedience to magistrates, that ' he is the minister of God, a revenger to execute wrath ' (namely, God's wrath on thee for sin), ' if thou do evil ; ' and then infers, ' Wherefore ye must needs be subject, not only for wrath, but also for conscience sake ; ' namely, to be subject to the magistrate for wrath's sake as your end ; yea, for the con- science to look up unto God, as he that pours out his wrath by him (as God speaks, 2 Chron. xii. 7, ' My wrath shall not be poured out by the hand of Shishak '). Yea, and by the same reason, to look upon him as God that will pour forth wrath himself immediately upon thee; thus, to eye God is not for conscience sake. This is but to eye his wrath and thyself, although God be objectively eyed in it. Therefore that respect which is left for conscience to eye in God, is God himself, as severed from that or the like respects. In opposition to that other of wrath, this is put, to obey for conscience sake. If you would be further satisfied herein, take and join with it 1 Peter ii. 19, 'This is thank-worthy, if for conscience towards God ye suffer grief.' He speaks to servants under froward masters, exhorting them to obey them (ver 18), as in the former place he spake to subjects to obey their magistrates, and in both singleth forth God as the chief motive, and that unto conscience. And what in the one he termeth obedience for conscience sake, in the other he termeth conscience of God, διὰ συνείδησιν Θεοῦ. Now it being evident that God subjectively hath not a conscience proper to him, his meaning therefore must be, that our consciences should be the consciences of God; that is, of God *tanquam objectum finale*, as respecting him as our end, whom our consciences should principally eye and look unto, which ver. 20 following expounds: 'This is acceptable with God' (says he), as presenting to us this motive, this will take God's heart, and be pleasing to him. So look, as sorrow, because it is moved chiefly by what concerns him, is called sorrow κατὰ Θεόν, 'sorrow for God;' or fear, when it is chiefly terminated on God, 'sanctifying and exalting God in our hearts' (as 1 Peter iii. 15) is styled the fear of God, as in like sense sincerity of heart is termed 'sincerity of God' (so in the Greek, 2 Cor. i. 12); in like manner, conscience, when it respects God chiefly, and fetcheth its motives from him, it is termed 'conscience of God,' as observing or respecting none else, or nothing else above him. It is God's conscience, in that respect, more than thine own. Yea, and if conscience had not had other respects to have been moved by, this distinction, 'conscience of God,' needed not to have been made; as not that about sorrow, which for the same cause the apostle maketh (2 Cor. vii. 9) 'sorrow for God.'

Now, this conclusion being thus firmly laid, those pretensions from the effects of natural conscience (whether that it prevaileth to carry the heart on unto action, or that not outward respects move, but principles and workings of conscience do) instantly fall to the ground upon the putting this one thing to the question, But is it 'conscience of God' that moves thee? This in general.

2. But more particularly, what do men take for what is done for conscience sake, and so judge it to be integrity?

1. Men ignorantly imagine that sincerity and integrity of heart lies in opposition to outward respects and worldly considerations. So that if a man's heart be not chiefly moved by such kind of motives, as if the wind of vainglory doth not set this mill a-going, nor the golden key of covetous desires turn not about the wards, but if they be motions from conscience within, then they think that their hearts must needs be sincere and right. But they do not consider,—

(1.) That the spring of conscience within will move not only without, but sometimes against, all such respects. So in Judas, and so in Balaam, who crossed their dearest worldly lusts; and yet the chief motive it useth shall not be taken from God himself.

2. Men will not see, nor are able to discern, that great beam that is in the eye of conscience itself, not only because it is in their own eye, but also because conscience itself is the supreme judge. They will not be brought

to imagine that self-love (that is the beam I mean) should be the predominant principle in conscience as well as in other faculties; but they think all that conscience acts must needs be sincere, not considering what that means, that there is a 'defiled conscience,' Titus i. 15, and that conscience, in its urging motives to obedience, shews itself as full of self as any other faculty. As Christ says in another case, first make thy conscience good, and then the effects will be good; otherwise, let it be conscience which prevails and acts thee, it will nothing avail thee as to salvation.

3. Again, 3dly. Men judge those only to be outward respects which are taken from things of this world, not dreaming that things of a higher order and nature (of which conscience alone is apprehensive) do become by-respects, when conscience of God is not the chief.

4. Again, men consider not that all motives moving us, or prevailing with us unto that which the inward bent and stream and current of the heart is against, are in a true sense extrinsecal and outward motives, as well as worldly, if they compare them with the movings and actings of a regenerate and renewed conscience, which works naturally, and with the joint concurrence of the rest of the faculties, as hath been said. That is properly an outward motive which is against the hair, against the nature of a thing, and *pondus* of its inclination, as when water is forced some way it would not run. Now if thy conscience moves thee (though it be thy conscience) to such duties as the frame of thine heart is wholly contrary and averse unto, as to pray, to read the word, to keep the Sabbath, unto which thou hast no inward genius nor inclination spiritual (these laws not being written in thine heart), in these thy conscience is a violent and forcible worker, as truly as when outward and worldly respects do move. You will all esteem the fear of men to be an outward motive and respect, and yet fear is an affection seated in our nature and within us, and so moves from within: and yet being pitched upon an object which overcomes us unto what else we would not do, we use to say an outward respect moves that man. The reason is the same of the motions of conscience, which is but such another principle within thee as fear is. If conscience, apprehending the wrath of God as an avenger, chiefly moves thee, thy heart is as much wrung and wrested (when thine inclination is contrary to the thing commanded) as when the fear of man doth move thee.

5. Again; men consider not that God himself and his law doth then only become an intrinsecal mover of thee in thy conscience, when thy whole soul hath first begun to own, entertain, and receive him as thy chiefest end, and so thou hast taken in his interest as natural to thee as thine own, when God is become *intimior intimo nostro*, then, and not till then, it is that conscience moves thee as an internal principle, and not before. But if God and thy soul remain still at a distance, as strangers, and thou hast not yet closed with him, all the motives that are fetched from him are foreign and outward unto thee, as much as if drawn from any worldly thing whatever.

A second mistake concerning what is done for conscience is, that men judge that what is done by means, or by the influence of conscience anyway, that it is done for conscience sake, whereas many things are done,

1. Upon the stirrings of conscience.

2. Upon respects which pertain some way unto conscience only, which yet fall short of conscience of God. And, therefore, although conscience be the principal mover and swayer of such effects, yet still in Scripture sense it is not said to be done for conscience sake. When the workings or stir-

rings and troubles of conscience set men a-work, and carry them on to actions, they then put such actions upon this account, that they are done for conscience sake ; and this falls out in two cases.

(1.) The first ordinary, when at the importunity and continual doggings and yawlings of their consciences they do what they do to satisfy their conscience, which is the heathen's phrase, *conscientiæ satisficiamus.* Conscience in many men continually lies at them to perform or do such or such a duty, and they do it. Conscience is as the disease of the wolf, if it be not fed daily with such and such duties performed, it will feed upon a man's own heart and breast. But this is not doing a thing for conscience sake, but indeed for quietness sake and for peace sake. As a man yields to, and doth many things to please a shrew, that is as a continual dropping in of rain ; a man in that case is not said to do it for her sake, but for a quiet life. Now many men have shrewish consciences, as Delilah prevailed with Samson, she wearied him of his life, Judges xvi. 16, and as that judge, Luke xviii., yielded not for the woman's sake, but for her importunity, because she wearied him. Some men love to be at ease, to have nothing lie upon their thoughts, to sleep quietly, and to keep a perpetual calm and serenity of mind ; and out of the same principle that they contrive to avoid other crosses, out of the same principle, and no other, they avoid being dogged by their consciences, take a great deal of pains to still the child. In this, though they act upon conscience, and obey conscience, yet still they do it not for God in their consciences. A master sends a constable to fetch home a runaway servant, and the constable hauls and pulls him along : he obeys properly neither the constable nor his master, but least of all his master. So it is here.

(2.) There are also over and above this ordinary working of the importunity of conscience from day to day, which prevails to action, some extraordinary terrors of conscience, which do seize upon men as arrests in the name of God, both calling upon us for arrears and non-payment of duties, as also restraining from evils we have formerly run into, and which, like a mighty stream, carry on our hearts in the current and channel of obedience ; which was Judas's case : when the wrath of God was upon his conscience, he repented, confessed, restored, and would have done anything. Now if he had lived, could he have pleaded, or at the latter day should that plea be accepted, I did all this for conscience sake ? No ; and yet all this was done upon the impulses and violent provocations of conscience. As for terrors from God, conscience is the only principle that is apprehensive of them, and all other faculties by means thereof: God is the ' Father of spirits,' and ' chastiseth men's spirits,' and conscience is that tender place which lies exposed to, and which is most sensible of his lash, and to be acted by this smart in doing, is but to be led by sense, as brutes are, and not by conscience, though conscience be that sensible part, the torture of which extorts it. Now this then is a manifest and gross mistake, that because conscience is the subject of such feelings and smarts, and therefore what men do hereupon they do for conscience sake ; that they abstain from such a sin for conscience, whenas the true English and proper sense you must resolve it into is the same with this :—a rogue dares not forswear himself for his ears' sake, nor a thief steal for his neck's sake ; so nor these men for their conscience sake, conscience being the part subjected to this punishment, anxiety, and disquietment, as those members mentioned in those other cases use to be.

To conclude ; In these cases, and of these men, it may be said, that conscience makes them do what they do, rather than that they make conscience of what is done, or of the doing of it; or they may be said to do these things for conscience, in a philosophical sense, because actings and stirrings in conscience are the efficient cause of them; but still not in a theological scripture sense, according to which (as hath been inculcated) a man is then only said to do a thing for conscience sake, when motives of God chiefly carry us on thereto.

The other head of mistakes mentioned was when such respects move us, as pertain only or properly unto conscience; and when men act upon such respects, they still think the action is done for conscience sake. This is distinct from the former; for the former speak of violent impulses of conscience efficiently, this speaks of conscionable considerations, or respects objectively. Now there are many conscionable respects which belong only to conscience below God, which act men: which yet when they find, they persuade themselves they do it for pure conscience sake.

As, 1. There is a rational principle of equity and morality. A man is alone: conscience prompts him, what thou wouldst not have another do to thee, do not to another. This is current reason. And the reason of this principle prevails with the man, and no outward respect. In this case it is certain that a mere conscionable respect prevailed. But how remote is this from conscience of God! This is conscience indeed of a just and good principle, but not of God. Men do much to stick to their own principles. Men will not be false to their own rules, nor conscious to themselves that they are so. The text here says of these Gentiles, that they were ' a law unto themselves;' and the truth is, that they made their own principles their God, and men are obedient to them as unto God, and satisfy themselves herewith.

2. Conscience of the superiority of the law, and the subjection the heart hath to it, moves men much, and is a conscientious respect beyond all outward respects. The reason of the law might and would move one, if the case were between equals, if we and the law were supposed such. Job says, chap. xxxi. 13, that he would hear his servants' cause when they spoke reason; but the law hath a natural authority, majesty, superiority over the conscience. It is the husband, the heart, the wife which (as Rom. vii. 1, 2) ' hath dominion over a man.' The mere sight of their masters, with the noise of their whips, put to flight a whole army of Russian slaves, and brought them to obedience; so upon the very hearing of a duty or a threatening, conscience acknowledgeth it ought to be subject. But still this is but conscience of the duty, or of the external part of the law, not conscience of God.

3. There is conscience of the excellency that is in virtuous actions to adorn a man; this is also a conscientious respect which natural conscience may apprehend. Plato said, that if virtue were seen with bodily eyes, it would ravish all men with the sight of it and the love of it. He saw something in it made him say so. Conscience may see and approve an excellency in many virtues, and judge and affect it as their excellency. So did Socrates. So Paul, Phil. iii. 7, accounted the righteousness of the law his excellency. He says he ' accounted it gain to him.' And therefore as the ermine, counting her white skin her excellency, when she is hunted, will die rather than go through a puddle to defile it; so will many men die rathe. than blemish or stain their innocency, as it is their excellency. And so is that of the heathen to be understood, *Oderunt peccare boni, virtutis amore*r And this men will not do though in secret; they will not be conscious of a

base act, they will not have occasion to think vilely of themselves. As a man that is of a curious, neat spirit, and affects it as an excellency, he will not do an uncomely act, no, not in secret; it is against his spirit to do it; so nor will men defile that excellency their conscience apprehends such. And it must be acknowledged that many of the heathen saw that in virtue which made them love it for its own excellency, and as it put an ornament on their souls. They professed to do things *virtutis amore*, for the love of virtue; they renounced vainglory and such outward respects in many of their actions.* This indeed was a conscientious respect in them, yet still it is not conscience of God. For if virtue be considered as an ornament (as conscience may apprehend it, which sets a man up in his own esteem and others') that adorns the mind, as learning doth, men may affect it, and love it, and seek it, but still so as it falls into the same sphere and account that glorying in any other particular doth, be it either honour or learning; yea, and if it could be supposed that a man prized true grace thus, chiefly as it is an ornament to a man's soul, but yet abstracted from God, and not directed in order to him, this would be as great a sin as those other lusts in men are, who value either honours or such other particular good things; for the reason were the same. And yet this was apparently the heathens' highest excellency, who thus left God out even in their highest attainments. But Peter speaking of a virtue (and in itself but a moral virtue), meekness, 1 Pet. iii. 4, says, that as it is directed to God, being taken up and exercised out of conscience of God, and as it is acceptable to him (as the same Peter speaks in his second chapter) so it is ' an ornament of great price with God.' And then God himself is respected in it; for nothing takes with God but what relates unto himself.

To conclude; In all these there is conscience of an idol (as Paul speaks), be it virtue for itself, be it grace, but not conscience of God. These are all conscionable respects, drugs only found in conscience's natural garden; but still the main ingredient that should set all a-work is wanting.

CHAPTER XI.

Another deficiency in natural conscience is, that it may eye the command, and yet not obey for the sake of the command, nor regard God as the utmost end in their obedience.

Another effect mentioned was that natural conscience, in its instigations to obedience, had a real respect unto God, and unto the command of God. Laban (Gen. xxxi. 29) forbare to hurt Jacob, having a respect to God's charge given over-night. So likewise did Balaam, Num. xxii. 18.

Of this I have spoken much before, what it is to have a conscience of God, and to do things from such a conscience. Yet here some things practical may be added for the discovery of this, both as to the difference in the thing itself, and also as to the deceits men run into in thinking they act for God and for his command. The foundation of which deceit lies in this, that corrupt nature in us thinks much at everything we do for God, and also having slight apprehensions and regards of God, we are apt to put him off with any kind of respects had to him; and we thereby so easily come to deceive ourselves in a conceit that we act and do for him, when it is nothing less.

1. For that respect which men may have to the command.

* Mallem famam boni viri perdere quam conscientiam.

(1.) Men may have an eye to the command, when yet they obey not for the sake of the command, and so (as one says) *Deo obtemperant, non obsequuntur*. If men take the command into their thoughts, if they look at the command as the material cause of their obedience, and the exemplary cause they are to square their actions to, they think they perform that regard to the command that is due to it, when yet they regard it not so as to do the thing because it is commanded. They look to it as their chart to direct, but not as the spring that should move and steer them in and unto their obedience. A slave may diligently repeat over and over in his thoughts, and be careful to remember exactly, the command of his master, as well as a son the command of his father ; but yet still in the slave it is not kindly obedience, such as is performed chiefly with respect to his command, as in a son it is ; whereas David, describing a godly man and his obedience, Ps. cxix. 1, 2, 3, at the 4th verse shews the ground he looks at in his obedience : ' Thou hast commanded me to keep thy precepts diligently.' Others do it out of conscience so commanding, but not out of conscience of the command, which usually appears in this, that conscience lets us alone in some commands when it is vehement in urging others.

(2.) In looking at God in their obedience, men are willing to deceive themselves many ways.

[1.] They may have a real regard unto God as the object of the service they perform, and with this they do but delude themselves, if it be not also superscribed and directed to him. Now in all duties of worship performed by us, God is the person to whom intentionally a man directeth it ; as in praying, the person spoken unto is God ; in hearing, the person that speaks to us is God, and we give him the hearing, as making account that a God speaks to us. Now, this may be, and yet still ourselves may be the final cause or end, for whose sake, and upon whose interest, the duty is performed. I may speak to a man, as the person to whom my speech is directed, when yet it is my own business for which it is intended, and so I speak but for myself. And thus a man may perform a service even to an enemy (as Laban and Balaam did), and intend and mind them as the object of their service, but not as the end. Conscience herein carries a man towards God, but this is not conscience of God. They pray toward him rather than to him. When it is said, Zech. vii. 5, ' They fast, but not to me,' it cannot be so understood as if God was not the object of the duty, or the person it was directed and addressed unto (for they could not take on them to fast but that they dealt with him, and made their supplications to him), but the defect or default that is found is, that they made him not the end of those duties. ' They fast,' says God, ' but not to me.' And yet men are content to run away with this, as that regard which is due to God, in being in some regard a real respect.

[2.] They may further look to God as the author and efficient of the command, and the rewarder of the performance of it, and the punisher of the breach of it, when still they respect him not in their obedience as the final cause. They look to him as from whom the command comes, but they obey it not for his sake, and so conscience moves from God, but not effectually for God. ' They return ' (says God) ' but not to the Most High,' Hosea vii. 16. An unregenerate man's conscience looks to God the commander, as well as a regenerate man's, but then it is either as a slave hath an eye to his master, which is termed eye-service, as not being done heartily for him (Col. iii. 22, 23, compared), or as an hireling on his master, or as a condemned man upon his judge. But a godly man looks at God as one whose interest he hath made his own, and is therefore glad that God will command him. A godly man loves the command the better because it comes from God, and loves God the better because he is pleased to command and use him. And when it is thus, then a man's works are said to be wrought in God, John iii. 21. The want of which is oppositely that which makes other men's works evil : ver 20, ' For every one that doeth evil, hateth the light, neither cometh to the light, lest his deeds should be reproved. But he that doeth truth cometh to the light, that his deeds may be made manifest that they are wrought in God.' Where you see to ' do the truth,' or to act sincerely, is all one as ' to work our works in God,' that is, chiefly upon his interest. It is termed, 2 Cor. i. 12, sincerity of God, as having respect to him, as if none else were concerned. And no other eyeing God in his commands, as appears by that place, will satisfy a regenerate conscience.

[3.] Men may have a real respect to the glory of God, when yet not to that glory which is due to his name (which the Psalmist calls for), and so not glorify him as God. Haters and persecutors of the people and children of God, and so haters of God, yet relieve themselves with this pretence (as having some respect thereto in their consciences) not only that ' they think they do God good service,' John xvi. 2, but farther, Isa. lxvi. 5, ' say, Let God be glorified.' ' Hear the word of the Lord, ye that tremble at his word. Your brethren that hated you, that cast you out for my name's sake, said, Let the Lord be glorified. But he shall appear to your joy, and they shall be ashamed.'

But, *first*, they do but say it, as there, and that faintly ; and when their great zeal is in the prosecution of their lusts of malice, they colour it over with taking that respect into their thoughts, and so relieve themselves with the pretence of it.

And *secondly ;* If the thought thereof rise up to a zeal of God, as in Paul and the Jews, Rom. x. 3, it did, and may do in others, in what is truly the service of God, yet it still comes in but secondarily, not as the predominant end and motive, but as an end taken in by the by. They act as a man that at once can pleasure himself and another, and who will be glad it falls out so well, that what is done for himself chiefly is also a kindness to another. And thus a man may be glad when he can pleasure an enemy when withal he serves himself, and will make the best of such a kindness, as if he did it for him.

Thirdly ; And again, men may aim at doing service to God, as far as they use to aim at serving men, as their king, as their country : as soldiers and subjects use to say that they do service to their king and country, as it is a common cause, magnified and cried up to do so ; and in this service they use to spend their bloods. And after the same manner was Paul zealous for God and the religion of the Jews, as a man would be for his king or the cause of religion, as it is a cause in common. But thus only to aim at serving God is too low for him. It is not enough to aim at God thus far in thy service, as much as thou wouldst aim at men. But if thou glorifiest not God as God, Rom. i. 21 ; that is, as such a great God ought to be glorified, and transcendently set up above all creatures, even above thyself; thou dost not glorify God as thou oughtest. Many aim at glorifying God as far as they would serve a man, a superior ; but they must glorify him as God ; that is, above all else, even themselves and all their own interests ; not only by going against their interests for him, but when both fall in, yet to be moved by his above their own.

Fourthly and lastly ; There is no deceit more general than is this, viz., that if in the motion to any duty, the considerations of God and his command were the first propounders or motioners thereof in a man's conscience, then the man thinks them to be the chiefest swaying motives. If these get but the start, and have but the priority of time, if they put forth the first hand out of the womb, men then put the birthright, the dominion, or prerogative upon them; and this they do, though worldly or other self-ends do carry the work on, and are the most effectual agents to bring it to the birth. You will find that when a man is to do any action that is good, upon the motion, twenty by-ends will come in about him, like so many beggars about a great man, if he offers to stir abroad. Now, the main repute of bringing forth the action will not be cast on that which was the first propounder, but on that which was the main and strongest stickler in it, and promoted it, and brought it forth to execution. Now, conscience is apt, in most such actions, if not to be the first in them, yet to shuffle in such considerations as wherein God should be respected, and then to cry, this is done for God. Jehu was indeed first moved and set a-work by a prophet, and by God and his conscience, to destroy idolatry and Ahab's house, but it was respect to his kingdom which maintained the action, and which fell in and carried him through in it. And yet, because conscience had some hand in it, he in his deceitful thoughts ascribes all to it, entitleth zeal for God to be the only author of it: 'See my zeal' (says he) 'for the Lord of hosts.' Conscience often doth but cast in the bill, and make the motion, and rule the suit; and worldly by-ends follow it, bear the charges, and are the great promoters in it; yet then it must needs be made an act of conscience, and the verdict is given in its name alone, as the foreman of that jury.

CHAPTER XII.

The deficiency of natural conscience in another of its effects, viz., in speaking peace to men upon their doing well.

2. The last effect of natural conscience in respect of what is good is, that it gives forth peace upon doing well, as God's commissioner. And of this tranquillity of mind, which accompanies doing virtuously, great things are spoken by heathens, and (as would seem) out of their own experience.

And truly in answer unto this I would in the first place readily grant, that God, even God himself, in and by an unregenerate man's conscience, doth for particular actions speak an approbation and encouragement when they do well. That outward blessings and outward peace in this life were dispensed under the Old Testament (and are now) even to carnal Jews and Gentiles, upon their outward doings that were righteous, few if any man denies; when yet their persons were, and are, for the same actions, liable to eternal wrath. Now that some inward peace from God should be vouchsafed their spirits upon such actings, by which he should so far appear to approve and own actions that are materially good, with a different respect from what are evil; this holds but a due proportion with that other dispensation of God. 'The judgment of God is according to truth' (says the apostle, Rom. ii. 2); that is, God will ever acknowledge a thing to be what in truth it is, and so will own what is good so far as it is good. Yea, even at the latter day, then when he pronounceth some actions to have been deficient, and in respect of the manner of performance deserving wrath and condemnation, yet then, as a righteous judge, he will acknowledge what was any way good therein, with any other sort of goodness. For every man shall be judged, with all the abatements his condition did or would afford, even where he perisheth : Rom. ii. 12, 'For as many as have sinned without law, shall also perish without law ; and as many as have sinned in the law, shall be judged by the law.' And conscience, as well in excusing (which is, when a man hath done a good action) as in accusing for what is evil, is said συμμαρτυρεῖν, to 'witness with,' Rom. ii. 15. Witness with whom ? Even with God in either, God in the one witnessing with the conscience as well as in the other. And as the directing light of conscience is from God (as hath been said), so also the excusing light may, *ad tantum*, that is, in some measure, be also ascribed unto him. I would but further propound Jehu's case, and instance to any sober man, for the confirmation both of this truth, and the reasons for it which I even now alleged : 2 Kings x. 30, it is expressly said that ' God said unto Jehu, Because that thou hast done well in executing that which was right in my eyes, and hast done unto the house of Ahab according to all that was in mine heart.' God, whether by himself, or by a prophet, or otherwise, I need not dispute, testified to him the approbation of this fact as good. Now hereupon I urge, that what God spake to his outward ears, the same thing this same God might, yea, and did speak to his conscience, which is the inward ear, apprehensive of what God doth speak. Yea, and further, God did speak this to shew his approbation of it, to the end that his conscience should know so much, and view it with comfort. And then God also makes an outward promise hereupon, ' Thy children of the fourth generation shall sit upon the throne of Israel.' This also his conscience, with a joy and contentment, might take in from God, as a reward of his well-doing ; which makes good the proposition of that reason afore alleged. I might say the like in the case of God's acknowledging Abimelech's integrity to himself, in that sense he apologizeth for himself, Gen. xx. 5, 6.

Yet, secondly, I say (that this concession may not be mistaken), that though God thus far doth witness with conscience, in approbation of what is good in the fact, yet natural conscience usually doth (as it is apt through the defilement of it) carry on its own testimony further than God ever intended.

(1.) Conscience proceeds too far in assuming and taking upon it this occasion to pronounce peace to the state of the person, which is as false a conclusion upon the premises in itself as pernicious to the man. Cain's conscience, when it was once struck and blasted from God with the guilt of killing his brother, ran out in a despairing conclusion, ' My sin is greater than that it may be forgiven,' Gen. iv. 13. This sense the original bears, and is so varied in the margin. Here conscience carried it on further than that which God had spoken to his conscience, for his sin was not such but it might have been forgiven ; so now, on the contrary, when God gives forth and speaks such an imperfect approbation of the fact for the outward performance of it, conscience runs away with it, and speaks peace to the state of the man, and from outward carriages pronounceth justification and eternal peace. Thus Paul once thought himself alive, from his doing the law ; and so they cry ' Peace, peace, when there is nó peace,' as the scripture speaks. And so here that distinction interpreters give, upon that of Abimelech's integrity, holds true. There is *integritas facti, et integritas personæ*, an approbation of the particular fact, where there is not so of the person and his state. I might give many instances of this kind, how when God speaks but so far to a thing, men's hearts, in the application and conclusion, fall into the greatest delusions. This is true in men godly as well as unregenerate. No man shall draw near to God but God will so far draw near to him. A temporary believer, that is not in the state of grace, if he doth come and pray to God fervently, God will put a joy into his heart, to encourage him to come again. No man shall set a step towards God but God will set a step towards him. But then men mistake, to the perdition of their own souls, that what is really intended but an encouragement, they draw and conclude to be an acceptation of their persons to eternal life, and account joy *from* God to be joy *in* God.

(2.) A second error which natural conscience runs into, is even concerning matters of fact, inasmuch as God approving the fact in and with conscience, but so as it is morally good ; conscience is apt to pronounce the same sentence, *super totum*, upon the whole of it, the carriage of the heart in it, and all, and often blesseth and applauds itself in it. This is evident in Jehu, whose conscience shewed itself unfaithful to God and him thus, that he overlooked the carriage of his heart in it, and the carnal ends he drave therein, and yet pronounced peace to himself upon the whole, both for matter and manner : ' Come, see my zeal,' says he, ' for the Lord of hosts ; ' whenas the same God pronounceth of the very same fact, in respect of his carnal ends, that were predominant in it, and acted him, that it was murder, Hos. i. 4. So that I may apply what befell that good Lord Protector in the reign of Edward the VI. (who was acquitted of treason, and yet condemned for felony), unto what befalls an unregenerate man in this respect, that, namely, whilst for the outward fact God in this life gives him such an answerable approbation as hath been spoken of, yet at the same time he binds over his person to eternal wrath for treason against himself, in not having made him his chiefest end therein, nor aimed at his glory, which is the highest treason againt the sovereign God.

This hath been spoken by way of concession herein, and to clear it from mistakes. I come now to a more set examination of the difference natural conscience gives, from that which a regenerate man hath. In the examination whereof I shall consider three things.

1. The differing well-springs and fountains, or originals, whence peace is fetched.

2. The ways of peace (as the Scripture phrase is) which natural conscience takes to fetch and bring in peace, differing from what the Spirit of God in a true believer carries on and directs the heart unto.

3. I shall cast in some differences concerning the peace itself.

1. For the source or originals of true peace and false, I shall fully couch my intendments in it under this following metaphor and allegory.

(1.) You may remember how in this discourse we have carried in our eye those two dividing covenants of grace and of works, under one of which all men are at present. Unregenerate men are under the covenant of works, regenerate under that of grace. And I have also shewn how each of these have a lordship or dominion over those that are under them, Rom. vi. 14, Rom. vii. 1. And so they have the power of life and death, peace or wrath, according as men demean themselves towards them. It was a royalty which the covenant of works once had, to give life and peace, and to pronounce the sentence hereof, which stood good in law : ' The commandment' (or covenant of works) ' was ordained' (originally) ' unto life,' says Paul, Rom. vii. 10, and ' The man that doeth them shall live in them,' Gal. iii. 12 ; and that is all one as to have peace, absolution, and justification from them.

And therefore in Scripture a covenant of peace, Isa. liv. 10, and a covenant of life and peace, Mal. ii. 5, are equivalent.

(2.) All royalty and dominions have, as you know, courts belonging to them, unto which the subjects of their homage come. Now, these two dominions have all their courts and judgment for justification, &c. By the same reason, 'speaking peace' is *verbum forensicum*, a forensical act, properly belonging to court proceedings, or holding analogy with sentence in a court; and this our divines, out of Scripture, against the papists, have largely shewn.

(3.) Each of these courts (which are first kept in the manor or mansion-house of every man's own soul, shall be more publicly held at the day of judgment) have their two offices, which, because we are speaking of peace, I may term 'justices of the peace,' or, if you will, two stewards of these courts, that are authorised to manage things in their names. Natural conscience is, by nature and legal inheritance, the steward of the covenant of works; but faith is by grace appointed to transact the affairs of the covenant of grace: Eph. ii. 8, 'By grace ye are saved, through faith.'

(4.) Every man in either state that is a seeker of peace (which I add, because some are so ignorant that they mind not any such thing; so the apostle speaks of the Gentiles, Rom. ix. 30, 'The Gentiles that sought not after righteousness'), doth seek to have his peace from that court to which he belongs. Look what his state is, or what the jurisdiction is which he is yet under, look what homage he belongs to, unto what he falls in his own spirit, and unto that court he secretly comes and hath recourse for a sentence of peace and life. If a man belongs still but to the covenant of works, although now, man being fallen, that covenant be utterly unable to give peace, yet this having been the ancient custom of this manor in Adam's time, when the covenant was in power and force unto such ends and purposes, and this being the natural law between the creature and Creator, thither therefore do poor deceived souls come all of them still to take up their copies for life and peace. And natural conscience being by nature constituted the supreme judge in that court, will hold its place; and being true to its lord and master's royalty, and having never yet submitted to the supreme jurisdiction of faith, and these poor souls knowing no better, they come and deal with conscience for life and peace; and conscience takes upon it to proceed according to the ancient rules and customs of that court, and so sets men on work a-doing, exacts the performances of such and such duties, then undertakes how it will thereupon issue out peace and comfort. Satisfy me, says conscience, by doing what I direct and instigate you to (and nothing will satisfy it but doing what it commands, nothing else will bribe it, no other pay passeth current with it), and thou shalt have inward peace from me. Yea, and further, if men be slack and negligent in those dues, it tortures, disquiets, and issues out writs of threatenings, &c. And thus, as it undertakes to sanctify by urging legal motives, so also to justify and pronounce peace in a legal way; for indeed it was once ordained to both.

(5.) But now, 5thly; On the contrary, this covenant being made void, and so God having given unto free grace the dominion for justification and true peace, Rom. v. 21, grace is said to reign to eternal life, and it hath taken the kingdom to itself. It is therefore now become the only true fountain of peace from God the Father, and from our Lord Jesus Christ. It is written on the frontispiece of every one of Paul's epistles, that by the inscription over the porch you may know to whom the dominion appertaineth, even unto grace from God and Christ, upon whom peace and life do hold.

(6.) This grace in God's heart will be applied unto us only by faith in our hearts, for it can trust no other principle within us. And though it be the lord of peace, yet it doth not issue forth a sentence of peace authenticly, but upon men's believing, and by faith; as lords do not give possession without their stewards: Rom. v. 1, 'Therefore being justified by faith, we have peace with God through Jesus Christ.'

(7.) Lastly, These two have divided the world, from the fall to this day, into parties, the one seeking righteousness of peace by the works of the law, the other seeking it by faith : Rom. ix. 30–32, 'What shall we say then ? That the Gentiles, which followed not after righteousness, have attained to righteousness, even the righteousness which is of faith : but Israel, which followed after the law of righteousness, hath not attained to the law of righteousness. Wherefore ? Because they sought it, not by faith, but as it were by the works of the law : for they stumbled at that stumbling-stone.'

This differing way of seeking peace by conscience or by the covenant of works one way, and by faith in another way, began in Abel and Cain, the two prototypes of regenerate and unregenerate men, Jude 11. Their way is called ' the way of Cain.' And the difference is evident by the 4th of Genesis and Heb. xi. 3; both sacrificed and worshipped God; but, Heb. xi. 3, ' Abel offered it up by faith;' that is, he looked not at the performance as that from whence he must have his peace and acceptation with God, but by faith, by believing, he looked on his free grace and promise of the Messiah given. But Cain erred in his heart, not knowing this way of peace, but thought to go the old way of works, when yet he wanted power to perform them, in which way natural conscience led him. He brought his sacrifice as a performance, and was so stout and stiff in his principle, that he was in a rage that God should give a manifest token he was not accepted. And God on the other side, perceiving him so angry, says to him, ' Why art thou wroth and sullen, Cain? I will deal with thee according to thine own principles.' And out of his own law and covenant of works, by which he thought he had the better of God, God confutes him : Gen. iv. 7, ' If thou dost well (or good), shalt thou not be accepted ? ' This is plainly thy covenant of works by doing good to be accepted; therefore, in the next words it is opposed to all sin, ' If thou dost not well, sin lies at the door.' He speaks to him in his own language, and yet beats his own weapon to his head, and bids his conscience for the time view over, and examine his own performances and ways, and particularly the frame of heart wherewith he did offer this sacrifice. ' The sacrifice of the wicked is an abomination to the Lord,' much more when he offers it with an evil mind, as Cain had done. And for time to come, God bids him to look to it that he did well in all things (seeing he stood upon it), or he could not look for acceptation. And thus God dealt with the Jews when they were sturdy in the opinion of their own righteousness : Ezek. xviii. from verse 5th to verse 10th, ' But if a man be just, and do that which is lawful and right, and hath not eaten upon the mountains, neither hath lifted up his eyes to the idols of the house of Israel, neither hath defiled his neighbour's wife, neither hath come near to a menstruous woman, and hath not oppressed any, but hath restored to the debtor his pledge, hath spoiled none by violence, hath given his bread to the hungry, and hath covered the naked with a garment; he that hath not given forth upon usury, neither hath taken any increase, that hath withdrawn his hand from iniquity, hath executed true judgment between man and man, hath walked in my statutes, and hath kept my judgments, to deal truly ; he is just, he shall surely live, saith the Lord God.' Wherein he offers to deal with them according to that covenant of works they trusted in, and puts them to it, thereby to shew them their inability to perform it.   Thus the division began, and so it went on to Paul's time, Rom. ix. 31, 32; and as it was then, so it is now, and will be to the end of the world.

These are the two contrary sources, and also ways of peace in the general set out; and this metaphor of a way the apostle takes up and follows, Rom. ix. 30, terming it a ' seeking' or a pursuance, by a metaphor from men's running in a way or race.

2. Let us now trace and follow each of these sorts of men in their several paths which they take, than which nothing more discovers the difference of them.   And because *rectum est index sui, et obliqui*, I will first set out in few words the way of peace by believing, or faith, as it runs in opposition to this high way and road of all mankind, which conscience will needs mislead them in.

If God means to give true peace to a poor soul by the tenor of the covenant of grace, the way he takes is this.

(1.) He breaks the old peace which conscience had spoken, and to that end comes in with a new light upon this heavy, dull-eyed conscience (that hath but half an eye by nature to discover to a man his sinfulness, and shews but the outside of it), and God by this new light gives a man a true and thorough sight into that condition he hath continued in, and gives him a view of the sinfulness of all his works and performances (yea, of those from which conscience hath been so bold as to speak peace formerly unto him), by discovering to him the defect, for manner and ends of them. Conscience plainly tells him, the true God thou hast not glorified (as Daniel told Belshazzar, Dan. v.), nor hadst him ever in thy thoughts, to mind and pursue as thy dearest interest.   And so conscience discovers how the inwards of his soul are very rottenness, and that he never did a good action (in respect of what should be the soul that gives life and spirit, that makes an action truly good), no, not one in his whole life.   A man hath a new light which runs through the inwards of all, as the Spirit that moved in the wheels.   I saw (saith Paul) that all concupiscence wrought in me, Rom. vii. 8 ; that the best and rightest actings of the law on my heart by my conscience had only this issue, to bring forth motions of sins; and now the law which I thought had been ordained for life, I found to be unto death. And, my brethren, because that natural conscience was the great misleader in this, therefore God's Spirit first assaults that, and storms conscience, the first of all those towers and faculties in men's souls, and makes the breach there.   Yea, God takes this law, and the true light of it, and cutteth conscience its throat first of all therewith ; and so the whole man dies, and all that false peace which conscience had given him expires for ever in him : Rom. vii. 9, ' When the commandment came into my soul' (as the light of the sun into a darkish room), this new light caused sin to revive in his conscience, namely, the proper state of the guilt of it ; ' And I died ' (saith he) ; and it was the commandment slew him, ver. 11.   And (saith he, Gal. ii. 19), ' I through the law am dead to the law.'   Yea, and conscience, which was the great deceiver of the whole man, and undertook to be the dictator and *conservator pacis*, the keeper of the peace of this old commonwealth, is that part of the soul that is made the rendezvous of all a man's sins, and all confusion and trouble for them. All a man's sins do quarter upon conscience, and now it pays for all, bears the load, the guilt of all. As in a man in a fever, though the other parts are in a distemper, yet head and heart most; and so here, though all in a man is in a disturbance, yet conscience is as the stomach, whither the humours are gathered which makes the man sick to death.

Now (2.), to be sure this man will never put trust in conscience for giving forth peace to him any more, in this former way ; nor will the heart ever come to its court to take it up, nor to have it upon those terms as it had wont to do. Upon this discovery, yea, by it, this court of conscience, the chancery is pulled down, and so ever dissolved, and that justly too, for it had run all a man's lifetime into a *præmunire*. And now all its decrees of life and peace are cashiered and cancelled for ever by that one sentence, which the soul now submits to, uttered by God upon man's having broken the covenant of works : that ' by the works of the law no flesh shall be justified,' Rom. iii. 20. The law is killed in the man : Rom. vii. 6, ' That being dead wherewith we were held ;' and the man is dead to the law : Gal. ii. 19, ' I am dead by the law to the law.' He speaks of the light and works of humiliation by which he was killed by the law : ' And I saw I had been so deceived by it' (says he, Rom. vii. 11), that I shall never trust the proceeding of it, or have recourse to that court for life and peace any more. It is dead and made void to me, as to any such relief, and my soul is as dead to it, and I have no heart, no spirit to have to do with it, or its agent conscience, upon the old terms, to get peace by doing any more.

(3.) Now let us see what way the soul is directed unto as the true way for peace. It is merely and entirely faith on Christ : Rom. iii. 24–26, ' Being justified freely by his grace, through the redemption that is in Jesus Christ; whom God hath set forth to be a propitiation through faith in his blood, to declare his righteousness for the remission of sins that are past, through the forbearance of God ; to declare, I say, at this time his righteousness ; that he might be just, and the justifier of him which believeth in Jesus.' Rom. iv. 5, ' But to him that worketh not, but believeth on him that justifieth the ungodly, his faith is counted for righteousness.' Rom. xv. 13, ' Now the God of hope fill you with all joy and peace through believing.' Rom. v. 1, ' Therefore, being justified by faith, we have peace with God, through our Lord Jesus Christ.'

Yea, now that this court of faith is in and by grace's prerogative set up to give forth peace, now even conscience itself, that was the great undertaker for peace afore, the great non-submitter to the righteousness and peace of faith (it is the phrase, Rom. x. 3), is now glad to come and appear in this court, and to make use of faith, and brings with it all the works that were the darlings of conscience, which it once judged good, but now sees to be but dead works ; as also all the sins whereof it is the drain, the sink (and therefore is called an evil conscience), all these it brings with it, and comes weary and heavy loaden to Christ, and cries out, Oh, sprinkle me, Lord, with thy blood, by faith ! Oh, give me joy and peace through believing ! The Scriptures are express : Heb. ix. 14, ' The blood of Christ purgeth your conscience from dead works,' when nothing else can do it. The opposition there shews how it is done : Heb. x. 22, ' Let us draw near with full assurance of faith, having our hearts sprinkled from an evil conscience.' And this is that very same conscience that once was counted so good, and spake so much peace once. And now this conscience, that hath been made the seat of humiliation, the rendezvous of all guilt, is now on the contrary made the seat of justification, the receptacle or cistern of Christ's blood, which runs into it through the pipe or conveyance of believing.

Quest. But will you say to me, Is there no use of a regenerate conscience in the matter of speaking peace after believing?

Ans. 1. I answer in general, when conscience its court is down, and itself put out of office of being the supreme judge, the room where the audit of gospel peace is held is the ear of faith, wherein and whereby God makes the soul to hear of peace and gladness, even the joyful sound; yet still that peace which faith alone brings in and settles in the whole soul, is that which quiets it, and establisheth its joy. And an eternal prohibition is given in against all proceedings for peace, according to the former custom of that court; and conscience itself hath thus submitted to faith's court, as to this supreme jurisdiction thereof. Indeed, conscience comes to be taken in again as an under-officer under faith, as an apparitor, as an appendix or subservient, and receives from faith a new commission: Gal. iii. 15, 17, there is a phrase used of the law, that it was 'added to the promises' of the gospel, added, that is, as a subservient to it; and as the law, its master, so conscience also is added to faith, to serve it in many offices, and among other in this of peace. It is not proper here to enlarge upon some offices it serves in, viz., to represent what sins are in the heart, also to instruct and direct to what is to be done by us, and instigate thereunto, or restrain from evil; it being as a rule in an artificer's hand to guide us in working. These are foreign to my scope; the matter of speaking peace, and the influence a regenerate conscience hath thereunto, is that which lies afore me.

Faith must be the sole judge to pronounce the sentence of peace, of justification; and conscience, if it could bring this verdict, 'I know nothing by myself' (as Paul speaks of himself); yet it must be silent in this respect, and only say, 'I am not thereby justified,' and leave it entirely to faith to transact the whole of justification another way.

Ans. 2. Yet conscience may come in as a witness in this court of faith, to confirm that sentence.

(1.) It is a great witness to the sovereign virtue that is in Christ's blood; as that blind man was to Christ himself, ' Whereas I was blind, sure I am, I now see, and this man hath opened mine eyes;' so conscience comes in and attests, Whereas I was wounded, blooded, and gashed with such deep and smarting abominations, as no medicines in heaven or earth could cure or assuage, I found that blood of my Redeemer, which faith alone applied to me, to give me ease, yea, cure and heal those wounds, and wash and purge out those stains, which no nitre nor fuller's soap could do. The waves rose high, the winds blustered, and the still voice of that blood speaking better things in me than Abel's did in Cain's conscience, calmed all. The sea and the winds obeyed it, and were stilled at it. Blood is made one, yea, and the first witness, 1 John v., which is no other than the blood of sprinkling, in its efficacy, upon the very sprinkling thereof, to make conscience as white as snow, though before it was as red as scarlet, with bold and bloody transgressions. Conscience is that faculty which gives the testimony of that blood, and correspondently, Heb. x. 22, ' washing with water,' which is the second witness in that of John, is mentioned and joined with the sprinkling of an evil conscience, as here in John the witness of blood and water in like manner are.

(2.) Conscience seconds and backs the sentence of faith, by giving in evidence of graces and gracious dispositions in the heart; and this in and by the Holy Ghost witnessing with them that we truly believe, and are persons justified by faith : 2 Cor. i. 12, 'For our rejoicing is this, the testimony of our conscience, that in simplicity and godly sincerity, not with fleshly wisdom, but by the grace of God, we have had our conversation in the world, and more abundantly to you-wards.' You see it was the testimony of his conscience, and it is but a secondary testimony, coming in to make good a higher sentence, and so still subordinate unto faith. And here I give these cautions.

Caution 1. That faith is left alone to treat for a man's peace, and justification, and that it alone goes to Christ to pronounce that sentence, only conscience gives a testimony unto faith and the truth thereof.

Caution 2. That the matter of regenerate conscience's testimony is not only fetched from outward facts or performances—these are natural conscience's court-rolls it hath recourse to to pronounce peace from—but regenerate conscience looks chiefly to the inward sincerity and carriage of the heart to God in a man's conversation, as matter of evidence. It regards inward and gracious dispositions in the heart, and regards not all outward performances, further than as it hath discerned inward sincerity aiming at God's glory to have been the companion, or rather ground of them. Conscience discerns and finds out gracious dispositions in the heart, and seeks after such chiefly ; and then faith finds out a promise to such dispositions, and the Holy Ghost bears witness with both.

Caution 3. A regenerate conscience witnessth not by or with these our graces, but as and when actuated by the Holy Ghost, who to be sure will not use or improve that testimony to the prejudice of believing. This eminent disposition in Paul's heart, in wishing to be accursed for his countrymen, he thus brings forth to light, ' My conscience bearing me witness in the Holy Ghost,' enlightening me in the discovery, and strengthening conscience to give that evidence. The truth is, conscience, so far as it is regenerated, and as thus commissionated anew by faith, is not, nor should not be, too forward to speak, lest it intrench upon what belongs to faith, but only to answer and give in testimony in a subordination to faith, whence it is called in to speak. It is termed rather ' the answer of a good conscience,' 1 Pet. iii. 21, than the proposition or claim of conscience first made of itself. And it is the answer of conscience, as spoken first itself unto, and having heard Christ's blood speaking better things than the blood of Abel, and as having heard faith first talk of Christ's death and resurrection for its justification (Rom. iv.) as the foundation of its answer and apology.

But now, let us see how contrary and remote from this true way of peace that way is, which natural conscience doth mislead men's spirits into, and how much and how many ways it endeavours to set a man out of the way. You may observe, Rom. iii. 17, in the catalogue or indictment of the particulars, or general heads rather, of men's corruptions, this inserted as one, ' the way of peace they have not known,' as not among themselves ; so nor to find it with God. Heb. iii. 10, 11, ' They do always err in their heart, and have not known my ways. So I sware in my wrath, they shall not enter into my rest.' Their erring, and erring always, this standing universal *errata* that is found in all editions and impressions of men's hearts, is by reason of their being thus addicted to the covenant of works, as the sworn creatures and vassals of it.

The working of this mystery of iniquity you may perceive through all states and conditions which the sons of men run through. For either,

1. Men were never enlightened, nor natural conscience ever yet awakened, which was Paul's case afore conversion—' I was alive without the law'—or before the revival of sin in his conscience ; or, 2. They come to be awakened by the law, and living also under the gospel, and being enlightened therein and instructed in the way of salvation ; and natural conscience plays a deceitful part in all.

The first sort, that were never struck, which were never troubled nor humbled under the sense of their lost condition at all, are the most of mankind. And either they are such,

1. As are regardless of peace of conscience or righteousness, in order to eternal life ; they know not what either of these mean ; either through want of a discovery of their sinfulness, or ignorance of a righteousness ordained to life eternal. And such were the most of the heathens, and such are the most of common Christians, that are ignorant and atheistical. It is said of the universality of the Gentiles, Rom. ix. 30, ' The Gentiles followed not after righteousness' as the Jews did, that is, they lived without the sense of any such thing, and so had it not in pursuit at all. These are said to sleep : 1 Thess. v. 6, ' Let us not sleep, as others,' namely, of mankind, do, they being ' in the night' (ver. 7), that is, the darkness of ignorance ; and cry ' Peace and safety' (ver. 3 of that chapter), as being ignorant of any danger they are in, in respect of another world. But this at the best is but quietness, not peace ; a freedom from being troubled. As if a man deep in debt is kept by them about him in ignorance of his estate, hears of no suits entered against him, no serjeant to attack him, no writ out for him ; he is in a senseless security, and not at peace with his adversaries. It is such a quiet as a man condemned to die next morning hath in his sleep over night. It is called a ' spirit of slumber,' Rom. xi. 8, when yet ' damnation slumbereth not,' as 2 Peter ii. 3.

Now, it is natural conscience is in the cause for this. For whereas its office is (as the prophet's was, Ezek. iii.) to ' discover to man his sinfulness,' and to give warning of the judgments of God (as Rom. i.) ; natural conscience that is thus betrusted seeks to hide, conceals all this, even from itself ; they ' wink with their eyes,' and are said to ' close their eyes, &c., lest they should see,' as the prophet, and Christ out of the prophet, speaks.

For if conscience at any time opens an eyelid half way, sees a little of a man's sin, a glimpse thereof, yet it will shut the same again presently, that it might not see what follows, and is the consequent of it, what is the next behind it, judgment and wrath, which if it comes in so quick as it cannot shut out the sight thereof, as the Gentiles could not, Rom. i. 32 ; yet it turns away the next thought, and cuts off the application thereof unto itself : Rom. i. 28, and chap. ii. 3, ' And thinkest thou this, O man, that judgest them which do such things, and doest the same, that thou shalt escape the judgment of God ?' Thus they ' shut their eyes lest they should see,' Mat. xiii. 15. Now this is wilful security of conscience, this is not peace. Now if men's consciences will use such tricks as these, when a man doth ill, to keep off the consideration thereof, or of the consequent of it, and to pocket up, and conceal the writs of judgment, and let them lie by and not open them (so Hosea vii. 2, ' They consider not in their hearts that I remember all their wickedness') ; and if when a man doth well (as he thinks), then to cry, Peace, peace ; that man shall be kept quiet all his days. But this is not so much as true, much less peace, but deceit and fraud. This is a making their hearts glad with lies.

Or, 2. Men's case is, that they set themselves a-work to follow after a righteousness in order to peace, as many of the Jews, Rom. ix. 30, 31, are said to do; and some few heathens, and many devout Christians among papists and ourselves, use to do.

Now, 1. For those few Gentiles that sought for any kind of righteousness above the rest, they withal professed to trust in themselves, upon three principles: 1, to obey right reason; 2, and that they obeyed God in obeying right reason; and 3, to trust in themselves, *sibi fidere.* These were the professed catholic maxims, or fundamental principles practical in their religion. And, which is strange, the very same proper character, in the same words, is attributed to the Jews, Luke xviii. 9, that 'they trusted in themselves,' with this addition, 'that they were righteous.' So then the same spirit and mystery of iniquity wrought the very same thing both in Jews and some heathens, and both from the same cause. A righteousness both sought, and peace therefrom; and that righteousness was in and from themselves, on which they trusted, with despising others. And this was their *sibi fidere,* their trusting in themselves. Which how contrary it is to the fundamental principle true Christianity teacheth every one's heart that is truly a Christian, Paul hath informed us, in making this one essential characteristical property of a true believer: Phil. iii. 3, 'Who rejoice in the Lord Jesus' (as trusted in, and complete to save), 'and put no confidence in the flesh.' And by flesh he eminently intends a man's own righteousness, which is of the law, opposite to that by faith, as by verses 6 and 9 is evident. And how difficult a lesson it is for us to learn, and how yet withal the main, and as it were the top, and the ultimate of all other God would bring us to, the same apostle Paul hath in his own example, after many years' proficiency in Christianity, taught us, 2 Cor i. 9, 'We had the sentence of death in ourselves, that we should not trust in ourselves,' neither for bodily life nor strength, nor righteousness, nor revelations, gifts nor grace, nor any thing we can call ours whatever.

But 2dly. As for the multitude of such as profess themselves Christians, which know the Scriptures, though they dare not in their doctrine make such a profession of principles, yet in their hearts they practise it.

For the papists and their devotionists, who profess Christ, and to trust in Christ, yet in the point of righteousness and like, you know what their doctrine is. And as they set up the pope, as holding all his power from Christ, yet exercising it against Christ, with profession it is in Christ's stead, so they set up their own righteousness, graces, and doings, though they profess to hold all of Christ, and that by his merit these were first given. So as nature in them, too, speaks out as far as it dares.

And 3dly. For the generality of such protestants as look after a righteousness for their peace, whilst they in doctrine profess to trust in Christ alone by faith only, and do at solemn times do homage to it, because of the doctrine generally professed, yet practically their hearts run the way of all flesh before them; and having never been struck with the sense of their natural condition and emptiness, their peace lies in satisfying their consciences with duties, which in the first and chief place raiseth up and maintaineth in them an opinion that they are truly religious and conscientious in their ways, and then they are bold to add thereto faith in Christ; yea, and the opinion they have obtained of themselves from their consciences, by complying with it in doing, is the foundation in their hearts of that their faith on Christ.

Now as for this peace of all these sorts of men, thus raised and maintained, it is sufficient by way of difference to say, that it hath been a peace hath grown up alone out of what is in themselves; and not made and founded anew, after a sight of their lost condition and of their being enemies; or which is equivalent to it, there is not an utter renouncing of their own righteousness as dung, and as being afraid to be found therein (as was Paul's case, Phil. iii.), but a peace it is that was never concluded upon a new treaty with God, and upon new offers of free grace. The old title remains, and they act for the maintaining of it. For they having taken it for granted that God and they have been at peace, conscience, which they have by nature, hath struck in to be the upholder, continuer, and maintainer of this peace, and the conceit hereof, by doing righteously and uprightly, ' so *keeping* peace' (I allude to that speech used of Christ, and indeed only proper to him, ' so *making* peace,' Eph. ii. 15), whereas true and sound peace is a peace anew created, as the word is, Isa. lvii. 19, 'I create the fruit of the lips, peace;' created as light out of darkness at first, so 2 Cor. iv. 6, or as creatures out of nothing. It brings a man's former light and peace into darkness and confusion, reducing the soul to nothing in itself, and in all its performances; and then God causing light to spring in by the face of Jesus Christ, it grows not up out of a man's own heart and conscience as a natural soil, as your ears of corn on the house tops; but its original comes from what is without the man, in God's heart and in Christ. It is a seed and fruit that drops from the lips of others preaching the gospel of peace either in their writings or sermons: ' I will create the fruit of the lips, peace;' which, Eph. ii. 17, Paul interprets of the preaching of the gospel of peace, as it is therefore termed. It is not such a peace as a man behind hand in the world holds with his creditors, paying a little here and a little there, in some things punctually keeping his word, and so endeavouring to satisfy and keep them off from arrests, and so thinking he holds up his credit still with them. But it is a peace which an utter bankrupt hath obtained after he is utterly broke, that hath the statute sued forth against him; and all his creditors come in and he hath nothing to pay; yea, further, is discovered to be a perfect cheat, coining himself, and then paying all he seemed to have. And what is the peace such a one can expect? But a total forgiveness of ten thousand talents out of mere compassion, as you have it in the parable, Mat. xviii. 24, 27. And most of all, a forgiveness of that treason and dishonour of which the man is guilty, in thinking to put God off with his false coin, his self-coined righteousness, that had not his stamp and image on it, Rom. v. 1, 11, compared. But the peace which a man justified by faith is said to have, is by his ' receiving the atonement:' a total discharge and acquittance through the alone satisfaction of Jesus Christ, pleaded, and had recourse unto, ' by whom we have now received the atonement.' The debt was sued out, the man ready to be cast in prison: ' Deliver him' (saith God), ' I have found a ransom;' and he receives it, as a matter that wholly is from without him, and which comes as a new gift, even as, Rom. ix. 30, the Gentiles are said to have apprehended, received a righteousness; so the word there used imports κατέλαβε, laid hold on righteousness, even the righteousness of faith, as a hand lays hold of a gift without itself, as, Rom. v. 17, this of righteousness is termed. Whereas the other thought to have wrought it out by doing, as men by running win a prize, as those other words διώκων and ἔφθασε import (v. 31).

In the conclusion of this part of my discourse, I cast in these three differences of true peace, from that which natural conscience gives.

Diff. 1. True peace is a peace comes from without you: but the peace of all these men by natural conscience is from within. Let me say it to you, brethren, and be not offended by my inverting Christ's word, the peace that is from within the man defiles, deceives the man. It is the peace that is wholly without, that saves and comforts the man. Only it is received within us by faith, or we could not be comforted by it. It is compared therefore unto a guard ; 'The peace of God, φρουρήσει, shall guard your minds ;' φρουρά is *præsidium militare*, a guard, it is the same word that is used, 1 Peter i. 5, when it is said, ' we are kept by the power of God unto salvation :' kept as with a garrison. Now look, as the power of God is a thing without us, and a garrison is a foreign external defence, brought in to defend a place, and keep peace in it, which else would be at divisions within itself, so is this true peace, the peace of God. It is therefore termed not a peace of conscience, but of God, Phil. iv. And also peace in the Holy Ghost, Rom. xiv. 17, and that ' good hope' (as the apostle calls it by way of distinction from false and untrue), Rom. xv. 13, it is from the God of hope, and through the power of the Holy Ghost. ' Now the God of all hope fill you with joy and peace in believing, that ye may abound in hope through the power of the Holy Ghost.' If thou hast not joy, thou mayest have peace : if not peace, thou mayest have hope. Well, but all this joy, peace, and hope come from without, from God, from the Holy Ghost, and therefore are taken in by the way of faith, which is a receiving faculty, it is all through believing. Yea, and they are brought in as foreigners are, by a mighty power, which, as it guards the soul to salvation, so it guards the heart to peace. Or if you will, take the word of Christ : ' *My* peace' (says he), by distinction. It is Christ's peace which the soul of a true believer seeks, and which Christ in that speech directs them to, in a double respect, and both of them exclusively spoken, as to the peace we ordinarily term peace of conscience.

1. Because he is the sole procurer and purchaser of, and matter of our peace. ' He is our peace,' is the common cry of all believers, Eph. ii. 14, through his alone merit, Rom. v. 1, 11, and accordingly a soul that seeks peace by faith, eyes what is in Christ as the object matter of his peace with God, and is taken up with that in its pursuit after peace : John xvi. 33, ' These things have I spoken, that in me you might have peace.' He had related in the late sermons what he was about to do for them in dying, and also what he would do for them in heaven. And let these things (says he) be matter of peace and comfort to your souls, when I am gone. And therefore ' through Jesus Christ' is everywhere added, where peace is spoken of, Rom. v. 1, Phil. iv. 6.

2. It is Christ's peace, my peace, and the peace of God, because it is such as God himself speaks and communicates when the heart is quieted by it. And so in that respect also it is a peace without us. It is not a peace which conscience speaketh (which is the speaker of the natural man's peace) but which Christ speaketh by faith to conscience, whom (Heb. xii. 25) the apostle termeth τὸν λαλοῦντα ἀπ᾽ οὐρανῶν. And so in that respect also it is Christ's peace. The Scripture knows no such phrase as ' peace of conscience.' It is indeed peace of conscience *subjectivè*, conscience being the principle it is spoken unto. But when it is spoken, it is so spoken as that it is the peace *of* God, and not peace *with* God only. Yea, and as a true believer seeks for it, it is the peace of God only. He seeks not only to be at peace with God, but to have the peace of God, which God immediately from himself gives and communicates ; this is that which a true believer seeks. He goes to God, and says, Lord, it is true I have walked thus and thus, and have these and these dispositions in me, but

it is not the peace which these offer to give me, and in which my natural spirit would rest in, that I wish for; but, Lord, I desire thee to speak it. ' I will hear what the Lord will speak' (says the Psalmist): ' he will speak peace to his people,' Ps. lxxxv.   Oh, let me hear himself speak.

Diff. 2. A second difference is in that testimony which is allowed unto regenerate conscience from within to give.   It eyes principally what is the sincerity of heart wherewith all hath been done in respecting God, and laying aside and renouncing carnal ends: 2 Cor. i. 12, ' This is our rejoicing, the testimony of our conscience.'   What was it which this grand jury founded its verdict upon, and witnessed as matter of rejoicing?   Even this, ' that in simplicity and sincerity of God, not with fleshly wisdom, but by the grace of God, we have had our conversation in the world.'   So then, his having sincerity, aimed at God as God (in so much as he called it sincerity of God), and his having been moved and guided, not by principles or ends which fleshly wisdom suggested, but by motives and persuasions fetched and drawn from the grace and love of God, sweetly and predominantly swaying his heart (for so the opposition of *by grace* there runs unto with *fleshly wisdom*, both being put in opposition as *in eodem genere causarum*, as two differing principles, yet of the same head or kind of causes, that is, inducing, moving causes both; that look, as fleshly wisdom moves and steers a carnal heart, so did the grace of God move Paul's heart), these are the things which his regenerate conscience was now taught to eye, or else (as in order unto salvation) he should not have had matter of rejoicing for any other thing within the cognizance of conscience, though he had done more, and laboured more than all the apostles.   On the contrary, his unregenerate conscience had eyed only the observation of the outwards of the law, ' serving in the letter,' Rom. vii. 5, 6, and a blamelessness in the law, and that was the matter of his rejoicing afore, Phil. iii., which confirmeth this difference.   By another scripture you may see what sort of actings his conscience by the Holy Ghost was intent upon; not matters of outward fact, as that he made so many sermons, &c., but a high and holy, elevated and sublimated, disposition of soul, even a continual heaviness and sorrow of heart, yea, even wishing to be accursed from Christ, for his brethren the Jews, Rom. ix. 1–3.   Observe what a preface he maketh to it; ' I say the truth in Christ, I lie not, my conscience also bearing me witness in the Holy Ghost;' that is, acted and enlightened, not by the common light which natural conscience is acted by, but a special and evident work of the Holy Ghost, and enlightened thereby to witness this.   His conscience, you see, singleth forth such a disposition of heart as was eminently characteristical of saving grace, and infallibly such, and is not found in any heart that shall perish.   ' I speak the truth in Christ,' that is, as one that is in Christ, and hath this evidence for it.   Thus also speaks Hezekiah, Isa. xxxviii. 3, ' Remember, O Lord, how I have walked before thee in truth, and with a perfect heart in thy sight.'   His conscience was it that gave this testimony.   Now it was not his outward walking he insists on, but his walking afore God in sincerity or truth, and with a perfect heart.   And this his own conscience was instructed to account and esteem to be that true goodness which is good in God's sight.   And the reason is, because when a man is regenerate, his conscience is filled with the genuine knowledge of God, as God.   And so he looks upon things with that light God doth, and so only values and reckons that to be good which God doth account good.   And God always, in judging of the action, takes in what the heart is, which was the spring of it: 1 Kings viii. 39, ' Thou

dost give to every man according to his ways, whose heart thou knowest.'
And by this rule doth regenerate conscience, his vicegerent, also judge.
This is the second difference.

Diff. 3. The peace which natural conscience speaks, is, at the height of
it, but a dull, flat, dead peace ; even as the original of it are themselves but
' dead works,' Heb. ix. 14. It is with them as with those that go with
and carry dead children in the wombs of their hearts, such living throes
they know not ; but, 1 Pet. i. 3, it is called ' living hope' we are begotten unto, and such a hope faith affords, at least in the object of it. And
it often riseth up to a peace which passeth or exceedeth the understanding,
Phil. iv. 6 ; whereas that which natural conscience gives, is but such as
riseth up from the understanding or practical reason ; but that of faith
cometh from heaven, and carries the heart to heaven : ' Being justified by
faith, we have peace with God,' Rom. v. 1, and ' rejoice in hope of glory,'
ver. 2 ; yea, ' rejoice in God,' ver. 11. And sometimes this peace riseth
up unto joy unspeakable, and full of glory, 1 Pet. i. 8, which though
Christians always attain not to, yet the object matter which their faith is
carried forth unto, out of themselves, hath all this in it. Yea, and the
faith itself that is in the soul is still working the heart up unto it, to seek
after this, not to be quiet without it, or rest in any peace besides it ; even
as every natural faculty seeks and pursues after some way or other the
highest perfection of that which is the proper object of it. And, on the
contrary, although the unregenerate man may have a further joy than that
of natural conscience, from a tasting of the powers of the world to come
(Heb. vi.), yet that joy is not from natural conscience, but an effect of supernatural enlightening in matters of faith, and that as it is a counterfeit of
faith, though not attaining unto true faith. And the differences of such joys
from that other joy believers attain unto, is not proper to this discourse,
which only treats here of the peace which natural conscience as such
affords, with difference to that which faith gives, or riseth up unto.

This Paul knowing full well, being trained up to the experiment thereof,
no means, no works, no testimony of conscience could avail of itself, unless
God speak peace. When therefore he would pray for peace, he frames his
prayer thus : that God himself would give it, 2 Thes. iii. 16. It is his
manner, you know, at the beginning or end of his epistles, to wish ' Grace
and peace from God the Father,' &c., and he had so at the beginning of that
epistle ; but at the latter end, being about to renew the same again in his
farewell, he as it were corrects his speech, and frames his prayer thus :
' Now the Lord of peace himself give you peace always by all means,' both
as knowing his wishes and all means else ineffectual to attain or procure
true peace, as also signifying what kind of peace it was that true hearts
desire and seek after. The Lord of peace himself giveth peace, and though
himself blesseth means whereby he doth it, and you are to use them, yet so
as he, the God of peace, must himself give it. Take the holiest and best
man in the world, whose conscience is the largest treasury of good done
by him, or wrought in him, and although conscience be a reflecting faculty
in all men, yet his conscience from all the good that is betrusted with it, and
it is privy unto, cannot testify a word for that man's peace and comfort
unless the Holy Ghost speaks in and unto conscience, by the light of faith,
with power. For though the spirit that is in man is said naturally to
know the things that are in a man, 1 Cor. ii., yet they are but those things
which we have as men. But such things as we have as good and holy
men, given us by the Holy Ghost, these the Holy Ghost must by a super-

natural act enable conscience to discern, or we do not, cannot, discern them. And therefore in the same chapter it is said, 'He hath given us his Spirit, that we might know the things that are given us of God.' And his graces in us are gifts, and special gifts of God's grace in us.

CHAPTER XIII.

The highest degree to which a temporary believer can possibly attain, described by the apostle Paul, Heb. vi., which yet falls short of that saving work, wrought in a sincere believer, there spoken of by him.

For it is impossible for those who were once enlightened, and have tasted of the heavenly gift, and were made partakers of the Holy Ghost, and have tasted the good word of God, and the powers of the world to come, if they shall fall away, to renew them again unto repentance ; seeing they crucify to themselves the Son of God afresh, and put him to an open shame. For the earth, which drinketh in the rain which cometh oft upon it, and bringeth forth herbs meet for them by whom it is dressed, receiveth blessing from God : but that which beareth thorns and briers is rejected, and is nigh unto cursing ; whose end is to be burned. But, beloved, we are persuaded better things of you, and things that accompany salvation, though we thus speak. For God is not unrighteous, to forget your work and labour of love, which ye have shewed toward his name, in that ye have ministered to the saints, and do minister.—Heb. VI. 4–10.

The apostle sets before these Hebrews the most dreadful things about a temporary work and condition that is to be found in the whole Scriptures, and yet in the occasion he took for it, he doth it with the greatest advantage for the comfort of the weakest sound Christian, and with the greatest tenderness that possibly so great a matter could be uttered in. The advantage he takes for it appears in this, that whereas one of the greatest objections that many sound believers have against themselves, that they are but temporaries, ariseth from manifold defects, and (some of which are but accidental to a Christian's state) the deadness of their hearts, the lowness of their graces, the want of growth, rebellion of lusts, and the like, for there are a thousand such might be instanced. They judged such like things, especially when of a long continuance, to argue them hypocrites ; which doubts of theirs they were the more strengthened in when withal they compared the soaring heights, the high enlightenings, the vehement and forward affections, tastes of things in the other world, which concerns men's salvations, that they had observed to have been in some that had utterly fallen away. Alas, thought they, when I compare what deadness is in my heart, what little or no proficiency my soul hath made in things heavenly for so long a time ; and, on the other hand, what wonderful enlightenings, quickness of affections, such as have fallen away have shot up into, I cannot but conclude that I much rather shall fall away too ; for, alas, I am far short of them in these things! The apostle therefore, intending to discourse this great point in this epistle, takes this strange advantage for it, and such a one as shall prevent the discouragement of the lowest saint. The course he takes is this.

1. He presents the worst and lowest case of a sound Christian that well can be supposed, and tells those Hebrews plainly that it was many of their

cases, chap. v., ver. 12, 13, ' For when for the time ye ought to have been teachers, ye have need that one teach you again, which be the first principles of the oracles of God, and are become such as have need of milk, and not of strong meat. For every one that useth milk is unskilful in the word of righteousness, for he is a babe.' He instanceth indeed only in point of defect in, and want of growth in knowledge ; but that must be proportionably supposed to have been accompanied with answerable flatness and deadness of holy affections, and colder exercise of grace. It is certain, if they did not grow in knowledge in so many years, they had not grown in grace : ' Grow in knowledge ' (says the apostle) ' and in grace.' And it is as certain, that if they had not grown in grace, there must have been a decay in grace and the exercises of it, and thereupon a worldly, fleshly frame and an overgrowing of many lusts would rise instead thereof. Whereby at last they grew nigh unto a curse from God, and were even at the very pit's brink, to have been given up by God to final hardness, &c. Yet knowledge is that thing which even hypocrites use to grow up into more than in any other endowment. In gifts of knowledge, and the exercise thereof, they are eminent. These are an excellency which corrupt nature affects, and seeks after above all other, that therefore such as were true Christians should not have sought to grow up in this ; what a strange thing and case was this ! And the ground thereof must needs be, because they had not had a great valuation of things heavenly, which if they had had, they would have sought to grow accordingly in the knowledge of them.

Now take their case as to knowledge, as the apostle here sets it out, it was very deplorable, ver. 12.

(1.) They seem to have lost of that spiritual capacity to take in spiritual things which they once had, and to have fallen from much of that spiritual favour and quickness of understanding in the fear of the Lord which they once had. This that word, ' *You are become such*,' &c., seems to import.

(2.) They are represented like men old, or men in a consumption, whose stomachs cannot digest strong meats (as they had wont), and are therefore glad to live on milk, and the weakest sort of food. ' You are become such' (says the apostle) ' as have need of milk, and not of strong meat.' Which the opposition, ver. 14, shews and explains ; ' But strong meat belongeth to them that are of full age, even those who by reason of use have their senses exercised to discern both good and evil.'

(3.) That word, *by reason of use*, implies that they had not exercised their graces, whereby their knowledge might have been put in use, and so enlarged thereby.

2. Having thus set them forth at the lowest, he describes the highest and quickest sort of workings, and operations and advances in matters of religion, made by some that yet fall away : chap. vi. ver. 4, 5, ' For it is impossible for those who were once enlightened, and have tasted of the heavenly gift, and were made partakers of the Holy Ghost, and have tasted the good word of God, and the powers of the world to come, if they shall fall away, to renew them again to repentance.'

3. And yet, thirdly, he concludes, ' That he hoped better things, and things that accompanied salvation,' or that ' have salvation in them :' ver. 9, ' But, beloved, we are persuaded better things of you, and things that accompany salvation, though we thus speak ;' ἐχόμενα τῆς σωτηρίας, according to that saying ' He that truly believes hath eternal life.' Of these, concerning whom he had afore spoken the worst things that could be spoken, he yet hopes, nay, is persuaded that such better things, or saving

graces, yet remained in them, than all those enlightenings specified had been in those other, as having been but such as never had true salvation in them, but had all the while been short of it, and not in the event only. And the ground of his persuasion was,

(1.) That they had wrought in them at first a sound and sincere love to God, his name, and his saints, which they had by deeds and labour therein given many real testimonies of.

(2.) And to this end he bids them call to remembrance,' &c.: chap. x. 32–35, ' Call to remembrance the former days, in which, after ye were illuminated, ye endured a great fight of afflictions; partly, whilst ye were made a gazing-stock both by reproaches and afflictions; and partly, whilst ye became companions of them that were so used. For ye had compassion of me in my bonds, and took joyfully the spoiling of your goods, knowing in yourselves that ye have in heaven a better and an enduring substance. Cast not away therefore your confidence, which hath great recompence of reward.' It went, it seems, very low with them at present, when, to persuade himself and them of their grace, he is fain to have recourse unto things so far back.

(3.) He elsewhere minds them also, that though they had never yet been called to martyrdom, ' nor resisted unto blood,' chap. xii. 4, yet they had continued to ' fight against sin,' and with much contest and hazard to keep themselves from the evils of the times, all which are a-fighting against sin, to keep a good conscience ; as also they had maintained and kept up a conflict against sin in their own hearts.

(4.) And those things they had continued (though in some low measure) to do for a long time from the first works upon them; and even there and then, ver. 12, whilst he blames them for their non-proficiency, yet those words, ' That when for the time ye might have been teachers,' &c., argues them to have been a long time converted; then again, chap. x. ver. 32, he bids to ' call to remembrance the former days,' &c., when first converted ; which had been long since past.

Obs. That in the conflicts and disquisition your spirits may have whether yourselves be temporary believers or no, consider that there are many things accidental to the state of grace, which you are not absolutely to conclude of your estates by.

(1.) Not by a great decay of what affections, and perhaps some principles of strictness you had at first, now much decayed and lessened. If these he wrote to had these as fresh in them when he wrote as at the first, he would not have remitted them to their experiments in former times,—' Call to remembrance,' says he, &c.—nor would he have comforted them with this, that God is not forgetful, &c., of what had been so long past, if fresher and better fruits, and more lively evidences, had of latter years been found in them.

(2.) Nor are you to judge of yourselves by a comparison of appearance made of yourselves, with some you have known or read of in the word to have gone so and so far, whom you verily think, as to your own view, whilst you compare yourselves with them, that they have fallen short. Alas! if these, among these Hebrews, should have compared their low present actings, enlightenings, workings of heart, &c., with those other in the appearance of them (as verses 4 and 5 he hath set them out), where would these poor ungrown Christians have appeared ? As it is an uncertain rule to judge a man's good, by comparing himself with others that are worse, so and so, fetching his comfort thence, so it is as uncertain a one to judge of myself and of my Christian estate, by comparing it with others whom I have thought better than myself, to have gone farther, who yet have proved apostates. For what do I know what was the frame of their hearts towards God, and the principles of their profession ? Thou dost not know the whole of the state and condition of such men, what it was. Bring then thy heart to God, and view all that hath been between him and thee, either of his love drawn forth to thee, or thine to him. Consider whether thy heart in some degree yet cleaves to God, and continues to pursue after him. So shalt thou have comfort from the Lord, who is not forgetful of any of these things. Cast not thy confidence away in such a case. If you let that go, you let all go ; hold fast the beginning of thy confidence to the end. Thus the apostle exhorts in this epistle again and again, chap. x. 35 : chap. iii. 6, ' But Christ as a Son over his own house ; whose house are we, if we hold fast the confidence and the rejoicing of the hope firm unto the end.'   This is what, above all else, the apostle exhorts unto, ver. 14. Some of these poor Hebrew Christians, that were sound-hearted, who had not fallen off and departed from Christ, as others had done, yet could not but have great doubts and disputes within themselves, whether they were not temporary believers, and that their latter end might be like unto theirs. For such a declining and ungrowing a condition could not but have been accompanied with such temptations, in a heart in any measure considerative or attentive to its own salvation. Yet you see the course the apostle takes with them.

[1.] He puts them not upon the dispute of this, which was a controversy and suit they could never have brought to an end, and which nothing but faith ends.

Nor [2.] doth he seek to work in them such a work of humbling or apprehension of their being in their natural condition, as useth to be at first ; wherein converts do cast away all that had been wrought hitherto as unsound, as if that were a necessary foundation in such unto a new saving work. He doth not direct them to make utterly a new beginning, as to their own apprehensions. But the case stands thus : that whereas sound believers use to have emptyings of themselves upon discovery of their wants and corruptions, which causeth them to apprehend, for the present, their conditions to be unregenerate, after which the Holy Ghost comes and takes the advantage out of themselves unto renewed acts of faith ; so these, having the convictions of their former unsoundness laid open to them by the Holy Ghost, are thereupon gently led into true and saving acts of faith, regenerating of them. And look, as afore this work, these temporaries had a work so like true grace as it was very hard to distinguish it from the true, so this very new saving work in them is hardly distinguishable from that renewed work on true believers upon and after such tentations.

[3.] He exhorts them to remember what had been wrought in them, and how God had drawn and won their hearts unto him, and accordingly that they should hold fast the beginning of their confidence to the end, and they would find themselves partakers of Christ. It is unto the way of renewing their faith he directs them ; for faith would only end it, and renew that often, says he : chap. iv. 11, ' Let us labour to enter into that rest, lest any man fall after the same example of unbelief.'   The word is, let us study that point, and to enter into rest is to believe, as the opposition, and likewise ver. 3, shew : ' For we which have believed do enter into rest.'

If any one object to me, Would you have me to recall my first work, and trust in that ? Suppose it were indeed not a saving work (as in many that are after made sound it is not), would you have me renew my confidence thereon ?

Ans. No ; that is not my meaning, nor Paul's. For if the work were never so good and sound, your confidence must not be upon that, much less when it may be a false one ; but this I say, renew the same acts of faith, and trust on the same God and Christ thou dealedst withal at first. Have recourse to them afresh, reiterate again and again thy faith on them immediately, as thou didst at first. In the original it is ' the *subsistence* of your confidence,' hold God and Christ afore thee as subsistent by faith to thee in thy treaties with them ; and if God continues to carry on thy heart thus to pursue after him, Christ cannot but save thee. For if thou continuest to cast thyself upon him, and still in all such disceptations about thy estate pliest him, and puttest thy salvation into his hands, Christ will not, cannot, depart from thee whilst he continues thy heart to trust him. He cannot but work savingly in the end on such a soul, if he hath not done it already. Remember then whence you are fallen, and do your first works and repent : Heb. vi. 11, ' And we desire that every one of you do shew the same diligence, to the full assurance of hope unto the end.' If you have slackened (as you have done), yet revive that diligence again, and you will find your first confidence will come in again, if true, with advantage and increase, even with full assurance of hope unto the end ; or if there was not a true faith at first, then a better will come in the room of it.

Only [4.] he severely cautions and admonisheth them to take heed lest there be in any of them an evil heart of unbelief, in departing from the living God : ' But exhort one another daily,' says he, ' while it is called to-day ; lest any of you be hardened through the deceitfulness of sin,' chap. iii. 12, 13 ; and ver. 15, ' While it is said, To-day, if you will hear his voice, harden not your hearts,' &c. He exhorts them to take heed of indulging their lusts : Heb. xii. 15–17, ' Looking diligently lest any man fail of the grace of God ; lest any root of bitterness springing up trouble you, and thereby many be defiled ; lest there be any fornicator or profane person, as Esau, who for one morsel of meat sold his birthright. For you know how that afterward, when he would have inherited the blessing, he was rejected : for he found no place of repentance, though he sought it carefully with tears.' He exhorts them to take heed of leaving off ordinances : Heb. x. 25, ' Not forsaking the assembling of ourselves, as the manner of some is ; but exhorting one another : and so much the more, as you see the day approaching.' And many such most earnest exhortations he makes, not only in relation to their neglect of particular duties, but in relation to their eternal estates and conditions.

BOOK VII.

*Of the difference of the works on temporary believers and those truly called,
and that they differ in their nature and kind.*

CHAPTER I.

That the apostle Peter, 2 Peter i. 3, 4 ; 2 Peter ii. 20, 21, makes a clear distinction between temporary professors and those truly called.

*According as his divine power hath given unto us all things that pertain unto
life and godliness, through the knowledge of him that hath called us to glory
and virtue: whereby are given unto us exceeding great and precious promises; that by these ye might be partakers of the divine nature, having
escaped the corruption that is in the world through lust.*—2 PET. I. 3, 4.

*For if after they have escaped the pollutions of the world, through the knowledge of the Lord and Saviour Jesus Christ, they are again entangled
therein, and overcome, the latter end is worse with them than the beginning.
For it had been better for them not to have known the way of righteousness,
than, after they have known it, to turn from the holy commandment delivered unto them.*—2 PET. II. 20, 21.

I HAVE set these two passages of the same epistle together, and by comparing the one with the other, you may easily discern that Peter would seem
to speak somewhat like, yet clear differing things of two several sorts of
professors, and two several works in those professors of religion. In the
second chapter, he speaks of such who professed religion, and had once a
work upon their hearts, which caused them at first so to do, and to break
forth from the world, ver. 18, and that ὄντως (as the word is), that is,
' *really* had escaped from them who live in error,' or the common error of
a natural condition, common to you with other men, but now were fallen
away, and their latter end was worse with them than the beginning, ver.
20–22. But in the first chapter, ver 1, he speaks of and unto such who
had obtained ' like precious faith with us,' namely, the apostles of Christ.
And of each of these he seems to speak like things (as on purpose), and
yet how distant are they in the reality !

1. Of both the one and the other he says, that ' they escaped the defilements of the world,' 2 Peter i. 3 ; ii. 20.

And 2. He tells us that both of them were wrought upon and induced to
this by one and the same means, ' through the knowledge of the Lord and
Saviour Jesus Christ ' (compare ver. 3 of chap. i. and ver. 20 of chap. ii.),
insomuch as both are enlightened with such a knowledge of Christ, as hath
a powerful impression upon their hearts, as it is said of these (2 Peter ii. 18)

that thus fall away, that they did *ὄντως*, really and indeed, and in earnest, forsake those sins.

Yet how differing is the state of these persons! The sum of which difference is reduced to this, that those (of whom he speaks in the first chapter) that were savingly wrought upon, had such a knowledge of Christ as had thoroughly altered and changed the frame of their hearts, their very natures and dispositions, turning and transforming them from sin to a divine nature.

1. It had prevailed to sever and part their souls from the power of inward lusts, as well as outward gross defilements, *ἀποφυγόντες τῆς ἐν ἐπιθυμίᾳ φθορᾶς*, 'that corruption that consisteth in lust or inward concupiscence.' The prevailing knowledge of Christ had destroyed and rent the indentures that had been between the soul and these corruptions; for the word *escaping* speaks and hath reference to freedom from the tyranny of a hard masster (or as it is, ver. 19 of chap. ii.), of being 'servants of corruption.' In these sincere believers, the divine power had cut the very heart-strings, ligaments, and ties between their souls and their lusts so far, that their inward man had really parted with, and was delivered from the strength and violence of lusts. But of those other, chap. ii., it is barely said they had escaped, *τὰ μιασμάτα*, 'the grosser defilements of the world,' ver. 20, that pollute men outwardly; in respect of which it is that they are said to have escaped from those that live in error, ver. 18. He mentions nothing to express that this work had reached to the destroying of lusts, or alteration of their sinful natures, but their case was as that of runaway servants. They had made an escape from their masters, but the inward bonds and indentures were not cancelled, and so they were fetched back again; ver. 19, 'While they promise them liberty, they themselves are servants of corruption: for of whom a man is overcome, of the same is he brought in bondage; which he affirms more plainly, ver. 22, comparing them to a sow that was once washed, which imports an external cleansing only, from the mire they wallowed in, which cleaves to the outward parts; but to escape the corruption that consists in lusts, to have the sinful nature, the inward radical constitution changed, this they wanted. The old man, or nature of man as it comes into the world, is said (Eph. iv. 22, like to what is here), to be 'corrupt in lusts;' that is, the formal being and essence of its corruption (as it is corrupt) is said to consist in lusts; and therefore to have escaped, through the knowledge of Christ, the corruption that is in lust, is to put off the old nature, to have the inward disposition altered; which there also the apostle affirms is done by such a knowledge of Christ as hath a difference in it from what is in ordinary professors: ver. 21, 'If so be ye have heard him, and been taught by him as the truth is in Jesus.' It imports a distinction from what is counterfeit, therefore, Gal. v. 24, those that are Christ's, are said to 'have crucified the lusts with the affections.'

2. Here is another difference, namely, the participation of a contrary divine nature. This divine nature clearly shews a change of nature; and so their having 'escaped the corruption that is in the world through lust,' 2 Peter i. 14, is the 'putting off the old nature, which is corrupt in lusts.' And on the other side, forasmuch that such a change from a state of natural corruption is specified with this divine nature as its opposite, it is evident that this participation of the divine nature is to be understood of the contrary divine qualities and principles, but now made natural to the soul, as lusts once were. But it is not the participation of the essence of God substantially, as some both of old and of late have offered to affirm.

My assertion is yet more clear, inasmuch as the apostle also calleth the communication of this new nature the ' giving of all things belonging to life and godliness ; ' that is, all inward principles, seeds, powers, and abilities of godliness, and a spiritual life, and those as the roots and habits of all actions made natural.   Now, look, as there is a different mercy or grace in God, out of which he bestows those gifts he vouchsafes unto men, whom in the issue he saveth not, different far from that mercy out of which he gives that grace and holiness which hath salvation accompanying it, so the like difference is to be found in the exertings of the degrees of his power, out of which he worketh either.   His mercies, that are over all his works, are styled common mercies, whereas to his elect, there are peculiar special mercies, called ' the sure mercies of David.'   Answerably the works on temporaries flow but from his common providential mercies, only farther heightened towards such than to others of mankind (these being choicer mercies in themselves than riches, honours, &c.), and are therefore styled common graces, as being in their general valuation cast but into the same heap with other common mercies.   But they are rather called common graces, because they bear the semblance and counterfeit of true and saving graces.

It is therefore a subject worth the prosecution, to shew the disproportion of power which is seen in these two works, that the measure of the one may be mutually taken from each other.   For the one, by the kind of it, will be found to be such a work as needeth not the exceeding greatness of God's power to be put forth to work it ; and the other, namely, the divine nature, is a work of that excellency, as requires the utmost of God's power to be stretched forth in the working of it, or it will not be effected.

CHAPTER II.

The usefulness of this doctrine concerning temporary believers to many holy ends and purposes.

The apostle farther, in this Heb. vi., sets forth the high and great workings which are in the hearts of temporary believers that fall away, and the dreadful event and issue of their so falling, ver. 8.   And as there were in those times the highest effusions of the Spirit and graces wrought in many true Christians in comparison of other times, so there were answerably the highest sort of temporaries (which verses 4, 5 doth speak of), and indeed the most sublimated that corrupt nature was capable of.

He adventures this doctrine among them, true believers that were weak and doubtful.   And notwithstanding there might be very many souls entangled in fears that they were of that number, yet this doctrine is good and profitable to men, as the apostle speaks in another case.

Obs. The doctrine and knowledge that there is only a temporary work in many professors, is useful to sincere Christians for many holy ends.   Peter declares it to those he wrote to : 2 Peter ii. 20–22, ' For if after they have escaped the pollutions of the world through the knowledge of the Lord and Saviour Jesus Christ, they are again entangled therein, and overcome, the latter end is worse with them than the beginning.   For it had been better for them not to have known the way of righteousness, than, after they have known it, to turn from the holy commandment delivered unto them.   But it is happened unto them according to the true proverb, The dog is turned to his own vomit again ; and the sow that was washed to her wallowing in the mire.' Jude also, upon occasion of men that had once professed the doctrine of grace, ver. 4, turned it unto wantonness, doth the like at ver. 5, ' I will put you in remembrance, though ye once knew this, how that the Lord, having saved the people out of the land of Egypt, afterward destroyed them that believed not.' The meaning whereof is, he would have them consider that the Israelites' coming out of Egypt was a type of our ' common salvation ' (as he hath called it, ver. 3) ; yea, many of them came forth through a work of God upon them, for they believed : Exod. iv. 31, ' And the people believed : and when they heard that the Lord had visited the children of Israel, and that he had looked upon their affliction, then they bowed their heads and worshipped.' They had been in great distress, and man's nature is apt to believe and embrace news of deliverance in such a case, which was a great ground of that faith in many of them ; but however, this, together with the sense of their bondage, moved them to come out of Egypt. You read of the like faith upon the great visible deliverance at the Red Sea ; Exod. xiv. 31, ' And Israel saw that great work which the Lord did upon the Egyptians : and the people feared the Lord, and believed the Lord, and his servant Moses.' But, says Jude, I would have you withal remember, that though their faith served to bring them out of Egypt, yet it was but a temporary faith, such as lasted not, nor served to bear the condition of a wilderness ; their faith failed them as to perseverance, cheerfully to go on into the good land. They would, if they could, have returned back into Egypt ; and you know the sins they fell into ; and concerning them Jude adds, that ' God afterwards destroyed them that thus believed not.' And this (saith he) though you know, yet I would have you remember and lay it to heart, as that which was God's aim and intendment in this dispensation, in relation to those their times, and the professors of it. It is of special use to you all ; for this is the case of multitudes of professors, that come out of a gross, sinful condition ; they see their former estate to be a state of bondage and damnation (which is as a coming out of Egypt), but their own lusts, in their progress in the wilderness of this life, ruins them. And what befell the Israelites as types, is for our instruction. 1 Cor. x. 11, ' Now all these things happened unto them for ensamples ; and they are written for our admonition, upon whom the ends of the world are come.'

And Jude tells them, that when he set himself to write of our ' common salvation,' ver. 3, the Holy Ghost, who dictated this epistle, presented this caution and discourse about such temporary professors first unto him to present unto them.

The like to this also doth Paul in his Epistle to the Hebrews, chap. iii. and iv., and 1 Cor. ix. 24 to the end : ' Know ye not that they which run in a race run all, but one receiveth the prize ? So run, that ye may obtain. And every man that striveth for the mastery is temperate in all things. Now they do it to obtain a corruptible crown, but we an incorruptible. I therefore so run, not as uncertainly ; so fight I, not as one that beateth the air : but I keep under my body, and bring it into subjection : lest that by any means, when I have preached to others, I myself should be a castaway.' He indeed in that chapter presents this under another scene, and similitudes of the Olympic games, in which many run, but one obtains ; and so in Christianity, many beat the air, and run but uncertainly.

And how much our Saviour insisted on this doctrine, you all know. How many parables did he spend upon it ? That parable of parables (as himself indigitates it to be) do you not understand to be, of all other, of the most concernment to you and others ? I mean that of the sower, and the several grounds ; and the parable likewise of those that built their house on the sand, when others built upon a rock ? Moreover, many speeches there are scattered up and down to this effect, that 'many are called, but few are chosen.' 'Enter in at the strait gate, for many will seek to enter in, and shall not be able,' Luke xiii. 24. The usefulness of this doctrine is,

1. To awaken dull professors, as our apostle terms those Hebrews, Heb. v. 11, to consider their estate. The wise virgins sleep, Mat. xxv. 4, as well as the foolish ; and the noise of this doctrine rouseth up such sooner than any other.

2. This doctrine is useful to quicken them to holiness, and to endeavour to make sure work. Thus it wrought with Paul himself, and Paul makes use thereof to quicken others. 1 Cor. ix. 26, 27, 'I therefore so run, not as uncertainly ; so fight I, not as one that beateth the air : but I keep under my body, and bring it unto subjection : lest that by any means, when I have preached to others, I myself should be a castaway.' He had this in his eye to the last, after he had done all : ver. 23, 'And this I do for the gospel's sake, that I might be partaker thereof with you.' The like use he makes of it unto all, in 2 Tim. ii. 19, &c. : 'Let every one that nameth the name of Christ depart from iniquity. But in a great house there are not only vessels of gold and of silver, but also of wood and of earth ; and some to honour, and some to dishonour. If a man therefore purge himself from these, he shall be a vessel unto honour, sanctified, and meet for the master's use, and prepared unto every good work.' It was upon the occasion of the examples of Hymeneus and Philetus, having gone so far, but now shipwrecked both in faith and conscience, that he thus wrote.

3. This doctrine exalts and magnifies unto us the grace of God towards us, as that which hath put so vast a difference between man and man in things that are so like to true grace, and that make men come so near to the kingdom of God. Who caused thee to differ (says the apostle) from another ? And that other perhaps had a mighty work upon him, which caused him to profess more than ever thou hadst done. Judas had a work upon him as well as Peter or the rest of the apostles; what put the difference ? God's free grace. 'Thine they were, and thou gavest them me; and I have lost none, but the son of perdition.'

4. As this doctrine is in these and many other respects useful to us, so God himself hath many holy and glorious ends in ordering such a dispensation to be found amongst professors.

(1.) It is for his greater honour and glory, as he is Lord over his church, which is his house, to have (as in great houses there use to be) 'vessels not only of gold and silver, but also of wood and of earth; and some to honour, and some to dishonour,' 2 Tim. ii. 20.

(2.) These dispensations of God, short of regenerating grace, do lay up matter for a great honour unto the man Christ Jesus, as he is to be the judge of all the world, and to give the exact account of every man's condition and ways and heart, and to judge of them accordingly. One would think that such a work of the Spirit as hath so great a likeness, and that with a reality joined with it, in the hearts and spirits of men, should make a great puzzle and blind at the latter day, how clearly to distinguish and discover to the men themselves, and all the world, that such professors as these were never truly regenerate, but this will turn to the greater glory to Christ: Heb. iv. 12, speaking of Christ, 'the Word' (as the close of his speech, ver. 13, shews, before the eyes of him 'with whom we have to do'); of him thus considered as the Word, he says, 'He, the Word of God, is quick and powerful, sharper than any two-edged sword, piercing even to the dividing asunder of soul and spirit, and of the joints and marrow, and is a discerner of the thoughts and intents of the heart. Neither is there any creature that is not manifest in his sight, but all things are naked and open to the eyes of him with whom we have to do.' He speaks this of him, as he is to be the judge of all men. 'All things are naked and open to the eyes of him,' πρὸς ὃν ὁ λόγος, 'to whom we must give the account.' And as in the next verses he represents him as a great high priest in all his compassions, and power 'to help in time of need,' so in these 12th and 13th verses he sets him out as a judge, with ability to detect all men to themselves; and he speaks this in a way of admonition, especially to such as were in danger to fall from a work of God upon them, and to become apostates. This the verse before shews us. 'Lest' (saith he) 'any man fall after the same example of unbelief,' of whom the Israelites in the wilderness were types. And because the discovery of all men's estates and conditions depends upon an exact dividing or differencing what is in the soul, what is in the spirit, and what are the joints all men's actions turn upon, and what is the marrow and intimate meaning and mind of every man's soul in his actions and ways and thoughts; and since such a discovery consists in laying open every man's ends and intents in his heart and thoughts and principles, hence therefore he compares the power of this judge unto such things as are most quick and powerful, as among metals mercury or quicksilver is, when it is put to other metals by them that are refiners. And though metals are blended and mingled one with another, or with dross never so much, yet this is so quick and so active as it will make every metal run a several way, and sever one from the other, and shew which is which. Thus the light that Christ shall then bring with him will do into all men's hearts, and all the thoughts and intents and principles, which are the foundations of men's actions, and which do difference them and give them their several kinds; these will all be clearly discovered; and though the creatures of our hearts (for so he compares our thoughts and intents and purposes, and the like) are for their kind unknown to us, because so like sometimes to the true goodness, yet the apostle says they are all manifest in Christ's sight, and all lie naked and open unto the eye of him; and he, when he comes to take the account, will lay them all open unto us, that let a man have never so fine-spun a work upon him, never so deep a counterfeit of what is true grace, the light that he will bring will make them all naked unto men themselves, as truly as they are to him. And it is certain that this manifestation and laying bare all men's hearts could be performed by none but him, or his Spirit, when he comes powerfully upon men to discover their estates to them. But the greatest difficulty of all lying in the similitude of these workings with those that are true and perfect, and hence the greatest difficulty in judging must needs lie here; therefore herein especially will Christ shew his glory and skill, and will give every man his accounts perfectly, and set all right and straight unto the least minute.

(3.) God dispenseth such lower workings, though short of regenerating grace, to make way for a fuller conviction of all sorts of wicked men at the latter day, and to justify himself in his condemnation of them. The great design God doth drive all along in this world upon the sons of men, is to clear himself at that day, and to confound them who shall be condemned ; at which day he will have a great deal to do with the hearts of men, to convince them, as ' Enoch the seventh from Adam in his prophecy, saying,' Jude 14, 15, ' Behold, the Lord cometh with ten thousand of his saints, to execute judgment upon all, and to convince all that are ungodly among them, of all their ungodly deeds, which they have ungodly committed, and of all their hard speeches which ungodly sinners have spoken against him.' The hardest speeches that men living under the gospel speak against him, are touching his ways and dispensations about grace ; and by this proceeding, he prepares both to confound the deepest practical opinions and sayings in men's hearts, and also the doctrinal opinions that men living under the gospel do take up hereabout.

1. As for the practical opinions in men's hearts, the greatest thing that God hath to do withal in all men's hearts, is this opinion, that they generally will not see nor believe that corrupt nature in themselves is so corrupt and disabled, to the attainment of that grace which only and necessarily must save them ; but on the contrary think, if they have anything that hath the appearance of good in them, that they can do and may do much to the salvation of themselves, especially if they shall be assisted and elevated by the Spirit of God, above what nature doth enable a man to do.   God hath on the one hand, as much to do with men in this point, as he hath, on the other hand, to do with men in the breaking forth of their lusts into grosser sins.   Men will not believe their own utter inability, and their dependence wholly upon free grace, and their total need of regenerating grace ; and therefore, by lesser experiments of the failure of lower and inferior workings of his upon them, God goes about to convince them of this their corruption and utter disability, and of the absolute necessity of their total dependence upon him, which yet they will not see ; and therefore God justly leaves them here, and works no further, and thereby lays a foundation of justifying his condemnation of them in their several proportions, and the rest of mankind, by the example of those that are wrought upon the highest.   And so God provides for nothing more than the conviction of men at the latter day, concerning the falsehood of their opinion of themselves in this respect.

(1.) Men's opinionativeness herein did cause even heathens to set up what light or virtues they found in themselves, as sufficient to bring them unto happiness.   We know the Stoics did set up *recta ratio*, right reason, for their rule, and their imagined perfection was, *vivere secundum naturam*, to live according to what seemed good in nature, either in light of conscience, or virtuous dispositions, or inclinations when acted and put in ure. Yea, so impudent hath the devil been, that he hath revived this, we see, in our days, in Quakers, yea, and caused them blasphemously to call this ' Christ within them.'   Hereupon, says God, and he says it justly, there shall be instances of some of you in the issue, to confute all the rest, in whom this light and these dispositions shall be tried to the utmost how far they will reach (as in Socrates, and Cato, and Aristides, &c.), and yet in the exercises of all these he leaves them, and gives them up unto that which shall convince them of an unregenerate estate ; as the apostle doth convince all those philosophers, that whilst they professed themselves wise they became fools, and glorified not God as God, nor were thankful ; and some of them were abandoned unto unnatural lusts, as Socrates to the love of Alcibiades, &c.   And however, if God hath not left them unto some great sort of wickedness or other, thereby to convince them, yet the discovery of the deficiency of all the light of their consciences, and of all their virtues and virtuous practices, and of the ends, intents, thoughts, and principles of their hearts, which shall be laid open at the latter day, will abundantly detect them, and leave this further conviction upon them herewith, that God had made trial of them in their sphere, how far corrupt nature could go, and yet how infinitely it fell short of true religion and happiness.

(2.) The Jews had a further addition both of knowledge and impressions that accompanied it. They had the knowledge of the law, and God did not deal so with any nation; and they had a zeal of God according to this knowledge, and they thought themselves sure to attain salvation if they set up with this new stock. I need not tell you, out of Rom. i. 6, how whilst they sought after righteousness with all this new raised stock, they did not attain unto the law of righteousness, ver. 31. And Paul's case, you know, Rom. vii., that what was ordained, as he thought, to life, he found to be unto death; and the conclusion which the apostle makes in Rom. viii. is this, 'that the law was weak through the flesh,' ver. 3; that is, all the assistance and energy which it could afford, through man's heart continuing still corrupt and flesh, remained ineffectual, like physic in a dead man's body; and the righteousness which they went about to establish, as the apostle says, they were not able to make it stand, though they attempted it again and again, no more than one is able to make a dead man stand, and to continue to do so, Rom. x. 3. So that we see that this addition also made unto the Jew would not do; and yet corrupt nature finding some assistance and strength come in thereby, they thought themselves sufficiently enabled for the attainment of salvation.

(3.) But then, thirdly, when Christ and the light of the gospel comes to be revealed to men, accompanied with divine enlightenings and tastes of the powers of the world to come, though still short of regeneration, men will presently be apt to say in their hearts, 'Who shall ascend to heaven? that is, to bring Christ down from above. Who shall descend into the deep? that is, to bring Christ again from the dead,' and to bring him into my heart. For still men think, and therefore say thus in their hearts, that by that new strength they may attain it (I take this to be the meaning of the place), and God affords them all helps towards it, inward and outward, true regenerating grace and a new principle of faith only excepted. Still he prosecutes the same design, that corrupt nature may see that when it attains unto the eleventh step of the twelve, and that men * not far off; yet corrupt nature, being corrupt nature still, though never so much assisted, falls short, and is weak and utterly unable. And these things God works once and twice, in a tendency to 'hide pride from man,' as Elihu speaks, that man might be emptied of that opinion of himself, and adore and give himself up to the grace of him who hath said, 'I will have mercy on whom I will have mercy;' and therefore it is 'not of him that wills, nor of him that runs, but of God that sheweth mercy,' Rom. ix. 15, 16. Paul, we see, there lays it upon that: God acts thus with men also, that they might see the absolute necessity of true regeneration and of a divine nature; but this men would not be brought to see, and therefore God justly leaves them to go on in their own way, and to enjoy their fond opinion to their destruction; because they would needs, against all these experiments, hold up this principle and self-opinion, in defiance of God's grace, and would be saved upon such terms as would make grace to be no grace. For if this opinion of self-working, though never so much assisted,

* Qu. 'even'?—Ed.

continues in the heart, the apostle tells us grace would be no more grace. And seeing that the glory of the grace of God would hereby be soiled, if God should save men upon such workings as these, though never so strict or high, he therefore justly, and with indignation, leaves them unto these their own counsels ; and hereupon it is that God and they do break off, whilst they are in the midst of a treaty with him for salvation. For they will never come off to receive God and his grace upon his own terms, nor set up God's banners of his free grace to them, and of sincere love to him, upon their turrets above self; and so by degrees the Lord withdraws his treaties from them, and they by degrees become revolters from him, and in the end return to some of their own rebellions, upon which God says, ' Which covenant and treaty they brake, and I regarded them not.'

Moreover, God by his discovering such as these never to have had true grace, under so high and eminent workings and actings, needs make but a short work (as to point of conviction) of all the rest; for all those who have lower works than these, of what kind soever, are with ease discovered to have had no grace, when these for a deficiency and want of a wedding garment, or marriage affection to God and Christ, are sent speechless to hell ; so then this design and dispensation of God is every way prepared for judging all men at the last day.

2. God hereby makes way to confound the corrupt doctrinal opinions that men have of grace. For this iniquity in practice hath come to be established in all ages by a law ; inasmuch as agreeably to men's deport-ment, according to their fond thoughts of corrupt nature's abilities in point of grace, they have framed doctrines, and drawn models of what they judge to be grace. All Pelagian, semi-Pelagian, and Jesuitical doctrines, and all Arminian tenets about converting grace, have in their several proportions arisen from what men in their own experience have taken to be true work-ings of grace in their own souls, or else from the pride of carnal wisdom, whereby men of learning and parts think to understand this (as Asaph hath it, Ps. lxxiii.), even as they think to comprehend anything else that is within the compass of man's understanding. And hence they think them-selves as sufficiently furnished to judge of matters of grace as of any other; yea, and would be thought of all things else to have skill in matters spi-ritual. Whereas, on the other hand, there are, and have been such, who, beside the doctrinal light they have had from the word in these points, have also had a deep and thorough experience of either sort of workings, both temporary, and of those other of saving, regenerating grace on them-selves ; and who, by comparing what the opinions of the Arminians are, and oppositely what are the orthodox doctrines, as they are stated in seve-ral columns in writings of either side, and then by comparing these with what hath been written on their hearts in those two several columns of workings (as I may so speak), have, and do clearly see and conclude that the Arminian doctrine about converting, sufficient grace hath been but a copy or model taken from the experience of a temporary work ; yea, and but for the most part of the lower sort, or of that of the stony ground. And though many persons that hold the Arminian doctrine in the point of conversion may and shall be saved (because they hold fundamental truths otherwise, and God works beyond and besides what men's speculative opi-nions are oftentimes), yet it is no thank to that doctrine of theirs in that particular point of conversion ; for if only such a work be wrought in any of them, that is no deeper nor higher than their doctrine requires, they would not be saved.

And the rule and measure these go by in drawing such draughts and schemes, either of conversion or of sufficient grace enabling to it, I say the rule and measure which misleads them is, that they set up free-will, and a grace attempered unto that kind of liberty of man's will which they have set up for themselves, to be essential to it as it is will, as they think, and by no means will permit such a doctrine of grace as shall detract from that kind of liberty as they conceive; which liberty, say they, can noway be saved, or stand with, or be preserved in that infusion of new principles, or an infallible, effectual working and overcoming the will, though done by all the power that is in God, and by an omnipotent sweetness that doth demulce it, as our doctrine of regeneration teacheth. So as they say and hold that free-will, set free by the light of the gospel, let into the understanding, may, and doth yield unto God savingly, with less power of grace than our doctrine requires; their bottom error lies in this, that they think if they should pitch upon that grace which we say is requisite, and absolutely necessary to salvation, then they must derogate from their *Diana* of free-will, and therefore they frame a doctrine that may stand with it. And then having made these draughts, they take liberty to rage and rant against our doctrine of free grace, either as it is in the workings of it in our hearts, or as we affirm it is in God's heart towards us, either in electing or regenerating grace, and representing God with our opinions herein, they take liberty to blaspheme him, that if he be such a God, he is so and so (not to repeat any). And it is wonderful to see what hard speeches they speak, as Jude says. And the bottom of the quarrel is free-will and self, as it is in man corrupted, which is set up as the great undertaker against God and his grace in all these things. They pretend and plead most outrageously, that if God will but take the shackles off, with which man's will is manacled, so as it be left to its own innate freedom, and if God will but move, and elevate, and assist it, and work upon the principles in it already, and strengthen them with an accessory and additional power of light and good motions, free-will shall then understand to will and run. And men will never be disputed out of their opinion of its ability to do thus, because they will not consider and acknowledge the bottom of corrupt nature, that it lies corrupt at the bottom, in the inward principles of it, in its foundations; and that let it be never so much assisted, if it be not regenerated and born again, it is never able so much as to see, much less to enter, or to put one step into the kingdom of God. They consider not, that without a regenerating passive principle wrought, the will itself and the affections, and all in man, remain corrupt as it was; and that the understanding may be enlightened to divine objects, and not be spiritualized, or endowed with a spiritual capacity of knowing spiritual things in their spiritual nature, and as they are in themselves; and such are the enlightenings here (Heb. vi.) spoken of. They do not consider how far this boasting will may be demulced, allured, and tolled on, and elevated to things of salvation, without having a principle of true love to God wrought in it: nor yet how far the affections may be moved and stirred with the cords of a man, that is, such as are suited to the principles in man, nor what good things there are in the promises, in Christ, in his righteousness and salvation, suited to work upon self in a man; and thereupon what tastes and joys may self be receptive of from all these. But all these workings will be found (as of the law it is said) weak through the flesh, through corruption of self remaining whole still at the bottom. And until this be inwardly mortified and deposed in the dominion of it, and the power of God come with that almightiness of working that raised Christ from the dead, putting in new principles of life and godliness, and making us partakers of the divine nature; until then, free-will, in all its conversions, whether to divine objects, or what else, is but as a door that turns upon its own hinges, moves but upon its own axle-tree, and within its own sphere, let it be moved and turned which way it will; and in these workings it is but (as I use to compare it) like a drop of water upon a board, which if you gently put your hot and dry finger to, and then as softly lift it, it will a while cleave and rise up; but if but a little farther, it falls down again to its own centre.

But oh! how severely doth God make way to confute and confound all these in their opinions! Wherein they deal most proudly, he goes beyond them, and is above them. Indeed, would there or could there any other course have been taken so effectually to stop their mouths, and so invincibly to convict them at the last day, as this?

1. He first in the world deals so with many of them, and with others of the sons of men, as to answer them according to the idol and stumbling-block of their opinions, and to that end tries to the utmost proportion in some or other, how far corrupt nature of itself, and left still to its innate corruption, will rise and go, and yet remain but corrupt nature and self at bottom still. He tries how far all in man may be so wrought upon, as hath been said; and yet so allays and moderates his workings, as their hearts still fall short of the glory of God, or of his regenerating grace flowing from election, which these men so despise. And herein free-will and self, which they adore so much, continues (even as they desire) with the same principles that by nature they have, and devoid of having an inward principle and root of grace; and this, according to their doctrine, is their desire also. So that indeed by these means, by making these experiments on corrupt nature, God doth but make way for the triumph of his grace over the proud conceits of self, which are in mankind, and which are most natural, and the most deeply rooted of any other.

Then, 2. When he, at the latter day, brings forth his true saints, and his workings upon them, and (as it is in the prophet) says, 'These are my witnesses,' and then lays open (what he hid from those other, the wise and prudent) what real, true, and uncounterfeit workings and experiments of his grace there were in their hearts, suitable unto the true doctrines of eternal love and invincible grace; when he displays what a new heart and new spirit he gave them, and how he wrote the law in their hearts, and taught them all anew to know him with a new and spiritual light, and put his Spirit in the midst of them, that should cause them to walk in his commandments, and put his fear into their hearts that they should not depart from him; and then shall produce what the word says, together with what hath been in their hearts and souls, beyond what all the doctrine of the adversaries of his grace taught; and when it shall be discovered, that the workings which these adversaries had, according to their doctrine; yet failed of the grace of God (as the apostle speaks), even for want of that farther power to be put forth by God, which they desired not of him to bestow upon them; what a fatal decision, though a final one, will this be, whereby God will put an end to their controversy!

For then, 3, he will come upon them with their own principles: Isa. v. 3, 4, 'And now judge, I pray you, betwixt me and my vineyard. What could have been done more to my vineyard, that I have not done in it? wherefore, when I looked that it should bring forth grapes, brought it forth wild grapes?' This is your sufficient grace, which yourselves desired, and

would have none other.   Much good may your free-will-grace do you!
You have had, many of you, enough of it; as God in that place of Isaiah
speaks those words unto proud man, that under the covenant of works
would be setting up his own abilities, which God, according to their principles, had assisted.   This (as I take it) is the true air of the interpretation
of that place.   He will, in like manner, plead against these at the latter
day; and then must all men fall down and acknowledge that it was the
grace of God alone could save, which before man would never understand
nor be brought unto.   In these men (whose work is deciphered here, Heb. vi.)
God did vouchsafe as full a sufficient grace, according to their principles,
as they do describe or desire in their low model of doctrines; for they will
needs argue these men to have been actually converted, and to have walked
as true and sincere Christians, which yet how short it was of saving grace,
I have out of the 9th and 10th verses shewn.   So then, God will be found
to have gone beyond their doctrines and demands; yea, and it will appear,
that because God did not farther work that in them which we say saving
grace must do (and those verses 9, 10 shew), that therefore, and therein,
they were short of grace.

CHAPTER III.

*That a genuine saving work of grace is specifically distinct from that which is
in a temporary believer, evidenced from a consideration of the state of the
thorny ground here, in Heb. vi., set in parallel with the parable of the
sower in the Evangelists.—Some observations on the whole.*

In prosecution of my discourse about the nature of the work wrought in
temporary believers, and to prove that the true work of grace wrought in
sincere believers is specifically distinct from it, I shall now consider the state
of the thorny ground, as represented in Heb. vi. 7, 8, ' For the earth which
drinketh in the rain that cometh oft upon it, and bringeth forth herbs meet
for them by whom it is dressed, receiveth blessing from God: but that
which beareth thorns and briers is rejected, and is nigh unto cursing;
whose end is to be burned.'
    1. I shall consider the parallel these words do hold with the thorny
ground in the parable of the sower, in respect of what each brings forth.
    2. I shall consider the allusion whereby the event or issue that in the
end befalleth these thorny-ground professors that fall away, is set forth in
those words: (1.) *Nigh unto cursing.*   (2.) *Whose end is to be burned.*
    3. I shall consider the import of the similitudes whereby the means by
which they are wrought upon are set out. (1.) Rain. (2.) The dressing.
    4. Some observations upon all.
    1. As for the parallel which this text, Heb. vi. 7, 8, holds with the
thorny ground in the parable of the sower, an allusion here seems expressly
to be intended.
    In the substance and reality of the things, the works here spoken of by
Paul, from which men fall away, are one and the same with those mentioned in the parable.   For he speaks here of the highest sort of workings
upon men that fall away, as the descriptions of the workings themselves
shew, viz., their being ' enlightened, and having tasted of the heavenly gift,
and being made partakers of the Holy Ghost, and having tasted the good
word of God, and the powers of the world to come.'   And as in the primi-

tive times there were in true believers the highest communications of graces and of the Holy Ghost, so there were then the highest elevations and raisings up of the principles in men unregenerate, and influences of the Spirit upon them; and here he mentioneth the highest of what are spoken anywhere in any other place of Scripture.

Now then in like manner, in the parable, the order of Christ's placing the thorny ground, and the works thereon, doth speak the highest work of them that fall away. For, as for the stony ground, that imports a lower degree of working upon it than that of the thorny; and there is no other work mentioned by our Saviour (whose scope was perfectly to set down all the several sorts of hearers and professors) beyond the thorny, but only the good ground, the good and honest heart that brings forth fruit with patience to the end. And therefore, this work on the thorny ground is, of temporary works, the highest, and so in reality is one and the same with this in Heb. vi.

But let us compare the analogy of the words and phrases, and so thereby of the things that are found in that parable, and in these words of Paul.

As there in the parable you find three hearts or hearers, compared in general unto the ground which seed is sown in, to the end to bring forth fruit, so here unto the earth which drinks in the rain from heaven, to the end to bring forth herbs, doth answer. For those words, ' The earth that drinks in the rain,' ver. 7, are to be carried down unto ver. 8, in common spoken both of good and bad, and are thus to be read in ver. 8, ' But that earth which drinks in the rain and bears the thorns,' &c. The comparison is in all unto the earth in bearing and bringing forth; this in general.

But secondly, and more particularly, the parallel here and there, as concerning the good ground, agrees perfectly in both, even in this, that the good heart or good ground there in the parable, is said to bring forth fruit to perfection : Mark iv. 8, ' And the other fell on good ground, and did yield fruit that sprang up and increased, and brought forth, some thirty, and some sixty, and some an hundred.' 1. It yielded fruit. 2. That sprang up. 3. And increased and brought forth ; that is, continued to bring forth, some thirty, &c., even till the harvest, and so from first to last had some fruit all along. But of the thorny ground it is oppositely spoken. 1. That it brought forth no fruit, Mark iv. 7. 2. That it became unfruitful, Mat. xiii. 22. 3. That it brought no fruit to perfection, Luke viii. 14. The meaning of all which comes to this, that it brought forth no true perfect fruit, for the kind of fruit, as also not fruit to the end of their days, unto the harvest, or unto maturity. Thus we have it in the parable. And answerably we have here, Heb. vi. 7, the difference between the two earths or soils : that the ground that is good, and blessed, is said, 1, to bring forth herbs meet for them by whom it is dressed ; 2, and to receive a blessing from God. The first imports that it brings forth true and wholesome herbs, meet for his use, for his taste, his gust, for his diet, as the margin varies it.

Yea, and critics have observed this difference between the two earths here in this place (which I make use of unto this correspondency with the parable), that concerning the good earth here, and of its bringing forth its herbs, the phrase used is τίκτουσα, it begets, and brings them forth as a mature birth ripened to perfection ; as when a woman goes forth her whole time. For in allusion unto a woman's bringing forth, is a womb ascribed unto this earth (as ordinarily it useth to be), and so a double metaphor is insinuated. But of the other earth (ver. 8, as prosecuting the same), it is said ἐκφέρουσα, they cast out their production as abortive births, and so their best fruits arrive not at perfection, but end in abortiveness. And indeed if we would study an expression whereby to set out the difference of a temporary and a saving work, or a holy calling, we could not do it more lively than to say, that the one is a ripe and perfect birth, the other but a *mola*, an abortive; and becomes such through and from the deficiency in the work itself from the first, as women's abortives usually are. However, the issue of this second parallel is this, that the actings and products of the thorny ground professors were never true fruit, for neither Christ nor the apostle here do vouchsafe them that name.

And I may strengthen this parallel from that of Jude, who speaks of the same sort, or of like professors. That those he so vehemently inveighs against once were professors, is many ways evident, as having been such as once had had some green fruit: ver. 12, ' Trees whose fruit withereth' (says he), and once had some life (why else are they called ' trees twice dead'), once in Adam, and then wrought on anew, and then dead a second time. And yet, lo, he plainly concludes of them, that they had no fruit. They are (saith he) ' trees whose fruit withereth, and are without fruit,' wherein he corrects his first, having said, ' whose fruit withereth,' because it might be thought thereupon that yet at least he acknowledged they once had some fruit, and that fresh and lively, and therein did honour them. Therefore he in this after-saying absolutely denies it, that they ever had any true fruit. No, ' they are without fruit,' says he.

The third parallel is, that in the very letter the apostle, ver. 8, doth describe these temporaries by the same similitude by which our Saviour sets out that third and highest sort of professors, that ' they both bring forth thorns.' And this is the most characteristical and most eminent decipher-ing whereby either of them did set them forth; and therefore, besides the reality in what is the main, they in the very letter agree.

And for the further illustration of either, I shall pursue this query, whether in the intendment both of the apostle here, and of Christ in the parable be, that the thorny earth in both places did bring nothing but thorns ?

1. In the intention of the apostle it is so to be understood; for not only he mentioneth no fruit at all, but thorns only ; but takes it in its compara-tive opposition unto the good earth's bringing forth good herbs, as in difference from this, and therefore this other earth brings forth no such herbs at all, but only these thorns instead thereof. And this sense is confirmed by this, that seeing the best earth, or hearts of the holiest upon earth, do bring forth thorns as plentifully as it doth herbs, therefore the point of difference in this opposition must lie in this, that this second earth brings forth nothing but thorns and briars, and no herbs at all; whereas that other did bring forth some herbs, for if it also brought forth no herbs, there would be no difference between them.

If it be said that he speaks of this bad earth, how that in the end it brings forth thorns, and so is cursed, but not so from the first,

The reply is, 1. That if this earth had brought forth herbs at first, as well as thorns, as the other earth doth, then it would have received a bless-ing from God upon such its bringing forth, so as to bring forth more, for that is also one difference put between the one and the other. 2. The apostle (in the 9th and 10th verses) shews in the persons and instances of these Hebrews, that the difference between them was not confined unto what was the event on either side, but extended unto what, from the very first of their being good earth, they had brought forth. This the apostle doth here, and also chap. x. ver. 32. In both he refers them to time past, yea, unto the first: chap. x. ver. 32, ' But call to remembrance the former days, in which, after ye were illuminated, ye endured a great fight of afflictions.' And he doth it also here, ver. 9, 10, ' But, beloved, we are persuaded better things of you, and things that accompany salvation, though we thus speak ; for God is not unrighteous to forget your work and labour of love, which ye have shewed towards his name, in that ye have ministered to the saints, and do minister.' Therefore oppositely (in this 8th verse), speaking of the other earth, his meaning must be, that for time past, yea, and from the first, these only had brought forth even thorns, and nothing else.

2. For the parable, I urge that in the Πρότασις, or forepart of it, there is this expression: Luke viii. 7, ' Some' (of the seeds, namely) ' fell among thorns, and the thorns sprang up with it.' Where,

(1.) The word συμφυεῖσαι, imports at least that from the very first, together with the word, there were thorns sprung up. This cannot be denied, and therefore take it as it is styled, a ' thorny ground' (in difference from the good ground), and it is to be understood to have been such as brought forth thorns from the first, in such a manner as the good ground did not ; for otherwise even the good ground doth bring forth some thorns from the first, and it cannot be otherwise ; but this of the thorns must be understood with difference.

(2.) That word also may, and doth sometimes import a coalescency, or a growing up into a oneness, or a becoming one (as Grotius hath observed,* and quotes this very phrase, Luke viii. 7, for that signification), as well as a springing up together from the first, or all along, and so implies that some of the thorns did at least coalesce and become one with what these men had received of the word, and as they received it ; for it is the same word that is used of our ingrafture into, and our being one with Christ as our root : Rom. vi. 5, ' If we have been planted together,' &c. The main emphasis of which speech lies not in this only, that all the saints are ingrafted together, but chiefly in this, that Christ and all and each saint are ' planted together,' and are σύμφυτοι, for it refers to it as explaining his foregoing speech : ver. 3, ' Know ye not that as many of us as were baptized into Jesus Christ,' which (here in ver. 5) he explaineth by our being ' planted together with him,' it having been into him, and therefore ' were baptized into his death' (which here in ver. 5 is explained by a being planted together into the likeness of his death, &c.), baptism being the sacrament signifying our ingrafture into Christ, ver. 3, and our being planted together with Christ into the same conformity, being the thing signified thereby, ver. 5. Now in the like sense here the thorns and the work of the word in the heart are said to grow into one, to be σύμφυτοι ; that is, the word they received was admitted by way of ingrafture upon some thorns or other in the heart, and thence all the actings of their spirits were but fruits of flesh, as the root of them, though conversant about spiritual objects ; and if so, then all such actings of spirits unrenewed are no other unto God than thorns in reality, although in view and in speciousness herbs and fruits.

And certainly the reason of the thing itself falls in fully for this, for to sow among thorns, or earth where thorns are unploughed up, or in the midst

---

* Græcis συμφύεσθαι dicuntur quæ in unum coalescunt, ut plantæ quædam, Luke viii. 7, &c.—*Grotius*, in Rom. vi. 5.

of thorns, ἐν μέσῳ (as the parable, Luke viii. 7, hath it), is all one in Scripture phrase as to sow seed upon a heart remaining still wholly unregenerate : Jer. iv. 3, 'Break up your fallow ground, and sow not among thorns,' which is interpreted to be, ver. 4, ' Circumcise yourselves to the Lord, and take away the foreskin of your hearts ;' so as to sow among thorns is to plant the word received in a heart that remains utterly flesh still.   And as this is the mind of the prophet's caution there, so it must be understood to be the mind of Christ here in the parable, that there were no other principles in the heart to receive that word into, so as to affect the heart, but what was flesh, and so there was an ingrafture of it upon, and a coalescency with, some root of thorns or other ; and it cannot be otherwise, if the heart remains thorny ground.

But here may this *objection* be made, That in the interpretation of the parable these thorns are said to enter in after the seed was received into the ground, Mark iv. 19, and so the whole sense of the parable is to be restrained thereunto.

I *answer*, That indeed there is one sort of thorns that do as it were anew arise, and so are said to enter in after the seed was received into these men's hearts ; and they are such as Christ (in that 19th verse) instances in, viz., either worldly lusts or gross sins, the tops whereof, by the power of the word, when it was received even into these men's hearts, were lopped off, so far as they grew above ground ; of which thing Calvin was well aware whilst he notes upon it, ' That though indeed evil lusts, before the word riseth up unto a stalk ' (in these men's hearts), ' did wholly possess the heart, that yet they did not seem to be predominant at the first beginnings ' (of such men's being so wrought upon), ' but to come or steal upon them by little and little, after the word is grown up into some blade, and where it promiseth some fruit.'   Yet still, say I, this noway lets but that there might be some other thorns that should rise up with the word received even from the first, which I will call in respect of their objects *spiritual thorns*, seeing in their root they are *fleshly*, and indeed but the affections and actings of self upon what is in the word suitable thereunto ; and my reason is, because these two speeches of Christ, the one of which is in Luke, ' They sprung up together with the word,' and the other is in Mark, which speaks of lusts entering in afterward, must be reconciled ; especially considering withal that these thorny professors were men unregenerate, and by their thorns so distinguished from the good ground at the very first, the reconciliation seems easy ; for that speech, ' They sprang up together,' expresseth and takes in the whole from first to last, as to this sense, that some were still springing up, and not at last only, but from the first, insomuch as there were some or other all along.   There were at first those spiritual thorns, and afterward those other worldly thorns, so as, what with the one and with the other, there was still a growing up of thorns all the while, which do both of them also tend to ' choke the word,' as it is there said, received in the heart.   For selfish affections unto spiritual things are still behind-hand with themselves, and do destroy themselves (as Aristotle says of vices), and through their intermingling with the word received do hinder and spoil the efficacy thereof, and turn all into sin.   And then again those other thorns, namely, worldly lusts, supervening, do more conspicuously choke that word, by sucking and drawing away all the sap and juice, and intention of the mind from those spiritual objects at first entertained.   And these latter are said to ' enter in,' as it were anew, because indeed the former growth of such lusts was (so far as before this new work they appeared above ground) in a great measure as then cut down; what through errors of conscience, sense of sin, tastings of the powers of the world to come, by which the intention of the mind was drawn out another way, yet still self remained in its full vigour the same, though diverted another way, and turned upon other objects.   Hence therefore all those worldly lusts do in their root remain still unstubbed up, for they are all seated in self, and if that be not mortified, then they all remain unmortified at the bottom, and will in the end rise up as much as ever; for worldly pleasures are the natural objects suited to the genius and disposition of self-love, as it is now corrupted, and are the natural channel for corrupt self to run in.   But, on the other hand, its diversion unto spiritual objects of the other world (whilst itself remains in its native strength) is but forced and with a violence offered upon it, and therefore will not continue; and for the same reason those other worldly lusts will sooner or later sprout and revive, as Job speaking of a tree says, Job xiv. 7, 8, 9, 'There is hope of a tree, if it be cut down, that it will sprout again, and that the tender branch thereof will not cease; though the root thereof was old in the earth, and the stock thereof die in the ground, yet through the scent of water it will bud, and bring forth boughs like a plant.'   Thus here, in the case before us, the general root of self is still as much alive as ever; and upon the fresh scent of former objects presenting themselves, who had been the old and natural acquaintance of their hearts, they obtain their wonted life and strength again, and overcome, as Peter says.

2. The second thing proposed is the dreadful issue that befalls the thorny ground professors, and the allusions it is set forth by.

(1.) In this life, *nigh unto cursing.*

(2.) *Whose end is to be burned,* in the world to come.

Our Saviour Christ in the parable doth not mention this dreadful issue, for his main scope was to shew the causes of each ground's unfruitfulness; but Paul's drift is mainly and farther to shew the end of such men.

(1.) They are *nigh unto cursing.* This hath relation and allusion to the condition of the earth afore the fall, and after the fall: I say the earth, for the *substratum*, or principal subject-matter or thing the comparison runs upon, is the earth, to which men and their hearts are compared: so ver. 7, 'The earth which brings forth,' &c.; ver. 8, but 'that earth,' namely, 'that brings forth thorns,' &c., it is that earth is nigh unto cursing; so as to make out the allusion we must find out some earth that was cursed; and what other earth do we find to have been cursed but that earth for Adam's sin? And so as Adam himself was a type of Christ (Rom. v.), and Adam's world afore his fall a type of the world to come (Heb. ii.), so upon Adam's falling, the curse of his earth was the type of such persons that should apostatize from Christ.   And so the allusion holds thus, that as before the fall the earth was so fruitful that with a small pains it would bring forth fruit, in comparison of what it did after the curse, as those words, 'In the sweat of thy brow,' &c., do shew.   But how it was after the fall accursed you read, Gen. iii. 17, 'The ground for thy sake is cursed; thorns also and thistles shall it bring forth to thee.'   Now to make up this comparison about the thing in hand.   Man's heart before the fall was a paradise to God, planted 'wholly a right seed,' as the prophet expresses it; and man himself was blessed of God, and God rejoiced in him, Gen. i. 31.   But now man, being fallen, is cursed, and brings forth nothing but thorns and briars.   Well, but yet the Lord comes again to cultivate and till the earth of some men's hearts a second time, sows his seed, and comes with rain, and sends dressers to manure it, but it still brings forth thorns; then it is nigh unto a final cursing, says he, as the earth was then cursed. See Isa. v. 1, 2, Jude, ver. 12, 'Trees twice dead,' once in Adam, and then after their fall some little life was put into them, but they brought forth thorns. And Peter, writing of the same sort of men (as you well know that Jude doth), his express sentence of them is, 2 Peter ii. 14, 'cursed children.'

(2.) *Whose end is to be burned.*

That the thorns are to be burned is not immediately said of them, but that the earth shall be burned, and therefore by consequent the thorns that are found growing thereupon; yea, and the thorns being set on fire, do help towards that fire that burneth the earth together with themselves. Now, the earth notifies the *man*, the person, and the thorns his *works* and fruits brought forth; but it is the man chiefly, for he is the earth. This I take to be an allusion to the land of Sodom and Gomorrah, with the inhabitants of all sorts on it. The soil of Sodom and Gomorrah, before its being burned, was, as you find Gen. xiii. 10, 'Behold all the plain of Jordan, that it was well watered everywhere, before the Lord destroyed Sodom and Gomorrah, even as the garden of the Lord.' It was like to paradise itself (which we spoke of before) before God destroyed it. Thus here the rain comes often upon this earth, and it is watered with better water than ever paradise was; but the effect of all being that it brings forth thorns, then follows that which is equivalent unto the curse of Sodom; for God comes upon that land with fire from heaven, and burned the very ground as well as all that were upon it. He did not only turn it into barrenness, as when it is said 'a fruitful land shall be turned into a desert' (so the psalmist), but it was turned into a lake, and that a sulphurous lake of fire and brimstone, out of which such vapours do arise as kill birds that fly over it; and the fruits that grow upon the banks do, through the heat and fire that is in the earth, turn to dust, which fruits are called proverbially 'the apples of Sodom.' The very rocks are blasted, and the ground smells of fire to this day. Now, to this earth are the hearts of apostates here compared, in their fatal and final punishment in the other world. And Jude's comparison, when he speaks of these, is the same: 'Even as Sodom and Gomorrah,' says he, 'and the cities about them, in like manner giving themselves over to fornication, and going after strange flesh, are set forth for an example, suffering the vengeance of eternal fire.' He speaks of such very apostates, and these that were trees twice dead. And on the contrary, he thereupon comforts and encourages the 'preserved in Jesus Christ;' as ver. 1, in a purposed opposition, he styles them, in reference to these apostates. Oh! bless God for election! that we were not left to be such professors as these, bringing forth nothing but thorns, whose end is to be burned; as, if he had left us to our own spirits, and had not changed our hearts, we had been: Rom. ix. 29, 'Except the Lord had left us a seed' (viz., of election), 'we had been as Sodom, and like unto Gomorrah.' It would have been the issue of us all, we should have been burned with our thorns.

3. We have next the rain falling on this earth, and its being dressed, spoken of. This is the third part of his comparison, wherein he compares the means of grace whereby men are wrought upon unto two things: (1.) The rain; (2.) The dressing of the earth. The rain I take to be inward means vouchsafed, viz., those illapses, enlightenings, good motions, and comings of the Spirit of God upon man's soul, falling immediately from heaven, as the rain does. The dressing is the outward means, as preaching of the word, and other ordinances, differing from and besides the rain, as when it is said that 'Paul plants, Apollos waters,' &c., 1 Cor. iii. 6,

there is the dressing; but the rain is the inward means, of which I understand that of James, when he speaks of the husbandman's waiting for the
harvest: James v. 7, says he, 'He hath long patience for it, until he receiveth the early and latter rain.' These come before the harvest, and are
those inward influences and refreshments which do accompany the outward
means. The Lord affords such rain to poor souls when they need it,
some at one time, which is the early rain, and some again at another
time, still as they need it; and all tends to ripen the fruit, and keep the
soul in heart, as the rain doth the earth. And then what man doth in the
outward ministry of the ordinances, that is the dressings or culture here
spoken of.

Now I come to the observations, which are of three sorts:

1. Upon the ground that is cursed.

2. Upon the ground that was fruitful.

3. Concerning the means, rain, &c. These two latter I shall put under
one head.

1. The first sort of observations is upon the ground that bore thorns,
and that was cursed. (1.) From that of the earth bearing thorns, although
the good word had been sown into it; and although the rain had come
upon it, and it had drunk in that rain, yet the heart remaining only carnal,
and the roots of thorns abiding (as hath been opened), it brought forth no
other product. Observe, that all means, inward and outward, and influences from heaven, do but nourish self, and but cause worldly lusts and
self-love to grow. Take a poisoned plant, plant it by another wholesome
herb in the same ground, and let the rain fall upon both, yet the rain and
the ground nourishes the poison in the one, and causes that to grow, as
well as a good plant in the other. So that we have no way but to turn to
God, and to get the thorns out, and new principles in their room. Yea,
in a regenerate man, so far forth as the roots of thorns remain, so far forth
all the actings of the spirit will be the actings of the flesh, and so but thorns.
The root is thorn, and the fruit will be like the root; as Christ says, that
the fruit was like the tree. They are all thorns to God; and carnal affections to spiritual things, or affections arising merely from self-love to divine
objects, will make fuel for hell, as well as worldly lusts; they are all thorns
in the eyes of God.

(2.) Observe, concerning these thorny professors, that God proceedeth
towards them in casting them off by degrees, and not presently upon the
first advantages against them, which is apparent out of the text.

For [1.] he continues the rain, the inward good motions, long to them;
for that which is said, ver. 7, 'the earth that oft drinks in the rain,' is to
be understood ἀπὸ κοινοῦ, and to be carried to the 8th verse, and applied to
this earth that brings forth thorns as well as to the good; for that is spoken
in common, both to the one that brings forth herbs, &c., and to that other
that is rejected.

[2.] After such a bringing forth of thorns for some long space of time,
he yet proceeds by degrees. As, *first*, though within himself and in his
own purpose he rejects them sooner, that is, he purposeth, if they persist
still to bring forth no other fruit than thorns, to have no more to do with
them: Luke xiii. 7, 'Then said he unto the dresser of his vineyard, Behold,
these three years I come seeking fruit on this fig-tree, and find none; cut
it down, why cumbereth it the ground?' He, after two years' expectation,
had his heart taken off from them, and began to have no pleasure in them,
as the Epistle to the Hebrews expresseth it, yet still continued a-dressing

of it: ver. 8, 'For he answering said unto him, Lord, let it alone this year also, till I shall dig about it, and dung it;' and withal God sends rain upon it as aforetime. But, *secondly*, after some further expectation, it becomes 'nigh unto cursing.' Now, what it is for God to curse finally, you may know by the contrary dispensation towards the good here in ver. 7, 'The earth that brings forth herbs,' &c., 'receives a blessing from God;' that is, so as to bring forth more herbs, which the parable calleth 'an increase,' and which Christ, John xv. 2, thus expresseth, 'Every branch that bringeth forth in me he purgeth it, to bring forth more fruit.' And that is the blessing it receives here in this world, nor can there be a greater blessing in this life vouchsafed; and yet still to be nigh unto cursing imports God's loathness and backwardness finally to pronounce it; only in the meanwhile he withdraws his influences, till—*Thirdly*, At the last he curseth them indeed, as he did those in 2 Pet. ii. 14, 'cursed children;' and as he did the fig-tree, Mat. xxi. 19, 'And when he saw a fig-tree in the way, he came to it, and found nothing thereon but leaves only, and said unto it, Let no fruit grow on thee henceforward for ever. And presently the fig-tree withered away.' Now, as Paul says, 'doth God take care of oxen?' No; his aim was further, at ministers in them. So here, doth Christ curse fig-trees? No; his aim is to shew how he curseth in the end fruitless souls. He says of such a soul, Let never fruit grow more on thee; and look, as that tree stood still in the same place, but yet none of its former fruit grew thereon, so men may profess religion after such a cursing of them, and continue in the church and under ordinances, but never a prayer with affection grows any more thereon, no more dews from heaven, or inward correspondences with God.

Use. Let us take heed therefore, and eye the withdrawings of God, and mourn presently, lest we grow nigh unto cursing; let us watch the rising up of thorns, for they will bring a curse of bringing forth worser and sharper thorns; and let us humble ourselves for them, and seek to root them out.

(3.) Observe God's dealings with these men, that having had workings on them, do fall away. You see how dreadful they are. Everywhere you find this dreadfulness expressed: 'He built his house' (says Christ) 'upon the sand, and the fall of that house was great.' All the sermons he had heard, and all the profession he had made, and all he had done, fell upon him and broke him to powder. Read Jude: you have black words given to such. The blackest words that ever fell from the Holy Ghost's pen, are to be found in Peter (2 Peter ii.) and in this Jude, concerning such men, for whom the blackness of darkness (he says) is reserved; read but that epistle. Then says Peter, 2 Peter ii., 'If they be again entangled and overcome of corruption, their latter end is worse than their beginning; for it had been better for them not to have known the way of righteousness,' &c. Men cannot profess religion at that rate they may profess other things.

The consideration of these things should awaken and quicken us to be observant how thorns grow in our hearts, viz., worldly lusts, cares, murmuring, unthankfulness, inordinate fancies of what in the world we would be. And we should be watchful to keep them from growing up in us, as also to observe narrowly any steps or beginnings of God's withdrawings from us; for they tend to cursing, and we should never be quiet in such a case.

II. The second sort of observations is, concerning the good earth, and the means vouchsafed.

1. Observe, even in good hearts that have a blessing from God, the fruit, or at least the increase of that fruit, doth not appear oftentimes of a long while. This is plain out of the text ; for of the good earth that brings forth herbs, it is said, ' The earth, which drinks in the rain that comes often upon it, brings forth herbs meet,' &c., and receives a blessing from God to bring forth more. If therefore thou dost bring forth herbs meet for God after the rain hath come oft upon thee, it is well ; thou art still within the compass of receiving a blessing from God. Affliction works the quiet fruit of righteousness, after we have been exercised thereby ; but it is afterward, not presently.

2. Observe, God's saving and through workings in the spirits of men are not always in violent ways, but in gentle, sweet, soaking dispensations. The word ὑετὸς here, signifies your mizzling rain, *molliores et minores guttas* (saith Hyperius), as the Israelites, 1 Cor. x. 2, were sprinkled in the cloud ; it was such a rain as falls in a mist. Multitudes of souls are not wrought upon by stormy showers of rain falling with thick drops. No. There comes your gentle rain, ' the early and the latter,' as the poor soul hath need thereof, and bedews his heart. He prays and goes to bed, and it may be in the morning finds some dew upon his heart. Now wilt thou comfort thyself, though thy work goes on but gently, yet it goes on surely. Thou hast not those high manifestations and sudden sensible comings in thou hearest others speak of, yet thou hast God's presence in a subsistence to thy heart, and thy heart drinks it in, and goes away strengthened and quickened. There is a still work that doth not make a noise, when some that are far greater works decay, and like a land-flood dry up. Of the sly husbandman that found the treasure in the field, it is said, that ' he did hide it,' but for joy thereof went and sold all he had for it, Mat. xiii. 44.

I shall answer but an objection or two which good and honest souls may make about themselves, upon occasion of these observations, and the doctrine that hath been delivered.

Obj. 1. My heart hath a world of thorns in it, and more of thorns than of what I can ever hope to be good herbs.

Ans. So hath every regenerate man a world of thorns in him : ay (says Calvin*), thick-set copses of them. Every one's grace is sown and continues amongst a wood of thorns. Yea ; but yet there is another root of something that grows up in thy heart, that is not thorns ; and there is a conflict against the thorns, an endeavour to stub them up ; and they are thorns in thy side. Therefore there is another principle in thee.

Obj. 2. Thou wilt again say ; I do not grow by reason of these thorns. But comfort thyself (says Calvin†), for he that brought forth the thirty-fold is by Christ reckoned with him that brought forth the hundred-fold. Christ puts them altogether, and dignifies them all alike with the common style of good ground ; and where the expectation of the husbandman (as he speaks) is not altogether frustrate, that little they have is accepted.

Obj. 3. But you will object, Alas ! my affections were mightily flushed at first, and now they wither, and worldly lusts grow up in their stead.

---

* Nemo est qui non ingenti spinarum copia et quasi densa sylva refertus sit. —*Calvin.*

† Quanquam mediocris erit profectus, quisquis tamen non degenerat a sincero Dei cultu, bona terra et fertilis censetur. Etenim etsi centupli respectu tenuis est ejus fertilitas quæ trigintacuplum reddit, terras tamen omnes simul Christus conjungit, quæ agricolæ laborem ac spem non prorsus frustrantur ; et communi bonitatis elogio interiores quoque dignatur.—*Calvin in verba.*

Ans. Shall I yet say to thee ? Doth God maintain a conflict in thee against sin, an endeavour to stub up the thorns ? Dost thou water those roots of bitterness with bitter tears and sorrow, and with the blood of Christ, to kill them ? Then still the root of the matter remains in thee.

Again, consider, when thou wert first converted to God, as thou hadst grace in thee, so thou wert a temporary believer at first, in respect of thy unregenerate part. All was stirred at first ; corrupt self-love was stirred at first, as well as what was truly gracious ; and when all was stirred, there must needs be a great flush of affection. This was my case at first, and then the stream was strong ; as take a little rivulet, which runs naturally and constantly, but as the prophet says, runs softly, with a slow and gentle current ; let a land-flood come upon it, it will prove a river, a strong and violent stream. But when that land-flood ceases, then the brook is not so swelled, though it goes on still, so much of it as was truly and naturally so, and had a spring. So it is here. At first, half thy heart, thy unregenerate part, was turned a temporary believer too ; and self-love, the great Simon Magus in thee, was wrought upon, and became a temporary believer ; but yet besides, and over and beyond that, there was a little fountain opened in thy heart, and this continues still to flow, when the land-flood ceases; and then look, what is true grace indeed holds out the conflict against itself in worldly lusts, and bears alone the stress of all ; and then worldly lusts begin to contend purely with this little grace in us, and that fights it out alone, and then is the truer trial of grace, though less discernible to sense than it was at first.

CHAPTER IV.

That the work of grace in true believers differs in kind from that which is in temporaries, proved, because true holiness of heart cannot be produced by any virtue of the covenant of works since the fall; but that it is peculiar to the covenant of grace to effect this.

God hath put that genius and disposition into the grace of the new covenant in us, as might answerably glorify the grace of God in Christ towards us, according to the tenor of that covenant. And the soul accordingly hath in it a radical disposedness to give up the soul to Christ, to be acted by him, and to be made sensible of its own insufficiency to act itself, and so to glorify Christ as its root for sanctification, as well as its Saviour for justification ; and accordingly, sooner or later, both through the inexperience of its own inability to act itself, and of that continual infused strength which from without it feels freely derived, as the Spirit pleaseth to dispense, and whereby it is carried on to motion ; especially when by the word, and the relation of that truth out of it, it is called upon to do this, it actually doth most readily submit, and followeth the truth revealed therein in a continual dependence upon Christ, to do all in him, and through him, as being that which glorifies Christ and debaseth itself, and so it practiseth accordingly. But I do withal conceive, that this giving up the soul to be acted only by Christ, doth arise rather from the grace of faith, unto which, of all graces in us, the predominancy and prime agency is committed under the new covenant, Rom. iv. 16, whose office it is to enervate and spoil all derived grace in us of its strength, by discovering its weakness and insufficiency, as also to carry them out of all to Christ, to abide in him as their only element, in which they move, and from whom also. And this faith also doth from its object revealed to it and apprehended by it; namely, that the tenor of this second covenant (under which the soul is now brought) is clean altered and changed, in respect of God's dispensing strength and motion, from what was in that first covenant with Adam, with whom the covenant was struck, being the covenant of nature. Hence God's concurrency with it was ordained suitable to the principles by nature bestowed, which were habitual graces; that is, to concur with them according to their kind, as in a free agent, as with other natural principles in their kind. And hence they had a strength to act from themselves, according to the freedom of man's will to use it. But now that power is forfeited, through the breach of that covenant, which was, as now the strength of sin (as the apostle speaks), so then of grace. And therefore the strength of grace to act under the second covenant can never be in grace itself, but in him who is the strength and foundation of that covenant, Jesus Christ. Faith being thus 'taught of God, the truth as it is in Jesus,' this lesson of dependence for motion, as well as that for justification, doth keep all those principles of graces in us from attempting to put forth in their own strength, and carries them out of themselves to Christ, and teacheth them to lay down their own abilities in subjection to his Spirit. Therefore this living in Christ is attributed to faith: Gal. ii. 20, 'The life I now lead is by the faith in the Son of God,' which evacuates still all the power of grace, any otherwise than as in Christ the fountain, and preserves the soul in a sense of its weakness under his second covenant, that so 'the power of Christ might rest upon it,' 2 Cor. xii. 9. Faith being herein to all graces that which moralists say that prudence is to all other virtues, their governor and tutor, was made thus the great officer in this second covenant, because it would give all to grace and Christ, Rom. iv. 16. Otherwise, I do not conceive that in the graces themselves there is any such peculiar inbred instinct, differing from what under the first covenant; and therefore the apostle Paul and all else have found it the hardest lesson to have their hearts brought to this dependence, and not to trust in themselves, and act from themselves; because grace was not at first brought up to it, to be of itself thus poor and beggarly, as this second covenant hath made it.

2. It is acknowledged that one essential difference between a temporary work and a saving is, that the one acts all from itself, though it be received, and that grace evangelical acts or is in disposition to act from Christ as a head, as well as to Christ as a lord, and accordingly is taught to depend at length for sanctification in working, as well as for justification, upon Christ; which I take to be the main difference intended in that 15th chapter of John, in the parable of the vine, and bringing forth 'fruit in Christ,' as the Syriac reads the words, through 'abiding in him,' in a continual sense that they of themselves can do nothing without him. And this fundamental principle did Christ teach his disciples then at his departure. So that Christ is 'made to us sanctification,' as well as justification, by a new covenant. Yet so as, 1. It may be a long while ere such true grace is taught distinctly and knowingly to itself thus to do, as may seem to have been the case of these his disciples, and of Peter, not long after this new lesson of their faith towards Christ; for this, as in other things of more concernment, was little or not so distinctly as yet exercised; as they exercised faith on God, but not so distinctly on Christ, John xiv. 1, therefore Christ calls for it. Thus also they had not prayed in his name—'Hitherto ye have asked nothing in my name'—nor yet so distinctly knew how they

were in him, and how he acted all in them, as appears by the 20th verse
of the 14th chapter of John ; and yet in the mean time that grace was
acted by Christ secretly. And herein it falls out, as Christ says to Peter,
John xiii. 7, in another case, ' What I do now thou knowest not, but thou
shalt know hereafter.' So it is with them ; that Christ doth all in them
they at present haply do not know, but when their union to him is cleared
up to them, and their faith taught more distinctly out of the word, of their
dependence upon Christ, they then more distinctly acknowledge all they
formerly did was from him, and give him the praise. And 2dly, In the
mean time, such souls do acknowledge all they have and do is not from
themselves, but Christ only, if they do any good ; which acknowledgment
(upon all occasion of their quickening) is to be taken *interpretativè ;* for this
doing all in Christ by faith is not always apprehended by many poor souls
that in a sense of their emptiness wait upon Christ for all, and do from
their souls desire to attribute all to Christ, and yet always discern not how
the strength to do all flows upon an act of faith fetching that virtue from
Christ, or from union with him, because that their union is yet doubted by
them.   They acknowledge both that Christ is and must needs be the fountain of all, and accordingly have recourse to him by acts of recumbency in
all, and virtue comes from him insensibly upon such acts put forth ; but
yet the connection between the cause and the effect they do not see, nor
can hang them together, the power that works in us being as secret as that
of the heavens on our bodies, and as strong as that of physic, which yet
is often not discerned ; and therefore the apostle prays for the Ephesians,
chapter i. 19, ' that their eyes might be opened to see that power wrought
in them.'

3. It is acknowledged that all the gifts and graces in temporaries,
whereby they conform to the law, &c., are all conveyed by the knowledge of
Christ ; for thereby it is said they conform to the holy commandment,
2 Peter ii. ; but yet these are by no other tenor conveyed, than as that
moral light and natural light which Christ sets up in the dark hearts of
all men, John i. 9 ; neither are they any more conveyed by a covenant, or
as the foundation of a covenant, than such light to heathens is or was,
although they be conveyed by the knowledge of the word, and of the covenant of works, set on by the Spirit of bondage, and also of the covenant,
which being indefinitely propounded to them, as well as to the elect, in the
ministry of it, Christ, for the magnifying of saving grace in and towards his
own the more, and many other ends, makes trial how far corrupt nature
remaining such may be induced, by working upon the principles therein,
and also by infusing such principles thereupon as may stand with nature
remaining still corrupt (though adorned and garnished), and how far it may
be carried on and invited by this indefinite revelation of the gospel, to close
with Christ and the grace of the gospel, and, as Christ's phrase is, how
' nigh the kingdom of God ' it may be brought, and accordingly be obedient,
which yet it ' falls short of ' (as the phrase is in the Hebrews). God meets
them in the indefinite promulgation of the gospel, as he did Balaam, and
enlightens them, and allures them ; and as he ' filled the Gentiles' hearts with
food and gladness,' and so ' left not himself without witness,' acts thereby
to lead them to repentance, Rom. ii., so he makes impressions of further
joys and sweetness from himself (though not in himself as their chiefest
good) upon the hearts of temporaries, to lead them to repentance and faith,
so that, though it be a work tending to salvation in this sense specified, yet

not saving, or which hath salvation annexed to it at any time, as, Heb. vi. 9, the apostle distinguisheth them.

4. It is acknowledged that such thus wrought upon, though by the gospel, do for their persons remain still under a covenant of works, or under the law, because they were created under it, and having been once thus married to the law, until they die to the law to be married to Christ, they according to the rule of law are never freed from this husband, but (as Rom. vii. 1–4, &c.) the law hath still power over them ; and hence also those graces and gifts they use in a legal way, though they be exercised about evangelical objects, and do turn (as my expression hath often been) the gospel and the acts required therein into law (their husband the law converting all its own way) ; yet they trust on their own righteousness, and upon their own acts of faith, repentance, &c., the counterfeits whereof are wrought in them ; and even the ordinances of the ceremonial law (which unto true believers were then evangelical, through their faith looking at Christ, and justification through him, Ps. li.) were yet all turned by the carnal Jews into pure legal performances, they going about in a legal way to expiate their sins by sacrifice, Ezek. xxxiii. 13 ; and so Rom. ix. 32, ' They sought righteousness as it were by the law,' says the apostle there ; so these seek a righteousness in their evangelical acts (such I call them in respect of their object), but ' as it were by the works of the law.' And as in point of justification they thus err, so also in acting of their graces, they do all as it were by the law, as Adam at first did, but by their own strength, and so bring not forth fruit in me, as Christ complains, John xv., and so are cut off, as there it is said.

5. I yield these graces and gifts given them to be a true real work, as reality is opposed to hypocrisy, taking hypocrisy for acting a part, and so that word ὄντως, speaking of the work on them really, 2 Peter ii. 18, implies ; yet still so as compared with true sanctification it is but counterfeit, as of aurichalcum we say that it is false gold, though it be true metal ; and of a brass shilling it is counterfeit coin, though true metal, and which otherwise may serve to many purposes ; and so I ever accounted it an expression not according to the word, to call them ' hypocrites,' but rather ' temporaries,' πρόσκαιροι.

6. Grant also I do, that through those gifts and habits they are enabled to perform duties of the law and gospel ; Herod heard gladly, did many things, and many others much more ; yet as the apostle says, Rom. ii., of the Gentiles, they do but τὰ τοῦ νόμου, ' the things of the law,' but not in doing do they obey the law, nor is the action legal, or such as the law requires, no, not for the kind of it ; but as the heathens did in civil things many things commanded by the law in the second table, by moral habits of virtues, which were yet when done splendida peccata, so these temporaries perform the religious duties of the first table in many things (by the like habits infused) ; but they serve God but ' in the oldness of the letter,' as the apostle says of the best of the Jews, Rom. vii. ; but still not ' in the newness of the Spirit,' as his distinction there is, that is, from a received principle of spirit, opposed to flesh ; so that indeed they conform not to the spiritual law, as the apostle calls it, which only truly is the law, as appears in that chapter ; ' the law is holy and spiritual,' and when he thus served God he yet says he was ' without the law,' ver. 9, because without the spiritual light of it in his understanding, and therefore without all true genuine spiritual dispositions suitable thereunto in his affections. And hence it appears to me (as many ways else) that the difference of their

specious holiness from true sanctification in the elect, should not only lie in acting of itself, or from another, though that be true, but in the materials themselves ; that is, that the one reacheth not to a true spiritual conformity to the holiness of the law in any degree, nor is such as was in Adam in innocency, whereas the other doth; neither is there true love to God, nor is God made the supreme end, until which be done there cannot be said to be true holiness in the heart or action till they be predominant. For holiness is a setting up God as the supreme end, or it is not holiness ; so until then self-love is the predominant principle, and so they remain wholly flesh still, though self is diverted from worldly to heavenly objects ; and so all their actions from these graces are deficient of legal righteousness, such as should be in them ; and without love to God as the predominant principle, there cannot be any true legal sanctification, for ' love is the fulfilling of the law,' and ' the end of the commandment is love out of a pure heart,' 1 Tim. i. 5. God requires a right manner and a right end, or else the command is not said to be done at all; so Deut. vi. 25, ' This is your righteousness, if you observe all these commandments as he hath commanded them ;' without which there is no more true legal righteousness, or anything of the image of God, than of the true image of a man in the body without the soul ; and bodily exercise and godliness are opposed by the apostle.

7. I acknowledge this work to have also a ' goodness' in it—so Hosea vi. 4, it is called—but yet which still falleth short of the goodness which is in the law, of which the apostle says, Rom. vii. 12, ' The law is holy, spiritual, and good,' for it is not the law written in the heart, but τὸ ἔργον τοῦ νόμου γραπτὸν, Rom. ii. 15 (so in the Gentiles), that is, something which produceth many effects of the law. And in the Jews it is called, ver. 20, μόρφωσις, ' a form of knowledge, and of the truth of the law,' which he had in his mind, which as it signifies a system or body of the law (as we say) in his mind, so withal insinuates the slightness of it for the kind ; it is but a form, a picture, in comparison of the real law itself, and so 2 Tim. iii. 5, μόρφωσις, ' a form of godliness,' is opposed to the power or reality of godliness, and so I confess it hath a goodness in it.   (1.) Natural, as it is a creature wrought by the Spirit. (2.) Moral, so far as the letter of the law may be called such, as in a picture there is a double truth and goodness, the one natural in the substance of the colours laid on, the other relative or artificial as it is a picture, and as more or less it comes near the life, but still so as it reacheth not that kind of goodness that is in the man himself. So hath this work, the more lively it is, the more goodness, but still not that which is in the law, which is holy, spiritual, and good. I call it a literal goodness, because it is the image of the letter, not spiritual. As a picture represents the outwards, so this ; and if it counterfeits the inwards (as in some of a finer thread), yet still it is but the picture thereof. And that not any such a kind of true righteousness was ever renewed in any that perish eternally, and that no man that is but under a covenant of works attains it, nor that ever the first covenant availed to work any such righteousness in any one since the fall, much less in all the Jews, I prove by these reasons among many other.

(1.) That is made the very fundamental difference between that first covenant, and that second of grace, that in the latter God ' writes the law in the heart,' by giving ' a new heart and a new spirit,' Jer. xxxi. 33, Heb. viii. 8–11 ; that is, a heart conformable to the law ; for the law written in the heart is imprinted dispositions suitable to the law, which is called 'the law of the mind.' That scripture, Heb. viii., being so express, and making this the difference of the two covenants, it seems that that which is made the difference of the latter covenant, cannot be made common to the first ; compare with this Heb. x., where it is said, Christ hath 'for ever perfected' (therefore none of them perish) 'them that are sanctified,' ver. 14. And what sanctification is it ? In the 15th and 16th verses he explains it by alleging the words of that second covenant, which at once interpret what it is to be 'perfected for ever,' and what to be 'sanctified :' to be perfected for ever, is to have your sins forgiven and remembered no more ; and to be sanctified, is to have the law written in the heart, ver. 16. What God hath thus put together for ever, let no man sever. The same is the difference that is put between the two covenants, 2 Cor. iii., through- out. The one wrote it upon men's consciences, but as in letters upon stone, there they might read it ; but the other in living letters, in disposi- tions suitable in their whole hearts. The gospel changeth into the same image, the law not so ; and this was by Moses himself put, when he came at the end of all to publish this second covenant, which he doth in the 29th and 30th chapters of Deuteronomy throughout. He tells them, verse 1, chapter xxix., that it was a covenant 'besides that made at Horeb,' which he did now publish, that is, the second covenant ; and ver. 12, 13, it was that covenant he swore to Abraham, and that was the second covenant, Heb. vi. 16–18. That covenant, made to Abraham with an oath, was to shew the immutability of his counsel to the heirs of life, that is, the elect ; and so Luke i. 72, 73, we have it. Again, the covenant there was the second covenant, for, Rom. x. 6, Paul, in opposition and distinction to the law, quotes the words of that covenant then promulged, in 30th chapter, as proper to the gospel ; 'The righteousness of faith speaks on this wise,' &c. Now chap. xxx. 6, among other promises peculiar to this covenant, this is one, to 'circumcise the heart,' and so to cut off the foreskin of flesh, and to 'give them an heart to love the Lord ;' and this is delivered as that which should be fulfilled under the New Testament, upon the Jews at their last call, because then it eminently takes place ; and in opposition to this he speaks of those Jews who had the first covenant, that God had not given them a heart to perceive to that day, by all he had wrought ; so chap. xxix. 4.

(2.) My second reason is, that to be 'under the law' is to be under the predominancy of sin, and so their state is distinguished (Rom. vi. 14) from that of grace. 'Sin shall not have dominion over you, for you are not under the law, but under grace.' Now if those, under such a work, have still a predominancy of sin, they cannot have true legal righteousness or holiness, which, if not predominant, at least is not holiness.

Again, (3.) In the seventh chapter, which follows, the apostle, in his own person, now, when evangelically sanctified, sets forth, as his corrupt part remaining, by 'the law of the members,' so the regenerate part in him by 'the law of the mind,' which is a conformity to the law of God in the inward man, approving it, delighting in it, and though the imperfection of it still drives him to Christ to deliver him, to whom he flies, ver. 25, yet so as he there doth abstractly and apart consider his grace in itself, as it is a created habit in the heart, and as it is a conformity to the moral law (of which he there speaks), as it is holy, spiritual, and good, verses 12, 14.

(4.) The fourth reason is, that in the highest instances of temporaries, they are still reckoned men unregenerate, and flesh, &c., and grace evan- gelical, as it is considered abstractly, a qualification conformable to the command, is mentioned as the difference from the work on them, and not only as it is acted by Christ in us, though that be true, John xv. 1, 2, &c., as I said before.

First, In the 6th of Hebrews, how are those enlightenings, tastings, &c., distinguished from true evangelical graces, which are called, ver. 9, ' better things' (that is, in themselves for the work and substance of them), and ' things that have salvation' (as the word is) annexed to them. We find the grace of love unto the saints in truth, and a labour of love thence issuing, to be the thing instanced in, and are mentioned to be in them oppositely to their enlightenings. Answerably, the thorny ground, the highest degree of temporaries, unto which these enlightened are compared, ver. 7, 8. How is it distinguished from the fourth ground, Luke xiii. 15, but by the change in the subject of the heart, ' a good and honest heart' receiving the word ; *honest*, as in not robbing Christ by taking anything to itself, so also in conforming itself to all the commands, as truly as laying hold on promises. And so the other, the stony ground, their fault was, that still they remained unrenewed at all ; for the stony ground wants root *in sese*, in themselves, that is, as they wanted Christ, so also a true principle of sanctification in themselves. But ' the root of the matter is in me,' says Job, pleading his own righteousness.

As in like manner, concerning the foolish virgins, the difference put between them and the wise is, that the wise had ' oil in the vessel,' habitual grace, which those other wanted, though they were acted for present performances, as a dead body is by angels for a fit, having oil in their lamps for present acts. And then the thorny ground was a heart, though humbled, yet never regenerated nor sanctified : for Jer. iv. 3, 4, the ' taking away the foreskin of the heart' is opposed to ' sowing among thorns ;' and our Saviour shuts up all that parable with this, ' From him that hath not, shall be taken what he hath ;' and in Luke xiii. it is explained ' what he seems to have ;' so as indeed it was not true sanctification, but seeming such. So these in 2 Pet. ii. 20, who really, ὄντως, escape from the world, embrace the holy commandment, through the knowledge of Christ, yet, 1. they are said but to escape, τὰ μιάσματα, not τὰς φθορὰς, that is, the defilements outward, and in that respect they are called virgins, Matt. xxv. But they escape not inward corruptions at all of lust, as, by being ' partakers of the divine nature,' the true believers are said to do (chap. i. ver. 4). In opposition to these ;—

Secondly, They are therefore called swine, for their natures still remaining as afore, though washed outwardly ; and the dogs vomiting out through present pain, yet with a stomach to the vomit, and therefore were never renewed into so much as true legal sanctification inward ; which, if they were, such expressions of differences could not be given them ; nay, they are on purpose given them to express the contrary. And for that expression of goats elsewhere, it seems not to note out any farther degree of men not saved, than such as these were, but rather seems to be put for all wicked men, placed at the left hand, in opposition to the sheep.

Obj. It may be objected, that they are said to be sanctified through Christ's blood, Heb. x.

I *answer*, 1st, In that sense, as elsewhere, they are said ' to believe,' and Judas to repent, Matt. xxvii. All graces have a counterfeit called by their name, as in herbs and stones, and as the picture of the king is called the king.

Ans. 2d, Shew me a place that they are justified (when yet a promise thereof is affirmed to belong to them), which being an act of God upon us, hath no counterfeit. Yea, or shew a place that they are said to be born again ; which, if they are not, they are still flesh, and so have no holiness begun.

Ans. 3. That is said to be sanctified, which is set apart from common uses, as the priests, the sabbaths, &c. So in men their graces, though not sanctifying their persons inwardly, yet they set them apart to God in many works done for him, and to his church in their gifts outwardly.

Ans. 4. Which being the purchase of Christ's blood, is said to be done by his blood : Eph. iv., He gives gifts ' to the rebellious also,' and being wrought by a knowledge of Christ's blood, as Peter speaks, and that as in the covenant of grace revealed, therefore they are said to be ' sanctified by the blood of the covenant.'

Obj. That instance of Abimelech, Gen. xx., may be objected, he having followed his conscience in the matter of Sarah, so as if he had known her to be Abraham's wife, he would not have taken her, and this act God acknowledgeth to be integrity.

Ans. 1. The answer is, that it is acknowledged such in the sense as Abimelech meant it, who pleads there his innocency in what he might seem to have been guilty of, speaks according to the judgment of his conscience, and such an integrity God acknowledgeth ; and the meaning is, Abimelech followed his principles in it, and so it was good in its kind, but not in that court God means to keep hereafter. So in that speech of Paul, Acts xxiii. 1, he speaking in a court of Pharisees, where he was to justify himself and his cause, he speaks according to their principles, ' I have kept a good conscience' (says he), and might well say so afore them, but not afore God. For in his estate of unregeneracy, whilst in the flesh, he says the affection of sins which were by the law, that is, stirred up by the light of the law in his conscience, had a force in his members to bring forth fruit unto death, that is, outward actions against conscience and that light of the law therein.

Ans. 2. There is a twofold integrity : 1. Absolute, which agrees with the first rule of the word. So this action of Abimelech, though he followed his conscience, was not integrity. But, 2, it might be comparative integrity ; namely, in that he followed his conscience, which was his immediate rule. Integrity, we know, is a conformity to its rule, and so conscience being a man's rule, when a man's actions are squared to it, they are said to have a kind of integrity in them ; but there being a rule above conscience, to which both conscience in the motives, matter, &c., ought to be conformed, from which natural conscience swerves, therefore an act which is wrong in such a respect it is not integrity. A man may honestly tell an untruth, because it agrees with what he thinks, yet it is an untruth ; and *veritas est conformitas cum suo archetypo ;* so is integrity.

And as I have thus proved, that no true spiritual holiness, regularly to act according to the law, was ever renewed in such temporaries, so that not any promises of life, justification, adoption, communion with Christ, or covenant, is made to any such works by God. And as in the former I granted some things, so in this. 1. That it is their persons and works are under a covenant of works, for all are either under the law, or under grace, Rom. vi. 14 ; yet it is but by reason of their first creation, when they were made under the law, and had it written in their hearts, unto which, in that respect, they are eternally subject till they die to that law, and are married to Christ, Rom. vii. And, 2, I think that in judging men at the latter day,

God will condescend to proceed with corrupt nature, not in the rigour of
that law, but according to what was by nature or otherwise revealed thereof
unto them, as appears, Rom. ii. 12, 16, God winking at much of their
ignorance, as it is in the Acts; and the rather, because Jesus Christ he is
their judge then, who may (for he hath paid for it) relax of that righteous
exaction of the law in a way of abatement, that they 'without the law
should be judged without the (written) law,' by the law written in their
hearts, by natural light, &c., and so punish them with less punishment,
who by reason of such work have had fewest sins; and as such a work is
a restrainer of corruption in them, so there will be a minoration of their
punishment, unless they have returned again unto their vomit, when their
latter end is worse than their beginning, as Peter speaks.   And, 3, I acknowledge that so far as any goodness is in it, it is respected and accepted by
God himself; and so far as it serves to any end, as God hath ordained, as
he did that act of Jehu, 2 Kings x. 30, God commends it, and says he had
done well, and all that was in his heart to do, and accepted it to a temporal
reward: but in any spiritual acceptation he rejected it, yea, in one of the
prophets* he calls it ' the murder of Jehu;' having his own ends in it.   No
man can bring forth fruit to God, which he accepteth, until he be married
to Christ, and dead to the law, Rom. vii. 4.

And so in this life, whilst Christ governs, he is pleased, I grant, to reward
such legal performances (and as he crowns other his graces, so those) with
rewards within their own sphere, as he did Ahab for humbling himself, and
in the parable, gave the penny to the labourer; and accordingly also forgiveness, namely, in a way of forbearance, to ' have patience' with sinners
(as in that parable of the evil servant, the forgiveness is expressed but by
no more), which forbearance is truly a forgiveness, in that he loseth so
much glory so long unrecovered on them, and spendeth riches of mercy, which
he will never reckon to them, farther than as they have abused them; yet
this is but so much as he vouchsafed the heathens, towards whom he
exercised riches of forbearance, Rom. ii. 4, 5.   But that he should work
these common graces in a way of any covenant, or make any such promises
of adoption, justification and forgiveness, the same for substance with these
to the elect, and these proportioned to that degree they shall act their
graces given; for this I see no footstep at all in the word, or in anything
written to prove it.   Neither can I see how, without a contradiction *in adjecto*,
any such covenant, though for Christ's sake, should or could be made with
creatures fallen and sinful, that had broken it already, how they could
come to be capable of promises of forgiveness, &c.; for the covenant of
works given to Adam, which we call *fœdus naturæ*, and the moral law
(the copy of it), promulged by Moses, says expressly, ' Cursed is he that
continueth not in all things,' Gal. iii., and already all mankind have not
continued in all things, having sinned in Adam, and so are incapable of any
promises of forgiveness, of life eternal, and communion with Christ in any
degree, upon condition of imperfect doing of the law, though never so
holily; for if any such promises be made, it must be supposed that this
first covenant of nature (now in the renewing of it to corrupt nature) was
attempered and allayed by Christ in the rigour of it; but how this is consistent with that sentence yet in force, ' Cursed is he that continues not in
all things contained in the book of the law to do them,' I cannot conceive.

The argument in show for it is, the renewing that covenant in Horeb with
the Jews, Exod. xx., and elsewhere; which, together with the ceremonial
_____
* The reference is probably to Hosea i. 4.—ED.

law joined with it, was sprinkled with blood, with glorious promises, that they should be to him ' an holy nation,' and ' of priests,' &c., and also God's saying, ' Do this and live :' when also it is said, that God sanctified that people to himself, and promised to be their God, and was present with them, &c.

For answer ; this covenant, which was *fœdus subserviens* to the gospel (as learned Cameron calls it), had many scopes and aspects ; but none of them is that scope which is here put upon it.

1. It was truly the promulgation of the covenant of nature made with Adam in paradise (in the moral part, the ten commandments), and did refer thereto, and so did call them to look but to that estate they once were in, and now were fallen from ; and because the story of Adam's righteousness was lost, what was written in his heart was there renewed, only delivered negatively, because man was turned against it—' Thou shalt not,' &c., which was written rather affirmatively, ' This thou shalt do,' &c., in Adam's heart ; and God delivers it now covenant-wise, because he presents himself as ready to perform his covenant—' Do this, and thou shalt live'—and calls on them to perform their part, they being born under the covenant as creatures ; hereby at once to convince man of his impotency to fulfil it, and withal to shew what God would have done for man if he had kept it ; and it was thus promulged with evangelical purposes to drive men to Christ. Neither did the promulgation of it convey any heart to them to do it in the least degree ; for God, when they promised to fulfil it, said, ' Oh that there were an heart within them !' &c., Deut. v. 29. And Joshua, at the same time when the covenant was renewed, intimates to them that the purpose of that covenant was not as if they could do anything of it, but to shew them rather their inability to do it, Joshua xxiv. 19. Thus Joshua, when he renewed it, told them, ' Ye cannot serve the Lord, for he is holy and jealous, and will not forgive your sins.' Yet they, in confidence of their strength, would take it as a covenant they were to perform, ver. 21. And Joshua tells them, ver. 22, that they were therein witnesses against themselves. So as both God and Joshua would have them understand by it, and the promise of life by it, their inability rather, which yet they were not brought to be sensible of. And so when Moses did so distinctly propound the second covenant, Deut. xxix. and xxx, he tells them, that by the former covenant God had not given them ears to hear, nor hearts to perceive, ver. 4, chap. xxix. ; and to propound it thus covenant-wise, was the most fit way to convince them of their inability, that in the attempting the obedience of it they might see ' the weakness of the law through the flesh,' that it could not do, as afore it did in Adam, not in the least degree, Rom. viii. 4. And answerably the ceremonial law annexed to it concurred in this very scope. It was given that they, now fallen, might under their own hand, as it were, acknowledge themselves debtors to this moral law, both as sinners fallen unto the curse of it, and yet the obedience of it obliged ; so Gal v. 3, ' He that is circumcised is a debtor to the whole law ;' and so to the curse of it, and Col. ii. 14, it is called ' The handwriting of ordinances against us.' God, at the same time he promulged the ten commandments, brought a bond for men to seal, and therein to acknowledge themselves bound and debtors to it.

And as this was one scope both these had, so the moral and ceremonial put together (both which put together, I have long observed as given the Jews to be reckoned one covenant, out of Heb. ix. 15–19 compared) became in the latter* of them, as to the outward performance, fit matter of an

* Qu. ' letter '?—ED.

outward covenant with these Jews, as they were a national church; and so considered as such a covenant, with promises suitable, I do acknowledge it given *de novo* to the Jews, though fallen, as they were a church; but this, being proper to the Jews, hath no influence or relation at all to temporaries under the gospel; and so, in all those places quoted, where the law was given, did they stand as a church to enter into covenant with God, as in that 19th Exodus, &c.; and the apostle calls the whole as thus considered, ' a carnal commandment,' Heb. vii. 6, because, besides their spiritual use, in typifying things heavenly to spiritual believers then, they had an outward carnal use to the whole nation, who became a church, and therefore called holy, as set apart from the nations, to be separated to God's service and worship prescribed in the law ceremonial and moral, and so as also a 'nation of priests,' wherein yet was typified out the spiritual assemblies of true saints and churches under the gospel, and is so applied by Peter, 1 Pet. ii. 5, 6. And this covenant was founded on a redemption and deliverance of that nation out of Egypt, as that of the gospel is upon our redemption through Christ; and yet they being sinners, how should they have access to God that was holy? They therefore had Moses, a typical mediator, Gal. iii. 19. The people stood afar off, and Moses only drew nigh; as by Christ we have access to the Father, Eph. ii.; and so it had a blood sprinkled upon the book, Heb. ix. 19, Exod. xxiv. 8, and answerably outward justifications, δικαιώματα, Heb. ix. 1, as well as the gospel, and a remission, ver. 12 of that chapter. But how? Not at all purifying the conscience from the guilt of sin, from dead works, or from the power of sin, but of the flesh and outward man; for that is the very difference that is put, ver. 13, 14, and therefore there was no promise of such a forgiveness as should clear the conscience, or reach it in the least to pacify or purify it, nor therefore of any true ground for any such legal faith, but a forgiveness of reprieval, not to be destroyed for their sin if they offered sacrifice, as it is expounded in the psalmist exegetically, Ps. lxxviii. 38, and was so limited by God and Moses their mediator also, Num. xiv. 19, 20. Pardon ' as until now '; that is, spare them at present; and God says, I have pardoned; that is, so far; but threatened to take vengeance, however, afterwards when he should visit; for as their church fellowship was outward, so their forgiveness, so their promises of blessedness, were outward annexed thereunto, which God fulfilled. And they had also sins which were no sins morally, as the touching the dead, and so had a sanctification and a justification which were not really such; that is, not of the heart and conscience from the guilt and power of sin. And they had ' promises' typical, Heb. viii. 5, 6, and in that respect those of the gospel are called ' better.' And they had an answerable communion with God in a church fellowship, and an outward presence of God amongst them in visible signs of a cloud and ark, and the observances of the ceremonial law were the expiations of the transgressions of the moral, in respect of the outward transgressions of it, so as the outward punishment (which else to the despisers of it without mercy had befallen him, Heb. x. 28), was remitted and they absolved, and stood *recti in curia* again, as we say. And they had promises of a life, that ' in doing they should live,' even in that good land of Canaan, the type of heaven, Deut. vi. 2, 18. And this covenant, promises, &c., considered in these two fore-mentioned scopes thereof, was truly, and *toto genere*, differing from that second covenant of the gospel given, Deut. 29th and 30th chapters, and was that old covenant God found fault with.

Yet so, 3dly, As the holy and great God had not made such an outward covenant with that nation as a church in such promises, such a justification, adoption, sanctification, outward and carnal, had not he therein had a farther scope in types, hereby to note out another covenant, church, promises, justification, sanctification, true and real, whereof he made this the shadow; and this he did for Christ's sake also, whom and whose covenant these things typified out, and so made this covenant and promises in the very terms of the thing signified, thereby to point out those glorious promises, that real holiness, justification, adoption of the gospel, Heb. ix. 21–23 compared, which true believers among them had in their eye, and had wrought in them, and they endeavoured after, so as to them it was gospel also, yet in this, differing from that delivered, Deut. xxix. 30, that there it is expressed clearly and directly in plain words, here it is unfolded in a parable, that had also another scope besides it unto the carnal Jew. And because this covenant had these several and various aspects (though some more, some less principal), hence though the carnal Jews should have literally performed the typical covenant in the letter, yet God finds fault with them, as wanting spiritual holiness, to which by the moral law they were obliged as creatures, and as a church redeemed, and which in the ceremonial law was typified out as that which was aimed at in those types; and hence were those continual complaints and finding faults by the prophets (who understood the spiritual intent of all) for their want herein.

Now then that covenant, those promises, that sanctification, thus understood, how far is it from any such scope as is put upon it by some men to convey a true sanctification by a mere legal covenant unto others of the Jews beside the elect? I acknowledge that, as it was an outward covenant, so it had an answerable grace went with it to some of the Jews not regenerate, to help them outwardly to keep the law, as it had in Paul, who was blameless in it through conscience enlightened by it, Phil. iii. But withal I have sometimes thought that those heavenly enlightenings, tastings of the powers of the world to come, &c., which are now in temporaries under the gospel, were never under that covenant wrought in the hearts of any unregenerate amongst them, because sinning against truth so acknowledged seems to be proper to the times of the gospel, and presumptuous sinners then did but sin against Moses's law, which is spoken oppositely to sinning against the truth of the gospel (Heb. x. 26, 28 compared), and temporaries now under the gospel are not to be church members if they could be known to be such; and the Jews were not in respect of any such work from the law as then members, but typically only. My reason is, because that churches are to consist of ' saints elect,' therefore only under the covenant of grace, 1 Pet. v. 13, and such as are so sanctified as that Christ will perfect the work, Phil. i. 5–7. That they are admitted *de facto*, is because the rules given saints in the word, whereby we are able to judge of others by, are but such as temporaries may seem to them to be true saints, and so they are bound to receive them; yet not if discerned such; for to them the seals of the second covenant (which they are not under) cannot belong; but such are our sacraments now, viz., the seals of the covenant of grace, ' This is the blood of the New Testament,' says Christ, and only so.

So as I add this for a conclusion, God hath made trial of corrupt nature, how far it might be wrought upon by several workings of his Spirit and truth, without attainment of true holiness. And this is manifested in three several degrees of the revelation of his truth, with workings of his Spirit proportioned thereunto.

1. He made, and still makes, trial how far the light of nature would go without the law (though not derived by nature, but from Christ, John i. 9), which light of nature is God's truth, so called Rom. i. 18; and ver. 19 it is also called God's manifestation of himself to them; and ' God's wisdom,' 1 Cor. i. 21, and which had that effect in the hearts of many of them the law hath in some things : Rom. ii. 15, τὸ ἔργον τοῦ νόμου, ' The effect of the law' it is there called, and the revelation of this truth had a spirit within them, as Seneca (the highest instance among them for knowledge moral that ever was) calls it, *Est spiritus in nobis qui ita nos tractat ut a nobis tractatur,* who made impressions of many moral virtues on their wills, and also in and to their consciences, for their consciences are said, συμμαρτυρεῖν, to witness; with whom ?   God in their consciences, who witnesseth also ; the same word that is used of the Spirit's witnessing with our spirits, Rom. viii. 16, revealed and then seconded that light with a bondage of accursing if they transgressed, and fed the fear of death, Heb. ii. 15, and excusing if they obeyed, Rom. ii. 15, which was a reward for so much integrity as was found in their actions; and the highest instance for practice I know, of how far corrupt nature might be empowered this way, was Socrates, who suffered for that truth of God manifested to him.

And 2. A further revelation of truth was made to the 'carnal Jew, who ' had a form of knowledge and of the truth of the law,' Rom. ii. 20 ; but, as I take it, without any perceivance of the truth of the gospel and the spiritual redemption by Christ, by reason of that carnal commandment, in the letter of which they rested, 2 Cor. iii. 13, 14, through the veil on Moses's face, and on their hearts, so as the glimmering notion thereof was peculiar to the elect during those times ; and this had a further measure of the Spirit (for Neh. ix., as he gave them on mount Sinai, good commandments, ver. 13, so also his ' good Spirit to instruct them,' ver. 20), who became a Spirit of bondage to them, Rom. viii. 15, and who (according as that covenant was literal and outward, so far as *de novo* struck with them) did accompany the revelation of it with the habits of devotion, and of a zeal of God misguided, with warmth, Rom. x. 2, and his worship, to serve God ' according to the oldness of the letter,' but not at all ' in the spirit,' which is to worship only ' in truth.'   And the highest instance I know that God held forth of this work was Paul, who was ' blameless as concerning ' that outward ' righteousness of the law,' Phil. iii. 6, and wherein he exceeded others of his companions, yet without the true holiness of the law as it is holy, for so he was ' without the law,' Rom. vii.

3. A farther discovery was made under the gospel, wherein as there is a plain revelation of Christ and the way of salvation in him (which is eminently called ' the truth') which is now common in the notion of it to carnal men, so God makes a further trial, and experiments the utmost how far corrupt nature may yet be wrought upon by the truths thereof, without his infusing or their attaining true faith and holiness; and answerably gives a further Spirit, Heb. vi. 4, called the ' Spirit of grace,' Heb. x. 29, that is, of the gospel, called grace, Tit. ii. 11, whereby they are partakers of further tastes than of outward blessings, and the comforts of an excusing conscience, even of ' the powers of the world to come,' which was not subject to the angels who gave the law (Heb. ii. 2, and 5 compared), and are ' partakers of an heavenly gift;' yea, they may receive a work on their hearts some way answerable to all the truth of the gospel; for as Junius and others have observed, and by comparing those six principles mentioned, ver. 1, 2 of Heb. vi. (the sum of the rest), and those works on them men-

tioned, ver. 4, 5, they one answer to the other, and yet these attain not to true holiness or any true qualifications or works truly such ; not to true love to the saints, and works thence issuing for Christ's sake, which is put by way of distinction, as better, ver. 9, than all that work upon them. And the work there mentioned I account the highest instance can be given of any temporaries. For which dealing of God with men I must refer the wonderment to the ' deepness of the riches both of the wisdom and knowledge of God : how unsearchable are his ways, and his judgments past finding out ! '

BOOK VIII.

That there are three parts of our regeneration : 1. *Humiliation for sin, and the necessity thereof in order to faith ;* 2. *Faith in Christ for justification ;* 3. *Turning from sin unto God, or holiness of heart and life, proved, from the work which our Lord Jesus Christ ascribes to the Holy Ghost, John* xvi. 7–11, *from the instances of conversion in the time when Job lived ; and of the conversion of the apostle Paul.—Of the subservience of humiliation unto faith.—Objections answered.—Of our turning from sin unto God, or of holiness in heart and life.*

CHAPTER I.

That conviction of sin, humiliation for it, faith on Jesus Christ, sanctification, or amendment of heart and life, are the parts of our conversion to God, is demonstrated from the work which our Lord Jesus Christ ascribes to the Holy Spirit, John xvi. 7–11.

*Nevertheless I tell you the truth ; It is expedient for you that I go away : for if I go not away, the Comforter will not come unto you ; but if I depart, I will send him unto you.   And when he is come, he will reprove the world of sin, and of righteousness, and of judgment : of sin, because they believe not on me : of righteousness, because I go to my Father, and ye see me no more : of judgment, because the prince of this world is judged.—*JOHN XVI. 7–11.

These words contain a summary of the work of the Holy Ghost in regeneration and conversion (of which in the general so much hath been premised) throughout all the parts thereof.   And the occasion of Christ's so distinct an enumeration of his several works, in all the parts thereof, was this.   In these his last sermons he had told them he was shortly to go away from them, and they in his absence to bear witness of him, by preaching him over all the world (as it is in the last verse of the former chapter), and withal that for that their message they should find but hard entertainment of it and of themselves at most of the world's hands (and this at the beginning of this chapter).   And because they began to be sorrowful at this, and to repine to be employed in a business of so much danger and trouble, therefore to comfort them he tells them it was ' expedient ' it should be so, both for theirs and his church's good.   ' It is expedient ' (says he) ' for you,' that is, you my apostles, even you in particular, for I going away ' will send you my Spirit,' who shall be a ' Comforter ' unto you in all those troubles which you are to meet withal.   Neither is it for you only that I shall send my Spirit to you, but for my elect's sakes, who are now to be called over all the world by your preaching ; and not only for those impaled within the church of the Jews, to whom only I have hitherto sent you, for my Spirit, ' when he is come ' (on you namely), ' shall convince the world,' that is, savingly convert my elect in all nations. And this work of conversion he sets out in all the parts of it. 1. By convincing the world is meant conversion, for so the word is used both in the Old and New Testament.

1. In the Old, when the prophet speaks of the conversion of the Gentiles, and establishing Christ's kingdom among them by his word and Spirit, you shall find the same word in the Hebrew that is used in the Greek here; thus, Isa. ii. 4 and Micah iv. 3, it is said, that ' the word going forth from Jerusalem ' (as it did then, when the apostles went to preach), Christ should ' judge among many people ;' that is, set up his kingdom among them, and rule them by the sceptre of his word. And how was it that this should come to pass? He should ' rebuke the nations.' *Rebuke, reprove, convince*, are all one, as interpreters observe, and it implies the opposition that is in men's hearts to receive that his word, so as they need rebuking and convincing before they will effectually yield unto it. And whereas other conquerors obtain their crowns by force of arms, he acquires his only by the conviction of his word and Spirit.

2. It is thus also used in the New Testament, 1 Cor. xiv. 24, 25, where the apostle, to shew the benefit of preaching above speaking with tongues, giveth this instance. Put the case, an unbeliever and ignorant person should come in ; by that means, says he, he might be ' convinced of all, that is, truly converted from his heathenism, ignorance, and unbelief, unto the profession and worship of the true God, as it is in the following words. In a word, Heb. xi. 1, 2, the apostle useth the very same word that is here to express saving faith by, which will appear, if you compare the original texts together, he there taking it in its common nature, as it hath all spiritual things for its object. The word there used is ἔλεγχος, *evidences* or *conviction*. And so here, ἐλέγξει, *he shall convince*. The words therefore are all one as if Christ should have said, I send you into the world to preach, and I send you my Spirit ; and though the world be drowned in ignorance and unbelief, and set in opposition against your doctrine, yet my Spirit, which I will send, shall convince them, and make them know, believe, and yield unto it. And because the apostles might further desire to know what doctrine were best to preach to convert them by, as also in what manner and order the Spirit would convert men, that they might accordingly apply themselves in their preaching, our Saviour Christ therefore at once sets forth a universal platform, both of the sum of their ministry, and of the Spirit's working in men's hearts, as the stamp doth the image that made it. That whereas there are three things necessary to be known and believed particularly and savingly of all that shall be saved, so in the true conviction of them conversion doth consist.

1. There is man's sinfulness and misery in himself out of Christ.

2. The way and means appointed by God to come out of this misery, Christ's righteousness.

3. What a man ought to do by way of thankfulness to Christ for that his delivery (unto which three heads our divines have reduced their catechisms and systems of theology). Our Saviour doth at once inform them how the Spirit in converting them should convince them of these three, and that in their conviction of these three the work of conversion is absolved ; and withal instructs them what particulars to insist on in their preaching, as being those things which the Spirit would make most use of to convert. So

that he at once delivers both the particulars of the work of the Spirit in conversion, as also the sum of Christian doctrine and the apostles' preaching, and the order and method to be used in both.

1. The Spirit will ' convince of sin,' that is, of that miserable and sinful estate which men live in my nature, so long as they are out of Christ, and which, without belief in him, will prove matter of condemnation to them, so that the Spirit will humble them, ' Because they believe not on Christ.'

2. He will convince them of 'righteousness, because I go to my Father,' says Christ; that is, the Spirit shall by faith reveal unto them the righteousness of me, who am to ascend up to heaven to be the only true means to be justified and saved by. He names his ascension (which includes his resurrection) because that declared his righteousness to be the true righteousness of God, else (had he been an impostor) God would never have suffered him to come to heaven.

3. He will convince of 'judgment, because the prince of this world is judged,' the meaning of which phrase that which is in John xii. 31 evidently explains : Christ there speaking of the fruit and efficacy of his death, as it were triumphing, says, ' Now is the judgment of this world ; and the prince of this world shall be cast out.' He there speaks of the conversion of the Gentiles : ' When I am lift up,' says he, ' I will draw all men unto me,' ver. 32.   Those whom Satan hath ruled and subjected to his kingdom, and who had lived according to his laws, now were to be reformed : ' Now is the judgment of this world ;'that is, there is now a great change and reformation to be made in the hearts and lives of men, for so the word 'judgment' signifies, namely, a reformation made according to some law or statute. And so Satan's kingdom is to be destroyed, and he cast out, and Christ by his laws to bear sway.   And thus Satan is judged ; so that to be convinced of judgment is to be convinced of that sanctification and true change of heart and life which believers ought to take up.   And so in Mat. xii. 18 (out of Isa. xlii. 1) it is said of Christ, that he should ' shew forth judgment to the Gentiles ' by his ministers ; that is, teach them true holiness and reformation of heart and life, and the right manner of serving and worshipping of God.   And at the 20th verse it is said he should ' bring forth judgment unto victory ;' that is, carry on the work of grace and sanctification (begun in the heart of any convert) unto victory and triumph, by upholding it and causing it to prevail, by subverting Satan's laws and holds in the hearts of men, and erecting his own.   And this is all one with ' convincing men of judgment,' as here, making them believe, submit, stoop to, embrace, and take up that strictness which he in his word requires.   And so in Zeph. ii. 3 the saints are said to be such as had ' wrought his judgment ;' that is, had endeavoured to reform their hearts and lives.

CHAPTER II.

In which it is proved that to convince us of sin, and to humble us in the sense of it, is the work of the Holy Ghost in converting us to God.

It is granted that in the humiliation of a sinner the vision and knowledge of Christ and his glorious righteousness strikes the greatest, the last, and most complete stroke.   But whether the first and single sight of it, without any work of the law before Christ revealed as a ground-colour to make this take upon the heart, is sufficient, this is the question between us, and those of the contrary opinion, of which the great and main ground is, that because the vision of Christ doth by reflection and comparison discover a man's sinfulness, that therefore there seems to be no need of any use of the law to do it.   But if this were so, then by the like reason also, because Christ's example is a complete rule fully directory to a Christian; therefore there needs no direction from the law, and so you wholly abolish the use of the law.   But that there should be a foregoing discovery of sin by the law, before faith and the revelation of Christ, and that it is an ordinance of God to this end, and a way of God's so to work, and so to that end that the law should be preached, is clearly evinced.

1. By that instance of the first work of conversion, and of the first sermon that ever was made in the world, by God the Father, who first gave the promise of the Son unto our first parents.   Yea, although Adam's natural conscience was already made sensible of his misery, so far as the light of that conscience left in him could work, Gen. iii. 7, 8 (for Adam confesseth to God his being afraid, and his sense of his own nakedness, ver. 10), yet God, ere he preacheth the gospel, and lets fall the promise of the seed, ver. 15, spends the first part of his sermon in a further convincing him of his sin by that law which he had given him, and which he had transgressed, thereby to convey the Spirit of bondage, to work a further conviction than natural conscience had wrought, expressly putting him in mind of the command which he had broken, ver. 11; and though he doth not terrify him with the curse annexed, because his natural conscience was already made sensible of it (for that was it which he feared), yet because this humiliation preparatory is mainly to be for sin as sin, and as a transgression of the law, which natural conscience, without a further work of the Spirit, is not apprehensive of; therefore that which God intends his conviction in, is the heinousness of his sin, by setting before his eyes himself as the commander—' which *I* commanded'—and the law itself commanded and broken, which discovery is the main and proper end of the law in its work.   If therefore a man, whose natural conscience was already awakened, needed yet a further distinct and more spiritual conviction of sin by the law ere it was fit to preach Christ unto him, then much more if we were to preach to Turks or pagans, who are ' past feeling,' as the apostle says, should we first awaken them ere we speak to them of Christ.   And God himself being the preacher to Adam, and appearing to him, if the vision of his glory alone would have done it, without a distinct discovery by the law first wrought, then surely God might have spared this legal discovery, rather than all the preachers that succeed him.

2. When Christ himself, the promised seed, came to preach the gospel, the first sermon Luke records, preached at his own town, was upon that text, Isa. lxii. 2, ' I am sent to preach the gospel unto the captives, and in prison' (' shut up under the law,' as Paul says), ' to heal the broken-hearted,' &c.; for to such only does the gospel belong.   And therefore he sent John before him, to ' prepare his way,' even to make way for the entertainment of his ministry, to break, and bruise, and shut up such as Christ might heal and enlarge; whose ministry, though it had gospel in it (for, Acts xix. 4, he bids the people believe, &c.), yet so as that came in but in the close and up-shut of his ministry, as the thing which his preaching made way for. But still the eminent impression of his ministry upon men's hearts was a sense of their sins, which legal humiliation still left.   Though a seed of faith was in the bud, and by his ministry begun, yet was it not blossomed,

but to be raised up to victory by him who breaketh not the bruised reed, and Christ's ministry was to raise assurance in them upon whom John had wrought; and therefore John is said to have come mourning, and to have preached repentance, and his baptism is called 'the baptism of repentance.' And these titles his ministry had given it, to shew what were the eminent effects which it was ordained to work. And accordingly, though it sowed a seed of faith by his pointing to the Messiah, yet it left his hearers and converts a greater impression of legal terrors still remaining upon their consciences, for Christ's ministry to take off from them by a more clear preaching the gospel. And in this respect John was said to 'prepare the way of the Lord;' and that by casting down mountains, filling valleys, and removing discouragements, so to make Christ's way level, and by causing men to see the vanity of all flesh, Isa. xl. 1–6. And in some of those sermons recorded of his, you shall observe his method to answer this, and so discern the better what was the scope of his ministry; for he first falls upon them and threatens them, and convinceth them of their estates, Luke iii. 7; he tells them of God's wrath, and takes away those false conceits which had kept them from being sensible of their estates, as if they were Abraham's seed, ver. 8. And further, to convince men of their particular sins, he tells them each of their especial bosom lusts (which is the distinct and special way to humble, observed also by Christ to the woman of Samaria, and by Paul to Felix); so, ver. 11, he tells the people of their want of charity, the publicans of their oppression, ver. 13, and the soldiers of their violence and rapine, ver. 14; and preacheth Christ, as it were, but by occasion of men's wondering whether he were the Christ, and that too after all these other passages in his ministry premised, ver. 15, 16.

3. God the Holy Ghost, who is to work with and second our sermons, and to deal with men's hearts, hath a peculiar office assigned him, which therefore must needs be necessary, as appears by that title given him, Rom. viii. 15, 'the Spirit of bondage;' and as such he is received ere he becomes a 'Spirit of adoption.' Which Spirit of bondage hath not relation to the bondage under the law, for he speaks it to the Romans, who were Gentiles, and not nurtured up under the law—'_Ye_ have not received'—nor to the bondage of natural conscience; for it is a Spirit 'received,' and a Spirit that returns no more to work fear, which in them that are converted natural conscience still doth, yea, even in many believers. But the Holy Ghost is a Spirit of bondage in conversion only; and in that it is said '_to fear again_,' it implies it was once received. The office of which Spirit appears by the opposite effect of the same Spirit as he is called 'the Spirit of adoption,' which is to witness adoption and sonship, as the other is to witness our slavery and bondage to sin and death.

4. As the Spirit hath an office designed him for such a work, so God hath appointed a word in the hand of this Spirit to work and 'engender bondage' by, as the phrase is, Gal. iv. 23, 24. And that the law was revealed to the world to this end, and that this is as proper a use of it as any other now since the fall, I will take that which the Epistle to the Romans affords for the proof of it.

I come to the more direct proofs out of that epistle; the very method the apostle takes up to promulge and lay open the gospel (which is the subject of that epistle) offers something to me clearly to evince this, which by the hand will bring me to what I aim at.

The epistle, you know, is an exact system or form of wholesome words, such as Paul would have Timothy keep by him. After salutations, from verse 1st to the 15th, he propounds the general subject and argument of his epistle, the gospel, ver. 15, 16, and the main argument of that gospel, ver. 17. Now, after he had declared the argument and drift of the whole, he enters upon this system and method of handling and revealing it. And to clear the way for it, he convinceth the Gentiles that they are under sin and wrath, chap. i. from verse 18 to the 9th verse of chap. ii., and then he convinceth the Jews that they also are under sin; and this he doth by taking away their false props, chap. ii. from verse 9 to the 9th verse of chap. iii. And then he enters into a proof that all, both Jew and Gentile, and all mankind, are wholly corrupted, from verse 10 to the 19th, where, ver. 19 and 20, he shews, that as the gospel was appointed to reveal Christ's righteousness, chap. i. 17, so the law to give 'the knowledge of sin.' True, you will say; but unto whom? Verse 19 answers us: 'To them that are under the law.' And therefore it is most properly given to discover to men unregenerate whilst under the law their sins: 'It saith,' that is, it preacheth to them. And to what end? To humble them, 'that every mouth may be stopped,' and so 'every one' (in their own apprehensions) 'become guilty before God.' And 'By this law,' says he, 'is the knowledge of sin.' And to what end is this knowledge of sin but to make way for the conviction of that righteousness which the gospel holds forth, and unto which all this tended? Verse 20, and so on to chap. v., where, at verse 12, he again proceeding to the discovery of the source of all that sinfulness, viz., Adam's sin, and of all that righteousness, viz., Christ's righteousness, he at the 13th verse shews that the end why God gave the law was to discover sin: 'Sin indeed was in the world before Moses, but was not imputed till the law came,' that is, not charged on men's consciences. And verse 20 more expressly says, 'The law entered that the offence might abound,' that is, in men's apprehensions. For though the law stirred up sin, as he shews, chap. vii., yet that was but an occasional and accidental end (as it is in the 8th verse of that 7th chapter), not the primary end of God's revealing it. And it entered not that sin might be more, but that it might be imputed; and so that the guilt which was already contracted might be charged upon men's consciences, and that the guilt imputed might abound, or appear above measure sinful; and this to the end to set up and to illustrate grace, and Christ's righteousness in their hearts who should be partakers of that grace: 'Where sin abounded, there grace abounded much more.'

If you will yet make question, whether that the first knowledge of sin is to come in by the law, so to make way for the abounding of grace, consider what is said in the 7th chapter, wherein the apostle (having proved that both justification and sanctification were from Christ alone, in the 3d, 4th, 5th, and 6th chapters, and having before professed, chap. iii. 31, that 'he did not make void the law, but established it') undertakes to shew the ends whereto the law now serveth unto men. And this to remove that great objection, that the law was made void by him. Whereof one primary and direct end unto which it serves is, to give in conversion the first knowledge of sin. So ver. 7 of that chapter, 'I had not known sin but by the law.' And what knowledge speaks he of, but that which humbled himself at his first conversion? For, ver. 9, he says, he was 'once alive without the law,' that is, without the knowledge of it; as the Gentiles are said to be 'without God in the world.' Now, Paul being a Pharisee, was never without the law, and some knowledge of it, he being educated in the law from a child; and therefore he must needs speak of that knowledge which he began to have when he was first converted, differencing it from his former pharisaical knowledge of it, in that he was alive notwithstanding that knowledge of it.   Nay, he calls that knowledge no knowledge in comparison of this, for he says he was 'without the commandment' when a Pharisee.   And that he speaks of his knowledge in or after conversion is evident by this, that he knew not original sin nor lust until then.   The Pharisees, as appears by Christ's sermon, Mat. v., thought it no sin.   But now Paul was humbled for it; he saw that in his state of unregeneracy the law had occasionally 'wrought all concupiscence,' ver. 8.   And that he speaks of his knowledge not after conversion, but in the work of humiliation, appears by this, that 'sin revived, and he died,' who in his own apprehension was once alive, and thought himself a living man and an heir of life, thinking to be justified by the law.   And so the law not only really put him into a state of death by occasioning sin, ver. 11, but stirred up in him apprehensions of his bondage unto death, ver. 13, by discovering it unto him; he finding himself deceived in thinking to attain life by the law, whenas it wrought death in him.   In all which, sin every way appeared to him above measure sinful.   And this effect of the law in his first conversion he brings to shew the proper use of the law, confirming it by his own example (as he doth the other ends of the law also), which he shews in that whole chapter, in three things, according to a threefold condition wherein men may be supposed to be :

First, Of an unregenerate man, having a common knowledge of the law, such as himself had whilst in the flesh, ver. 5, which knowledge did then enrage his lusts; which yet (to excuse the law) he shews, ver. 8, to have been but 'occasional.'   And this condition he sets down from verses 5th to the 7th.

The *second* condition he mentions is, when men come to have a spiritual conviction of their sin by the law, to bring them out of that estate by being humbled.   To which end the law serveth more directly to give them the knowledge of sin; not such as stirs up lust, as afore, but such as humbles them, and lays them for dead.   And this also he shews by the effect it had in himself, verses 7, 9, 10, and 13, his purpose being to confirm all by his own example throughout the chapter.

And, *thirdly*, after his conversion he shews the use of the law to a man regenerate, to discover sin and his captivity under it, by the spiritualness of it, from verse 14th to the 24th, so as to drive them to Christ for help ; verses 24, 25.

All which I take to be the true analysis of the chapter.   For all which uses he brings his own example, speaking in his own person as a pattern herein.   Now if his own particular instance before conversion and after, be brought as a common example to shew the use of the law in common, and after conversion, then also in conversion it must be taken as a common pattern also.   Whose conversion thus by the law, had it not been extraordinary, it had not been a fit instance to vindicate and clear the law, that it hath still its use subservient to the gospel, and particularly in this, to discover men's sinfulness when first converted.

And I will add but this, that if the vision and conviction that Christ was the Messiah and Saviour of sinners, be ordained to humble alone at first without the law, then of all other Paul needed not to have had this revelation by the law added.   For who ever had such a conviction and vision of Christ upon the first moment of his conversion as Paul had from heaven ?   If, therefore, he was notwithstanding by a legal humiliation converted, how much more then we ?   Yea, he plainly says, that he ' had not known sin, but by the law.'

CHAPTER III.

In which it is proved, from the instances of conversion in the time of Job, long before Christ came, from the instance of the apostle Paul's conversion, after Christ's coming in the flesh, that a converted soul must be convinced of sin, be humbled for it, and believe on Christ for righteousness and salvation.

Set narrations of solemn conversions are rarely found in the Old Testament among the Jews.   We read not how or by what means Isaac, or Jacob, or Moses, or David, were wrought upon, and turned unto God ; but here, among the records of those that were not of that genealogy, or of the Jewish line, and so not members of that church, and yet circumcised, and retaining the profession of the true God, being Esau's seed, we find in a book of greatest antiquity, a lively description thereof, taken from the experimental observations of Elihu.   He spreads them afore Job (chap. xxxiii.) for his encouragement and hopes of mercy from God, notwithstanding his great sinfulness, which Elihu had charged him withal, in the former chapters ; or maugre those deep afflictions God had visited him withal in his body, his mind, and outward condition.   It hath rejoiced me to have met with so ancient footsteps of the same doctrine, of ways, and means, and operations in conversions so long ago, to have been for substance much one and the same, as under the gospel we have seen, and is frequently exemplified in these last days.

The means Elihu relates to have been several dispensations of God ; as by awakenings and inspirations, in dreams and visions in the night, which then, when the word was not put into writing, but conveyed either by tradition or immediate revelation, was more ordinary in those times.   And with this means he therefore begins : Job xxxiii. 15–17, ' In a dream, in a vision of the night, when deep sleep falleth upon men, in slumberings upon the bed ; then he openeth the ears of men, and sealeth their instruction, that he may withdraw man from his purpose, and hide pride from man.' He instanceth likewise in God's visiting men with ' great and sore sickness' unto death's door ; and when humbled thereby, and not knowing what to do to be saved, he sends a messenger to open and make known God's mind to them, to shew and instruct such a one in the right way of salvation.   This you may see in ver. 19 unto ver. 27.   And a seasonable word coming upon apprehensions of death, God often, both then as now, blesseth wonderfully, to work upon men savingly.   And Elihu shuts up these instances (which are but a few of many, and instead of all the rest he might have produced) with this conclusion, ver. 28, 29, ' Lo, all these things,' that is, both these and divers other ways and means, which he names not, ' doth God work by;' as also all these operations by those several means doth God work.   Ere I draw forth the particulars of these workings of God with this sick man, I premise two generals.

1. That these instances do set forth the workings of saving conversion unto God ; both initial at first, or renewed conversions after great sinnings ; yet initial especially, and most directly, as the circumstances instanced in do carry it.   Although in the intended or useful aims in them to Job (who was converted already), they are directed as a prescript for him to take

the same course that new converts are said here to do, to be restored to
the favour of God again, by the same ways which new converts are at first
admitted into. And, indeed, initial conversion, and renewed, come all to
one in the substantial operations of either : ' All these things' God works
in all and every convert, whether at first, or after in repeated repentances ;
the operations are the same in both ; like as in the original draught of a
picture, the first drawing gives all the substantial lineaments, and the after-
draughts go but over the same rudiments, in additions more to the life. And
that such an original draught is intended principally, is evident from the
series of Elihu's discourse ; in that from the instances he draws this conclusion from the premises, viz., a gracious invitation made to all, or any
man ; and an encouragement given them in like manner to come in, and
turn to God, with promises of like grace and mercy ; and that he plainly
infers this is a corollary brought of, and deduced from the example of
this sick man's conversion ; and that the grace that God had manifested
in saving him, should be shewn to any other convert, is apparent in those
words, ver. 27, 28, ' He (that is, God) ' looketh upon men, and if any
say, I have sinned, and perverted that which was right, and it profited me
not, he will deliver his soul from going into the pit, and his life shall see
the light.'

This is a general proposition which concerns the sons of men; so involves
those that never as yet had been wrought upon, as well as those that
had been ; Elihu declaring that God would in like manner upon faith and
repentance be gracious to them ; ' to deliver his soul from going into the
pit.' And the argument or encouragement, from the conversions of men
unregenerate afore, must needs have more force and persuasive power in it,
to prevail with others that are still such. For it is not only the same case,
but if the same instance had only intended men actually wrought upon
already, the encouragement and hopes given had been capable of this grand
exception, that those that had been in grace already, and had a seed of God
still abiding in them, would be easily received into God's favour, and grace
renewed in him ; as a charcoal that hath been dried will easily take fire.
Oh, but an unregenerate soul might say, I who have lived all my days in
such a condition of sinning, and have provoked God with so long continued
a course of sins, without any the least spark of good in me, how shall I
hope to have it begun, and my person to be renewed ? But when he shall
hear of so great and so long hardened sinners, who have been converted,
and that God hath been gracious to them, as if they had never sinned
against him ; and not only so, but that they have been admitted into his
presence, and ' seen his face with joy' (and such sinners as have utterly
been strangers to God, do need the highest inducements, and widest door
of hope set open to them) ; such an example as this must needs be wonderfully inviting, and give abundant hope to them. For the condition of these
is just the same with their own. Yea, the sick man instanced in seems, by
his manner of speech, to be one who had hitherto been ignorant of the way
of salvation until then. That providentially some messenger, and he one
of a thousand, doth shew and discover to him that uprightness and way
whereby men must be saved, as good news to him, which he knew not of
till then : ' If there be with him an interpreter to shew to man his uprightness.' And any intelligent soul, that knows what it is to be converted, will
be ready to acknowledge by descrying, upon view of them, several of the
most eminent lines and lineaments of such a work drawn in this dark
ancient piece ; as, namely, in general it is described to be an efficacious

'working,' signified by the phrase of ' opening the ear,' in the Old Testament : Isa. l. 5, ' The Lord God hath opened my ear, and I was not rebellious, neither turned away my back.'

In the New Testament it is an ' opening the heart,' as Lydia's, to attend to the things delivered ; as likewise by a ' sealing of the instruction given,' ver. 16, impressing them as effectually on the soul, as the seal doth on the wax the image engraven on it, so as finally they resist not, but become obedient thereunto, ver. 16.   But particularly, 1. God worketh so as to ' withdraw a man from his former purpose' of going on in sin, and ' hides pride from man,' by convincing him of his sins and sinful estate, and thereby ' breaking the staff of pride of a man's spirit,' in the sense of his sinful and woeful condition, in the ignorance of which he had stoutly gone on in the height and pride of carnal excellencies, but now is emptied of them all, and of that his conceited righteousness he was opinionated of in his former estate, and ' brought low' (as James's word is), humbled to the dust in the sight of his sin and misery he lies in, and thereby, 2. the soul is wrought on, for its receiving and accepting by faith Christ's righteousness and ransom, or redemption, which was to be given him out of the free grace of God : ver. 24, ' Then he is gracious, and saith, Deliver him from going down into the pit : I have found a ransom ; ' which righteousness is the principal part of that blessed message, which that messenger or interpreter from God brings him then, when, 3, he closeth with and betakes himself wholly unto that, for his alone righteousness, found and provided by God for him ; he also, 4, is brought in, and represented to have prayed and supplicated God for the obtaining of these, prayer being the first fruits of faith ; and, 5, the consequent of that is, God's gracious acceptation, and ' seeing God's face with joy,' as the words of the 23d, 24th, and 26th verses manifestly shew : ' If there be a messenger with him, an interpreter, one of a thousand, to shew unto man his uprightness : then he is gracious unto him, and saith, Deliver him from going down to the pit : I have found a ransom. He shall pray unto God, and he will be favourable unto him : and he shall see his face with joy ; ' 6, He withal confessing and forsaking his sin, and pursuing after that uprightness of holiness in heart and life, which is the other part of that message the interpreter makes known unto him.   It involveth also the renewed conversion of a man that is declined, and hath grievously sinned, and heinously perverted that which is right, whom God recovers and brings to himself again by some great affliction, by which the Spirit works conviction of his sin, and reneweth faith on the Messiah's righteousness.   Whereupon God restores him to his former comforts out of his graciousness, through the redemption of the Messiah ; and from the instance of such an one brought so low, and by this means so raised again, Elihu (who directs all this personally to Job in his condition) would give him ground of hopes of grace and mercy from God under this deplorable affliction that he was in.*   And thus in this parable here, Elihu, callidè (as Sanctius's word is), presents himself as a messenger from God, directing Job to the only true means whereby God is pacified, viz., the Messiah's ransom and righteousness, and the right course he was to take to recover the favour of God, and remove that evil that lay upon him ; namely, by having recourse to that ransom of the Messiah, and free grace of God by faith, both which he points unto, ver. 24, joined with repentance, in confession of sin, and turning from it, as ver. 27.

Both or either of these serve to this scope, but eminently the first, viz.,

* See the Dutch Annotators.

the conversion of one unregenerate, as being the greater example of mercy and grace, which might give the more abundant hopes to Job in this his case, who had long been savingly himself wrought upon, though, as Elihu thought, greatly fallen into sin; the recovery of a believer fallen but as the renewal of friendship of one who had long been in friendship with another, whom he had unworthily provoked. But the other is as the first beginning of friendship of one that had continued an utter enemy all his days till now.

2. The second premise is this general rule, for the understanding the workings upon this sick convert his heart (which example I make my special centre of the particulars that follow, drawing all the lines thereto); look, what in other parts of this discourse he makes to be the inward workings upon him, he mentions afore to have been wrought upon, ver. 15–17, the same must be taken in and attributed unto this sick man's conversion also, and he to have had the same inward operations in his soul also which that other by dreams had. And the reason is clear; for although the outward means God used was differing, as a dream or a vision to the first, and a great sickness, &c., to this other, yet conversion from sin being said to be the effect that was wrought thereby, this is common to either, as to any true convert else in the world. And therefore, when it is said, ver. 26, 'Then he openeth the ears of men, and sealeth their instruction,' it is to be conceived that this sick man, when humbled by his sickness and apprehensions of death, and that a messenger from God had further instructed and informed him, 'that then God also opened this man's ear, and sealed up in his heart effectually' those instructions that messenger had delivered to him, he did hear and obey; and therefore it is said, ver. 24, '*Then* God is gracious to him also.' These were but differing ways, and instruments, and occasions of working, but the effect the same in both; so when, in ver. 17, he declares God's end to be 'that he may withdraw man from his purpose, and hide pride from man;' that is, to turn a man from his sinful way and course of life he was resolved to have persisted in; this must in like manner be supposed to have been the end and effectual issue in this sick man's case, for this is common to all converts. When, likewise, he further adds in the same verse, and 'hide pride from man;' that is, to work pride out of his heart, to bury it (as Calvin's word is), extinguisheth it, which consists chiefly (as in New Testament language) in the 'pulling down of strongholds, casting down imaginations, and every high thing that exalteth itself against the knowledge of God, and bringing into captivity every thought to the obedience of Christ,' 2 Cor. x. 5, it is that universal pride in man's heart that is opposite to conversion or subjection to Christ, and not only or chiefly the pulling down the plumes of that particular sin of pride before and towards men. But this is to 'break the staff of the pride of man's heart' by nature, which bears men up in self-confidence of one's own righteousness, and creature-confidence, to work poverty of spirit in a man. Now, the same is to be understood the issue and effect that is in this sick man's heart, and here intended; they are the essentials of conversion he sets forth, only mentioneth one piece or strain of spirit wrought in the one instance, another in the other; even as in the New Testament, in relating conversion instances, we find them in like manner scatteredly narrated, some in one, other effects in another, which, when gathered together, give us a description of the whole work completely.

This general rule I desire may not be understood, as if I meant that God did not use sundry means, as that one threatening brought home to one

man's heart, another to another man's, to humble them; as likewise several promises brought home to work faith, &c., yet still there is the same
effects, or 'things wrought' in the hearts of all, and common to all; as to
be humbled for sin, to confess and forsake it, to repent and turn to God,
to believe in Christ and God's free grace, for they are the essentials, the
inwards of the new creature, as every child born into the world hath alike
the same inwards; and of such substantials, and none other but such,
doth Elihu make mention as works in the soul, in the whole of this his
discourse.

I come to draw out the particular workings themselves, as they are represented, either in the instances, or any other part of his discourse.

The parts of conversion our Saviour reduceth unto three, as I have
shewed in opening John xvi. 8.

1. The conviction of sin, which we call humiliation.

2. Of Christ's righteousness, with faith thereon.

3. Of judgment, or reformation of heart and life.

Let us consider if the substantials of these are not to be descried in, or
fairly to be collected from out of the aforesaid instances; as, namely, of
the sick man, and the circumstances whereby Elihu sets forth the story of
him, or from other parts of the discourse.

1. They shew a conviction of sin, and of a sinful estate that they had
formerly continued in; so the visionist had his ear opened, and this instruction set home, that the 'work' (as some translate it), 'his purpose'
(as others) is sinful and wicked, and to be forsaken, or else he will utterly
perish; this ver. 17, 18 declare; in ver. 17, God instructs him, 'That he
may withdraw man from his purpose,' or, his work; which denotes his
course and way, and him to have been a worker of iniquity, a committer of
iniquity in Christ's and the apostle's sense; translated therefore, 'his purpose,' namely, of continuing in his sin. He sees likewise the danger of
'going to the pit,' and of perishing, ver. 18. And by these, as persuasives
set on upon his heart, he is induced to leave, and 'break off' his sin' (as
Daniel's phrase is), as being the way to hell and destruction. This was
'an instruction sealed' upon his mind. But more expressly in ver. 27,
'If any man say I have sinned, and perverted that which was right,' and
perversion there notes out great and grievous sinnings; these the convert
is brought to see, and confesseth.

And when the sick man hath also his sin, and unrighteousness laid open
to him; for these words of ver. 27, 'If any say I have sinned,' &c., (which
is the first A. B. C. of true repentance), thereby is strongly implied, yea,
declared, that the same was in this sick man's heart—for it is an inference
drawn from his example in particular; teaching all men to do, even as
this man had done : to lay to heart his sin. It had not been an opposite[*]
general inference, unless we suppose it to have been in that man's spirit,
who is proposed as the particular example or pattern that it is drawn from.

And if any object and say, that this would then have been expressed in
words, in relating the sick man's case ; the answer is, that it needed not.
It was enough to be set down in the inference, and needless to have been
repeated over and over in both. And such manner of implications are
frequent in the Scriptures, and especially to be observed in the Proverbs.

Yea, many interpreters, eminently skilled and versed in the Hebrew, do
understand and read the words of that 27th verse, as if they were the
speech of that sick penitent's, when restored ; and it is so varied in the

Qu. 'apposite'?—ED.

margin as to this sense. That *he*, the now penitent convert, looks upon men, other men, as occasionally he meets with any, and proposeth to them his own example and says, ' I had sinned, and perverted that which was right, and it profited me not,' but brought upon myself therewith, the danger of death, and guilt of hell upon me. But *he*, namely God, hath, upon my repentance, ' delivered my soul from going into the pit :' and therefore do you all in like manner repent, as I have done. And it is certain that the Hebrew will bear either readings, though I prefer that which our translators have given far before it. For this reason, that phrase, *He looks upon men*, &c., is most properly used of God, who from heaven looks down upon men, and observes whether they repent.

Neither was this sick man only brought to be sensible of his sin, but being brought to death's door, is made apprehensive of hell too, which is ' the wages of sin,' ' the second death ;' ver. 22, ' Yea his soul draweth near unto the grave, and his life to the destroyers ;' which words serve not simply to set out his danger, as it was in the reality, or as it was in the thing itself, but also to shew that he had apprehensions of it. And how often hell is called that pit, in the Proverbs by Solomon, and in other Old Testament Scripture, I need not insist on ; in the New, that ' bottomless pit ;' Rev. ix. 11, ' The angel of the bottomless pit,' the devil is called. Which is likewise as often termed destruction, and is joined with hell, to signify it, Prov. xxvii. 20. And the word here translated *pit*, in general signifies *corruption*. And the dread of this for his sin, is the great distress which this sick man's soul is brought to. And this was it which gave the advantage to this interpreter, ' one of a thousand,' who took the opportunity to strike whilst the iron was hot. Even when his soul ' drew nigh to the grave, and his life to the destroyers' in his own fears ; that is, to the devils ; who (as Christ said of that rich fool, ' this night *they*'—the angels of this pit—' shall take away thy soul') carry it to that pit of destruction, whereof he hath the power, Heb. ii. ; and he hath his name from thence of Apollyon, and Abaddon, in the foresaid Rev. ix. 11, that is, *destroyer ;* and at death stands ready by an unregenerate man's bed-side, to take away his soul. And as the *grave*, and *pit*, and *destruction*, are used to express *hell*, the thing itself, so in the Old Testament, a man that is filled with such apprehensions about this, is brought in as using the like phrases to these, thereby to express his sentiments thereof. Thus Heman in trouble, and terrors of conscience for sin, and God's wrath, speaks of himself as of a man in hell, when yet he was not sick in body ; in like language to what Elihu speaks of this sick man here : Ps. lxxxviii. 3, 4, ' My soul is full of troubles, and my life draweth nigh to the grave : I am counted with them that go down into the pit. And again, ver. 5, ' Free among the dead, cut off from thy hand ; whom thou rememberest no more ;' and verses 6, 7, ' Thou hast laid me in the lowest pit, in darkness, in the deeps : thy wrath lieth hard upon me ; and thou hast afflicted me with all thy waves. Selah.' This was not sickness bodily, or danger of the grave. For he speaks of himself as a man already ' laid in the lowest pit,' and that all the waves of God's wrath had gone over him. And how often is it that the approaches of death to a man's view, and fore-thoughts of these things, awaken men's hearts, and possess them with such apprehensions, experience abundantly shews. Men's consciences naturally being ' subject to the fear of death all their life long,' Heb. ii. 15, much more at the sight of death's approachment to them, who have heard and known that hell immediately doth follow, as in Rev. vi. 8.

But further, in this juncture of time, here comes 'a messenger, who is one of a thousand,' as it is spoken of him. He will be sure faithfully to second this voice of conscience, by a further laying open his sinful estate to him, and the spiritual danger he is in of the second death, 'if he turn not.' And when he is said to 'shew to man his uprightness,' even whilst it is a-doing, a man withal is shewn what he ought to be, and what he ought to have been, and what righteousness he must get and obtain. This, when done, will withal effectually discover unto a man his own uprightness, far more than natural conscience alone doth do. For this man speaks the holy and spiritual word, and mind of God ; and sets a man's secret sins in the light of God's countenance, afore the man's conscience ; which natural conscience could not reach to. And the Spirit of God, joining with both these, as he did in the heart of the jailor, Acts xvi., 'convinceth him of sin,' and thus humbleth, and prepareth him, which, by God's ordination, is the first work in men's conversion.

And truly that joyful word ('joyful sound' the psalmist calls it) 'Deliver him,' ver. 24, may very rationally be judged to relate to the many fears his soul was in, from the sight of his sins and apprehensions of damnation, upon his apprehensions of death ; and that God, in and by that blessed word 'deliver him,' pronounced his absolution from his sins and hell. Especially it being followed and strengthened by those promises that follow, that God would favourably 'accept him,' as the word is, and he should 'see God's face with joy,' in ver. 26, both which in conjunction speak that kind of God's manifesting of his face, which is by 'lifting up the light of his countenance' immediately upon the soul ; which gives 'more joy,' as the psalmist his experience assures us, 'than oil and wine,' or all temporal mercies whatsoever. These speeches are too big to express the mercies of this life only. They are promises, though *in* this life, yet not *of* this life, but the beginnings of that which is to come. And those speeches of 'seeing God's face,' and 'accepting with favour,' do refer unto it. And indeed many of those interpreters that would understand these phrases of deliverance only from bodily death, in a great sickness, yet withal acknowledge this sick man to have been delivered therefrom, upon his true conversion unto God in the sight of his sins, his true faith, and sincere repentance, and prayer unto God for the continuance of his life in this world. And this every verse and circumstance in the story do abundantly declare. And further, that the sight of his sins, and the sense of death's approach, being not sufficient of themselves to work faith and conversion in him, that therefore God afforded the spiritual assistance of a messenger, &c., whose errand must be supposed to be, to discover and press upon his soul such things as are most persuasive and productive to draw on true faith and repentance in him. And those things, or motives, we know are such as belong to the other world after death, and mainly of 'hell that follows it,' Rev. vi. 8 ; which all that die in their sins will immediately be carried into, when they turn not from them. This messenger also, by declaring and laying open the rich mercies that are in God, gives him hopes, not of recovery only out of sickness, but teacheth him to pray unto God, as ver. 26, for pardon and forgiveness of his sins, deliverance from hell, acceptation of his person, and seeing God's face. And had there not been this use of such a soul-messenger to instruct, guide, and direct him in these great concerns of his soul ; a physician or worker of miracles that could have raised the sick, had been more useful and proper to have been sent. than such an interpreter, if restoring unto natural light only had been all the intent.   Nor are the simple concerns of this life, as deliverance from bodily death, and bestowing temporal blessings of this life, without the mixture of the motives from, and knowledge of the things of the other, sufficient to work spiritual conversion, faith, and repentance in men, which were wrought in this man here ; and which serve not only for such low things as those of this world are, but for the great things of the other world, pardon of sin, acceptation of our persons into grace and favour.   For pardon of sins is that special mercy, that great grace and spiritual blessing appertaining to the other world : Eph. i. 7, ' In whom we have redemption through his blood, the forgiveness of sins, according to the riches of his grace.'   And therefore it is not bodily life only, or bodily death simply, that are ultimately here intended in those words with which he concludes ; ver. 39, 40, ' Lo, all these things worketh God oftentimes with man, to bring back his soul from the pit, to be enlightened with the light of the living.'   And although it often falls out that, together with pardon of sins, &c., God vouchsafes a present deliverance from bodily death, and from out of such or such a sickness, and that through Christ's ransom ; yet they are but some small things added, as Christ's word is, and cast into the bargain, which is therefore mentioned, ver. 25, ' Then shall his flesh come as the flesh of a child,' &c., yet this were but a small thing, and for a moment. But that God should produce and bring forth his hidden treasures, and allege that infinite price of redemption laid down for men's souls, when it is so rarely spoken of in the Old Testament, upon occasion of delivering a man only from a sickness, &c., this holds no decorum or proportion.   That had been a ' light thing,' as Christ in the prophet speaks of the reward of his redemption ; but to be delivered from sin, and sins infinite in their weight, and infinite in number, to be delivered from hell and eternal death ; to be discharged at once for ever, so as never to see death, nor set a foot in the pit, not to enter into condemnation—and he that undertook for, and paid this price, and knew best the estimate of both, thus sets out this deliverance and redemption purchased to believers, and promised from the time of their regeneration that ' he that believes in me shall never die,' John xi.—this is something indeed, this is a redemption some way worthy of, that is, suitable and answerable to, so great a ransom, and worthy of such a mention, so rare, and so unwonted.

And then by that other phrase, to be ' enlightened with the light of the living,' is meant, that through those gracious workings upon the soul God gives and brings a man into the light of life eternal, which is begun here, and with which a man is enlightened at first conversion, and thereby brought into a new world, and to see the kingdom of God : ' Arise from the dead, and Christ shall give thee light.'   They do therefore very ill that would limit these phrases, and the issues of these workings, to be a temporal deliverance (and that only), and restoring a penitent sinner to natural life.   And therefore many interpreters * that seem to verge that way, interpose and inject in their expositions of these phrases, à morte utráque, from both deaths ; or à morte æternâ, from eternal death ; and cannot forbear to do it, though literally they expound them otherwise.

---

* Mercer on the 30th verse ; Piscator on verse 24.   *Redime eum, id est, a morte æterna.*—Calvin on verse 18.   ' He pulleth back from the grave or pit,' these words (says he) concerns not only bodily death, but by a similitude.   The everlasting damnation is termed here a *grave* or *pit*.   And in his 125th sermon, interpreting that of verse 24, ' Deliver him from the pit.'   The case here standeth not only upon temporal death, but upon damnation.   And thus divers others.

Thus much for the conviction of sin, and of the soul thus prepared, and humbled, and ' chastised' for his sin (as in verse 19), which word signifies also ' instructed ;' for his chastising thus even to death, helps forward the instructing man in these things.

2. I come to the second work, to effect which, indeed, is the main errand of this interpreter, to whom God had committed the word of reconciliation of such a soul to God ; and here his part begins, and God's effectual working therewith.

Verse 23. ' If there be a messenger with him, an interpreter, one of a thousand, to shew unto man his uprightness.'

I will analyse the words into these parts or heads.

1. I will consider what kind of person this messenger is, with some observations thereupcn. It is a fond and utterly unwarranted interpretation, that it should be some good angel sent from heaven, as Mercer, misled by his Jewish Rabbis, would put this upon ; to whom I refer the reader. For that which follows will not agree therewith, as not to say of an angel sent from heaven, he is ' one of a thousand ;' for in comparison unto what other angels is it that this is spoken ? To be sure, not of devils, the destroyers. It were a dishonour to any of these elect angels to have any comparison made with them, to set forth their excellencies thereby ; and if with others, the good, certainly any one of those glorious creatures, coming with a message from God, would have had the same efficacy on this man's heart, and would have been sufficient, if that had been the meaning. Nor do we find that God used in those times their ministry to convert, and to work saving faith in any, though with other messages they were entrusted. They gave the law, but that is the ministration of death. No ; God hath betrusted the ministry of reconciliation unto us men, and not angels. Much less not to be mediators between God and souls, and to present their prayers to God, or to be employed to carry news of their faith and repentance, that thereupon God should then say to that angel, ' Deliver him, I have found a ransom,' as these interpreters would have it. But men eminently holy, or else prophets, teachers, and instructors of others, employed by God for the conversion and salvation of souls, are styled angels, that is, God's messengers. Thus, in the Old Testament, John the Baptist, Mal. iii. 1, and indeed the whole tribe of Levi, the priesthood to whom was betrusted by covenant, Mal. ii. 5, the law of God, the conversion of souls, ver. 6, he, or the whole fraternity of them, are styled ' the angel' (as here), or ' the messenger of the Lord,' ver. 7. In the New, the ministers or bishops of those seven churches are so dignified. And souls that are truly wrought upon by them, do ' reverence them as an angel of God,' as the apostle, Gal. iv. 14. And these are called angels or messengers, because ' sent' by God to work faith in men :' as Rom. x. 15, ' How shall they preach except they be sent ? as it is written, How beautiful are the feet of them that preach the gospel of peace, and bring glad tidings of good things.'

By an interpreter is meant an expounder of God's mind and will in this covenant of grace, touching men's salvation, and of the way to be taken by man for the obtaining it : ' To shew unto man his uprightness,' is the matter of the message here. And he is ' one of a thousand ' who is able to reveal the things of God touching man's salvation, and give right directions unto such disconsolate souls that are unfeigned, * and taken quite off from all their false supports and confidences, and their ignorant carnal pleas that

* Qu. ' unhinged '?—ED.

their estates were good and blessed; to settle such souls upon a right, sound, and new basis, and bottom of unhinged * faith and thorough repentance. This is not every man's skill, that yet is learned in many other great mysteries, but of one who is experimentally versed in soul work, to whom God hath ' given the tongue of the learned, to speak a word in season, unto him that is weary,' and hit his case and condition home, and ' speak to his heart,' and apply the word aright; and whose spirit God's presence accompanieth with the power and spirit of the gospel.   Such an one is ' one of a thousand.'   ' He that converteth souls is wise,' Prov. xi. 30.

Obs. 1. That natural knowledge, though improved and quickened to the height, is not sufficient to be effectual to work regeneration in men.   The inhabitants of those countries where Job and Elihu lived were the most raised in natural knowledge, participating of all what their bordering neighbours of Chaldea, Egypt, and Phœnicia had. Witness the many golden sands, and ore of such knowledge, dispersed and inserted up and down in this book.   This raised these indwellers in those regions to a greater height than Greece, which lighted their candles with the light of these.   Likewise that natural knowledge these had, though impregnated and actuated to the height by the apparent approach of death, when conscience is awakened, when sin that lay at the door, as a dog asleep, comes in and takes a man by the throat; when ' the iniquity of a man's heels does compass him about,' as the Psalmist speaks, and the other world is near to view, and but as the land that is on the other side of a narrow river; yet all these were not found sufficient savingly to work in any of them.   It may conduce to convince, as such apprehensions did the jailor, Acts xvi.   But the work stays there, yea, turns into despair, if there be not a messenger, an interpreter of God's mind from heaven, and he one of a thousand too, ' to shew to man his uprightness,' the right way of salvation, which natural light is utterly ignorant of, so far as may effectually bring men into God's favour, the state of grace.   There must be a revelation for this, a shewing it to a man by a farther means than nature.   Job himself had in a large harangue discoursed this in chap. xxviii. throughout, in the midst of which he cries out, ver. 12, ' But where shall wisdom be found ?' true wisdom, ' the fear of the Lord,' as he expounds himself, ver. 28, by which eulogy that religion which only is saving was still signified under the Old Testament.   And ver. 20, 21, ' Whence then cometh wisdom ?   And where is the place of understanding ?   seeing it is hid from the eyes of all the living, and kept close from the fowls of the air.   It is God alone that understandeth the way thereof,' ver. 23, that invented it of old; ver. 27, ' Then did he see it, and declare it; he prepared it, yea, and searched it out.'   He searched it out, ' and prepared it for them that love him ;' and no man knows it, so as to be saved by it, but that man to whom he reveals it: ' God said unto man,' &c., ver. 28.

Obs. 2. We see God used then the ministry of man; that is, of men that are interpreters of God's mind, to open and declare his will; ' teachers of righteousness,' as Noah is called ' a preacher of righteousness' afore the flood.   And the like we see hereafter continued, and to be the ordinary converters of souls; and the word the means of conversion: Ps. xix. 7, ' The law of the Lord is perfect, converting the soul; the testimony of the Lord is sure, making wise the simple.'   And the same course he continueth to this day, to work saving faith in men: Rom. x. 14, 15, ' How shall they then call on him in whom they have not believed? and how shall they

* Qu. ' unfeigned '?—ED.

believe in him of whom they have not heard? and how shall they hear without a preacher? And how shall they preach except they be sent?' Conversion was the same then that now, and his ordination of instruction from the word by man's ministry is the same. And the apostle there concludes, ver. 17, ' So then faith cometh by hearing, and hearing by the word of God,' that is, by the appointment of God.

2. I come to the matter of the message itself, the discovery of which is used as the means of this man's salvation and conversion. It is ' summed up in one word,' as the apostle speaks of the law, Gal. v. 14, ' to shew to man his uprightness,' which is no other than the word of reconciliation under the New, 2 Cor. v. 19, revealing both on God's part how he comes to be reconciled to us ; to wit, ' God was in Christ reconciling the world to himself, by making Christ sin for us ;' and, on our part, how we are reconciled to God, by laying hold on this by faith, that thereby ' we might be made the righteousness of God in him,' and therewith turning unto God, out of love wrought by faith, apprehending that righteousness. These words, ' to shew to man his uprightness,' comprehending both these, were the message committed to this interpreter's trust ; even as the word of reconciliation under the New is unto ours in these expressions, ' the word of truth,' ' the gospel of salvation :' Eph. i. 13, ' By which word,' God out ' of his own will doth beget all ' that are begotten of him ; James i. 18, this one word, *man his uprightness*, comprehends both. And indeed those in the Old Testament ' were saved by the same grace of the Lord Jesus,' though darkly and afar off revealed, ' as we' under the New, Acts xv. 11. And the shewing this, for the substance of it, which is the Old Testament phrase here and elsewhere also, though in a more obscure manner ; and man's hearing and closing with it, and obeying of this message, was that which saved them then, as well as the clearer revelation of it (which is the New Testament phrase) doth us now.

The great inquiry then must be, What is to be understood by ' man's uprightness' ? the hearing of which shewn and declared to him by this interpreter, and this sick man's soul closing with and obeying of it, then saved him. What that is, the papists carry it to a man's own merits ; our latter protestant interpreters unto that duty on man's part, consisting in faith and repentance, and upright walking. But Calvin in his sermons on Job, published in French the year afore his death, hath clearly and fully pitched it on the righteousness of justification, whereby God, pardoning our sins, accepts us for righteous for his Son's sake, and through his ransom and redemption. ' This is the righteousness,' says he, ' which is spoken of in this place.' Thus in Sermon 126, and again in Sermon 127. His reason is, because Elihu speaks it ' of a wretched creature in trouble, that feels God's wrath and vengeance ; and there is no way to comfort him but this ; that it is not that men are righteous in themselves, or that they are able to stand before God, but that his righteousness is that whereby God burieth all their sins in the blood of Jesus Christ ; and the shewing man his righteousness is his shewing good remedy for us to be discharged of the bond of death wherein we were bound. Which remedy is to put our whole trust in the death and passion of our Lord Jesus.' Thus he. I join to him John Cotton, an interpreter one of a thousand, in those imperfect notes of exposition on the 1st Epistle of John, upon those words, chap. ii. 29, ' If ye know that he is righteous.' ' A ground,' says he, ' of wonderful consolation to every poor soul that is burdened with his own unrighteousness. This comfort Elihu gives to a man in extremity of body and soul, Job xxxiii. 23, to declare where his righteousness is to be found; that is, it is not to be found in himself. God will say of such a soul, " Deliver him from going down to the pit; I have found a ransom." ' I forbear to mention others who speak near to this. But of late Mr Caryl, in his complete and accurate comment on that book, on these words, doth ultimately come fully up to the righteousness of justification chiefly (as his word is), though he takes in the whole of a man's duty in all other parts of uprightness in himself.

And I like well enough, and exclude not any part of the duty of uprightness on a man's part towards God. For unto justification by Christ's righteousness, faith, or an act of closing with it, and reliance upon it, for a man's particular justification, is necessary; which is the ' duty of ᵐan,' and yet requisite on man's part to his justification; though, as such, justification itself is not attributed unto it, otherwise than in respect unto Christ its object, and as apprehended by it. And as for repentance, and man's turning to God in his first conversion, and his future obedience, that I acknowledge to be intended also, provided that this righteousness on God's and Christ's part for justifying a sinner be first served, according to the merit thereof, and the sole honour thereof in justifying be kept inviolable in the prerogative thereof. And then I take both in, although these two be different righteousnesses, because the Holy Ghost, choosing out but one word to express the whole errand and matter of this interpreter's exhortation, that came to instruct him in what was necessary to his salvation, it was meet it should be such an one as was most comprehensive. And therefore we are to involve all that may any way be justly understood and signified thereby, and are consistent together, the word *righteousness* being used to express both Christ's righteousness, viz., made ours by faith only, and our own righteousness inherent also, and both requisite to, and concurrent in conversion, though in various ways, and to differing purposes; and conversion being the subject of Elihu's discourse, it is apposite to take in both.

I begin first to shew that the righteousness of justification through Christ's righteousness is here intended, and this may several ways appear out of the text.

1. Uprightness or rectitude (which Piscator says ought to be retained, and Vatablus so renders it) are all one with righteousness in Scripture phrase: Eccles. vii. 29, ' God made man upright,' that is, righteous; and so here, only there it is used to express the righteousness of man in his first creation, whose righteousness of justification and of holiness was but one single righteousness, and the whole of it was in himself; but here in Job is meant the righteousness of man fallen, with which he must appear afore God's tribunal, and which must be the righteousness of Christ alone. And indeed that *righteousness*, in ver. 26, that flows,* and *uprightness* here, are in Elihu's intention one and the same, appears by comparing both ver. 23 and 26, what is man his *uprightness* in ver. 23, is in ver. 26 ' man his *righteousness*;' the *thing* is the same, though the *words* are not the same; so then righteousness it is.

2. This must be understood to be such a righteousness as this sick, sinful, dying man might with boldness appear afore God withal, at the bar of his strict justice and judgment. It must also be a righteousness which this sick man lays hold of, when now he is made sensible of his sin, the heinousness, the multitudes of them, and of hell the desert of them, which he sees he can no way escape by himself, or anything in himself; he looks to die,

* Qu. ' follows '?—Ed.

and expects no other, and then follows judgment ; and where shall such a righteousness be found to come afore God with ?   Not any righteousness of a man's own, Phil. iii., either *past*, for in unregeneracy a man hath nothing but unrighteousness ; or *present*, that is, his present repentance ; or *to come*, that is, his filial obedience.   No ; David cuts off all pleas : Ps. cxliii. 2, ' Enter not into judgment with thy servant, for in thy sight shall no man living be justified.'   No ; none of his best and dearest servants dare venture or stand at that bar in their own obedience nor righteousness, either at or after conversion ; and yet appear before God they must, and be justified by some such righteousness, or they will be condemned ; ' and where shall such a righteousness be found ? ' as Job says of wisdom.   Nowhere but in Christ, to be prehended and pleaded by faith, looking out of a man's self to Christ as a Saviour for righteousness and justification thereby.   These are express in Isaiah, speaking of Christ : chap. xli., ' A just God and a Saviour ; there is none beside me,' ver. 21 ; ' There is no Saviour but me, and therefore look unto me (alone) and be saved, all ye ends of the earth ; for I am God, and there is none besides me,' ver. 22.   And this is our Christ, as appears by what follows : ver. 23, ' I have sworn by myself, that unto me every knee shall bow, and every tongue shall swear ;' which is punctually applied to Christ, and that twice, in the New Testament : Rom. xiv. 10, ' We shall all stand before the judgment seat of Christ ' (to be justified, namely, as was said, or condemned), ' For it is written, Every knee shall bow to me,' &c.   And again, Phil. ii. 10, 11, this, as distinct from the Father, is spoken of there, ' That at the name of Jesus every knee should bow, and that every tongue should confess that Jesus Christ is Lord, to the glory of God the Father.'   And what, both in this world and at the judgment seat, shall the righteous confess, for their righteousness, the prophet goes on to tell you : ver. 24, ' Surely shall one say ' (all men shall not say this, though all shall bow, &c.), ' In the Lord I have righteousness and strength, and to him shall men come ' (for both these), ver. 25.   Will you have it yet plainer ?   ' In the Lord shall all the seed of Israel be justified, and shall glory.'   Now here is a messenger, one of a thousand, from God, on purpose to shew a poor wretch wherein the righteousness of fallen man doth lie.   And what other righteousness can he allege and produce to make void that *caveat* and bar put in against him (whenever he comes afore God's judgment-seat), and all men living, yea, against the best servants God ever had on earth, which he finds written over the door of that court, at the very entrance : ' Enter not into judgment, O Lord ;' seconded with this as the unalterable ground thereof : ' Cursed is he that continues not in all things to do them.'   Now wherewith shall the clamours that his soul is filled withal be quieted, but by this perfect and alone righteousness of Christ's, current (we see by Isaiah) under the Old Testament ; God's free grace accepting it for this man, ' without works ;' ' but now the righteousness of God, without the law, is manifested,' Rom. iii. 21, ' being witnessed by the law and the prophets ' (and one of these prophets that testifies to is this Elihu, and that is this very speech of his in Job, who testifies it with the rest), ' even the righteousness of God, which is by faith of Jesus Christ, unto all, and upon all them that believe,' for there is no difference, ver. 22.   That it is said ' *but now* is manifest,' in ver. 21, respects the times of the New Testament, when this is most broadly and openly, and clearly revealed, but was darkly afore, and whispered in the times of the law and the prophets ; and as in the dark, was yet catched hold of by souls that were saved ; it was the current

righteousness among the godly then; one and the same righteousness, and
but one and the same both in the Old and the New ; so as we may conclude, that this messenger had not deserved the character of ' one of a
thousand,' or of some ' prophet' (by which interpreters frequently notify
him), had he not mentioned and spoken of this righteousness above all; he
had otherwise fallen short of his undertaking to relieve this forlorn soul, if
this had been left out.

As the nature, necessity, and reason of the matter, or thing itself, and
these circumstances touching the person in the text, even now specified,
requireth this interpretation, so three words there are, and three sayings
spoken of in the text, which duly examined, in the reference or aspect which
those speeches of them do cast one upon the other, will prove them to be
one and the same thing, and that thing to be Christ's ransom, and our
righteousness or justification thereby.   And so as if one of the three prove
to be Christ's righteousness and redemption, then the other two also are
to be understood to be the same, and all one thereupon.   These three
words or things spoken of are, 1. man his *uprightness;* 2. *ransom;* 3. man
his *righteousness.*   The three things or sayings spoken of them are, 1. ' *to
shew* to man his *uprightness,*' in ver. 23, which is done by the messenger
and interpreter, and with that sentence he begins the round to the other
two.   2. Christ's ' *ransom,*' or price of redemption 'found' by God, and
the saying or sentence concerning this is God's, ' He himself says, *I have
found* a ransom,' ver. 24, and owneth it to be a satisfactory ransom for
righteousness, for and unto that man ; and herein himself doth second and
verify that word spoken by his messenger, who had shewn the man that a
righteousness there was to be found with God for man fallen ; and together
therewith a righteousness which might be obtained by this man, if he would
seek out for it ; which righteousness having been first laid open by the
messenger, God himself seconds him in it, and explains to be a ransom of
redemption which himself hath found.   3. There is to man his ' righteousness rendered,' ver. 26, and the saying or thing spoken thereof is Elihu's,
uttered of God, ' For he will *render* to man his righteousness ;' but still
uttered of this same God, who in those words afore had himself said, ' I
have found a ransom ;' and Elihu hereupon says, for he ' renders,' or gives
it forth to whom it belongs as his due upon his conversion, and laying hold
upon it, and renders it as his due, which cannot be withheld from him.
So then, in reality, these three are one and the same thing put into three
distinct words, *uprightness, ransom, righteousness;* and these sentences
about them do, in their mutual aspects and references one to another,
' agree in one,' and utter this harmonious sound jointly, that man's
righteousness for his justification is Christ's ransom and redemption ; at
least it is included and aimed at in them all, though uprightness, ver. 23,
and righteousness, ver. 26, may perhaps secondarily involve something on
our parts besides it.

1. They are one : this is proved by two parts.   1. That uprightness,
shewn to that poor man, ver. 23, is one with righteousness *rendered,* ver. 26,
not only because uprightness is used to express righteousness (which was
afore observed), but that addition in both places of ' *to man his* righteousness,' and ' shew *to man his* uprightness,' thus set to both, doth apparently
argue them to be one thing in Elihu's intention ; for that addition is appro-
priative to man, and as distinguishing it from the righteousness of angels.
2. That middle word, ' a ransom,' is as plainly comprehended in that of
uprightness, shewn by the messenger, ver. 22, for these words, ' I have

found a ransom,' are not only God's own verifying and acknowledgment that he had indeed ' found,' as this messenger had told him that God had favour to him, and shewn the man that it was to be found with God, and to be had from him for his deliverance and salvation; but in this return and answer of God's upon it, God particularizeth more distinctly what manner of thing that righteousness, whereby man is saved and delivered, is; it is a deliverance by way of ransom, a redemption of him from sin, hell, and the grave, procured by a price of redemption laid down for him by another, whom he procured to lay it down for him. Christ is ' made sin, that we might be made the righteousness of God in him;' and by calling it a ransom, he beats man off from vain imagination of his own righteousness, for that is nowhere called a ransom. No; ' the redemption of the soul is more precious' than so, as the psalmist speaks: no; it was so far from that dream, that such way by ransom at the full rate and *quantum* of it, as should satisfy for sin, could never have entered into a sinner's heart or thought to perform; it was ' past his finding out,' as the aspect intimates: but *I* (says God) have found this ransom, and therefore give me the glory of that. God was the founder, or procurer, and Christ the finder, as we use to speak of the price as paid in another. And then this middle word and speech, ' for I have found a ransom,' hath such a correspondency with the third and last word and sentence of the three, that shews that ransom placed in the middle of the other two, to be included in that righteousness specified at the close spoken by Elihu upon it; ' He shall render,' &c., and refers clearly to God's saying, ' I have found;' and is but as if he had said, that God had found it for that man as a price paid for him by another redeemer, which God will surely render and give forth to that man; and that otherwise God should retain from man, that which himself acknowledgeth he had found for him, in ver. 24, and Elihu, in the 26th verse, calls that which God renders to man, the man's righteousness; and therefore *ransom* and *righteousness* are one also.

The other instance I shall give of a converted soul's having a sight and sense of sin, is the conversion of the apostle Paul.

There are many accounts of it of several kinds: the history of it in the book of the Acts, related two or three several times; the infinite riches of grace that were in it: 1 Tim. i., the work of faith and love wrought in him thereby towards Jesus Christ at his first turning; also in his being delivered from the power of the law, and married to Christ, in Rom. vii., with a narrative of his humiliation for sin, which in him was a saving work: in Rom. vii. ver. 4, 5, he there involving his own example when he was in the flesh; ver. 5, 6, and from ver. 7th of that chapter, and so on, he professedly applies it unto his own conversion; and again the same, Gal. ii. 19, 20, ' For I through the law am dead to the law, that I might live unto God. I am crucified with Christ: nevertheless I live; yet not I, but Christ liveth in me: and the life which I now live in the flesh I live by the faith of the Son of God, who loved me, and gave himself for me.'

The only question that I know may be raised is, whether these words, ' I am dead to the law by the law,' which are spoken of the work of humiliation in him at conversion, be to be understood of a saving sanctifying work begun to be wrought in him, yea or no. Now that it was part of a work of that kind is clear by the 9th verse, where that he speaks of that work which was the beginning of his conversion out of unregeneracy, is evident; for (says he) ' I was alive without the law once.' Those words note the whole time of his unregeneracy, which he had lived in until this turn, unto which those other words, ver. 19, 'I am dead by the law to the law,' do refer; alive before once, but now dead, his death and his life must be measured to be of one and the same kind of life and death.   Now, the life he had before was an opinion of himself to have been alive by the works of the law, and the death he mentions must be from the contrary apprehension, which did strike him dead in his spirit.   And, secondly, during his former time, when he speaks of that *once*, he says he was without the commandment: Rom. vii. 9, 'I was alive without the law once; but when the commandment came, sin revived, and I died.'   How was Paul without the law in that former time of his, but in this respect, that that which was the soul and spirit of the law he was wanting in, he had not the due apprehension and the right knowledge of it, so that he reckoned as not the law, all that he apprehended about it in the time of his pharisaism?   He says he had lived without law all that time, who yet had been so zealous for the law, as elsewhere you read; but he wanted the true soul and spirit of it, which makes it the law.   He tells us in the 7th verse, 'I had not known sin but by the law, for I had not known lust unless the law had said, Thou shalt not covet;' for the knowledge of this inward corruption was that which killed him, and he calls it the law.   'I had not known sin,' says he, 'but by the law,' but by the light of this one notion let into his soul.   He now saw, looking back upon his former estate, this inbred sin inherent in his own nature had taken occasion by the commandment, and had wrought in him all manner of concupiscence, for without the law sin was dead.   And, thirdly, I call this sight of sin, as it had been wrought in himself, 'the spirit of the law;' for in the 14th verse he says, 'We know that the law is spiritual, but I am carnal, sold under sin,' even after he was converted.   He speaks this of himself after his conversion, and he speaks the same of the law at the 10th verse; of that law, the knowledge whereof he now had, and not before; 'wherefore the law is holy, and the commandment holy,' which had discovered lust to be sin, to be sin to him. And the knowledge of this law was that which did convert him, that struck him dead, and put him out of his jolly life he had led, which was from the thought and apprehensions that he should have been justified by the outward performance of the law, in which he was deceived: 'And so the commandment, which was ordained to life,' says he, 'I found to be but unto death.'   And this was effected in him when the commandment came, that is, that which was, in the true light of it, the commandment itself, that never came before; 'and so sin revived,' like the snake in the fable, that was brought in benumbed with cold, but laid by the fire, the heat revived it, 'and I died,' says he; sin revived, and stung me to death.   And this sin, he afterwards tells us, was that sin that dwelt in him: ver. 20, that 'sin that dwelleth in me,' which causeth me to do that which I would not, and is opposed by another self opposite thereto.   In respect whereof he says, 'It is no more I that do it,' which opposes the corrupt self in me, which he calls 'sin that dwelleth in me,' ver. 20.

From hence I gather, that a true and spiritual sight of lust to be sin, mingling itself with all a man's ways, is from a spirit of holiness begun to be wrought in the mind.   For such a light as this was Paul's, wrought in the entrance into his conversion, and such must therefore be the light in any one that hath it; and true conversion follows upon it, as it did in Paul.   And I give this reason for it, that out of that principle by which we see the spiritual evil of sin, whereof this was the light that gave the knowledge of it, it is that any man sees the spiritual good, in opposition to lust, to be in him. For as the same visive faculty in man, the same eye whereby a man discerns one contrary, it also discerns the other, as the same eye that sees white also discerns what is black, or *è contra;* so the same light that discerns grace in the spiritual nature of it, discerns sin, and on the contrary in like manner. And this principle the apostle's discourse in this chapter clearly runs upon.

CHAPTER IV.

The use and subservience of conviction of sin, and humiliation for it, to induce the soul to believe on Jesus Christ for salvation.

I shall now give you an account of conviction of sin and humiliation, not in the general only, but of every particular mentioned, to let you see the reason, the use they serve to, viz., to advance God himself as man's chiefest good, and to set up Christ and his righteousness, and his own free grace in justifying, sanctifying, and in all.

First, That the soul should be wounded with sin as sin, and as in itself the greatest misery, to what a blessed end tends it!

1. By this work of humiliation, the heart is for ever weaned from the comfort that is in sin, or in any creature, so as never to be quiet till it meets with God, the God of comforts. For if this apprehension, that sin is the greatest evil, season but a man's spirit once, it sours all pleasant things with him, they have lost their taste for ever; and nothing can be so good to him as sin is evil, but only God; for nothing is so good as sin is evil, but only he. And then a man will take God and his favour for a comfort alone; all he can ever look for, or hope to find, it must be in him, his comfort in sin and all things else is everlastingly spoiled and marred; so Hosea ii. 14. When God would allure and win his church's heart to him, what doth he? He 'brings her into the wilderness,' into a barrenness of all comforts, and then ' speaks comfortably to her.' A man convinced of sin and lost state is like a man condemned to die, the pleasure which may be had in the green pasture he goes through to execution, affects him not, so nor can this man take content in anything, till he hath the favour of that God he hath offended. God only can speak comfort to such a soul, and nothing else.

And 2dly, Hereby it is made restless after Christ and his righteousness, as the means of bringing him into favour with God. If it were wrath, or trouble of conscience thereby, were all his grief, ease would content him; but it being sin, nothing but Christ and his righteousness will do it. As the hart wounded rests not till it comes to such an herb as cures it, so nor he that is wounded ean take delight in anything till he spies Christ out, and sighs and pants incessantly after him.

2. For a man to see himself an unbeliever, and without faith, without Christ, it is also exceedingly necessary, John xvi. 10.

(1.) Because it tends to bring in the guilt of all his sins upon him, to serve the inquest against him; for when the conscience is charged with oaths, adulteries, &c., it pleads a presumptuous sinner's pretensions of a believer—I am in Christ, and I believe—and so sin cannot fasten on him, but he puts it off and slights it, and walks outfacing it and all its bills; but when he is convinced of unbelief, which is the protector of all sin, then every commandment may bring out its bill and be heard, and serve a writ upon him. Convince him of this, and you will convince him of all.

(2.) Because they may be convinced what is the main thing necessary, and the first thing they are to do, the next course they are to take ; for if men should not be convinced of unbelief as the great sin of all the rest, they would not be pitched upon faith as the only and full remedy of their evil. Hereby they see the necessity of faith, the stead it must stand them in ; and their aim will be to get it.

And (3dly) hereby, and for want of faith, seeing themselves out of Christ, they will be pitched upon what is the especial aim of faith, union with him, as the foundation of all good they must receive from him. Many being humbled for want of duties, pitch upon performing them, and so are eased ; but when unbelief is the main sin, and want of union with Christ the greatest misery, then union with him is the first aim of faith, and the soul is convinced that it must have his person, as Paul, Philip. iii., ' that I may win Christ,' and then have righteousness and all else. I must believe, and I must have Christ, or nothing is accepted, says the soul. Then,

(4.) By seeing a man's self to have been an ungodly person, and to have done no good, and by seeing the inwards of actions, and the carriage of the heart in them, the soul is convinced that this is true, that no good thing dwells in a man ; and this moves the soul to go to Christ both for justification and sanctification, and without it a man is in danger to err in both.

For [1.] if he sees not that there is no good in him, he will certainly trust in himself, and not go wholly to Christ for righteousness ; if it hath any of its own, it will trust partly in Christ, and partly in itself ; and, like the ship in the Acts, be part aground, and part in the water, and so be broken a-pieces when the waves of temptation come. Go to the first working of faith, God will have a man apprehend himself an ungodly person : Rom. iv. 5, ' To him that worketh not, but believeth on him that justifieth the ungodly, his faith is accounted for righteousness.' And after faith wrought, though a man sees some good wrought in him, yet it hinders not his attributing all to Christ in justification. Yet in the first working of faith, it is clean otherwise upon a different reason : for that good which is wrought after faith, is wrought by faith, that fetched all from Christ. And so sanctification, being but borrowed by faith, hinders not faith ; the daughter hinders not the mother. But if a man should see any good before, it being not wrought by faith, nor fetched from Christ, the heart would rest in it, and oppose the work of faith and going out to Christ. It being from a man's self, a man would rest in it, and not seek abroad for righteousness, whilst he hath any at home. As any one sin preserves the power of sin in the heart, though a man parts with all other, so any good, or unrighteousness ungiven up, preserves self-confidence, and hinders justification, as the other doth sanctification. There is no remedy therefore, but that all our supposed good be discovered to be naught and rotten ; that every burrow be stopped, ere these poor helpless creatures will go to the rock.

[2.] The want of such conviction will hinder sanctification ; for it would not renew the man throughout, but piece new grace to old, false grace to true, and make the rent worse ; for he would rest in some false good. Christ will have ' all old things pass away, and all to become new ;' every stud pulled down, and nothing in the new building that was in the old. Yea, it hinders Christ from working it. He will shew his skill in drawing his image upon a plain board, and so wipes out all afore. Bring to a curious painter, that would shew his skill, a board with a picture falsely drawn, and he will not go about to mend it; he can make no work of it, but he will take his pencil and dash all out, and shew his art in a new one; and so doth Christ. Bring a bell to a founder that hath a crack in it, and he will not go about to solder that up, and so let it go, but dash all in pieces and melt and cast it anew; and so doth Christ with those who have the seeming cast of goodness, and that by letting us see the falseness of it; for that is his end in breaking and melting the heart, to cause us to apprehend all is naught.

[3.] A man's sight and sense of his utter sinfulness, both in his life, heart and nature, the multitude of sins, and the strength of sin, is necessary.

First, Because, though God pardons, he will have us know what he pardons; as he, Mat. xviii. 23, though he meant to pardon his servants, yet would take account of them, that pardon might be the more sweet to them. When a man's soul draweth near to the grave, then for God to say, ' Deliver him, I have found a ransom,' Job xxxiii., how welcome is it!

Secondly, A sight of sin is needful, to constrain us to make use of Christ's righteousness, and every part of it, to search thoroughly into it, and every parcel of it, and to see the necessity of all the holiness of his nature, life, &c., that nothing could be spared. Men that are confusedly convinced that they are sinners, their faith is answerably as confused; they believe in Christ as a Saviour, and that is all; but their faith improves not his righteousness to the uttermost, nor do they search into the riches of Christ's active and passive obedience, and the holiness of his nature, as necessary to obtain their acceptance with God.

Thirdly, It is necessary that we may not rest in a false sanctification. Men that see but the corruption of their outward actions, content themselves with an outward reformation. But men that see their lusts, rest not till they be mortified; they bend their force against them. A convinced soul sees his nature corrupted, and the spring of all defiled, he will not rest till he hath a new nature; as the power of corruption he sees lies there, so the power of godliness, he will see, lies in cleansing that fountain. Paul seeing a law of death in his members, rests not till the law of life in Christ condemns it.

Fourthly, A conviction of our sinfulness is needful, that we may see an utter helplessness and hopelessness in ourselves for time to come. The heart is ready to account it can do something for time to come, though it can do nothing rightly; yea, when it is stripped of self-righteousness for time past, yet not self-ability for time to come; but now it thinks and casts with itself, I will go fast, and go pray, and go meditate on Christ and a promise, and I will get him ere I have done; which resolutions are good, when in sense of a man's own emptiness they are stirred up and maintained by a dependance upon God, to work faith; but the heart naturally secretly projects this cut of itself, as they in James iv. 13, and not, ' if God enable me,' &c. They reckon without him; and in hopes of this the heart rests, and thinks in the end to get faith to come. Among other steps and degrees of our misery, this is made one, that a man is not only ' ungodly, but without strength,' Rom. v. 6. A man that hath no money in his purse, yet whilst he hath hands to work, he makes no such reckoning of want; and so men, when they see they want all good for the time past, yet they hope to work it out; they have hands left, and with them they fall to work; but when a man shall see hands cut off too, and nothing but stumps left, which are as unfit and unable to lay hold on Christ, as a man's arm without hands is upon a rope to save him; and God must not only find him Christ, but his grace

must give him hands to lay hold on him also : that the apprehension of
this serves both to drive him out of himself, and to magnify God's free
grace in working faith.　For if any pretended power in himself were able
to help him, he would never go out of himself to Christ, nor would he attribute all wholly unto grace, which is that God intends to have exalted ;
Eph. ii. 8, ' You are saved by grace, through faith.'　Might some think, we
shall acknowledge grace enough, if we acknowledge that grace pardons all,
and effects all, though faith be of our own working : ' No (says the apostle),
' and that not of yourselves,' not so much as faith, ' it is the gift of God.'
And so Paul, to magnify Christ's grace, he says Christ died not only for
men, and ungodly persons, but also for persons ' without strength,' Rom. v.
This you must apprehend and find, and then grace will be grace indeed,
and nothing but grace ; and then when you despair of yourselves, you will
rejoice wholly in Christ.　What says Paul, Phil iii. ?　' We have no confidence in the flesh,' but despair utterly of all in us, and ' rejoice in Christ
Jesus,' acknowledging that he is all, and doth all.　God cures one contrary
by another ; self-confidence cannot be cured but by despair.　God glorifies
not, till the body be dead and rotten in the grave ; and he sanctifies not till
the heart be dead to itself, and unable to stir, to move no more to Christ
than the earth can towards heaven.　If the sun come nigh it, well and good,
but it cannot move nigher to it.　Or as Luther compares it, the barren
earth may gape for rain, but it cannot procure it, till heaven pour it freely
down into her lap.　And so he calls this righteousness of faith a passive
righteousness, and faith a mere receiving grace.

CHAPTER V.

*In which answers are given to several objections made against the usefulness of
conviction and humiliation, to bring the soul to believe on Christ.*

My next work is to answer the objections and cavils which men make
against conviction of or humiliation for sin, not only as needless, but dangerous, and that to trouble men's consciences for sin is to drive them to
despair.

1. They call it a doctrine teaching men to despair, and that the issue of
such troubling tender consciences is despair.

2. That ministers or others, who on men's deathbeds endeavour to discover, to men that have been civil or formal, their estates, are miserable
comforters, as Job's friends were, who would persuade him all was naught.

3. That men's aim in urging this work, as first necessary, is, by troubling
men's consciences, to bring them to their bent, and to make them willing
to be of their mind and faction, to entertain willingly their dictates and
opinions, and so to tyrannise over their consciences.

4. If men cavil not at this work, yet they deny it, cannot see any reason
why it should be so necessary to the power of godliness.　If I acknowledge
myself ever to have been a sinner, and to have failings in all I do, having
always believed in Christ, is not this (say they) enough ?

Unto the end both to answer these cavils, as also to vindicate the doctrine the more, I propose these following assertions.

1. That to bring men to such apprehensions as these is not to bring men
to despair, but the contrary.　To make this good, we will go over all the
particulars.

(1.) To make men apprehensive that sin is the greatest evil, is not to

drive them to despair; Paul, Rom. vii. 13, saw it to be above measure sinful, when first converted, and you can never be enough convinced of it, not
so much as you should, though the sight of it scares you, and fears you,
and this you may see without despair; yea, where that sight is, that soul
shall never despair, for it directly leads the soul to Christ, and causeth it
to see a beauty in grace.   If, indeed, we taught it were necessary to have
such horror and anguish of soul as Spira had, or if we endeavoured to
make impression of such deep terrors from the wrath of God as Judas and
Cain had, then you might have reason to think that this work tended to
despair, though many have had them, and have not despaired.   But we
profess, that as ravishing joy is not necessary and essential to faith, so nor
deep vexing gashes and impressions of wrath are necessary to humiliation,
though they often accompany it; as the one is but the overflow of faith, so
the other of humiliation.   But as to see Christ the greatest good is essential to faith, so to see sin the greatest evil is essential to humiliation, and
this is the main.   The damned indeed, who are plunged in wrath in hell,
they despair through extremity and everlastingness of torment.   But they
are far from what we urge as requisite to humiliation, from seeing the evil
of sin in itself.   And as far are they that see sin as sin, to be the greatest
evil, from despair, as the damned, that feel nothing but wrath, are from
true humiliation.

And (2.) if some drops of wrath and fears of damnation be mingled with
this cup, yet it is far from despair, for it is a work of the Spirit of God, who,
before he becomes a Spirit of adoption to save, becomes a Spirit of bondage
to cause men to fear, Rom. viii. 15.

(3.) To bring men to apprehend all their former estate to have been
hitherto throughout sinful and damnable, and out of Christ, is not to bring
men to despair.

For, 1st, to apprehend that a man's person is simply damned, this indeed causeth despair; but to apprehend that my person is in a damnable
condition, and such as if I remain in, I cannot be saved, is far from despair; for Paul apprehended himself once a child of wrath as well as others,
Eph. ii. 2.

2dly, To apprehend their condition to be thus, is not to believe that there
is no mercy reserved for them, or that they are not capable of it; if so,
then indeed it would make men despair; but, as Peter says, 1 Peter ii. 10,
' which in time past had not obtained mercy,' so to apprehend that as long
as I remain in this condition I do not obtain mercy, is not to despair, but
to apprehend the truth.   For as it follows there, ' Those who once had not
obtained mercy, have now obtained mercy.'   And so we say he may obtain
mercy, whose condition is most sinful.

Nor, 3dly, to apprehend thyself out of Christ in the condition thou art
in is not to despair; for then the Ephesians, when they saw their former
condition to have been, as (Eph. ii. 12) it is said once it was, and who are
exhorted to remember that they were once without Christ, and without the
promises, should have despaired.   But there is yet hope left for the greatest sinners, that for time to come they may be in Christ, as those Ephesians
after conversion were.   To apprehend that I am absolutely excluded from
the benefit of Christ's death, that will cause despair; but that humiliation
teacheth not.   But to apprehend that it is not yet applied to me, that it is
as yet to me as if Christ had not died, and if I die in such a condition, I
should die in my sin, this is not to despair.

4thly, Again, to apprehend my estate to be helpless and hopeless, in regard of any duties I have or can perform, or in respect of any power in me, or any creature to help me, is not to despair. It is indeed to despair of thyself, and all the creatures, and to have no confidence in the flesh; and that is a good despair. But to despair, is to despair of God and his mercy for time to come; to say that he will never be merciful, never give me faith and Christ. I may rightly make use of that in 2 Cor. i. 8–10 to illustrate this, which, though spoken in regard of despairing of his natural life, yet for the same reason there used, will hold good of this despair of eternal life. We were so pressed, says he, that we despaired of life, and had the sentence of death in ourselves; so far as by any means of ourselves we could use, we saw no way but death. But, says Paul, it was 'that we should not trust in ourselves, but in God that raiseth the dead;' that is, though we despaired, yet it was not of God's power to help us, but we despaired in ourselves. And thus God deals with men, and dealt with Paul about eternal life; he passed a sentence of death on him, and Paul saw no help in himself to believe, or come out of his misery; Rom. vii. 10, 'I was alive, but when the commandment came, I died;' that is, received the sentence of death, and saw no way to escape it by anything he could do. This was, that he should not trust in himself, but this was not that he should despair of God's shewing mercy for time to come.

5thly, Again, understand aright whence despair ariseth: not from the greatness or heinousness of a man's sins, or insufficiency of a man to help himself, but from stubbornness of heart, not to go out to Christ for sufficiency in him, that is the work of despair: 'Ye will not come to me that ye may be saved,' as Christ told the Jews.

6thly, Again, poor souls that are in this condition, God hath an especial care of to keep them from despair, when they have renounced themselves and their former condition. Though their souls be a *Tohu* and *Bohu*, and as that first matter, Gen. i. 2, without form, and so of themselves would sink into nothing, yet God's Spirit broods upon it and upholds it. They shall fail between those two rocks, blockishness and despair, so as the convinced sinner shall be terrified, and yet God will keep him secretly. God hath an especial eye upon such a soul: Isa. lxvi. 2, 'To this man will I look, to him that is poor and contrite, and trembleth at my word,' and I will so look to him as he shall not despair. Isa. lvii. 16, 'I will not always contend, for the spirit would fail before me,' and I will not suffer it. Though he melts it, yet he will not suffer it, when melted, to boil over into the fire, and to be cast down and spilt into hell fire irrecoverably. No; but though he be shut up and sees no help by anything he can do to get out, Gal. iii. 23, yet he opens a door of hope, Hosea ii. 15, when the soul is in the valley of Achor, of starving; when sins fly about a man's ears, yet God opens there a door of hope. And again,

(4.) To let men go on without knowing their condition, is the way to despair at last. For when men come to die, and then have their eyes opened, and their consciences convinced, to see their estate out of Christ wholly sinful, and themselves not able to lay hold on Christ, or believe, and that now they have but a few hours to get oil and grace in, then they despair indeed. Isa. l. 11, the prophet shews that trusting in false righteousness, sparks of their own kindling, will bring them to despair in the end, they shall lie down in sorrow; whereas a timely discovery of this prevents it, gives them time to use their endeavour, and to wait on Christ. To lie at God's feet, and refer thyself to him, to damn or save, is not to despair, but argues the greatest ingenuity that may be, and argues some trust and hope in God begun, that a man will refer himself to him, as David did: 2 Sam. xv. 26, ' Here I am ; if he thus say, I have no delight in thee, let him do what seemeth good in his eyes.' And whom a man would choose as an umpire to cast his life upon, and to be his judge, he hath some confidence in him ; this is not despair.

We come to the second cavil, viz., that the issue of this work in many is despair, and well nigh undoing themselves.

1. When the jailor was humbled for his sins, he had well nigh killed himself ; shall we condemn that work was then upon his heart, that led him to Christ, and brought him to ask, ' What shall I do to be saved ? ' No.

For, 2, such stories and conclusions are the devil's work, to discredit the work of the Spirit ; he enters upon God's work to spoil it. As when the incestuous Corinthian was excommunicated, 2 Cor. ii., which was an ordinance to humble him, Satan was ready to take the advantage to have swallowed him up of sorrow, ver. 7. ' And we are not ignorant,' says the apostle, ' of his devices,' ver. 11. Shall we condemn that ordinance, because Satan might abuse it ? And so, shall we decry this work of humiliation, because Satan adds fearful conclusions to it ? There is no work of the Spirit but he adds false conclusions to it if he can. If the Spirit comforts, he endeavours to make the soul presumptuous ; if he casts into bondage only, the devil labours to cast into despair. But as we may not condemn assurance, because sometimes it hath such an issue, so, nor humiliation.

3. If any do miscarry, they are but such as would ever have perished, whatever course in preaching had been held.

The third cavil is, that when we labour to humble men, our aim is only to bring them to our bent, and so impose on them what we please.

I answer, 1st, Then Peter might be charged with the same, when he endeavoured to humble the Jews for their sin in crucifying Christ ; when he brought them to such a pass that they, being pricked in their hearts, cry out, ' Men and brethren, what shall we do to be saved ? ' Acts ii. 37. But Peter's aim was orderly to bring them to sound repentance, and to believe in Christ ; and that is all that we aim at also, and all the remedy we prescribe. Mark xvi. 16, Christ bids them preach, that ' he that believes not shall be damned.' One part of their office was to humble men, and discover their estates out of Christ ; and to what end ? Mat. xxviii. 19, you shall find it was to make them disciples, as the word signifies ; but of whom ? Not of themselves, but of Christ, and to bring them to universal obedience, which without this work they will never come to : ' Teaching them to do whatever I have commanded,' ver. 20. And as Christ's promise is to be with us to the end of the world, so this must be our course to the end of the world.

And 2dly, If we did indeed, as the friars of old, who preached the law, and, stinging men's consciences, took the advantage of it to bring the people to auricular confession, and get their secret sins out, and so make them obnoxious to them, and then took money for pardons and absolutions ; and set them about building this convent and that convent, for satisfaction ; if we did it thus to make a gain of you, as Paul says, 2 Cor. xii. 17, you might suspect us in it. But we speak before God in Christ, ' we do all things for your edifying,' as Paul says, ver. 19. It is to set up Christ in your hearts that we endeavour to humble you ; that you may see your need of him ; and that you may see your own emptiness and his fulness, to make him precious to you, and to drive your souls to him, and to bring every thought into the obedience of Christ ; to make you sensible of sin, that you may make conscience of it, and know what Christ hath done for you. And if the duties that are required be not duty, the sins discovered be not proved to be sins, your humiliation will not bring you to make conscience of them. It is our Master's advantage and your edifying is our aim ; ' we seek not yours, but you.'

And 3dly, If we were minded to gain a party out of the world, and to gain your ear, it were a better course to soothe you up in a good opinion of your estates, to sew pillows under your elbows, and cry Peace, peace, when there is no peace, as the false prophets did.* But to go about to persuade men that their estates are bad, and to urge a necessity of apprehending it such, this is the way to exasperate men. This provoked the Pharisees against Christ ; brought the world about Paul's ears, as Paul says, Gal. i., ' Do we persuade men or God ?' that is, for God. This doctrine crosseth the world, sets up God, and gains but few ; for men will and do stand out ; and where one is throughly humbled, thousands presume, and will do so.

For, indeed, 4thly, it is a mighty work of the Spirit to convince. And so, when the apostles were sent out, the Spirit is promised, and he ' shall convince the world of sin,' John xvi. 8. We could never do it, and the devil he would never trouble men, for he keeps all in peace, and as I said, enters upon the Spirit's work to spoil it. So of all projects and courses this were the vainest, if it were not God's way, and he did not go forth with us in it.

And whereas, 5thly, men complain that such are miserable comforters to convince and humble men for sin, like Job's friends, and that it is cruelty in men to deal so with poor souls.

1. Consider that such a comforter is the Holy Ghost himself, John xvi. He is promised to come as a comforter ; and what should he do for to comfort ? ' He should convince the world of sin, because they believe not in me ;' for this makes way for comfort. And so, Rom. viii. 15, ere he becomes the Spirit of adoption, he becomes a Spirit of bondage ; for none else are fit for comfort but those that are broken : Isa. lxi. 1–3, ' The Spirit is upon me, to preach glad tidings to the meek, and comfort those that mourn,' &c.

And 2dly, It is cruelty indeed to break the bruised reed, to smite him whom God hath smitten, as David says ; to break him in pieces whose bones are broken. But if men's joints are set wrong, it is not cruelty to break them in pieces, for else they cannot be set right.

CHAPTER VI.

Of the last part of our conversion, which is our turning from our evil thoughts and ways unto God.

Holiness in the heart is the main and ultimate birth brought forth in regeneration ; and to make us partakers of God's holiness is the sum and scope of all towards us, both of his election, Eph. i., and of all his dealings afterwards, Heb. xii. 10 ; and without which, ver. 14, no man shall see

---

* It is Augustine's argument, Libro de Pastoribus, tom. ix., p. 1333. Absit ut dicamus vobis, Vivite ut vultis, securi estote, Deus neminem perdit : tantummodo fidem Christianam tenete ; non perdit ille quod redemit. Hæc si dixerimus, congregabimus turbas ampliores, et si sint quidam qui nos sentiunt hoc dicentes non recte sapere, paucos offendimus, sed multitudinem conciliamus.

God. Now the essential holiness that is in God we cannot be partakers of, neither by imputation, as Osiander dreamed, much less by real transubstantiation to be 'Goded' with God, as some have arrogantly asserted. We can be no otherwise partakers of it than in the image thereof, Eph. iv. 24, 'which after God' (as pattern or prototype) 'is created in righteousness and true holiness.' You have the same, Col. iii. 10, 'After the image of him that created him.'

Now man being fallen, and having lost this image, which was at the first immediately given, without any instrumental means then used by him to stamp it on the soul, God was pleased, in restoring and renewing this image in man's heart a second time, to set up mediate instruments that should have his image stamped upon them first; and by the means thereof to communicate to us this holiness first imparted to those. Now these patterns or middle instruments, on which God first stamped his holiness, are, 1. His word or law evangelised; 2. The man Christ Jesus; and both in this respect are termed ὁ λόγος, the word of God: the first, viz., God's word, bearing a doctrinal image of God's holiness; the other, viz., Christ, being a living, transcendent image of it. Therefore you shall find in the Scriptures of the New Testament our sanctification or holiness set out to us, 1. By a change or conformity in the heart to the written word and whole law of God, Rom. vi. 17, Heb. x. 16, James i. 21; and, 2dly, it is set forth by a conforming or changing the heart into the image of Christ: 2 Cor. iii. 18, 'But we all with open face beholding, as in a glass, the glory of the Lord, are changed into the same image, from glory to glory, as by the Spirit of the Lord.'

Now we must know that a real conformity to the word and law of God is true saving holiness and sanctification, as a conformity to Christ in his death, resurrection, and ascension; and though all these are never separate each from the other, yet the first is more discerned by us at first than the latter. Many in regeneration at first find a suitableness in their hearts to the duties and rules of the word, whatever they know of it, when yet they are ignorant of, or at least attend not unto, that holiness in them as it is the image of Christ in his death and resurrection. And even that other is true holiness, and whoever hath it shall be saved. For which my ground is in Heb. x. 14–16, 'For by one offering he hath perfected for ever them that are sanctified. Whereof the Holy Ghost also is a witness to us: for after that he hath said before, This is the covenant that I will make with them, after those days saith the Lord, I will put my laws into their hearts, and in their minds will I write them.' Where we see the sanctification of those Christ hath for ever perfected, and whose sins are forgiven, are set out by their having the law written in their hearts, &c. And therefore Paul, for the comfort and support of weak believers, doth in his own person, Rom. vii., set forth the holiness of a believer, as it is the law of God written in the heart, which, ver. 23, he termeth the 'law of the mind,' by which 'he consents to the spiritual law of God in the inner man,' ver. 22, which law, ver. 25, he serveth, and would fain obey, and have no other in his mind, even then, when 'with the flesh he serves the law of sin.' So then this is true sanctification, though not the *tota ratio*, or the whole notion of a Christian's sanctification, who also is changed into a more glorious image of Christ, which at least is as the varnish to this other conformity to the word as the groundwork of it. And accordingly it is made part of the covenant of grace, in difference from the old covenant, that the law is written in the heart: Heb. viii. 9, 10, 'Not according to the covenant that

I made with their fathers in the day that I took them by the hand to lead them out of the land of Egypt; because they continued not in my covenant, and I regarded them not, saith the Lord. For this is the covenant that I will make with the house of Israel after those days, saith the Lord; I will put my laws into their mind, and write them in their hearts, and I will be to them a God, and they shall be to me a people.' And David's instance in that medal of a gracious heart, and the copy of his own (Ps. cxix., throughout) shews how it stood pointed to the law of God. And answerably it is the general description of the saints in the Old Testament, who were taken into the covenant of grace: Isa. li. 7, 'The people in whose heart is my law;' yea, of Christ, and by Christ, it is said, Ps. xl., 'Thy law is in my heart.'

For though this holiness be legal, in respect of the materials and pattern of it, the law of God, yet it is not legal in respect of the subject or state of the person that hath it begun, or in respect of the tenure of the covenant, or of the virtue efficient that wrought it. For the person that hath it is the subject of the covenant of grace, belongs to that division and jurisdiction, and hath it wrought in him by virtue of Christ's death and resurrection, though as yet he picks not out in his own discerning that this is the image of Christ in him.

Now those mataphors or similitudes which the Holy Ghost hath chosen forth to express that change of heart, as it is an inward conformity to the law and word of God, are especially three : 1. Casting the heart as in a mould into the same image of spiritual holiness that is stamped on, and found in the word. 2. Ingraffing the word on the heart, and so changing the stock (the heart) into the same nature. 3. Writing the law in the heart. All which we have implied in Rom. vi. 17, 'But ye have obeyed from the heart that form of doctrine into which ye were delivered.'

The words in the Greek are εἰς ὃν παρεδόθητε τύπον διδαχῆς, 'That form of doctrine into which ye were delivered;' and so out of the Greek the margin varies them.

The substance of his comparison comes to this, that their hearts having been first, in the inward inclinations and dispositions of it, framed and changed into what the word requires, they then obeyed the same word from the heart naturally, willingly; and the commandments were not grievous, because the heart was framed and moulded thereunto. The heart must be made good ere men can obey from the heart; and to this end he elegantly first compares the doctrine of law and gospel delivered them unto a pattern or sampler, which having in their eye, they framed and squared their actings and doings unto it. And he secondly compares the same doctrine unto a mould or matrix, into which metals being delivered have the same figure or form left on them which the mould itself had; and this is spoken in respect of their hearts. Therefore this word τύπος is a common word, and will serve both these purposes and aims, both which in common signifies the express image, *effigies*, form, or first draught of a thing unto which another is to be framed or fashioned, whether it be in a mould into which metals or clay is cast, and so have the same stamp or print upon them, as we see in goldsmiths' work and other trades (and this suits to the stamp in their hearts wrought thereby), or whether it be after a copy, pattern, or sampler which one having in his view before him, frames and fashions his work unto it, as Moses framed all things according to the pattern in the mount. And this suits the expression of their obedience from the heart; and this he clearly intends, for the words are, εἰς ὃν παραδόθητε, 'into which ye were delivered,' rather than 'which was delivered you,' as our translation was pleased to render it.   Other arts and sciences are said to be *nobis traditæ*, delivered to us ; but of this doctrine it is said that ' we are delivered unto it,' to be framed and conformed to it.   And this is that which I have afore me, that the work of sanctification is a work framing and casting the heart itself into the word of God (as metals use to be in a mould); so that the heart is made of the same stamp and disposition with the word.   This similitude being opened from the Scriptures will afford some light unto us.   There are four things for the opening of it.

I. That the word and law of God evangelised may truly be compared to such a mould.

II. That our hearts must be fashioned unto it ere they can be saved.

III. I shall shew the way how the heart is moulded to it.

IV. I shall explain the work itself, what it is to have the heart truly moulded to it.

I. The word may truly be compared to such a mould.   A mould, you know, is an instrument that hath the representation or shape of something engraven in it, to the end to leave the same stamp and fashion upon the things that are cast in it.   Now such an instrument hath God appointed his word to be.   For,

1. It hath the representation of his holiness in it.   For whereas man had raised and defaced that image or likeness to God in holiness and righteousness, wherein he was at first created ; and so that living copy of the law was lost (that written in men's hearts by nature being imperfect, and but some footsteps of some outward parts of this outward letter of the law remaining), God therefore writ out the copy of that image in his most holy word ; that, as Adam's heart had then the perfect image of God, so this doctrine hath that absolute form upon it now.   And therefore this law is called holy and righteous, which are the attributes of God himself, and which are the parts of God's image whereof it consists, Eph. iv. 22.   Adam was the real image, this the verbal ; but both have the same form, God being the archetype of both.

2. It hath not this image on it, only for man to look on, and so to see the picture of his estate in innocency, and bewail it as now lost, as James says of a negligent hearer of the word, that he beholds his face therein as in a glass, for the present, but forgets it ; no, but God hath appointed it, in the virtue of the gospel, to be, as the common standing mould, instrumental through the knowledge of it, to renew that his image again in man, and to cast all his people's hearts into it.   That whereas there are but two especial ways more eminent to work the image of anything in another solidly and substantially, the one by way of engraving or sculpture by the hand of some artificer on some stone, metal, or other material ; the other by way of casting metals or plaster into a mould, so as they are fashioned unto the figure of it, without losing any of their materials ; now God having once at first created his image on man's heart by way of engraving, as by his own finger, and the soul having now lost that image and being changed into another, namely, that of sin and wickedness (the image of Satan), God therefore does now rather take this second course, and new casts the heart again, using the artifice of his Spirit ; and his word is as the instrumental cause or mould, bearing that former image, and fashioning the heart thereunto.

II. Let us see why the heart must needs be thus new cast in such a mould ; the reasons of it are,

Reason 1. Because we are by nature cast into the devil's image. For if we would draw the devil's picture we would draw pride and malice, revenge, lying, and murder, and all sinful dispositions. Now Adam's sin, by its virtue, does at our first birth mould us into this image ; so says David, Ps. li. 5, ' I was shapen in iniquity,' *formatus*, as Immins* and others read it. All the limbs of sin are fashioned in our hearts, and our hearts to them ; Gen. vi. 5, ' The fiction,' or ' fashion,' or ' frame of the heart is evil,' as the word signifies. And we coming thus into the world with this shape on us, and thus cast, our hearts are also daily more hardened in this sinful fashion by the examples of men. Therefore we are said ' to live to the lusts of men,' 1 Peter iv. 2 ; that is, we apply ourselves and our desires unto the common sin of others, suffering them to mould us also ; which the apostle thus expresseth, ' living according to the course of the world,' Eph. ii. 1. And the same apostle says, Rom. xii. 2, ' Fashion not yourselves to the world,' μὴ συσχηματίζεσθε, *ne accommodetis vos ad hujus seculi figuram*, to the figure or fashion of this world, so Erasmus paraphraseth it. Seeing therefore you are thus by nature cast into a sinful frame, and are more and more in that estate moulded by the fashion and mould of others' bad examples : upon that account the apostle there requires a change, or metamorphosis μεταμορφοῦσθε, that is, get the form and fashion of your hearts altered, for so the word signifies, a transforming or changing of a thing from one form to another. Men's hearts that are shaped like to devils—' the lusts of your father' (says Christ) ' you will do '—being cast anew in the word, are made ' partakers of the divine nature,' 2 Peter i. 4. So that by it we come to be like to God, and have his image again renewed in us, which that mould bears, without which image of holiness thus imprinted by the word upon our hearts, we can never come to receive happiness from him.

Reason 2. Unless our hearts be thus new moulded, we remain ' vessels of dishonour,' and not ' fit for our master's service.' What is it that chiefly makes one vessel differ from another, but the fashion of it ? You have vessels made of the same matter, whereof one, because it is cast in the mould and fashion of a baser utensil, is therefore used about dishonourable employments. But now another that is cast in another mould, though of the same metal, is served up to the table, and used in honourable services. Nothing puts a difference between these two except the fashion, that they are cast in a several mould. This is part of the scope of the apostle's comparison, 2 Tim. ii. 20, 21, ' In a great house, there are some vessels of honour, and some of dishonour.' Now the vessels of honour are described to be such as are ' sanctified and prepared to every good work, and meet for the master's use.' Fitness to be employed in God's service is that which makes any one to be a vessel of honour, and that fitness it hath is from its being sanctified ; which sanctification is a new casting of it, and a giving the heart new dispositions, such as the word requires. Until, therefore, the word hath changed thy heart, thou art a vessel of dishonour. Thou mayest indeed be gilt over with civility and formal profession, but till thy fashion be altered, that is, the frame of thy inward parts, thou remainest a vessel of dishonour, and fit for nought but wrath, Rom. xix. 22. These reasons, you see, are suited to the expression or similitude used in the text.

III. In the third place, I will shew you how this is done and wrought, so far as this metaphor will, out of the Scripture, give us light.

1. God begins to work by humiliation and contrition, and breaks the

* Qu. ' Junius ' ?—Ed.

heart all in pieces by the word.   A founder that hath a statue or image to make of some hard metal that hath a contrary form on it (as suppose a horse to be cast into a man's shape) will first knock that metal in pieces. And so had our hearts need be dealt withal, they not only bearing the image of the devil, but that image being seated in our inward parts, and not only in the superficies or outside, as artificial forms are, yea, and being as brass and iron hardened in that fashion : Isa. xlviii. 4, ' I know thou art obstinate, thy neck is as an iron sinew, and thy brow as brass ;' so that the heart will not yield or apply itself to the fashion and mould of the word. Ministers may preach to you long enough, and your hearts still retain the same dispositions, because they are not broken with a sense of your sinful estate, and the curse due unto it ; for the ' heart is enmity against God, and cannot be subject to God,' Rom. viii. 7.   It will not yield to the mould, therefore it must first be broken.   Hence in Jer. xxiii. 29, the prophet compares the word to a hammer, that breaks the rocky hearts of men in pieces.

Yet 2. That is not enough, for it must be melted also ; therefore it is not only a sense of your misery that will prepare you for this new moulding, but a melting also.   Hence, as the word is like a hammer to break your hearts, so it is like fire to dissolve your hearts and make them soft and pliable, and so fit to take any impression.   Thus Jer. xxiii. 29, and thus 2 Chron. xxxiv. 27, Josiah's heart was melted, and became tender at the reading of the law.   And this similitude the prophet alludes to when shewing the inefficaciousness of the word upon their rebellious spirits, not praying into* conversion.   He says, ' The bellows are burnt, the founder melteth ' (or endeavours to melt their hearts) ' in vain.   Reprobate silver shall men call them,' Jer. vi. 30.   And this melting of the heart thus contains two things.

(1.) It imports the separating the corrupt dispositions and lusts of it (as the dross and scum useth to be in the melting of metals) which before were blended with it, ' their dross, till then, remaining within them,' as the prophet speaks.   But now he purgeth it from the midst of them, ' by the spirit of burning,' Isa. iv. 4, or (as it is in Mal. iii. 3) ' They are purified as gold is purified ;' the very inward dispositions to sin being mourned for, complained of, hated, and cast out with loathing.

(2.) And as this melting fetcheth out the dross, so, 2dly, it softeneth the good metal ; it makes all the faculties pliable, and apt to receive the impressions of the word ' with meekness,' as James speaks of receiving the word.   It maketh it a meek heart, an heart of such a temper as will be content to do anything that God shall command.   It can suffer exhortation and suffer reproof, Heb. xiii. 22.   It suffers the word to frame it which way it will, and to that end urgeth it, presseth it, stamps it upon itself again and again in private, till an indelible impression be made, and till it finds the same dispositions wrought to obedience which the word requires.

(3.) This transformation is done by the intervention of knowledge or faith.   The mind being enabled to conceive what is that good, perfect, and acceptable will of God, and so approving of it as good for him, the whole man is thereby fashioned ; so Rom. xii. 2, we are said to be ' transformed by the renewing of our minds, to prove what is that good, perfect, and acceptable will of God.'   And Col. iii. 10, ' The image of God ' is said to be ' renewed by knowledge.'   For we are not wrought on as a piece of dead clay, but according to the nature of the soul, which being an under-

* Qu. 'prevailing unto' ?—ED.

standing creature, the heart is wrought upon by means of it. Faith believing, approving, applying the word as good, the will and affections are presently fashioned to it, and so there is a change wrought in the whole man.

IV. Now, fourthly, for the work itself, if it be asked what this transformation of the heart into the word is, I answer, It is a universal frame and temper of all the faculties of the soul, whereby each, in their proportion, are respectively made suitable to the word in their inward several dispositions, and prepared and fitted to do whatever the word commands.

1. It is a change, though not of the substance or faculties of the soul, yet of the temper, frame, and disposition of it. For a thing moulded remains the same metal it was before, only the frame and fashion of it is altered ; and yet the alteration of that fashion works a great change in it, both in its name and nature. And the metal that once was a dish being turned into a pot, hath a new name given it ; and *in genere artificialium*, the spirit of it is altered. So when a man's heart is changed by the word, though the same nature of man remain in him still, yet he receives a new name, Rev. iii. 12, and is a new man ; and so called because the fashion of his heart is altered, and *in genere spiritualium*, he is another man, differing from what he was before.

2. By this change all the faculties are made suitable to the word. Even as you see the mould and the thing moulded fit one another, as the seal and the wax do so too, so the heart, which before was enmity to every commandment, now is moulded in and by the word. It delights in the law according to the inner man, and finds an agreeableness between the law and its own disposition, there being answerable dispositions wrought in all the faculties of the soul to what the word requires. If God says, ' Fear me,' the heart answers, ' I desire to fear thy name,' as it is said of them, Nehem. i. 11. If the word says, ' Keep the Sabbath,' the heart can say, ' The Sabbath is my delight,' Isa. lviii. 13. If the law says, ' Love the brethren,' why the heart finds an instinct begotten in itself to do it (as there is in birds to love their young) ; thus believers are said to be ' taught of God to love one another,' 1 Thes. iv. 9.

3. There is a change in all the faculties, according to their several tendencies and poises.

(1.) There is a change in the understanding or judgment, and when it is thus changed, there will be an ability, δοκιμάζειν, to try what is the acceptable will of God, to judge and know how he ought acceptably to be served. Such a renewed mind is ' quick in the fear of the Lord,' Isa. xi. 3, to try it as the touchstone doth gold, and also to consent to the law that it is good, and good for him, Rom. vii., and to esteem every commandment concerning all things as right, Ps. cxix. 128, and to set an high price on every ordinance and every duty, as being matters of great moment. And so it is ready likewise to disallow and ' hate every false way,' as you have it expressed in the aforesaid psalm, and also in Rom. vii.

(2.) The print of this mould in the conscience will be a quick, vigorous light, so as the motives that are spiritual, and for the glory of God, shall naturally rise up in the mind and move the heart : 1 Peter v. 2, ' Feed the flock, not for lucre, &c., but of a ready mind.'

(3.) The stamp of it in the will, will be a propensity to choose the things that please God (as it is said of those eunuchs, Isa. lvi. 4), those things that most of all please God, will be most of all pleasing to a holy soul too, and he will walk in them to choose. The will being thus transformed, the mind needs not be wrought off by selfish ends unto holy duties, but will be willing (as the apostle's phrase is, 1 Peter v. 2) 'in a ready mind, to feed the flock.' Taking care for them 'naturally' (as Paul says, Phil. ii. 20), even as a nurse for the child. And thus Paul makes to be more than obedience itself, when the heart is thus framed : 2 Cor. viii. 10, 'Not only to do, but to be willing.' Also part of this stamp and impression lies in the will's having a strong bent and bias upon it, forcibly carrying it in all the turnings of a man's life towards the commandment, and obedience unto it, and causing the will to incline to, and follow the command, and likewise to stick unto it ; even as the iron doth move with, follow, and apply itself to the loadstone. 'I have sworn, and I will perform it,' says David, Ps. cxix. 106.

(4.) So answerably this stamp of inward holiness is set on the affections, when every affection, according to the nature of it, is exercised in and about the law, and the things thereof. Even 'sorrow' is 'after a godly sort,' for the breach thereof, and for sin as committed against a holy God. Also hatred is raised against the things therein forbidden, and a love to the things commanded, and joy in the performance. See Ps. cxix. throughout, where all sorts of such affections as these towards the law of God are recorded. Thus when every faculty is seasoned with a new disposition towards God's precepts, and the obeying of them ; when there is an universal conformity of all faculties according to their several kinds and offices, and also their subordinations one to another, with a natural fitness and disposedness unto what the law requires, then is the heart moulded in the word.

4. There is a preparedness unto all duties revealed in the word, and a facile readiness to be employed in them, so that (as is said 2 Chron. xxx. 19) the whole heart is prepared for every duty. And this the similitude implies, for it is the end of casting metals into this or that form, that they may be serviceable to such or such an use. Now when the soul is cast into such a frame that the heart is as a 'vessel meet and prepared for the master's use' (as it is said, 2 Tim. ii. 21), then it may be said to be moulded in the word ; even when all the powers and faculties of the soul are become weapons of righteousness (as the apostle's other similitude in this chapter is), as being made on purpose for righteous uses. And it is the fashion in a weapon that gives it the fitness for such a use, as a spade, by reason of the fashion of it, is fit to dig the earth, but not to cut with, a bowl to drink in, and a sword to fight with. Not but that a godly man's heart may at some times be dulled, but still as in a weapon there is an habitual fitness, which it hath from the fashion of it, as in a sword or knife to cut, and there is an actual fitness, namely an edge, which though it be blunted, yet the habitual fitness is not taken away, so it is in a godly man's heart, though the frame and fashion of it still remains the same. Thus there is an habitual preparedness to good duties, yet the edge and actual vigour may be wanting, till it be whetted again, Deut. vi. 7 ; his heart may be hacked and battered, and so at the present made unfit, yet the fashion is still the same, and one good prayer or sermon whets it again, and brings its edge again. Now wicked men want both these fitnesses. Indeed, in the furnace they will bow to any fashion (as the heart of Saul and of Pharaoh did), but when they are once out of it, they will return to their own frame again.

5. This inward stamp of holiness is both an universal and proportionable impression upon the heart, which the mould of the word leaves upon it.

(1.) It is universal. There is no small scratch or raze in the mould, but it will appear in the thing cast in it. Therefore civil men that have impressions of the second table, and few or none of the first, were never truly moulded in the word.

(2.) It is proportionable. Look what cuts and engravings are deepest in the mould, these will make the highest and fairest embossments on the things cast in them, the very smallest and shallowest being visible too: so it is with one converted by the word, and who hath his heart moulded in it. The stamps of those duties which God most of all requires of him in his particular and general calling, will be most eminent upon his heart. The great things of the law will be the great desires of his heart to fulfil, and not be taken up about mint and cummin only, Mat. xxiii. 23.

The second similitude the holy God is pleased to use to express the change of the heart into the word and law of God, is this of ' engrafting the word upon the heart,' as a graff on a stock, with ability to save and change it: James i. 21, ' Wherefore lay apart all filthiness and superfluity of naughtiness, and receive with meekness the engrafted word, which is able to save your souls.' I must first fix the interpretation, because this translation is controverted by some interpretors, although not many.

1. Some say that the word ἔμφυτος imports that which is natural, and is so far from signifying the engrafted word, that it is opposed thereto ; so ' natural branches are to be engrafted,' Rom. xi. And the Greek scholiast kept so close to that meaning, that he plainly interprets the engrafted word here to be the natural light of reason. But this interpretation is manifestly false ; for, 1st, this word is to be *received*, and therefore is not by nature, nor any thing natural ; and, 2dly, it is said to be ' able to save our souls,' which the light of nature is not.

2. Others would have the word of God called ἔμφυτος, in this sense, that it is native and genuine, which signification is opposed unto what is artificial, affected, adulterate, or counterfeit : as if you should call a true virtue ἐμφύτην ἀρετὴν, that is, a genuine true virtue, not acted or counterfeited. And so ἔμφυτος λόγος would signify the pure naked word in its simplicity, unmixed, unadulterate with man's inventions ; and so it would be all one (as they urge it) with what this same apostle had called it, ' the word of truth :' ver. 18, ' With the word of truth he begat you.' For God useth not falsehood nor error to beget men to himself. And I confess I was tempted to this interpretation, by paralleling it with 1 Pet. ii. 2, where he exhorts them to desire ' the sincere milk of the word,' ἄδολον λόγον, without deceit, but as it comes from the dug, not mixed with medicines or waters. The like to which also you have 2 Cor. ii. 17. And that which further strengthens it is, that in the other words and phrases, in coherence with these in either places, both in Peter and James, there seems to be a parallel, and therefore in this also, both James and Peter using the same words in either.*
The one says, ' laying aside all naughtiness, receive this word ;' the other says, ' laying aside all superfluity of naughtiness, desire the sincere milk of the word.' And thus the meaning of James's exhortation should be as if he had said, ' You that were begotten at first by the word of truth' (that is, the sincere word), ' take heed you receive that only which is the true, pure, and genuine word of truth ;' as that which is only able ' to save your souls.'

---

* Ἀποθέμενοι πᾶσαν κακίαν,—so Pet., ver. 1. Ἀποθέμενοι πᾶσαν περισσείαν κακίας,—so James.

For as it was that pure word which begat you at first, so that alone must build you up to life.

But that which I have to say concerning this interpretation is,

1. That it is not called the word of truth, James i., ver. 18, in opposition to error and falsehood, so much as by way of eminency, as it is thus called too : Eph. i. 13, ' The word of truth, the gospel of your salvation.' It is too low an epithet to say it is styled the word of truth in opposition to what is erroneous, feigned, and false, or devised, for that is but what is common with it to every philosophical truth.   But it is so called for the eminency of truth in it ; with which also that eulogium of Paul concurreth, ' This is a faithful saying, worthy of all acceptation.'

2. Whenever the word ἔμφυτος is used to signify that which is genuine in their sense, yet then withal it is applied to, and made the epithet of, some inward quality or disposition of the mind of man, which is inbred and inherent therein, as when it is applied to virtues and the like.   And so according to this meaning of it, if we would suppose the word of God were termed ἔμφυτος, as noting forth purity, sincerity, or truth of it, yet still withal it would connotate and import this other interpretation also ; namely, inherent or inbred, in our hearts and minds ; or that which is ordained to be inwrought or engrafted in us.

I come, therefore, to the third and most usual interpretation, which our translators have chosen, namely, that it signifies the ' engrafted,' or rather ' engraftable word' (for it is *nomen verbale*, not *participium*) ; that is, it is that word whose end, use, intent, and ordination by God, is to be engrafted, inbred, and ingenerated into the souls of men, and is to be received to that end.   And so it is a metaphorical allusion to seed or a plant that is sown, engrafted, or inoculated either in ground, or into a stock, and especially the latter.   That look, as the word σύμφυτος, used Rom. vi. 5, which is akin to this, and of the same stock (as I may so speak), and which, as there used, signifies ' planted together ;' being there spoken of Christ and his members, being planted together in one, as two twigs growing, or set in one common stock, becoming and growing up into one tree ; so ἔμφυτος, here spoken of the word of God, signifies planted, or plantable within us, these two words differing but in this, that the word there is a compound with συν, that is, *together with*, but this here is compounded with ἐν, or in, and so the one signifies *grafted*, or *planted together one with another;* this other here signifies *planted in :* the first being spoken of Christ and us, and our being planted together in one ; this latter being spoken of the word of God as planted, or to be planted, in our hearts.

Obj. But some urge that this interpretation cannot stand, because the same word cannot signify both what is *natural* and what is *engrafted* too, for these two are opposed, Rom. xi. 17. 21.   The natural branches are opposed to those grafted in.   Now it is evident (say they) that the word ἔμφυτος doth signify (at least sometimes) that which is natural.

Ans. 1. But first, I answer, the word in Rom. xi. used for *engrafted*, is not ἔμφυτος, but another word, and so prejudgeth not this sanctification* here.

Ans. 2. The word ἔμφυτος in common imports whatsoever is inbred and seated in the inwards, whether it be by nature, or otherwise set in, so as that it becomes as nature.   And thus the Latin word *insitum* answers to it in the like large signification ; or as we say in English, implanted in one, whereby we express, not only what hath been by nature, but as well what

* Qu. ' signification '?—ED.

otherwise is inwrought, though acquired by education, breeding, or habitual custom.* So then this word, though upon other occasions it may be used for what is originally natural, and inbred by nature; yet withal, it still allows us that other signification of what is inwrought by an engrafture, or otherwise acquired. In the book of Wisdom, chap. xii., ver. 10, μίσος ἔμφυτον is put to signify an inbred hatred, or grudge, not that which was by nature, which we call an antipathy; but that which had been inbred by injuries, and yet was so deeply rooted, that it is as if it were natural. And thus, ἔμφυτον is all one with ἐγκάρδιον, that is, ' seated in the heart: so that this word ἔμφυτος may well bear either sense.

This being cleared, it is evident that the apostle James's comparison and allusion is to liken the word to seed cast into the earth, or to a graft or more noble plant set into a stock, being ordained to take root, or to be inoculated and made co-natural with, and so to bear fruit in the heart according to its kind; which interpretation is most natural to this place.

For, 1. This interpretation excludes not that other of being natural, taking it in respect of what the word doth *consequenter*, and in the event become to the heart by its engrafture; for thereby it doth become natural and inbred in, and genuine to the heart, and as a new nature.

2. It agrees in this sense with the coherence and scope of the apostle, and his foregoing passages, for,

(1.) Whereas he had declared, ver. 18, how they had been ' begotten by the word,' as of seed (which is formed into and becomes the substance of the new creature), now in the 21st verse he exhorts them to receive this word they had been thus begotten by, so as to grow up more and more, and to bring forth fruit; which he expresseth by being ' doers of the word,' in the following 22d verse. Only in carrying on of this exhortation, he takes up this other metaphor as genuine to this scope, as that other of begetting was to the former, namely, comparing the same word of God in that respect unto seed sown in a soil, or to a graft engrafted on a stock, which by becoming one nature with our hearts, and by changing the stock thereof into its own nature, doth increase our graces in us more and more, and causeth us to bring forth fruit, which he termeth doing of the word. And this is withal a better parallel with that place of Peter fore-mentioned, and his scope, than the former interpretation. For even just thus: Peter had spoken of the word first, as the means of begetting us, chap. i. 23, ' Being born again, not of corruptible seed, by the word of God.' And then, chap. ii. ver. 2, he exhorts them under a new metaphor, as ' new-born babes to desire that word as milk to grow thereby;' even as we have the like.

(2.) He had indeed begun and laid a foundation for this very allusion in ver. 18, in styling believers, and men begotten again, the first-fruits of God's creation, as ordained to be so after regeneration: ' He begat us,' says he, ' that we should be a kind of first-fruits of his creation' (even as, 1 Cor. xv. 23, Christ is termed ' the first-fruits of them that sleep'); alluding to Jer. ii. 3, ' Israel is holiness to the Lord, the first-fruits of his increase.' They are then begotten to that end, that in their future course of life themselves and all their actions might be consecrated to God as the first-fruits of the creation (holiness in one man being more to God than all the creation without it). Now, then, in answer to and prosecution of this

---

* Even as σύμφυτευσθαι. (which is of the same kindred) imports both engrafted with another; and withal what is together in nature with another, *simul naturâ*. See Stephan, *in* σύμφυτευω.

allusion there begun, to the end to exhort them to accomplish this, what could be more proper than to make use of this new comparison of the word of God unto a graft ordained to be engrafted on their hearts; and accordingly to exhort them to receive it as such into their souls, unto the end that they might in the sequel of their lives be consecrated wholly to God, in bringing forth fruits to be offered up unto God, as the first-fruits were.

(3.) The very words here used, 'receive,' and 'receive with meekness,' these words comply evidently with that sense of engrafting rather than any other. The phrase to *receive* is proper thereto, for we say the stock *receives* the graft as let into it; and the words 'with meekness' are added, for it is received into such a stock, man's heart, as hath the life of sense in it. And also because that in order to this receiving the word by an engrafture, the corruption of the heart is to be parted with, yea, and cut off, as the old top is, to make way for the new graft. He might well add 'with meekness,' for thus to cut off lusts is painful and troublesome. Christ tells us it is to cut off members, to cut off hands, and pull out eyes; and this tree to be lopped is the heart of a man.

(4.) Other scriptures do fall in to confirm this metaphor (here used) of the engrafture or sowing the word of God in our hearts, in order to the bringing forth of fruit in us: 1 Cor. iii. 9, 'You are God's husbandry, and we are labourers together with God;' which work or labour is in the verses aforegoing said to be 'planting and watering,' ver. 6, 7. Again, John xv. 16, Christ sending forth his disciples to preach the word, and to convert souls, and to build them up to life, expresseth it thus, 'I have chosen you, that you should go forth' (namely, to preach), 'and bring forth fruit;' therein comparing their preaching to sowing seed or engrafting plants which should bring forth fruit. Again, Col. i. 6, 'the word of truth,' as thus planted by the apostles, is said to bring forth fruit in them, and in all the world. Moreover, in the same 15th chapter of John, Christ is not only said to bear fruit in us by our 'abiding in him,' as the vine, but also by 'his word abiding in us.' For as at the 1st and 4th verses he had said, 'The branch bringeth not forth fruit unless it abide in the vine,' so at the 7th verse he says, 'If you abide in me, and my words abide in you.' So then where we, that is, our persons, are said to be engrafted into Christ, even there also it is said, that in order to bringing forth fruit, his word must be engrafted into us also, as we are into him, he expressing the one as well as the other by one and the same word of 'abiding in.' And thus James his ἔμφυτος, spoken of the word, and Paul's σύμφυτοι, Rom. vi., spoken of Christ and us, do well agree in one and the same kind of allusion. Thus I have fixed the interpretation.

To come now to the opening of the particulars contained and implied in the metaphor.

1. God (whose word this is) is tacitly compared unto a tree, who hath all excellencies, perfections of holiness, justice, wisdom, truth, righteousness, goodness in him essentially.

2. His word is as the seed, or as twigs growing out of the tree, fit to be sown, inoculated or engrafted in the hearts of men.

3. And look, as seed or twigs plucked or fallen from a tree hath virtually all the perfections of the tree it comes from, and being planted or inoculated, spreads forth into the same likeness, and brings forth like fruits; so this word of truth, fallen from God, containeth in it all his perfections communicable to us, holiness, mercy, goodness, &c. The law, or his commandment, is holy, spiritual, just, and good, Rom. vii. 12, 14, as God

himself is ; and the gospel hath the mind of God and of Christ in it, 1 Cor. ii. 16.

Only, 4, look, as seed or a graft brings forth no fruit if it remains alone, unset, but it must be engrafted into some stock, or sown in some soil, if it brings forth fruit, so this word of truth remains as a dead letter, un-fruitful, unless it be received into men's hearts, and there takes root, and abides ; even as Christ says the branch cannot bring forth fruit of itself unless it abide in the vine, John xv., so the word brings not forth fruit unless engrafted into us ; yea, to that end it was ordained and delivered by God, and preached by us. The epithet here given it imports this end and ordination of it. It is called ' the engraftable word,' and so termed as it is in itself in respect of this its end and ordination, ere that yet it is received into the heart ; for he thereupon founds his exhortation to them to receive it as such, as being the word that is ordained, intended for this, and whose end is to be engrafted, to be insititious as the perfection thereof (it is a noun, not a participle) ; as when we say, a child-bearing woman, that phrase im-ports not so much one actually with child, as fit in respect of age or condi-tion for it.

5. To be engrafted is not barely to be outwardly let into the ear or un-derstanding, but to be let into the heart, there to be recreated, there to abide and become one therewith, and (if you will) to be naturalised into the heart. The graft, if it take on the stock, is let into the very pith ; so must the word be, and then it is that it becomes λόγος ἔμψυχος. Then is the word ensouled (ἔμφυτος and ἐγκάρδιος are used for one) ; and so the in-terpretation of natural comes fitly in, the word and the heart becoming one in nature. The word is not only received into the conscience, to be a guide or rule of life, but also into the heart, as a graft that doth naturally coalesce with the stock. Other scriptures express this under other meta-phors, comparing the word to milk and meat, which, received into the stomach, are turned by the digestive faculty into the spirits, blood, bones, flesh, &c. And this is the true import of that phrase in Heb. iv. 2, μὴ συγκεκραμένος τῇ πίστει, speaking of the word, that it profiteth not, because it was not digested by faith, and so turned into blood and nourishment.

6. And lastly, It imports not barely its being made natural to the soul, as meat is with the body, when turned into flesh and blood, for the meat turns not man's nature into its nature, but the man's nature assimilates it unto itself. But this metaphor further imports, that the word turns the soul of man and the dispositions of it into the nature of itself, as a noble plant doth a more wild stock, Isa. lv. 11. He speaks of his word and the power thereof, which ' shall prosper to the ends he sends it,' whereof one end is, ver. 13, that ' instead of the thorn shall come up the fir tree ; in-stead of the briar shall come up the myrtle tree ;' that is, the nature of the trees themselves shall be changed by it. Again, in meat digested, the nature of man useth all the blood and spirits gotten by it according to its own will and temper, which still remains the same ; but this word, engrafted into the heart, converts all the sap and strength in the stock to bring forth fruit according to its own kind, for the virtue of it overrules all, and it brings forth according to the kind of itself. And therefore in that, Col. i., the word is said to bring forth fruit in us, and not so much we ourselves to do it. Grace is the word concocted, and the fruit of holiness is but the word brought forth into the life.

Use. Therefore be exhorted to get the word thus received into your hearts, or it will not save your souls. ' The engrafted word' (says James)

' is able to save your souls.' It saves only as it is engrafted; else the whole word of God is not able to save you, but will condemn you. Men that hear the word and are enlightened by it, either receive it as ' the earth doth the rain, and brings forth thorns and briars,' Heb. vi., the very rain making lust more fruitful, or else they ' receive it as engrafted' (as James speaks), and that is, when it changeth the heart, and then it saves. Whereas, of the other it is said, ' that they are near to cursing, whose end is to be burned.' Nor is it having the graft tied about with a thread, or the word to stand in the memory or outward profession, but it must take root and become one with thy heart.

The third similitude whereby the Holy Ghost expresseth sanctification to be conformity to the word or law of God is here, in Heb. x. 14, 16, ' For by one offering he hath perfected for ever them that are sanctified;' ver. 16, ' This is the covenant that I will make with them after those days, saith the Lord; I will put my laws into their hearts, and in their minds will I write them.' 1. He says, ' I will put my law into their hearts.' 2. ' And in their minds will I write them.' And thereby he intendeth to express sanctification as differing from justification. For so he distinguisheth them in the prophet's intention. For having said (ver. 14), that ' by one offering Christ had perfected for ever them that are sanctified;' he allegeth the saying of the prophet, as in one including sufficient proof of this assertion, and punctually allegeth both for the subject and predicate thereof. The subject is ' them that are sanctified,' to which he applies these words, ' Those in whose hearts he puts and writes his laws,' that is, those whom he sanctifies; such he hath ' perfected for ever,' in respect of justification, by that one offering; which he proves from these words of the prophet which follow, ver. 17, ' And their sins and iniquities will I remember no more,' and therefore they are perfected for ever. So then writing the law in the heart is true and genuine sanctification. It is such, that to the persons that have it justification belongeth. Now let us consider these two phrases.

1. Putting the laws into their hearts.

2. Writing the laws in their minds, which still aim both at one meaning.

1. He is said to put the law into their hearts, which you may conceive by what he did to Adam at the first, into whose heart he put his law. Now what was that law, as it was put into Adam's heart, but all sorts of holy instincts, properties, and inclinations unto whatever God did command; and an antipathy against whatever God did forbid? This was the law of nature in his heart. The laws of God in Adam were Adam's original nature, and the constitution of his soul and spirit; which we may all easily apprehend by what we conceive to be the law of nature in beasts, and other creatures, which God hath put into them to act according to their kind, as to beasts to love their young, to birds to build their nests at such a season, with skill to do it. When God created man at first, he gave him not an outward law written in letters, or delivered by words; but an inward law put into his heart, and concreated with him, and wrought in the frame of his soul. And the whole substance of this law of God, the mass of it, was not barely dictates or beams of light in his understanding, directing what to do; but also real, lively, and spiritual dispositions, and inclinations in his will and affections, carrying him on to what was so directed, as to pray, to love God and fear him, to seek his glory in a spiritual and holy manner. They were inward abilities suitable to every duty. And as an evidence of the law having been Adam's nature, we have the shadow of it in the hearts of all men, which evinceth it. For they do by nature τὰ τοῦ νόμου, Rom. ii. 14,

' the things of the law ;' though the inward part of the law, the holiness and spiritualness of it, be blotted out, which was then Adam's nature.　And the remainder of this, even in corrupt nature, and by nature without outward revelation of the law, is an evidence that this spiritual part (which is that of the law which is lost) was once in man as his nature ; as we know what corn the earth once bore, by the stubble that is found upon the field.　So then, that just, and holy, and spiritual law we now have extant in the word, is but *historia Adami*, the story of Adam's heart, viz., of those instincts and properties which were once there ; as Pliny's *Natural History*, or Aristotle's *Historia Animalium*, is the story of the several instincts, properties, and living dispositions, and postures of all sorts of living creatures, painting out in a lifeless story that which (when you come to see these several creatures) you shall perceive naturally acted by them.　And because the same law is renewed again in the soul, it is termed the law of the mind, which serves and observes the law of God, as the heliotrope doth the sun, or the needle the loadstone, being pointed and touched by it.　The law of God is become the law of the new nature, and so the law of nature anew ; and commands as a law (even as sin is termed the law of the members, Rom. vii. 23), ruling also as a law useth to do.

2. The second phrase is in Heb. x. 16, ' Writing the law in the heart,' which imports the very same thing.　And one contrary serving to explain another, we may fitly understand what it is to have God's law written in the heart, by what is meant by the writing its contrary, namely, sin and corruption, in the heart, Jer. xvii. 1.　There sin is said to be written in their hearts, as with the point of a diamond, that is, deeply engraven.　Now what manner of letters these are wherewith sin is written on our hearts, we have woful and daily experience of.　They are letters suitable to the paper they are writ on.　The soul is a living, active creature, never resting, and these letters are answerably strong, vigorous, active, and lively inclinations and provocations unto what is evil and wicked, in all the varieties of it which naturally arise.　Such answerably are those holy characters written on a living soul; and this the apostle expresseth, 2 Cor. iii. 3, ' Forasmuch as ye are manifestly declared to be the epistle of Christ ministered by us, written not with ink, but with the Spirit of the living God ; not in tables of stone, but in fleshly tables of the heart.'　His scope is to clear that different writing of the word of God, by the power of Christ, in regenerate men's hearts, from what it is in unregenerate men's hearts, who also have the law written in a sort in them.　He compares the latter to that writing the law by God at first on a stone, or by Moses on a book.　So, comparatively, it is written on unrenewed hearts, where, when written in their understandings, memories, and consciences, it appears and remains, yet for the powerful efficacy of it, it is but as if it were written on stone.　There, indeed, he that hath it may read it written, for in the letter of it it shews itself, but yet it is but written on a stone or in a book.　But now, says the apostle, suppose you see the same law, by the power and finger of God written on flesh, on a creature active and living, if you see this law thus written by the same power and finger of God which first put laws into living creatures to act so and so, what difference would there be evident between the former writing and this ?　Such is the writing the law in regenerate men's hearts (says the apostle), ' It is written, not with ink, but with the Spirit of the living God ; not in tables of stone, but in the fleshly tables of the heart ; ' that is (says he), you must understand these letters and characters of the word written to be answerable to the Spirit with which they are written.

Now, this is the Spirit of the living God, who is a pure and mere act, and his life is holiness and righteousness, and he acts accordingly ; and these letters, therefore, are such dispositions of life (like unto God's) as shall incline the creature, by a vital principle, to act holily. The letters are spirit and life in the soul, and not dead characters as on stone, such as in unregenerate men's minds the law makes.

They are also written there as on fleshly tables ; that is, suppose you should see the living God would say he would write on a living heart, these letters wrote must bear a likeness to the subject or paper written on, and so have living impressions suited to every faculty and power in the soul, expressing the outward letter in living and active energies and virtues, according to the capacity of each faculty. Conceive it thus: if you should see the statue of a man completely cut out in stone (which is one part of the apostle's comparison to which he compares unregenerate men's hearts), having all outward members, yea, and the inward parts also, cut by a dead tool by the same artificer, and you should hear God (who is the Father of life, and is able to raise out of stones children to Abraham) say, You behold this man of stone, this dead nose, eyes, &c., which bear the resemblance of a man ; come, you shall see what manner of man I, that am the living God, will make of him, after my image ; what would you expect, but such a man as now you see yourselves to be, having all the members answerable to those in that man of stone, and also not only the outward shape of a dead eye carved in stone, but a living, quick, sparkling, sprightful eye, that could discover this world and all things in it out of a vital principle ? What would you expect to see but a heart likewise and pulse beating, veins full of blood, the arteries of spirits, a living fleshly man, having all members like to that man in stone, but living and acting according to their several offices and properties, enlivened with a restless soul that enflames them ? So it is here. Paul, when a pharisee, had the law carved forth in all the lineaments of it on his conscience and understanding. He had a form of truth and knowledge in the law ; but when Paul became a believer, he had all this form and the members of it turned into spirit and life in him, into properties and instincts answerable to that outward form, as hath been expressed.

BOOK IX.

Of the eminency of mercy and grace discovered in this work of regeneration, comparatively with other works wrought in us.—Of the greatness of the power which God manifests in regenerating us.—Of the influence which Christ's resurrection hath on our regeneration.

CHAPTER I.

The eminent mercy of God towards us in our regeneration evidenced, because it is the first apparent discovery to us of our election.—And because this work alone makes an alteration in our state, doth it once for all, brings us into an eternal state of happiness, and alone makes a specifical change in us.

I HAVE discoursed of the nature of the work wrought in us by God in regenerating us, and of the several parts in it; the next thing to be considered is the eminency of mercy, which is shewn in this work. So eminent it is, that it hath singularly obtained the title of mercy, and obtaining mercy: 'I who before' (says Paul, 1 Tim. i. 13) 'was a blasphemer, and a persecutor, and injurious, but I obtained mercy.' He speaks of his conversion : 'And the grace of our Lord was exceeding abundant' (namely, in that first work, in working faith and love, as it follows), 'with faith and love which is in Christ Jesus.' And thereupon he breaks forth into that high celebration of God for the mercy in it : ver. 17, 'Now unto the King eternal, immortal, invisible, the only wise God, be honour and glory, for ever and ever !'

There are three sorts of works whereby our salvation is completed and accomplished.

1. *Immanent* in God towards us, as his eternal love set and passed *upon* us, out of which he chose us, and designed this and all blessings to us.

2. *Transient*, in Christ done *for* us ; in all he did or suffered representing of us, and in our stead.

3. *Applicatory*, wrought *in* us and upon us, in the endowing us with all those blessings by the Spirit ; as calling, justification, sanctification, glorification.

My purpose is not to institute a comparison of this work in us with those two mentioned, transacted towards us or for us by God and Christ, but only with those other of the latter sort, wrought in us after conversion. And so compared, this first work, and the concomitants of it at first, have some things therein which may and should cause us to look upon it as a most abounding mercy, surpassing those other fore-mentioned that follow after it.

1. Because it is the first discovery, appearance, and manifestation of the first two, election and redemption, in the persons to whom they were in-

tended : Tit. iii. 4, ' When the kindness and love of God appeared.' And
how, and when, did it appear ?   Ver. 5, ' According to his mercy he saved
us, by the washing of regeneration,' &c.   God's eternal love, like a mighty
river, had from everlasting ran, as it were, underground ; and when Christ
came, it took its course through his heart, hiddenly ran through it, he
bearing when on the cross the names of them whom God had given him ;
but was yet still hidden here as to us, and our knowledge of it.   But the
first breaking of it forth, and particular appearing of it in and to the persons, is when we are converted, and is as the first opening of a fountain,
whereto the calling of the elect Jews in the last days is compared, Zech.
xiii. 1.   And accordingly, in the first of the Galatians, Paul expresseth his
conversion to be the first revealing Christ in him, and of God's grace towards him : ' But when it pleased God, who called me by his grace, to
reveal his Son in me,' chap. i. 15, 16.

2. There is no other spiritual mercy we can lay claim to as ours before
this, or without this ; but upon it we are led unto all mercies.   This Peter
(first epistle, chap. ii. ver. 9, 10) expresseth, both in the negative and affirmative thereof : the negative, in saying that afore their calling (of which,
in the words afore, he speaks) ' they had not obtained mercy ;' the affirmative, ' but now' (namely, upon calling) ' they had obtained mercy.'   Whilst
a man lives without regeneration, he is also without promise : Eph. ii. 12,
' He hath now quickened you, who in times past were strangers to the covenant of grace.' *   And what are promises but the golden veins or rivulets
that mercies run into, as the dust and sand of the purest gold use in several
rills to do ?   Which promises, though they were bequeathed before by God's
eternal decrees, and purchased by Christ's death, yet the right to them, the
seisin, the possession of them, is given at conversion : 2 Pet. i. 3, 4, after
he had said that ' his divine power had given to them all things belonging
to life and godliness' (that is, furnished us with all requisite abilities thereunto), ' through the knowledge of him that called us to glory and virtue,'
he adds, ' Whereby are given to us' (delivery of seisin thereby is made)
' exceeding great and precious promises ;' so as the youngest convert may
upon regeneration go over and run through all the Scriptures, and view and
lay claim to whatever is promised of spiritual blessings therein.   And oftentimes all the promises are brought by the Spirit in unto this young heir,
upon his first birth, for them to do homage, at least to own him, and acknowledge him as their heir.

3. Then it is that both the first and the greatest sum of pardoning mercy
is granted and expended on us, in the forgiving both of more sins, and of
them at once, than perhaps ever after at several times.   All the sins a man
had committed for twenty, thirty, or perhaps more years, lay on heaps ;
and forgiveness had not been given forth, not so much as for one of them,
all that time.   And every commandment brought in his bill, which the
Spirit reduced unto heads, and made catalogues of particulars under each
head : ' I was a blasphemer' (says Paul, and had blasphemed times without number), ' a persecutor, injurious.'   And God forgave them all at
once, as it is said Mat. xviii. 24, 27, even ten thousand talents at once.
All the debt and arrears that had run on score so many years, were then
acquitted.   In the last chapter of James, and the last verse, the apostle,
exhorting to convert souls to God, says, ' He that converts a soul,' though
but one soul, ' hides a multitude of sins ;' for all his sins, till then, lay
unforgiven.   This you have Col. iii. 13, where, setting forth the mercy of

* Qu. ' promise ' ? -ED.

their calling out of their unregenerate condition, which he describes in these words, 'And you being dead in your sins, and the uncircumcision of your flesh;' and going on, 'You hath he quickened together with him' (there is their first conversion); then follows, 'having forgiven you all trespasses;' all, and at once together, namely, then when quickened. Which great debts in that former estate had been so long contracting.

I need not here debate that point, whether all the sins Christ died for are at that time forgiven, though that forgiveness be renewed every day, when pardon for new sins is asked by us, and so is to be sought for every day, as our Lord in his prayer hath taught us. It is enough for the proof of my assertion, and acknowledged by all, that then it is, that such a multitude of sins past, so long continued in, come first to be actually forgiven; and that after calling he gives them forth pardon by the day, every day for the sins of the day, *peccata quotidianæ incursionis*. He that is in the state of grace asketh pardon every day for the sins of the day, as he committeth them; as well as we do pray for daily bread (as in the Lord's prayer we are taught). And we daily 'confessing our sins, he is faithful and just to forgive them,' 1 John i. 7, 9, 'And Christ's blood still cleanseth us from all sin.' All along he speaks of it, as of the continuation of a continual act that cleanseth; as a running fountain doth what defiled things are brought to it: as in that respect it is compared to a 'fountain opened for sin and uncleanness,' Zech. xiii. Fountains are called 'living waters,' because they continually run, after their first springing, and cease not; and thus the blood of Christ doth, and washes from the sinful flowings of that original uncleanness which is continually bubbling up in us. Yet, at this first opening of it, it may be compared unto a sea, in that respect we are now upon, of pardoning us at first, as Micah vii. 19, God's pardoning mercies are compared; but in respect unto the continual cleansing us, it is compared unto a fountain that always runs. And the difference of these two may be thus illustrated. There is a father that spares and forgives a son that serves him every day, and dischargeth his dribbling debts (as I may, in comparison of the ten thousand talents at first, term them) still as he runs into them: but God's first forgiveness is as that of the father of the prodigal, who had spent all his stock given him, and run out of cash millions; or as a father that hath a son that is a merchant, who breaks and is found thousands in debt, and he at once dischargeth all, and gives him a new stock to set up, and to begin the world anew with. A father brings forth his bags at such a time, and layeth forth more mercy at one clap, than by daily supplies all a man's life after.

4. This work of regeneration doth alone make that great alteration mentioned, of a man's state before God for all, and that for ever. That this makes the alteration of a man's state, I have shewn. The apostle Paul hath it, Titus iii. 5, 'Hath saved us by the washing of regeneration.'

(1.) That this alone doth make the alteration of the state is evident, because all other alterations after, are gradual, and additions of degrees, within the compass of the same state. Yea, even that great change from grace to glory is but from faith to sight, from imperfect to perfect. We know but in part (yet in part), as 1 Cor. xiii. 12, 'Now we see through a glass darkly, but then face to face; now I know in part, but then I shall know even as I am known.' The same things which we believe, and know in part, we shall then see the whole and full of it. And it is but instead of seeing them in a glass as now, then to see them face to face. The state of the man is one and the same, as to the grace of God, when a Christian liveth, and after when he dies.   To be the Lord's, is the state of the man in both.   The fellowship the same, it is but the change of place, not company.   Rom. xiv. 8, ' Whether we live or die, we are the Lord's.'   Faith itself hath eternal life in it, 1 John v. 11, 13.   And not in hopes only, but it is in part ' abiding in him,' 1 John iii. 15.   Death and heaven are accounted the great changes.   As Job xiv. 14, ' I will wait till my change will come.'   But this is a greater, ' a turning from darkness to light, from Satan to God,' Acts xxvi. 18.   Yea, indeed, God then actually gives the whole right of all, that ever he gives forth afterwards ; then in the lump, afterwards by parcels.   The Scripture calls it salvation, and being saved, speaking in the great and the whole of it.

And (2.) this great change is made but *once*.   There is but ' one baptism,' as ' one faith ;' and as the faith was but once delivered to the saints, Jude 2, so baptism is but once to be administered.   And why ?   Because the thing signified, sealed up thereby, which is regeneration, is but once wrought (but the Lord's supper is often celebrated, 1 Cor. xi., ' As oft as ye receive'), which is therefore called a ' baptizing into the likeness of his death and resurrection,' Rom. vi. 4, 5.   And that in two respects, which are the same with those before.   1. Inasmuch as Christ died but once, and rose but once, Heb. vii. 27, and Heb. ix. 26, 27, ' Once in the end of the world he died, and offered up himself, even as it is appointed for men once to die.'   And 2. That the estate he rose into is an eternal state of life : Heb. x. 12, ' He for ever sat down on the right hand of God.'   Now both these the apostle applies in that Rom. vi., unto men regenerated, and baptized into Christ, by instituting the parallel between our state by regeneration, signified by baptism into Christ's death and resurrection, and Christ's death and resurrection itself, in both these very respects fore-mentioned, in these words, ver. 9, 10, 11, ' Knowing that Christ being raised from the dead, dieth no more ; death hath no more dominion over him.   For in that he died, he died unto sin once, but in that he liveth, he liveth unto God.   Likewise reckon ye also yourselves to be dead indeed unto sin, but alive unto God through Jesus Christ our Lord.'   From whence he infers, ver. 12, that ' sin shall not reign.'   It is a promise, as well as a command.   And those words, ' Likewise reckon yourselves,' import the parallel to lie in this, that as Christ died but once, and rose but once, so we are planted by baptism and regeneration (which work bears the resemblance of his death and resurrection, and whereof baptism is the sign) but only once.   And thus as, in Heb. ix., we heard the apostle saying, that Christ died ' but once,' so in Heb. x. 26 we read, that for that very reason it is, that ' those that have been illuminated, and made partakers of the Holy Ghost,' &c. (of whom you read in the 6th chapter of that epistle), that if they shall ' sin wilfully, after they have received the knowledge of the truth, there remaineth no more sacrifice for sin :' which is all one as to have said on Christ's part for us, ' for Christ died but once.'   And it is once, therefore answerably hereunto, there cannot be a new repetition of the work of regeneration, which they professed to have received at their baptism ; which that 6th chapter of the Hebrews, verse 6, had given a clearer explanation of ; that ' those who have been enlightened, and tasted of the good word of God, and have been partakers of the heavenly gift, &c., if they shall fall away, it is impossible to renew them again unto repentance.'

And why ?   But because as Christ died but once, so men are renewed but once.   And therefore those that hold total falling away from regeneration, must either hold no second regeneration for such, which is to put them into despair ; or they must say, that regeneration is often reiterated, and then that baptism, the sign of it, ought also to be repeated (even as the Lord's supper is), and then Christ's death reiterated also ; for these are parallels in the apostle's intention.

5. As the change wrought in regeneration is once for all, so the estate we are brought into thereby is an eternal estate, never to be changed. As Christ died once, and lives ever, and death hath no more dominion over him, likewise reckon yourselves. This second Adam, Christ, that came to restore us, being immutable, and his state unchangeable, such is the state and condition of the members of him, 1 Cor. xv. 45. And they are called Christ's fellows, Ps. xlv. 7, being made partakers of fellowship with him, in his death, and in the virtues and glories of his resurrection, Phil. iii. 10 ; and regeneration (whereof baptism is the sign), is their admission into that society. And they are admitted *in socios perpetuos*. ‘ In that they live, they live unto God ; and sin hath no more dominion over them.’

Now then, all this put together : 1. Regeneration changeth the state of a man ; 2. this alone doth it ; 3. once for all ; 4. brings him into a perpetual estate ; all this (I say) put together, argues the mercy transcendent. And further, by how much the misery of that estate *from which* may be greatened, or the privilege of that estate *into which* we are by regeneration brought, may be aggrandised (which is not my scope), by so much is the mercy of this new birth to be estimated by us.

6. This alone makes the specifical change. All other changes that follow are but gradual. I intend to make this branch distinct from the former, as to my purpose in hand (though I confess it may be made one branch, involved in the foregone), the change of a man's state of salvation is mainly a moral, legal, forensical change ; as that change which of a man condemned to die, unto a state of life ; or that of a servant, to a son (which out of Rom. vi. was instanced in) ; of an heir of hell, to be an heir of eternal life. And the greatest change of our estate lies in such privileges ; or, as John expresseth it, John i. 13, in giving us ‘ authority to be the sons of God.’ But over and above such as these, there is a physical change, which is more properly the impress of regeneration, which is a work in us. The other changes are the consequents or concomitants thereof ; and that is it that makes a specifical change, as all births, and generations, and corruptions are said to do. Other changes, by growings up in grace, are but gradual, from faith to faith, Rom. i. 17 ; from strength to strength, Ps. lxxxiv. 7 ; from glory to glory, 2 Cor. iii. 18. It is true, the substance of a man's nature, as a man, is one and the same afore and after. It is therefore called but ‘ putting off an old man, and putting on a new ;’ even as you cast off or put on another garment. And also that holiness, or the divine nature, is but a quality, which, as it is more worth than a man's soul devoid of it, so doth raise the soul into another kind or species of man, taking it together with that indwelling and information of the Holy Ghost, who dwells in that inner man, Eph. iii. 16, as another soul in our souls. Nay, the very body, the animal part, is said to be the temple of the Holy Ghost. And it is added, ‘ who is in you,’ in your souls, namely, by a nearer conjunction than in your bodies. John xiv. 17, ‘ He dwelleth with you, and shall be in you.’ And the conclusion of both is, that take this new creature, with this indwelling of the Holy Ghost in it, and the old man, with the inhabitation of Satan in him, and it makes, *analogicè*, a greater change in kind than if a beast were made a man, a clod of earth a star.

If the spiritual body and the natural body (of which the apostle speaks, 1 Cor. xv. 44), if the heavenly man, Christ, and those that appertain to him ; and the earthly man, Adam, and his earthly ones, ver. 47, 48, may by the apostle's arguings and comparisons (and so in his account and intentions) be said to differ, like the several species of creatures, which you reckon differing in kind, ver. 39. By these differing species, he sets out the difference of the natural and spiritual body, ver. 44, whenas that is but the change of qualities in them, which yet is said to make this vast difference. A vaster difference must needs hold much more in this transmutation of our souls we treat of. The one is natural, the other is spiritual. The persons are in the Scripture termed another generation of men. Peter distinguisheth those that are disobedient, 1st Epistle, chap. ii., ver. 8, and those born again, ver. 9, with a *but* of discrimination. ' *But* ye are a chosen generation.' Christ calls the other a generation of vipers. The psalmist says, ' These are the generation of them that seek thee.' And to the other a distinct generation is attributed by Christ, as in that speech, ' They are wiser in their generation than the children of light,' who are of another sort. And hence it comes to pass that the change made by the new birth is in Scripture expressed by such changes ; or, as the apostle's word is, Rom. xii. 2, by such a μεταμόρφωσις, ' Be transformed by the renewing of your minds.' It is a word which the poets used to express those changes which they feigned, from men to beasts, or beasts to men. The reality of which in this work might by many scriptures be made good, by shewing how the specifical properties of men's spirits are altered ; like as if a lion were made a lamb, and such like. And this change the new birth makes at first, and that alone, in wholly beginning that new kind, which was not before.

CHAPTER II.

The eminency of God's mercy in our regeneration evidenced from these considerations: that no motives from us can be supposed to incite God to do this for us ; that we do not so much as concur to the work, but are merely passive to it.—The uses of the doctrine.

Unto all that hath been said, this may be added further, that there can be supposed no motives inciting God to bestow this blessed change. It is not according to works of righteousness which we had done. In giving other mercies, after he hath begotten us, he may at least take occasion from something in us to move him ; as, to give perseverance, for he that hath begun a good work will perfect it : for *artifex amat opus ;* and he is faithful that hath begun it, to finish it. So to him that hath brought forth fruit already, he is therefore moved to purge him, that he may bring forth more fruit, John xv. 2. ' And to him that hath, shall be given,' as Mat. xxv., and often elsewhere. He crowns his own works in us with a farther increase. But before regeneration, there is neither any work of ours by us, nor work of his own in us, to move him. In giving glory, though he doth not bestow it *propter opera*, for our work, yet *secundum opera*, according to works. I speak as to degrees of glory ; so everywhere up and down in Scriptures. Only in this work of regeneration there is neither *propter* nor *secundum*. Even according to works is excluded. No *secundum*, but of his mercy. 'According to mercy' (so Paul). 'According to his abundant mercy' (so Peter) 'hath he renewed us.'

2. The lesser concurrence man himself may be supposed to have in any work done by God for us, the greater, the entirer is the mercy shewn in it, for then it is wholly God's. Now of all things, whatever may be supposed we can do for ourselves, we cannot beget ourselves; as not at first could we have created ourselves. Neither can any creature do this for us. So John i. 13, 'Who were born' (says the evangelist), 'not of blood, nor of flesh, nor of the will of man, but of God.' This birth goes not by blood. Neither that we are born of great parents, or of good. Therefore 'say not' (says Christ) 'you have Abraham to your father.' Nor is it of the will of the flesh, the power of man's corrupt will, who is born nothing but flesh. Water may as soon of itself attain the form of fire, as the will of the flesh, that is, the will as acted and informed by flesh, elevate itself, or be elevated (remaining flesh) into the least disposition or act of holiness. It is not in him that wills or runs, but in God that shews mercy. Nor is it in the will of man, nor of our parents or friends, that use all means to do us good; nor of the holiest, through their prayers or endeavours, to work it. Abraham would have had Ishmael, but God would not. No power or will of any creature whatsoever can regenerate us; but it is God who of his own will begetteth us, as it is James i. 18.

And the reason of this is founded upon this observation, which holds in nature, that the more noble the birth is, the more God hath a hand in it; and this being the most noble, and wholly divine and heavenly, therefore it is alone from God. Animals are only said to be begotten. Now beasts being more ignoble creatures, unto their begetting God concurs but by the ordinary way of providence, for they traduce both soul and body. But the birth of man, being of the most noble creature, God therefore reserves the main immediate stroke in it unto himself; and the parents having prepared the body through that *plastica et prolifica seminis vis*, God comes and infuses the soul. And therefore, Heb. xii. 9, he is called 'the Father of spirits,' and they but 'the parents of our bodies.' *Sol et homo generant hominem*, says the philosopher, that is, God and man do beget man. But in this new birth, because the most noble of all, God doth all, and all is to be ascribed to him: James i. 17, 'Every good gift and every perfect gift is from above, and cometh down from the Father of lights, with whom is no variableness, neither shadow of turning.' And then he instanceth in this of regeneration, 'Of his own will he begat us.' The coherence evidently argues this to be so noble and so perfect a work of God's, and of such a kind as is wholly heavenly and divine, and from him as the Father of lights. That as nothing but the sun itself, that is, the visible Father of lights, can cause a true genuine likeness or image of itself, whether in the eye or in a glass, or in a parhelion in the clouds, so none but God alone can and doth frame the true image of himself in the hearts of men. This rich and noble begetting us of his will is therefore wholly heavenly and from above; for it is a perfect birth, a good and perfect gift, and so entirely descended from above; whereas the works raised in the hearts of temporary believers are made up, partly through the influence of heaven, partly from self-love stirred up and excited thereby, and so are but imperfect gifts; like those creatures begotten by the sun warming and shining on mud, as frogs and other creeping things, whose form is raised and educed out of that corrupt matter the beams of the sun fell on.

I add, that take the substantials of it, we contribute nothing, but are merely passive. Therefore an infant is as capable of all the essentials of regeneration as a man grown up is ; and therefore of baptism. For what are the essentials of regeneration ?

1. Christ's apprehending us, ere we him, Phil. 3. Thus children are capable of being apprehended by Christ ; even as children in the womb are comprehended by the mother, though they hang, as the earth, in the middle, not laying hold on her.

2. The Holy Ghost shed down into the heart, as here in the text. This children are capable of, for John Baptist was 'filled with the Holy Ghost from the womb,' Luke i. 15.

3. The new creature, in all the principles of it, the habits of holiness wrought, the workmanship (as it is called) which children are also as capable of ; for as they are capable of all the evil dispositions of sin, and inclinations to it, so of holiness ; yea, and therefore of sin now, because once of holiness. So as in receiving all these, a man may be wholly passive ; and yet these are the substantials. All that follow are but the actings, by the Spirit, of that new creature in us, and our apprehending that for which we are comprehended (as the apostle speaks) ; yea and it is as certain that ere any man can be born of Christ, he must be apprehended of Christ ; and ere he have spirit or divine nature begotten in him, he must have the Spirit come upon him ; as also ere he can put forth the least act of holiness, he must have the principle of holiness ; as no man that hath not a principle of life can stir a finger, or that hath not an eye can see. So then, in receiving all these a man of riper years is passive, and the receiving of all depends upon no foregoing actings of his. ' Turn me' (say they in the prophet) ' and I shall be turned,' Jer. xxxi. 18. Whereas afterwards *acti agimus* : Rom. viii. 13, ' We by the Spirit do mortify the deeds of the flesh.' Not the Spirit alone, but we by the Spirit, who in our prayers is said to ' help our infirmities,' ver. 26. And therefore they are said to be our prayers, as well as the Spirit's in us. When the lamp is once lighted, put oil to it and it burns, but who shall light it ? When the wheel is made round, an easy touch sets it a-going ; but who shall round it ? In this therefore we are merely passives ; though when thus turned, we also turn to God, Jer. xxxi. 18.

Even of all the good works we are enabled afterwards to do, this is the womb, the foundation ; so as without this one work first begun in thee, no work thou doest or canst do, hath the name of good ; even as all evil thoughts and lusts in the heart proceed from that corrupt nature we had at our birth. That is the mother of all abominations, which David in his confession, Ps. li., had recourse unto. So is this seed of God, the divine nature at first put into us, the seed abiding, whence all that is good and acceptable springeth. They are all fruits of the Spirit, as the other of the flesh, Gal. v. All the good we bear is from the root. First (says Christ) make the tree good. In some trades there is required frames of workmanship to be set up, or cast, ere they can work ; as to a printer, a press ; to him that will cast letters, a matrix (as they call it) ; to a weaver, a loom ; to a smith, a forge ; to a goldsmith, &c., moulds to cast metals in, from whence they receive their fashion. And the whole actings in their callings afterwards do depend on such workmanships and fabrics at first erected. Now so is it here, as in two places to follow these metaphors the apostle holds forth. The one Eph. ii. 10, ' Ye are his workmanship, created to good works.' A new workmanship must be created ere any good work will be effected. The other text is Rom. vi. 17, ' You have obeyed from the heart that form, mould, or pattern of doctrine ye were delivered into, τύπον εἰς ὃν παρεδόθητε. The word of God he compares both to a pattern or sampler of obedience, and to a mould or matrix which their hearts were first cast in themselves, that so they might become a meet, fitted, and prepared womb, in which and from which all obedience might receive its formation and shape, and there be cast. Now you know that such as the mould is, such are the things cast therein ; if they be misshapen, then are all the metals cast therein spoiled, as in some wombs the formation of children also is. Thou mayest perform works of all sorts that are good ; but let me tell thee, unless thou hast thine own heart first made a new workmanship, a workmanship created and forged by the Spirit anew, as a principle thereunto, thou spoilest all in the doing, thou marrest all in the making. This for the reasons of this point.

Use 1. Let the saints bless God in a more special manner for this work of conversion and regeneration wrought in them. Study the riches of that mercy which have been shewn in it. Put this eminently and usually into that catalogue of mercies which thou givest thanks to God for. Two things are not reminded enough by us, our first birth-sin, to humble us in our confessions ; our first birth-mercy to make us thankful ; wherein abundance of mercy is shewn, there God looks for abundance of thanksgiving. Many years after Peter remembers it, to bless God for it, and stirs up them to it, and puts himself into the number ; ' who hath begotten us.' So Paul also speaks (who delights and takes often occasion to tell that story), ' To the King immortal,' &c., 1 Tim. i. The links of that chain, ' Whom he hath predestinated, them he hath called ; them he hath justified ; them he hath glorified,' we should always wear about our hearts, to oblige us to thankfulness and obedience. Kings usually owe more to their births, in which they were mere passives, than to all their after achievements. Kings are therefore wont to celebrate their births. At the beginning and the laying the first foundation of God's great works of wonder, the angels are still brought in singing and rejoicing ; at the foundation of the earth, Job xxxviii. 7, ' When the morning stars sang together, and all the sons of God shouted for joy.' So at the birth of Christ, an heavenly host, a multitude sang. We read not so at his resurrection. Again, at the conversion of a sinner, there is joy amongst all the angels. Heaven rings of it that a new heir, a new prince, is born. And besides the substance of the mercy itself, if thou canst find out any peculiarity of mercies that environ it in the circumstances of it, consider them, and bless God for them, this work being one of the greatest acts that ever God did about thee, or towards thee. God sometimes plots to set forth the mercy of it, to make his hand and love in it the more eminent and remarkable. Christ's birth was accompanied with a star, which made it observed by the wise men ; and all Jerusalem was troubled at it. And as our late chronologers undertake, it fell out in the four thousandth year of the world, as the finishing the temple, his type, in the three thousandth ; and also at a time of general and universal peace. Some circumstances or other, perhaps, thou mayest discern in thy new birth, if thou hast had the advantage to discern the time or occasion of it. I shall mention some that are not merely circumstantial ; whereof, though some one may be different from the other, yet in their variety they have some peculiarity of mercies.

1. The longer thou didst live before God turned thee, and yet did it, and the more sinful thou wert, this in one respect wonderfully heightens the mercy of it. Christ encountered Paul as a man would do an enemy in the

open field, unhorsed him in full career, when his heart was more than ever set to mischief, and near the place of doing it.

2. On the contrary, the sooner God turned thee, if in thy youth, this was mercy to thee, for God had thy virginity, ' thy first love,' before lovers had bruised thy breasts. ' I remember' (says God) ' the kindness of thy youth, when thou wentest after me in the wilderness,' Jer. ii. 2. Paul in this respect complains of it as a disadvantage to him, that he was ' born out of time,' 1 Cor. xv. 8, and like a truant had been put to this school or academy long after other apostles, who had the start of him. He seems to mention it with a little holy envy at the honour others had before him, ' who were' (says he) ' afore me in Christ,' Rom. xvi. 7, and thereby were elder disciples than himself.

3. If God at thy conversion gives thee a greater stock and measure of grace, brings thee forth in a fuller stature in Christ the first day, herein is great mercy shewn. Thus Paul was recompensed. He was born a strong man the first hour, insomuch as being the chief of the apostles added nothing to him in experience or knowledge, Gal. ii. Many are born weaklings in comparison, and are long a-growing up to what thou perhaps at first receivedst.

4. If when God began to work it he did effect it speedily, in this he was kind to thee,—Hos. xiii. 13, ' Ephraim is an unwise son, he stayed long in the place of the breaking forth of children,'—if as Matthew, we come at the first call The rude and barbarous jailor had quick despatch. He came in trembling at midnight to Paul, and was converted with joy before break of day, yea, the same hour, Acts xvi. 25–34. The Philippians, the first day they heard it, Phil. i. 5. If as Paul, immediately thou conferrest not with flesh and blood, Gal. i. 16. If as soon as God called thou heardst, and wert not rebellious, but openedst thine ear, this is an effect of God's peculiar love to thee.

5. If God put thee to less trouble and horror, brought thee forth with less pains, in this his mercy appears. Some souls have very hard labour. Paul lay but three days, and Christ from heaven pities him, and sends Ananias to him. The stone in some men's hearts God dissolves, when others are cut for it, and lie roaring night and day. Lydia's heart was gently opened, and by faith closed up again (as Adam's was for Eve) ere she was aware. Though sometimes it falls out, the lesser fine, the more there is in rent after, in greater temptations.

6. Greater mercy is displayed to thee if God came in then with much joy, whenas he deals so roughly with others, as Joseph did with his brethren; but no sooner thou hadst begun to confess and open thy mouth to speak to him for his love, but he fell on thy neck and kissed thee, yea, came and kissed thee sleeping, and with joys first awakened thee; and instead of shewing thee the rack, the dungeon, the everlasting chains of wrath, and shutting thee up under the law, he had thee down into his wine cellar, and brought thee to a banquet. The Thessalonians were thus dealt with : 1 Thes. i. 6, ' Ye became followers of the Lord, having received the word with joy in the Holy Ghost,' &c. In a thousand of these varieties doth he deal with souls, and playeth with us in his wooings, that his ways should be past finding out. And if all the stories of souls converted in this as well as in the primitive times were written, you would admire Christ for nothing more than his art of love, and the variety of his artifices in wooing, and his manifold wisdom in contriving mercies in conversions.

7. The more exemplary our conversion was, the more peculiar was the

mercy shewn in it.   And such was that of those fore-named Thessalonians:
1 Thes. i. 7, 8, 'Ye were ensamples to all that believe, and in every place
your faith to God-ward was spread abroad.'   Such likewise was that of the
Romans, Rom. i. 8; and of the Ephesians, so Eph. ii. 7.   And thus
Paul also speaks of his conversion : that he was 'a pattern of mercy to
them that should afterward believe.'   And thus much shall serve to shew
the greatness of this work, from the abundance of mercy that God shews
forth in it.

Use 2. You that have received this mercy from God, shew mercy to
others ; if in anything, in endeavours what in you lies to beget men to God.
Though God alone doth it, yet he useth means ; though means contribute
nothing, yet God useth them, as the clay to open the eyes.   Hast thou a
chamber-fellow, a pupil, a friend, a brother still in their natural state ?
Oh, if thou hast received mercy from God, endeavour to bring them in to
obtain like mercy with thyself !   'On some have compassion, save them
with fear, pulling them out of the fire,' Jude 22, 23, with fear lest they
should die ere converted, snatching them with all violence   Can you endure
to see men burn ?   Hear what James also says in his last words : 'If any
of you do err from the truth, and one convert him, let him know, that he
which converteth the sinner from the error of his way shall save a soul
from death, and shall hide a multitude of sins.'   Let him know ; he
speaks of it as a matter of such high worth and moment as few consider
the worth, the greatness of such a work.   'Let him know he saves a soul
from death,' and whom would not that move ?   And it is a means of forgiving innumerable sins.   Who, with speaking a word, would not get a man
in debt for thousands freed ?   A man that converts another (though he contribute so little that God doth all), yet the person converted owes himself
to him, Phil. i. 9.   Oh, what do we then owe to Christ ?   And we have
nothing but ourselves to give to him.

Use 3. Despise not the ministry nor work of it.   It is to convert souls,
and therefore it is the best calling in the world : 1 Tim. i. 12, 'And I
thank Jesus our Lord, who hath enabled me, for that he counted me faithful, putting me into the ministry ;' the despised ministry, that few of you
now-a-days will be of that calling.   The wares it deals in is souls, men and
their salvation : 1 Tim. iv. 16, 'Thou shalt save thyself, and them that
hear thee.'   He could not give a greater motive unto any work.   God had
but one Son, and he made him a minister : Rom. xv. 8, 'Christ was a
minister of the circumcision for the truth of God,' which he preached
among the Jews, through all their cities.   One of his royal titles is, 'a
bishop of souls,' 1 Pet. ii. 25 ; only he is the chief, the arch-bishop, 1 Pet.
v. 4, and we under-shepherds.

Use 4. Lastly, What is then the glory of the church, and so should be
of universities ?   Even this, that multitudes of converts are born again
therein, and they filled with such.   In the 87th Psalm, 3–6, the psalmist
enters into a comparison, in this very respect, of the surpassing glory of
Sion and Jerusalem, the mother of us all, above all those nations and cities
that were then renowned in the world, as Babylon, Tyre, Egypt, &c., who
boasted of those worthies and heroes that they had brought forth and been
the mothers of, their Belus. Trismegistus.   'Glorious things' (says he) 'are
spoken of thee, O city of God,' and far more glorious than all the nations.
'I will make mention of Rahab and Babylon to them that know me : behold
Philistia, and Tyre, with Ethiopia ; this man was born there.'   Among
their familiars they used to boast and brag of their brave and gallant men

as born among them. ' But of Sion it shall be said, This and that man was born in her.' If he had intended to vie and compare Sion with Babylon and Egypt, in respect of an outward birth and nobleness in that respect, or for worldly excellencies, that make men renowned, they might have excelled Sion, at least equalled her sons in that respect. But Sion, considered here as the city of God, her glory spiritual, her children here spoken of born of the Spirit, and she a spiritual mother of them (as, Gal. iv. 25–29, the apostle speaks), and so their birth answerable and suitable to the dignity of the mother, that she brought forth every day multitudes of saints and regenerate men, children and citizens of that Jerusalem and Sion that is above, the mother of us ; her glory in God's account was ten thousand times greater than what the flower of all other nations could pretend to. And therefore he adds that God, when he makes up his catalogue of those whom he accounts of, should pass by all theirs, and leave them out, and set them only that were regenerate and born in Sion, as the only excellent ones of the earth. As it follows, ' The Lord himself shall establish her' (as having such a royal generation for her race and progeny), ' the Lord shall write, when he counts up the people, that this man was born there.' All which the apostle alludes to, speaking of this heavenly city and her children : ' Ye are come to mount Sion, the city of the living God, the heavenly Jerusalem, the first-born which are written in heaven,' Heb. xii. 22, 23. And this was Sion's glory and establishment then : Ps. cxxvii., ' As arrows in the hand of a mighty man, such were the children of her youth' as these. O that such may be yours ! And whilst former times have boasted they have sent forth out of such a college so many bishops, deans, &c., or famous writers, men of such and such learning and renown, the memory of whom you continue in your windows, let the glory which you affect be, that such and such a man was born again here ; and blessed are the colleges that have their quiver full of them, as the psalmist there goes on. And these shall more speak for you, with your enemies in the gate, than all other arguments. ' Yea, God himself will establish you,' and these that cry, Down with her, down with her, shall not dare to attempt it, much less to effect it.

CHAPTER III.

The eminent mercy of God in our regeneration appears, inasmuch as all three persons concur in it, though it be attributed, efficiently, more eminently to the Holy Ghost.

I shall farther demonstrate this truth from the solemnity that is in heaven at the effecting of this work of regeneration, in a set distinct concurrence and appearance of all three persons, Father, Son, and Holy Ghost therein ; which will yet further shew the greatness of divine mercy in this work.

This great and happy conjunction appears in Titus iii. 4–6 : ' But after that the kindness and love of God our Saviour towards man appeared, not by works of righteousness which we have done, but according to his mercy he saved us, by the washing of regeneration, and renewing of the Holy Ghost ; which he shed on us abundantly through Jesus Christ our Saviour.' There is a distinct and conspicuous appearance of these three. The word used in the text is ἐπεφάνη, ' After that the love and kindness of God *appeared.*' When our Lord and Saviour was born, it is said his star appeared, Mat. ii. 7. The same word is used; and the remembrance thereof, the church called ἐπιφανία, the *Epiphany* unto this day. But here is a greater Epiphany than that was, an appearance, not of one star, but of three, the three persons; not a constellation, but a great conjunction in the heaven of heavens.

1. There is the Father, who in the 4th verse is called ' God our Saviour,' as a distinct person from Christ, who is also called ' our Saviour,' ver. 6. And of the Father it must be meant that it is said, that ' He hath saved us,' and that ' He hath shed on us the Holy Ghost, through Christ our Saviour :' the Father is spoken of as distinct from those two.

2. There is the Holy Ghost's appearance, who is said to be ' richly,' or ' abundantly shed,' which in those times often was visible: Peter and the rest having received the Holy Ghost, he doth appear to the senses of the standers by: Acts ii. 33, ' He hath shed forth this' (namely, the Holy Ghost, mentioned and spoken of in the very words afore) ' which we see and hear.' ، Your senses may inform and convince you; it was so evident an appearance, both in the shapes of tongues, as also in the gifts and graces on a sudden poured forth upon illiterate and sinful men. The same appearance of the Holy Ghost you have in Cornelius, Acts x. 44, which was conspicuous to standers by; that it is said, ver. 45, ' They of the circumcision were astonished, because on the Gentiles also was poured out the gift of the Holy Ghost. For they heard them speak with tongues, and glorify God,' ver. 46.

And 3. Here is Christ's concurrence also: ' which he shed on us through Christ,' says the text. For upon the preaching of Christ, and upon mentioning of his name, did the Holy Ghost fall upon men. Peter preaching Christ, and peace by him (Acts x., ver. 36 to ver. 44), when he had centred his discourse in ver. 43, ' That to this Christ all the prophets gave witness, that through his name whosoever believeth in him shall receive remission of sins,' the next words tell us, ' That whilst Peter yet spake these words, the Holy Ghost fell on all them which heard the word.' The Holy Ghost took that very cue (as we say) to come in and enter upon the stage; that is, then to fall down on all that heard the word; thereby witnessing, that as remission of sins was through his name only, so that the Holy Ghost, to work faith in his name, was poured forth, through his name also. As the same Peter had before in that Acts ii. 33, informed his hearers, that ' Christ, being exalted at the right hand of God, having received of the Father the promise of the Holy Ghost, hath shed forth this.'

For explication of this. It is true there is a joint concurrence of all three persons in every action that is done; for *opera Trinitatis ad extra sunt indivisa.* But then of such lesser works and appearances of God, you read the mention of their concurrence but singly in several and scattered places of Scriptures. So it is scatteredly attributed to the Father to create, and to the Word, and to the Spirit. But where and when in any work you find at once and together all three appear, all mentioned in a chapter, as here in the text for regeneration, that work is ever some eminent work, and hath a *not only* upon it, a solemnity in it. Yea, and thereby is signified, that over and above their ordinary and common influence, they have a special, distinct, and extraordinary hand and operation. As God's presence was ordinarily in the pillar of fire, and the cloud in the wilderness; but if the glory of God at any time appeared over and above upon the tabernacle, then some great thing was in hand, either of judgment or mercy. Perhaps many other instances might be brought, wherein these three great persons are together brought in as met in the like near conjunction. I shall instance but in two, the greatest of all other, and but in these because they hold some parallel with the work of our regeneration, and are patterns of it. They both of them appertain to our Lord Christ our head, to whose image we are ordained to be conformed, and so will serve to illustrate the like done towards us in this regenerating of us.

1. What was the greatest work of wonder that ever God did in the world ? It was the incarnation of the Son of God : Jer. xxxi. 22, ' God hath created ' (says the prophet, speaking of it) ' a new thing in the earth,' viz., that a woman should encompass in her womb that Gheber, that strong and giant-like man, Christ, God and man, without the help of man.

Now at the instant time and moment when this was to be done, there was a manifestation and declaration of all three persons in it. A record is extant how all, though invisibly, concurred in it, not darkly, with an *us* in general words, as at the creation, ' Let *us* make man,' but clearly and distinctly. And as at the transfiguration of Christ (which Peter maketh the solemnest and most glorious manifestation of God that ever he had been an eye and ear-witness of, 2 Peter i. 16, 17) you find, to grace the solemnity of it, Moses, Christ, and Elias talking and conferring together ; so here, there is the very conference recorded. A set and solemn conference it was in heaven, and the words spoken set down at the instant of Christ's conception ; the Father declaring his decree about it to the Son, and the Son speaking to the Father of his willingness to it. Paul hath recorded and set down the very words as a great secret, as it must be accounted : Heb. x. 5, ' When he comes into the world he says ;' it is the Son of God he speaks of, as existing afore he took man's nature ; and the words that follow, spoken by him, are expressly said to be at the time, instant, or moment of his coming into the world, and his being made flesh when he came into the world, as prophesied of by David ; and Paul affirms he then did utter them. This his taking flesh was a going forth from his Father (as himself styles it in John), the setting out upon the greatest adventure and design that ever was. And therefore Christ, at the time of his first setting forth, thought fit to speak something about it, as a distinct person from his Father, as he that should be interested in it (for none was to be made a sacrifice but he), to let him know upon what ground it was he undertook it, merely in obedience to his will. The like he did when he suffered : ' Not my will, but thine be done,' which was his motto from first to last. ' Sacrifice and offering thou' (as speaking to his Father) ' wouldest not, but a body hast thou prepared me.'

Now as Christ is thus expressly introduced, so it is to be noticed that his Father had given the occasion, having first declared to him and revived the remembrance of his everlasting decrees and prophecies about it. For the speech of Christ, ver. 7, ' Then said I, Lo I come to do thy will,' is evidently in answer to another speech first uttered and declared to him by his Father, which he repeats, ver. 6, ' When in burnt offerings and sacrifices for sins, thou,' O Father, ' hadst had no pleasure, then or thereupon said I, Lo, I come ;' reviewing* also the memory of God's decree, and an old record about it : ' In the volume of the book it is written of me to do thy will, O God.' God the Father hath declared his will, both *viva voce, et scriptis ;* and the Son his, and the Holy Ghost, the secretary of heaven, is brought

* Qu. ' reviving ' ?—ED

in as a recorder of all this : ver. 15, ' Whereof the Holy Ghost is a witness.' That word *also* bids us take in this allegation of Christ's speech, as that which is referred to, as well as to that quotation which followed. And he was in a peculiar manner in this, for none else could have told it as uttered at that very time but he.

And for this Christ hath expressly told us, that as he and his Father do confer together about the great transactions of man's salvation, so that the Spirit hears all that passeth, John xvi. 13. Nor yet did he stand by as a bare witness to relate it and confirm it to us, but was sent down by both as a principal actor, that had the great and ultimate hand in effecting, of it.

The Son of God speaks of a body prepared by the Father for him to take up : ' A body hast thou prepared me.' The Father had a hand in it then, but by whom ? By the Holy Ghost ; so expressly, Luke i. 35, ' The Holy Ghost shall come upon thee, and the power of the Highest shall overshadow thee : therefore shall that holy thing that shall be born of thee be called the Son of God.' Here is, then, if not a visible Θεοφανία, as our divines call that at his baptism, yet an evident record of an invisible and distinct conjunction of all three persons at the instant of Christ's conception, bearing their parts in it.

1. The Father declaring it as his will, both to the Son and the Spirit.

2. The Holy Ghost, as the person sent by the Father, to perform and fashion that body in Mary's womb ; this tabernacle being of another building, which God pitched, and not man, Heb. ix. 11 and viii. 2.

And 3. The Son, as the person that owns and assumes that body so prepared for him to dwell in it, as in a tabernacle, as the author to the Hebrews terms it : ' Lo I come ' into the world ; which was only done by his taking that body to himself, into one person with him.

And this great and eminent concurrence of all three may perhaps more clearly be gathered from the story of the angel's coming to Mary, Luke i. 26, 27, &c.

1. God the Father sent his angel. ' The angel Gabriel was sent from God unto a city of Galilee, named Nazareth, to a virgin espoused to a man whose name was Joseph, of the house of David ; and the virgin's name was Mary.' God the Father gave his angel his commission, and a particular note of all the circumstances, as punctually as any one that sends a messenger of an errand. God sent him to a city of Galilee, and by name Nazareth, to a virgin espoused, and her husband's name is in the note ; a man whose name is Joseph, and his lineage of the house of David. You see God the Father was deeply in it.

2. The Holy Ghost, he was sent, as was observed, ver. 35, ' The Holy Ghost shall come upon thee.'

3. God the Son must needs be supposed most in it of all three. For by virtue of his assuming unto one person that holy thing which was conceived in her, it was, that, ver. 32, ' He was called the Son of the Highest.' And if he had not actually assumed, married into one person with himself, that which was formed in her womb by the Holy Ghost, it had not been called the Son of God, as ver. 35 it is. He it was who put on and wore, and married this flesh made of a woman, and therefore his consent was of all other most explicit.

And thus began the New Testament (as became it) with the discovery of the three persons in that great work, at which the era of the New Testament itself began. And this so distinct a discovery of the three at the incarnation, being thus express and eminent, hath not been enough noticed

by our divines, nor added, in handling this argument, unto those other at
Christ's baptism and transfiguration. How this at Christ's conception, and
that happy contract, and espousal, and union made between the human
and divine nature, will conduce to illustrate the like at our regeneration, I
shall shew when I have added another conjunction, more famous, because
more visible, namely, at Christ's baptism, where usually our divines begin
the discovery of the three out of the New Testament. And this I shall also
speak (though more briefly) unto, because both these put together will
have their joint virtual influence of tending to clear the point in hand.

The meeting of the three persons at his conception was invisible, for the
formation and union of his human nature was, as ours, ' in the lower parts
of the earth,' hidden and under ground, as the psalmist speaks. And unto
which, speaking of Christ's formation in the womb of a virgin, the apostle
alludes, Eph. iv. 9. But what was as then uttered and transacted between
the three persons in secret, was at his baptism to be proclaimed upon the
house-top. It was the public owning, inauguration, and instalment of the
Son of God. It was the solemnisation of that marriage between the two
natures, human and divine, which had been carried more privately, yet by
all the same three witnesses. And accordingly, God took a time for this,
when all the people were baptized and standing by (so Luke iii. 21, Mat.
iii. 5), who had come out of Jerusalem, and all Judea, and the region about
Jordan, when they were all thus standing by. ' And Jesus was baptized,
and praying,' ver. 21, ' heaven opened,' which is the greatest outward
miracle in the heavens, as an earthquake, or opening of the earth, is on the
earth. And heaven opened to let down the revelation of the greatest mystery, which only could be *cœlitus*, or from heaven revealed. A light comes
down from the throne of God, and all three persons make an outward
manifestation of themselves. *Pater in voce, Filius in homine, Spiritus Sanctus
in columba.** And what is the business they appear about ? But to own
their former act and work. To proclaim that Christ. They had met to
make the Christ at his conception, now they meet openly to proclaim him
to be the Messiah and Son of God ; yea, and to seal up and give testimony to the human nature itself (who had lived thirty years without any
such extraordinary revelation) that he was indeed the Son of God ; that
this holy thing born of that virgin was the Son of the most high God, as
the angel told Mary. And unto both these testimonies and transactions
of God the Father, Son, and Holy Ghost, both at his conception and baptism, doth that triple testimony of the three in heaven refer, mentioned
by John the apostle, 1 John v. 5, 7, even to this, that Christ is the Son
of God.

But have I told this long story merely to this general purpose, to shew
that in God's greatest works of wonder there is a distinct appearance of the
three ? or withal, to add a new instance of the Θεοφανία of the three, and
indeed the first mentioned in the New Testament, and upon the greatest
occasion ? No ; not to these ends only or chiefly have I told this story, as
singly to be considered ; but further, as more particularly conjunct with
the thing in hand, as parallel withal, though transcending this of our new
birth, and first conception of the new creature in us, or that other work, the
manifestation of it at the sealing of salvation, or the revealing of Christ in
us (as it is called, Gal. i. 16), the forming the new creature for Christ and
the three persons to dwell therein.

There is nothing in Christ, or of Christ, but it is set up as an image or

* August., Tract 6, in Johan.

pattern of the like to be done to us in our measure, 'being predestinated to be conformed to the image of his Son,' Rom. viii.   As he was circumcised, so we have a circumcision ordained for us, Col. ii.   We have a crucifying, burial, resurrection, as he had; we have a conception, a forming Christ in us, an uniting us to Christ.   As in him there was the union of two natures, there is a time wherein we are made adopted sons, as well as there was a time in which he was born the natural Son.   I might quote scriptures for all these, but you know them.   In the 4th of the Galatians, the 4th and 6th verses compared, the apostle seems to institute a parallel between God ' sending forth his Son, made of a woman,' and his sending forth (for he useth that word of both in common) ' the Spirit of his Son into our hearts, crying, Abba, Father ; ' ' But when the fulness of time was come, God sent forth his Son, made of a woman, made under the law. And because ye are sons, God hath sent forth the Spirit of his Son into your hearts, crying, Abba, Father ; ' thus clearly paralleling the conception of the human nature and union with the natural Son of God, and our being made adopted sons by the coming of the Holy Ghost into our hearts. Observe the parallel in this respect by comparing scriptures.

1. As there was a fulness of time, an instant of time, when the Son of God was to be made flesh, and so be admitted a member of this world, so there is a fulness of time, a set time to send down his Spirit into the heart to regenerate it.   Gal. i. 15, 16, ' But when it pleased God to reveal his Son in me ' (says Paul).   God let me run on much of my time, of which he speaks ver. 13, 14; but having chosen me before, and separated me from the womb, he had a set time when to reveal his Son in me.

2. When that set time is come, set by the Father, of whom Paul there speaks, the Father begins and sets all a-work in the conversion of that soul.   This Christ expresseth in the 6th of John, where Christ, giving the reason why some souls come to him and not others, he resolves it into his Father's act and will, as the main (verses 64, 65, which is the conclusion of his discourse about it), ' But there are some of you that believe not. For Jesus knew from the beginning who they were that believed not, and who should betray him.   And he said, Therefore said I unto you, that no man can come unto me, except it were given unto him of my Father.' Now he attributes to his Father a double hand or stroke in it, one towards the soul itself, the other unto Christ himself, that is to be married now to it.

(1.) There is God the Father's actual drawing the soul to Christ, a whispering to the heart to persuade it to take his Son; himself secretly woos the heart for him, ver. 44, 45, ' No man can come unto me, except the Father, which hath sent me, draw him : and I will raise him up at the last day.   It is written in the prophets, And they shall be taught of God. Every man therefore that hath heard, and hath learned of the Father, cometh unto me.'   Of this you read, Psa. xlv., what kind of words he speaks, and what counsel he gives a soul that is brought to Christ; as ver. 14, ' Hearken, O daughter, and give ear,' even as he had spoken to his Son to make himself a sacrifice.

(2.) As he thus actually draws the soul to Christ (and the Father is at that work, and at the cord's end), so he actually gives the soul unto Christ, that Christ would both take the soul and own it when it cometh to him. Thus, ver. 37, ' All my Father giveth me shall come to me ; and him that cometh to me I will in no wise cast out.'   And he speaks this as the reason why some believe and some not, though they hear the same sermon, and have the same means. So ver. 36, 'But I said unto you, That ye also have seen me, and believe not.' Now, Christ giving these as reasons why some came and some not, and why he receives those that come because the Father draws, and the Father gives, speaks of both as of two like acts of the Father done by him at conversion ; then it is the Father thus gives, and the Father thus draws. And though God had given them to the Son of God from everlasting (as John xvii., ' Thine they were, and thou gavest them me'), yet now he renews that act of giving them to Christ. Therefore, *de præsenti*, Christ useth the present tense : ' All that the Father *gives* me ; ' it is a giving *de præsenti*, as a drawing *de præsenti*, to distinguish it from that from everlasting. And so as Christ resolved it into his Father's will, Heb. 10 (as you heard), why he came into the world at all, so, ver. 38, he resolves the reason why he owns and receives them that come to him unto his Father's will in like manner. ' For I came down from heaven, not to do my own will, but the will of him that sent me.' And this gift or donation is as if then and at that time the Father should rise up in heaven and say to his Son, ' Yonder is a soul which I gave thee from everlasting, whom thou diedst for upon the cross ; and now is the fulness of time written in my book, the set time appointed by me to have mercy on him, for him to come unto thee ; now take him for thine, take hold of him, and draw him to thyself,' and so joins with Christ in drawing him. This is the Father's work in regenerating us.

2. The Son's work is as follows :—

(1.) Of himself he says, John x. 14, 15, ' I am the good shepherd, and know my sheep, and am known of mine. As the Father knoweth me, even so know I the Father : and I lay down my life for the sheep.' He knows them particularly and personally, as they know him, even by name. And as he loves us, ere we love him, so he knows us ere we can know him ; yea, look, as distinctly as the Father knows him, and he knows the Father, even so distinctly doth he know and take notice of all his sheep, and this when he is to bring them to himself, as ver. 16.

(2.) At that time he first takes and apprehends that soul as his, and to be his for ever, in answer to that gift of his Father then made, Philip. iii. 12, ' I follow after, if that I may apprehend that for which also I am apprehended of Christ Jesus.' He speaks of that act put forth by Christ in apprehending him first, ere he did him, which is the fundamental act of union. As Christ loves first, so he apprehends first. And as he had compared before his Christian life to a race which he was to run, so here he tells us how Christ took him first by the hand, and held him when he first entered into that race. However, he means it of that act of Christ's at his first conversion, which is the foundation of all that we afterward pursue after. And herein you see the parallel runs on as at Christ's conception ; as then the Son of God his work was to take to that body fitted for him (Heb. ii. 16, ' He took not to,' or ' he took not hold of angels, but the seed of Abraham'), so us at our conversion, and thus works the union.

3. The Spirit's work hath been discoursed of before. I shall now only mention that text in Gal. iv. 6, ' Because ye are sons' (namely, by election), ' God hath sent forth the Spirit of his Son into your hearts, crying, Abba, Father.' And this Spirit works faith in us, which is hands, and feet, and all. It is seminally the whole new creature ; hands to lay hold on Christ again, and we embrace him, Heb. xi., and embrace him gladly, Acts ii. 41.

4. As all three persons thus between and among themselves deal secretly, and treat with each other for us, the Father giving and recommending, the

Son apprehending, both sending the Holy Ghost into the heart ; so in our coming to God, both first and last, we have our pass from one person to the other, and have distinctly to deal with them all; which is contained in one verse, Eph. ii. 18, ' For through him we both have access by one Spirit unto the Father.' And this is more open and more sensible to us, as the other more secret. The word in the original is προσαγωγὴν. The Spirit, being come into the heart, leads us by the hand back again to Christ ; and Christ leads us to the Father.

I will give you but one instance of one conversion, which I have had recourse to hitherto all along, and which is Paul's, who professeth himself converted, as for the substance of it, εἰς τύπον, for a pattern, 1 Tim. i. 16. And though his story hath this extraordinary in it, that Christ visibly apprehended him, and the Holy Ghost fell on him in laying on of hands upon him, yet for substance the same things are done in heaven for us by the three, who love us as they loved him. Even as at Christ's baptism all three appeared, but at ours not, yet we are baptized in the name of all the three. In the substance of salvation, conversion, faith, &c., the apostles had not any privilege that we have not.

1. The Father's good pleasure appeared in Paul's conversion, as you have it expressed, Gal. i. 15, 16, ' When it pleased God, who separated me from the womb, to reveal his Son in me.'

2. Of Jesus Christ you may read twice in the Acts, chapter ix., from the 6th verse, and chapter xxvi., how Christ bestirred himself at his conversion. He meets him in the way, at the place and time appointed. And himself speaks to him, ver. 5, 6, ' And he said, Who art thou, Lord ? And the Lord said, I am Jesus whom thou persecutest : it is hard for thee to kick against the pricks. And he trembling and astonished said, Lord, what wilt thou have me to do ? And the Lord said unto him, Arise, and go into the city, and it shall be told thee what thou shalt do.' And Christ directed him what to do. And not only so, but speaks himself to Ananias : ver. 11, ' And the Lord said unto him, Arise, and go into the street which is called Straight, and inquire in the house of Judas for one called Saul of Tarsus : for, behold, he prayeth.' You see he gives as particular directions as God the Father did to the angel, when he sent him about the conception of his Son. It is to shew what notice he takes of all the circumstances of a soul's conversion. No kind husband could more bestir himself at his wife's labour, than Christ did at Paul's travail in the new birth. He calls up Ananias at midnight, as it were, bids him go in all haste to help him : ' Behold' (says he), ' he prays,' ver. 11 ; he is in his throes.

3. The Holy Ghost (ver. 17, 18) wholly falls upon him, and this at his laying on of hands, and his being baptized.

Use. You that are regenerate, and born again, the saints and children of God, shall I affect your hearts a little ? Whom would not this love move ? There was a time, though perhaps thou knowest it not, when all this ado was in heaven about thee, unknown to thee, when thou wert first married unto Christ, the greatest espousal that ever was transacted, one alone excepted, and that was when the human nature and divine were espoused together in Christ. And the same kind of stir that was for Paul was also for thee ; what was done extraordinarily and visibly by him, was as effectually and strongly carried on and done for thee. He was directed by Christ what to do, and Ananias directed to go to him, and his condition made known to him, that he might know what to speak unto him. Now the same hand did secretly guide and direct thee ; perhaps to go to such a congregation which thou hadst no mind unto, or for fashion-sake frequent-edest ; or thou fellest into such or such a company, of such or such persons, who spake so or so unto thee ; or such and such an accident befell thee as thou wert going such or such a journey ; as Saul, in seeking his father's asses, was met by Samuel in the way, and he is anointed unto a kingdom ; and so wert thou taken in the heat of the pursuit of vanities. And as his secret providence directed thee, so perhaps the minister or person that spake unto thee when thou wert first drawn to believe or close with Christ, had such a word put by God into his mouth, as if he had known thy very heart and condition, such promises as most nearly concerned and suited thy spirit, and condition, and temptations ; even as he directed Ananias to speak to Paul what most concerned him. And when by this invisible con-duct he had brought thy heart and his word together, he then shed forth his Spirit upon thee, who made that good word effectual to thee ; and it returned not empty to him that sent it, but had that blessed effect that he intended. Or perhaps when thou wert first humbled and stricken for sin, God took a keen arrow out of the quiver of his word, and put it into the hand of an able minister or friend, which shot by him at random (as when Ahab was stuck), was carried home by the wind of the Spirit, that went with it into the heart and wounded it. And such circumstances as these may move thee to acknowledge that good hand that was the mover and orderer of them in heaven, in analogy to his dealings with Paul. But above all, the three persons affect thy heart with the love of God the Father unto thee. At such a time when thou wert in the church, in the midst of the crowd, first the Father he spied thee out there, and remembers it was the time, the full time to have mercy on thee, which he had written in his book ; and thereupon riseth up (as it were) in heaven, and saith unto his Son (as Christ upon the cross did to his mother, ' Woman, behold thy Son ') ' See, Son,' says he, ' behold thy spouse, designed unto thee from ever-lasting. Take him and apprehend him for thine at my hand : I will see you married, and the indissoluble knot tied ere he stir from hence.' Which is more than as if the greatest king on earth should espy, in the midst of multitudes, a beggar standing in rags, and say to the prince, his eldest son, Go, marry her here afore me. And then when he had bespoke Christ's heart, he also bespake thine. He let down a cord of love into it, which took hold thereof, and drew thee by it to his Son and to himself.

And when Jesus Christ had thy soul actually anew commended to him by his Father, he; looking on thee, said with himself, That soul ! surely I should know it. This is the very same that my Father presented unto me from everlasting, says the second person, in all that glorious array which I am to be the endower of her with, which made her appear so lovely, as it then took my heart ; but it is so much altered since, I scarce can know it, being defiled with so many sins. And yet again, saith the man Christ Jesus, it is the same was presented unto me by name, with all these very sins, when I was to suffer. I know her sure enough by a good token ; for she was brought and presented to me in the garden, and hanging on the cross, with these very sins she is now guilty of ; and I have the remembrance in scars upon my soul, which these sins made, when my soul was made an offering for sin. And so he takes her for his. And then he sends his Spirit into thy heart ; and what the Spirit wrought upon thee when he drew thee unto Christ, I leave that to thine own experience to bring to mind.

Now the joy that was thereupon in the breast and bosom of God the Father, Son, and Holy Ghost, was not contained alone in this transaction, but to make the solemnity the greater, it was diffused throughout the heavens. Not one, but two parables are made on purpose by our Lord Christ to express this jubilee unto us, in Luke xv. First, there is a man that sought his lost sheep; then a poor woman that sought her lost groat. The stir and zeal each shewed about it is sufficiently expressed, as deciphering the heart of God and Christ therein to such a soul, in that he leaves ninety-nine to seek such a soul, long before it thinks of seeking him, which it doth not, but is prevented by him. And he goes out with that resolution, not to give over seeking until he hath found it, come what will. And this eager resolution is expressed, ver. 4, 'He leaves the ninety-nine in the wilderness, and goes after that which is lost, until he find it. And then, when he hath found it, he lays it on his shoulders rejoicing.' What doth this signify, but his own abundant gladness? He hath at last found it, with care to keep it. And this action of laying it on his shoulders speaks his heart, as saying within himself, Have I now got you with all this trouble and pursuit? I will now make sure work of letting you run away again, or giving me any more the slip. So doth he rejoice; and so careful is he, that he lays it on his shoulders; he doth not venture to drive it afore him. No, he will not trust it so loosely. He doth not only hold it in his hands, though therein (as Christ says) it is safe enough, for 'my sheep none shall pull out of my hands;' but puts himself to some trouble and care about it, lays it on his shoulders, rejoicing. Oh, how full of joy is God's heart and Christ's heart, that he cannot contain it in his own breast, but makes a solemnity of it! calls together a parliament of 'his neighbours and of his friends,' ver. 6, and makes such a matter and story of it, saying unto them, 'Rejoice with me; for I have found my sheep that was lost.' So then, its having been lost is that which increaseth his joy. And yet, when all is done, it is but a ragged, scabby sheep all this ado is about. Oh, but God loves it; Christ hath laid down his life for it. For who is this sheep? Ver. 7, it is a sinner that repents. And who are those friends God calls together thus to rejoice? Ver. 10, 'There is joy in the presence of the angels of God.' The higher house of heaven is called together on purpose to rejoice, though the lower house regards not such a poor soul.

Well, but it will be said, it may be thus at so great a shoal of converts as in the conversion of the Jews shall fall out, or when three thousand in a day are converted, as Acts ii. Nay, but this is at the conversion of one sinner. And as Abraham made a feast at Isaac's weaning, so God feasts the angels with the conversion of each and every sinner. And it is emphatically said, 'the angels of God,' even those that have God to rejoice in, have their joy yet more full by the addition. But it carries with it this reason, that it is because they are friends. The account is, ver. 6, God and Christ are so well pleased with it, as the angels know and perceive full well their nearness and oneness with God, and ingratiate themselves by joyful acclamations at their conversion.

CHAPTER IV.

That there is an exceeding greatness of God's power apparent in our regeneration.—This is demonstrated from the nature of the work in general.

There is not only infinite mercy, but the almighty power of God manifested in our regeneration. It is exceeding greatness of God's power, no less than that which raised Christ up to glory, which is necessary to work faith and grace in the heart of every true believer. I desire that all those who in their opinions and expressions do lessen and extenuate God's work herein, as Arminians do ; or others who, in the secret sayings of their hearts, and practice in their lives, make the work of grace very easy, and in their own power, and therefore refer their repentance to their own leisure ; would but come and consider what the Spirit of God tells us : Eph. i. 19, 20, 'And what is the exceeding greatness of his power to us-ward who believe, according to the working of his mighty power,' ver. 20, 'which he wrought in Christ, when he raised him from the dead, and set him at his own right hand in the heavenly places.' Whatsoever low, and mean, and slight conceit we, not knowing the power of God's grace, may have of it, yet let us but consider,

1. Who it is that let fall these words ; it was not only Paul (who had the deepest experience and insight into a work of grace, more than all the discoursers in the world), whose authority were enough in the case ; but it is the Spirit of God in Paul from whom they dropped, 2 Pet. i. 10, compared with the chap. iii., ver. 15, 16. Now it is this Spirit of God that gave out these words, who is the great agent in the business, and employed in it, Luke i. 35. It is the power of the Highest (as it is called, Luke i. 35), who works it ; who hath been the converter of the apostle Paul, and of many millions of souls, that expressly says there is thus much power goes to it. If at any time God will convert any soul, he must put forth the exceeding greatness of his power. If we would know how much force goes to the effecting of anything, the surest way is to hear the agent himself speak. The standers by, nay, nor the patient itself, doth not so fully discern it often : when Christ healed the woman of the bloody flux, and that but by the touch of the garment, the standers by, the disciples, they discerned nothing ; but hear Christ himself speak, δύναμις, power or virtue (says he) is gone out from me. He could tell, and best might, what pains went to effect that miracle ; because it went from him. So now also for the work of grace, because it is despatched often and done in a trice, as we see in Paul and the thief, and done as it were by the touch or striking of the words of a weak man at the ears of another, therefore the standers by think there is no great power goes to all this ; but ask him whose work it is, and he tells you, it is the exceeding greatness of his power, &c. If a strong man lift up a great weight, and doth it slightly, the standers by are not competent judges what force goes to it, but only the man himself that felt the stress put to it. So it is here. Indeed the Spirit of God clothes and hides this exceeding greatness of power working in believers' hearts, by using such sweet persuasive motives, and gentle, rational inducements, as cords to draw men's hearts, as the word of God hath in it ; which is the reason why some bring down all this great power spoken of to moral persuasion, making the working power of the Spirit of God in drawing men's hearts but as an engineer that draws and winds up some heavy weight by ropes fastened to it ; as in cranes and the like artifices : so as the ropes bear the stress, and all is done by their force ; and if the weight be too heavy, it cracks them, and down falls all again ; and so the Spirit works not but by those moral persuasions in the word, by enlightening, fastening them to the heart ; and if the poise of the will, and weight of sin (which so presseth down, Heb. xii. 1), if it breaks those bands asunder, all the Spirit's work is lost ; the heart falls down and settles again in the same estate it was. Which, if it were true, wherein should this exceeding greatness of God's power be spent ? Doth the Spirit make more of it than it

is ? If the Spirit effected but by his power concurring with the force of such twine threads only in themselves, why should such big words be used about it ? You see, in such kind of working, the power of a child is able to wind up great weights, if the cords hold. But the truth is, my brethren, that the Spirit, willing to hide the greatness of his power, immediately working, and having hold on the heart (the work of grace being the only standing miracle in the church), useth these instruments in the working of it, yet doth it not according to the strength and force of these, but according to the exceeding greatness of his power alone. As when the angel stirred the water of the pool, it was not the angel's stirring that healed, but the immediate power of God then extended, and by that means. So nor is it the stirring of God's Spirit of the heart by good motions, or moral persuasions, though these be used, that work grace ; but the exceeding greatness of God's power extended in and by these, working beyond the sphere of their power and activity. And that this is so, will be evident if you consider,

2. Secondly, the instance given. It is said to be the same power that wrought in Jesus Christ, in raising him from the dead. Now to raise any one from the dead, is an act of the immediate power of God. Christ, in raising up Lazarus, said indeed, ' Lazarus, come forth,' John xi. 45. But was it the word, think we, or the power of God that went with this word, raised him ? And so the Spirit useth persuasions to the heart, but there is a farther power goes with them ; but yet if you observe the words of the text, the working of God's power here in believers' hearts, is not simply paralleled with the power of raising Christ from death to life, but from death even to that glorious estate he now in the heavens enjoys, which is a work of further power than the raising up of Lazarus and any dead man. For there is a great distance between death and life, so as it must be a great power to raise one from the one to the other ; but between glory and life, there is yet a hundred times a vaster difference. So that now to raise Jesus Christ, so low laid in the grave, and subdued by death, not to life only, but far above principalities, &c., to that top of glory in heaven : this is the exceeding greatness of God's power indeed. Therefore, Rom. i. 4, this work of raising himself thus up is made the greatest that ever God did by his power, and which, of all other manifested, to the utmost, that Christ was the Son of God ; put that out of the question, more than all his miracles : he was ' declared to be the Son of God with power, by the resurrection from the dead ;' such was the power shewn in that work above all else. And therefore the Holy Ghost singles out that, to express his power in raising men from sin to grace ; a greater distance being between them, than simply the natural death and life ; even as much as between the estate of Christ humbled in the grave, and glorified in heaven ; and the like exceeding greatness of power worketh in the one and other.

Again, 3. Consider the great superlative expressions the Holy Ghost useth, besides the paralleling it with the instance given. It is not only great power, but greatness of power, and that exceeding greatness. Now such superlative expressions are never used concerning any attribute, but when it is manifested in some work of God to the utmost, and more than in other former works of his ; in comparison of which, these superlative expressions are used and taken up. And indeed you shall find them only used in the expressing his works of grace ; which being as it were *nova scena et ultima representatio*, the last stage whereon his attributes are to shew themselves, and act their parts ; therefore every attribute that appears on this stage in any act doth its utmost, most superlatively, beyond what was done in former works of creation, providence, &c., and therefore every attribute that bears a part herein, hath superlative expressions of it. Take any attribute, viz., his mercy, which he shews in other works ; when he speaks of them as shewn in other works, it is in the positive degree, simply thus, ' His mercy is over all his works ;' that is, shewed in, and to them all. But when he comes to speak of the mercy and love shewn in the work of grace, he contents not simply so to express it, but he tells us of ' the riches of his glory,' and ' the height, breadth, &c., of his love, which passeth knowledge,' Eph. iii. 16, 18, 19. And he speaks of ' God who is rich in mercy, according to the great love whereby he hath loved us,' Eph. ii. 4. See what superlative terms he here useth, that are in no work of common mercy, because indeed more mercy is shewn to one poor redeemed soul, than to all the world besides. The like is of his power here, expressed in other works of creation, it is expressed in the positive degree, Rom. i. 20, ' They' (says the apostle) ' express his power and Godhead.' But when he comes to speak of the power shewn in the working of grace and second creation, then nothing serves to express it, you see, but ' the exceeding greatness of his power.' For it being a new creation, his last work and way of manifesting his attributes, so every attribute must exceed in it ; for that is God's manner, that his last works, if he do any, should be greater, and clean put down the former. He observes it in deliverances, Jer. xxiii. 7, and so in all other works. So as if he shewed power in creating at first ; if he come to create again, he will have it be such a work wherein much more power shall be shewn, even ' the exceeding greatness of his power ;' for every wise agent, if he doth a thing over again, will be sure to exceed ; he reserves the greatest to the last. Now, therefore, will you set the work of creation by this work, and equal God's power in that with this here, see how it equals it. Creation is a making something out of nothing. Why, this work is a creation also ; it is called, 2 Cor. v. 17, ' a creature,' and we are said, Eph. ii. 10, to be ' created to good works.' But yet there is something more, for it is said to be ' a new creature.' Now as in the case of the covenants, Heb. viii. 13, speaking of the new covenant, he hath made the first old, so this phrase, the *new creature*, implies, that there was an abolishing of some old thing first ; and so the next words do certify us, 2 Cor. v. 17, ' Old things are passed away, all are become new.' Behold, here is a greater work than was at the first creation, in that there was but a making something out of nothing ; here are old things first to be destroyed, to pass away, that is, come to nothing ; which to do, requires as much power as to create ; and then new to be made. There is a great building, old things pulled down, and abundance of rubbish to be pulled down and carried away, and then a new erected ; yea, all old things must be done away, and all must be made new ; not a stick or stud that goes to old building, will serve in the new. And yet this is not all ; for in the first creation, only nothing was before, and nothing that opposed it ; though all made of nothing, yet nothing against it ; but now in this work, these old things do mightily oppose it, 2 Cor. x. 4, 5, Rom. viii. 7 : God hath much more therefore to do, not only to destroy old things before he make new, but old things that are enmity.

There is not only a changing of water into wine, which is done daily in the grape, as John ii., but of contrary into contrary ; of hearts of stone into flesh, and wolves into lambs, Ezek. xxxvi. 26, Isa. xi. 6. This is greater than any miracle Christ shewed, and therefore he tells his apostles, that were workers with God, as it were, in this work, that greater works than he did, they should do ; even as great as the greatest and last work Christ ever did, in raising himself from death to glory.

Use. Is there such an exceeding greatness of power in the saving work of God's grace, which interests us in the rich inheritance of glory ? Why, methinks, this should begin to rouse and startle many of us, and make every one of us, that look for a part and portion in that inheritance, to consider with himself whether there is such a work of grace in his heart as bears proportion, correspondency, and in the working of it answers to such an exceeding greatness of power, so as necessarily it should draw forth so much power from God to work it. For we cannot imagine God doth overdo anything without imputation of folly : no wise agent will put more strength to the working and effecting of a business than will necessarily work it, for there would be so much strength as is overplus spent in vain, as the prophet complains. A king will not stretch out his prerogative royal, or send an absolute mandate, use his extraordinary power, when the bare intimation of his pleasure will do it ; and therefore certainly God, who is said to do all things in weight and measure, and who doth always proportion his power to the work, will never exert such an exceeding greatness of power, if less would serve the turn. Conclude therefore we must, that the true work of grace hath all this power spoken of necessarily drawn out to work it ; and therefore we should all do well to examine whether we have had such a working on our hearts as bears proportion with such a power, so as we can conclude and say, I feel such a work wrought in me, which no power but the power of God, thus mightily unbared and manifested, could ever have wrought ; and the prints of such a work we may safely build on, as a note of election, as the apostle makes it : 1 Thess. vi. 4, 5, ' Knowing your election, for that the word came to you in power,' &c. And, indeed, I know no better way to distinguish the common workings of the Spirit, which so many falsely take for notes of election, than by this truth now in hand ; for though they be all works of the Holy Ghost, and works of power also, yet not such as the exceeding greatness of power here spoken of, and no less, should be engaged in them ; and therefore now, to lay aside such as have had no working on the hearts by the Spirit more than nature, who as those, Acts xix. 2, cannot tell by any working that they have felt of the word and Spirit, whether there be any Holy Ghost, yea or no ; and who are resembled unto the highway side, to let them pass as those in Jude 10, ' who as brute beasts' know no more than nature : let us examine you that think you have some work of grace to shew for heaven.

First, Some will say, I am no adulterer, no drunkard, no unjust person, but sober, chaste, &c. ; and is not this a work of God's power in me, and of his grace, being more than nature ?

For answer,

1. I grant it is a work of God more than nature, man's nature being as fully prone to these sins as any other, and the Scriptures telling expressly that God restrains such dispositions in men ; God kept Abimelech from adultery, Gen. xx. 2, and Laban from hurting Jacob, Gen. xxxi. 34, &c.

Yea, and 2. I grant it to be a work of power, as great as to say to the proud waves of the sea, Stay here your waves, and overflow not ; or as it was to chain up the power of the fire from singeing the garments of the three children ; so to say effectually to the pride, malice, and envy, &c., of a wicked man, Boil not over, requires as great power ; and not only so, but to work and stamp light impressions and tinctures of moral virtues, is a work of great power. Yet,

3. It is not comparable to that power which wrought in Jesus Christ, in raising him from the dead.

(1.) Because the instance of restraining grace alleged, is but keeping the dead body from stinking, and putrefying so much as else it would, and causing it to retain some of the colours a living body hath, though wan and lifeless, which embalming of a dead body will do for many a year. And so indeed that men are kept from stinking, and retain some colours of justice, chastity, &c., is from an answerable embalming power of the Spirit; but this is far from that power which puts a new principle of life into a dead man, and raiseth him up to life.

(2.) Restraining grace is but keeping in and restraining sin in men, yet so as still there is not the less of it in a man's heart, as there is not the less water in the sea, for bridling the foaming and raging waves of it; whereas in the work of grace there is an abolition or annihilation in part begun of old things, so as they pass away and cease to be; now that is a power equal to creating.

And 2. There is an alteration of corrupt nature, inasmuch as a new creature, and contrary workmanship wrought, so as the dross is turned into pure gold throughout; but those tinctures of moral virtues are not a new creature in nature, changing it throughout, but a slight and superficiary gilding of the dross, corrupt nature remaining so still; which impressions also are wrought and maintained, even by the help of what is left in corrupt nature, namely, the natural conscience, in which stamps of law are written, and natural wisdom improved, both which stirred up, and actuated by these apprehensions that vice is evil, virtue good, and that in wisdom it is best, in a man's carriage here, to shun the one and follow the other; and that it is of profit and good report amongst men; by means of these thoughts, I say, such restraint, and the impressions of virtues are easily wrought, even by the help of what is left in nature itself. Whereas now, in the work of grace, the Spirit doth create anew by his immediate power, and therefore it is called a new creature, and this made out of nothing that was in the heart before to further the work.

To conclude: This stirring up of moral virtues, &c., is but as a new dressing of an old garment, which though it may deceive some, and make them think it is a new creature, yet there is nothing added to it that was not, or might not be in it before; only by the help of conscience and natural wisdom some tufts of good are stirred up; but in the work of grace there is not only a new dressing of corrupt nature, but a putting it off, and then a new man created, and that put on, Eph. iv. 22, 24, not a gilding only, but a renewing throughout, changing us in the spirit of the mind, turning the metal into gold to the bottom, ver. 23. But as for the superficiary tincture in such civil men, if not in time worn off, as gilding is, and though it appears in their ordinary carriages of their lives, as set in such and such a condition, yet let them be melted a little, and tried, put upon some new temptation, cast into another fashion, then the base metal, the corruption and naughtiness of their hearts, appear. Whereas a godly man, whose heart is throughout changed, try him how you will, cast him into what mould you will, yet the grace appears. I therefore earnestly desire those that find no further work of power on their hearts than restraint from evil, and slight dispositions to moral virtues, to consider of their estates.

I come to a second sort of men, and to a further work. For some will now plead, I find not only my heart thus embalmed, as you call it, by the Spirit, and the corrupt lusts of the old and dead man, as they are called, Eph. iv. 22, kept from stinking and putrefying, together with some additions of moral virtues ; but I find some lively warmth wrought in my heart and affections by the word and Spirit, even to such things, and by such motives as the word delivers.   In hearing and praying, &c., my eyes are enlightened to understand and assent to those spiritual truths in the word, my heart so far wrought on, and such stirrage of affections upon the consideration of the truths delivered therein, as I can sorrow for my sin, tremble at the threatenings, joy in the promises, and flickerings also of good purposes, desires to obey, and some endeavours ; and I hope you will say, that it is impossible, but that such a work as this should be only from the exceeding greatness of God's power, a mere supernatural work of the Spirit of Christ, above the power of nature in itself, as it is for a dead man to have warmth, or move, or speak ; and one now that hath such a work of power will presently say, as the magicians did, Exod. viii. 19, ' This surely is the finger of God ;' a work of the greatness of God's power ; such as this no wicked man can have, that is dead in trespasses and sins.

1. I grant it is a work of the Spirit, and above the sphere of nature, and its activity in itself alone, for it is a sure rule the apostle gives, 1 Cor. xii. 3, that no man says Jesus is the Lord without the Spirit ; that is, no man can have his understanding brought to assent to, and profess Christ to be the Lord and Saviour, or any other truth preached in the gospel, unless the Spirit persuade his judgment of it ; much more to have the heart wrought upon, and stirred up to good by such truths, is a work above nature, and therefore of the Spirit.   Why, but yet this is little for a man's comfort, for the apostle in that place, as the rest of the chapter, speaks of common gifts of the Spirit, communicable to reprobates, as that of healing, &c. ; and besides the insurance * shews, that many wicked in the church, even such as sin against the Holy Ghost, have had a supernatural working of the Spirit, for they are convinced of the truth of religion and ways of grace, which by nature they could never be, but by the Holy Ghost, which therefore they are said to sin against ; so that a man, you see, may have a supernatural working of the Spirit in him and upon him, and yet not a work of saving grace ; the very insensible creatures have workings of the Spirit on them : Gen. i. 2, it is said, ' The Spirit of God moved upon the waters ;' and suppose he moves upon the surface of thy heart, and hath some supernatural working upon it, doth it presently follow then that thou art in the estate of grace ?   No more than it doth that the waters are.

2. I grant that it is the work of power, and that more extended and greater than the former.   For the former was but a power restraining corrupt nature, but this is an elevating, raising it to such acts as are simply, and of itself, above its reach and own pitch ; and therefore, Heb. vi. 4, it is so expressed and called, ' a tasting of the power of the world to come ;' that is, the apprehensions of the world to come : as heaven, hell, the day of judgment, of things belonging to another world, have powerful workings on men's affections, being enlightened by the Spirit to apprehend them in some measure and sort ; insomuch as in Felix, Acts xxiv. 26, the discourse of judgment to come made him tremble, so powerfully it wrought on him, it shook his heart as a mighty wind doth an aspen leaf ; so King Agrippa's heart, at the hearing of Paul's conversion and of Christ's sufferings and rising from the dead, Acts xxvi., began to be stirred to have provocations

* Qu. ' ensuance '? or ' inference '?—ED.

to become a Christian.   I forbear instances any more, and yet it doth not follow that such a work as this holds proportion with the exceeding greatness of God's power.

(1.) For though it be a work of the Spirit, yet it doth not follow it is saving grace.   Indeed, if the Spirit of God were a mere natural agent in working, and always did work *ad ultimum potentiæ suæ*, to the utmost of his power, as fire, which when it burns must needs burn as much as in it can ; and the sun when it shines shineth according to the fulness of its strength ; then indeed every man that had any working of the Spirit of God upon his heart might certainly conclude that he wrought it by the exceeding greatness of his power ; but the Spirit of God is a free and voluntary agent, who therefore may and doth moderate his power in his works ; puts more or less to according to the working of his good pleasure, and hence now it comes to pass that every man, who is yet partaker of the Holy Ghost and of his workings, hath not yet a saving work wrought in him, such an one as draws forth the exceeding greatness of his power ; for though it is the same Spirit that is in the regenerate, and works thus mightily, yet you must learn to know from the apostle, 1 Cor. xii. 6, that there may be ' diversities of operations,' though the same God which worketh all in all; ' and all these worketh the selfsame Spirit, according as he will,' ver. 10, 11.   And that you may see the truth of this, viz., that you may be partakers of the Holy Ghost, and have your judgments thus wrought on by enlightenings and affections stirred by supernatural objects, and yet all this not be a saving work, take only one instance, which is that of Balaam, that remained a wizard, a wretch, a devil, who went after the wages of unrighteousness, 2 Pet. ii. 15, Num. xxiv.   First, the Spirit of the Lord came on him ; secondly, marvellously enlightened his eyes to see some glimmerings of the true God, ver. 3, 4, and of the blessed estate of God's people ; witness his expression, ver. 5, 6, to the 9th, and that so also as his heart was wrought upon and stirred to desire that condition : chap. xxiii. 10, ' Let me die the death of the righteous,' &c., and yet who will say his heart was changed ?

There may be such a work upon a man's heart, and yet not the exceeding greatness of God's power go to work it.

(1.) As in the former instance of restraining power, so here in the Spirit's elevating power, as I may so call it.   Let us suppose a dead body lay before you; it is in the power of a man bringing it to a fire, or by rubbing, to stir up warmth in it.   Let an angel come, he can take it up, inform it, act it, so as it shall serve to move, speak, and perform the like actions of life. And yet this body is not all this while raised up from death to life, nor can all the ' sole-rubbing, or all simple moving it so by all the power of angels, ever do it.   So now, my brethren, is it in the point in hand; besides the enabling or restraining men's corrupt lusts, there is a farther working on corrupt nature to perform acts of life in show, and as it were the Spirit enlightening, warming, rubbing on men's affections by the word, and the things revealed therein, moving them and carrying them on to good purposes, endeavours ; and yet still this heart may be in itself dead, no new principle of life put in, besides the present actings of the Spirit; no new breath of life as was breathed into Adam, who, 1 Cor. xv. 45, ' was made a living soul;' and therefore now when the Spirit ceaseth to move on this heart, as the angel sometimes did on the waters of the pool, all symptoms of life vanish. warmth is gone, and the heart is as dead as a log, as ever it was; as Balaam's also was out of that good mood; so that you see this is far short of the working of his power, which wrought on Jesus Christ when he was raised from the dead; a less power than this goes to the working of it.   For such a raising of dead bodies the devil hath often practised, carrying dead bodies out of their graves.   There is no such exceeding greatness of power goes to such a work.

(2.) In reason also it may appear, that to the effecting such a work as this in man's heart, there needed not such an exceeding greatness of power be drawn forth.   For there need not any new principle, any new soul or life, be created or infused into man's heart to make it capable of such a work as this is.   For there are principles remaining in corrupt nature, which if but stirred, acted, elevated by the Spirit of God, are capable of all this; and simply to stir those principles up, and propound objects to them, and so to act and affect them, is not a work of the exceeding greatness of God's power.

First, I will shew this in the work of enlightening ; and *secondly*, in the work of being affected with the things that the word delivers.

First, For the work of enlightening, there is in every man an eye of understanding and conscience, which, though sin-shot (that I may allude to the phrase of *blood-shot* in the eye) and defiled, Tit. i. 15, by reason of which defilement it cannot indeed see the spiritual goodness as it is in spiritual things themselves, 1 Cor. ii. 14 ; yet even this blood-shot eye being able truly and really to apprehend the fearfulness of God's wrath, and the torments in hell which come by sin, is therefore by consequence capable to see an accidental goodness in Christ and the ways of God, viz., that by them this misery may be escaped.   And this defiled understanding is capable to apprehend that the estate of the righteous after this life is glorious and blessed (as Balaam did), though indeed and in truth, if once they came to partake of it in heaven, the presence of God would be hell to them.   Man's understanding being naturally in the dark, to make it apprehensive of the goodness of spiritual things thus far, there must be not only a propounding these objects to it, but also a new light brought into it, which may make manifest this accidental goodness, this goodness of them in the general spoken ; for we are darkness, and it is light makes all things manifest ; and therefore those that taste of the powers of the world to come (Heb. vi.) are said to be enlightened ; that is, there is a new light brought in which did not shine about their minds before.   But now to bring barely a new light into the mind is not a work of the exceeding greatness of God's power on the mind itself ; for it is but extrinsecal and outward, no more than to bring a candle into a room to a man that hath some sight already, whereby he sees new things, which being in the dark before, he saw not ; but there is thereby no intrinsecal principle put into the eye of the man, no alteration wrought in it by this, as in a new creation and in a resurrection (to which this work of grace is paralleled) there must be supposed to be ; and yet in some degree or other God vouchsafes to every man that comes into the world (John i. 9) some light wherewith their minds are enlightened.

But you will say, What is there further wrought on the understanding of a regenerate man, which will hold proportion with the power manifested in creation, and the resurrection of Jesus Christ ?

I answer, That besides shining upon the mind with a new supernatural light, there is a new principle, a new eye, as I may call it ; a new power of discerning put into and created in the understanding of a man, whereby he is further enabled to see the intrinsecal spiritual goodness which is in Christ and grace ; to see the beauty, the goodness of holiness of God's face and

presence, which never entered into the heart of any carnal man. Therefore to this enlightening there is not only the Spirit of revelation given
(Eph. i. 18); that is, the Holy Ghost coming with a new external light,
making them manifest; but there is also given an inward Spirit of wisdom
created in the mind itself, a new habit and principle of spiritual discerning
and of the wisdom of the just (for so Spirit is taken often in Scripture),
whereas the other are barely said to be enlightened.   There is a new eye
created εἰς ἐπίγνωσιν, on purpose to know them (Col. iii. 10), so it is in the
original ; there is a new principle of life put in, as in a resurrection there
useth to be.   For so Christ expresseth it, John viii. 12, calling it the light
of life, that is, such a light as hath a new principle of light* joined with it,
and enableth a man to see spiritual things as a living, spiritual man should
see them, which is spiritually, 1 Cor. ii. 14 ; so that such a work as this
holds, you see, in Scripture expressions, proportion with the creation and
resurrection of Christ, to annihilate and bring to nothing flesh and corruption in the judgment, &c. ; and in the room a new spirit of judging things
aright is created, a new principle of discerning spiritual things spiritually
(Eph. i. 17), called a ' Spirit of wisdom.'   Spirit is taken for a new habit
or principle of judging wisely of things, and herein now the exceeding greatness of God's power is manifested in a work in and upon the judgment
itself, in taking away that sin which covering it made it as a dead eye, in
regard of a right discerning of spiritual things, and then putting a new
principle of seeing things as a living man sees them, called therefore by
Christ, as distinguishing it from the light of wicked men, John viii. 12, ' the
light of life.'   Here now is a work holds proportion with the power spoken
of, raising up a dead man to life ; whereas in the enlightening of a wicked
man there is no renewing of the judgment, but barely a light brought in,
actuating and elevating it to see and discern, so far as sin and that veil which
covers it will suffer it ; and to that no such greatness of power is required,
for there is not a new living eye put in, but only a new light, there being
a principle of seeing and understanding in a man by nature, already able,
by the help of the Spirit shining upon it, to have some glimmerings of
spiritual things.

And *Secondly*, For the work of good motions of joy, fear, and good purposes in the will and affections, there is a principle already also in the will
and affections of a carnal heart, which, if it be but awakened by such
enlightenings, stirs up such good motions and purposes in carnal men.   If
you ask what this principle is ? I answer, it is self-love, which is the general
that commands the will and affections, and rouseth them ; but it and all the
affections are set afloat and raised up only to those objects which a man by
self-love apprehends to be hurtful or good for him.   Nay, then, when by
such common enlightenings a man's carnal understanding apprehends hell
to be a dangerous condition, and that sin is the way to it ; that heaven is
an excellent condition, and that to leave sin and do good, &c., is the way
to it ; and by those moral persuasions are in the word, self-love is once
awakened, as easily it is ; a man's affections are set a-work to fear hell as an
evil, to sorrow for sin, that will bring him to it; to rejoice in the news of
heaven as attainable, and to desire and begin to endeavour to take such
courses as will bring a man to it ; and so that affection of joy, sorrow, fear,
desire, may be elevated, lifted up, to be conversant about spiritual objects,
such as are sin and good duties, heaven and hell ; and yet not the exceeding
greatness of God's power go to work it, because there is already a principle

* Qu. 'life'?—ED.

even in a carnal heart which may be stirred with the apprehension of these, and so set all these a-work, namely, self-love. So as the Spirit, to work such good motions, shall not need to stretch forth the greatness of his power to change the heart, and to create anything anew in it, as he doth in a regenerate man; but the old heart remaining carnal still, may by persuasions, such as are in the word, and such considerations of being damned and saved and the like, be stirred to all this, and to move only by such persuasions and considerations, and to propound them in such a manner as they should move, is no such great work of power. A good orator will do as much in another case. So as the Spirit doth no more upon the heart, in this case, than the light and heat of the sun doth upon a dunghill, shining upon it and heating of it, by the power of both which it elevates and raises up vapours in it, which yet were in it before; to a higher place indeed than of themselves they would ascend, namely, into the air; yet these vapours are not changed, they are as stinking as before. So now is it in the working of the Spirit. John the Baptist preaching the kingdom of heaven was at hand, the Spirit of God went with this news to men's hearts; both darted in beams of light to understand some goodness in that kingdom preached, and also warmed men's hearts and affections with the apprehensions of it; there went both light and heat with it, John v. 35, both which raised up and elevated their understandings with the light to some glimmering apprehensions of heaven's goodness, and their affections, yea, and wills also (for it is said they rejoiced willingly, &c.) with the warmth to desire, and joy in the news of so great a happiness. Here indeed both were elevated to a higher object than ever of themselves, without the concurrence and existence of this light and heat from the Spirit, they would have ascended, yet without any powerful change wrought in men's hearts themselves, or any new principle put into the heart, only the carnal heart, still so remaining, by self-love stirred up; for in the 43d verse he says, that though they rejoiced thus in John's ministry, yet they would not believe in him, and in ver. 42, that though they did thus, out of love to themselves, rejoice in the news of heaven as good for them, yet they had not the love of God in them to seek his honour only and principally, and not their own, ver. 44; and certain it is that their affections of joy and desire, which out of self-love were stirred to desire honour from men rather than from God, the same affections out of the same principle of self-love were stirred then to desire and rejoice in that kingdom of heaven offered; and yet still the heart was as carnal, as unchanged, as empty of the law of God as before, it being self-love only that set afloat both the one and the other. And so in Felix (Acts xxiv. 20) the same principle of self-love that would have made his carnal heart have trembled at the news of being brought to Cæsar's judgment-seat, made his heart, remaining still as carnal, tremble at Paul's preaching of Christ's judgment to come. And so in Esau, Heb. xii. 17, the self-same carnal affection of sorrow, which self-love would have stirred up in him for the loss of any outward thing, was stirred up in him to sorrow and weep for the loss of his birthright and blessing, types to him of heaven; and all in vain, for want of true repentance, as some interpret, which he found no place for, though he sought it with tears. And therefore thus to stir men's affections is not simply in itself a work which argues the exceeding greatness of God's power, seeing there needs no new principle be created in the heart which was not there before, only the old ones stirred up and elevated and acted to a higher pitch; neither is there any true and intrinsecal change and alteration wrought on men's hearts, or the affections themselves, only a setting them afloat about new propounded objects, such as heaven and hell, they remaining still the same. There is indeed a new working upon the heart which was not on it before. You will ask then what is it that is wrought beyond this, which is an effect of this great power ?

I answer, *first*, by paralleling it with the power shewn in the creation; Eph. ii. 10, it is a workmanship created, as it were, a-purpose to good works ; the difference of which from the former, I express by this similitude. An old clock that is out of frame, and set wrong, may be brought to move about without any new workmanship bestowed upon it, merely by new weights hung on it ; and so may the old man, the carnal, remaining so ; and the wheels, affections thereof, be stirred by the moral persuasions and considerations of heaven and hell, hung on by the Spirit ; and this is but an artificial kind of working, which argues no great power in the agent, but a skill rather that knows how to apply things will move it. But now when the exceeding greatness of God's power comes to work, he takes the old frame in pieces, and creates and sets up a new frame, a new piece of workmanship, created on purpose for good works, by changing the heart intrinsecally, putting new principles of life and motion to what is good ; and though indeed those weights and considerations which move the carnal heart, make it move the faster to what is good, yet this in itself is a frame made on purpose, 'created to good works ;' which phrase implies and imports a principle of motion inclining the heart that way of itself ; for when God is said to create things to such and such an action, as the heaven to move, the fire to burn, the ground to bring forth herbs, the meaning is, he hath put such principles into it as tend to produce such actions; and so to create a workmanship to good works, is to endow the heart with such abilities, ard *actus primi*, as they are called, as should enliven the heart to good works, as *actus secundi*. And therefore this difference will evidently appear between the work of good motions on a carnal heart only, and a work of the greatness of God's power creating a new workmanship, namely by this, that when such considerations are taken off, then the heart stands still, hath no inclinations towards what is good in it ; when the Spirit ceaseth thus sensibly to move and act the dead heart, it lies as a log, without any principle or symptom of life in it ; whereas now a changed heart, even in the greatest desertions, hath still a new workmanship in it, the bent whereof is contrary to what is evil ; and if the weights of sin wring it to what is evil, Heb. xii. 1, yet it is as winding the frame of a watch the wrong way ; and the inward frame and constitution whereof still is for what is good and holy, and God and the law commands. And why ? Because this workmanship, though not stirred about, yet was created for good works. And it is against the inward framing of it to be moved the other way.

In the *second* place, I answer, by paralleling it with the power shewn in raising up Christ from death to glory, which is the instance in the text, and which I mean principally to prosecute and insist on ; only I take the other also for further confirmation sake, and because the Scripture instanceth in that also, as an expression of the power which worketh in this work of grace, calling it a creation. For now, if it be asked what new principle it is which is thus created and brought into the soul, I answer, it is a principle of new life, which, as another soul, raiseth it. For the satisfaction of such I will therefore add this, before I come to what I have further to deliver ; and it is a difference answering to, and serving further to discover in what this exceeding greatness of power consists, for no other must here be handled ; and in brief it is this. If thou findest another and a further principle than self-love stirring in, and raising up these thy affections; namely, godliness and respect to God ; then the exceeding great-ness of his power hath been, and doth work in thy heart.   First mark the reason and ground of this, for the thing in hand.   He tells you the exceed-ing greatness of God's power is seen in this, in putting in and creating a new principle and soul of spiritual life into the heart, and not simply in stirring up the old one of self-love ; now what think you is this new principle of life which this great power puts in besides that of self-love ?   Look into 2 Peter i. 4, ' According as his divine power hath given' (mark here, he speaks of a work of the exceeding greatness of his power) ' us all things to life ;' that is, *all* the exceeding greatness of his power, *all* things to life ; and what is that ?   It is energetically explained in the next words, ' godli-ness.'   Herein then consists the working of such a power as raised Christ to life and glory ; giving or putting certain powers and abilities of a new life, namely, godliness, into the soul ; and indeed to work this there must be stretched forth such a power, for though there be a principle of selfness, as I may so call it, which makes the carnal heart respect the good of itself, and to be affected with joy or sorrow about that which tends to the hurt or happiness of a man's self, yet in that vast ocean of man's heart, by nature, there is not the least drop or disposition of godliness to be found, which should stir a man's affections and raise them so high as to be answerably affected with those things which touch simply upon God, have relation purely to him.   And therefore now, though the heart of a carnal man may be stirred at the consideration of such things out of the word as are suitable to, and apt, and fitted to stir self-love ; and thus it may be more violently and turbulently than one who is sincere, yet in regard of godliness his heart is dead ; such considerations wherein God is involved, and his glory and cause is the principal ingredient, these lie in their hearts and affections, like pills in a dead man's body; they stir not the humours, nor these the affections ; or if they work, yet no further than their own heart or happiness is enwrapped up with the other ; for why, there is no suitable principle of life and godliness to work upon.   Wouldst thou there-fore now distinguish thy affections of sorrow or joy at the hearing of the word, or at other times, in thy own meditations, from those in a carnal heart ?   Mark if there be any drops or strains and dispositions of pure godliness mingled with a great deal of flesh and corruption in the affections ; for as oil, a few drops of it, keep themselves severed from the water, though jumbled with them, so will small drops of godliness, and the having respect to God, keep themselves pure in a sea of corruption, in thy affections. There is a meaning in every affection ; as of the good, Rom. viii. 27, so also of bad ; when thou art stirred to sorrow or joy in meditating or hear-ing of the word, observe the full meaning of those affections, upon what kind of considerations they are thus set afloat.   And that you may see this difference between carnal affections and sincere renewed ones, under this very notion grounded upon Scripture, and so may more distinctly know how to apply it : 2 Cor. vii. 9, Paul had sent a letter, wherein he had sharply reproved the Corinthians for a sin committed and suffered amongst them ; by which this affection of sorrow for sin was much stirred in them ; now mark how Paul, in this second epistle, speaks of this their sorrow : ' Now I rejoice ' (says he), ' not that you were made sorry ' (not simply that their affection of sorrow was stirred for the sin ; that it might have been, and they never the better), ' but that ye were made sorry after a godly manner.'   Mark it, here comes in this very distinction, even to this very purpose in hand ; if, when a man sorrows for sin, it be the consideration of God's dishonour that is wounded by it, that is thus laid to heart ; and if such motives as lay open God's interest and relation in it that wounded the heart, that raised up this sorrow in any measure in truth to God ; so as it is not for that misery only which sin would bring on a man, that makes him sorrow ; but that it is done against his God, whose favour he accounts more than his life, and whom to displease is as death to him ;—as they, Zech. xii. 10, that are not said to mourn so much for sin, or themselves, as for God, whom they had offended, and Christ, whom they had pierced ;—then thy sorrow is after a godly sort. Which sorrow being for thy offence against God, so much the more increaseth by how much thou apprehendest he is pacified towards thee (as they, Ezek. xvi. 63) ; and though thy heart should not apprehend so much, yet there are some relentings in it for offending him whom thy soul loves ; so as, if now the sentence of death were passed against thee, as at the latter day, and thou wert out of hope, yet at thy doleful farewell from him, thou couldst find in thy heart to down on thy knees and ask him forgiveness first for all the wrongs thou hast done him. Is there any such whisperings of such a meaning in thy sorrow ? This is from a new principle of life and godliness infused into it, which nothing but the exceeding greatness of his power could have infused ; so also for thy joys, dost not only rejoice in the hopes of glory, which thou conceivedst as good for thyself (as it is Rom. v. 2), but also (mark the gradation, ver. 11 of that chapter), not only so, but also thou rejoicest in God, apprehending thy heaven to consist in him, and communion with him, as one who is suitable to thy inward man, with whom therefore thou shouldst find in thy heart to live and die ; and this barely for those excellencies of holiness, wisdom, goodness, and lovingkindness that is in him ; this being the top of thy joy, that he is such a God, so holy, &c., and that he is a God to whom thou hast a relation and a reference, and in whom thou hast an interest. If there be the least drop of such dispositions running in thy joys, and discovering themselves in them, then is there something pertaining to life and godliness wrought in thee by his divine power ; for there is no principle at all left in corrupt nature which could ever elevate thy joys so high, but it ariseth from a divine nature infused, which in the same place, 2 Pet. i. 4, he says the same power of God makes us partakers of ; for only *simile gaudet simili.* And so, lastly, for thy good purposes and designs to fear and obey his commandments : are they stirred up in thee only because sin is the way to death, and good duties the way to life ? Or is there some further meaning in thy desires, so as hypocrite or not hypocrite, heaven or not heaven in the end, thou desirest and purposest to obey him ; and though in the end thy labour should be lost to thyself, yet if God be a gainer by thee, thou shouldst not altogether be sorry ; but yet sorry truly for this, thou canst do no more ; are there any the least part of such dispositions covered and taken up in thy desires and purposes ? There then hath been the exceeding greatness of God's power dealing and tampering with thy heart, putting in a new principle of godliness and life, to which thy nature is as truly dead as Christ's body was in the grave. Such small drops and sparks as these cost the Lord more power than creating the whole frame of heaven and earth ; and sooner shall they be dissolved than the least iota of these shall utterly perish, if all the power that is in God can preserve them to salvation. Believe it, and build upon it ; such dispositions and such tangs of godliness seasoning thy sorrows, joys, and desires shall never go to hell with thee, nor thou with them. Therefore now, to conclude this, as Paul speaks of the Corinthians' sorrow, so do I of all affections and good motions, rejoice not simply in this, that you feel such affections stirred in you when you hear sermons, &c., but if you find them stirring in the least measure according to God, that he be aimed at in them, then rejoice; by which principle of godliness also a man sets up God in his heart above himself, is willing to deny himself, so God may be exalted.

If, then, thou hast found a work of God in thee, which hath took thee off from, and hath prevented thee in all thy natural designs, purposes, and intents of thy heart, which thou hadst for thyself; and hath wrought thee another way, hath disposed thee to another end, set all that is in thee a-work for God and his glory; this is godliness, this is a mighty power, as much as bringing in a new soul into a body, for a new end, is a new form. Thus Paul was prevented of all his natural aims taken off from him, and he makes it an evidence of his conversion, Gal. i., when he was most hot in the pursuit of eminency in learning, credit among his nation, ver. 13, then did God (says he), who had separated me, ver. 15, that is, appointed and destined me to another end, ' call me by his grace.' ' And the life I now lead is not my own,' chap. ii. 20; ' it is not I, but Christ lives in me.' As when he sins, he says, ' It is not I, but sin ;' so here, ' It is not I, but Christ,' when any good is done; that is, I am not guided by the principles and ends of my former life, when I did all for myself; but all is from Christ, and for Christ; he is the beginning and the end. That whereas all were dead, 2 Cor. v. 14, 15, he quickens them with a new principle of life and godliness, whereby they live not to themselves; that is, they make not themselves their end, but they ' live to him that died and rose again for them ;' and this life is godliness. Whereas every man that is born into the world begins, as Paul did, to trade for himself, and is bound some-whither, where he thinks happiness is to be had; and he takes in loading accordingly, with thick clay or pleasures, &c., fills himself with a thousand vanities ; but when thou art converted to God, a contrary wind takes thee, as it did Paul, and defeateth thee utterly of all thine own purposes, carries thee strongly to another haven, to have another loadstar in thy eye ; a new principle sets thee a-work to be a factor as much for God as ever thou wert for thyself; and to that end thou throwest out all those vanities which will tend no way to his advantage, as being bound for a port where thou canst vend none of those thy former wares ; and this not as merchants do their lading, in a storm, because they may sink thee into the bottomless lake, but because they are unprofitable for God ; and as willingly as ever thou tookest them in, thou throwest them out. Thy heart can know what wares will be most for God's advantage, using thy wisdom to see what will bring him in most glory, and thou dealest accordingly in such things as may increase his revenue ; and though thou losest, yet art sure he shall be no loser, being made as faithful to God as once thou wert for thyself. This is godliness, this is a new life, a new principle, and as great a power must go to this as to raise up Christ from the grave to glory ; for this raiseth thy soul from earth to heaven, out of thyself to God ; and is as much as to turn the sun in its course, or to invert the order of nature. Thus nothing but an almighty power can thus advance a man's aims out of himself, and make all in a man subordinate to another. There is no principle in nature, if not informed by godliness, can reach thus high, much less in corrupt nature. Only let me add this, that the principle of self-love still remains in the heart of a godly man, sets his affections afloat, and is a weight makes the wheels move, and acts him in his actions also, and it ought to do; yet so as there is a farther principle of godliness, which elevates self-love higher, and makes it subordinate. For as, when the reasonable soul is infused and annexed to the sensitive, the acts of reason do not extinguish the acts of sense; nay, the senses are helped and perfected much by them, and they subordinately concur and join together in most; yet still so as the acts of reason reach higher, and do guide and moderate the other: so this new created principle, and fountain of life and godliness, infused into the soul by God's power, doth not destroy the acts of self-love, only winds up the will and affections to have higher reaches, even as high as God, in whose glory our happiness lies, and so guides and moderates this other. But now, it may be said, that though indeed to put in and to create in the soul such a new principle of life and godliness argues great power indeed, and as much as was spent in the creation of the world, but yet no more, if this were all; for simply to infuse and introduce into the soul this new life, is no more than the breathing the breath of life into Adam, whereby he was made a living soul. But this is not simply a creation, as I said before, but a *new* creation, wherein not only a new life is put in, but old things, which resist the bringing in of this life, are to be destroyed also. Yea, further, it is paralleled, we see, with the resurrection of Jesus Christ, wherein there was more than ordinary power spent, more than in the resurrection of others we read of; for, Rom. i. 4, he was thereby with power mightily declared to be the Son of God. Wherein, then, was this exceeding greatness of power spent? Was it simply in bringing his soul into, or joining it unto his dead body again? This much power must and did go to the raising again of Lazarus, of him also who was raised by the prophet's bones. There was something else, therefore, which in his rising drew forth this exceeding greatness of power spoken of, for which I refer you to Acts ii. 24, where Peter, proving to the Jews that Jesus was the Messiah and Son of God, he argues it from the power manifested in his rising again, and that power not simply shewn in bringing his soul into his body, or raising him up, but principally in rescuing his soul first, and 'loosing it from the pains of death,' which, if it had been possible, would have held him, but it was impossible they should. There were certain pains then which hindered, and with much power would have detained, had not the exceeding greatness of his power broken their power, and in breaking this their power lay the miracle. 'God raised him up,' says the text, 'having (first) loosed the pains of death,' &c. Now, what pains of death means he? Bodily death only? Those the soul is rescued from in dying, and from these also were they rescued who were raised before Christ. The word is ὠδῖνας, the throes and pangs of a woman in travail, which, Isa. liii. 11, are called the travail of his soul, he in his soul bearing that wrath which was due to us, verse 5 of that 53d chapter, which pangs, because they tended unto death, and would have carried his soul to hell with them, would have stabbed him outright, and sped it for ever rising again; therefore they are called the pains of death; which pains, had they seized upon any of our souls, would have for ever killed them and detained them, for they had the power of death in them; for if it had been possible, they would have held him, but that they were encountered by the power of his Godhead. They light upon one who was more than a creature, who was backed by the almighty power of God, by which power he was rescued from them, they and his soul were loosened, their power being first subdued; and therefore Peter, out of the Psalms, at the 27th verse, speaks of a resurrection of his soul out of hell, and then a resurrection of his body from corruption in the grave. These pains encountered his soul whilst it was in his body, but God left it not to their power, but raised it up to paradise, and then put it into his body again, and therein principally was this great transcendent power seen, which was declared by the rising of his body; and therefore he says, 'Death is swallowed up in victory;' now there is never a victory gotten but where there is a contrary power opposing, and that power subdued, crushed, swallowed up; so says that text, 'If it had been possible, they would have held him.'

Answerably now, in this great work of grace, that which draws forth this exceeding greatness of God's power here spoken of, is not merely putting in a new principle of life and godliness into the soul, but it lies in dissolving the works of the devil, 1 John iii. 8, as in the other the pains of death were loosened. For there are certain strong potent detainers, allurers of the soul, to keep it in the estate of death, answerable to the pains of death, which have a mighty power, oversway, and interest in the heart of man, which nothing but the like power to that wrought in Christ could dissolve and subdue, which, when God doth begin to work effectually, do put forth their power, and if possible would hold him, but that a stronger comes and subdues, conquers, and destroys that power, and so loosens them and the soul, and rescues the soul from them. This you shall find expressed Col. i. 13, where the apostle, with thanks, ascribes it to the power of God the Father, that 'we are translated into the kingdom of his Son, and delivered from the powers of darkness.' For all lies not in bare translating us into the kingdom of his Son. There must first be a delivering out of the powers of darkness; which words tell us, *first*, that sin is nothing but darkness, and Satan the prince of darkness hath a power over, and a kingdom in a man, and such a power as will not easily give up and yield up a man's heart to God, but will strive to hold a man as long as they have any power left; for so, *secondly*, the word *delivering* implies, namely, signifying a forcible snatching out and rescuing from the enemies' hands; it must be by a greater power encountering that power. Sin will not part with a man without blows, and stronger than the strong man must come and bind him, yea, disarm him, kill, subdue, and destroy this power, or it will never yield.

For it is with this delivering out of the power of darkness as it was in delivering Israel out of Egypt (which was a type of this), God is said to have brought them out of Egypt 'with a strong hand, and a stretched-out arm;' that is, with power drawn forth. Now, what was it drew out his power? Not barely carrying them out, but that he did it maugre the opposition of Pharaoh, and all the power of Egypt, which withstood it to the utmost; therefore it is said, Rom. ix. 17, 'Even for this same purpose have I raised thee (O Pharaoh) up, that I might shew my power on thee.' That he rescued them out of Pharaoh's hands by destroying his power, therein was the stretching out of his arm seen. Answerably is it in the work of conversion; the power of darkness is set up to draw forth the exceeding greatness of his power in destroying it. For as God sent messages to Pharaoh by Moses to let his people go, so God deals first with the heart, by his word and Spirit, striving and persuading to let the soul go free, and to turn to him, but the power of sin denies it, and will not let the heart to turn; God then sends judgment after judgment, and what? Will you yet let the soul go? The pleasures of sin say no, and though some slight flitting resolutions are often wrought, and purposes to turn, yet as Pharaoh still returned to hardness, and Israel was undelivered, so do those purposes vanish, and still the heart is kept under the power of darkness; and if it were possible to hold the heart, sin and Satan would. Well, but in the end God comes with his almighty power, and kills and subdues the first-born, that is, the strength of sin (for so the first-born is called, Gen. xlix. 3), snatcheth a man out ; and yet when the heart is a-going once in good earnest, Satan and sin in the heart muster up all the power and forces that Egypt can make, to stop the heart and detain it, and bring it back again, as Pharaoh did. Then all the strength sin hath begins to bestir itself and make out after it. And then is that great and main battle fought (even at the first conversion), and the main and famous victory gotten, and great overthrow given to the power of hell and darkness in a man. By this exceeding greatness of God's power, subduing, killing, and giving it a deadly wound, and destroying it, as he did the Egyptians in the Red Sea, the soul is rescued and delivered from the dominion of them. This we may note in the general, to help us to discern a true work of grace, wherein the exceeding greatness of God's power is drawn, from those inferior works of the Spirit formerly spoken of, namely, that the true work of grace is such a work as wherein there was and is the utmost opposition that sin can make shewn, and yet a foil given, a victory, a conquest gotten, which is not so in those inferior works of the Spirit. There is not a delivering out of the power of darkness in them ; that is, sin doth not shew its utmost opposition against the inferior works of the Spirit, and so is not foiled, having that power broken, as in this great work it is ; for otherwise, this exceeding greatness of power would not be seen, for the power of the conqueror is not drawn forth but by bringing forth the strength of the adversary and subduing it.

Now in those other lesser works of the Spirit, whether of restraining, enlightening, and enlarging grace, it is not so. For those works are not directly contrary to corrupt nature, though indeed above it, and elevating it higher than of itself it could reach, yet not changing it by destroying corruption. It is *supra*, not *contra ;* for it works upon those principles that are left in it, namely, of conscience and self-love, and so insinuates itself, and therefore is not contrary to it, as heat and fire is to cold and water, which, when they meet, do fight to the utmost to destroy each other, and shew their utmost power in opposing the conquest of the other ; but they are in corrupt nature rather as those qualities the philosophers call symbolical, namely, as moisture stands with cold in water ; and therefore a form of godliness stands with the power of sin, and often of some particular masterlust. However, though the work of enlightening may procure a combat in the conscience against the power of sin, in other faculties, yet not such as raiseth the utmost of the power of sin, and then foils it ; neither doth it fight against corrupt nature, but acts with motives suitable to self-love in corrupt nature, drawn from such inconveniences as self-love in corrupt nature is sensible of, as shame, and hell, &c., so as it sets but self-love against itself, by raising carnal desires after heaven, and to avoid hell, or desires of the world. So as there is not stirred up a full, a direct, and high opposition *in summo gradu ;* corrupt nature is not provoked to bring forth its utmost forces. Neither indeed doth the Spirit work in those inferior works, by delivering the soul out of the power of darkness, making an insurrection against its working, but by restraining it only ; wherein therefore corrupt nature puts not forth much resistance. It is but binding of the strong man, and simply to be bound, he will endure and suffer it, and resists not, as Samson did not ; and a strong man laid asleep may be easily bound and be kept under by a child, when he doth not put forth his strength ; and so the Spirit, in those workings in civil men and others, layeth lusts asleep and binds them with purposes and resolutions to leave them, and they resist not; so as to do this, there needs not the exceeding greatness of God's power. But now true grace and the power of God coming in, the work of it is to deliver a man out of the power of darkness by destroying it, and by coming to set up and introduce into the heart a contrary principle of godliness in the soul, to which corrupt nature is, *in summo gradu,* contrary, and is called ' enmity;' and therefore a man's lusts, and all the power of sin, fortify themselves against it, shew their utmost power, as Samson, though being asleep, was bound ; yet when the Philistines, his enemies, came upon him to take him and kill him, he stirs up himself and his utmost strength, and the devil knows all lies upon that battle; so that by this you may know whether it be such a work as in proportion of power answers to Christ's resurrection, by this, if in thy conversion thou didst feel the power of sin to the utmost opposing it, so as thou didst not think it had half so much power and inte- rest in thy heart as then thou sawest it had (for when one comes to grapple with one, then he knows his strength); and yet, for all that, thy sin and lusts were backed by the power of hell, so as, had it been possible, they would have detained thee; yet thou didst find they had the foil in thy heart, lost ground, and God and Christ was set up as king there, so as thou feltest thy heart loosened from them, and that as willingly and freely as ever thou wert subject to it, then know this power hath wrought in thee.

CHAPTER V.

The greatness of divine power in our regeneration manifested from instances of the several parts of that work.

But you will say unto me, Shew us (as he said to Samson) in what things principally this great power lieth, what there is in the heart thus strongly to detain it, answerable to the pains of death, which God's power is to en- counter with, and loosen the soul from, and which to subdue, this exceed- ing greatness of power must be drawn forth.

1. The first particular instance we find, 2 Cor. i. 4; and we have it there brought in just to our purpose in hand. For speaking of the mighty power of God working with the word, he illustrates and sets forth that power by shewing the powerful opposition it meets with and overcomes. The weapons of our warfare are ' mighty through God.' And wherein is their might seen? ' In pulling down strongholds,' &c. You see there is such opposition in the heart to be converted, as useth to be in a besieged town of war, which will hold out as long as possibly it can, and to that end it builds and casteth up strongholds and high forts, strong and high, which the heart sticks to and will not be beaten from till they be beaten down; ' To the pulling down,' &c., says the text; for yield it will not, till they be pulled down. Now the particulars he there instanceth in are reasonings and imaginations. Some translate the one, some the other, that is, secret dislikings, or not fancying the ways of God, with secret objections and argu- ments against them and the subjection to them; as also high thoughts that exalt themselves, high, proud, contrary thoughts of enmity; two great and mighty armies to overcome, and the Spirit had need to come against them with no less than the exceeding greatness of his power. For you must know that when the Spirit effectually converts any soul, he brings Jesus

Christ into his heart, and sets up Jesus Christ there as king, and causeth this fundamental law to pass, and be enacted by the consent of the whole heart and greater party, in all the faculties, as the predominant rule and principle to guide a man's whole life ; that it is absolutely best to obey Christ in every particular passage of life, in every thought, in all conditions; that this, I say, is absolutely best for him, and necessary to begin presently. This you have in the following words expressed, ' To bring every thought into the obedience of Christ ;' this conclusion hath been irremoveably and irrevocably laid and fixed in the hearts of all the saints.   So in the apostles, as you may see by their expressing their resolution in a case of the greatest difficulty when they were most strongly tempted.

2. Another particular instance of the greatness of God's power in our regeneration, is his breaking off a man's heart from the pleasures of sin and inordinate lusts.   A man is as unwilling to part with them as with life ; and therefore all the power that is in the heart resists what would loosen them and the soul, and raise it out of that estate of spiritual death ; as anything would resist what would take life from it.   And as death is a strong thing, so is life also, and the law of it.   And therefore the law of pleasures is strong in all men that lie buried in them, we being by nature ' lovers of pleasures more than of God,' 2 Tim. iii. 4.   Pleasures are so powerful, because so suitable to the disposition of a man's heart, that a man hath not the power, because not the heart, to resist them.   And therefore you shall find that men will say (and the Scripture expresseth it in their own phrase) that such a pleasure they cannot leave.   It is as the life to them, and they can no more part with it than be willing to cease to live.   So unclean wantons : 2 Pet. ii. 14, 'Eyes have they full of adultery, which cannot cease from sin ;' such power, interest, and sway it hath in their hearts.   So, Luke xiv. 20, when one who had lately married a wife was invited, he professeth plainly, without any excuse, 'I have married a wife, and I cannot come.'   The inordinancy of his pleasure in her had such hold in and power over his heart, that though he be damned for it, and lose heaven for it, he could not part with it.   So that the same power which rescued Christ's soul from the pains of death to that glorious life in heaven, must work to raise that dead soul from the pleasure of sin unto the participation of the life oí God, and to delight himself in the pleasures thereof (for without pleasure the creature cannot live), from which, by reason of those sinful pleasures, he is estranged.   Therefore our Saviour Christ, speaking of the power and prevalency that the pleasure and sweetness of riches (for gain hath its sweetness) have in the heart, says, Mat. xix. 24, 'It is as easy for a camel to go through the eye of a needle, as for a man that trusts in his riches' (as, Mark x. 24, it is expounded) 'to enter into heaven,' riches being also one of a man's strongholds or towers formerly spoken of.   So Solomon says, Prov. xviii. 11, possessing the midst of the heart, and so commanding the whole heart, as holds use to do the cities they are in, and chaining all the munition and strength of the heart, as it is reckoned an impossibility to scale these forts and break the heart from them, therefore the apostles, apprehending that every man had some dear pleasure or other, even poor men as well as rich, which was as dear to them, they stand amazed and ask, 'Who then shall be saved?'   And our Saviour Christ goes not back from his word, only by way of distinction adds, that ' with man this is impossible indeed ;' that is, all the power that is in man, all the reasons, all the motives and persuasions he can be made apprehensive of, cannot ever effect this, divorce the heart and them ; but subjoins,

that with God all things are possible. Shewing plainly, as the greater
power pleasures have in the heart, so what power it is must go to work a
separation between the heart and them; no less than that power to which
all things are possible, even the greatest impossibilities. If God could not
do all things, he could not do this. And, my brethren, do you know what
it is to part with the pleasure of a sin? Which there is none knows but
he who has done it indeed; and he that hath done it finds a greater
strength working in him than all the creatures have in them. It is not all
the persuasions of angels and men, not all the offers of eternity, can make
a man forego the bird in the hand, the present pleasures of sin, though
but for a season. And till a man come to part with them in earnest, he
never knew the greatness of their strength, and what power they have in
him. For then all the pleasure that ever a man did enjoy by and in a
lust, and all that he might do still, will be united and collected into one
temptation, to make it work the more effectually. And that which is of all
most dear will the devil set upon a man, as his last and strongest means
to prevail with him; as uncleanness did with Augustine (as in his case
thus he relates it). It came to me, says he, when I was resolving to turn
to God, and plucked me by the sleeve, and casting the most pleasing
countenance that ever he saw, said, What! will you forego me, and that
for ever? Now, therefore, to find so mighty a power in a man, as with
Ephraim to say at thy conversion, 'What have I to do with idols?' so
with all the pleasures thou hast doated on; and to part with them as freely
as ever thou didst follow them, even as young commencers do with their
money, as we use to say; then know this exceeding greatness of power
hath begun to work in thy heart.

3. The third particular which, to loosen the heart from it, and to overcome it in the heart, draws forth this great power, is the world. For we
are 'dead in sins and trespasses,' and yet 'walk according to the course
of this world,' Eph. ii. 1, 2, and live to the lusts of men, 1 Pet. iv. 2.
And this world hath a mighty power in it to detain a man in the grave of
death. The men of the world, and the things of the world, are as grave-
clothes, as our coffins, as the mould of earth that covers us, and hinders
us from rising, as the great stone did Christ. And that a great power
comes and says, Arise, and stand up from the dead! must be that power
which wrought in Christ when he was raised from death to life: John
v. 4, 'Whosoever is born of God overcometh the world.' Which argueth
the world hath a great power it puts forth to hold a man; for where there
is no army, no fight, no power put forth, there is no overcoming, no victory. And what is the power by which we are enabled thus to overcome
the world? 1 John iv. 4, 'Stronger is he who is in you than he who is
in the world.' The world hath a great power in you, and such a power as
none but God's Spirit could overcome and encounter with, and scatter;
and therefore conversion is called, Gal. i. 4, 'a delivering us out of this
present evil world' by the Lord Christ, who having overcome the world for
us, overcame it also in us. For both the things of the world, and the men
of the world, have a great power in our hearts; the good things of it, and
the bad things of it. The good things of it: the world is a large shop of
vanities, and every man's eye is fastened upon something, which works
and draws mightily. His heart stands as Jael at the door of her tent,
with milk in her hand, and cries, 'Come in, my lord.' And we have all
as thirsty hearts as he had after the flattering courtesies, the honour of the
world, and the good opinion and good word of the world. What strong

biases are all these to draw a man out of his way and course into the ways of the world! Receiving honour from men, how did it hinder the Jews from Christ! John v. 44. And so the disgraces and discouragements from the world, from carnal friends that have power over us, as parents, masters, husbands, very much prevail. Many would have believed, but that they should have been cast out of the synagogues. There is a corrupt strain and fashion of the world, which the apostle calls 'the course of the world,' which men are carried away with as men in a dream; which not to conform unto is accounted matter of greatest shame, and thought the greatest folly. And then also there are many entanglements and correspondencies with carnal companions, and with those we have been by many kindnesses endeared to, which are most powerful bands and ties to ingenuous natures. And all these doth the god of this world represent, at a man's conversion usually, as he did to Christ when he tempted him with the glory of all the good things of it. And he knows how to varnish, and paint, and set them forth in their best splendour; and so also the disgraces, discouragements, and dangers from the world, and these he represents in their worst visor. Now, to be able to look upon all these goodly things as crucified things, and as dead flowers which the Spirit of God hath blown upon—to choose rather to suffer afflictions with a few poor despised ones in the world, who are not of it—to get and stand out of the crowd as a man wondered at—to be able to swim against the stream and tide of the multitude, the rage and fury of oppressors—to have strength to break through all those weeds of correspondencies with men, though never so great—to break off the strongest leagues and treaties with them, and to venture all their enmity—if wife and children (which are as hostages given to the world of amity with it) hang about thy neck (as Jerome says in his first epistle), if father and mother down upon their knees—to fling away the one and trample upon the other—if thy friend, which is as thy own soul, entice thee (Deut. xiii. 6) to forsake him—to have a heart and strength to do all this, and not to be overcome, is from the cords of God's almighty power drawing the heart. And yet the child of God finds such power working in him, as if all the world lay between Christ and him, Christ would draw his heart through. Nothing can hold him from Christ.

4. You have seen how the exceeding greatness of God's power is drawn out in the work of sanctification; let us see it also a little in the work of true justifying faith; which though to carnal men seems of all things the most easy, yet to educe and bring forth the least act of it requires as great a power as hath been spoken of, and therefore it is called, 1 Thess. i. 3, τό ἔργον πιστέως, the work of faith, for the difficulty of it, the same τό ἔργον, the work of God, κατ᾽ ἐξοχην, John vi. 29, which he especially commands, and shews most power in working of; yea, the same power that was shewn in creating the world, and raising up Jesus Christ. We have an express place for this: Col. ii. 12, 'We are risen with him through faith of the operation of God, who hath raised him from the dead.' Faith, you see, is a work of God's power only, 'faith of the operation of God;' as you say of things that some one man only can make, it is an instrument of such a man's making; so because God only can make true faith, it is called, by way of distinction from false faith, a work of the operation of God. And if you would know what power goeth to work and effect it, he adds, it is of that God who raised up Christ; for no less goes to make faith, whereby indeed a resurrection is wrought likewise in the soul; for he says, 'We are risen with him through faith;' that is, in believing there is a work

wrought in your soul resembling the resurrection of Christ, which therefore must have the same power drawn forth to work it. But you will say, Wherein ?

1. To open this. Consider, that the raising one is putting life into a dead man. Therefore faith, you know, is a new principle of life put into the soul. ' The just shall live by faith ;' as our life lay in doing, under the covenant of works, ' Do this and thou shalt live' ; so now in believing. ' The life that I now live is by faith of the Son of God,' Gal. ii. 20. It is a principle of living in another, and fetching life from another, even from Christ, in whom our life is hid, a going out of a man's self, for life, to him.

2. Consider, that every man by nature would and doth live in himself, and that also by doing still ; though indeed and in truth all hope of life by works of righteousness is cut off, though all our works are ' dead works,' yet we would live of our own, though it be less ; are loath to go out of ourselves for life to another, to depend upon another, in so great a matter as life is ; to have the breath we live with, breathed out of another. Nature is averse to nothing more than to this. Though Adam lost this power of living in himself, yet as Samson, though his strength was gone, thought to do as in former times, so do we, though dead and lost, think to live in ourselves still ; to live by our hands, by doing still. And therefore all the righteousness we have of our own, every good inclination, every good performance, maintains an opinion of life in us. As that church had a name she lived, when she was dead, so we have an opinion we live, when we are dead. So says Paul, Rom. vii., ' I was alive,' says he, when I was a Pharisee. He thought himself a living man in God's sight, by reason of what righteousness he had of his own, which he thought living works.

3. Now therefore, that we may be driven out of ourselves, to seek life in another by faith, it is necessary we should be killed in ourselves, and see, and apprehend ourselves dead men, and all our works dead works. So says Paul in the verse before that, 20th verse of the 2d chapter, lately quoted to this purpose : ' I through the law am dead to the law, that I might live unto God ;' I must be dead first in myself (he speaks it in point of justification, as appears by the scope of the place), that I might live in another : and therefore he adds, ' Nevertheless I live ; and the life I now live is by faith ;' which life of faith can never come to be in the soul, till the opinion of living in myself, and in my own righteousness, be destroyed. And therefore says Paul in the same Rom. vii., ' I was alive indeed,' says he, thought myself a living man ; ' but when the law came, sin revived, and I died :' that is, when I came to see the spiritual meaning of the law, and what true holiness it required to life, I saw, that all my works were unholy, dead works. That was one death, he saw he had no true life of godliness in him, no ability to bring forth a living work ; and so could not live by doing. But there was a second death worse than this : for ' sin revived ;' he before had looked upon all this sin as small matters that would never hurt him, no more than dead serpents would, and had regarded his own righteousness as living works, which would maintain him eternally ; but now, when God opened his eyes, sin revived ; he saw an eternal abounding guilt in the least sin, which stabbed and wounded his soul, for it condemned him ; and, says he, ' then I died ;' I was so far from thinking myself a living man, that I received the sentence of death in myself, and thought that if there had been no more men in the world, I should have been damned ; and I saw no hope of life in myself, and no more power to attain to it, than is in a dead man.

4. Now then to infuse into this man, a new power of believing, a new principle of life, namely, faith, by which he may see himself ' twice dead, plucked up by the roots ;' dead in regard of any work of righteousness, whereby to be justified, or to live in God's favour ; dead in regard of millions of transgressions, the guilt of which like poisoned arrows have wounded him ; and seeing himself thus dead, he is engrafted into another, and comes to apprehend and believe himself an heir of life, and to live in God's sight ; from him to suck life and power to bring forth new works of life : thus to raise him up when once laid for dead, is a work of God's mighty power. For as soon may a dead tree engraft and join itself to a living root, or being set in, as soon may it draw life from that root, and live again, and bring forth fruit, as this man can come to live by faith in Christ. It is exceeding great power to bring a man that is alive in himself, to see he is dead ; we are so conceited of our own righteousness, as to take anything as a sign of life ; and as men fight and strive for life, so do moral and civil men against that word that would kill them, and bring them out of conceit with themselves. But when once the soul apprehends itself dead in itself, it is ten thousand times harder to raise it up to fetch life from Christ, to get it set into Christ. As before a man is humbled, there are many carnal pleas the heart hath for itself, that make a man think he is a living man ; so when a man is once humbled, there are as many pleas against the work of faith, that do detain a man in the estate and opinion of death and condemnation, especially when he is deeply wounded and stabbed with the guilt of sin ; for the wounds of the guilt of sin are as incurable as the wounds of the power of sin : so Ps. lxxxviii. 10, says Heman (being wounded within, and apprehending himself thus, a condemned man), ' Wilt thou shew wonders to the dead ?' that is, wilt thou ever raise my poor soul up to live in thy sight, pardon and heal all these sins ? It is a wonder, says he, if ever this be done ; as great a wonder as to raise up a dead man to life, or a man out of hell ; for as the pains of death detained Christ's soul from rising, so the guilt of sin coming upon the conscience, with a thousand fears and objections, keep a man's thoughts from ever daring to think that he shall yet live, and that God will accept him. Even to raise up the soul to the lowest act of faith, this power is required ; even to believe a man's sins to be pardonable, this is required. For before he believes this, he must be made partaker of God's vast thoughts in pardoning, Isa. lv. 8. A man must forsake his own thoughts ; and therefore a man that comes to believe the pardon of his sins, must not bring the thoughts of a man with him (for in that sense also he may be said to forsake his thoughts), for they can never imagine God will pardon so much, till they be enlarged by a new principle. Now the most in the world, having never been laid for dead thus, think it nothing to believe ; but those that have, find nothing harder and of greater difficulty. It is not in us to apprehend what infinite, vast thoughts of mercy there are in God. And though this seems easy, yet when a man is once enlightened to see the sinfulness of sin to be above measure sinful, Rom. vii. 13, and that for multitude, they are as piles heaped up as high as heaven, and as low as hell ; then to be enabled to see, and be convinced that there are such thoughts of mercy in God, as will swallow up all these sins, as the heavens do the earth, and that they are but a point, in comparison, to think that God thinks, when he looks upon these sins, that though there are millions of them, yet he can pass by them, can find mercy enough to pardon them ; and upon these thoughts, to rest and stay a man's self ; and so to seek him, as not to be denied ; these thoughts are

as far above man's thoughts, as the heavens are above the earth.　There-fore doth the apostle pray, Eph. iii. 17–20, that they might have faith, and so be grounded in love ; that they might be able to comprehend the height, depth, breadth of God's love and mercy, pardoning and swallowing a man's sins up, 'which passeth knowledge ;' that is, above the reach of natural men : it can never enter into their hearts, that there is such a depth, until God elevates them to such thoughts of it; and therefore the apostle farther adds, ' Now unto him that is able to do abundantly,' &c.

I will demonstrate this exceeding great power in working, in paralleling it also with the work of creation, as I did the other.　To which end con-sider, that to see the least creature arise and start out of nothing, argues an almighty power : so also to lay and found so great and weighty a bulk as is that of the earth, upon mere nothing, that the axle-tree and hinges of it should be nothing, is one of those great works of wonder whereby God in Scripture sets forth his glorious power to us.　Now, such is the work of faith whereby I believe Christ made all things to me, and in him all things to be mine ; for it ariseth out of nothing, is founded upon nothing in a man's self, which is the greatest miracle in the world.　But you will ask me what my meaning is, that true faith is founded on nothing, and how I demonstrate it ?

For answer ; When God, and where God means to work true faith, he first brings the heart unto nothing ; to nothing in its own righteousness, to nothing in its own abilities; that is, to see and apprehend itself mere nothing. By nature we all apprehend ourselves to be something, and to have some-thing, out of that self-flattery which is in us: Rev. iii. 17, ' Thou sayest, I am rich, and increased with goods, and have need of nothing, and knowest not that thou art wretched, and miserable, and poor, and naked.'　Now ere God works faith in us he makes us know and apprehend this our nothing, which the Scripture calleth ' poverty of spirit.'　And this is the nothing which I mean, not *in statu entitatis*, as in the rank of creatures ; but nothing as *in statu gratiæ*, nothing in righteousness, nothing in abilities, ever to please God ; nothing in the new world, though something in the old.　The soul sees itself to be worth nothing, as to what is to be possessed in the new creation, unable to purchase anything which is to be enjoyed there, to have interest in nothing but sin and hell.　God by saving ' things, that are not,' confoundeth ' things that are,' 1 Cor. i. 28; that is, he confounds the carnal men in the world which think they are something in wisdom, in power, in righteousness, and have a subsistence within themselves, and on their own bottom.　These he confounds by things that are not, whom he brings to apprehend and profess themselves nothing : ' That no flesh should rejoice in his sight,' ver. 29 ; that they might have a new being and sub-sistence in Christ : ver. 30, ' Of him ye are in Christ Jesus, who of God is made unto us righteousness, wisdom, sanctification, and redemption.' When we are thus annihilated in ourselves, he makes Christ ours, and in him we see all things made ours.　That which makes these things real, and to have a being and a subsistence to me, is my faith, Heb. xi. 1, which is therefore called ' the subsistence of things hoped for, and evidence of things not seen,' and therefore a mighty power must concur with it to effect this. Then, 2 Cor. iv. 6, he compareth that power, which God shewed in creating the first perfect and glorious creature, light : ' God, who commanded light to shine out of darkness, hath shined in our hearts, to give the light of the knowledge of the glory of God in the face of Jesus Christ.'　What was before the light was made ?　You shall find nothing but a rude, void chaos, a darkness and emptiness of all form; a *Tohu* and *Bohu*, which was next door to nothing, which the Spirit immediately sustained and hatched; it had vanished to nothing else. And God said there, ' Let there be light, and there was light.' Any one that reads this will say that God here manifested the exceeding greatness of his power. Just so doth God deal in creating faith in our hearts, which are nothing but darkness in themselves. He brings them first to a *Tohu* and *Bohu*, an apprehension of their own emptiness of grace, as that was of form ; to be nothing but darkness in thine own apprehension, so as the soul is sinking, falling, going into nothing; and then didst thou feel the Spirit of God moving upon thy heart, working in thee, and commanding light to shine out of thy heart ; even the knowledge of God's free grace making Christ to be righteousness, sanctification, and all things to thee. But now the common mock-faith, which is in the world, which is so easy, which comes up alone of itself, riseth still out of something in a man's self, is not thus founded upon nothing; their hearts never having been thoroughly emptied of themselves, nor humbled, nor brought to nothing, their faith stands not on the power of God, but upon themselves, and therefore they think it so easy. Their own natural righteousness, goodness of nature, justness of dealing, every good motion, holy duty performed, emboldeneth them to believe and think they shall be saved. And they are deluded by that self-flattery which is in men's hearts, whereby they are apt to believe good news, or anything which may make for themselves, and whereby they think well of themselves, and are loath to think so harshly that they shall be damned. And therefore they are light of belief to think salvation theirs, and to take anything as an evidence of it ; even as Haman, when he heard that the king would honour a man, presently he thought, out of his pride and self-flattery, that he was the man whom the king would honour ; so says every man's heart naturally, as soon as he hears of such good news as the gospel, I am the man whom God will save. If there were but one to be saved, self-love should easily persuade him he was the man. For pride makes him think better, and hope better, and believe better of himself than of any one else ; especially if he hath any natural goodness or acts of righteousness to shew for it, which, being his own, he thinks well of. And this is the foundation and rise of common faith, which is engendered out of the principles of self-flattery in a man's self, and nourished, and backed, and fed by the righteousness which is in a man's self; and what great power is there in working this ? Nothing is more easy ; nay, nothing is more hard than to beat a man off from believing thus well of himself. But if this were true faith, a man should have wherewith to boast. God therefore, in those whom he means to save, works true faith, which shall ascribe all to Christ and his free grace ; blows down all the building of presumption : the foundation whereof was laid in self-flattery, and natural pride, and good opinion of a man's self; the walls whereof were doubled with untempered mortar of a man's own righteousness (for the heart gets all the rubbish it can to maintain and strengthen itself in a good opinion of itself), and God razeth down all these to the very foundation, puts a man clean out of conceit with himself, that instead of thinking he is the man whom God will save, he begins to think that, of all men in the world, he is the man must die, and sees more reason for it than why all the men in the world should be damned ; and, instead of having any good in him, he sees he is an ungodly person, void of all grace and goodness, Rom. iv. 3–5, and that he is without all ability or strength to help himself; no more able to believe than to climb up to heaven. When he is thus brought to nothing in himself, and to see no reason why he, of all men else, should be saved, a mighty power is necessary to draw him to believe on him that justified the ungodly, Rom. iv. 5, and to build his faith upon nothing in himself, but upon God's free grace in Christ, and so to raise his soul plunged into a gulf of misery, bladders pricked, no hands to swim, that it can stand on 'the rock that is higher than I,' as David says, Christ, and find footing on him, and so is raised out of apprehension of nothing, now to be all things, and to have all things, in Jesus Christ. The power of God working in that great work, τό ἔργον πιστέως, the work of faith, is declared to be as great as to create the world by these three things.

1. By raising up a soul, sinking in its own apprehension into nothing, to believe seriously, that yet he is and may be all things in Christ; and though he hath nothing of righteousness, wisdom, &c., yet that he possesseth all things, as Paul speaks, 2 Cor. vi. 10, that out of such low annihilating thoughts a man's heart should be raised to such vast and high thoughts, that once a man should dare to think that Christ and all his righteousness is his, that sanctification, heaven, redemption is his, who even now was nothing but sin, hell, wrath, and destruction; this is a work of almighty power, greater than the creation of the world, for here is all things come into the room of nothing.

2. Yea, and further; whereas all the things Christ is made to me by faith, as righteousness, &c., are all 'things not seen,' Heb. xi. 1, things out of a man's self, yea, out of a man's ken and reach by nature, and so are to all carnal men in the world as if they were not, and so they reckon them as nothing, because not seen; reckon them as empty notions, that have no being, no subsistence, because none in view; that all these absent things not seen should, by an unheard of art and way, be presented all before me as real, present, subsisting things, to have a being to me and in me, as true, and real, and sensible a being to faith as the sun which I see before me, John xiv. 21, as the meat which I eat (as Christ says, John vi. 55), as real as the things I handle or embrace, Heb. xi. 13; that faith should thus be the evidence of things not seen, and the subsistence of things absent and hoped for, and cause therefore the heart to part with all things at the present he enjoys and sees; to be made a possessor of these, such reality doth he find in them; what mighty power, think we, must accompany the work of faith, that works so great a wonder and miracle, as to make absent things present, things hoped for to subsist, things afar off to be in a man's heart?

3. Whereas a man hath no power to go out of himself to lay hold on these things, thus presented and offered to him, finds in himself no more ability to embrace, and grasp, and reach them, than to lay hold on yonder star, or upon the sun, and a man truly sees he hath no strength, Rom. v. 6, but is like one falling from a high pinnacle of self-confidence and presumption, which is blown down from under him; and though looking up to heaven, he sees righteousness, glory, all things in Christ, offered to be his if he could catch hold upon them, yet, alas! he is not only sinking and falling down headlong further and further from them, but wants hands to lay hold on them if he were at them, and nigh them—in this case now, to have a man's soul drawn and wound up by the power of God, John vi. 44, and carried up by the wings of the Spirit to the throne of Christ in heaven, and to have new hands of faith given him, to embrace and apprehend him of whom he is comprehended; all these are so many wonders in the work

of faith, which requires as much power to effect as was seen in the creation of the world.

And if any have not observed this power working thus in their hearts at first, in bringing them first to nothing (God working upon some insensibly and by degrees), yet they may discern the power of God working in their faith, in continuing, backing, strengthening, and preserving of it ; for he fulfilleth the work of faith with power, as well as he begins it with power ; and if man lives not by bread only, but by God's command and power, then the life of faith is much more continued with power. And indeed, if we would define faith, what is it but the power of God drawing the heart to Christ, and holding it to him ? John vi. 44 ; and 1 Peter i. 5, ' Ye are kept by the power of God through faith ;' that is, the power of God is seen in faith, and that in temptation especially, ver. 6, 7 ; and though in ordinary passages of a man's life, when faith is not put to it, a man will scarce discern this power backing it, when signs, and the witness of the Spirit, and assistance in duties, do take part with faith, yet in time of temptation this will more evidently appear, when the spurious faith, that is but a fruit of the flesh, will fail ; but if true, he that maintained the oil in the cruse, that it decayed not in the time of the famine, he will maintain that little drop of faith in the time of temptation. For this is a sure rule, that which backs thy faith in temptation was the begetter of it. As the woman, when her child was like to be divided, laboured to save it, because it was her child, so will God preserve that faith that is begotten by himself, when it is like to be overborne. And know this, that if thy faith be true, it will be tempted. Satan hath desired to ' winnow thee, but I have prayed' (says Christ) ' that thy faith fail not ;' faith being that thing that Satan desires most to winnow. Dost thou therefore feel the power of God backing, strengthening, joining with thy faith, drawing thy heart to cleave to Christ, maugre all temptations ? Dost thou feel faith an invincible thing, that will never be nonplussed ? It is because God's power is in it. Let a flood of temptations come in, yet faith, like a small drop of oil, will be above them all ; and like a man hanging upon the top of a pinnacle, though ordinarily he hath a stool to ease his hand, yet when the stool is taken away, still he hangs ; so faith, when temptation takes all signs and props away, then upholdeth the heart ; though the devil not only plucks the stool away, but also strikes at the hand that holds it, yet still faith cleaves to Christ, and that so as sometimes the hand is benumbed also, and feels not that it holds it.

Use 1. The first use is to convince those, who defer repentance, of their low and light esteem of the work of grace, they ' erring herein, not knowing the power of God ;' whereas if men apprehended that this work is as much as to dissolve the world to nothing, and make it new again ; and that it is as impossible for them, by their own power, to repent, as to do this, they would set all aside, and think this one thing necessary, as Mary did, and immediately begin to seek to God for it, and think that little time they have to live were little enough for to beg so great a thing at God's hands, and be glad if they could obtain it at last. But such is the foolish wisdom of men, that think to grasp both the pleasures of sin here and heaven in the end, that think to go beyond God and the devil also, thinking to put God off with any repentance at their cast-away leisure, after the strength and flower of their youth and years are spent in the service of sin ; and after a long apprenticeship served to the devil, who takes them captive at his will, think yet to give him at last the slip, to knock off his fetters, and to escape ; as if repentance were within their own power, so playing with it as the cat with its silly prey, thinking that one sudden leap will translate them at once from death to life; between which yet there is as great a gulf as between heaven and hell. Away, you foolish sinners, that say in your hearts as he, Deut. xxix. 19, ' We shall have peace,' &c. Go on to make your own ghests* (as they, James iv. 13–15), chalk out what ways of pleasures this day and the next you mean to walk in, at last meaning (as your hearts tell you) to turn in and see where true repentance dwells, I tell you (as James says, in matters of far less dependence, and more in your own power than repentance is), you reckon without your host; it must be the exceeding greatness of God's power must work it. If you dare yet think it in your own power, go on and prosper, set your own times, put off God still, who it may be now offers and begins to work it, and in your own deceitful hearts appoint and take a longer day, and then break it and perish for ever; do. But if you think it be in God's power only (as, if this text be true, it is), tremble to have such a thought; take his time who hath appointed a time for every work under the sun, the grass to grow, flowers to spring, trees to blossom, and all in their season; which when past, dung and water, and use what means you will, they appear no more.

But you will say, If the greatness of his power work it, then he is able to do it as well at one time as another; and so no time is past with him.

I answer, That his power is regulated by his will, for his power working anything, is his will. ' He worketh all things according to his good pleasure,' and the ' counsel of his will;' therefore, speaking of works of regeneration, it is said, ' Of his will he begat us,' James i. 18. He is a free agent, breathing when and where he pleaseth; and therefore presume not on his power at all times, unless thou beest sure of his will at all times. Now that thou art not; for after that day appointed, he swears in his wrath, ' they shall never enter,' Heb. iii. 18. As he dealt with Saul in the matter of his kingdom, 1 Sam. xiii. 13–15, so with men for matter of grace, Ezek. xxiv. 13 : When I would, they would not ; therefore I will not, says God.

But you will say, I will seek him, and that earnestly.

I answer, Remember Esau, who in this is made a type of all neglecters of grace offered in the gospel, Heb. xii. 17, as the birthright is made a type of the grace offered in the gospel; so his father is a type of God offering it, he having sold it, as men do the offer of grace, for their lusts ; his father could not change his mind, though he sought it with tears ; he found no place for repentance : weep thy eyes out, it will do no good.

But you will say, I will then turn from my sins, take up new purposes and resolutions to forsake them and confess them, and then I hope he will repent and have mercy on me.

To this I answer, I confess you may do so ; only take this with you, that there is a kind of repentance which is partly in your own power, such as Ahab had, who mourned and went softly; such as Judas, Matt. xxvii., who repented himself, confessed, and restored ; such as they performed, Hosea vii. 16, ' They returned, but not to God,' not doing it out of a changed heart, which moves not God; but to have a changed heart, a new life of godliness put in, is not in thy power. For thou canst not make a hair black or white, nor can a blackamore alter his colour, though his blackness be but in his skin ; and canst thou change thy heart, thinkest thou, sin being incorporated and blended with thy nature, so baked into thy bones and the spirit of thy mind ? Tell me, can this heavy, massy lump,

* From the connection, the meaning must be, ' arrangements,' or ' plans.'—ED.

the dregs of the world, the earth fastened in its own centre, can it remove itself and become a star ? Can all the creatures, angels, men, if they set their shoulders to it, with all engines, move it a jot off the hinges it hangs on ? No more can thy heart move itself, being as averse to what is good as the earth is to move upward, as fixed upon sin as the earth upon its centre ; and as great a distance is there between the state of grace and nature as between heaven and earth.

But you will say, I will send for a minister or some good man to help me, and speak peace to me at my death.

Still this doctrine answers you ; it is God's power only can do it. Send for all the angels from heaven, the whole college of physicians, let them come with all their balms, yet as he said, 2 Kings vi. 27, if God do not help thee, they cannot ; for this birth is, John i. 13, not of itself, or the will of man, but of God. Though the minister preach then the gospel of peace to thee, yet unless God makes an echo to thy heart, they are but tinkling cymbals : Isa. lvii. 19, ' I create the fruit of the lips, peace ;' talk they of peace never so much, unless God speak peace, and create it, as the fruit of those words, by an almighty power, thou canst not have peace. ' The wicked are as the troubled sea, which cannot rest ;' when the sea was troubled, Matt. viii. 24, could all the disciples still it ? Could all their anchors save the ship and stay it ? No ; ver. 27, Christ only did it. So when thy conscience is tossed at death, and when the waves of thy sins arise, and the devils, as the winds, are let loose to join with those waves, who can command them silent ? Sooner mayest thou command the thunder silent, that roars in the midst of heaven ; and then thou, poor wicked wretch, art tossed, overwhelmed, and no anchor will hold or stay thee ; no prince of peace comfort thee ; and suppose now all men speak things of peace to thee, yet ' there is no peace to the wicked, says my God ;' and if he says no, his word will stand.

But thou wilt say, I am of an ingenuous temper, and soft to the impressions of good, so as at any time when I consider things, I find my heart moved.

I answer, Suppose it ; yet if this be true that God's power must work it, thou, for all thy good nature, art as far off as another in regard of any active concurrence to it ; as take a piece of soft wax, and another of hard, the soft is no more able of itself to work the image and impression of any thing upon it than the hard, but a hand and seal must stamp the one as well as the other. So is a good nature, as you use to call it, as empty of the image of God as the crookedest, and as unable to stamp that image as the most perverse. It must be God's Spirit (for it is the seal of God, and so called, Eph. iv. 30) must stamp and work an impression, as well as upon the hardest heart, upon thy soft heart : this you may see in the example of the young man, who was ingenuous, soft, pliable, and Christ loved him ; yet of him Christ says, and upon occasion of him, that it was as easy for a camel to go through the eye of a needle, as for a rich man to go to heaven.

But some will say, If I should now set myself to turn, I fear my case is desperate, and there is no hope, I am so hardened in evil.

Ans. The power of God being it which must do it, thou mayest come to repentance, though thy heart be never so hard. At the latter day the earth and elements shall melt with fervent heat, and is he not able to melt thy heart ? Look now on the frosty weather : though all men could not thaw it, yet stay, thou shalt see it thawed ; and cannot he dissolve thy heart ?

But thou wilt say, My heart is full of sin, and of the works of the devil in it, and hath so long lain in them, that it cannot be healed.

I answer, He raised Lazarus, though dead four days, and he stunk ; and why not thee also, though thou art not only dead, but stinkest in thy sins?

CHAPTER VI.

That the virtual cause of regeneration is the resurrection of Jesus Christ.— What influence it hath to raise us to a newness of life.

Blessed be the God and Father of our Lord Jesus Christ, which, according to his abundant mercy, hath begotten us again unto a lively hope, by the resurrection of Jesus Christ from the dead.—1 Peter I. 3.

By the resurrection of Jesus Christ from the dead. The next thing to be considered is the virtual cause of regeneration, namely, the resurrection of Christ.

The words may, *first*, either refer to our hope, as being the cause of it : for in that Christ is risen and ascended, lies our hope that we also shall, as the apostle connects them, 1 Cor. xv. 17, 20, and it is the inference which the apostle makes, Col. iii. 1, 3, 4 compared, that he, being risen, ver. 1, and being our life, ver. 4, therefore when he appears in glory, we shall appear with him. And this it was that made the primitive Christians (as with good news) thus to salute one another, ' Christ is risen, Christ is risen.' ' Because I live' (says Christ), ' you shall live also,' John xiv. 19 ; and therefore, 1 Tim. i., Christ is called ' our hope.'

Or else, 2, it refers to being begotten again. And this seems here to be the most probable reference. Only this is a rule I take in interpreting scriptures, that when any passage relates to two things, I take them both. But here I shall only speak of the last reference, because the dependence between Christ's resurrection and the new birth is the most difficult to discern. To shew the affinity of these two, and to explain this in general, I shall say two things.

(1.) That Christ's own resurrection is called his being begotten; so, Acts xiii. 33, that place in the 2d Psalm is applied to his resurrection, ' This day have I begotten thee,' &c. The reason whereof I take to be this, because when the human nature first entered into that estate, which primitively was ordained for him by his Father (for he should not have come into this world clothed with infirmities but for sin, Rom. viii. 3. But the world to come was ordained for him, as this world was for the first Adam) ; his first entrance into that his world being at his resurrection, it may truly be called his begetting, as being then first brought forth into that his world. And so I understand the coherence of those two verses, Heb. i. 5, 6. That begetting spoken of, ver. 5, was his resurrection, which was that his first ' coming into the world' mentioned, ver. 6, namely, that world which is called ' the world to come,' chap. ii. 5. Now, as his resurrection is called his begetting again, so our resurrection is called our regeneration. So you have it in those words of Christ, Mat. xix. 28, ' Those that follow me, in *the regeneration* shall sit on twelve thrones,' &c., which refer rather to the time of the resurrection, which is the restitution of all things (as Peter calls it), than to the time of following Christ here, although they may relate to both. And therefore we find, Luke xx. 36, the children of God are called by a new title, which ariseth from God's raising them up, it being a begetting them anew as his children.   The words are observable, for they are said to be 'the children of God, they being the children of the resurrection,' or peculiarly for this, that they are raised up by God.   And there is this particular reason in it: for in their first begetting, as men, God was but 'the Father of their spirits,' they hav-ing other bodily 'parents of their bodies and flesh,' Heb. xii. 9 ; but now, in the resurrection, God becomes a father anew unto their bodies, and the whole man, raising them up, and joining both body and soul together; and so they become 'the children of God, being the children of the resurrec-tion.'   And therefore also it is that the redemption at the resurrection of the body is called 'the adoption,' Rom. viii.   And to this purpose also is that phrase, Col. i. 18, where Christ is called 'the first-begotten of the dead ;' the resurrection being a begetting both unto him and them, and because they are raised by virtue of his resurrection, therefore he is called 'the first-begotten.'   Wherefore, that there should be some special affinity between Christ's resurrection and our new birth is not unlikely.   But more expressly those two places, Col. ii. 12 and 1 Peter iii. 21, do ascribe the new birth of a believer unto the resurrection of Jesus Christ.   'The like figure whereunto even baptism doth now save us, by the resurrection of Jesus Christ.'   Baptism is the sacrament of regeneration ; and when the apostle says, 'Baptism saves,' his meaning is, that the grace in baptism, which is regeneration (for that is the thing sealed up) wrought by Christ's resurrection, doth save us.   And the like to this is that in Col. ii. 12.

(2.) The second thing in general to be observed is, that though all the works of Christ for us have an influence into his works in us and upon us, yet so as some are more especially attributed to some work of Christ than to another, and some things in every work in us, more peculiarly to some of his works for us than to others.   That being true of Christ's work for us, that is of the works of the trinity, that though all works are common to all the persons, yet some are more peculiarly attributed to the Father, as election ; some to the Son, as redemption, &c. ; and likewise in every work something more peculiarly attributed to one than to another: as in conversion, drawing us to Christ is attributed to the Father, John vi. 44, and sanctification to the Holy Ghost.   And answerably is it in the thing in hand, the work of regeneration, wherein mortification, or destroying the body of sin, which is one part of it, is attributed to his death, Rom. vi. 4, and the begetting, or infusing a new principle of life into us, unto his re-surrection, ver. 5 of the same chapter.   And thus likewise in justification; the matter of our righteousness which is imputed is Christ's obedience unto death, but the imputation itself is ascribed to his resurrection, Rom. iv. 25. And so, Rom. v. 10, our reconciliation is attributed to his death, but our preservation in that estate unto his life and intercession.

And then, to shew why this new birth is thus peculiarly attributed to his resurrection.

1. It is not by way of merit only, for the merit or price laid down was fully accomplished and paid at that instant when he arose out of the grave (which was the last part of his satisfaction, and when he arose out of de-basement), but his resurrection was the entrance and first step into his glorified condition.

Neither, 2, is it simply in respect of application ; that he arose again to live and send the Spirit to work regeneration in us (as Rom. v. 10, where we are said to be 'saved by his life').   For in this respect, his resurrection hath but the same common influence which it hath into all other works, as upon justification, &c. And indeed, to speak properly, his death is the *meritorious* cause, his intercession the *applicatory* cause. But his resurrection is the *virtual* cause, as by virtue of which it is wrought. And, therefore, Phil. iii. 10, it is called 'the virtue of his reconciliation.' A dew comes from his resurrection, like the 'dew of herbs,' as the prophet Isaiah calls it in the 26th chapter of his prophecy, ver. 19, which (as there) causeth the conversion and calling of the Jews, and their resurrection unto life, even as the dew from heaven causeth the herbs to grow out of the dead womb of the earth. Therefore Christ is called 'a quickening Spirit,' as Adam 'a living soul,' 1 Cor. xv. 45, Adam being able indeed to convey life, but not to quicken dead hearts, as Christ doth. Now, this virtue consisteth in, or ariseth from, two things, or rather shews itself in two things.

(1.) In that the very same power that wrought in Christ when he was raised up works in us to beget us again. So Eph. i. 19, 20, it is expressly said, that 'the same power that wrought in Christ when he was raised from the dead, works in them that believe.' It is no less, yea, it is the same; and this to work faith, Col. ii. 12. And so, Rom. viii. 11, the same Spirit that raised up Christ raiseth us up; our souls here, and our bodies hereafter. And it not only required the same power (as I have elsewhere shewn), but the same power was engaged by his resurrection to work this new birth in us. For Christ rose not as a private man, but as a head, and as 'the first fruits of them that sleep,' 1 Cor. xv. 20, and 'the first-begotten of the dead;' and so, in a way of representing their persons therein, thereby engaging the same power to work in them the members, that wrought in him the head, because he rose with them considered as in him, and he having that power for their sakes, to shew that first in his natural body, which afterward he was to shew in his mystical.

(2.) Christ's resurrection is the exemplary cause of our regeneration, according to which, the Spirit, or that same power that wrought in him, works a work in us conformable to his resurrection, as the pattern of it. And so, although an exemplary cause hath of all ordinary causes the least influence, yet this hath more than such ordinary causes use to have; and that by virtue of a decree, or ordinance given out by God, that we should as well 'bear the image of the heavenly, as of the earthly Adam.' This law was given to grace, as well as nature, and so gives force to Christ's actions, to conform us and ours unto them; as it did to Adam's actions, to transform our nature unto his (as his corruption doth, by the law of nature). And thus our begetting again (which is by the infusion of a new life) bears the image of Christ's resurrection, and so is attributed unto it; the rule being, that that in Christ should have an influence more special to work in us that which was most like thereto. Thus, Rom. vi. 5, it is expressly said, 'We shall be baptized into the likeness of his resurrection.' Now baptism is the sacrament of regeneration, which resembles, in the dipping under water and coming forth again, our burial with Christ in his grave, and our rising again by faith and a new life: Col. ii. 12. Now then, I shall let you see in general the similitude between Christ's resurrection and our regeneration.

1. As the resurrection of Christ was the great 'declaration of him to be the Son of God, with power,' Rom. i. 4; so is the regeneration of a believer the first declaration of his being a son of God, and the first discovery of his election.

2. As Christ's resurrection was the first step unto his glory, and to that

exaltation that followed that his resurrection, so regeneration is the foundation and first step unto all those privileges of a Christian that follow upon the state of grace, whereunto this is the door, or first entrance.   I might shew this more particularly in the principal parts of regeneration ; as,

(1.) In the work of faith, in a rising from under the guilt of sin.

(2.) In the work of sanctification, in a rising from under the power of sin.   For we are dead in respect of both ; dead in respect of guilt, as a man condemned is said to be a dead man, bound over to death ; dead in respect of the power of sin, as a man whose soul is gone is dead, he being unable to move or stir, because he wants a principle of life.   It is faith which raiseth us to a life of justification, as, Rom. v. 18, it is called.   And this it doth, as really from the state of condemnation, which change is called a ' passing from death to life,' so also apprehensively ; that is, from the apprehension of being under the guilt and condemnation of sin ; which apprehension is wrought by humiliation, wherein the Spirit condemns a man, and binds him over to guilt and death (and therefore, Rom. viii. 15, he is called ' the Spirit of bondage'), and also gives a man up to the law, which shuts a man up with a guard or garrison, as one condemned, until faith comes, Gal. iii. 22.   For therein God's dealing with the Jews was a type of his proceeding by a Spirit of bondage, wrought in those God means to convert.   And so the Romans are said to have received the Spirit of bondage.   God also stayeth the sinner with that guilt : Rom. vii. 10, 11, ' Sin revived, and I died,' says Paul, when he was humbled.   And out of this death doth faith raise the soul up to a ' justification of life.'   Therefore, Col. ii. 12, it is said, ' You are risen with him through faith of the operation of God, who hath raised him from the dead.'   For it is faith which makes a man live in God's sight, and enjoy his favour, which is the life of the soul.

BOOK X.

*Of the two essential properties of inherent holiness and sanctification.—That a
regenerate man makes God his chiefest good.—That he also sets up God and
his glory as his chiefest end.—A trial of difference between a regenerate and
unregenerate man herein.—That there is also an eminent disposition in the
new creature, inclining a regenerate man earnestly to desire, and endeavour
to convert others to God.*

CHAPTER I.

*That every man hath something which he makes his chiefest good.—What men
unregenerate place their chief good and happiness in, and in what the regenerate place theirs.—That there are two chief treasuries in which the good
things of men are laid, viz., heaven and earth.*

*But Abraham said, Son, remember that thou in thy lifetime receivedst thy good
things, and likewise Lazarus evil things : but now he is comforted, and thou
art tormented.—*LUKE XVI. 25.
*Lay not up for yourselves treasures upon earth, where moth and rust doth
corrupt, and where thieves break through and steal : but lay up for yourselves treasures in heaven, where neither moth nor rust doth corrupt, and
where thieves do not break through nor steal ; for where your treasure is,
there will your heart be also.—*MAT. VI. 19–21.

ALL creatures are said to have their life, motion, and being in God, Acts
xvii. 28. But this is only as he is their efficient cause, and upholder of
them by his power. It is in like manner said, that ' God hath made all
things for himself, even the wicked,' Prov. xvi. 4, namely, as the *finis cui*,
or external end. He by his power and wisdom ordered all their beings and
motions to his own glory. But it is the privilege, yea, essential constitution of the new creature, to hold of God by a more near and intrinsecal
tenure or copy, even for its very being, to have its life bound up in God,
and that in a double further respect unto him. Namely,

1. To have its life, actuation, and motion, and stirrings of all within itself
to lie and consist in God himself, as known and loved by itself as the close
object and matter of its happiness and comfort. And

2. To have God made unto it, from the inward constitution and tendency
of itself, its proper, natural, principal end, its own intrinsecal end or *finis
cujus*, and more intrinsecal unto it than itself is to itself He is the loadstar that guides, and loadstone which quickens all the motions and tendencies of all within it, and which draws them all into, and carries them
along with, itself.

And look, as the understanding and will are two essential faculties in the soul, so to make a man's chiefest good, and a man's chiefest end, these are the two essential properties of the new nature that do constitute it such, and are proper thereunto. The soul was originally made for God, so as both to glorify him, and also to be made happy in him ; and holiness in the soul, and that principle alone, doth fit it for, and elevate it unto both these. Therefore in some scriptures you find it termed, ' the life of God,' as Eph. iv. 18 ; sometimes ' the glory of God,' Rom. iii. 23.

The first of these is my present subject in design, and to call all your souls to an account, what it is you account your chiefest good. All men of knowledge, brought up under the light we enjoy, out of ordinary conviction of what God is, and out of common experience of the vanity of the creature, do acknowledge and profess this God to be the chiefest good as to the speculative part; but that which we seek after is a discovery of what men do herein practically and really in the daily actings and motions of their souls towards God, and into God, and not what men profess him to be in reason. All will say, We hope for happiness from God in the other world, when they can live no longer, though all their lives here they live in the creatures. But the inquisition is, what men do make here in this life their chiefest good, and do live upon it, and are taken up therewith, either in the pursuance or enjoyment of it, and this with difference from all carnal men in the world.

It is uttered as the common cry and voice of the many or multitude : Ps. iv. 6, ' The many will say, Who will shew us any good ?' That is the common voice and cry of nature, common to good and bad ; but how then are wicked and godly men differenced and distinguished ? Even by this, what good things their souls make their good things. There are multitudes of scriptures to evidence this ; Luke xvi., Christ's chief scope indeed was to shew the vastly differing conditions of a rich wicked man, and of a poor saint in this world, and in that to come. How plentifully the rich man lived, and what he enjoyed according to the opinion and desire of his own heart, the 19th verse relates : ' There was a certain rich man, which was clothed in purple and fine linen, and fared sumptuously every day.' And how miserable the poor man was : ver. 20, 21, ' And there was a certain beggar named Lazarus, which was laid at his gate, full of sores, and desiring to be fed with the crumbs which fell from the rich man's table : moreover, the dogs came and licked his sores.' He was in his body full of sores, and so in continual tortures, unable to stir, for he was laid at the rich man's outward gate, not having to sustain nature, for he desired crumbs, which are the allowance of dogs, and these were denied him ; and on the contrary, the rich man's dogs licked and sucked his blood, refreshing themselves therewith, a dead carcass, he unable so much as to drive them away. This difference is in their lives.

The other is in their death. Poor Lazarus dies, and ' the angels carry his soul to feast in heaven,' which Christ elsewhere expresseth by ' sitting down with Abraham, Isaac, and Jacob,' as at a feast ; and here, by his being placed in Abraham's bosom, as next guests to him, it being the manner at feasts to lean on the bosom of him that was next him, as John did in Christ's, John xiii. 23. ' The rich man dies,' and hath a stately funeral ; ' he was buried,' that is added, which you may observe is not spoken of the other ; but withal, the next news you hear of him is his being in hell, where, in the words of my text, he is upbraided with and reminded of this, ' Remember thou receivedst thy good things in thy lifetime, but

Lazarus evil things.' Souls in hell meditate and perfectly remember what in this world they had been and what sins they committed, what pleasures they enjoyed, and in the conscience and remembrance of such things does lie ' that worm that never dieth ;' and the 21st verse of the 50th Psalm tells us that ' their sins are set in order,' or martial array, ' afore them.'

Nor is it simply said, ' Thou receivedst good things,' as of Lazarus, it is said he ' received evil,' as if that were the rule God went by. No ; for even this very Abraham, who is here brought in speaking this to him, is an undeniable instance to the contrary. And the rich man had had from thence wherewith to have retorted to him. Gen. xiii. 2, ' Abraham was very rich in cattle, in silver, and in gold.' And this was spoken of him many years afore he died, and it is to be supposed he increased therein. The sting therefore which he sets and leaves in this rich man's heart lies in this word, ' *thy* good things ;' that is, which thy soul pitched upon as such, as the chief object of its desires, the darling of thy delights, or (as it is uttered by God to the inhabitants of that great city, when in like manner destroyed and cast to hell, Rev. xviii. 14), ' The fruits which thy soul lusted after, and all things that were dainty and goodly ' (namely, in thine own eyes), ' are departed from thee.' And this the very text, with difference, puts the emphasis upon. For of Lazarus he says that he ' received evil things ; but thou, *thy* good things.'

So then carnal men make the good things that are in this life their chief and only good things which their souls lust after, and live upon. And the reason is in Eph. vi. 18, ' They being estranged from God, and the life of God, through ignorance and unbelief, they know no better.' And all men's souls cry out, ' Who will shew us any good ? ' And therefore they, as the prodigal (whose story is the living type of this), being ready to starve, and no saving intercourse being betwixt God and them, they content themselves with what is afore them, though but husks. Nor can they relish, or take in, or delight in any other, and so are confined and shut up to these.

And 2. In that other Scripture, Mat. xvi. 19–21, Christ holds forth as to this point in hand these two things : 1. That every man hath something or other he accounts his treasure, which in like manner, speaking to every man, he calls their treasure : ' Where *your* treasure is, there will your hearts be.' Every man that hath a heart hath also some treasure. For it will be taken up with something or other ; and the reason is, because every man hath self to provide for and lay up for. Christ hath expressed it in these very words : Luke xii. 21, ' A man laying up treasure,' says he, ' for himself ;' and of what his heart judgeth best, and finds naturally most content in, it lays out for such things. It is not riches only that are the treasures of the sons of men (though some men's), but whatever thing the heart fancies and is set upon as its chiefest good. The poorest have their treasure in this respect, of what is in their sphere and compass ; it is that on which their hearts are, as the phrase is, ver. 21 ; that is, which he values and esteems as his chiefest good. So then, ' thy good things ' in Luke, is all one with ' thy treasure ' in Matthew ; only the one is a real expression, the other only a metaphorical. A treasure hath this addition, that it is some eminent good thing, which he accounts such, and so his chiefest good. Treasure, you know, is of what a man counts most precious. Rich and covetous men (from whom the metaphor is taken) heap not up for treasures iron, lead, or pebbles, but gold, precious stones, the world, which in common estimation hath turned up trump. We may approve of many things in their kind which we make not our treasure, but treasure is still the choicest and the chiefest, and so here is put to express what a man hath pitched on as his chiefest good. A godly man accounts the things of this life good, for he useth them ; yet he reckons them not as his treasure. And a wicked man may acknowledge, and cannot but say of the things of the other world, God, and Christ, and grace, that they are things that are good ; yet he makes them not his treasure.

The second thing that Christ holds out is, that there are two differing treasuries or storehouses, repositories or places, in which the chief good things of the sons of men are found, and but two ; and they are earth and heaven. These are the two great staples of differing commodities. Look, as heaven and hell will one day make a perfect dichotomy, disjunction, or a single division of men's persons hereafter ; so here, on earth, and on heaven, do men's hearts and affections divide.

Now, as the general reason afore given was, that every man hath a self to provide for ; so the reason of this different treasure and provision is the difference of that self that is in men. Some have nothing but an earthly self. All their affections, and inclinations of their souls, are through sin become ' members upon earth,' Col. iii. 5, and earth will to earth. But a man born again hath another self begun in him. For what is it else that is born again but another self, by this second birth (as the product thereof), as that former self was by the other birth ? and is therefore called the ' new creature,' as that which is made for and fitted to the things of another world. And these things on earth will no more make that self happy, than meat and drink, and clothes or beauty, would conduce to make an angel or a separated spirit happy, or contribute to their well-being.

I need not open to you these two vast treasuries ; they are known to you all. The world is a large shop of vanity, and one heart hath a mind to this thing, another to that, viz., beauty, credit, learning, wit, conversation, riches, honour, power ;—' Soul, thou hast goods for many years,' Luke xii. 19 ; ' eat, drink, and be merry ;'—which, because the world generally knows no better, and uttering their very hearts, they use to give the name of *goods* unto ; yea, and of *substance* forsooth, it being so to them ; and therefore John is fain to distinguish them, upon the mention of them, from the true good, terming them the world's good, 1 John iii. 17 ; that is, which they count such. It is the name the world gave ; and in the other part of the distinction, or rather in opposition thereto, Luke xvi. 11, the other are termed ' the true riches ' by Christ, and, chap. xii. 21, ' riches to God ;' that is, in God's account and valuation such, whereas the others are such in the world's.

But not riches only, but anything else more mental and aerial, as honours, learning, yea, legal righteousness itself, outward privileges and duties of Christians (when God is not made a man's chief end in the performance or enjoyment of them), come under this inventory of men's treasuries, Philip. iii. 5, 6, ' Circumcised the eighth day, of the stock of Israel, of the tribe of Benjamin, an Hebrew of the Hebrews ; touching the law, a Pharisee ; concerning zeal, persecuting the church ; touching the righteousness that is in the law, blameless.' Now he counted these his excellency and his gain : he useth both expressions in what follows, ver. 7, 8, ' What things were gain to me, I accounted loss, for the excellency of the knowledge of Christ.' Yea, put in ' all things,' for so Paul doth : ' I account all things now but loss.' Or,

Heaven's treasury you have set out under that notion (for I shall quote no other than such as speak in the language of this metaphor) ; ' I am thy exceeding great reward,' says God to Abraham, Gen. xv. 1, after he had refused the spoil of five kings. By this metaphor are set forth—

1. God, who in Job xxii. 25 is termed a righteous man's best gold. See the margin.

2. Christ, in whom are 'unsearchable riches,' Eph. iii. 8.

3. The promises, which are the veins, the mines, those treasures are laid up in. They are 'great and precious,' 2 Pet. i. 4.

4. The graces that do interest us in these riches, as faith, it is called 'precious faith,' 2 Pet. i. 1 ; yea, 'much more precious than gold,' 1 Pet. i. 7. So wisdom also is styled, whether you understand it of Christ, or the wisdom to salvation, through faith in him: Prov. viii. 19, 20, 21, 'My fruit is better than gold, yea, than fine gold ; and my revenue than choice silver. I lead in the way of righteousness, in the midst of the paths of judgment : that I may cause those that love me to inherit substance ; and I will fill their treasure.'

And 2. That the soul of a man born again is thus framed as to place in God, and these things of God, his chiefest and sole supreme comfort, and this by way of difference from wicked men, the Scripture throughout sheweth. David is a sufficient instance, who utters this disposition of his both absolutely, or singly, as also comparatively, or with difference to what wicked men account their chiefest good.

(1.) Absolutely or singly : Ps. lxxiii. 25, 'Whom have I in heaven but thee ? Or in earth in comparison of thee ?'

(2.) Comparatively, with wicked men, as a difference from them : Ps. iv. 6, 'There be many that will say, Who will shew us any good ? Lord, lift up the light of thy countenance upon us. Thou hast put gladness in my heart, more than when their corn and their wine increased :' where, 1, He brings in the common cry of all mankind, as hunger-starved creatures, 'Who will shew us any good ?' Then, 2, shews what chief good the option of himself and of all the saints is, in whose name he uttereth it, as Paul, in the like case, instancing in his own persuasion, but speaking in this name of the whole us of believers: Rom. viii. 37–39, 'Nay, in all these things we are more than conquerors through him that loved us :' ver. 38, 'For I am persuaded, that neither death, nor life, nor angels, nor principalities, nor powers, nor things present, nor things to come, nor height, nor depth, nor any other creature, shall be able to separate us from the love of God, which is in Christ Jesus our Lord.' 'Lord, lift upon us the light of thy countenance ;' this we have pitched on as that in which our joy and happiness lies ; and the light or communication thereof unto us is the pursuit of us all which are the chosen of God : ver. 3, 'Know that the Lord hath set apart him that is godly for himself, 'to enjoy himself,' to be made happy in himself, ordained him and singled him out to communicate himself unto ; and accordingly hath given him a principle of godliness suited to himself. He hath set out him that is godly for himself, making him capable of himself, as the faculty is of its natural object, and the eye of colours, &c. Whereas wicked men (says he) have their corn and wine. Observe how he calls it their corn, &c. Had not David corn and wine too ? Oh but these were these men's chief good things, which their souls had seized upon, as the bee doth on the flowers, to suck honey out of.

Again ; You find the same request with this very difference, Ps. xvii. 14, 'The men of the world' (says he) 'which have their portion in this life.' There is the one sort, who have their name from the things they affect : 'The men of this world ;' that look, as things of this world, in relation to their adherence to them, are called 'the goods of this world,' 1 John iii. 17, so David calls carnal men ' the men of this world.' They have their denomination and distinction from what their hearts are set on and addicted unto ; even as Esau is called 'a man of the field,' like as the birds are called ' the birds of the air,' because that is the element they live in. ' And their portion is in this life :' their portion, that is, that which themselves seek and choose. ' Remember thou hadst thy good things in thy lifetime.' The prodigal's portion was that which himself desired, Luke xvi. 12, of which, Mat. vi. 2, Christ speaks ; that as they seek glory from men, so they have their reward ; still it is called theirs ; that is, what they pitched on, expected, desired, covenanted for.

Now, how doth David ? As a godly man he distinguished himself from these, it follows, ver. 15, ' As for me, I will behold thy face in righteousness.' He severs himself from them, as a man of another genius. It is as when we say, *For my part ;* so he speaks to God, The happiness I look for lies in thy face, in thyself ; that is, in thy person and favour (as face is taken) ; this I pursue after in this life, upon the glimpse I have of it. And in expectation of that, my desires grow dead and flat to all other things here. So as though the chief of my affections towards it here are but desires, yet when I awake from the dust, Isa. xxiv. 19, I shall be satisfied with thy image, the light, sight, and knowledge of thee, and of him whom thou hast sent, Christ, the express image of thy person. That desire or aim of Paul's, Phil. iii. 11, did fully interpret this. He looked not to ' things that are seen, which are temporal, but his eyes were upon things that are not seen, but are eternal,' as himself speaks, 2 Cor. iv. 18.

So that in philsophy we say, *Potentiæ distinguuntur per actus et objecta,* as sight from hearing, as having colours for its object, whereas hearing hath sounds ; so shall the distinction of persons and their fatal conditions at the latter day be fetched from the objects their souls pursued after, as their chiefest good, as that which they enjoy or hope to arrive at, Ps. xxiv. 6. They are ' a generation ;' that is, a sort or kind of men whose differencing property is this, that ' they seek thy face.' ' This is the generation of them that seek him, that seek thy face,' in opposition to which, Christ using the same denomination David had done, termeth the other sort ' the children of this world ;' and then adds, ' who are wiser in their generation,' Luke xvi. 8 ; thus terming them in that very respect, a generation distinct from the children of light, insomuch as this distinction riseth up to be an essential difference, and to make a several kind and generation of men, Ps. xxiv. 6.

CHAPTER II.

That we may know what we make our chiefest good, let us inquire in what things we take most pleasure and delight.

Let us all narrowly inquire in what good things our treasury doth lie, which will be the great inquest at the latter day. Hell, you see, gets those that do make the good things of this life their good things. It is that which stops the mouth of one in hell : ' Thou receivedst thy good things in thy life.' And at the latter day, when men shall see what a good and glorious God they have neglected, for the desires of, or pursuit after these low vanities, all men's mouths will be stopped, and have nothing to say.

That therefore which I put to the question is, in what dost thou place thy treasure ?   I examine not the particulars; let thy conscience do that.   But deal impartially ; to what world doth it belong ?   Wherein lies it, and what is it your hearts do trade for ?   Every man is a merchantman. Rome's customers are termed ' merchants upon earth,' Rev. xviii. 11. And of the commodities they traffic for, you have the bill of trade in the 12th and 13th verses : ' The merchandise of gold, and silver, and precious stones, and of pearls, and fine linen, and purple, and silk, and scarlet, and all thyine wood, and all manner of vessels of ivory, and all manner of vessels of most precious wood, and of brass, and iron, and marble, and cinnamon, and odours, and ointments, and 'frankincense, and wine, and oil, and fine flour, and wheat, and beasts, and sheep, and horses, and chariots, and slaves, and souls of men.'   The other are termed, on the contrary, merchants for heaven ; and the commodities of that kingdom you have, Mat. xiii. 45 : ' The kingdom of heaven is like a merchantman who sought out good pearls.'   And I may say, the pearls of that kingdom are good; as it was said of the gold in the land of Havilah, Gen. ii. 12.   Now Christ tells us it is the heart that lays up this treasure.   And the heart is deep, and of all things else treasures are the most hidden things in the heart. Men seek to hide them ; God is said to have hid his in the field, and so do men.   Ps. xvii., their treasure is called the ' hid treasure.'   Yet the heart knows where it is, and what it is, for they are buried there.   As therefore searchers into mines have long borers or wimbles, which, put down into the bowels of the earth, do bring up some of the ore with them, and discover what mine is there ; so there is a *virgula divina* will go down into the bottom of your hearts.   Two ways I shall now proceed in it, according to the differing language of these texts.   1. The real naked question, What are thy good things ?   2. The metaphorical one, What is thy treasure ?

1. For the real part of this question, I shall propound two trials.

(1.) What things doth thy soul favour and relish most ?   The things of this world, or God, and the things of the other world ?   The truth of this sign is evident ; for whatever is good and convenient to any creature, it hath a suitableness thereto.   And if it be a sensitive or natural creature, it hath a favouring or relishing thereof; for *omnis vita gustu ducitur*, is maintained by a drawing in unto itself, and by a pleasing tasting of what is that good thing is appointed for it.   As thou hast a soul (which is of itself a mere empty stomach), so that soul hath a palate to savour and relish what is good for itself; which is fitted to take in the sweetness of some good thing or other.   And as that palate is affected or possessed with its native soundness of taste, or with a vitiated humour (as we see in sickness), accordingly it doth savour and relish things, in the like difference with which men in health or sickness use to do.   Now, upon that which is the palate of the soul of man, there is by the fall contracted vitiated humour, which maketh sin and the good things of this world only pleasing to it : Job xx. 12, wickedness is said to be sweet in his mouth.   I might give you this difference out of Rom. viii. 5, ' For they that are after the flesh do mind the things of the flesh ; but they that are after the Spirit the things of the Spirit.'   They do mind, or savour, or relish, as the word is translated, Mark viii. 33.   Those two scriptures are sufficient, the one spoken of carnal professors, 2 Tim. iii. 4, ' Lovers of pleasure more than God ;' of pleasure, namely, in other things than in God, that are besides God.   The other scripture speaks of every babe in Christ.   Let a man be but a Christian of a day's standing, and a new palate is given him, clean

altered to the taste of things: 1 Pet. ii. 2, 3, ' As new-born babes, desire
the sincere milk of the word; if so be that ye have tasted that the Lord is
gracious.' I take the connection thus; I cannot say it is a mere *exegesis*,
that is, explaining the same thing in new words. Nor is it yet a new
argument drawn from a further experiment. As if he should first urge,
if you be babes, then, 2, if afterwards in process of God's dealings with
you, you have further tasted, &c. (thus most carry it.) But it is a most
vehement indigitation of what is the true ground and reason why, if they
were but even new-born babes, they must needs desire the sincere milk of
the word, drawn from what is the first and essential property accompanying that new estate, even to taste how good the Lord is; and is as if we
should say, As you are a man; and add, If you so be, you have reason in
you, which is proper to a man as a man; so urging them with what is
most immediate and essential to them. So as Peter's scope is, that they
must renounce their being so much as babes, if they have not found something of this faculty and act of tasting in them. Lawyers give this evidence
of a child that is new born, its being alive, that it cries. Peter here gives
another as characteristical of this new birth, that it hath a taste to discern
how good the Lord is. And whereas here in Peter it is that the Lord is
gracious, there is therein an allusion unto that of David: Ps. xxxiv. 8,
' O taste and see how good the Lord is.' The Septuagint renders it
χρηστός, gracious, but the Hebrew *tob*, how good; and because to a soul
new born that part of God's goodness which allures his heart to him is his
free grace, and lets in all his goodness into the soul, and so it is as that
pap or dug the soul sucks his goodness by and through, therefore Peter
chooseth rather to · say, If ye have tasted how gracious the Lord is; and
so, as new-born babes, have this desire in you. For taste, we know, is the
foundation of the most eager desires and imports; that look, as a child
come new out of the womb, though there it never had occasion to exercise
the faculty of taste, for it took its nourishment at the navel, yet being
come into the world, it instantly seeks after milk, and tastes it, and in it
the mother's blood, which argues the constitution thereof so framed as it
hath such a faculty of tasting congenite, whereof it had before no use whilst
in the womb. Now, thus constituted, says Peter, is the new creature towards God. There is such a faculty of taste in every new-born babe, framed
to things of the other world by its new birth, unto which world it is on
purpose now new brought. And one of the first spiritual senses it exerciseth is a tasting how good the Lord is. Are the pleasures of sin yet more
to thee, and so have been hitherto all thy days, more than all that goodness that is in God (who is a sea of honey), whereof yet thou sayest, as
Solomon of his old man doth, ' I have no pleasure in them'? It is an
evident sign thou retainest wholly still the old man, and hast nothing of
the new babe in thee. Or as Barzillai, 2 Sam. xix. 32, thou sayest, Can
I taste what I hear in sermons or prayers, or read in the word? Yea,
perhaps thou hast no more taste of these things than thou findest, as Job
speaks, in the white of an egg, Job vi. 6. Thou art not yet so much as a babe.

But now whilst I make this so great a difference between a regenerate and
unregenerate man, the objection will be, that regenerate men find a sweetness in the good things of this life; yea, often in the pleasures of sin. And
unregenerate men, that fall away, do taste of the powers of the world to come.

I shall endeavour to answer this objection by parts.

1. For a regenerate man's tasting the pleasures of sin. There are indeed
fits and paroxysms, in which, as in a man's body that is in an ague (and the

state of the most regenerate is but made up of such a mixture), corrupt
humours overflow and prevail, and vitiate and distemper this renewed
palate ; which when they do, no wonder if God and spiritual things be out
of taste with him, and he relisheth things worldly, yea, simple.* It may
strike, and yet withal comfort, the hearts of the best here to hear Christ
our Lord and Saviour speak of Peter, that holy apostle (as to that present
prevailing frame of his spirit), such sharp and strange language as once
upon occasion he utters of him, such as worse could not be given an unregenerate man : Mat. xvi. 23, ' Get thee behind me, Satan.' For Satan
then possessed his soul, and suggested that wicked speech he tempted
Christ withal, as the devil could not have uttered a worse. Neither doth
Christ lay all the fault on Satan (as we should not), for Peter's own heart
was in a prevailing distemper, overflown with the gall or jaundice ; so as
it follows, ' Thou savourest not the things of God, but those that are of
men.' At present his palate was in savouring these rendered as carnal as
an unregenerate man's. It was so to Christ that knew his heart, and
therefore might be so to his own sense. Yea, a man in an ague or fever
thinks he shall never relish his meat again. Here is the very distinction I
have put : 1. The things of God ; 2. The things of man, that is, which are
suited to the corrupt nature of man, which is nothing but flesh (and therefore to be carnal, and to walk as man, is made all one, 1 Cor. iii. 3). But
this was but a fit, a paroxysm for the present ; Peter's taste came to him
again : John vi. 68, ' Whither shall we go ? thou hast the words of eternal
life.' The foot of his soul was here taken off from all other between, and
knew not where else to rest itself. So then this is but as the fit of a man
that is of a sound constitution.

2. The delight he takes in sin is but a broken delight, for the principle is
broken and wounded. And *læsa principia habent læsas operationes*, as a man
that walks with a bone out of joint, he doth it lamely. If he chews the bread
of wickedness, or as the psalmist, ' the dainties of the wicked,' Ps. cxli. 4 ;—
Yet, 1, it is as with a broken tooth.

Or, 2, not so as to swallow it down (as they, Prov. xix. 28, the mouth
of the wicked, is said to devour iniquity), not so as to return to a greediness, as Eph. iv. 19, but though he tastes, he soon spits it out again, as
they did that broth of which they cried, ' There is death in the pot.'

Or, 3, if he takes it down for a fit, he comes not to take that pleasure in
it for the future as to retain it as a sweet bit, which of a wicked man is said
that he ' rolls it under his tongue,' to the end to protract his pleasure in it
all his life (as children will do sugar-candy all day long) ; which also ' he
hides, and forsakes not,' as Job xx. 12 ; but this man soon casts it out again
with the deepest detestation.

4. The heart is never wholly ' overcome with it,' as Peter's phrase is,
2 Pet. ii. 20. Overcome he may be to an act the grossest, and in the hour
of temptation the major part of his will must needs be for it, or he would
not act ; but so as to make it his rest, to sit down in it as the swine, to
wallow in the mire, which is Peter's character of one so overcome in his
sense, to centre in it as the chief pleasure of his life, he can never come to
do it any more. The impressions he hath had of God and Christ, which
are indelible in his soul, and the remembrance from whence he is fallen or
falling, as Rev. ii. 5, brings his heart off and about again. He still says
the old wine is better, as Christ speaks, or as Hosea ii. 7, ' I will return to
my first husband, for it was better with me then than now.'

* Qu. ' sinful ' ?—ED.

For the second part of the objection, that unregenerate men taste of the powers of the world to come.   The only answer I shall now give is,

That a right and true parallel between a godly man in tasting the pleasures of sin after regeneration, there remaining a radical constitution of soundness in him, and an unregenerate man's tasting the powers of the other world, doth help to clear this, and indeed each one doth illustrate the other.   To make forth which I express myself thus.   The palate of such an unregenerate man remains in the inward constitution and temper of it still wholly corrupt, namely, in respect of this radical corruption of it, wherein the bottom of man's corruption doth consist, and that is *self;* whatever object it relisheth and pitcheth upon, it is only such as is suited unto self.   Now in the things revealed in the gospel there are two sorts or kinds of goodness ; the one is the essential, substantial goodness of things themselves, the other is an accidental goodness cleaving hereunto, over and above the substantial goodness of them ; and this latter suiteth self-love that is in every man's heart.   The promise of heaven, taken in under the notion of a happiness to a man's self, is in that respect an object suited to self in a man ; and any man, in respect of self-love in him, is thereby capable to be inveigled with it, and struck with the news of it as to listen after it, to taste and relish, to be taken with what can be said of it, so far as it may suit that principle.   Though, take heaven substantially, as it is the enjoyment of God himself,—heirs with Christ of God, as the apostle says, Rom. viii.; for God himself is Christ's inheritance, as avowedly himself speaks, Ps. xvi.; —so conceived it is suited only to a heart regenerate.   The Holy Ghost may set on the former, as he did on Balaam, and give or convey unto self in a man a taste of a supernatural sweetness ; to toil on and entice the creature to himself, when yet that taste and sweetness is not of God himself as pitched upon alone as our happiness.   I might make the like distinction of Christ as a Saviour only, and Christ as in himself, as I have done of heaven.

So then, in such a heart, the competition betwixt the taste which self merely hath had of that accidental goodness in the things of the other world, so far as it is capable thereof, and the same self in a man as it is still naturally rooted and set in this world, and hath tasted the pleasures of this world, and is suited unto them.   Now mark it, the things of the other world (take them in their own nature, and own proper notion), these no ways suit a man's heart at all, but all within him is enmity and averseness to the things themselves.   And it is nothing else, for he is in his root and conjugal constitution as a man of this world.   And so look, as it is only accidental goodness which is in the things which he tasteth, so his own natural and radical disposition verging wholly another way, these his motions and elevations towards them are in like manner but accidental to his spirit ; that is, only as he is set in such and such circumstances of distress of conscience or fear of wrath, and is influenced by such apprehensions as comes upon him for the present ; all which are but foreign and extrinsecal to his genial constitution or inward nature.   And thus self in him is but forcedly raised up to that joy he hath in the things of the other world, even as they come so to be set home, as to amuse self a while with the strange news of happiness, as in another country to be had.   But his joy in things in this world is natural, congenial.   Now that which is natural, and agrees with the whole inward constitution of anything, must needs be stronger, and so eat out what is but forced and extrinsecal.   For what is good naturally to a man is always so, and is so *per se.*   What is good accidentally holds only in such a distress, in such a case or circumstance, or apprehension as man is in, and so wears off, as colours laid on use to do. The stony ground received the word with joy (namely, in this sense as hath been explained), but their defect is noted to be the same that I have said, that ' they wanted root in themselves,' Mat. xiii. 20, 21; that is, a congenial, natural principle suited to things heavenly. Self was taken a while with the hearsay of them; but the root of their hearts and natures remained still fixed in the things of this world, in earth. And the root went on to bring forth according to its kind, and to draw the juice of the earth it was fixed in to itself, which dried up that moisture that fed those plants which were adventitious, and set in made earth for a while. So likewise of the thorny ground, it is said (ver. 22 compared with Mark iv. 19), ' The cares of this world, and the lusts of other things entering again' (which are and were natural to the heart and the soil of it), ' choke the word' that was superficially cast in ; for why, the heart is wholly a stepmother to the one, and a natural mother to the other ; and so the heart in the end returns to itself. But now in regeneration we affirm, that a man receives a heavenly nature, which is a noble plant of the Lord's planting, naturally rooted in heaven and things heavenly, as in its proper soil it is to grow up and thrive in. And although there is another root, that is seated on earth, that remains still in the heart, yet it is a-dying, and that heavenly plant is that which is deepest in and nearest the heart, as the inner man, and the other but as the outward.

Hence then the parallel runs clear between these two, in an opposite way, (though I acknowledge a difference in one respect) ; that look, as an unregenerate man may taste (as hath been explained) of the accidental goodness that is in things heavenly, yet all that while his inward natural constitution in him remaining wholly disposed to things in this world of itself, and to them for themselves ; hence, let him have what tastes he so remaining is capable of concerning things heavenly, that you can or will suppose, yet he is overcome again of what is natural to him. For it is certain that *actiones sequuntur animi constitutionem*, and the remembrance of former pleasures entering in, do wither and shale off again all accidental joy and sweetness in things heavenly, which are to him also and to his radical constitution but accidental.

The contrary falls out in a regenerate man, that though he hath that corruption in him which may make the pleasures of sin sweet to him, and he may again taste of their dainties, yet he having a new divine nature, which God upholds, and will bring forth to victory, as Christ speaks, as being ordained for eternity, and which is now become a man's self, and is as health is in a temper made sound, that hath yet some humour remaining, and the things of the other world (which it is now rooted in, and is naturally suited unto) being of such a greatness and glory in themselves, they still leave those impressions behind them upon his heart, that upon the least reviving of them by the Spirit the heart is fetched off from the pleasures of sin, as the other is by his sin drawn off from tasting the powers of the world to come. I may say, as Christ says, John iv. 13, ' Whoever drinketh' and tasteth of heavenly things (but only as unregenerate men have been said to do), ' he will thirst again' after earthly, and be overcome of them ; and this I speak by way of allusion; but what follows, ver. 14, is really true and intended by Christ of a man regenerate, ' Whosoever drinketh of the water Christ shall give him, he shall never thirst ;' that is, never come to have that impetuousness of full desire, and so not that pleasure or delight in other things carnal and outward (which Christ resembles the water of that well to) as he formerly had. He shall never 'add drunkenness to thirst' (as Moses speaks): his thirst thereto will be, by the taste of this water Christ gives him, allayed; that that vehemency and greediness he formerly had is for ever taken off and abated, and this because the water which Christ gives him becomes 'a well of water, springing up in him to eternal life;' so it follows in the same verse; it is not adventitious, as water in a cistern, but as in a spring, and it continually aspires to things above. And though it may be dammed up with that earth that environs it, yet it works out that earth, and overflows in the heart again.

To the third part of the objection, concerning a godly man's finding comfort in things outward that are lawful.

The answer is, and it is a great invitement to religion, that he may (and it is his own fault if he does not) find more comfort even in them than carnal men use to do: Ps. xxxvii. 16, 'A little that the righteous hath is better than the riches of many wicked.' He opposeth, 1, a *little* unto *riches* and abundance; and 2, the little of *one man* to the riches of *many men*, whereof each are rich. So as if one man alone had the riches that many great rich men have, yet a righteous man, that hath but a little, hath more comfort in it than he, yea, than all those rich men have, put their comforts all together. Therefore 'godliness' is said, 'with contentment, to be great gain,' for it alone brings contentment. For though the creature is (taken in itself alone) more vain to a godly man than to another, and so if he should go about to seek his contentment from it, as carnal men do, I may then invert it that the little which a wicked man hath is more to him than all abundance would be to the other. Solomon that pursued this, being a godly man, could best write of the vanity of these things; but yet when the heart is set a-work to seek God, and hath the scent of him, as I may so say, mingled with the outward things he doth enjoy, or if it have the light of his countenance, it puts a fulness into the creature. A dinner of herbs, sauced with his love and served up by him, is more than the greatest feast. And surely God traineth up his children one way or other unto this. The more a man truly godly will seek to find comfort in the creatures, the more thorns he shall find in his way, Hosea ii. 6, 7, the more comfortless they will be to him than to another, because his soul is used to better fare. His faculties have been widened and extended by having tasted, or by having had impressions of the sweetness and goodness that is in the Lord. And so the creature in itself is more emptiness and vexation than to another man. And therefore a godly man, if he will live, and but keep up the comfort of his life, and not fall lower in this respect, nor live at a lower rate than he did in his natural condition, he must necessarily (even for his daily comfort) seek after God, and hold up intercourse and communion with him; so to fill up that *chasma* that is otherwise made, the creature is rendered more vain to him than afore.

CHAPTER III.

If we would know whether we make God our chiefest and supreme good, let us observe by what things the comfort of our lives is principally maintained and upheld.

Inquire by what things the comfort of thy life is principally maintained and upheld from day to day. For it is that which is good in this life whereby the comfort of one's life is nourished, as fire by fuel. We all live here in a miserable world, and our life is a pilgrimage of many a weary step ; and the soul must have baitings and refreshings, or it will faint and fail, and not hold out to its journey's end. The comfort of a man's soul in Scripture is termed ' a man's life,' Luke xii. 15. ' Life,' says Christ, ' consists not in abundance ;' by *life* there, he means the comfort and joy of life, which all abundance of outward things cannot give. And in this very respect, when comfort in outward things is gone and departed, the ' heart dies,' as 1 Sam. xxv. 37, Nabal's soul is said to ' die within him,' though he was merry over night ; yet when he fell into the fear of losing all by David's plundering him, he having provoked him, it is said that his heart died within him. He lived ten days after, ver. 38, but his heart died, and became ' as a stone,' says the text ; that look, as if you had beheld Lot's wife when her soul went out, and she was metamorphosed to a stone, or rather a pillar of salt, such was, in respect of the life of comfort, this man's condition. Look, as the body is not able to sustain and support itself without the soul ; so, nor is the soul, which is mere emptiness, able to sustain itself in life without some good thing it hath conjunction and commerce with. Now then, what is the element thy soul lives in ? It is certain that in him that is truly born again, his conversion wrought these two things in him : 1. His soul was struck dead, as to the making the comforts of this life his chiefest good. And this humiliation usually doth work : Rom. vii. 9, ' I was once alive, but I died.' Gal. ii. 19, ' I through the law am dead to the law, that I might live unto God ;' and ver. 20, ' I am crucified with Christ.' There are these more eminent parts of humiliation : 1. To bring a man to nothing in his own righteousness (as 1 Cor. i., last verses), and to kill and slay a man thereunto, that so he may be brought to accept of God's righteousness in Christ prepared for him, and to live thereby. 2. To bring the soul to nothing in outward comforts in sins, or in the creatures. And this also is the work of the law, through the cross of Christ, which goes with it. Isa. xl. 7, it is made the effect of John Baptist's ministry, of which ver. 3 speaks, ' The voice of him that crieth in the wilderness, Prepare ye the way of the Lord, make straight in the desert a high way for our God ;' that at his voice ' the grass withered, the flower faded, because the Spirit of the Lord had blown upon it.' He speaks not simply of the vanity of the creature in itself, but what it became to his hearers, that received the Spirit of bondage from his ministry, as those words that follow do shew, ' because the Spirit of the Lord,' namely, in his ministry, ' had blown upon them all,' and was *ventus*, a wind that blasted and withered all their good things to them ; so as now they looked upon them all as withered flowers. And therefore Paul in the next verse in that Gal. ii., says he was ' crucified with Christ ' also ; which, Gal. vi. 14, he interprets among other things to be a crucifying of the world to him, which was done by the power of the cross virtually, though by the law humbling a man instrumentally, as that Gal. ii. to me evidently importeth.

Now the end why God thus kills man by humiliation to his own righteousness and to all comforts, so as never to have help to his soul in them, is to the end he may live anew, and have a new life in both. 1. To live by going out to Christ for righteousness, ' the just shall live by faith.' And 2. To cause the soul to pitch upon God for ever as his chiefest good ; and all that desired good it ever looks for in this world, or the world to come. So you have it, Ps. xvi. 5, 6, ' The Lord is the portion of mine inheritance, and of my cup : thou maintainest my lot. The lines are fallen unto me in pleasant places ; yea, I have a goodly heritage.' And this is done by faith, as it sanctifies, and by instinct of the new creature. 1 Cor. i. 3, Paul termeth God both ' the Father of mercies,' as in relation to justification and pardon, and then the ' God of all comfort.' It is an attribute he hath taken on him, as he is an object of his people's hearts ; and thus, in respect of sanctification, all the comfort we look for is from him.

Use. Improve and take the light of these trials, and go down into your hearts and take the keys of them and ransack your private cupboards, and narrowly observe what junkets your souls have hitherto lived upon, and gone behind the door and there secretly and stoutly have made a meal of them. Delights are secret things, Prov. xiv. 10, as treasures are. As dogs (and carnal men are so compared) have bones they hide, and secretly steal forth to gnaw upon ; so men have sins they hide under their tongues as sweet bits, Job xx. 12. But examine what your comforts principally consist in.

Now if you would further know how it may be discerned in what your chief comforts lie,

1. Look what in distress your souls have recourse unto for relief and support.

2. In ordinary cases take this division to help you. A survey either, 1. Of things present : 2. Past ; 3. To come. For in and from all these, men take up their comforts.

1. Observe what your hearts have their ordinary recourse unto in cases of distress, or the ordinary discomfitures of this life, which God in a man's race layeth on purpose even in every man's way. Men's expectations are usually and often disappointed, especially at times, and then their hearts and spirits fail. And look, as in fears, or in a swoon, men's vital spirits run to the heart to comfort it ; so in distress the heart runs out to some-thing else, which it is inured unto, to comfort it as a cordial and consola-tion. And as the otter, when in times of frost it is kept under water by the ice, yet by its breath keeps open some place as a breathing-hole, so doth the heart. Now watch and observe the haunts and breathing-holes which in distress thy soul keeps open to itself, to fetch in fresh air from ; or look, as if you should see a company of rabbits grazing in a sunshiny day, and a man come by whom they fear, or a storm, you shall see them all instantly run into their several burrows, which are proper to them ; and by the place whither each of them doth run, you may discern which is pro-per to each : now thus in distress doth the heart run to its holes. The like men do in times of war to their several forts and garrisons, and so you may know what party they belong to : Prov. xviii. 10, ' The name of the Lord is a strong tower, and the righteous runs to it, and is safe ;' that is, if he be a righteous man, that is his refuge, as Jer. xvi. 19, ' O Lord, my strength and my fortress, and my refuge in the day of affliction, the Gentiles shall come unto thee from the ends of the earth, and shall say, Surely our fathers have inherited lies, vanity, and things wherein there is no profit.' On the contrary, take a carnal rich man who puts trust in his riches ; he also in ordinary distresses runs to his tower, from the same place of the Proverbs : ver. 11, ' The substance of the rich man is his strong city.' If a cross in other things befall him, discredit, hatred of men, as an oppressor, yet he is still counting with himself, reckoning *nummos in arca*, the moneys in his chest, or out at use, or in revenue, *populus sibi sibulet : aut mihi plaudo ;* he the next morning, when he wakes, bids good morrow to his gold. And thus, if one comfort be gone, he runs to another, as the prophet told that

wretched man he should ' run from chamber to chamber for his life.' You may see this difference amplified in Esau and Jacob, Saul and David ; the first pair compeers for a birthright, the other for a kingdom. Esau, Gen. xxvii., when he had that great loss befallen him as ever befell a man, namely, the loss of his birthright, and himself made apprehensive of it (witness his tears), what doth he comfort himself withal ? Ver. 42, says Rebecca to Jacob, ' Behold thy brother comforteth himself, purposing to kill thee.' It was revenge ; which, to a man of his constitution, an hairy man of the field, is the sweetest lust in the world to accomplish. But Jacob, on the contrary, when he was distressed greatly, Gen. xxxii. 7, as the text there says, ' whither hath he recourse ? Even to God,' so ver. 9 ; and you may see by his prayer and hopes in God's promise, ver. 12, that God would surely do him good.

See it also in Saul and David ; Saul was made sensible by Samuel, that he had lost a kingdom : 1 Sam. xv. 30, ' Yet honour me' (says he) ' afore the people.' David lost all at Ziklag, wives, estate, and was put into as great a ground of fear, of hazard of life (and so of his kingdom promised) as man could probably be in (for the people spake of stoning him). And in this case what had David recourse unto ? The story tells you, 1 Sam. xxx. 6, ' David encouraged himself in his God.' So elsewhere David says, ' My heart fails, and my flesh fails, but God is the strength of my heart,' Ps. lxxiii. 26 : and Ps. cxix. 92, ' Unless thy word had been my delight, I had perished in my affliction.'

2. Observe whence your comforts come in ; which is discerned by the heart's recourse, either unto things present, past, or to come.

(1.) For things present. Men use to take an inventory of their present things afore them, to comfort their hearts with. So doth the rich man in the gospel : ' Soul, take thine ease ; thou hast' (now at present by thee) ' goods laid up for many years.' As rich men count their estates with themselves, and love to do it, so doth the soul in secret reckon up its comforts and opportunities to satisfy its lusts. In a morning when men wake, their souls look out what sports, pleasures, are ready to wait upon them that day. So they in the prophet, ' To-day shall be as to-morrow,* and much more abundant.' Whereas if a godly man hath the sense of the favour of God, he triumphs in it, and ' makes his boast in God all the day long,' Ps. xliv. 8. He often counts with himself, I shall hear a good sermon this day, and receive the sacraments, meet with my Saviour, my Lord and husband, when the day comes, and longs for it aforehand.

Again (2d), Men's souls have recourse for comfort unto what is past. Thus a scholar, that is low and mean in his outward condition, takes a pleasing survey of what credit he got by such a performance, at such a time ; how he was applauded, and in the contemplation thereof his soul bears up itself. When other straits and wants to satisfy other lusts do depress him, he swims and floats in his own conceits by means of these bladders, and his soul is thereby kept up from sinking. Yea, he is carried aloft (as he vainly thinks) on the breaths and opinions of men, as feathers and bubbles which children make for their pastime on them. Thus also men make and revive in their fancies the actings of former pleasures and dalliances, &c., whereas a godly man, in the present want of outward comforts, yea, the present sense of the withdrawings of God's love, hath recourse to times past, ' the days of old,' as David recounts with himself, what ' songs had been sung in the night,' between God and him, what earnest desires :

* ' To-morrow shall be as to-day.'—ED.

' My soul hath longed for thee in the night.'   What love and joys, sweet intercourse and communion, hath been between God and him, at such and such a time.

(3.) And especially you may discover this, by what recourse the soul hath to things to come in future hopes, and what kind of good things those are the soul hath thus recourse unto.   Men's souls do live by hopes, as much and more than by anything past or present; and we use to take up our comforts beforehand.   The miserablest man that is, hath yet usually a loop-hole of hope to look out of, a door of hope for his soul to go out at, and relieve itself.   Now, 1 Cor. xv. 19, the hopes of a godly and carnal man are distinguished.   ' If we' (that are believers) ' had hopes only in this life' (as all carnal worldlings have), ' we were of all men the most miserable;' as having given up this world for grace, both in the present and the future; and betaken ourselves to what is in the other world, by which we relieve and comfort ourselves against the miseries of this world, that befall us every day more than they do other men.   Christ is our hope (so 1 Tim. i. 1), that is generally of all Christians, and ' our life is hid in God with him'; whereas a carnal man makes his gold (or some like worldly comfort or other) his hope, Job xxxi. 24.

I shall, to clear this point further, remove one scruple, which good souls who are left to a dry faith, and to follow after God in a barren land, may and will, upon hearsay of this, be apt unto, and to say, This doctrine strikes me dead, for I have not, nor cannot yet find, any comfortable relish or enjoyment of God, but a great deal of carnal relish of things of the world, and deeper and more impressions of sweetness from thence, than these impressions are which the word or thing of another world brings in; and how is God my chiefest good ?

Ans. 1. It is a false rule, which will deceive, to measure out what is our chiefest good by what our enjoyments, possessions of, or delights are, in that which we pitch upon as our chiefest good.   The rule would fail us, whether we be carnal or regenerate men.   This is common to both, that in respect of enjoyment they have their disappointments, even the most godly, in this life, of him whom their souls desire.   A soul that hath pitched its happiness on such an outward worldly comfort, may yet perhaps never have come to enjoy it, as in men that desire to be rich, and are disappointed in their hopes, &c., we see it verified, so as the case of the one comes all to one, and holds true as well as in the other.   And a man that is carnal, lustful, worldly, may as well say he makes not preferment, or riches, or beauty his greatest good, because still he hath been kept under and disappointed; and sensible sweetness ariseth always from enjoyment.

Ans. 2. But hast thou not had thy heart emptied of all these earthly enjoyments, by what light and taste thou hast had from God ?   Hast thou not had such a spiritual appetite as all created comforts can never fill or quiet, instead of himself ?   So as thou pursuest after him with the strong intent of this, day and night.   What is it thy soul hath set up in its eye, as thy mark thou intendedst for (as Paul speaks) ?   Is it not God's favour which thou prizest, seekest for with thy greatest contention ?   Affections are to be measured by what we labour after day and night to arrive at.

Ans. 3. In the mean time thou sayest, Of all outward comforts, what good will all these do me ?   And what are they, if I want thy favour ?   As a man looking diligently for a pearl or jewel meets with many things that may entertain him; but still says his soul, This is not the pearl I seek for. Now, as in Heb. xi. 14, the apostle says of the patriarchs, that ' they which say such things declare plainly that they seek a country ;' so say I of thee, the discomfort of whose life lies in the want of God, who canst not sit down in anything on this side of him, these longings of thy soul do declare plainly that thy rest is not here in the world.   Yea, if worldly things court thee, and come in upon thee, so as thou couldst (as to outward advantages) return to make and patch up a life of comfort in them, yet still thou canst never do it.   So, ver. 15, of the patriarchs, the same apostle speaks ; ' If they had been mindful of the country' (and the comforts of it) 'from whence they came out, they might have had opportunities to have returned ;' but they would not, as their children would have done into Egypt.   Therefore, upon this demonstration, he concludes, ver. 16, ' But now ' (that is, having such a frame of spirit) 'they desired a better country : wherefore God is not ashamed to be called their God.'   For he was the chiefest and choicest of their desires, and nothing else would satisfy ; and therefore he was their chiefest good.   God is much glorified as thy chiefest good in such desires that can rest nowhere else but in him : he is equally glorified by thee, who waitest thus for him, and canst find no sweetness but in him, as he is by another in their enjoyments of him.   For the affections stir as well one way as the other towards him, and from either glory ariseth alike unto him. And what affections of love the one soul shews in joy, and in sweet enjoyments of his goodness, the other shews in restless desires after his goodness.

CHAPTER IV.

If we would know whether we make God our chief good, we must inquire what are the things which we value as our dearest treasures.

Thus much as to such signs, which that plain and simple expression, ' What are thy good things ?' hath afforded.   I come to the second, as the same thing is represented under this metaphor of What is thy treasure ?

The first sign as to this head is that which Christ, Mat. vi. 21, holds forth, who is to be our judge, Heb. iv. 12, and who is a discerner of the thoughts and intents of the heart.

Now ' where your treasure is ' (says Christ, Mat. vi. 21), ' there will your hearts be also.'   No man's heart is in his own keeping ; but his treasure, be it what it will, or take it away from him, yet the heart will be where it loves.   If God be made a man's treasure, he calls for the heart : Prov. xxiii. 26, ' My son, give me thy heart.'   And let any earthly thing be a man's treasure, and it takes the heart away without asking leave : Hosea iv. 11, ' Whoredom and wine ' (says God) ' take away the heart ;' Ezek. xxxiii. 31, ' Their hearts go after their covetousness.'

1. What hath thy heart, hath thy thoughts most ?   The chiefest and the dearest of thy thoughts are spent upon what is thy treasure.   Now therefore go down into thy heart, and examine what thing it is takes up and engrosseth to itself the musings and devisings of thy soul ; what it is the eyes of the mind still are glancing, yea, fixed upon, with dearest contentment, and scarce ever off.   That is thy treasure, and that hath thine heart. Thus, as a passionate lover delights to revive, in his captivated fancy, the image and likeness of the party he loves, draws pictures of her in his fancies ; and as the thoughts are the only means to bring things absent and the heart together : so the soul feeds and increaseth the love it hath to a thing it desires, by thinking of it.   Affections chain the thoughts, and

fasten the mind and intention of it to the thing they affect; and such a thing is certainly a treasure to thee. For take but the exemplification of it in outward treasures. You may observe it in men that have treasures, any jewels, &c. They will still be unlocking the casket, and viewing of them, eyeing of them. They love still to be opening the bags, and telling and counting of what is within. And so it is with the mind; what the heart hath pitched upon as its treasure, it ever and anon reviews and visits with its thoughts. For there is a fresh contentment and security ariseth to the mind thereby. Be it 'goods laid up for many years,' the thoughts of this give an ease to the mind. Be it the credit of something past, men love to chew the cud of it in their thoughts, and run it over all again in their minds. Or be it the pleasure of some sin to come, as a sin of uncleanness, how do men anticipate the pleasure of it in their fancies, rolling it over and over again, act it over again and again, ere they do it, as players do their parts. And this we all find, that the chiefest pleasure of our lives is brought us in by our thoughts; and when we enjoy not the things we desire, we please ourselves with our own fancies and ideas of them, which help to entertain the soul till it doth enjoy them. And we may observe it in Scripture, that men are differenced by the objects of their thoughts, and of the musings of the heart, as well as by anything else: Isa. xxxii. 7, 8, ' A covetous man deviseth wicked things, but the liberal liberal things.' Such as the things are men spend their devisings upon, it is certain such are the men. If they mind chiefly earthly things, as it is, Philip. iii. 19, then they are earthly men, 'whose end is damnation.' And in the first Psalm it is made a distinctive note of a godly man from a wicked, that ' he meditates in the law day and night.' The scope of David is to distinguish men; and there is good reason why men may be differenced by their thoughts, and the things they are conversant about. For, 1, *Noscitur ex socio.* A man's disposition may be known by his companion whom he is most entire and familiar with. Now those things a man thinks on most, he makes his most familiar friends, is most entire with. By our thoughts we have the entirest acquaintance that we can have with anything, the closest that we can any way arrive at; for it takes the things into our bosom. And therefore Solomon, Prov. vi. 22, speaking of meditating in the law, when a man wakes in the morning, compares it to a familiar friend talking with a man: ' When thou awakest, it shall talk with thee.' And a man is therefore termed a ' friend to the world,' James iv. 1–4.

2. The thoughts do most distinguish men's hearts, because they are the freest acts of the mind, wherein the mind is the most itself, and acts itself else: Prov. xxiii. 7, ' For as he thinketh in his heart, so is he.' And therefore the proverb is, that ' thoughts are free.' And in this sense it is true that of all acts else they are the least enforced, which do follow the free disposition of the heart. Men cannot speak what they would, or do what they would: these are subject to enforcement. And therefore, in judging by speeches and by actions, there may be deceit. But a man may think what he will; and, indeed, usually men do pore on that which pleaseth them; in their thoughts they act themselves, whatsoever they do in their actions. We do not know the disposition of players as acting their parts upon the stage, but look into the tiring-house, and there you may see them act themselves, their own base and lewd dispositions. The thoughts are the tiring-room of the soul, the privy chamber of it.

3. They are the immediate acts of the soul, and therefore shew what temper it is of. For the thoughts (as I may so say) are as they came new

from the heart; they are the figments of it, and so the image of the heart is fresh on them as coming new out of the mint. If you would taste a grape, take the juice as it is new squeezed out into the wine-press, and before adulterated with other mixtures.

4. Thoughts are the most continual actings of the soul of any else, which the soul abounds in most, and therefore discovers the heart most, for of all faculties that is always a-work. The thinking faculty is as that little wheel in a jack, that moves twenty times faster than any of the rest. And when we have not liberty to satisfy our desires, yet our thoughts are working, so as the heart cannot be kept off from thinking of what it would enjoy. Christ calls the thoughts the treasure both of a good and bad man, for the abundance there is of them; as in that speech, ' A good man out of the good treasure of his heart brings forth good, an evil man evil.' Mat. xii. 34, 35, ' For out of the abundance of the heart the mouth speaketh. A good man, out of the good treasure of the heart, bringeth forth good things : and an evil man, out of the evil treasure, bringeth forth evil things.' Christ, you see, when he would give a reason why men might be distinguished by their speeches, and with what kind men abound therein most, he reduceth it to the heart as the fountain : ' For out of the abundance of the heart' (says he) ' the mouth speaketh,' that is, out of the abundance of the thoughts. Some persons have many restraints, even of speaking good, and are disadvantaged when yet their hearts are working upon them. Therefore look, what thoughts the heart abounds in (it is the sure rule), such is the heart. There is no good man but he hath a treasure and a spring of good thoughts within him, which no wicked man in the world hath. And though there is a spring of mud and filth runs with them, of vain thoughts, and sinful thoughts, which intermingles itself with the current of them at the best, and which doth often stop the current of them ; yet this spring works itself out again, the current riseth up again, and though with many windings and turnings, keeps its course. And as rivers run into the sea, so there is a spring in his heart tends God-ward. Another man, though he may have a land-flood of good thoughts, in a good mode, yet they are soon dried up again ; there is not a spring of them. Prov. xii. 2d and 5th verses compared together. A wicked man is called ' a man of wicked devices or imaginations,' that is, a man of wicked thoughts, as it were, made up of them, whereas, in the 5th verse, a godly man's thoughts, in opposition, are termed right : ' The thoughts of the righteous are right ;' that is, for the tendency, the current of them, they are exercised about righteous things. Therefore David, Ps. cxxxix. 17, 18, says not only that the thoughts of God are precious to him, but for multitude more than the sand. It may be interpreted of his thoughts of God, which he could not tell the total sum of ; for, says he, ' every morning when I awake, I am with thee.' Whereas, of a wicked man, Ps. x. 4, it is said, ' God is scarce in all his thoughts.' And, Jer. ii. 32, God, upbraiding the people of Israel, says, ' Can a maid forget her ornaments,' not go abroad but be sure to be dressed ; and when she hath pricked up herself, her mind is still on them ? But ' my people hath forgotten me' (says he) ' days without number.' But, in Prov. vi. 14, it is said of a wicked man's heart, ' it forgeth mischief continually,' as a smith forgeth iron, he is still hammering of it. And because vain are all their thoughts, therefore a wicked man's heart is said to be little worth. Prov. x. 20.

There are two scruples and objections which, as to this branch of trial, some, yea, most good souls may and do make.

Obj. 1. The swarming of evil, vain, or foolish thoughts, that are so frequent and such familiars, that they are bold to knock and draw the latch when we have separated ourselves the most solemnly, and shut ourselves up for God in holy duties and on the Sabbath days.   If, therefore, I should judge by my thoughts, the world and a thousand vanities are my treasure.

Ans. 1. A man is not to judge herein by the crowd and swarming, or barely by the multitude, the noise, the humming, the buzzing they keep. For these will and do arise naturally out of the heart, as Christ says.   And ' the imagination of man's heart is evil continually.'   And it is certain that the bulk or quantity of the unregenerate part in most Christians is far more and greater than the regenerate part, though that be *major virtute*, greater in power, in carrying the heart on against corruptions, and strong steering a man in his course ; especially in the great turns of his life, and in the end Christ bringing it forth to victory ; so that if a man would go to measure by the bulk, or by the bushel, every man's heart would be found to have quarters of chaff, the flying thoughts which rise up in it, unto a peck of good grain and true corn ; but thou must take estimate by the entertainment, which vain and worldly thoughts, after they have risen, have in thy heart, by their taking root again through its indulgency to them, nourishing of them and intention upon them, and delight in them, Jer. iv. 14, ' How long shall vain thoughts lodge within thee ?' lodge, and nest, and find the most pleasing welcome and harbour ? lodge as thy best friends and pleasantest companions ; that lie down with thee, when thou liest down to sleep, and thou invitest them to bed with thee ; that talk with thee, when thou awakest, with deepest pleasure and delight ?   God's speech in Jeremiah is all one, as if God or a father should say to his son, a riotous entertainer of lewd company, How long shall thy vain companions lodge with thee, that eat thee out of house or home, consume that provision which thy wife and children should have ?   So here, ' How long shall thy vain thoughts lodge with thee,' that prey upon the best of thy heart and dearest of thy affections ?   The regenerate part in a man is in that condition, in respect of his thoughts, that a man is in that walks in the midst of dust continually raised about him, or of little flies that in summer swarm, against which he shuts his eyes and holds his breath, but cannot hinder their coming about him, though he carries boughs in his hands, or the like, to keep them off. Thus it is with a regenerate man ; but to another man these vain thoughts are as the free air which he breathes in with contentment and refreshment. They are his element.

The thoughts a man hath of his treasure are the thoughts of greatest delight and contentment ; not dry thoughts, but drenched and soaked deep in the whole of the affections, and they hug and entwine about them ; and of which the affections say, ' Whither you go, we will go ; whom you will bring with you, we will entertain.'   They may and do come into a good man's heart, as gipsies, by swarms, but by his good will they should not lodge there ; he goes often to God for a passport, and for a whip to send them away.   And these may trouble thee most in holy duties, which the unregenerate part doth naturally hinder and disturb.   It is strange that afore prayer a man would fain have recalled and remembered them, but could not ; as soon as a man falls down to prayer, they come in instantly. And the devil waits that occasion for injections also ; to be sure, what is like to strike the affections deepest, and to stick there, and so to hurry away the heart in the instant, that will be cast in at such cue and nick, when the heart is coming to such passages in prayer as his present condition hath most need of, and which he longs most to be at; so as the heart is carried out of the common stream into a creek or rivulet ere he is aware, insomuch as sometimes a man keeps but (I use to say) a negative Sabbath, the negative part of an holy duty; that is, it is his task upon that day, or in that duty, to keep a ward or court of guard against the troopings of vain thoughts; or (if you will) to keep the doors, either so as vain thoughts should not crowd in, or if they do, still to be turning them forth. So as it often befalls the sons of Abraham in prayer, &c., in respect of inward disturbances, as it befell our father Abraham when he was offering a sacrifice to God, in respect of outward disturbance, Gen. xv. 11. The fowls still ever and anon came down upon the carcasses. For it is said, 'when the fowls came down, Abraham drave them away.' He hunted them away with his breath, as the original imports, or crying out with a noise upon them, when he should have had his mind wholly intent on prayer and divine meditation which that solemn duty called for. Then his work must be to hoot away the fowls which came flying down upon the sacrifices. And at that time they did it especially, for there was prey for them. And Abraham could not hinder their coming down; for fowls fly aloft, and the same individual birds would come again and again, and he could not help it, that was not in his power; but when they came he could drive them away, and that was all he could do to them; yea, it took up his time when he was to have been at his devotion, it was his main work. And so it is here, the best of souls cannot help nor hinder these unclean and ravenous fowls from coming down upon the sacrifices, but they still endeavour to drive them away, &c.

Ans. 2. A second thing I would say, in answer to this, is, that although vain thoughts may be more by far, yet the heart of regenerate man (take the whole course) follows God, and returns to him and keeps its way. A spaniel that follows his master in a journey, runs out after every bird, after every flock of sheep, which he sees in his way; and in such goings out, runs over ten or twenty times more ground, spends more pains in them, than in the way his master goes in, or than it comes to; yet still he is sure to have an eye to his master, returns again to him, and follows him to the journey's end. And so it is with the soul in this respect.

Obj. 2. Are not godly men's thoughts to be taken up with their worldly business? Are not men to contrive and devise and mould what they are therein to do, especially in some callings, and therefore to spend the most of their thoughts thereon? How then can we make a judgment by our thoughts?

Ans. 1. A good man must do diligently that business to which he may be called: 'And whatever work thy hand finds to do, thou oughtest to do with all thy might,' Eccl. ix. 10.

Ans. 2. Yet, 2, there may be, and is, an habitual fear runs along and poiseth the heart all day long: Prov. xxiii. 17, 'Be thou in the fear of the Lord all the day long.' These two commands of the same pen cross not one the other; an inferior that hath business to do in a room, where his master, or one eminently superior, is present all day, he may be all along intent and sufficiently thoughtful on his business, and that in respect unto his master. For there is withal an habitual reverence, which all along doth awe and poise his mind to act nothing unseemly of such a presence as he is afore.

Ans. 3. But, observe what thoughts return upon thee, when the mill of thy calling stands still; at such times when thy heart is left free; as at spare hours, a-mornings, when thou liest awake, &c. Observe the vergencies and the haunts of thy heart at such times, as thou wouldst of a servant or an apprentice, who though whilst he is kept at home works diligently, yet the free time he hath, or if he can but steal forth, he is still at such an house, if he be sent out of an errand, he steps in there ; in like manner, watch thou the haunts of thine heart, when thou art retired, when the shop windows of thy calling are shut, and thou art free in thy thoughts to enjoy what thou pleasest ; then see what secret treasury thy thoughts steal to unlock and to view with contentment. ' The wicked imagine mischief on their beds,' they sleep not till they have wallowed and tumbled in such fancies as naturally suit their spirits. For these lighten their spirits, and make way for sleep. ' But with my soul,' saith the church, ' I have desired thee in the night,' Isa. xxvi. 9. David remembers the sweet songs in the night God and he had together: ' When I awake, I am still with thee,' Ps. cxxxix. 18 ; and Prov. vi. 22, ' When thou awakest, the law of God, as a companion, it shall talk with thee.'

Ans. 4. Last of all, if thou beest overwhelmed with such thoughts as keep thee off from the free air to breathe up to God, thou wilt find thy heart like a mole under ground, heaving and working upwards, tossing up the earth that keeps it under, till thou art above ground.

As to the rest of those signs that follow, I must premise (as in relation to that part, namely, what carnal men do make their treasure), that some sinners' treasures (I term them such, because they are such to their hearts and the affections thereof, though not to their judgments), lie in things more base, more vile, as in debauched courses of uncleanness, drunkenness, vain company, joviality, mirth, &c., which are so base, that, if you ask their consciences, or their judgments, they must acknowledge such things to be their shame. Some are swine, and wallow in open mire which stinks in all men's nostrils ; and yet as to their hearts and affections, they are that chiefest good they doat on ; like beasts, in what they know naturally, they corrupt themselves. Others are more clean, as dogs and goats ; to which those others of wicked men are compared, that feed more clean, and yet are beasts. These put the treasure of their hearts in things outwardly commendable, as riches, honours, learning, wit, reputation, quick conversation, &c. ; yea, sometimes in outward righteousness, and a fair deportment in this world. And yet, not making God their treasure, and not subordinating all these to him, and not preferring him, and the things of God, to the chief of their joy, they evidently lay but up treasures on earth. I shall leave the first sort, as self-convicted, as judged wicked by the world itself, and as sentenced by such cutting sayings of the word : 1 Cor. vi. 9, 10, ' Neither fornicators, nor adulterers, nor effeminate, nor abusers of themselves with mankind, nor thieves, nor covetous, nor revilers, nor extortioners, shall inherit the kingdom of God.'

But as touching the second sort, who place their good things in what the world highly esteems, as Christ says ; to convince them, and to comfort the hearts of the godly, by distinguishing and separating them from them, I shall give these following evidences or discoveries, which shall be fitted to the metaphor of a treasure, or what a man really makes his treasure.

I shall premise this, that in the hearts and lives of many saints, yea, in all more or less, there are corruptions answering unto what I shall instance in, to convince wicked men by, that such and such things on earth are their treasure : that yet a man truly holy doth still in the pursuit, and valuation, and endeavours, and reaching forth of the soul, make God his chief treasure (notwithstanding those corruptions), in comparison of all things else.

1. Examine thy practical esteem and valuation of things ; that is, what is it that is most precious to thee. That is thy treasure, 1 Peter ii. 7, ' Unto you, that believe, Christ is precious.' As in himself such, verse 4, ' A stone chosen of God and precious,' so in the esteem of believers ; ' Unto you he is precious.' And he speaks it by way of discrimination from carnal men, that have not true faith. ' But to them,' says he, ' that be disobedient, he is a rock of offence,' verse 7. Why doth he in this opposition give the title of *disobedient* to them, rather than of unbelievers, which is the opposite term unto the former, ' You that believe'? But because the valuation of Christ, or undervaluing him, is seen and discovered, as in the pursuit after him, so in the obedience to him, or in disobedience. Thus David, Ps. cxix. 14, ' I have rejoiced in the way of thy testimonies, as much as in all riches.' Even in the way of them ; mark it, because they did lead to God, as a man would do in a way, though never so craggy, that did certainly lead him to an hidden treasure : and in the way to them, in the pursuance towards God, he delighted as much and above riches in present possession. Yea, and above *all* riches too, of what sort soever, that men count riches ; which is not in money only. So then he esteemed God his treasure, and manifested this by diligence in the way unto him, the way of his testimonies. Thus of Hezekiah, of whom interpreters do understand that passage, it is said, Isa. xxxiii. 6, ' The fear of the Lord is his treasure.' So of Moses, Heb. xi. 26, it is said that he ' esteemed the very reproach of Christ greater riches than the treasures of Egypt.' With other men, how doth the market go ? It is apparent, 1, that they undervalue God and Christ, and those things of the other world, and hold them at the rate of common things ; so in the original the expression is, Heb. x. 29, though it is rendered ' an unholy thing'; which though there uttered of men that sin against the Holy Ghost, with the highest contempt of Christ's blood, and was therefore so rendered, yet to esteem Christ and his blood a common ordinary thing, is common with them and other wicked men, as their respect thereunto manifests. In comparison of other things, a wicked man is ' a profane person, as Esau, who, for one morsel of meat sold his birthright,' Heb. xii. 16 ; and for this his so manifest a demonstration of his undervaluing it to a mess of pottage (and the pleasure of lust is but just like it), he is termed a profane person, who is one which esteemeth holy things, and precious things, as common, for that is properly profanation.

And 2. Instead of these, what are their dainties ? Sins, and the pleasures of them : Ps. cxli. 4, ' Incline not mine heart to any evil thing, to practise wicked works with men that work iniquity : and let me not eat of their dainties.' And so the good things of this world, Rev. xviii. 12–14, were dainty and goodly in their esteem, and so (as there) their souls lusted after them. Now, then, let us examine ourselves hereby.

1. This thy esteem of God and Christ, if true, and in any proportion rising up to the worth of the things themselves, will shew itself : as in thy first conversion, in selling all for them, Mat. xiii. 45, so after conversion, in thy diligent pursuit after them. Treasures lie buried under ground to a great depth often. Therefore, says Solomon, speaking of Christ and all his graces (by which we come to have interest in him) under the name of Wisdom, Prov. ii. 4, ' If thou seek for her as silver, and searchest as for hidden treasure.' The mind of the similitude is, that as God, in his common providence, hath hidden the mines of rich metals in the bowels of the earth,

because he would have men take pains for them, so, in the course of his dispensations to his children, he hath hidden his Christ, whom he so values, in himself: 'your life is hid with Christ in God,' Col. iii. 3. And all the riches of Christ, which are unsearchable, they are hid in God, Eph. iii. 10, and hidden deep. They are the deep things of God, 1 Cor. ii. 10, to the end he may be treated with by every soul that will have them. And although he gives them freely, and sells them not for any or all of our endeavours; and therefore, 'say not in your hearts,' that is, think not within yourselves (as Paul interprets Moses) 'who shall ascend up into heaven?' as if any may by his endeavours 'bring down Christ from thence;' 'or who shall descend into the deep?' Rom. x. 7; yet before he usually brings Christ down into the heart, or discovers his own heart and face, he orders it so that men shall take the utmost pains, and use the utmost diligence, to the end to shew their valuation of these things. 'Many shall strive,' says Christ. You must do more, work as at a mine: 'If thou search for her as silver.' To work in mines is the toilsomest work in the world. The Romans of old, and the Spaniards now in the West Indies, condemn their slaves thereto. And indeed, what a man values and esteems precious, his desire will set all in him a-work to seek: Pro. xviii. 1, 'Through desire a man, having separated himself, he seeketh and intermeddleth with all wisdom.' Others read (as also the margin varies it) 'intermeddleth with every matter.' That is, what a man strongly desires and esteems, it will make him separate, or set himself apart wholly to it. He will deal in every matter, that is, way or course, whereby it is to be attained. He will turn every stone, or (which is all one, as we read it) will intermeddle with all wisdom. He will use all his wits to cast with himself how it may be compassed. Now go down into your own hearts, think, and think seriously, what doth the strength of thy intention run out upon? Is it after God and the things of that other world, or things in this? If thou hast been truly wrought upon, perhaps at the first thou wert so affected, as wholly to separate thyself through desire after God and his favour, because thou didst thus judge, It is not necessary for me to be eminently learned or rich, &c., but to be saved is that one thing necessary, and so didst nothing else with thy heart, until thy spirit was settled and quieted in some good measure. Then afterward thou wast settled, and so that present and absolute necessity thy soul was put upon at first, as in respect to that distress and unsettlement, is not the same as before, yet thy esteem continues such to the things themselves. As, though thou spendest not the greatest outward bulk of thy diligence, because thy outward calling in this world calls for it, yet the greatest strength of thy intentness of spirit and heedfulness is spent upon them, so as not to lose thy interest in them. And to that end a godly man will intermeddle with every duty, and he will deal in all ordinances, take the advantage of all opportunities.

On the other hand, my brethren, what is the reason that men search for learning as for silver, and dig for it as for gold, separate themselves unto it, intermeddle with every author, as the bee with every flower, and yet neglect God days without number? Or if not that way given (I would it were so commonly), men spend their intention and diligence (what it is) in idleness, vain company, which we term passing away the time. But as for God and Christ, and the ways of holiness, they are so far off from separating themselves unto them through desire, that they scarce intermeddle with them in a week, a month. These, as pebbles in the streets, they are so far from digging for them, that they trample as swine upon them (as Christ speaks), or at least stoop not to take them up. They think they may have them at any time for stooping for, at their cast-away leisure, or on their deathbed. What is the reason of this? Even because they are not their treasure. God hath not yet given thee a heart to value them at their own rate. Suppose thou hadst lived in Solomon's times, when gold and silver were as stones in the streets, or wert in the Indies, where, at least for the seeking or digging for them, thou mightest have enough, and yet all thy time were spent to load thy poor back with peacocks' feathers, which you read of also in Solomon's times (which were indeed those glorious birds we now-a-days see brought from the hotter climates), would any man think, or couldst thou in reason think, that thou didst make gold and silver thy treasure in such a case?

Consider, you live in times and places in which the unsearchable riches of Christ are shovelled up to your hands, every day offered, tendered, yea, put (as it were) into your hands. The word we preach is nigh thee, even in thy ears and heart; and yet, as Solomon says, Prov. xvii. 16, 'A fool hath a price in his hand, only wants a heart towards it.' Go home and consider with thyself, these things are not yet my treasure, nor hath as yet God given me a heart to make them such.

Again, if these had been thy treasure, thou wouldst have parted with all for them; sold all thou hast, as Christ speaks of that good pearl. For all men will do so for what is precious to them. What says God, Isa. xliii. 4? 'Since thou wert precious to me, I gave nations for thy life.' And so wouldst thou have done for Christ ere this, and never have repented of your bargain. It is repentance never to be repented of. 'I have accounted all things loss,' Phil. iii., 'and I do account them so still,' says Paul. And still he pressed forward to attain them with the greatest diligence. But thou partest for unworthy courses, uncleanness, drunkenness, or such petty base lusts, which the best part of thee, the speculative part of thy mind, is so far from reckoning a treasure, as they are thy shame; yet to the practical part, they are really thy precious things thou in thy great wisdom seekest after. Thou canst sell all for them, as Esau his birthright, thy soul, thy books, thy good name, the hopes of preferment in the place thou art in, thy health, thy strength, thy wits, thy favour, expectations, and joy thy friends might have in thee, to pursue them. A goodly treasure sure! Are they not? Yet they must be reckoned thine.

2. Wherein, or in what, dost thou account thy greatest gains and thy greatest losses to lie? That, in the valuation of thine heart, is thy treasure.

You find, 1. Tim. vi. 6, Paul speaking of the opposite disposition of a man truly godly, and who 'seeks the things of Jesus Christ,' from his that is carnal, he expresseth it with a but. 'But godliness with contentment is great gain;' or, as the word is, 'self-sufficiency,' μετ' αὐταρκείας; that is, godliness hath such a sufficiency in itself, that, with or through that sufficiency, it alone is great gain to him in whose heart it is placed, and by whose spirit it is truly valued. And he speaks this in perfect opposition to the spirit of carnal gospellers and professors, of whom he had spoken the verse afore, and which was the occasion of the saying annexed. Men of corrupt minds, supposing that gain is godliness; that is their secret opinion and esteem, that gain in outward things is the best religion in the world. But our religion, which we profess, is to serve him that is God; now, Phil. iii. 19, Paul, speaking of the same sort of persons (for of those of the circumcision he speaks in both places), 'whose god is their belly,' he compares the lusts and appetites of natural men's hearts unto those of the belly; that is, the furious desire to the pleasures thereof; and such are theirs to earthly things, as it follows, 'who mind earthly things.' Unto which, Ps. xvii. 14 accords : 'The men of this world' (says David), 'who have their portion in this life, whose belly thou fillest with thy hid treasure,' namely, of the earth (which also speaks home to the metaphor of the text). So then, earthly things were their god ; that is, their chiefest good, instead of God.   And the eager pursuit with which they adored their god, he as justly terms their religion, especially when under the pretence of religion they serve those ends.

The result is this (which is the thing in hand), that earthly things are, in the valuation of carnal men professing religion, their gain; and their religion also, supposing gain is godliness.   But to godly men godliness is great true gain, having a sufficiency in it.   Unto which accords that also of Solomon, Prov. iii. 14, 'The merchandise thereof is better than the merchandise of silver, and the gain thereof than of fine gold.'   Hast thou ever been brought to such dispositions of heart and spirit as these ?

1. To suffer (in thine own resolutions and account) the loss of all things, that thou mightest win or gain Christ.   It is Paul who is your pattern, Phil. iii. 7, 8, 'What things were gain to me, that I accounted loss for Christ; for whom I suffered the loss of all things, that I might win Christ.' Conversion to God is a great shipwreck of an old man, and all his goods and appurtenance.   I do not know how conversion goes now a-days, when you may judge the world favours religion ; but I will tell you how the price of the market went in our days.   A man's conversation* was such as not only some things, but all things he most valued, he was fain to bring it and lay it down at Christ's feet, as they did their money at the apostles', and by wholesale give it up to him.   For he knew not but that, for the sincere profession of Christ, he might lose all presently.   Take a scholar in the university, whose education was as Paul's, profiting in the Jewish learning above his equals ; yet the learning then cried up, and the way of preaching, in quotations of fathers, poets, apophthegms, stories, &c., was such as when a man had profited therein seven or ten years, and had a dispute† with or above his equals ; if he were humbled for sin and came to Christ for righteousness, and treated with God for salvation, God would say to him, What advantage or use will all this your learning, you have counted your treasure, be of to me ?   This poor soul was fain to give it all up for ever as lost, and was turned into the world a dunce, stripped of all his plumes ; for the other was loss and useless, and all this to win Christ.   And then his carnal friends would come upon him too, and say they had lost all their hopes, their cost upon him.   Thus a proud scholar was at once undone by bankrupt.‡   Again, his heart was swollen with hopes of preferment, his sails filled with the wind of it ; and he had ordered his studies, his comportment accordingly ; taken in commodities for that port.   And as he, in Habakkuk, had in his conceits gathered to himself all nations, all sorts of preferments as his prey ; but when he came truly to turn to Christ and enter into a profession of strictness, he was brought in his own resolution to lay down all he was in hopes of, and all which he had laid up as gains, towards the procuring of it ; and to be a poor schoolmaster, or a Levite in a private gentleman's house, was what in his future projections or expectations this man was brought to.   Conversion was a great shipwreck.   And sure it is, and will be to every one that turns to Christ still in something or other.

2. Again, after thou art turned, wherein dost thou reckon thy comings

* Qu. 'conversion'?—Ed.   † Qu 'repute'?—Ed.   ‡ That is, 'bankruptcy.'—Ed.

in to lie, and thy truest gains ?   Paul being a preacher of the gospel, as
before a persecutor (to instance therein), what were the chiefest of his gains
he looked at ? What, to get livings ? &c.   No ; but that he might win some
souls converted or quickened by his ministry, he accounted his treasure.
' What is our crown' (says he, 1 Thes. ii. 19, 20), ' but even ye, in the
presence of the Lord ?'   He acknowledged every such soul added as a
' ewel to his crown ; and every degree of grace that was added to those souls,
us so many carats in diamonds, which increaseth their value.   Thou hast
an outward man with many appurtenances, a name and repute in the world,
outward comforts about thee, health, vigour, the world fair on thy side.
All these in Scripture language are termed the outward man.   Well, and
thou pretendest to have an inward man in thee ; that is, to have a repute
and acceptation with God, made to enjoy communion with him every day ;
unto which the things and comforts of another world do as properly and
as suitably belong, as the other to that outward.   To instance first in that
part of thy outward man thy good name, God comes and makes a breach
upon thy name ; and this party of men, they report this, another that ; yea,
and pervert thy best and sincerest actions to thy reproach, turn thy glory
into shame.   And these losses and revilings daily come in like Job's messengers, upon the neck of one another.   These are shrewd losses.   But
what dost thou reckon thy gains ?   All this while thou findest God draw
near to thee, own thee, testify thy sincerity to thee.   Thou hast an inward
man, whose praise is with God, and not with men.   And thou hast further
a name in thy eye, at the latter day, above every name that is in this world.
Yea, and every reproach will turn to increase it at that day.   ' Even this
shall turn to my salvation,' Phil. i. 19.   Every thing written or spoken
against thee will then be a crown about thine head, as Job xxxi. 36, and
every scoff and contempt a fence.   And thine heart all this while finds a
self-sufficiency in godliness, betwixt God and thee, in which thou rejoicest,
and reckonest all these things thy gains, and secretly rejoicest heartily
herein upon this account.   Thus it was with Moses : Heb. xi. 26, ' He
esteemed the reproach of Christ,' or for Christ's sake, ' greater riches.'
He looked on them as his gains.

    And thus it is in all other kinds of outward losses, which are of the
appurtenances of the outward man.   See Paul's spirit, 2 Cor. iv. 16,
' Though our outward man perish, yet, I thank God, my inward man is
renewed day by day.'   I find comings in more or less every day thereby,
and what do I lose by that then ?   And therefore I value not my losses of
this kind, whilst a gain comes in the other way.

    Yea, upon this account all afflictions are therefore but light, and so all
losses of all sorts whatever, because they work for us an exceeding weight
of glory.   So it follows, verse. 17.

    And reason good why we should thus judge : For the things we lose are
but things temporal ; but the things we have in exchange for them are
things eternal.   So again it follows, ver. 18, ' We look not at the things
which are seen, but at the things which are not seen : for the things which
are seen are temporal ; but the things which are not seen are eternal.'
That true believers do really and in the private estimation of their souls
thus judge, you may also see by the instance of the believing Hebrews,
whose hearts Paul cuts up : Heb. x. 33, 34, ' Ye were made a gazing-stock
by reproaches and afflictions, and took joyfully the spoiling of your goods,'
as great losses as can be supposed to befall men.   What should be the
reason of this ?   They knew that they were gainers, that they got well by

it. ' Knowing in yourselves' (mark that) ' that you have in heaven a better and an enduring substance' (which as Paul told us even now), is wrought and increased by all these losses a hundred fold, as Christ speaks. It was the knowledge and actual application of this, caused them to rejoice as well as they might. But how did they know it ? The text says, ' In themselves.' When the great providence of God took away these, or any-thing from them, God was graciously pleased still to seal to them a bill of exchange in their own hearts ; to return instead thereof, so much better and enduring substance by way of exchange in the other world ; and he wrote this bill in their hearts, they had it themselves, the earnest of it (as 1 John v., ' he that believes ' is said to ' have the witness in himself) ; and look, as all a man's actions are written in a man's conscience, which he shall not be able to deny, so all such impressions from God are also written in the heart. And God will own all these his bills of exchange at the latter day. So then a Christian accounts these his greatest gains. And well he may, for if one should come into your house and take all your pewter and all your brass, and melt it before your face, but then come and sprinkle some of the elixir upon it (which you call the philosopher's stone) and turn it all into gold, I pray, what loss had you ? Yea, what gains ! And truly thus by faith you may—and in the issue, in experience, all you true Christians must—look upon all afflictions and losses whatever. By faith you may aforehand, as knowing this will be the issue ; therefore says James, chap. i. 2, ' Count it all joy, when ye fall into divers temptations ;' observe his *when*, not when after ye are fallen, but at first, when you do fall. Re-joice thus aforehand. Suppose thy afflictions be for thy sins, no matter ; wait and thou shall gain by them. They bring forth a quiet fruit of righteousness, that is, that issue which so quiets, as it causeth the soul to say, I am satisfied ; it was well for me I was thus afflicted. Thou losest a child dear to thee, for it is thine image, and God renews (upon the occasion and by the affliction of it) his own image, or some member of it, more fair and fresh than ever. What are a hundred thousand children to the least degree of grace ? The comings in by one good prayer is worth them. God takes a pin off thy sleeve, and puts into thine heart the white stone which hath a new name on it. ' It was good for me I was afflicted,' says David ; that is, he reckoned it his gains. To be kept but from one sin by an affliction is greater gain than this world hath to afford. ' I went astray,' says David, ' afore I was afflicted.' Crosses which break other men's hearts, and which they can never get off, but are sunk with the burden of to their graves, they are made light to a believer, as Paul speaks ; they bring him nearer to God, and he blesseth God that ever it befell him. It is true, indeed, he desires rather, and he is to seek it, that God would sanctify mercies to him ; yet if there be no other way to be made a partaker of God's holiness (as the apostle speaks) but this, he would not care what God did with him. ' If by any means I may attain the resurrection of the dead,' says Paul, Phil. iii. 11. He speaks it in respect of the holiness that will be in that state. Let God take what course he will, what means he will, he should be glad. It was because he reckoned God and the things of God his treasure, and so his gains to lie there. By these two dealings of God with thee put together, thou mayest make forth a great and mighty evidence of thy election.

1. That however God deals with thee in what thy flesh and outward man desires, whether rich or poor, despised or in repute, &c., yet still thou canst and mayest observe that by all such dispensations God seasonably keeps

thee, or breaks thee off from sin, draws thee nearer, and puts thee upon praying and crying out to him. What is this but that his eternal love hath taken care of an inward man in thee, which he doth renew from day to day (if thy crosses be such), or from month to month, from week to week ; and therefore will not let thee go on in such a sin as others do, or in that dead frame, but it shall cost thee this affliction or that, a loss in this thing or that thing which is dear to thee ; another piece of thy name must go for it, or the other child, or some of thy estate. This is a sign eternal love carries on its design towards thee, and not common or providential love.

2. Then, secondly, dost thou find this still, upon all such losses and perishings of thy outward man, thy heart to have some quietness and rejoicing from this, that though God hath dealt thus bitterly with me, yet he hath made it up by a supply of his Spirit some way or other, either in preserving from sin, stirring up conscience, quickening to prayer, exercising faith, waiting submission. And then with all thy heart thou dost value these more than all thy losses, and dost say, howsoever, I see it was good and best for me I got by such a sickness brokenness of heart, both off from and for such a lust ; and though I cannot say I have grown much, yet my inward man hath been renewed, some life of graces have been kept in ure hereby, so as I would not for all the world but God should have dealt thus with me ; I would not have been rich, or great, or honourable instead thereof, though still what God will do with me at last I know not. I tell thee, such thoughts and dispositions as these do manifestly declare that thy treasure lies not on this side of heaven, but it is in the other world, which appears by thine own audit-book, in which losses and gains are written ; that is, what things they are thou esteemest thy greatest losses and thy greatest gains. Thy gains in this case lie in things of the other world.

Now, further, to give you an evidence that not in this world, but in the other, a Christian's treasure lies ; not only that he accounts the afflictions of this present life gains, but even death itself, concerning which other men's hearts say, When I am gone, all is gone. Death is the great murderer ; like a sweeping rain, despoils a man of all in this world at once. But what says Paul ? Phil. i. 21, ' To me to die is gain.' So a good soul looks upon the thing in itself. And oh! that I had assurance, that I might account it so for me ; yet such it is in his estimation, in his hopes, though not in his particular confidence. Oh, says he, I heartily value the things of that world, so as that I would not care if I were well there ; this wife, these good houses, children, credit, honours, what will they do me ? Whom have I, in affection, in heaven but thee ? In earth I have too many harlotry things which draw away my heart from thee. Oh, would I were with thee, and in thy bosom ! So he prays and sighs. And why is this ? Because the true treasure thy heart values is laid up there, and there is an enduring substance. And then says the heart, If I die, I should go and receive all my bills of exchange, into which all the comforts I have had first or last have been one way or other turned. I shall meet with every prayer, tear, sigh, groan, and have all mine afflictions returned me with infinite advantage. ' To me to live is Christ, and to die is gain.'

Again, I shall add, What dost thou endeavour to add to daily ? Therein lies the gains, and that is thy treasure. It is in the text : What is a man's treasure, he will lay up, and be still adding to that heap. For a treasure lies in an abundance which a man seeks to heap up ; whereas of other things he only provides so much as barely serves his present use, as coals for firing, &c. Of the believing Corinthians Paul gives this testimony, and withal this motive, which he knew would take with their hearts : 2 Cor. viii. 7, ' Therefore, as ye abound in everything, in faith, in utterance, in knowledge, and in your love to us ; see that ye abound in this grace also.' Wherein lay the force of this exhortation, but that they accounted the graces of the Spirit their treasure ? and so had a principle provoking them to abound in all sorts of them.   The like exhortation you have, 1 Cor xv. 58, ' Always abounding in the work of the Lord ;' that is, in some good thing or other that is for God, ' knowing your labour is not in vain ;' for the more you abound, the more treasure you lay up in heaven.   Consider, therefore, what heap thou art endeavouring to add unto as thy treasure.   I do not say which of the heaps are bigger, thy good works or thy sins ; but which heap is it thou seekest to add to, and to abound in ?   Dost thou go on reck- lessly to add sin to sin, Isa. xxx. 1, till the measure of thine iniquity is full ?   Thou and thy companions say (as Isa. lvi.), ' Come, to-day shall be as to-morrow,* and much more abundant.'   Abundance of sin, and pleasure by sin, is that thou seekest ; adding drunkenness to thirst, as (Deut. xxix. 19) Moses his phrase is ; that is, a full satisfaction to every lust thou hast a mind to : if covetous, seekest to add land to land ; if a scholar, notion to notion ; but neglectest, yea, valuest not to add grace to grace, one good prayer to another, as Peter exhorts, 2 Peter i. 5.   Dost thou give all diligence to add grace to grace, to that end that you may be rich in faith, James ii. 5, rich in good works, in good speeches, good thoughts, as account- ing these your treasure ?   Then God is the chief portion and treasure.   And this by so much the more as thou hast formerly added sin to sin.   And if thou sayest, Alas, my lusts abound, and deadness and unfruitfulness ; well, but then thou aboundest in complaints hereof, and addest complaint to com- plaint ; and it makes thy life bitter to thee, as a sorer vanity than any Solo- mon instanceth in.

Again, What times of thy life dost thou look upon as lost time, or else as most precious and gainful to thee ?   Days of greatest receipts of what is one's treasure, he reckons his best days.   A man counts that time lost, in which what he principally intends goes not forward.   A scholar that makes haste to be rich in knowledge, as others to be rich in estates, looks upon times that conscience puts him upon holy duties in, as interruptions, which he thinks much at, as impediments to his main end.   So of the Sabbath ; when will it be gone ? as they in the prophet ; or, as the heathens scoffed the Jews, that they lost the seventh part of their lives. Dost thou so ?   It is because thou makest not God, nor the things of God, thy treasure.   What made David account ' one day in God's house better than a thousand' ? Ps. lxxxiv. 10.   What makes one day better than another, but that gain which the day brings in ?   Oh, say they that run into excess of riot, What a gallant night had we of it ! when their wits and spirits were flushed with wine and joviality   But on the contrary, what says a good and holy soul ?   I have had a good day of it, or a good night of it, when God hath been near him in a private prayer, or at meeting with others, Isa. lviii. 13.   To a godly man a fast-day or a Sabbath-day is said to be honour- able, that is, precious and high in his esteem.   Hence when a man comes to turn to God, he accounts all the time before, however spent, to be lost time.   You have therefore Paul complaining that he was converted later than the rest of the apostles ; 1 Cor. xv. 8, that he was born out of time, as a scholar that is kept from school, or from going to the university till twenty years old or upwards, bewails his loss, or his having been a truant.

* Qu. ' To-morrow shall be as to-day ' ?—ED.

And yet Paul had spent his time well in the Jewish learning, and profited therein above measure. Yea, but I knew not Christ, says he, for the excellent knowledge of whom I account all things loss. To this also refers that speech of Christ: Mat. xx. 3, 6, ' Why stand ye here idle all the day long in the market place ?' And therefore a godly man also looking back upon the times past after his conversion, those days wherein (though under bitter temptations) yet he sought God much, and with the utmost intentions of his soul ; or wherein there was a quick trade and intercourse between God and him, or others and him in the things of God, he notes them in his almanack with a white stone. And these wherein he considers that the world and vain thoughts have, as the lean years, eaten up the fat, he looks on these with sadness, and with bitterness cries out, *Amici! perdidimus diem*, 'Friends, we have lost a day,' in which he hath not made some addition to his treasure. This is the great rule in Moses his arithmetic, which he hath taught us, to ' number our days, by applying our hearts to wisdom.' Which rule by proportion holds and instructs for time past, as well as time to come, that a man reckons that time lost, in which he hath not applied his heart to wisdom.

CHAPTER V.

To know whether we make God our chiefest good, we must state the account upon what it is that we most value ourselves or other men.

The last head of signs from this metaphorical expression, *What is thy treasure ?* is, What thou dost value and estimate thyself by, as also other men ?

This note differs from the former. For when I asked what was precious to thee, it signified what valuation thou hadst of the things in themselves, which is a direct act of valuation. But this query is by what things you put a value upon yourselves or others, which is as the reflex act, as in other cases we use to distinguish. That I may give a right stating of this note, that it may be fitted for all sorts to apply it without mistake of what I intend, or disquietment to their own souls, I shall premise these things by way of explication.

1. That this note holds in an affirmative, a positive sense, true of unregenerate men, who may be convinced by this what their hearts do really value themselves by, when it is found to be some earthly excellency or other, which therefore is their treasure.

2. Of godly men it holds true negatively, as to what they have learned not to value themselves by, not by earthly and worldly excellencies ; that rate-book is cancelled in a great measure with them. And as for a positive valuing carnal self in a way of being lift up, they have learned to be as cyphers in their own hearts, to be nothing in a man's self. This is the A. B. C. in Christianity, though we are always a-learning it. Ask a humble soul, what dost thou value thyself by ? He will readily answer (as to what he is of himself, and in himself), Alas, by nothing. Thus Paul, in divers places, two especially : 1 Cor. xv. 9, ' I am the least of the apostles, that am not meet to be called an apostle.' Again, 2 Cor. xii. 11, ' I am nothing.'

And yet, 3, for all this, you shall find the same apostle value himself as he was a man in Christ, and according to what he had by grace, as he had lived in and to Christ, and acted for Christ, he doth value himself thereby ;

yet still vailing and attributing all unto that grace of God which had done it for him, even at the same time and with the same breath with which he lays himself thus low. Which is sufficient ground to the note in hand, that even regenerate men have also that treasure of another kind belonging to them, which they do and may value themselves by, even whilst they really profess themselves as nothing; as in respect both to themselves as in themselves, and unto the grace of God working in them and with them, which is one branch of the point in hand. Consult we for this the places cited: 1 Cor. xv., 'I am the least of the apostles.' So, ver. 9. But then at the tenth verse he riseth again : ' But by the grace of God I am what I am.' Well, and what was he ? It follows : ' I laboured more abundantly than they all ;' there he pulls forth his treasure. Yet still (lest he should have said too much) he distinguisheth again upon it : ' Yet not I, but the grace of God that was with me.' And in 2 Cor. xii. 11, with the same breath with which before he had said, ' I am nothing,' he boldly premiseth this, ' In nothing am I behind the very chiefest apostles, though I be nothing.' Paul had then wherewith he valued himself, you see. And in the same chapter he gives you that other part of the distinction I mentioned, ver. 2, 5, ' I knew a man in Christ. Of such a man I will glory : but of myself I will not glory, but of mine infirmities,' as in that respect, and yet it was himself he speaks of. So then take himself as in himself, and so carnal men never thoroughly humbled never do; and of that self, abstracted from any relation to Christ, says he, ' I profess myself nothing.' But of such a man, and so of myself as conjunct with Christ, what I am in Christ, I may and will glory. So then the right state of this note of difference between a godly and an ungodly man lies fair afore us.

1. That a carnal unregenerate man doth positively value himself and others by some excellency that is earthly, if he have any to value himself by. Or if not, he values others by what his heart accounts truly a treasure.

2. A godly man hath learned not to value neither himself nor others chiefly by such things.

But 3. His heart being pitched upon living upon God in Christ, he values himself, if he hath assurance of his being in Christ, by what he is in Christ, and by the grace of God, as by a rich treasure still with vailing to grace, and distinguishing himself as in Christ from himself as in himself.

And 4. So far as he wants assurance, and so can value himself by nothing as assuredly his own, yet what his heart truly maketh its treasure may be discovered in him, and by himself, in this, what things they are he values others by. It being thus stated, let us come to the proof and application of it.

The reason why carnal men value themselves by outward excellencies is, that man naturally would not be a mere cypher to himself and others. He must be somebody, a μέγας τίς, as it is said of Simon Magus, Acts viii. 9. Now the souls of men, upon the same account that Aristotle calls them *abrasæ tabulæ*, in point of motion and intellectual species, may be called cyphers, considered as separated from all outward excellencies and encowments, as wit, learning, estates, beauty, riches, power, or some such things. And they stand and appear to themselves as cyphers in comparison of others. But look, as any of these things are added to them, which they see are in high esteem with men in the world, then this poor naked cypher will begin to reckon itself a number, and still the more that is added the greater number it goes on to think itself to be ; as the more figures, the more the value of a cypher is increased.   You may see the truth of this too true a similitude in the instance of Saul.   When Saul was young and a stripling, and a private person, Samuel reminds him, ' Thou wert little in thine own eyes,' 1 Sam. xv. 17.   The cypher had but a few figures then set or belonging to it.   And he was, though something, as the word *little* imports (according to what he then possessed when he went to seek his father's asses), yet little then in comparison of what the value of himself did rise to when a kingdom, with all its glories and privileges, were added to him.   A kingdom, set to original sin, hust and blew him up, so that he thought himself worth no less than all the kingdom besides (as we have heard and seen other kings have been wont to do), he grew too great for God himself to rule, and to have respect to his commands ; to intimate which to his conscience was Samuel's scope.

The prince of Tyre is another instance, Ezek. xxviii. 2-6 verses.   It seems he was a man eminent in wisdom and knowledge, as ver. 4 : ' With thy wisdom and understanding thou hast gotten thee riches, and gold and silver into thy treasures.   And by reason of all this (as ver. 2) thy heart is lifted up ;' as the ark was, as the waters that bore it did rise and increase. Well, and how big was this cypher, this mote, this atom, this less than nothing, lift up ?   Even as high as the throne of God.   So God, the searcher of hearts, chargeth him : ver. 2, ' Thus saith the Lord God, Because thy heart is lifted up, and thou hast said, I am God, I sit in the seat of God, in the midst of the seas, yet thou art a man and not God, though thou set thine heart as the heart of God.'   Oh, how big did this toad swell in his own imagination !   Therefore God, to confute him, and to bring him to his native cypherhood, threateneth to bring a sword against him and all his glory, that should strip him of all his excellencies he valued himself by, and should slay him, ver. 7, 8.   And then says God (and it was as great a sarcasm as that shot at our first parents, ' Man is become as one of us '), ver. 9 : ' Wilt thou say before him that slayeth thee, I am God ?'   He will make but a poor god of thee.   God pricked the toad, and he fell to nothing.   As also he did Herod, Acts xii., when swollen with the flattering breath of the people for his eloquent oration.   God sent his angel to cut the bladder, and how did it fall !   I have instanced in kings, because they are suns of the greatest magnitude any of the cyphers of man-kind grow to.   But it holds proportionably in all men else.   If a man scrape together a little riches, and scraps of wit and learning, men's souls presently value themselves thereby : 1 Tim. vi. 17, ' Charge them that are rich in this world, that they be not high minded.'   As riches increase, the heart increaseth.   This is one reason why a carnal man comes to value himself by things outward.

2. If you will see a reason of the difference of the second thing pro-pounded, viz., how it comes to pass that a godly man and a carnal do differ thus in the valuation of themselves, among others there are two several rate-books, or books of valuation, which according as men have eyes given them to discern, and spirits impartially to view themselves in, and guided to judge themselves by, accordingly will they come to rate and value them-selves with this vast difference spoken of.

There is the world's book, which is that common esteem which the gene-rality of men have of things, and do cry up and magnify them by.   Now what things do bear a rate and value with the world but things worldly ? Ps. xii. 8, Vanity with mortal man highly is extolled.   And Christ, Luke

xvi. 15, hath this expression of it, ' Things highly esteemed by men.' Now a worldly natural man, having the spirit of this world as yet predominant in him (1 Cor. ii. 12, which is especially there spoken in relation to his judging of persons and things, for he exposeth* it there to the spiritual man's judging of things spiritually) ; such a man therefore jumps with the carnal world in his judgment, both about men and things, looks upon himself and all things with the world's eye, and is said to walk according to the course of the world, Eph. ii. 2 ; and so rates and values himself by the world's book, that is, by the common opinion and price which things by the world are taken up at.

On the contrary, there is God's book (as you say, ' the king's book,' by which you know the value of livings). It is *Doomsday Book* if you will, in which the rate of all persons and things are laid down, according as the value of things shall go at the latter day. And this was written to that end, to correct and amend the common account of things, that men might ' judge righteous judgment,' and learn to esteem of themselves as they are indeed. And this book heightens the price of the things of the other world, which carnal men undervalue ; sets down a thousand where the world sets down nothing ; ' Vanity of vanities,' ' Dung,' ' Dross,' where they write down a hundred. And therefore in that Luke xvi. 15 it is said, ' that what is in high esteem with men is an abomination unto God.' So Christ there exposeth and sets at distance God's esteem of things and man's. You find the same opposition of these two in Paul's spirit : 1 Cor. iv. 3, ' I care not to be judged by man's day' (as in the Greek), translated ' man's judgment.' God hath a day of judgment, and man hath his day of judging things, so called, because man's judgment carries it from God. Men are clerks of this market, the prizers of this dead world's goods. Now what God's judgment is of things and persons, his own book doth perfectly serve to inform us, and so how to value ourselves and others, so as the greatest monarch in the world, whose glory and greatness this world adores, if he comes, as Hezekiah, to read himself in God's book, he finds himself nothing, of no value therein. And in Deut. xvii., you find that God hath written this book in a special manner, for this very end ; ver. 18, ' It shall be when he sits on the throne of his kingdom' (speaking of their kings, as they should be surrounded with all things which make them great and glorious), ' that he shall write a copy of this law in a book, and he shall read therein all the days of his life.' And one end is, ver. 20, ' That his heart be not lifted up above his brethren.' If he looks upon himself as he stands in the world's book, he will rate himself worth more than ten thousand others ; but when he comes unto God's book, which presents unto him, as in a glass, how persons stand in God's eye (who ' judgeth without respect of persons,' Acts x. 34 ; that is, without those outward garbs of conditions men are in. For in the sun, a beggar and a king have both the same shadow), therein a king, reading, with the Spirit of God enlightening him, falls as low as the poorest beggar, yea, lower, if he hath grace. Now, a godly man ' hath not received the spirit of the world, but the Spirit which is of God. That we may know the things which are freely given us of God,' 1 Cor. ii. 12, so as, ver. 16, ' we have the mind of Christ,' and do look upon things with that light, in our measure, wherewith he doth. And hence comes that great change and alteration in a godly man in judging of himself, valuing himself by what he is in Christ, by the things he hath received of God. David, who knew himself designed unto a kingdom, made

* Qu. ' opposeth '?- -ED.

that Psalm cxxxi., on purpose to shew the frame of his heart this way. 'Lord' (says he, appealing to him that knew the heart), 'mine heart is not haughty, nor mine eyes lofty.' It is a strange level that grace makes in the view and prospect of him that hath it. It makes, as John's ministry, the mountains, in the world's eye, valleys; and fills up the valleys that were low and empty, in the apprehensions of those men that have it. And this is perfectly James's scope, chap. i. 9, 10, 'Let a brother of low degree rejoice in that he is exalted: but the rich, in that he is made low.' Which when converted, the light of God discovers to him. James wrote to comfort poor believers, and to humble the rich professors (whereof many being but temporary believers, despised the poor, chap. ii. 6). This you may see run along, as a vein, throughout his epistle; chap. i. 9–12, chap. ii. ver. 1–6, chap iv. and chap. v. And because in the world's light and eyes, and afore regeneration, there appears so mighty a distance and disproportion in a poor man's condition and in a rich, he therefore sets afore them what the true saving light of Christianity works in the apprehensions and valuations of men converted, whether poor or rich. He supposeth to be aforehand both to a poor man that is godly, and a rich man that is godly; supposing such a brother a believer, as ver. 9 shews. A rich man, afore conversion, looked upon the poor man with a lofty eye, as one so far above him, and a poor man looked upon himself as mean and ordained to misery, in comparison, and calls the rich happy. Well, the Spirit comes and converts the one and the other. And then the wheel turns (as the poets feigned of fortune), the world is turned upside down. Saith the poor man when converted, I that had nothing to betake to in this world, nor much hopes of being anything, I find I am an heir of glory, and higher than all the kings and great ones of the earth. 'Hath not God chosen the poor of this world rich in faith, heirs of the kingdom?' chap. ii. 5. This therefore gives the poor man ground to rejoice, as well he may, that he is exalted. 'Let the brother of low degree rejoice' (says James) 'in that he is exalted.' And let him value himself with joy unspeakable and glorious, by what he reads and finds himself to be in that other world. On the contrary, a rich man, when converted to God, and he begins first to be humbled, he, as he is a rich man, is as much cast down and dejected. For seeing his sinfulness and nothingness through the light of the Spirit and the word, and his obnoxiousness to eternal death, thinks he, the poor man that hath but grace, and an interest in Christ, is infinitely happier than I. He lies low and puts his mouth in the dust, if there may be hope. And when faith and assurance of the other world comes in, he rejoiceth in this his happy misfortune he hath had, to be humbled and levelled in his outward condition with the poorest cobbler, whom if he have more grace than he, he looks upon as a better man than himself. And with this high and differing valuation (as it is kept up in their spirits) do these two look upon things and persons for ever after. A bondman, a slave, was taught not to care, for he is Christ's freeman. Masters were taught that they have a master in heaven, who 'hath no respect of persons,' Eph. vi. 9, The new creature teacheth a man to 'know no man after the flesh,' 2 Cor. v. 16, that is, to estimate no man from outward things, that is, with that high valuation and admiration a man had wont to do. Had any man any special, spiritual privilege, Paul learnt to value that man by it, and that foare himself. Such an one 'was in Christ afore me' (says he). He is my elder, and of more standing in grace, and he gave them a reverence accordingly; yea, take a poor soul that dares not yet say that it is in Christ, and so cannot value itself thereby, yet this true valuation is seen by what it hath of others. When he sees the greatest king in the world living in his natural estate, and swimming in greatness, he would not change conditions with him for ten thousand worlds. For although his own being in the estate of grace is yet uncertain to him, yet the other's (supposed in his natural condition) is certainly at present damnable. Also every one he looks upon as godly are the precious ones of the earth with him, as the psalmist speaks. And oh (says he) that I were but an hired servant amongst them, in the meanest condition, so one of that number, as the prodigal convert wished. And what is the reason of all this? Because his esteem and valuation of things is altered.

Now then, for the application of all this, consider by what principles the valuation or disvaluation of thyself is measured or guided. To what beam or balance dost thou come to weigh thyself; whether in the balance of the sanctuary or the balance of common opinion which is hung up in the world's great market-place? Thou mayest be great, and happy, and honourable in thine own eyes, as also the world's, when thou art miserable and abominable in God's. Thus a rich man, or one in power, men account a great man. But what is that greatness, but such as a man that is fat and pursy hath? And so men weigh fat and all, and account a man great. So Nabal, 1 Sam. xxv. 2, is termed ' a great man,' because ' he had three thousand sheep and a thousand goats,' which was a great estate in those days. But this kind of greatness God and his word regards not. Therefore God pronounceth of Belshazzar, though he had the whole Babylonian monarchy, and all the glory and the riches of it, environing of him, to put into the scale, ' Thou hast been weighed, and art found too light.' Here we might, for our help, run over all sorts of instances, of things of value, either worldly or heavenly, as the Scripture sets the one against the other ; and how thereby this difference in godly men's hearts and others may evidently appear unto themselves.

1. There is that which is honour in the world's esteem, and that which is truly and indeed such with God. Hast thou an ambitious heart? (God allows an ambition, pitched right, as we see in Paul's speech of his ambition to preach the gospel.) There is an honour to satisfy it. And doth thy valuation thereof carry forth thy spirit thereto? Christ gives us the distinction : John v. 44, ' How can ye believe, which receive honour of one another, and seek not the honour which cometh from God only ?' Here is honour from God only, and honours from men, and men's estate distinguished by their pursuit after them. The glory of God himself, and the seeking thereof, in aiming at him, that is not here meant ; but it is that honour which is from God, and with God, and which by approving a man's self to him alone, obtains with him. God's favour is true honour in such a man's esteem : Isa. xliii. 4, ' Since thou wast precious in my sight, thou hast been honourable, and I have loved thee : therefore will I give men for thee, and people for thy life.' So that, though before, a man hath valued himself by those things which have brought him in honour from men, yet when converted, he takes another account, knowing that God's favourites only, and whom he loves, are only truly honourable, and that his ways are only honourable (as the Sabbath is called, Isa. lviii. 13), and that to ' lay hold of his covenant and keep his Sabbaths,' purchaseth himself a ' better name,' and more lasting, than ' sons and daughters,' as it is, Isa. lvi. 4–6. On the contrary, he looks on others as vile persons. ' God abhorring them,' Ps. x. 3, he abhorreth them also ; whereas a wicked man ' blesseth the

covetous, whom God abhorreth.' And so for things he once made his glory, and valued himself by, he now accounts to have been his shame, Phil. iii. 19, and that would bring him to confusion of face.

So also, 2, this holds in wisdom (hence that distinction, 1 Cor. ii. 6, 7, ' The wisdom of the world, that comes to nought,' and ' the wisdom of God.' ' Wisdom to salvation,' as in Timothy) ; so that a man who hath valued himself by his learning, knowledge, wits, parts, and policy, when he comes to be converted, finds (as Rom. i. 22) that whilst he hath professed and thought himself wise (as of the philosophers it is said there), he is become a fool ; and he finds that the word proves him so to be, and he thinks so of himself; that he hath but even studied all his life to be a fool, because he wants true wisdom to save his soul. Which wisdom now he magnifies, for this wisdom is justified and magnified of all her children, and is glad to become a fool that he may be wise ; and on the contrary, with carnal men, worldly ' wisdom is justified of her children,' and this unto salvation is counted foolishness, 1 Cor. ii. 14.

So also, 3, is it in riches, which is another thing men use to value themselves by. Take that distinction of Christ, Luke xvi. 9, of ' the unrighteous mammon ' and ' true riches.' So that a man that hath thought himself a rich man in the world's books, upon conversion, becomes a beggar in his own eyes. It is therefore called ' poverty of spirit.' For why, as Christ says, Luke xii. 21, ' He that lays up this as treasure for himself, is not rich towards God ; ' he thought himself ' rich and increased with goods,' as the church of Laodicea says of herself; Rev. iii. 17, ' Thou sayest I am rich, and increased with goods,' whenas God knows and says it, and the soul now finds it, that it is ' wretched, miserable, poor, and naked.' Whereas God values him as rich that hath faith and good works : Rev. ii. 9, ' I know thy poverty, but thou art rich.' And so now a fair woman, whose treasure lay in her face and good clothes, by which she once rated herself when she looked into the world's glass, because all men ran doating and wondering after such an one, as the world once did after the beast, Rev. xiii. 3, when she comes to take account of the word, and to look thereunto, she finds another beauty, which is so in God's esteem ; 1 Peter iii. 3, 4, ' Whose adorning let it not be in the outward plaiting of the hair,' &c. ' But let it be of the hidden man of the heart, the ornament of a meek and quiet spirit' (which is a lasting ornament, the other decays), ' which in the sight of God is of great price.' I might instance in many more. Further, take a note or two.

1. That by which thou valuest thyself by most thou gloriest most in, makest it thy glory, either in the secret applaudings of thine own heart, or else it may be of others, Phil. iii. 19. Among other expressions which the apostle hath to express the over-valuing of earthly things by earthly-minded men, one is, ' whose glory is their shame, who mind earthly things.' Hence you find boasting in riches spoken of Ps. xlix. 6 and lii. 7. You also have that example of Nebuchadnezzar, Dan. iv, 30, who, walking in his gallery, and, as it may seem, alone, you find him, like a fool, talking to himself, ' Is not this the great Babel which I have built by the might of my power, and for the honour of my majesty ? ' As many a scholar in his own heart saith, Was it not such an act I kept, or disputation I performed, such an oration that I made ? That one place more is enough, and fit for this purpose ; Jer. ix. 23, ' Let not the wise man glory in his wisdom, nor the rich man in his riches, nor the mighty or potent man in his might and power.' God speaks thus severally, for men make any of these their treasure, and

will glory of these; and in these do men glory, if they know not God. But if he be a godly man, what doth he glory in? It follows, 'Let him glory in this, that he knows me: that I am the Lord, that shews him mercy,' and am his God and treasure. 'And of thee,' say they in Ps. xliv. 8, and our interest in thee, 'O God, will we make our boast all the day long.' Carnal men, says the apostle, glory in outward appearances; but, says he, Gal. vi. 14, ' God forbid I should glory, save in the cross of Christ.' And why might not Paul glory in the flesh and in the world as well as others? (It is well known he had wherewithal to do it, as he tells us elsewhere.) Why, he answers, that the cross of Christ, and the power thereof in him, had ' crucified the world to him,' had spoiled all the gloss of it to his heart, wiped the varnish off. For who values a dead man, a crucified man, at anything? Thus, Jesus Christ being a crucified man, Isa. liii. 2, 3, he is said to have ' no form nor comeliness in him.' And when we shall see him, he will have no beauty to a carnal eye, why it should desire him, being a despised and rejected man. Now, so says the apostle, ' The world is to me a crucified thing, through grace wrought in me by the cross of Christ.' Again, had not Paul many outward excellencies to make him glorious in the world's eyes, and might he not glory in them? Yes, that he had as great a confluence of all excellencies of learning, know-ledge, &c., as any, and was so accounted too. ' If I would glory,' says he, 2 Cor. xi. 21, ' I could too.' But his turning Christian spoiled all, cruci-fied them, marred the splendour of them in the world's eyes, so that, if he would have boasted of them now, he could not. For they had lost their grace and colour; grace had foiled them. And now, though he could vie learning with the best of them in anything, yet his being of that new sect, his professing the cross of Christ, which was foolishness to the world, spoiled all, made him be thought a mad man by him that thought he had learning enough, and too much, so that it was no booty to glory in any of these, though he would; and besides, says he in the next verse, ' Nothing avails but the new creature; ' neither circumcision nor uncircumcision (he means the greatest privileges, by a *synechdoche* of those which the Jews or Gentiles had and boasted of). And he says, ' they avail not,' they are little worth, of little value, as being able to do little, nay, just nothing with God, with whom we have to do. They are *nullius pretii* with him, and therefore with me also. But, being a new creature, that is worth having indeed, because it did interest him into Christ, and avails much with God in him. And yet not simply the new creature neither, as in itself, for so it avails nothing, as other things do, though it be an excellency; but ' *in Christ Jesus* a new creature' avails; that is, as it is in Christ. So a man may glory of it, and so Paul did, 2 Cor. xii. 1, 2, 5, speaking of his reve-lations and raptures, he would not simply glory in those as in themselves, or in himself as having these. But, says he, at verse 2, ' And of such a man I will glory, though of myself I will not glory,' and yet it was himself. And chap. xi., ver. 16, 17, ' What I speak,' says he of other things, ' I speak as it were foolishly in boasting.' He was ashamed to do it, but they despising him, he would shew that he could vie with the best of them in those things they made their chiefest glory. Yet still so as he is ashamed to do it; and therefore, in the midst of all, at ver. 23, he comes in with this parenthesis, ' I am a fool,' says he, ' to stand boasting thus.' For he thought them all not worth talking of in themselves. Yea, and he glories, to choose, in his infirmities, as of more value than all his sermons, because in them he was debased for Christ, in the other filled and assisted by Christ.

CHAPTER VI.

How the new creature makes God and his glory its utmost end.

Give unto the Lord, O ye mighty, give unto the Lord glory and strength.
Give unto the Lord the glory due unto his name; worship the Lord in the
beauty of holiness.—Ps. XXIX. 1, 2.

First, Here is the duty, ' Give glory unto God.' *Secondly,* upon the
most just reason, for it is *due unto his name.* Of all duties it is the most
large and comprehensive ; for it includes all obedience in it : praise, blessing,
thankfulness, are contained in it. But I will confine my discourse of it to
some such particulars, which the Scripture mentions under the notion of
giving glory to God.

I shall do two things.

1. Give reasons of this duty and disposition.

2. Insist on those particulars wherein especially we are to give, and the
new creature doth give, glory to God.

Reason 1. The first reason is in the text, ' Glory is due unto his name,'
because he is most glorious ; it is the reason given, Ps. cxxxviii. 5, ' For
great is the glory of the Lord ;' yea, his is glory, and his alone. Glory is
the superlative effulgence of goodness. Many things are good ; yea, many
things are excellent, which are not glorious. To things which are good,
praise and commendation are due ; to things which are more excellent than
ourselves, honour is due, so to superiors and magistrates, Rom. xiii. 7 ; but
such things as do super-excel to wonderment and amazement, such things
are only glorious. Thus the sun is called glorious, because it dazzleth the
eye, it is excellently sensible ; and such is God to the heart : his name is
glorious, because he is above all excellency, Neh. ix. 5, and Ps. viii. 1. It
is not simply said, ' Thy name is excellent,' but ' How excellent is thy
name !' It is above all expression. Therefore he is called ' God of glory,'
Acts vii. 2 ; ' King of glory,' Ps. xxiv. 10. For as kings are the fountain
of all nobility, so is God of glory. He is the father of all the glory which
Christ hath : therefore Christ prays to him for it, John xvii. 1.

(1.) God is most glorious in himself, though no creature had been to
glorify him. He was as glorious when there was no world as now he is.
Men's honours depend upon the opinion and apprehensions of them that
honour them. Where is the glory of a king, but in the multitude of his
subjects ? But God the Father, Son, and Holy Ghost, are sufficient to
glorify each other, if there were no creatures. ' If thou art righteous, what
dost thou ?' Job xxxv. 7. How do wise men contemn the approbation and
praises of the weak and foolish ? God might much more despise the
adoration and praise of us wretched creatures. We are therefore the more
engaged to give him all glory, upon this consideration, that though he needs
it not, yet he condescends to receive the inconsiderable tribute from us.

(2.) All things which are in him are all glorious. Take the best and
excellentest of the creatures, and still it is said of them that one particular
part in them is their excellency and glory, but all in them is not so, but
other things in them are but common and mean, to set off their excellencies.
So in men, so in the members of man, his tongue is called his glory, Ps.
lvii. 8 ; but that it may appear to be so, other parts must be mean, ' less
honourable,' as Paul says, 1 Cor. xii. 23. But all in God are, and that all

alike, glorious; his whole name, and all the letters in it.   Exod. xxxiii. 18,
'Shew me thy glory,' says Moses; 'I will proclaim my name before ye,'
says God, ver. 19.   His mercy is called 'riches of glory,' Rom. ix. 23.
His holiness also is glorious : thus when Isaiah saw his glory, the angels
cried, 'Holy, holy,' Isa. vi. 3.   His power is glorious, Rom. vi. 4; his
grace is glorious, Eph. vi.

(3.) When he would manifest this his glory to others, all that comes
from him is glorious; all his works are glorious.   1. The earth is full of
his glory, as it shews forth his glory, which yet is but his footstool, Isa.
lxvi. 1, much more his own habitation, Isa. lxiii. 15, which by Peter is
styled, 2 Pet. i. 17, 'the excellent glory.'   2. His word, both law and
gospel, are most glorious, 2 Cor. iv. 4.   Much more all his saints; his
servants, his courtiers are 'all glorious within,' Ps. xlv. 13.   His image,
whether substantial (as his Son is called the brightness of his glory, Heb.
i. 2), or representative, or similitudinary, as grace in his saints, his image
in Adam is called glory; 2 Cor. iii. 18, we are said to be changed 'from
glory to glory;' and he being thus glorious, to glorify him is a due to his
name, Ps. xxix. 2.   As we cannot but love things beautiful, and love is a
due to them, so is honour to things honourable.   Rom. xiii. 7, 'Render
honour to whom honour is due;' and therefore glorify God, who is so
glorious.

Reason 2.   As it is a due *to him*, as he is the glorious God, so it is due
from us, his creatures.

(1.) He made all creatures for himself, Prov. xvi. 4.   It is reason, if all
things be *of him*, they should be *to him*, Rom. xi. 36; therefore he there
adds, 'To him be glory for ever.'   But in a more special manner he made
us reasonable creatures for himself.

The unreasonable creatures are in some sort said to glorify him : Ps.
xix. 1, 'The heavens declare the glory of God.'   How?   They give occasion and afford matter whence we may take hints to glorify him.   As in
music there are the notes set out in the book, and the tongue that sings,
or hand that plays, which make the music.   The creatures are the notes,
or music, that is set, and have the notes, the keys, and characters of the
harmonious glory of God stamped upon them, Rom. i. 20.   But then there
must be an understanding creature, that hath skill and ability, to utter forth
the music and harmony of all these.   Therefore between the reflection, or
shine of God's glory from the creatures, and the glory he hath from us who
are reasonable creatures, there is as much difference as between the glory
of the sun appearing in its shining upon a wall, and in a looking-glass.
Now such hath God made our understandings, in comparison of other creatures, or as the eye is to the sun, on purpose that we might see his glory
as it is, John xvii. 24, and to reflect and beat it back again to him, so that
after God had emblazoned his rich and glorious power and wisdom in all
the frame of heaven and earth, as in a coat of arms, yet still there wanted
heralds to conceive of, and proclaim and adore his glorious name; and
therefore he created reasonable creatures, whose sole and adequate end was
to reflect glory upon him, even as the sole end of a mirror is to reflect the
image of things presented to it; and therefore, 1 Cor. xi. 7, man is said to
be 'the glory of God.'

Reason 3.   But especially this is required of his saints: Ps. cxlv. 10, 11,
'All thy works shall praise thee, O Lord, and thy saints shall bless thee.'
Ver. 11, 'They shall speak of the glory of thy kingdom, and talk of thy
power.'   Not only their making as creatures, but their whole formation, °s

new creatures, is to this end; for this they were elected, to be 'to the praise of the glory of his grace,' Eph. i. 6. To this end were they redeemed, yea, were 'bought with a price' (therefore, says the apostle, 'Glorify God in your bodies, and in your spirits'), a price which was paid by laying down and debasing Christ's glory, Phil. ii. 7. Therefore we should endeavour to restore it to him; we should glorify God, that was in our nature debased for us. To this end we are made and created new creatures. Isa. lxi. 3, 'They are the planting of the Lord, that he may be glorified.' Isa. xliii. 7.

Reason 4. They shall be glorified of God for ever, and should therefore here glorify God. Christ argues it, 'I have glorified thee on earth, now glorify me,' John xvii. Much more may it be urged on us, that if we pray that he would glorify us hereafter, we should glorify him here. And the rather, because here only is an opportunity of glorifying him actively; hereafter we are rather glorified of him, than do glorify him; as we are said to be rather known of him, than to know him.

Reason 5. All three persons do mutually endeavour to give glory each to other, and shall not we their creatures? 'The Father hath committed all judgment to the Son, that all might honour the Son as the Father,' John v. 22, 23. The Son he honoured the Father: John xvii. 4, 'I have glorified thee on earth,' &c. And the Holy Ghost glorifies the Son: John xvi. 14, 'He shall glorify me; for he shall receive of mine.' For he is continually magnifying Christ and his love unto believers' hearts. Now if they do so, shall not we? If they do it, who are equal to each other, shall not we who are so inferior, made for them? If one king honours another, shall not their subjects?

Reason 6. God is infinitely desirous of it, and exacts it. If a man looks for respect, and is worthy of it, and assumes not above his desert, those under him are the more careful to give it him. Others value a man as he sets a due and reasonable value on himself; but if he degrades himself, they give him the less respect. Now God, with the highest reason, doth value himself above all things, and will accordingly be glorified. 'Glory is mine,' says he, Isa. xlii. 8. He is so desirous of it, that he lays a tribute of glory upon every action: 1 Cor. x. 31, 'Whatsoever you do, eating and drinking, do all to the glory of God.'

Reason 7. Glory is all that God doth require of us, for all we receive from him. He would freely have us to take all the comfort that is to be had out of his blessings; but the glory of all, and for all, he reserves to himself: 1 Chron. xxix. 11, 12, 'Both riches and honour come of thee; thine is the glory,' &c. That is, though riches and all good blessings are of him, yet are so his, that they are ours also; but the glory of them all is his. This is his prerogative, his crown, wherein no subject shall partake with him. As Pharaoh said to Joseph, 'I am Pharaoh, and all Egypt is thine,' Gen. xli. 44; and ver. 40, 'Only in the throne will I be greater than thou:' so says God, I am God, and all the world, my Son, my self, are thine; all things are yours. But the glory of all is mine; that is, my throne, my crown. It is not your prayers, nor is it your duties he regards; but to be glorified in all these. Therefore in the Lord's prayer, the first petition is, 'Hallowed,' or 'Glorified be thy name.' That should be the main thing that should run through all the rest that follow, and which the heart should primarily fall upon, and eye in all. And as he teacheth them to begin, so also to end with an acknowledgment, 'Thine is the kingdom, power, and glory.' The end of all duties of God's worship are, 1. Com-

munion with God, and in God, on our part; and 2. Glorifying and sanctifying God in our hearts, on his part.   And as we are not to rest in a peace
of conscience, simply from having performed duties, but upon account of
communion and meeting with God in them; so, in like manner, we are
much less to rest in having done them for the satisfaction of our consciences, but so as to give in our heart that glory that is due to God,
whom we deal with in them.   And without this God reckons all but as
dung.   In the second of Malachi, God had called upon the priests who
brought sacrifices to him, to give glory to him therein, verse 2.   In the
3d verse he threatens them that, ' if you will not, I will fling back your
sacrifices as dung in your faces ;'—you know they sacrificed beasts then.
To shew how abominable to him without this these sacrifices were to him,
he compares them to dung, that is found in the belly, or ventricle of those
beasts they offered; and to express his abomination of such duties and
services, he says he would fling them as dung in their faces.   To fling
dung in one's face, is a note of the highest indignation and rejection.   Men,
in applying themselves to those they desire to approve themselves unto,
diligently use to observe what they look for, and expect, and what is their
disposition.   If a prince be covetous, they about him project always to
bring him money in; if vain-glorious, to flatter him, &c.   Thus let us apply
ourselves to God.   He is not taken with riches, nor duties, nor tears; with
nothing but glory.

Reason 8. Therefore, if this tribute be not paid, God will curse all good
blessings to us.   So it follows in that Mal. ii. 2.   Says God to the priests,
' If you will not lay it to heart, to give glory to my name, I will send a
curse upon you, and will curse your blessings.'   For should we hold all of
God, and his due be withholden from him ?   The kings' rents and customs
are still most strictly exacted, upon the greatest forfeitures.   If a man steals
custom and be taken in it, he forfeits all.   So do we our blessings, if God's
due, his glory, be not rendered him.   ' The God in whose hands are thy
breath and thy ways, hast thou not glorified.'   Dan. v. 23, ' Thy kingdom is
departed, and given to others,' in the following verses, said God to Belshazzar.

Reason 9. God will be sure to recover it on us, some other way ; if he
be not glorified by us, he will be glorified on us.   He will be sure not to lose
by any of his creatures ; if we are not active, he will make us passively to
glorify him.   He will have it out of us; we must pay the utmost farthing.
And seeing his tribute lies in glory, there are two ways of bringing of it,
or whence it riseth.   1. In and by our free giving it to him.   2. By his
vindicating it upon us.   To be glorified on us, is as much to him as our
obedience, and brings him in as much ; for his wrath, his power, his justice,
his holiness, &c., are enacted, made known and acknowledged that way, as
much as by our giving glory to him ; so as it is all one to him.   And therefore he calls this a glorifying of himself, as well as the other.   Thus he
spake of Pharaoh, whom Moses had long called upon to give glory to God.
Exod. xiv. 17, 18, ' I will get honour,' or be glorified ' upon Pharaoh.'   So
Ezek. xxviii. 22, ' I will set my face against Zidon, and I will be glorified
in the midst of thee : and they shall know that I am the Lord, when I have
executed judgment in her, and I shall be sanctified in her.'   His glory is
the making known of his name and attributes ; which he doth in punishing
as well as any other way, and he is said to be sanctified therein : Rom.
ix. 22, ' What if God, willing to shew his wrath, and to make his power
known, endured with much long-suffering the vessels of wrath fitted to destruction ?'   Therefore, Rev. xv., it is said, ' Give glory to God, for his

judgments are made manifest,' because his attributes being therein manifested, he is adored in men's hearts. So Lev. x. 3, when he brought the punishment on Nadab and Abihu, he gives this reason of it, ' I will be sanctified in them that draw nigh to me ;' either sanctified in their own hearts by themselves, or on them in the view of others. So as punishment on us executed, is as much to God as our holiness in us. And therefore in the prophet, the destruction of wicked men is called a sacrifice to God. He expresseth it by the same name he doth that worship he had then, as being as pleasing to him ; so that indeed the one is as much unto God as the other, if we do but consider the concernment of his glory. It is true, that out of his further goodness unto the creature, and his respects unto it, he declares himself more desirous of obedience from them, than their destruction ; but otherwise, as for his glory, it is all one to him ; for he is sanctified in either, and will be the one way, if not the other, as that speech implies. Oh, how much better is it for us so to glorify him, as to be glorified of him and in him (as we find both joined, 2 Thes. i. 12, where he prays they may be holy, verse 11, ' that the name of Christ may be glorified in them, and they in him'), than for him to glorify himself on us, in our confusion. The one or the other must be : it is all one to him which ; and if it be done by your destruction, ' this is unprofitable for you.'

2. I now come to enumerate some dispositions and duties of the new creature, by which it ought to reflect glory on God.

(1.) It ought to endeavour to know him, and to conceive aright of him, and to have such thoughts of him as become him. So Moses desires to see his glory ; that is, to know him and the excellencies which were in him. So David and all the saints desired to see him in the beauty of holiness, to see his face, and to have the light of his countenance lifted up, as Ps. lxiii. 2 ; so to rejoice, as Jer. ix. 24, ' in that we know God, which exerciseth loving-kindness in the earth.' And that thus to do is to glorify him, is evident ; for, Rom. i., when the Gentiles are said not to have glorified God, they are said, ver. 28, not to ' have liked to retain God in their knowledge.' And if his manifestative glory be the reflection of it, upon the understanding of another, then when we are ignorant of him, and conceive amiss of him, so much of his glory is lost, and therefore the Gentiles, which know him not, are said to live ' without God in the world,' being ' estranged from him through ignorance.' Ignorance makes him as no God to thee, and therefore thou dishonourest him in the highest degree ; if thou knowest him not, thou makest him no God to thee. On the contrary, to endeavour to know him, and think much of ' im, is a glorifying of him ; Ps. xlvi. 10, ' Be still, and know me : and I will be exalted.' If we spend many thoughts upon and do study a man's worth, we honour him exceedingly thereby in our thoughts. If we study any man's writings much, and preserve every note of his, we honour him exceedingly. So we honour God if we think of God much, and labour and desire to know him still better, more and better for the excellencies' sake that are in him ; and study his works that we may know him, and knowing him we may honour him in our thoughts, and glorify him.

(2.) When we admire him in all we know by him, and stand aghast at him, then we glorify him. And therefore in 2 Thes. i. 10, to be ' glorified' and ' made wonderful' are joined together ; things we wonder at we glorify ; and therefore, Rev. xiii. 4, to wonder at the beast is made all one as to worship him, saying, ' Who is like unto the beast, or able to make war with him ?' &c. So it is an honour to God to stand and to wonder at God, and every part of his name, which is called Wonderful, as David did : Ps. viii. 1, 'How excellent is thy name in all the earth!' To wonder at his mercy; as they, Micah vii. 18, 'Who is a God like to thee, in pardoning iniquity, transgression, and sin?' So likewise to advance his infinite wisdom, as David doth, Ps. cxlvii. 5; and 'his goodness is unsearchable,' Ps. cxlv. 3. To stand admiring a man's picture, or a piece of his workmanship, magnifies the workman that made it. Beauty, if not looked upon, thinks itself contemned; so doth God account himself neglected, if you do not know him.

(3.) We glorify God when we speak much of him to others, as of what we wonder at we use to do; for with men then a thing is said to be glorious, when it is spoken of much, when the world rings of it; and God's glory is such a great glory, as it is able to fill all the world, and all mouths with it. 'A good name is as a box of ointment,' says Solomon; which, when broken, fills the whole house. Now, God's name is a box of such ointment as may fill all the world, Ps. cxiii. 3. It is to be praised from one end of the world to the other, yea, and from one generation to another; it fills all time also; so ver. 4 of the 145th Psalm. Therefore the saints should have their mouths filled with his praise, Ps. lxxi. 8. But his saints bless him; all his works praise him, by talking of his power and mighty acts, Ps. cxlv. 12. And therefore the tongue is called man's glory, Ps. lvii. 8, because it is the instrument to set forth God's glory: 'therewith bless we God,' says James.

(4.) We glorify God when we ascribe all to him. So David did : 1 Chron. xxix. 11, 12, 'Thine is all,' says he, 'and all comes of thee; we have given thee but thine own.' And so Isa. xxvi. 18, 'We have not wrought any deliverance;' but, ver. 12, 'thou hast wrought all our works in us and for us.' So if thou prayest, acknowledge thou canst not as thou oughtest; but it is the Spirit helps thine infirmities. Before we do anything, we should by faith draw all power from him; and then when we have done, we shall ascribe all to him: Ps. cxv. 1, 'Not to us, not to us, but unto thy name be the glory.' They speak like those that refuse a bribe, and shew the greatest vehemence against the very offering of one. Their corrupt part in them suggesting thoughts of assuming to themselves; but they cry out, 'Not unto us.' I will give you the highest instance that can be given, to be an example unto you. The Holy Ghost, when he works anything in us, though the power be essentially his own, yet 'he glorifies the Son, by taking of his,' John xvi. 14, and working through him. How much more should we, when all we have is received! When Joab would honour David, and let him have the honour of the victory, he sends for him to take the city and wear the crown, 2 Sam. xii. 28; and yet it was but David's men and money did it, but Joab's wisdom and valour had a hand in it. Wouldst thou honour God? Send for him into thine heart, after a serious prayer; and give him the glory, for with his might thou didst it. Paul, that did more than all the apostles, yet says he had done nothing, but the grace of God that was with him.

(5.) We glorify God when we suffer for him: 1 Pet. iv. 14, 16, he is 'on your part glorified.' So the three children glorified God (in Daniel) when they said, that God they served was able to deliver them; if he would not, they would not go against his command. Nebuchadnezzar, that glorious king, could not have found one in all his dominions would have glorified him so; therefore Christ, by suffering for God, is said to glorify him, John xii. 23.

(6.) We glorify God by getting his image into our hearts, and imitating him. Imitation of any one is a great glory to him ; to have a great man's picture is his honour. If a great man be in favour, all follow his fashion, and therein they shew they honour him. And therefore (1 Cor. xi. 7) the man is said to be the image and glory of God. Both are joined ; get therefore the image of God into thy heart ; be holy, even as he is holy ; kind, as he is kind ; as he is patient and long-suffering, shew them forth in thy life ; shew forth the praises of him who hath called you : Mat. v. 16, ' Let your light so shine, that you may glorify your Father.' When the stars shine they glorify the sun, because they shine with his light ; thus a Christian glorifies God, when he lets any grace shine forth.

(7.) We glorify God by glorying in him, and boasting of our portion and happiness in him, 1 Chron. xvi. 10 and Ps. xliv. 8 ; for as they are his glory, so he is theirs, Ps. iii. 3.

(8.) We glorify God by living according to his will, and abounding in the fruits of holiness. So saith Christ, ' Hereby is my Father glorified, if you bring forth much fruit,' John xv.

(9.) We glorify God by doing all things for his glory as the end, 1 Cor. x. 31. This is more than all the rest (you may imitate kings, and suffer for friends, and yet you make not them your end), for it is to acknowledge that nothing in the world is so worthy as he, no, not yourselves ; and not only so, but that we are so infinitely below him, so dependent on him, and he so glorious, as we are not only subject to him, but made for him, and that all else are made for him. For therefore is all for him, because by him, Rom. xi. 36 ; and therefore glory be to him, and of all the greatest. And in this sense the woman is said to be the glory of the man, because made for him, 1 Cor. xi. 7, 8 ; and so man of God.

(10.) Unto that of doing all to God's glory as our end, must be added doing all we do in Christ. God hath made Christ the partner of his glory, his will being that men should honour the Son as the Father. And men honour the Son by offering up all they do to his glory through Christ and his name : Philip. i. 11, the fruits of righteousness that please God must be ' by Jesus Christ, to the glory of God ;' and, Philip. ii. 8, 10, 11, ' God hath given Christ that great name above every name, that every knee should bow to him,' that is, all was to be done to him, and through him, ' to the glory of the Father,' ver. 11 ; which is an exceeding great favour, that God would accept of no glory given him, but through him. For in one place you hear God say of him, ' This is my beloved Son, in whom I am well pleased,' and with all others in him ; so in another, ' This is my servant, in whom I will be glorified,' and by others through him, so Isa. xlix. 3. And God hath stamped upon his face his glory, that we might behold it ; and hath ordained him his servant, through whose hands he will receive glory again. Therefore, Ps. xxii. 22, 23, after Christ's death is there prophesied of, and his declaring his name in the great congregation, all are called to glorify God and praise him ; for without Christ, God had had none of mankind to fear him and worship him. And, Isa. lv. 3, God inviting men to the covenant of grace, which he calls ' the sure mercies of David,' that is, of Christ (as, Acts xiii., they are interpreted), he makes this promise of Christ, that ' nations should come' to Christ, because ' God had glorified him ;' that is, ordained him to be the mediator through whom he would convey all to us, and receive all from us : whom therefore he made a co-partner with him therein.

(11.) We glorify God by repenting and turning to him, when he punisheth and afflicts us. Rev. xvi. 19, when the fourth vial was poured out, it is said, ' They repented not, to give God the glory.' Repentance, and turning from a man's evil ways, bring in much glory to God : by confessing our sins, and acknowledging our deserts, we magnify his patience, and long-suffering, and justice on us, and wisdom in finding us out. ' Confess ' (says Joshua), ' and give glory to God.' By being vile in our own eyes, we exalt him. The most proper way a sinner that hath dishonoured him hath to glorify him again, is by debasing himself for that his dishonour of him ; and by turning from our evil ways upon his punishing us, we yield and subject to him, which gives him honour, as much as obeying him. The submission and coming in again of rebels establisheth and exalteth the honour of a king as much, if not more, than the continued obedience of good subjects. For it is glory with a victory, a conquest. And to hate sin because it ' provokes the eyes of his glory,' as the phrase is, Isa. iii. 8, is to glorify him, as those that respect a superior, a prince, shew it, by doing nothing before him which might be unworthy the presence of such a majesty, to give him the least distaste. The lesser the thing is we forbear in such a respect, the more respect give we them.

(12.) We glorify God by calling upon him in time of trouble, and praising him for delivering us out of it, Ps. l. 15, ' Thou shalt call upon me in the day of trouble ; and I will deliver thee, and thou shalt glorify me ;' to make God our refuge afore trouble, and to acknowledge him after, exceedingly honours him. How glorious doth it make a prince to take part with the oppressed, and to vindicate them upon their cry, Isa. xxv. 3, 4, ' There-fore shall the strong people glorify thee, &c. For thou hast been a strength to the poor, a strength to the needy in his distress, a refuge from the storm,' &c.

(13.) By believing on him we give glory to him. Of Abraham it is said, Rom. iv. 20, ' He was strong in faith, giving glory to God.' No man thinks himself more honoured than when he is trusted ; and in trusting on God, especially for salvation, we give him the glory of all his attributes at once, for there all attributes meet ; if any were wanting in its concurrence, we could not be saved. That 115th Psalm is a psalm on purpose made to call upon people to trust in God, as appears ver. 8–11 ; and from the 12th verse to the end, he expresseth nothing but peremptory conclusions of faith. ' God hath been mindful of us, and would bless us,' &c. And how begins he that psalm ? ' Not unto us, but unto thy name give glory, for thy mercy and truth's sake.' It is the pure voice of faith ; it is a self-emptying grace. ' Not unto us,' and it refuseth again to take anything to himself ; ' not unto us, but unto thy name give glory, for thy mercy and thy truth's sake.' Those two attributes faith gives especial glory unto. They are what faith rests in, and they are what God especially desires the glory of. Therefore, Exod. xxxiv., his mercy and truth are those attributes he only or chiefly proclaims when he shews Moses his glory. 1. The Scriptures call mercy the ' riches of his glory,' Rom. ix. 23. If it be the ' glory of a man to pass by an offence,' as Prov. xix. 11, then it is the glory of God to pass by so many. ' For all the promises are yea and amen,' that is, truth, ' to the glory of God,' 2 Cor. i. 20. God engageth at once not his truth only, but all his attributes, his whole glory, to perform them ; and therefore to believe them gives this glory to him ; and therefore, upon believing, God is said to shew his glory, John xi. 40.

(14.) We glorify God by fearing God above all : Rev. xiv. 7, ' Fear God, and give glory to him.' To fear God, that can cast body and soul into hell, in opposition to man, whose breath is in his nostrils, how doth it exalt him ?   Deut. xxviii. 58, it is called fearing his ' fearful and glorious name.'   All glory carries an awe and reverence with it ; they are therefore joined ; and by reverence we give an honour unto majesty.

(15.) We glorify God by joining ourselves unto the assemblies of his saints, and in the public duties and ordinances of his worship, Isa. lx. 7–9. He calls it ' the house of his glory,' speaking of the flocking of God's people as doves to the windows, or as clouds, ver. 8, unto the house of his glory ; with sacrifices, ver. 7 ; and he speaks of the times of the gospel, when the Gentiles were converted.   Now he says they should fly as a cloud, which removes sometimes from far, from one country to another, above the mountains that might hinder their course, and all impediments ; so they move to enjoy ordinances, and fly as doves to their windows or dove-houses, which especially they do when a storm is towards ; for God's house is the best shelter and dove-house against a storm.   And thither they come, as to the house of God's glory, ver. 7, so called, because, 1, there they see the glory of God.   So David desired, Ps. lxiii. 2, ' To see thy power and thy glory, as I have seen thee in thy sanctuary.'   And 2. There this glory is spoken of : Ps. xxix. 9, ' In his temple doth every one speak of his glory.' And 3. There they worship and glorify him.   So David foretells, Ps. xxii. 23, 24, &c., and Ps. xviii.   Where, when all are saints and holy ones, and none else admitted, his glory is the more set up, as Isa. lx., ver. 21, ' They shall also be all righteous, &c., that I may be glorified.'   For it is a dis-honour to him that persons profane and unrighteous should have com-munion with him, and eat at his table.   He is a glorious God, Ps. v. 4–7, and so ' hath no pleasure in unrighteousness : neither shall evil dwell with thee, or stand before thee.   But as for me, I will come into thy house,' &c.   For he will be sanctified or glorified (as the Septuagint renders it) in all that draw near to him, Lev. x. 3.   He puts an emphasis there, specially of the priests, Mal. ii. 1, 3.   This commandment, says he, ver. 1, ' is for you, O priests.'   And the command is, ver. 3, to give glory to God; that is, this most of all concerns or lies upon you.   A king looks more espe-cially to be honoured of his nearest servants and followers.   The gospel they preach is for their glory, 1 Cor. ii., and they therefore should be for God's.

Obs. 2. That in glorifying God we must give him the glory ' due unto his name,' or which is some way suitable and worthy of it.   God hath much glory and worship given him in the world, but it is not such as be-comes the great God to have, or which is due unto his name.   In Rom. i. 21 the Gentiles are found fault with, that they ' glorified not God *as God.*' There is a respecting of him, a doing something for him, and in relation to him, performed by many, but it is not a glorifying of him as God.   The Philistines, 1 Sam. vi. 5, when they made images of their punishments inflicted, and consecrated them to God, they thought it ' a giving glory to the God of Israel.'   But they glorified him not as that great God that made heaven and earth, with a glory due unto his name.   He will be served by us as a God ; and if our service falls short of this, he rejects it.

Reason 1. For otherwise it satisfies not his aim in his designs of glory which he looks for.   He would not at all have gone about a-glorifying of himself in his works, but to shew himself a God in them ; and so, nor would he have exacted it as a duty of us, to glorify him, if he had not de-signed that it should be done to a God so great, so glorious.   As that king said to Alexander, when he asked him how he would be used, Βασιλικῶς,

says he, 'Like a king.' So if you ask the word of God how he will be worshipped, 'Like a God,' says it. He stands upon it, and takes upon him
in it, as Ps. xlvi. 10, 'Be still, and know that I am God : I will be exalted
among the heathen, I will be exalted in the earth.' It is a phrase of one
exacting respect due to him in his place ; as if a master should take on him
and say, Know I am your master; or as if a king should exact obedience
of his subjects that slighted him, Know I am your king, and I will be
obeyed. So says God. It is not a little respect will satisfy a king, and it
is not a little slight respect will satisfy God. All things must be carried to
a king suitably to majesty, in speeches, in gestures, &c.; and all must be
carried unto God as God. God stands upon it as much as any of them :
he in his place, as they in theirs : Mal. i. 6, 'If I be a father, where is my
honour ? If I be a master, where is my fear ?' They served him but with
the lame, the sick, and the blind, ver. 8, and thought to put him off with
anything ; but how doth he confute them ? ' Offer it now to thy governor '
(they had then no king), and yet he, though no king, would not accept
such a present from you, says God ; and will you serve your God with it ?
will he accept it ? In the original it is, 'If he will accept,' IF being put
for NOT ; as often in the Hebrew ; as, 'If they shall enter into my rest;'
that is, they shall not enter ; and therefore, ver. 14, he takes upon him and
says, 'I am a great king, and my name is dreadful among the heathen;'
and therefore I will be worshipped accordingly. How do kings stand upon
points and terms of honour, and will not lower them ? How jealous are
they to preserve their prerogative, state, &c., in its height ? They are not
so in matter of money ; they will give away of that, but not abate of their
power and state, because it is proper to them as kings, it is that which
constitutes them such ; and thus is the God of glory a jealous God : he
will abate no whit there ; he will be God. ' My glory I will not give ' (says
he) ' to another,' Isa. xlii. 8. He cares not to give away kingdoms, and
worlds, heaven, his Son ; but not an iota of glory.

Reason 2. Because if he be not glorified as God, he is dishonoured. If
respect be given to a man, but not such as his place requires, he thinks
himself slighted ; to honour a king as a justice of peace, were to dishonour
him. For honour lies in a proportion, a suitableness, a comeliness, as beauty,
&c., doth. And therefore in that fore-named place, Mal. i., when they served
him thus below his worth, he says, they ' despised his name,' ver. 6, and
made ' his table contemptible,' ver. 7.

Reason 3. If we glorify not God as God, it is not godliness, but bodily
exercise, or selfness, natural devotion, hypocrisy ; for godliness is that which
exalts God as God. Thence it hath its name and denomination, which
applies itself to God and all his attributes, as becomes the creature to do ;
that is, godliness, if it be allied with anything that makes God less than a
God to a man's heart, it is debased, and is not godliness. As in justification, if we leave never so little to works, it is not faith ; for then the grace
we relied on is no more grace, as the apostle says. So in sanctification, if
we bow and bend our religion to any lower principles than what exalt God
wholly as God, it is no longer godliness.

Use. You have heard one of the truest and exactest trials of your grace
and religion ; and that is, whether you glorify God as a God. It holds
universally true that all men's religion, and the God they serve, are proportioned the one to the other. The religion the word requires sets up our
God as God. And so do all they in whose heart the law is written, and
who have faith. To know God as God, is indeed revealed in his word (so

you have it Jer. xxxi. 33, 34); and the taking in of God by faith, under the true and real notion of him, moulds all in a man to glorify him according as he is apprehended; and as men fall short of honour in their apprehensions, through unbelief of this God, accordingly do they fall short in that service and devotion they honour him with. And it is as certain that all carnal men in the world do, through atheism and unbelief, take into their hearts a false God, or false apprehensions of the true God, that he is not to them as God, and so accordingly they worship him. The Jews, who had the same revelation of God in his word as we have, yet still, through atheism, they took in such low apprehensions of him as they mistook the way of serving him. They glorified him not as God. When Joshua (chap. xxiv.) pressed them to serve the Lord and fear him, they thought with themselves that they would, and hoped to please him too; and far be it from us, say they, to forsake him, ver. 16–18. But Joshua tells them, ver. 19, they were mistaken in him; if you knew what a God he is, saith he, you would see that this service you think to please him with would not be sufficient. ' Ye cannot serve the Lord, for he is an holy God,' and so requires to be worshipped not outwardly or formally, but to be made your end, your guide, and to have all within you subject to him, according to all his glorious attributes; and such service your carnal hearts can never perform unto him. The like instance you have, Ps. 1. A formalist there thought to serve him full well with sacrifices, with the blood of bulls and goats, whereas he took liberty to live in known sins. What was the reason? He thought God would be pleased with such a form of religion. It all arose from mistakes of God: ver. 21, ' Thou didst think,' says God, ' that I was like thee.' This heart, through atheism, framed a God to his own frame of spirit, one that was of his mind, and his religion. And as David was a man after God's own heart, so they make a God after their hearts. They so temper their thoughts of him, and his mercy, justice, holiness, &c., in such a sense and interpretation as may stand with their ways and courses, and which doth indeed make him no God, or not as that God the word sets him out. What is the reason that men living in the church, and hearing all the glory of the great God set forth, yet worship this God with no more devotion in their hearts, nor obedience in their lives, than the Turks worship Mahomet with, and the heathens did their gods with? It is because they, in the interpretations their atheism puts upon all is said of him, make him but as one of their gods. And not only they, but those who are most enlightened (if not with a saving light) as their apprehension of God falls short, so the principles which they walk by (whatever they may profess) in the course of their lives to serve this God with, fall short also. Their conceits of him and about him are tempered so as to make him approving their ways, though in all the obedience they perform to him they seek themselves, and make themselves an end; and so bow God to their ends, and make a bridge of him, and go about but to serve their turns of him, which, did they spiritually conceive how holy a God he is, they durst not make bold to do, but would seek salvation from him, as aiming at him in all, and submitting themselves, their own ends and salvation, to him. Men do with God as the Venetians do with their duke. They set him up in all matters of state-attendance as a sovereign prince, but level his power so low that he is no more than an ordinary senator, for in the carriage of affairs of state, when anything comes to be done, they overrule him, bow him to their suffrages, contradict his will; and yet all the conclusions made go forth in his name, as if he were a sovereign prince. Thus do men give unto God all titles of respect, acknowledge him in all his glorious attributes to be as great a God as he proclaims himself in his word ; yet in the secret senate-house of the understanding, will, &c., where all actions are concluded, con-sulted on, and published, they un-god him again, walk by such principles therein as take all away again from him, setting up themselves in his room, making themselves their end, yea, carry things against him ; and yet when any good is done, they cry still as they, Isa. lxvi. 5, ' Let God be glorified,' when yet they cast out the saints for his name's sake, as there it is said. Men haply will shew as much respect to God as they would do to a man like themselves whom they reverence, or conceive thus or thus well of ; but we are to glorify him as a God, as he shews himself as God, and more than man, in his dispensations towards us, which are such as none but a God so great, so merciful, &c., would continue to dispense, to forbear us so as he does, as Hosea xi. 9, ' I will not execute the fierceness of my wrath, for I am God, and not man.'   So must we respect him as God, and not as we would a man only endued with such perfections.

If we trust him, we must trust him as God, and not so far as we would a faithful man only, though never so honest; put our souls' salvation, obedi-ence, and all into his hands. For ' grace is his faithfulness.' We must so sub-mit to him as to suffer him to alter all a man's ways and thoughts, and over-turn all his spirits in obedience and dependence on him.

When we come for pardon to him, seeing the greatness and multitudes of our sins, we must think higher thoughts of pardoning to be in him than in a man.   My thoughts are as far above them, says God, Isa. lv. (he speaks of pardoning) as the heavens are above the earth, for ' I will multiply to pardon,' or as we read it, I am the great pardoner.

If any business be to be done, any deliverance be to be wrought, let us trust his power, beyond that of second causes ; trust him as a God that can do what-ever he will on the earth and in the sea, and not limit the holy one, as the people of Israel did, when they said, ' Can he provide a table in the wilder-ness, to provide for so great a multitude ?'

If we love him, let us love him as God, for as Christ says, ' He that hates not father and mother for my sake is not worthy of me.'

If we fear him, let us fear him more than man, never so great or power-ful ; as Moses did, in whose eyes the wrath of Pharaoh was but, in com-parison of God, as a rod of straws in the hand of a child, to a rod of iron in the hands of a giant.   ' Who hath known the power of his wrath ?' says Moses, Ps. xc., ' As is our fear, so great is thy displeasure,' and greater. ' Fear not them,' says Christ, ' that can but kill the body, but him that can cast body and soul into hell.'   ' Who art thou, that thou shouldst be afraid of a man that shall die ; and forgettest the Lord thy maker, that hath stretched forth the heaven ?' Isa. li. 12.

So if we know his holiness and sovereignty, we would submit to him more than to any man ; in all afflictions, in all our dependences upon his pleasure, yea, in the matter of salvation itself.

We should also live to him, so as we do to no one else ; turn all our causes for him, take all our hearts and ends in pieces, and mould them all to him.

To conclude ; this is certain, that all the principles we take up to serve God by, and which we walk by (if our hearts be right), are such and so framed as to set God up as God, or all is naught ; we should put an estimate upon sin, by his greatness we sin against, and should say and hold to the conclusion which Joseph did, ' How shall I do this and sin against God ?'   We should not slight him in the least, or think any fear or care herein, too much strictness for him.   Nor would men sin in private if men thought him omniscient, nor would our consciences be content with obedience, without making God our chiefest end, if we know him in his holiness, which makes him exact all from the creature for himself, and justly too, seeing he is their maker and end.   Nor would men rest in duties of his worship, without communion apprehended or sought for, with him above all.   If they made him their chiefest good in worshipping him, men would worship him only according to his own will and word, and not teach his fear by the principles of men, as Mark vii. 7–9, for can men tell what will please the great God ?   The heathens thought that their gods were to be worshipped according to their own prescriptions.   So those that were placed in the room of the ten tribes, 2 Kings xvii. 26, thought that they must worship the god of the land after his own manner, they should not make a god of him else.   So, ver. 27, the king of Assyria said, ' Let them take a priest to go and dwell there, and teach them the manner of the god of the land ;' and ver. 28, 'he taught them how they should fear the Lord.' And as for matter, so for manner ; men would worship him in spirit, if they knew him to be a Spirit, as Christ says, and would bring living sacrifices, not dead formal performances, if they knew him the living God.   There are three cautions I will add to explain my meaning in this point.

1. When I say the glory due to God is to be given him, the meaning is not that which is simply due to so great a majesty ; *that* no creature can give him, but such, as in your condition, creatures sanctified can return to him.

2. That in the best there is an unregenerate part, which is a very atheist, and doth say, ' There is no God,' but denies all of him, as unregenerate men do ; for which men judging their estates must give allowance, yet so as there is a regenerate whole man in them, that sets God up as God.   Thus,

3. This setting God thus up as God, is best discerned by those principles which we habitually have taken up to ourselves to live by, which we will not leave, but stick unto, which lie in the heart, continually drawing up the whole man to them, moulding all according to them, and of which when we fall short, through the atheism of the unregenerate part, we judge ourselves. Now if so, then still God is then set and acknowledged as God, either when we keep to them or when we fall short ; when we pass sentence on all that pass, according to such laws as stand in force, enacted in our hearts.

CHAPTER VII.

That one eminent disposition immediately flowing from the new creature is a desire to convert and beget others to God.

Then will I teach transgressors thy ways ; and sinners shall be converted unto thee.—Ps. LI. 13.

In this psalm you have the lively workings and beatings of a holy heart recovering from a great fall and lapse into gross sins.   Which is also a renewed draught, or going over again of the first work of conversion of the soul unto God.   And you have them as lively represented as if you should behold an animal or living beast, cut up and dissected alive, and therein see the circulation of the blood, the beatings and pantings of the heart, the motion of the pulse, &c. As *first*, How deeply he humbled himself for his sin actual, ver. 4, and original, ver. 5. *Secondly*, Seeketh pardon and justification, as under the types of the old law it was signified, which David full well understood : ' Purge me with hyssop, and I shall be clean : wash me, and I shall be whiter than snow.' *Thirdly*, You have him seeking the assurance and joy of this to his own soul, and the shining of God's countenance (now eclipsed) again, ver. 8, 9. The prophet, as the story shews, had told him infallibly that his sin was pardoned ; and he believed it, but yet that satisfied him not. His spirit had been used to another's voice, even of the Spirit of God speaking peace in his own soul immediately. And I would hear God speaking it (says he). The ingenuity of his heart could not bear that God should be strange to him, though he knew his sin was pardoned, ver. 9. *Fourthly*, He seeks both, 1. For the renewal of that inward principle of grace and holiness in the heart ; ver. 10, ' Create in me a clean heart, O God ; and renew a right spirit within me.' 2. The continuance of the Holy Ghost's dwelling in him, as the fountain, and author, and actor of all grace, and giver of all joy, ver. 11. And this I observe : he frames not the matter of his petition into a positive request, as in all the other, as ' Give me thy Holy Spirit ;' but negative, ' Take not,' &c., ' Cast me not,' &c. The cause of which was, 1. He had seen by woeful experience that God had taken his Spirit away from his predecessor Saul, for smaller sins, 1 Sam. xv. 23, 26, chap. xvi. 14, chap. xviii. 12. And 2. He shews what of all else would be most dreadful to befall him, either to be cast forth of God's presence, and God and he part, or that God should call back his Holy Spirit, as he had done from Saul.

The rest of the Psalm, from the 13th verse, is most spent in holy resolutions and vows of what he would do for the future, if God would thus restore and equip him again ; which to do is the manner and duty of sinners turning or returning unto God.

As 1. He would teach sinners the ways of God, in order and aim at their conversion.

2. He makes returns of high praise, and loud thanksgivings and celebrations of God's mercy ; ver. 14, 15, ' Deliver me from blood-guiltiness, O God, thou God of my salvation : and my tongue shall sing aloud of thy righteousness. O Lord, open thou my lips ; and my mouth shall shew forth thy praise.'

3. He would present unto him what he knew would most of all please him, not sacrifices, but a broken heart : ver. 16, 17, ' For thou desirest not sacrifice, else would I give it ; thou delightest not in burnt-offering. The sacrifices of God are a broken spirit : a broken and a contrite heart, O God, thou wilt not despise ;' and ver. 19, ' With the sacrifices of righteousness.' Then closing up the psalm with the remembrance of the church, even when himself was in this deep distress, such as one would think should have swallowed all the intentions of his prayers for his own particular, yet he forgets not her : ' Do good in thy good pleasure to Zion : build thou the walls of Jerusalem.'

In my text you see the first-born of those resolutions, and most genuine dispositions that spring up in him ; to be teaching sinners God's ways, in order to their conversion.

For the opening which, in order to what I am to make observation of upon it.

1. This redintegration of love betwixt God and him he in every passage utters in the language, at least in the materials, of a new conversion, such

as the soul hath at first; yet so expressed as they carry with them strong and pregnant insinuations that the former work was not wholly extinct, nor the Spirit of God wholly taken from him, ver. 11. Recovery after great falls hath in it all the transactions and workings that is in a new conversion, and is indeed the same work acted over anew in a man's spirit. And therefore, says Christ to Peter, ' When thou art converted ' (speaking of the recovery of him from his relapse), Luke xxii. 32. To manifest this by particulars.

(1.) Here is the same humiliation or conviction of sin, sense of, and burden for it (ver. 3, 4, ' My sin is ever afore me '); together with a renewed sight and view of the original of all natural corruption (ver. 5, ' Behold, I was shapen in iniquity, and in sin did my mother conceive me '). And also of the deceits in the heart, and spiritual contrarieties to holiness, which, ver. 6, he termeth ' truth in the inward parts,' which looking into his own spirit he discerned all sorts of contrarieties thereunto: ver. 6, ' Behold, thou desirest truth in the inward parts.' He speaks it as having turned his eye, come new from the sight of his own corruption, ver. 5, to the purity of God and his spiritual law. And oh, how opposite is my heart from that sincerity thou requirest ! Then you may observe also self-emptiness, and brokenness of spirit (which is the bottom-work of humiliation) in discerning his own nothingness, ver. 17, which Christ terms, ' poverty of spirit.' This for the work of humiliation.

(2.) As for the works of faith for justification, here is a fresh and vehement goings out, and longings for washings by Christ's blood (ver. 2, ' Wash me thoroughly from mine iniquity, and cleanse me from my sin.' And ver. 7, ' Purge me with hyssop, and I shall be clean; wash me, and I shall be whiter than snow '), as ever were in a poor soul when it first lay at the footstool of God's throne of grace, imploring pardon as a condemned man to die. And here is not only begging the thing itself, but the renewed assurance of it to his soul : ver. 8, 9, ' Make me to hear joy and gladness, that the bones thou hast broken may rejoice. Hide thy face from my sins, and blot out all my iniquities.' And also, ver. 12, ' Restore unto me the joy of thy salvation, and uphold me with thy free Spirit.' Which few converts at first do. But David had been inured to it. Here is also as impetuous seeking after the face and presence of God, ver. 11. ' Hide thy face from my sins,' ver. 9. But turn it upon me, and ' cast me not out of thy presence,' ver. 11 ; that is, ' Let me see thy face.' This for the workings of faith.

(3.) For sanctification and holiness. He having seen the bottom corruption of his nature, ver. 6, he experimentally seeketh for a sanctification of his nature of the right kind ; even the contrary frame of heart to his natural uncleanness, ' Create in me a clean heart,' and give me grace of the true and right kind and breed. ' Renew a right spirit within me.' ' Truth in the inward parts, Lord.' Nothing else would content him, not outward sacrifices, nor performances, as you may perceive by ver. 16. Yea, and he seeks this in a sense of his own inability to effect it in himself. And so gives up his heart in acknowledgment of his utter and total dependence upon God's grace and power to work it : ' Create in me, O God.' Do thou do it, for I am no more able to work it, or the least degree thereof, than to create a world. And as he prays for habitual holiness in his nature, so for the Holy Ghost to abide in him, ver. 11, to act that grace and uphold him. Whom, ver. 12, he termeth the principal Spirit, or his leading Spirit. It is read either of them by some, as in distinction from inherent grace, which, ver. 10, he had termed 'spirit.' And the fruits and effects of it follow, seeking to turn others. This he did by opening his mouth in holy conference, to set out God's praise, praying for the saints and church of God, and studying and searching forth what would please God most, to the end to offer it up to him. These are all the dispositions of hearts truly and newly converted, and wrought upon. And such conversions as these, and renewals of the whole work upon us, we must have in our lives if we go to heaven; if not upon falls, yet upon some occasions or other. 'Except ye be converted,' says Christ to his disciples, that were converted already, 'ye cannot enter into the kingdom of God.' And these kind of workings you have now heard of in David's heart, may both help us to judge of ourselves, whether we have been converted, or rightly recovered after relapses, and comfort ourselves if we have found the like, as face answering to face in water. For David was a grown Christian before, and yet this great and second work upon him (greater than his first) rose up but to such dispositions as these. For God's second works always exceeded the former, and in all he is made a pattern of a man after God's heart. 2. This having been every way as a new conversion to him, look, what was the most natural disposition and motion of spirit in him, the same (in their proportion) is in others converted to God. Now in David you see the very first bud that puts forth in this fresh spring (for he had been as a tree in winter), in seeking to convert others. And he being further a prophet, and endowed with abilities to teach (as also Solomon his son after him), this gracious disposition, the spring of which is common to him and all other converts, the stream of it seeks vent, and most gladly and greedily runs out into this channel of teaching others, to convert them, whereunto he had the advantage by his gifts and calling.

The text hath three parts :

1st. A gracious disposition and resolution of spirit, flowing from conversion, to convert others to God.

2d. The most proper means to effect it; teaching men God's ways.

3d. The promise of success, 'and they shall be converted.'

From the first, the observation is, that in every truly converted soul to God, this is one of the most natural and genuine dispositions and desires, according to its ability and opportunity, to convert and win others to God.

The second observation is, that teaching men, and teaching them the ways and dealings of God with souls, in converting of them, or in recovering them fallen, is the most effectual way sanctified by God to effect conversion.

For the third, 'And they shall be converted unto me,' observe, that God more especially useth and blesseth the endeavours of such as himself hath already converted, to turn others to God.

Fourthly, That he useth such, notwithstanding their falls and corruptions. David still promiseth to himself, that God would yet use him and succeed his endeavours, and bless his example, yea, and perhaps more than ever afore.

For the first, I shall handle it as it is a common disposition in the hearts of all men converted, and even all having some ability and opportunity of doing good to some or other they converse with this way, though according to proportion of talents, calling, opportunities. In men set apart to the ministry of the word, this is chiefly incumbent upon them.

Now for the proof of how great and strong a disposition in the heart of a saint this is, I give that scripture, 1 Tim. iv. 16, 'For in doing this, thou shalt save thyself, and them that hear thee.'

These words have two parts. 1. A summary of the instructions given afore, 'Take heed to thyself,' and thy personal conversation. And 2. 'To thy doctrine,' or preaching; for I take it by a metonymy that is it he intends. And this is the epitome of all afore ver. 12, 13, &c., together with an exhortation to persevere in doing both. 2. The motives hereto, the greatest that can be. (1.) 'Thou shalt save thyself;' (2.) 'Those that hear thee.' Now, though the gift of preaching was not common, yet these motions are but such as are common to all saints; and upon these common motions doth Paul work upon Timothy's heart, and no other, to diligence herein. Salvation of a man's self is *suprema lex*, in nature. The salvation of others is the supreme law in the new creature. Therefore two greater motives cannot be spoken. First, for saving a man's self; if it were alone the privative part of salvation, that is, to be saved and delivered from the misery sin deserves, all in nature would put a man to choose it. If a man were in danger of being drowned, and had a crown thrown him, with a title annexed to it of being king of all the world, and at the same time throw him but a poor rope or cord, he will lay hold on the rope and let go the crown, because that it will (though but) save him. 'So shalt thou save thyself.' And to save others is the supremest law in the new creature. The title of being a Saviour did toll and woo Christ down from heaven to earth. And the name *Jesus*, or Saviour, is the highest name in heaven or earth. And this title, by discharging thy duty faithfully, shalt thou partake with him in; thou shalt have both the name and reward of being a Saviour to others instrumentally, and Christ himself could have no greater. Paul's instance argues the desire here of one of the supremest laws in the new creature. Rom. ix. 1–3, 'I say the truth in Christ, I lie not, my conscience also bearing me witness in the Holy Ghost, that I have great heaviness and continual sorrow in my heart. For I could wish that myself were accursed from Christ for my brethren, my kinsmen according to the flesh.' For both love to God and love to others, do, in the fullest stream and channel, meet in this. It was the salvation of such a bulk of mankind, in whom God's name was interested, as were the Jews, and the continuance of the gospel to them in future ages, for their salvation, that he here prefers to his own salvation. He wisheth himself accursed from Christ; and because, to have the new creature wound up to so high a note, without cracking and breaking nature itself, that the prerogative law thereof should so prevail and overrule the supreme law of nature itself, would (as he knew) be a wonder, and incredible to the most of Christians, he therefore makes the solemnest protestation, that this was real in his heart, that ever was made by man. 1. 'I speak the truth;' 2. 'I lie not;' 3. 'My conscience bearing me witness;' 4. And that *that* deceives him not, he calls in Christ and the Holy Ghost as witnesses of it. If ever Paul spake truth, he spake truth now; and what was it he utters? 'I could wish myself accursed from Christ.' What, Paul! Think what thou sayest; accursed from Christ! We will give thee leave to be in sorrow and heaviness, for so are we when we see men go to hell; but, to be accursed from Christ, and that Paul should say it! You find him in all his epistles breathing more after Christ than in the Acts you read he had ever breathed forth threatenings against his church. What? From Christ! 'To me to live is Christ, to die is gain,' says he, Phil. i. And again, chap. iii. 8, 'Doubtless' (there is no demur upon it), 'I account all things but loss for the excellency of the knowledge of Christ Jesus my Lord: for whom I have suffered the loss of all things, and do count them but dung, that I may win Christ.' What? And part with Christ! Yea, be accursed from Christ! His meaning is not, I wish the condition of the damned, in respect of despair, revenge, blasphemy, &c., that had been a sin to wish; but look, what state towards God Christ himself was in, in separation from God and sense of wrath, when he was made a curse to save me; that condition, says he, I could be content to be in, having those exercises of such graces, submission to God's will, which Christ then also had. Well, but Paul, think out, and think out again; why, says Paul, I have; I speak the truth, I speak the truth again; he seconds it with 'I lie not.' Well, but Paul, let that be granted, which yet perhaps some of us could do, to submit to it, if God would say it were his pleasure, that if we would be accursed, such and such should be saved. No, says Paul, that is not all; I find I could heartily wish it, to choose it should be my option. The highest instance that ever I have heard of any other was on the contrary. A tender mother, that had prayed long for her son, once was brought to this, to think that she should rejoice one day in his damnation; and it converted him. But still, Paul's is higher; he says, I would follow Christ, and Christ was made a curse from God for me, and I would imitate him, and do the like for others. It was well he spake this in Christ, as a new creature created in Christ Jesus. I am assured the first creature, the image of God in Adam, would not have been drawn up so high. The spirit of elixir would have cracked his earthen vessel; that earthly man, as the apostle calls him, 1 Cor. xv. It is a note beyond his *Elah*.* And the truth is, take all the mass of other Christians, God would but by this one instance of Paul's show what is in the root, and may be extracted out of the new creature, which is in them all; but Paul alone herein followed Christ. The highest note of the new creature, but far below this (as it was also of another kind), was that of a godly, tender-hearted mother,† who, having prayed long, as Monica for Austin, for a debauched son, and seeing no fruit of her prayers, but the contrary in the highest, at last was by God brought unto this, that if God for his own glory would rather damn him than save him, her heart was put into that disposition it should be in at the day of judgment, to think that she should one day rejoice to see him damned, even him whom she loved so dearly, and had prayed so much for. And the relating of this speech to her son, when he was in the height of his rebellion, broke his heart and turned him. But still, Paul's here exceeds hers, and all others' else. Yea, here when he speaks of Timothy, than whom he found none other like-minded, in naturally taking care of the souls of others, Phil. ii. 20, he winds not Timothy up so high as himself was wound up, and the new creature would bear. He prefers this motive of self, and puts it first: 'So shalt thou save thyself;' only next unto it adds, 'and those that hear thee.' So as this we may gain warrantably from it, as suiting the spirit and disposition of every man regenerate, especially ministers, that next to saving themselves, the conversion and salvation of others is the greatest and noblest argument that can be used.

I shall give you the reasons of it, the common foundation of which lies in this, that grace, which is a new divine nature, partakes of it (as the nature of all things doth with those of a like kind) in some analogy with it.

Now, 1. It is the natural property of every good thing to diffuse and

---

* The highest note in the musical scale then in use. See Adams's Works, vol. I., p. 472.—ED.

† This is simply a repetition of the same story, through inadvertence on the part of the author, or of the original editors.—ED.

communicate itself, and as it excels in goodness, so it exceeds in that desire. God, who is goodness and blessedness itself, hath delighted himself from all eternity to think of his communicating his blessedness to some of his creatures, whom himself would set himself to love. His delights were with the sons of men, Prov. viii.; and Exod. xxxiii. 19, 'I will make all my goodness pass before thee, and will be gracious to whom I will be gracious.' He would not enjoy his happiness alone, but have his creatures the better for him. And the inferior creatures, that partake of a portion of goodness from him, partake therewith of the like property ; fire to diffuse its heat ; the sun its light. Now, grace in the souls of men is in that manner the image of God's goodness, love, grace, mercy, &c., that the common goodness in the creatures is not. And therefore, answerably to the measure of its excelling them, it must needs excel in this, wherein a man comes nearest to God ; which, as the heathen Cicero said, is nothing more than in doing good to others. Yea, and we find in Scripture the new creature compared unto all things that are diffusive of themselves, as partaking with them in this, which is the common property. Thus, it is compared to fire ; one coal that hath fire in it enkindles another. And every man is either a dead or living coal. 'Thy word,' says Jeremiah, 'it was a fire in my bones, and I could not stay,' chap. xx. 9. It is also compared to light in a room, or set upon a hill, to give light to all in it ; to precious ointment, which, as that of Mary's did, diffuseth its odour to the whole room.

2. It is the nature of every thing begotten by another, to beget and propagate another of the same. It is the vehementest and strongest desire in nature : *opus naturalissimum ;* implanted as instinct by virtue of that law and command given forth by God : Gen. i. 22, 'Be fruitful and multiply,' according to their kind. The angels were not ordained to beget in their kind, for they gave not in marriage ; but of all creatures that are to multiply in their kind, the more excellent the kind is, the stronger is the inclination. Now the saints are a royal generation, 1 Pet. ii., the first fruits of God's creation, as being begotten of God : James i. 18, 'Of his own will begat he us, with the word of truth, that we should be a kind of first fruits of his creatures.' Every one that is born of God hath the seed of God in him ; that is, a 'divine nature,' 1 John iii. 9 ; and the Holy Ghost is also in that new nature to provoke him hereunto. Yea, and therefore it is in them from the first, which is not in other creatures. As soon as Paul was converted, he consulted not with flesh and blood, but went to preach the gospel, Gal. i. 16 ; and this is proper to men truly converted.

3. Grace hath, besides these properties common to it with other creatures, a transcendent elevation of it to the glory of God. 'Hallowed be thy name,' is the first petition the heart is taught to fall upon in the Lord's Prayer ; and 'Thy kingdom come,' is the next. Now it is Christ's coming into the hearts of men is the foundation of all his kingdom, for it brings in willing subjects. When many men are converted unto Christ, in so many men's hearts is the glory of God set up as their chiefest end, and they are vessels and instruments of his glory to all eternity. The glory of a king consists in the multitude of his subjects, Prov. xiv. 28. Now Christ is King of saints, Rev. xv., and in the multitude of them lies his honour.

4. In the regenerate there is love to Christ, and pity to the souls of others. I join them both together, for God himself hath joined them together in our salvation. And, 2 Cor. v. 11 and 14 verses, Paul joineth them together as motives to him to persuade men to turn to God : ver. 11, 'Knowing therefore the terror of the Lord,'—that is, what an

infinite treasure of wrath is laid up for men that die in their sins, we cannot but tell and persuade men, as Lot did his kindred, to come out of Sodom;—' we persuade men,' ver. 14, ' for the love of Christ constrains us.' And this was a motive over and above the necessity of his office. And he farther instructs others, Col. iii. 12, ' Put on, as the elect of God, bowels of mercy.' Now, to the elect of God, wherein are the bowels of God's mercy shewn ? In mercy, delivering them from the greatest misery, and that is, the saving men from sin, and wrath, and hell : Christ's love lay in this. Answerably, you that have received mercy from God, wherein is your mercy to be shewn most towards others ? In endeavouring to pull them out of hell, and save them from wrath to come. Christ, in Mat. v., enumerates the most inward dispositions of converted souls, and perhaps in order as they are wrought. He reckons up these two near one another : ver. 7, ' Blessed are the merciful ;' and ver. 9, ' Blessed are the peacemakers,' that is, who out of a sense of mercy, or seeing their need of it, do seek it at God's hands for themselves, and laying to heart the danger and misery others are in, endeavour to make peace between an offended God and them, or seeing the terror of the Lord, persuade men, as you heard Paul speaking his own disposition of spirit. In like manner, speaks Jude 22, 23, ' of some have compassion, making a difference, and others save with fear, pulling them out of the fire.' The allusion seems to be to one's seeing poor children, or impotent creatures, falling into the fire, out of which they have no heart or power to deliver themselves ; and it is an outcry in such a case. If you have any compassion in you, O save them ; and with fear, as knowing the terror of the Lord : for fear, lest ere you could persuade them, the wrath of God should seize upon them. And it is such an exclamation as would be in a family or room, wherein one in a lethargy or falling sickness is cast into the fire ; in which case men leave all business, as of lesser moment, and run speedily to pull out such. And this word, ' pull them out of the fire,' imports violence ; as Christ said, ' Compel them to come in,' so snatch them out by strong hands. Alas, they, poor creatures, are asleep and feel nothing ; yea, they struggle against it ; therefore pluck them out. My brethren, the terror of God is such as even those that are in hell (as Luke xvi.), have so much compassion in them as to desire their friends may not come thither. How much more should this work in your hearts (that have tasted of the mercies of God yourselves, that are escaped through that mercy) a compassion to the souls of others.

I might add, 5thly, out of Jude, what follows in these words, ' hating the garment spotted with the flesh ;' that is, if no more should move you, let this, viz., the destruction of what you hate. ' You that love the Lord, hate evil ;' and if you do, seek to destroy it in those you love.

Use 1. Observe whether, out of such principles as these in thy soul, thou hast found this so truly noble, generous, and natural disposition in thee. Is this thy aim, thy set desire and endeavour ? Hast thou not a spirit inclining, but also provoking thee unto it, out of a bleeding heart, over other men's conditions ? Is it the very delight of thy soul to have any opportunity of doing good this way, when thou seest any hopefulness or comingness in any ? Dost thou feel thy soul rejoice as much, or more, than in the addition of personal comforts to thee ? This was meat and drink to Christ, John iv. When he found a poor woman at Samaria, who began to listen to his doctrine, he says, it was meat and drink to him to do this will of his Father in this particular, John iv. 32, 34. It is spoken upon that occasion, for this he afterwards owns to be the eminent will and command of his Father, to bring in those he had given him; so John vi. 37–39. And Paul, who followed Christ, became all to all; he would stoop to any thing, and that to win but some. You see, Acts xxvi., when he was at the bar, and his particular interest was to plead for his life, he minds it not, but falls a-persuading Agrippa, before whom he appears, and his courtiers, to turn to God; and when he was somewhat stirred and persuaded half-way, and said, ' Thou hast persuaded me almost to be a Christian;' what? Do you speak of it only as *almost?* says Paul. And what? of yourself alone? Though he had caught the great fish, a king, yet it was not the saving of a king's soul contented him; his desires were larger. ' I wish' (says he) ' not only that thou, but all that hear me, were not almost, but altogether as I am, excepting these bonds.' The truth and strength of this desire is one of the most sure and certain signs of regeneration, and being begotten again, of any other. For besides that it is certain that Satan's kingdom is not divided against itself, nor can heartily desire the ruin of itself, and members of a body use to defend one another, and men may be zealous to convert men to particular opinions: it is more certain that to make disciples, and bring men thoroughly to Christ, to turn from all sin, to glorify God, and delight in doing this, and seeing it done, as in their own salvation, is the distinguishing character of a son of God: Mat. v. 9, ' Blessed are the peace-makers, for they shall be called the children of God.' This is proper to one begotten. The spurious spawn of professors, hatched out of self-love, are not acquainted with such vehement desires, that yearning of bowels, that pity to men's estates; it is not the ultimate end and scope of their speeches or profession. Grace shews itself strongest in this, and that more early than in other dispositions. Commonly as soon as a believer comes into the new world himself, and as one affrighted out of his natural condition, is brought into this marvellous light, and is environed about with it, he hath all things new in his sight, and apprehends with an edge of affection the danger of his former condition, and God's free grace reached forth to pull him out: and the light of these things is fresh, strong, and vigorous in him; and he sees and wonders how all about him are running headlong towards hell. If he casts, but though meekly in speech, but a word to stop any one, yet with a strong apprehension doth he speak it, and thinks that things that are so clear to him, and move himself so much, should also move others, and wonders if they do not. He thinks, sure he should convert the whole world if he had but the opportunity of speaking with them. The early buddings of this you see in Philip towards Nathanael, John i. 45, and chap. iv., in that woman of Samaria towards that whole city. So it was in Paul, who consulted not with flesh and blood, but fell a-preaching presently.

Use 2. The second use is of exhortation, to all that profess themselves born again; that in their capacity and opportunity they would set upon this work, especially where there is a heap of living coals in a society together. This exhortation is not to ministers only, but to you all, young as well as those of riper years. Oh! see, if possible, that none of you appear at the day of judgment afore God, without bringing some Benjamin or other with you. The apostle persuades a poor believing wife to dwell with and cohabit with an unbelieving, churlish Nabal, and to bear all the burdens of so unequal a yoke, even with the hope of so great a consequent, if it so fall out: 1 Cor. vii. 16, ' For what knowest thou, O wife, whether thou shalt save thy husband? or how knowest thou, O man, whether thou shalt save thy wife?' It is a great encouragement in James v. 19, 20, 'Brethren, if any of you do err from the truth, and one convert him; let him know, that he which converteth the sinner from the error of his way shall save a soul from death, and shall hide a multitude of sins.' And it is spoken not to ministers only, but to private Christians, even to brethren in common. And his motives are strong: 1. That he shall save a soul from death; which also Paul useth to Timothy, 1 Tim. iv. 16. If a man had a mortal disease, and a word of thy mouth would save him, what tender heart would not effect it? He will owe himself to thee, as Paul speaks of Onesimus. And, 2, he covers a multitude of sins; gets God's book crossed of debts, contracted from the beginning of his days. And what a great matter is that; and yet, unto that end thou mayest win others to God, and God may bless and succeed thee;—

1. Be holy in all manner of conversation; else, as Lot's kindred thought of his speeches, men will think thou art not in earnest. A dart thrown receives its force from the strength of the arm that throws it. 1 Pet. iii. 1, 2, he exhorteth wives to express a holy chastity in converse with their husbands, that they may be won thereby: 'Likewise, ye wives, be in subjection to your own husbands; that, if any obey not the word, they also may without the word be won by the conversation of the wives; whilst they behold your chaste conversation coupled with fear.' Chastity is but a moral virtue, as is also that fear or reverence wives are to express towards their husbands; yet it may be held forth and managed with such a spirit of holiness as may convey and dart into their consciences beams of the image of God, and enkindle the same into their hearts it shines into. Walk in light, that is, according to the spiritual light God hath given thee; and hold forth that light in the midst of a froward and crooked generation, Phil. ii. 15. Shew other ends in common actions than other men do.

2. Be fruitful in conference, dropping good and holy speeches: Prov. xi. 30, 'The fruit of the righteous is a tree of life;' such as the fruit that grew on the tree of life, that grew in paradise, of which God said, after man was fallen, 'lest he eat it and live for ever.' If you had a tree had such fruit grew on it as would restore dead men to life, how would you prize and value that tree, and the fruit of it; and the more it bare, the more would you esteem it. Such are the lips of a righteous man in order to conversion: so it follows, 'He that winneth souls is wise.' And though thou seest not a present effect of it, yet wait. The kingdom of God is as a sower that went out to sow, and the seed grew up from blade to ear, he knew not how. A man little thinks what God doth with occasional speeches, and to what use he puts them, both for conviction and conversion. A man hears of them, as of bread sown on the waters, many days after. You may have heard of a crow flying to let fall an ash key, which hath afterwards proved a tree. Yet wait, and see how thy sowing good seed doth take and thrive, as one doth a plant or seed sown in a garden. How often do they visit it, water it, and see how it thrives! The husbandman waits, says James, chap. v. 7, 8, for the precious seed its coming up, and loseth the sight of it when a winter and cold frost nip it; yet he waits for its precious seed, more precious than all the gold and silver mines or rocks of diamonds in the world, for mankind could not live on them; but if the seed corn should fail to come up, a universal famine would be in the world. Now, every holy truth and gracious speech is much more precious than seed corn, and proves a plant that shall never be

rooted up, but grows up to eternal life. Yea, if men oppose, yet still wait. So you are directed: 2 Tim. ii. 25, 'Instruct those that oppose themselves, if peradventure God will give them repentance.' Opposition is often a sign that the pill works. And suppose thou never shouldst convert them (as the apostle gives not a certainty, only a 'what knowest thou?' 1 Cor. vii. 16, a peradventure), yet know that as thou prayest for them, so thy instructions unto them shall return in grace into thine own bosom; as, Mat. x., their peace is said to do; and thou wilt glorify God in the day of their visitation.'

Use 3. You that are young students, and God hath turned your hearts unto him, you have in this doctrine a foundation laid of the greatest encouragement to the work of the ministry. For if to endeavour to convert souls be the most natural and pleasant work to the new creature, and the noblest endowment in you, and this suited even to the very essential constitution of it, then to have this work to be your very calling, and a proper work of the ministry which you are set apart thereby unto, must needs render it most acceptable and comfortable to you. For you see that parents use to observe what callings the natural genius of their children inclines unto, and when they set them in that which is most suitable thereto, they do therein work with pleasantness, and prove eminent in it. Now, as your education helps to fit you with abilities, so your conversion, and the *impetus* of the new creature, you see, carries your heart this way. David, though a king, yet having the spirit of teaching, dedicates much of his time and pains this way, and makes a vow of it; yea, the first-born of his vows, upon this so eminent a conversion. Whilst others are exercised in this world to get and heap up great estates, in killing men, overturning nations, and perhaps doing what they knew not, whether acceptable or not, you have the best, the surest, the comfortablest, the honourablest trade of winning souls; and may heap up souls, bring in great riches and treasure to Christ, and a greater account to your own souls, though in the world you may have contempt; and it is fit it should be so, for it is mercy enough to be a minister.

Obs. 2. That teaching God's ways and gracious dealings with men in converting and recovering sinners, is specially sanctified by God.

1. By God's ways sometimes all his works *ad extra* are meant. So Prov. viii., 'In the beginning of thy ways;' so Behemoth is 'the chief of God's ways;' but here the ways revealed by the word are meant. And therein, 1, in a more large sense, all the laws and statutes he hath commanded men to walk in. So often and usually, Deut. viii. 6 and x. 12.

2. The right way of true religion, and how a soul shall be saved, is called a way, and God's way, Acts xix. 23; and the way of God, Acts xviii. 26; 'the way of righteousness,' 2 Pet. ii. 21.

3. Sometimes, more strictly, the ways of God's dealings with or wooing sinners to himself (as Solomon calls the wooings of a lover, gaining the heart of his beloved, 'The ways of a man with a maid'). Thus here; for David refers to those experiments of God's grace which his soul had and should get by God's recovering him again, and converting him anew, which he would lay open to others, even all his gracious dealings to his: Ps. xxv. 10, 'All his paths are mercy and truth towards his.' Thus the mercies of God in justifying and pardoning sinners, God termeth his ways: Isa. lv. 6–9, 'Seek the Lord while he may be found, call ye upon him while he is near: let the wicked forsake his way, and the unrighteous man his thoughts: and let him return unto the Lord, and he will have mercy upon him; and

to our God, for he will abundantly pardon. For my thoughts are not your thoughts, neither are your ways my ways, saith the Lord. For as the heavens are higher than the earth, so are my ways higher than your ways, and my thoughts than your thoughts.'

4. The new birth and obedience that follows upon it, is the narrow gate, and the way that leads to life. Mat. vii. 14, Isa. xxxv. 8, ' an high way, a way, and a way of holiness.'

5. And the Israelites are said to have erred in their hearts, and not to have known his ways; where by *ways*, he means what was more eminently the object of saving faith, for Heb. iii., where this is cited, it is interpreted of unbelief, verses 10, 12, and 19 compared.

Christ, speaking of himself, says, ' I am the way ;' and his flesh crucified and torn, is that new and living way God found out into the holy of holies, Heb. x. So then, to teach men God's ways, in order unto their conversion, is 1. To discover to them their natural condition and unbelief to be a way of error, and of death : James v. 19, ' That converts a sinner from the error of his way.' For by nature it is spoken of all men, that ' the way of peace they have not known,' Rom. iii. ; ' erring in their hearts, and not having known his way.' 2. To teach them Christ, and the way of faith, and believing on him, and closing with the free mercies of God in pardoning. 3. To set out unto them the high-way of true holiness and obedience, of sanctification and the new birth. 4. To shew them all the errors, the by and crooked ways men turn aside into, both in believing and in turning unto God, and walking with him, which is called teaching them the good and right way : 1 Sam. xii. 20–24, ' And Samuel said unto the people, Fear not (ye have done all this wickedness : yet turn not aside from following the Lord, but serve the Lord with all your heart ; and turn ye not aside : for then should ye go after vain things, which cannot profit nor deliver ; for they are vain) : for the Lord will not forsake his people for his great name's sake : because it hath pleased the Lord to make you his people. Moreover, as for me, God forbid that I should sin against the Lord in ceasing to pray for you : but I will teach you the good and the right way : only fear the Lord, and serve him in truth with all your heart : for consider how great things he hath done for you.' And these were the ordinary subjects of Christ's discourses, especially in the first fruits of his ministry ; in his first sermon he speaks of faith and repentance, Mark i. 14, unto which two, Paul also reduceth the sum of his preaching, Acts xx. 20, 21, ' And how I kept back nothing that was profitable to you, but have shewed you, and have taught you publicly, and from house to house ;' verse 21, ' Testifying both to the Jews, and also the Greeks, repentance toward God, and faith toward our Lord Jesus Christ.' And, Titus iii. 8, he says, ' This is a faithful saying, and these I will that thou affirm constantly. These things are good and profitable to men.' And the true reason why men profit not, nor bring in men's souls, is, that they divert from these great, substantial, and necessary truths : Jer. xxiii. 22, ' If they had stood in my counsel, and had caused my people to hear my words, then they should have turned from their evil way, and from the evil of their doings.' In their discourses they tithe the mint and cummin of the Scriptures, and insist not on these great and necessary principles of religion. When our Saviour Christ was to send his disciples forth to preach the gospel to all the world, he promiseth the Spirit, as a comforter to their persons, and an assistant to them in their ministry, John xvi. And to shew what doctrines that Spirit would bless and go with to the hearts of men in converting of them, to the end that they accordingly should learn, in preaching to the nations, to insist thereon, he enumerates the work of the Spirit in men's hearts, in all the parts thereof, setting it out by the object matter of each work ; thereby withal pointing to them what subjects to treat on in their sermons, the Spirit using doctrines suitable to the work he is to do.

3. Observe that, in converting others, God more specially useth the endeavours of those himself hath turned.

(1.) The Holy Ghost dwelling in them, he is more easily communicated ; for themselves are anointed with him. Acts xii. 24, it is said of Barnabas, that ' he was a good man, and full of the Holy Ghost, and of faith ; and much people was added unto the Lord.'

(2.) Though God may, and sometime doth, use others, to shew his liberty, yet God delights to use them in it, and usually doth, who are themselves converted ; and this he doth out of choice: Mal. ii. 5, 6, ' My covenant' (says God, speaking of Levi) ' was with him of life and peace ; and I gave them to him, for the fear wherewith he feared me, and was afraid before my name. The law of truth was in his mouth, and iniquity was not found in his lips : he walked with me in peace and equity, and did turn many away from iniquity.' Even as it was with Abraham, whom being faithful himself, God chose to be the father of many nations. ' I gave them to him,' says God.

(3.) God rather useth such, because they have the art of doing. For God useth meet instruments for the work he employs them in. Now there is an art in converting souls, an eminent one. Therefore, says Solomon, Prov. xi. 30, ' He that winneth souls is wise.' Now a holy man is more wise in it, because he hath experience in the ways of God, in converting, comforting, recovering souls. ' Then shall I teach sinners thy ways,' says David, Ps. li. 13, namely, which I myself have had experience of : as Paul was able to comfort others with the comforts he had received ; and as Christ said to Peter, Luke xxii. 32, ' Peter, when thou art converted, strengthen thy brethren ;' he then knew how to do it. Such an one knows the heart of man, and the windings of it, by his own, and so knows how to make a key to unlock it, and that shall pass the wards of it.

4. Observe, that neither sins afore nor after regeneration should prejudice one in the ministry of the gospel, that truly returns to God, and recovers, as David here did. The instances are clear ; God used David to pen scripture, as he did this psalm, after his murder and adultery, and he promiseth himself as much success in doing good to others as ever. Solomon also the son, you know how he fell, yet God still used him to write scriptures, and to teach the people. Witness that book of Ecclesiastes, which he entitleth ' The Preacher,' after his great and long departure from God. Peter also, you know how he denied Christ, and also at Antioch dissembled, yet God converted by his preaching, after that first great fall of his, three thousand at one sermon, and poured forth his Spirit upon him notwithstanding, and used him to the end of his days, to write scripture fuller of holiness, that is, stronger incitements to holiness, than any other, and to preach and stir men up to remembrance. And the reasons are,

1. The gifts of God, even those given his elect, to do good to others, are of high value, and God will not lose the use and improvement of them for their sins, but will humble them for them, and so go on still to use and bless them.

2. His pardons are free-grace-pardons, such as they shall not invalidate by their sins. Free grace is still the same towards them.

3. Their hearts are the same to God upon repentance, and often more enlarged than before. They shew themselves clear in that matter by repenting, as, 2 Cor. vii., the apostle speaks. And so God forgives and man forgives, and they are both as afore.

And 4. Have gained more feeling experience, and deep and quick sense of God's love and gracious dealings than at first, converted by renewed repentance ; and so are more able, as Peter was, to strengthen their brethren.

Use. If such returning sinners are, both in respect of use and their gifts, the same to God, they should be so to men. Men should not be prejudiced when God is not ; specially seeing it is true of any that themselves also may be tempted. Now this takes away a great discouragement from what is in one's own person, as well as what prejudice useth to be in others' hearts towards one, especially from sins gross and scandalous after regeneration. This ought not, nor should not, upon and after manifest renewed repentance, discourage any one in this work, as to think that God will ever after such sins leave him, and not use him more ; nor should it be a prejudice in the hearts of others, for receiving what, out of experience from such falls, God shall give forth by such an one.

END OF VOL. VI.